CYBERSECURITY, PRIVACY AND DATA PROTECTION IN EU LAW

Is it possible to achieve cybersecurity while safeguarding the fundamental rights to privacy and data protection? Addressing this question is crucial for contemporary societies, where network and information technologies have taken centre stage in all areas of communal life. This timely book answers the question with a comprehensive approach that combines legal, policy and technological perspectives to capture the essence of the relationship between cybersecurity, privacy and data protection in EU law.

The book explores the values, interconnections and tensions inherent to cybersecurity, privacy and data protection within the EU constitutional architecture and its digital agendas. The work's novel analysis looks at the interplay between digital policies, instruments including the GDPR, NIS Directive, cybercrime legislation, e-evidence and cyber-diplomacy measures, and technology as a regulatory object and implementing tool. This original approach, which factors in the connections between engineering principles and the layered configuration of fundamental rights, outlines all possible combinations of the relationship between cybersecurity, privacy and data protection in EU law, from clash to complete reconciliation.

An essential read for scholars, legal practitioners and policymakers alike, the book demonstrates that reconciliation between cybersecurity, privacy and data protection relies on explicit and brave political choices that require an active engagement with technology, so as to preserve human flourishing, autonomy and democracy.

Hart Studies in Information Law and Regulation: Volume 2

Hart Studies in Information Law and Regulation

Series Editors
Tanya Aplin (General Editor)
Perry Keller (Advisory Editor)

This series concerns the transformative effects of the digital technology revolution on information law and regulation. Information law embraces multiple areas of law that affect the control and reuse of information – intellectual property, data protection, privacy, freedom of information, state security, tort, contract and competition law. 'Regulation' is a similarly extensive concept in that it encompasses non-legal modes of control, including technological design and codes of practice. The series provides cross-cutting analysis and exploration of the complex and pressing issues that arise when massive quantities of digital information are shared globally. These include, but are not limited to, sharing, reuse and access to data; open source and public sector data; propertisation of data and digital tools; privacy and freedom of expression; and the role of the state and private entities in safeguarding the public interest in the uses of data. In the spirit of representing the diverse nature of its topics, the series embraces various methodologies: empirical, doctrinal, theoretical and socio-legal, and publishes both monographs and edited collections.

Recent titles in this series:

Constitutionalising Social Media
Edited by Edoardo Celeste, Amélie Heldt and Clara Iglesias Keller

Cybersecurity, Privacy and Data Protection in EU Law: A Law, Policy and Technology Analysis
Maria Grazia Porcedda

Cybersecurity, Privacy and Data Protection in EU Law

A Law, Policy and Technology Analysis

Maria Grazia Porcedda

•HART•
OXFORD • LONDON • NEW YORK • NEW DELHI • SYDNEY

HART PUBLISHING

Bloomsbury Publishing Plc

Kemp House, Chawley Park, Cumnor Hill, Oxford, OX2 9PH, UK

1385 Broadway, New York, NY 10018, USA

29 Earlsfort Terrace, Dublin 2, Ireland

HART PUBLISHING, the Hart/Stag logo, BLOOMSBURY and the Diana logo are
trademarks of Bloomsbury Publishing Plc

First published in Great Britain 2023

First published in hardback, 2023

Paperback edition, 2024

Copyright © Maria Grazia Porcedda, 2023

Maria Grazia Porcedda has asserted her right under the Copyright, Designs and
Patents Act 1988 to be identified as Author of this work.

All rights reserved. No part of this publication may be reproduced or transmitted in any form or by any means, electronic or mechanical, including photocopying, recording, or any information storage or retrieval system, without prior permission in writing from the publishers.

While every care has been taken to ensure the accuracy of this work, no responsibility for loss or damage occasioned to any person acting or refraining from action as a result of any statement in it can be accepted by the authors, editors or publishers.

All UK Government legislation and other public sector information used in the work is Crown Copyright ©.
All House of Lords and House of Commons information used in the work is Parliamentary Copyright ©.
This information is reused under the terms of the Open Government Licence v3.0
(http://www.nationalarchives.gov.uk/doc/open-government-licence/version/3) except where otherwise stated.

All Eur-lex material used in the work is © European Union, http://eur-lex.europa.eu/, 1998–2024.

A catalogue record for this book is available from the British Library.

Library of Congress Cataloging-in-Publication data

Names: Porcedda, Maria Grazia, author.
Title: Cybersecurity, privacy and data protection in EU law : a law, policy and technology analysis / Maria Grazia Porcedda.
Other titles: Cybersecurity, privacy and data protection in European Union law
Description: Oxford ; New York : Hart, 2023. | Series: Hart studies in information law and regulation ; volume 2 | Based on author's thesis (doctoral – European University Institute, 2017) issued under title: Cybersecurity and privacy rights in EU law : moving beyond the trade-off model to appraise the role of technology. | Includes bibliographical references and index. | Summary: "Is it possible to achieve cybersecurity while safeguarding the fundamental rights to privacy and data protection? Addressing this question is crucial for European democratic societies, where information technologies have taken centre stage in all areas of communal life. This timely book answers the question with a comprehensive approach that combines legal, policy and technological perspectives to capture the essence of the relationship between cybersecurity, privacy and data protection in EU law. The book identifies tensions inherent in the EU cybersecurity policy and its implementation, the reach of cyberspace and its security, the meaning of 'data', as well as the value of privacy and data protection. The book's novel analysis looks at the interplay between the design of the technology implementing the applicable law, such as the GDPR and the NIS Directive, and the layered configuration of fundamental rights in EU law. This original analysis outlines the possible combinations of the relationship between cybersecurity, privacy and data protection in EU law, from outright clash to complementarity. An essential read for scholars and practitioners of IT law alike, the book demonstrates that reconciliation between cybersecurity, privacy and data protection relies on explicit and brave political choices, which require deciding what needs to be protected, and how"—Provided by publisher.
Identifiers: LCCN 2022046030 | ISBN 9781509939398 (hardback) | ISBN 9781509966080 (paperback) | ISBN 9781509939404 (pdf) | ISBN 9781509939411 (Epub)
Subjects: LCSH: Data protection—Law and legislation—European Union countries. | Computer security—Law and legislation—European Union countries. | Privacy, Right of—European Union countries.
Classification: LCC KJE1626 .P67 2023 | DDC 342.2408/58—dc23/eng/20221201
LC record available at https://lccn.loc.gov/2022046030

ISBN: PB: 978-1-50996-608-0
       ePDF: 978-1-50993-940-4
       ePub: 978-1-50993-941-1

Typeset by Compuscript Ltd, Shannon

To find out more about our authors and books visit www.hartpublishing.co.uk. Here you will find extracts, author information, details of forthcoming events and the option to sign up for our newsletters.

ACKNOWLEDGEMENTS

This book is dedicated to my parents, Erminio and Loredana, and is written in memory of Giovanni Buttarelli, European Data Protection Supervisor.

My first expression of gratitude goes to Professor Marise Cremona, my doctoral supervisor, for encouraging me to finish the PhD and warmly recommending to turn it into a monograph, alongside examining board members Professors Deirdre Curtin, Anne Flanagan and Ronald Leenes. I am thankful to all colleagues and friends who offered feedback on the proposal and on single chapters: Professor Mark Bell, Dr Sara Benidi, Professor David Churchill, Professor Louise Ellison, Bénédicte Havelange, Dr Justin Jütte, Dr Luigi Lonardo, Professor Marise Cremona, Professor Dagmar Shieck and Antony Haynes. I am also grateful to Professor Perry Keller and especially Professor Tanya Aplin, editors of the Hart Studies in Law and Regulation series, whose peer-reviews greatly improved this work. The exchanges with the many bright students of the Cybersecurity Law and Policy and IT Law modules I teach at Trinity College Dublin also helped shaping this work. As is customary, all mistakes are mine.

I wish to acknowledge the support and patience of Dr Roberta Bassi, Rosie Mearns and Linda Goss at Hart Publishing as well as Chris Harrison throughout the drafting of this book. Initial research for this work was funded by the Prize Ruffini of the Italian Lyncean Academy and the European Union's Seventh Framework Programme under grant agreements no. 284725 (SURVEILLE) and no. 285492 (SurPRISE) sponsoring my doctoral studies. The monograph incorporates original research funded by Enterprise Ireland grant no. CS20202036 and Trinity College Dublin's FAHSS 2020/2021 buy-out and partly carried out at the Historical Archives of the European Union in Florence. Many thanks to Nastos Pandelis for his help at the Archives and to Silvia Vailati for research assistance within the EI grant.

On a personal note, thanks to Oran and George for offering a safe haven in Dublin and to Audrey and Les for always taking an interest in this work. I am forever grateful to Martyn, my partner, without whose unconditional love and unfaltering encouragement the thesis first and then the book would have not seen the light of day. This book is dedicated to my mum and dad, in gratitude for all their love and support throughout many challenging years and their many sacrifices on my and my brother's behalf. Their generosity made it possible for me to finish my PhD, as did the resilience and resolution I learnt through the examples they set. My final thought goes to Giovanni Buttarelli, late European Data Protection Supervisor, in the memory of whom this book is written; it means a lot to me, as one of the trainees who was assigned to his mentorship at the EDPS, to testify that his inspirational leadership, kind teaching and remarkable legacy will long outlast him.

CONTENTS

Acknowledgements .... *v*
Abbreviations .... *xi*
Tables and Figures .... *xv*
Table of Cases .... *xvii*
Table of Legislation .... *xxiii*

Introduction 1
    I.   Investigating the Relationship of the Triad 2
    II.   Plan of the Book 5

PART 1
INTRODUCING CYBERSECURITY, PRIVACY AND DATA PROTECTION LAW AND THEIR INTERPLAY

1. Cybersecurity, Privacy and Data Protection: An Analytical Framework 9
    I.   Studying the Relationship between Cybersecurity, Privacy and
         Data Protection 10
         A.   Introducing Cybersecurity, Privacy and Data Protection
             (the Triad) 10
         B.   The Ambivalent Relationship of the Triad 15
         C.   Towards an Analytical Framework to Study the Reconciliation
             of the Triad 22
    II.   The Triad within the EU Constitutional Architecture: A Policy,
         Law and Technology Analysis 26
         A.   The EU Constitutional Architecture as a Constraint on the
             Relationship between Cybersecurity, Privacy and Data
             Protection 27
         B.   Cybersecurity, Privacy and Data Protection as Situated
             Objects: Law, Policy and Technology 36
    III. Conclusion: An Analytical Framework to Study the Relationship
         of the Triad 38

viii Contents

2. **The EU Cybersecurity Policy** 40
    I. The Development of the EU Cybersecurity Policy 40
        A. The EU's Approach to the Security of Cyberspace before 2013 40
        B. The Adoption of the EU Cybersecurity Policy 45
        C. The 2017 'Update' to the Cybersecurity Policy 48
        D. The 2020 Cybersecurity Policy 50
    II. The EU Cybersecurity Policy and Law Landscape 52
        A. Network and Information Security (NIS) and the DSM 53
        B. Cybercrime, e-Evidence and the AFSJ 57
        C. Cyber Defence, Diplomacy, Trade and the EA 62
    III. Conclusion: Tensions within Cybersecurity and the
         Way Forward 66

3. **Privacy: The Right to Respect for Private and Family Life** 68
    I. Sources and Scope of Article 7 CFR 68
        A. Determination of the Relevant Sources to Interpret
            Article 7 CFR 69
        B. The Correspondence between Articles 8 ECHR and 7 CFR 71
    II. Essential Components of Article 7 of the Charter 77
        A. 'Everyone has the Right to' 77
        B. 'Respect for': Vertical and Horizontal Obligations 78
        C. 'His or Her Private … Life' 80
        D. Family Life (The 'Inner Circle') 88
        E. Home 90
        F. (Confidential) Communications 91
    III. Conclusion: Essential Components of Article 7 CFR, Essence 94

4. **The Right to the Protection of Personal Data** 97
    I. Sources of Article 8 CFR 97
        A. EU Sources 98
        B. Council of Europe Instruments: The ECHR and Convention 108 102
        C. Other Relevant Sources 110
    II. Essential Components of Article 8 CFR 111
        A. Paragraph One: An Inclusive Right to Data Protection 111
        B. Paragraph Two: Obligation to Process Data Fairly, Purpose
            Limitation as Essence and Data Subjects' Rights 119
        C. Everyone has the Right of Access to Data which has been
            Collected Concerning Him or Her, and the Right to have
            it Rectified 122
        D. Paragraph Three: Control by an Independent Authority
            Ensuring Compliance 123
    III. Conclusion: Essential Components of Article 8 CFR, Essence 125

PART 2
TECHNOLOGY AND THE TRIAD IN THE DSM,
THE AFSJ AND THE EA

5. **Cybersecurity, Privacy and Data Protection as Techno-Legal Objects: Investigating the Role of Technology** 129
   I. Leveraging Technology to Appraise the Reconciliation of the Triad 130
      A. Technology: Security Properties, Threat Modelling, Protection Goals and Design Strategies 130
      B. Linking Technological and Legal Notions of Cybersecurity, Privacy and Data Protection 132
      C. Mode of Reconciliation of the Triad: From Overlap to Indeterminacy 138
   II. Technology as a Regulatory Target: The Effacement of Technology from the Law and its Consequences 141
      A. The Principle of Technology Neutrality 142
      B. The Principle of 'By Design' 144
      C. TN and By Design in Practice: TOMs, SoA, Standards and the New Legislative Framework 146
      D. Interim Conclusions: Technology Effacement and Indeterminacy 152
   III. Courts, the Effacement of Technology and the Indeterminacy Loop 152
   IV. Conclusion 155

6. **The DSM: Network and Information Security (NIS), Privacy and Data Protection** 157
   I. Reconciliation of Network and Information Security, Privacy and Data Protection: Policy 158
   II. Reconciliation of NIS, Privacy and Data Protection: Law 160
      A. Overview of Legal Instruments Relevant to NIS 161
      B. Comparative Analysis of Selected Instruments 162
      C. Interim Conclusion: Strong Reconciliation of NIS with Privacy and Data Protection in the Law 176
   III. Reconciliation of NIS, Privacy and Data Protection: Technology 177
      A. State-of-the-Art ToMs and the Regulation of ICT Products, Services and Processes: Strong Reconciliation (Im)possible? 178
      B. State of the Art Technical Measures: The Example of Deep Packet Inspection (DPI) 182
   IV. Conclusion: Strong Reconciliation of NIS with Privacy and Data Protection Challenged by Technology 193

x   Contents

7. **The AFSJ: The Fight against Cybercrime, e-Evidence, Privacy and Data Protection** 195
    I. Reconciliation of the Fight against Cybercrime, e-Evidence, Privacy and Data Protection: Policy 196
    II. Reconciliation of the Fight against Cybercrime, e-Evidence, Privacy and Data Protection: Law 200
        A. Reconciling the Fight against Cybercrimes with Privacy and Data Protection 202
        B. How the Collection of e-Evidence Affects the Reconciliation of the Fight against Cybercrime with Privacy and Data Protection 219
    III. Reconciliation of the Fight against Cybercrime, E-evidence, Privacy and Data Protection: Technology 229
        A. 'Use of Tools' and Implicit Reference to Technology Neutrality (TN) 230
        B. Deep Packet Inspection (DPI) in the Fight against Cybercrimes 232
        C. Beyond DPI: Technical Measures to Fight Cybercrime and Visions of Reconciliation Through Technology 237
    IV. Conclusion: Weak Reconciliation of the Fight against Cybercrime, e-Evidence, Privacy and Data Protection Challenged by Technology 239

8. **The EA: 'Cyber' External Action, Privacy and Data Protection** 240
    I. Reconciliation of Cybersecurity, Privacy and Data Protection in the EA: Policy 241
    II. Reconciliation of Cybersecurity, Privacy and Data Protection in the EA: Law 244
        A. The Overarching Framework for the Relationship between the Triad in the EA 245
        B. The Cyber Diplomacy Toolbox with a Focus on Cyber-Related Restrictive Measures 248
        C. Reconciliation of Cybersecurity, Privacy and Data Protection in EA Law 254
    III. Technology 255
        A. The Importance of Technical Attribution for RMs and Some Considerations on Deep Packet Inspection 256
        B. The Effacement of Technology: International Flow of Values, Norms, Ideas and Impact on the Triad 257
    IV. Conclusion: Weak Reconciliation of Cyber External Action, Privacy and Data Protection Challenged by Technology 259

Conclusion 261
    I. Summary of Findings 261
    II. Research Trajectories and the Future of the Triad 267

Bibliography 270
Index 293

ABBREVIATIONS

AFSJ	Area of Freedom, Security and Justice
BEREC	Body of the European Regulators of Electronic Communications
CDPF	Cyber Defence Policy Framework
CI	Critical Infrastructure
CII	Critical Information Infrastructure
CIA	Confidentiality, Integrity and Availability
CFR(EU)	Charter of Fundamental Rights (of the European Union)
CFSP	Common Foreign and Security Policy
CJEU	Court of Justice of the European Union
CoE	Council of Europe
CSA	Cybersecurity Act (Regulation (EU) 2019/881)
CSAM	Child Sexual Abuse Material
CSADir	Combating Child Sexual Abuse Directive (2011/93/EU)
CSAReg	Combating Child Sexual Abuse Regulation ((EU) 2021/1232)
CSDP	Common Security and Defence Policy
CTDir	Combating Terrorism Directive ((EU) 2017/541)
(D)DoS	(Distributed) Denial of Service
DNS	Domain Name System
DPAs	Data Protection Authorities
DPbD	Data Protection By Design
DPD	Data Protection Directive (95/46/EC)
DPI	Deep Packet Inspection
DRD	Data Retention Directive (2006/24/EC)
DS	Design Strategy
DSPs	Digital Service Providers

DSM	Digital Single Market
EA	External Action
EEA	European Economic Area
EEAS	European External Action Service
ECD	Electronic Commerce Directive (2000/31/EC)
EDA	European Defence Agency
ECtHR	European Court of Human Rights
ECHR	European Convention on Human Rights
ECS(s)	Electronic Communications Service(s)
EDPB	European Data Protection Board
EDPS	European Data Protection Supervisor
EDPSR	European Data Protection Supervisor Regulation (45/2001/EC)
EDPSR2	European Data Protection Supervisor Regulation ((EU) 2018/1725)
EECC	European Electronic Communications Code Directive ((EU) 2018/1972)
EHS	European Harmonised Standard
eIDASR	Electronic Identity and Assurance Services Regulation ((EU) 910/2014)
EIO	European Investigation Order
EIOD	European Investigation Order Directive (2014/41/EU)
ENISA	European Network and Information Security Agency (European Union Agency for Cybsersecurity)
EPD	Electronic Privacy Directive (2002/58/EC)
EP	European Parliament
EPR	Proposed Electronic Privacy Regulation (COM (2017) 10 final)
EPPOR	Proposed European Regulation on the Production and Preservation Orders (COM (2018) 225 final COD)
ESDC	European Security and Defence College
EU	European Union
ECCG	European Cybersecurity Certification Group
FCD	Fraud and Counterfeiting Directive ((EU) 2019/713)
FIP(P)(s)	Fair Information Practice(s) (Principles)

GDPR	General Data Protection Regulation ((EU) 2016/679)
IAS	Internet Access Service
ICCPR	International Covenant on Civil and Political Rights
ICT	Information and Communication Technology
IETF	International Engineering Task Force
INTCEN	European Union Intelligence and Situation Centre
IoT	Internet of Things
IP	Internet Protocol
ISO	International Standardisation Organisation
ISS	Information Society Service(s)
ISS	Internal Security Strategy
IT	Information Technology
ITU	International Telecommunication Union
JHA	Justice and Home Affairs
LED	Law Enforcement Directive ((EU) 2016/680)
NIS	Network and Information Security
NISD	Network and Information Systems Directive ((EU) 2016/1148)
NIS2	Proposed Network and Information Systems Directive 2 (COM (2020) 823 final)
NLF	New Legislative Framework (New Approach)
OIR	Open Internet (Access) Regulation ((EU) 2015/2120)
OES	Operator of Essential Services
PbD	Privacy by Design
PESCO	Permanent Structured Cooperation
PET	Privacy Enhancing Technology
PG	Protection Goal
PSD2	Payment Services Directive 2 ((EU) 2015/2366)
RMs	Restrictive Measures
RoL	Rule of Law
SbD	Security by Design

SDOs	Standards Developing Organisations
SoA	State of the Art
SP	Security Property
SSOs	Standards Setting Organisations
TCP	Transmission Control Protocol
T-CY	CoE Cybercrime Convention Committee
TEU	Treaty on European Union
TFEU	Treaty on the Functioning of European Union
TOMs	Technical and Organisational Measures
UDHR	Universal Declaration of Human Rights
UN	United Nations
UN GGE	United Nations Group of Governmental Experts
URL	Unique Resource Identifier
WP29	Article 29 Data Protection Working Party

TABLES AND FIGURES

Tables

Chapter 2

Table 1 NIS-related instruments 56
Table 2 Cybercrime-related Instruments 60
Table 3 Cyber defence, diplomacy and trade-related Instruments 65

Chapter 3

Table 1 Summary of essential components of the right to respect for private and
family life 94

Chapter 4

Table 1 Summary of essential components and essence of the right to
respect for data protection 125

Chapter 5

Table 1 Definitions of security properties, protection goals and design
strategies 133
Table 2 Technical and legal understandings of the right to privacy
(Article 7 CFR) 135
Table 3 Technical and legal understandings of the right to data protection
(article 8 CFR) 137

Figures

Introduction

Figure 1 Modes of reconciliation of cybersecurity, privacy and data protection
(the triad) 2

Chapter 1

Figure 1 Modes of reconciliation of cybersecurity, privacy and data protection
(the triad) 22

Chapter 2

Figure 1 The three-pronged approach, COM (2001) 298, 3 43
Figure 2 Overview of the objectives of the Cybersecurity Strategy 47
Figure 3 The integration between NIS, LEAs and defence 48

Chapter 6
Figure 1   Meaning of 'content' of a packet (OSI and TCP/IP architecture)
              following interpretation by the EDPB 190

Conclusion
Figure 1   Modes of reconciliation of the triad 261

TABLE OF CASES

Court of Justice of the European Union: alphabetical order

A, B, and C, C-148/13 to C-150/13, EU:C:2014:2406 .... 74, 84–85
Åkerberg Fransson, C-617/10, EU:C :2013:105 .... 31, 68–70
Al Assad v Council, T-202/12, EU:T:2014:113 .... 80, 253
ASNEF and FECEDM, C-468/10 and C-469/10, EU:C:2011:777 .... 105–06, 121
Asociaţia de Proprietari bloc M5A-ScaraA, C-708/18, EU:C:2019:1064 .... 35, 104
Avis 2/13, Opinion of the Court, EU:C:2014:2454 .... 24, 102
Ayadi v Commission, C-183/12 P, EU:C:2013:369 .... 85, 89, 253
Bauer and Willemorth, C-569/16 and C-570/16, EU:C:2018:871 79
Bavarian Lager Ltd, C-28/08 P, EU:C:2010:378 .... 82, 100, 104, 121
Belgium v Facebook, C-645/19, EU:C:2021:483 105
Bodil Lindqvist, C-101/01, EU:C:2003:596 .... 105, 111, 119
Breyer, C-582/14, EU:C:2016:779 .... 111–14, 186, 191
CA, B, and C, C-148/13 to C-150/13, EU:C:2014:2111, Opinion
  of AG Sharpston 74
Chakroun, C-578/08, EU:C:2010:117 .... 69, 89
Commission v Austria, C-28/09, EU:C:2011:854 74
Commission v Austria, C-614/10, EU:C:2012:631 123–24
Commission v CAS Succhi di Frutta, C-496/99 P, EU:C:2004:236 29
Commission v Hungary, C-288/12, EU:C:2014:237 124
Commissioner of the Garda Síochána e.a, C-140/20, EU:C:2022:258 ..... 214, 221–22, 225
Commissioner of the Garda Síochána e.a, C-140/20, EU:C:2022:941,
  Opinion of AG Sánchez-Bordona 225
Coty Germany, C-580/13, EU:C:2015:485 34
Dennekamp v Parliament, T-115/13, EU :T :2015 :497 80
Dereci and others v Bundesministerium für Inneres, C-256/11,
  EU:C:2011:734 .... 31, 71–72
Deutsche Telekom, C-543/09, EU:C:2011:279 .... 100, 104–05, 120–21
Digital Rights Ireland and Seitlinger and Others,
  C-293/12 and C-594/12, EU:C:2014:238 .... 34, 71, 80, 82, 86, 92, 104–06,
    115–17, 121, 125, 139, 153, 163,
    177, 185–86, 189, 219, 234–35
État luxembourgeois, C-245/19 and C-246/19, EU:C:2020:795 .... 34, 96
European Commission v Federal Republic of Germany, C-518/07,
  EU:C:2010:125 .... 29, 80
European Parliament v Council, C-658/11, EU:C:2014:41, Opinion
  of Advocate General Bot 247

xviii Table of Cases

F, C-473/16, EU:2018:36 85
Facebook Ireland and Others, C-645/19, EU:C:2021:483 123–25
Fisher, C-369/98, EU:C:2000:443 36
GC and Others (De-referencing of sensitive data), C-136/17,
    EU:C:2019:773 .... 103, 115, 122
Glawischnig-Piesczek, C-18/18, EU:C:2019:821 188
Google (Territorial scope of de-referencing), C-507/17, EU:C:2019:15,
    Opinion of AG Szpunar 100, 103, 119
Google (Territorial scope of de-referencing), C-507/17,
    EU:C:2019:772 .... 85, 100, 105, 113, 120, 122
Google Spain and Google, C-131/12, EU:C:2014:317 .... 85, 100, 105, 112,
                                                                                                         117, 119–20, 122
Google, C-193/18, EU:C:2019:498 235
Hauer v Land Rheinland-Pfalz, C-44/79, EU:C:1979:290 33
Hungary v Slovakia, C-364/10, EU:C:2012:630 29
Ilonka Sayn-Wittgenstein v Landeshauptmann von Wien, C-208/09,
    EU:C:2010:806 .... 30, 35, 84–85
Ireland v Parliament and Council, C-301/06, EU:C:2009:68
    (Data Retention I) 153, 214
James Elliot, C-613/14, EU:C:2016:63, Opinion of AG Sanchez-Bordona 148
James Elliot, C-613/14, EU:C:2016:821 .... 148–49, 151, 154
Jehovan Todistajat, C-25/17, EU:C:2018:551 113
Kadi and Al Barakaat International Foundation v Council and
    Commission (Kadi I), C-402/05 P and C-415/05, EU:C:2008:461 253
Karlsson and Others, C-292/97, EU:C:2000:202 .... 33, 76
La Quadrature du Net and Others, C-511/18, EU:C:2020:791 .... 71–72, 76, 86, 154,
                                                                                                         185–86, 188, 190–91,
                                                                                                         201, 214, 220–22, 225–26,
                                                                                                         230–31, 233–35
Latvijas Republikas Saeima (Points de pénalité), C-439/19,
    EU:C:2020:1054, Opinion of AG Szpunar 106, 114–15, 117
Latvijas Republikas Saeima (Points de pénalité), C-439/19,
    EU:C:2021:504 .... 106, 114–15, 117
Les Verts v Parliament, C-294/83, EU:C:1986:166 .... 24, 27
Mircom, C-597/19, EU:C:2021:492 .... 71, 79, 112–14, 186
National Panasonic v Commission, C-136/79 EU:C:1980:169 36
Nold KG v European Commission, C-4/73, EU:C:1974:51 32
Opinion 1/15 of 26 July 2017 pursuant to Article 218(11) TFEU
    EU:C:2017:592 .... 34–35, 77, 80, 117, 121,
                                                                                                         139, 185, 189, 235, 244
Österreichischer Rundfunk and Others, C-465/00, C-138/01
    and C-139/01, EU:C:2003:294 105
Parliament v Council, C-130/10,1 EU:C:2012:472 247
Parliament v Council, C-263/14, EU:C:2016:435 247
Parliament v Council, C-317/04 and C-318/04, EU:C:2006:346 33
Patrick Breyer, C-582/14, EU:C:2016:339, Opinion of AG Sanchez-Bordona 107

Table of Cases xix

Planet 49, C-673/17, EU:C :2019:801..88
Poland v Parliament and Council, C-157/21, EU:C:2022:98......................................27–28
Poland v Parliament and Council, C-401/19, EU:C:2022:297.................................186, 188
PPU McB, C-400/10, EU:C:2010:582...71–72, 88–89
PPU Mercredi, C-497/10. EU:C:2010:829..89
Privacy International, C-623/17, EU:C:2020:5, Opinion
  of AG Sanchez-Bordona..101
Privacy International, C-623/17, EU:C:2020:790 ....69, 72, 86, 91–92, 101
Prokuratuur, C-746/18, EU:C:2021:152 221
Promusicae, C-275/06, EU:C:2008:54..104
Rīgas satiksme, C-13/16, EU:C:2017:336..120
Runevič-Vardyn and Wardyn, C-391/09, EU:C:2011:291 .... 36, 84–85, 89
Ryneš, C-212/13, EU:C :2014:2428...104–05, 111, 113
Sabam, C-360/10, EU:C:2012:85...105, 153, 186, 188, 191
Sánchez Morcillo and Abril García, C-539/14, EU:C:2015:508 (Order).......................90
Satakunnan and Satamedia, C-73/07, EU:C:2008:727 ....76, 119
Scarlet Extended, C-70/10, EU:C:2011:255, Opinion of AG Villalón............ 153–54, 191
Scarlet Extended, C-70/10, EU:C:2011:771 ....105, 154, 186, 188, 191
Schecke and Eifert, C-92/09 and C-93/09, EU:C:2010:662.................................76, 81, 85,
  104–05, 114, 119
Schmidberger, C-112/00, EU:C:2003:333 33
Schrems, C-362/14, EU:C:2015:627, Opinion of AG Bot..34–35
Schrems, C-362/14, EU:C:2015:650...34–35, 92, 100, 105,
  109, 123–24, 230, 244
Schwarz, C-291/12, EU:C:2013:670 .... 32, 75, 83, 153
Sergejs Buivids, C-345/17, EU:C:2019 :122..111
Sergejs Buivids, C-345/17, EU:C:2018:780 Opinion of AG Sharpstone 102, 112, 114
Skype Communications, C-142/18, EU:C:2019:460.............................. 161, 163, 222, 235
Stichting Rookpreventie Jeugd and others, C-160/20, EU:C:2022:101 .... 148–50, 154
Tele2 Sverige and Watson and others, C-203/15 and C-698/15,
  EU:C:2016:572, Opinion of AG Saugmandsgaard Øe.......................................71, 103
Tele2 Sverige and Watson and others, C-203/15 and C-698/15,
  EU:C:2016:970 .... 69, 71, 103
Telenor Magyarország, C-807/18, EU:C:2020:708 187
U, C-101/13, EU:C:2014:2249...84, 122
UPC DTH, C-475/12, EU:C:2014:285..163
UPC Telekabel Wien, C-314/12, EU:C:2014:192..188
Van Duyn v Home Office, C-41/74, EU:C:1974:133..30
W. Ż. And des affaires publiques de la Cour suprême, C-487/19,
  EU:C:2021:289,Opinion of AG Tanchev..35
Wachauf v Bundesamt Für Ernährung Und Forstwirtschaft, C-5/88,
  EU:C:1989:321 29
WebMindLicenses, C-419/14, EC:C:2015:832 ....32, 77, 91, 235
Weltimmo, C-230/14, EU:C:2015:639 ....119, 125
Willems, C-446/12 to C-449/12, EU:C:2015:238..83, 153
Worten, C-342/12 EU:C:2013:355...119–20

xx *Table of Cases*

X and Others, C-199/12 to C-201/1, EU:C:2013:720 .... 85, 94
X, C-486/12, EU:C :2013:836 .... 105, 122
YS and others, C-141/12 and C-372/12, EU:C:2014:2081 .... 80, 100, 105, 122
ZZ, C-300/11, EU:C:2013:363 30

European Court of Human Rights: alphabetical order

Bernh Larsen Holding As and Others v Norway, App no 24117/08,
    CE:ECHR:2013:0314JUD002411708 90
Berrehab v The Netherlands, App no 10730/84, CE:ECHR:1988:
    0621JUD001073084 89
Big Brother and Watch v UK, App no 58170/13, partly Concurring, partly
    dissenting Opinion of Judge Pinto de Albuquerque 87
Big Brother Watch and Others v UK, App no 58170/13, 62322/14
    and 24960/15, CE:ECHR:2018:0913JUD005817013 .... 16, 31–32, 163, 223
Big Brother Watch and Others v UK, App nos 58170/13, 62322/14
    and 24960/15, CE:ECHR:2021:0525JUD005817013 .... 75, 223, 225
C. v Belgium, App no 21794/93, CE:ECHR:1996:0807JUD002179493 89
Chiragov and Others v Armenia, App no 13216/05,
    CE:ECHR:2015:0616JUD001321605 .... 81, 88, 90
Copland v the United Kingdom, App no 62617/00, CE:ECHR:2007:
    0403JUD006261700 .... 92, 163, 185–86
Eriksson v Sweden, App no 11373/85, CE:ECHR:1989:0622JUD001137385 90
Golder v the United Kingdom, App no 4451/70, CE:ECHR:1975:
    0221JUD000445170 92
Halford v the United Kingdom, App no 20605/92, CE:ECHR:1997:
    0625JUD002060592 92
Herbecq and the Association 'Ligue Des Droits De L'homme' v Belgium,
    App no 32200/96 and 32201/96, CE:ECHR:1998:0114DEC003220096 103
Herczegfalvy v Austria, App no 10533/83, CE:ECHR:1992:0924JUD001053383 92
Iordachi and Others v Moldova, App no 25198/02, CE:ECHR:2009:
    0210JUD002519802 75
K.U. v Finland, App no 2872/02, CE:ECHR:2008:1202JUD000287202 92
Klass and others v Germany, App no 5029/71, CE:ECHR:1978:
    0906JUD000502971 .... 75, 87
Leander v Sweden, App no 9248/81, CE:ECHR:1987:0326JUD000924881 75
Lopez Ribalda v Spain, App nos 1874/13 and 8567/13,
    CE:ECHR:2019:1017JUD000187413 .... 79, 83, 87, 103
M. C. v Bulgaria, App no 39272/98, CE:ECHR:2003:1204JUD003927298 83
Malone v the United Kingdom, App no 8691/79, CE:ECHR:1985:
    0426JUD000869179, concurring opinion of Judge Pettiti 87
Marckx v Belgium, App no 6833/74, CE:ECHR:1979:0613JUD000683374 .... 78, 87, 89
Mikulić v Croatia, App no 53176/99, CE:ECHR:2002:0207JUD005317699 84
Moustaquim v Belgium, App no 12313/86, CE:ECHR:1991:0218JUD001231386 90

Niemietz v Germany, App no 13710/88, CE:ECHR:1992:
1216JUD001371088 ....75, 81, 87, 90, 185, 189
Olsson v Sweden, App no 13441/87, CE:ECHR:1992:1127JUD001344187 90
P.G. and J.H. v the United Kingdom, App no. 44787/98,
CE:ECHR:2001:0925JUD004478798 .... 75–76, 92
Peck v the United Kingdom, App no 44647/98, CE:ECHR:2003:
0128JUD004464798 .... 75–76, 87, 92
Perry v the United Kingdom, App no 3737/00, CE:ECHR:2003:
0717JUD006373700 76
Pretty v the United Kingdom, App no 2346/02, CE:ECHR:2002:
0429JUD00234602 (tentative) 81–82, 86
Rotaru v Romania, App no 28341/95, CE:ECHR:2000:
0504JUD002834195 .... 81, 108, 186
S. and Marper v the United Kingdom, App nos 30562/04
and 30566/04, CE:ECHR:2008:1204JUD003056204 ....82, 139, 223, 225–26
Shimovolos v Russia, App no 30194/09, CE:ECHR:2011:0621JUD003019409 186
Stolyarova v Russia, App no 15711/13, CE:ECHR:2015:0129JUD001571113................ 90
X and Y v the Netherlands, App no 8978/80, CE:ECHR:1985:
0326JUD000897880 .... 79, 81, 83, 214
X and Others v Austria, App no 19010/07 CE:ECHR:2013:0219JUD001901007 89
Z. v Finland, App no 22009/93, CE:ECHR:1997:0225JUD002200993 108

German Federal Constitutional Court (Bundesverfassungsgericht)

BVerfG, Judgment of the First Senate of 27 February 2008,
1 BvR 370/07, DE:BVerfG:2008:rs20080227.1bvr037007 .... 13, 237
BVerfG, Judgment of the Second Senate of 30 June 2009, 2 BvE 2/08,
DE:BVerfG:2009:es20090630.2bve000208 .... 25, 62

United Nations

Human Rights Committee (CCPR), *General Comment no 16. Article 17
(The right to Respect of Privacy, Family, Home and Correspondence,
and Protection of Honour and Reputation)* (1988) 78
Singh Bhinder v Canada, Communication no 208/1986, CCPR/C/37/D/208/1986 83
Sayadi and Vinck v Belgium, Communication no 1472/2006,
CCPR/C/94/D/1472/2006 .... 85, 253

TABLE OF LEGISLATION

Council of Europe

Additional Protocol to the Convention for the Protection of Individuals with regard to Automatic Processing of Personal Data, regarding supervisory authorities and trans-border data flows, Council of Europe, ETS No181, 8 November 2001 108
Additional Protocol to the Convention on Cybercrime Concerning the Criminalisation of Acts of a Racist and Xenophobic Nature Committed through Computer Systems, Council of Europe, ETS No 189, 28 January 2003 58
Convention for the Protection of Human Rights and Fundamental Freedoms (as amended by Protocols No 1-16), ETS No 005, 4 November 1950 69
Convention for the Protection of Individuals with regard to Automatic Processing of Personal Data, ETS No 108, 28 January 1981 98
Convention on Cybercrime, ETS No 185, 23 November 2001 .... 43, 197
Explanatory Memorandum of Convention for the Protection of Individuals with regard to Automatic Processing of Personal Data, Council of Europe 108
Memorandum of Understanding between the Council of Europe and the European Union CM(2007)74 1 (117th Session of the Committee of Ministers, 2007) 28
Parliamentary Assembly, *Recommendation 2067 (2015) on Mass Surveillance* (2015) 16–17
Protocol amending the Convention for the Protection of Individuals with regard to Automatic Processing of Personal Data (Convention 108+), CETS No 223, 10 October 2018 108
Second Additional Protocol to the Convention on Cybercrime on enhanced co-operation and disclosure of electronic evidence CETS No. 224, 12 May 2022 .... 227, 245

European Union

Charter of Fundamental Rights of the European Union
  [2016] OJ C 202/2 ....26, 33–34, 37, 45, 68–81, 84–85,
  88, 90–92, 94–126, 132, 135–39, 145,
  150, 185–87, 189–91, 193, 197–98, 215,
  220–21, 226, 228, 235–36, 242,
  244, 248, 253–54, 257, 259, 260, 262

Commission Decision of 5 July 2016 on the signing of an arrangement
  on a public-private partnership for cybersecurity industrial and innovation
  between the European Union, represented by the Commission,
  and the Stakeholder Organisation [2016] C(2016) 4400 final 50, 56, 59–60
Commission Directive 2008/63/EC of 20 June 2008 on competition
  in the markets in telecommunications terminal equipment [2008] OJ L162 161
Commission Recommendation (EU) 2017/1584 of 13 September 2017
  on coordinated response to large-scale cybersecurity incidents
  and crises [2017] OJ C239/36 .... 56, 252, 256
Commission Regulation 611/2013/EU of 24 June 2013 on the measures
  applicable to the notification of personal data breaches under
  Directive 2002/58/EC of the European Parliament and of the Council
  on Privacy and Electronic Communications (Commission
  Regulation on Data Breaches) [2013] OJ L172/2 .... 140, 145, 170–71, 173
Consolidated versions of the Treaty on European Union (TEU)
  and the Treaty on the Functioning of the European Union (TFEU)
  [2016] OJ C202/1, 7 June 2016 (Lisbon Treaty) 24, 27, 33, 37, 45,
  71, 98, 198, 240, 247
Council Decision (EU) 2019/797 of 17 May 2019 concerning restrictive
  measures against cyber-attacks threatening the Union or its
  Member States [2019] OJ L1291/13 .... 65, 245, 250–57
Council Directive 2008/114/EC of 8 December 2008 on the Identification
  and Designation of European Critical Infrastructures and the Assessment
  of the Need to Improve their Protection [2008] OJ L345/75 .... 54, 56
Council Framework Decision 2001/413/JHA of 28 May 2001 combating fraud
  and counterfeiting of non-cash means of payment [2001] OJ L149/1 208
Council Framework Decision 2005/222/JHA of 24 February 2005 on attacks
  against information systems [2005] OJ L69/67 .... 43, 202
Council Framework Decision 2006/960/JHA of 18 December 2006
  on simplifying the exchange of information and intelligence between
  law enforcement authorities of the Member States of the European Union
  [2006] OJ L386/89 218
Council Implementing Regulation (EU) 2020/1125 of 30 July 2020
  implementing Regulation (EU) 2019/796 concerning restrictive measures
  against cyber-attacks threatening the Union or its Member States
  [2020] OJ L246/4 251
Council Regulation (EU) 2019/796 of 17 May 2019 concerning restrictive
  measures against cyber-attacks threatening the Union or its
  Member States [2019] OJ L1291/1 .... 65, 245, 250–56
Council, 'Draft implementing guidelines for the Framework on a Joint
  EU Diplomatic Response to Malicious Cyber Activities 13007/17' 249
Decision (EU) 2022/480 of the European Parliament setting up a committee
  of inquiry to investigate the use of the Pegasus and equivalent surveillance
  spyware, and defining the subject of the inquiry, as well as the
  responsibilities, numerical strength and term of office of the committee
  [2022] OJ L98/72 .... 1, 10

Directive (EU) 2015/1535 of the European Parliament and of the Council
of 9 September 2015 laying down a procedure for the provision of
information in the field of technical regulations and of rules on information
society services (codification) [2015] OJ L241 ....56, 163

Directive (EU) 2015/2366 of the European Parliament and of the Council
of 25 November 2015 on payment services in the Internal Market,
amending Directives 2002/65/EC, 2009/110/EC and 2013/36/EU and
Regulation (EU) No 1093/2010, and repealing Directive 2007/64/EC
[2015] OJ L337/35 .... 56, 157, 160, 162, 171–72,
174, 177, 210–11, 218

Directive (EU) 2016/1148 of the European Parliament and of the Council
of 6 July 2016 concerning measures for a high common level of security
of network and information systems across the Union
[2016] OJ L194/1 ....49–50, 52–55, 157, 160–62,
164–65, 170–71, 173–75, 180, 186–87,
206, 210, 244–45, 249, 252, 258

Directive (EU) 2016/680 of the European Parliament and of the Council
of 27 April 2016 on the protection of natural persons with regard to the
processing of personal data by competent authorities for the purposes
of the prevention, investigation, detection or prosecution of criminal
offences or the execution of criminal penalties, and on the free movement
of such data, and Repealing Council Framework Decision 2008/977/JHA
[2016] OJ L119/89 (Law Enforcement Directive) 59–60, 69, 72, 101,
109, 111, 116–17, 120–22,
124, 195–96, 198, 202,
207, 211, 215–16, 219,
222, 228–30, 233, 247–48

Directive (EU) 2017/541 of the European Parliament and of the Council
of 15 March 2017 on combating terrorism and replacing Council
Framework Decision 2002/475/JHA and amending Council
Decision 2005/671/JHA [2017] OJ L88/6 .... 59, 202, 216–17, 227, 230

Directive (EU) 2018/1972 of the European Parliament and of the Council
of 11 December 2018 establishing the European Electronic
Communications Code (Recast) [2018] OJ L321/36.....................56, 93, 157, 160–66,
168, 170–75, 186–87,
189, 213, 235

Directive (EU) 2019/713 of the European Parliament and of the Council
of 17 April 2019 on combating fraud and counterfeiting of non-cash
means of payment and replacing Council Framework
Decision 2001/413/JHA [2019] OJ L123/18 ....58, 60, 202, 208–11,
227, 230, 239, 252

Directive 2000/31/EC of the European Parliament and of the Council
of 8 June 2000 on Certain Legal Aspects of Information Society Services,
in Particular Electronic Commerce, in the Internal Market
(Directive on Electronic Commerce) [2002] OJ L178/1 .... 56, 186, 188,
191, 217, 220, 226, 235

Directive 2002/58/EC of the European Parliament and of the Council
of 12 July 2002 Concerning the Processing of Personal Data and the
Protection of Privacy in the Electronic Communications Sector,
as amended by Directive 2009/136/EC of 25 November 2009
[2002] OJ L201/37 (Directive on privacy and Electronic
communications) 20, 56, 69, 77–79, 86, 88, 91, 93, 100–01,
105–06, 111, 114, 117, 139–40, 157, 160–66,
168–71, 173–74, 177, 185–87, 189, 191,
207, 213, 215, 220–22, 226, 228, 232, 234

Directive 2006/24/EC of the European Parliament and of the Council
of 15 March 2006 on the retention of data generated or processed
in connection with the provision of publicly available electronic
communications services or of public communications networks
and amending Directive 2002/58/EC [2006] OJ L105/54
(Data Retention Directive) (invalidated) 44, 86, 153, 198, 219–20

Directive 2009/136/EC of the European Parliament and of the Council
of 25 November 2009 amending Directive 2002/22/EC on universal
service and users' rights relating to electronic communications networks
and services, Directive 2002/58/EC concerning the processing of personal
data and the protection of privacy in the electronic communications sector
and regulation (EC) No 2006/2004 on cooperation between national
authorities responsible for the enforcement of consumer protection laws
(Citizens' Rights Directive) [2009] OJ L337/11 .... 56, 171

Directive 2011/36/EU of the European Parliament and of the Council
of 5 April 2011 on preventing and combating trafficking in human beings
and protecting its victims, and replacing Council Framework
Decision 2002/629/JHA [2011] OJ L101/1 .... 60, 218

Directive 2011/93/EU of the European Parliament and of the Council
of 13 December 2011 on combating the sexual abuse and sexual exploitation
of children and child pornography, and replacing Council Framework
Decision 2004/68/JHA [2011] OJ L335/1 .... 58–60, 202, 211–17,
222, 230, 233

Directive 2013/40/EU of the European Parliament and the Council
of 12 August 2013 on attacks against information systems and replacing
Council Framework Decision 2005/222/JHA [2013] OJ L218/8 .... 57–58, 60–61,
147, 200–10, 216, 226,
232, 239, 245, 251–52

Directive 2014/41/EU of the European Parliament and of the Council
of 3 April 2014 regarding the European Investigation Order in
criminal matters [2014] OJ L130/1 .... 60, 219, 226–27, 233

Directive 95/46/EC of the European Parliament and of the Council
of 24 October 1995 on the protection of individuals with regard to the
processing of personal data and on the free movement of such data
[1995] OJ L281/31 (Data Protection Directive)(repealed) 35, 42–43, 99–102,
105–06, 108–09, 112, 114,
119, 122, 124–25, 132,
150, 167, 191, 244, 263

Explanations relating to the Charter of Fundamental Rights
 [2007] OJ C 303/02 (Explanations to the Charter)............................ 33, 69, 71, 74, 76,
 79, 97–100, 112
Notice for the attention of the data subjects to whom the restrictive measures
 provided for in Council Decision (CFSP) 2019/797 and Council
 Regulation (EU) 2019/796 concerning restrictive measures against
 cyber-attacks threatening the Union or its Member States 2021/C 192/05
 [2021] OJ C192/6 254
Regulation (EU) 2015/2120 of the European Parliament and of the Council
 of 25 November 2015 laying down measures concerning open internet
 access and amending Directive 2002/22/EC on universal service and users'
 rights relating to electronic communications networks and services and
 regulation (EU) 531/2012 on roaming on public mobile communications
 networks within the Union [2015] OJ L310/1 ....56, 162, 186–89,
 192, 232, 234–35
Regulation (EU) 2016/794 of the European Parliament and of the Council
 of 11 May 2016 on the European Union Agency for Law Enforcement
 Cooperation (Europol) and replacing and repealing Council
 Decisions 2009/371/JHA, 2009/934/JHA, 2009/935/JHA, 2009/936/JHA
 and 2009/968/JHA [2016] OJ L135/53 ....60, 218
Regulation (EU) 2018/1725 of the European Parliament and of the Council
 of 23 October 2018 on the protection of natural persons with regard to the
 processing of personal data by the Union institutions, bodies, offices and
 agencies and on the free movement of such data, and repealing
 Regulation (EC) No 45/2001 and Decision No 1247/2002/EC
 [2018] OJ L295/39 .... 101, 111, 247, 251, 253–54
Regulation (EU) 2019/517 of the European Parliament and Council
 of 19 March 2019 on the implementation and functioning of the .eu
 top-level domain name and amending and repealing Regulation (EC)
 No 733/2002 and repealing Commission Regulation (EC) No 874/2004
 [2019] OJ L91/25 ....56, 255
Regulation (EU) 2019/881 of the European Parliament and of the Council
 of 17 April 2019 on ENISA (the European Union Agency for Cybersecurity)
 and on information and communications technology cybersecurity
 certification and repealing Regulation (EU) No 526/2013
 (Cybersecurity Act) [2019] OJ L151/15 .... 54, 56, 145, 157,
 160–62, 164–66, 168–71,
 173, 176–78, 181, 245
Regulation (EU) 2021/1232 of the European Parliament and of the Council
 of 14 July 2021 on a temporary derogation from certain provisions of
 Directive 2002/58/EC as regards the use of technologies by providers
 of number-independent interpersonal communications services for the
 processing of personal and other data for the purpose of combating
 online child sexual abuse [2021] OJ L274/41 .... 60, 211–17, 230–31, 233
Regulation (EU) 2021/784 of the European Parliament and of the Council
 of 29 April 2021 on addressing the dissemination of terrorist content
 online [2021] OJ L172/79 .... 60, 216, 230

Regulation (EU) 2021/821 of the European Parliament and of the Council
of 20 May 2021 setting up a Union regime for the control of exports,
brokering, technical assistance, transit and transfer of dual-use
items (recast) [2019] OJ L206/1 (Dual-use Regulation) 65, 241, 245,
254–55, 257
Regulation (EU) 2022/868 of the European Parliament and of the Council
of 30 May 2022 on European data governance and amending
Regulation (EU) 2018/1724 (Data Governance Act) [2022] OJ L152/1 .... 4, 56,
177, 267
Regulation (EU) 2022/2065 of the European Parliament and of the Council
on a Single Market For Digital Services (Digital Services Act)
[2022] OJ L277/1 .... 56, 217
Regulation (EU) 526/2013 of the European Parliament and the Council
of 21 May 2013 concerning the European Union Agency for Network and
Information Security (ENISA) and repealing regulation (EC) No 460/2004
[2013] OJ L165/41 (repealed) 165
Regulation (EU) 910/2014 of 23 July 2014 on electronic identification and trust
services for electronic transactions in the internal market and repealing
Directive 1999/93/EC [2014] OJ L257/73 .... 56, 157, 160–62, 164–67,
170–71, 173–76, 211
Regulation (EU) 1025/2012 of 25 October 2012 on European standardisation,
amending Council Directives 89/686/EEC and 93/15/EEC and
Directives 94/9/EC, 94/25/EC, 95/16/EC, 97/23/EC, 98/34/EC, 2004/22/EC,
2007/23/EC, 2009/23/EC and 2009/105/EC of the European Parliament
and of the Council and repealing Council Decision 87/95/EEC and
Decision No 1673/2006/EC of the European Parliament and of the
Council [2012] OJ L316/12 .... 143, 146–47,
180–81, 263–64
Regulation 45/2001/EC of the European Parliament and of the Council
of 18 December 2000 on the Protection of Individuals with regard to the
Processing of Personal data by the Community institutions and Bodies
and on the Free Movement of such Data [2001] OJ L8/1 .... 99–101, 251

European Union Bills and Drafts

Council, Regulation on Privacy and Electronic Communications
2017/0003(COD). Mandate for negotiations with EP, 6087/21 (2021) 78, 174
European Commission, 'Proposal for a Regulation amending Regulation (EU)
No 910/2014 as regards establishing a framework for a European Digital
Identity' COM (2021) 281 ....160, 175
——, 'Proposal for a Regulation of the European Parliament and of the Council
on the Protection of Individuals with Regard to the Processing of Personal
Data and on the Free Movement of such Data (General Data Protection
Regulation)' COM (2012) 11 final 114

——, 'Proposal for a Directive on combating terrorism and replacing
    Council Framework Decision 2002/475/JHA on combating terrorism'
    COM (2015) 625 final..216
——, 'Proposal for a Regulation of the European Parliament and of the Council
    concerning the respect for private life and the protection of personal
    data in electronic communications and repealing Directive 2002/58/EC
    (Regulation on Privacy and Electronic Communications)'
    COM (2017) 10 final.. 69, 101, 160,
——, 'Proposal for a Regulation on European Production and Preservation
    Orders for electronic evidence in criminal matters'
    COM (2018) 225 final... 60, 220, 226–27, 230, 245
——, 'Proposal for a Directive laying down harmonised rules on the
    appointment of legal representatives for the purpose of gathering evidence
    in criminal proceedings' COM (2018) 226 final 60, 220
——, 'Proposal for a Directive of the European Parliament and of the
    Council on measures for a high common level of cybersecurity across
    the Union, repealing Directive (EU) 2016/1148'
    COM (2020) 823 final.. 160, 175–76, 178, 193
——, 'Proposal for a Regulation of the European Parliament and of the
    Council on contestable and fair markets in the digital sector
    (Digital Markets Act)' COM (2020) 842 final 267
——, 'Proposal for a Regulation amending Regulation (EU) No 910/2014
    as regards establishing a framework for a European Digital Identity'
    COM (2021) 281 final... 175, 211
——, 'Proposal for a Regulation of the European Parliament and of the
    Council laying down harmonised rules on Artificial Intelligence (AI Act)
    and amending certain Union legislative acts' COM (2021) 206 final 4, 267
——, 'Proposal for a Regulation on general product safety, amending
    Regulation (EU) No 1025/2012 of the European Parliament and of the Council,
    and repealing Council Directive 87/357/EEC and Directive 2001/95/EC of the
    European Parliament and of the Council' COM (2021) 346 final 151
——, 'Proposal for a Regulation amending Regulation (EU) No 1025/2012 as regards
    the decisions of European standardisation organisations concerning European
    standards and European standardisation deliverables' COM (2022) 32 final........ 149
——, 'Proposal for a Directive on liability for Defective Products'
    COM (2022) 495 final..55
European Parliament and Council, 'Political Agreement on the NIS 2 Directive,
    10193/22 (17 June 2022)'... 175

Other

Organisation for Economic Cooperation and Development, *Recommendation
    on Guidelines for the Security of Information and Networks. Towards a Culture
    of Security* (2002) 46, 110

xxx   Table of Legislation

——, *OECD Council Recommendation on Principles for Internet Policy Making* (2011).. 142
——, Recommendation of the Council Concerning Guidelines Governing the Protection of Privacy and Transborder Flows of Personal Data, C(80)58/FINAL, as amended on 11 July 2013 by C(2013)79................................. 102
Organisation for Security and Cooperation in Europe, Permanent Council Decision No 1106 on the initial set of OSCE confidence-building measures to reduce the risks of conflict stemming from the use of information and communication technologies of 3 December 2013 63
The Wassenaar Agreement on Export Controls for Conventional Arms and Dual-Use Goods and Technologies 255

Standards

International Telecommunication Union (ITU-T), *Requirements for deep packet inspection in next generation networks, Recommendation ITU-T Y.2770* (2012)... 182
——, *Recommendation X.1205. Overview of Cybersecurity* (2008)........................... 13
International Telecommunication Union (ITU) and International Organization for Standarization (ISO), *International Standard ISO/IEC 17788, Information Technology – Cloud computing – Overview and vocabulary, Recommendation ITU/T Y.3500* (International Telecommunications Union 2014) 41
Internet Engineering Task Force (IETF), *Internet Security Glossary, v.2. Request for Comments (RFC) 4949* (2007) 139
——, *Pervasive Monitoring Is an Attack. Request for Comments (RFC) 7258* (2014)..236
——, *Privacy Considerations for Internet Protocols. Request for Comments (RFC) 6973* (2022).. 131

United Nations

General Assembly, 'UNCITRAL Model Law on Electronic Commerce. Resolution A/51/628'... 143
——, 'Universal Declaration of Human Rights (UDHR). Resolution 217', 10 December 1948...70
International Covenant on Civil and Political Rights, I-14668, UNTS No 999 (ICCPR)..69–71, 77–81, 84, 86, 89, 111, 139

Introduction

When I first began the research for the thesis on which this book is based, 'cybersecurity' was not a term of current use in European Union (EU) law. Notwithstanding the fact that a Member State had already suffered from a debilitating cyber-attack,[1] the attention of Union institutions and Member States was focused on the long tail of the war on terror, migration and the unravelling of the global economic order. My research then was motivated by the desire to think outside of zero-sum frameworks and investigate the possibility of reconciling cybersecurity, privacy and data protection in EU law, on account of their importance to human flourishing, autonomy and the maintenance of democratic societies.

It did not take long, however, for the security of network and information systems to gain political relevance. A succession of 'revelations', including the uncovering of mass surveillance by Edward Snowden and disclosures of electoral interference,[2] exposed how our societies have become dependent on vulnerable cyberspace and its infrastructure, to the detriment of human flourishing, autonomy and democracy, as presciently argued by early cyberspace scholars.[3]

In the space of a decade, cybersecurity has taken centre stage, inspiring a spate of legislative initiatives that cut across markets, law enforcement, defence and diplomacy, initiatives that are placed under constant pressure by the pace of technological change and frequent revelations of mass surveillance. At the time of writing, the attention of legislators is on the use of Pegasus spyware, a malicious software capable of silently self-installing on smartphones and used for spying on journalists and politicians in Europe and elsewhere.[4] Against this background, reconciling cybersecurity, privacy and data protection ('the triad') becomes an imperative; the challenge though is to understand 'how'.

---

[1] S Brenner, *Cyberthreats and the Decline of the Nation-state* (London, Routledge, 2014) 18–21, 75–87.

[2] See generally European Parliament, *LIBE Committee Inquiry on the Electronic Mass Surveillance of EU Citizens: Protecting Fundamental Rights in a Digital Age. Proceedings, Outcome and Background Documents* (2014); RRsC Mueller, *Report on the Investigation into Russian Interference in the 2016 Presidential Election. Submitted Pursuant to 28 C.F.R. § 600.8(c)* (2019); Information Commissioner's Office, *Investigation into the use of Data Analytics in Political Campaigns. A Report to Parliament* (2018).

[3] In 1999, Wertheim wondered if, 'rather than bringing to mind the new Jerusalem … cyberspace will be more like a new Gomorrah'. M Wertheim, *The Pearly Gates of Cyberspace. A History of Space from Dante to the Internet* (New York, WW Norton & Company Inc. 1999) 298. See especially G Giacomello, *National Governments and Control of the Internet. A Digital Challenge* (London, Routledge, 2005); M Dunn, 'Securing the Digital Age. The Challenges of Complexity for Critical Infrastructure Protection and IR theory', in J Eriksson and G Giacomello (eds), *International Relations in the Digital Age* (London, Routledge, 2007).

[4] Decision (EU) 2022/480 of the European Parliament setting up a committee of inquiry to investigate the use of the Pegasus and equivalent surveillance spyware, and defining the subject of the inquiry, as well as the responsibilities, numerical strength and term of office of the committee [2022] OJ L98/22.

Introduction

With this book I investigate how cybersecurity, privacy and data protection can be reconciled in EU law. This is no easy task. The shockwaves caused by multiple revelations laid bare the ambiguous nature of their relationship which can simultaneously clash and converge, creating a complex web of interactions that unfold in markets, policing, defence and diplomacy and are permeable to geopolitical and economic dynamics. A testament to the Internet's global nature is that the security of network and information technologies has become part and parcel of the relationship between states and other relevant actors.

The potential for contradictory approaches is inherent in policy areas which harbour different values,[5] creating domino effects in their interaction. While this investigation is supported by the abundance of sectoral literature on cybersecurity and its different dimensions, EU law and its main areas of policymaking as well as privacy and data protection, there are no works that investigate their interplay across EU law. The research challenge I take on in this book is standing on the shoulders of giants to distinguish the trends that influence such a relationship and formulate a framework to investigate the triad's modes of co-existence. As such, I do not build on a single interpretive framework, but rather select additional literatures on human rights, international relations, law and technology, policymaking and regulation that help my appraisal of the relationship of the triad.

I. Investigating the Relationship of the Triad

How are cybersecurity, privacy and data protection reconciled in EU law? To investigate the ambiguous relationship of the triad, I construct a conceptual axis, shown in Figure 1, ranging from no to complete reconciliation, and represented by five relational modes.

Figure 1 Modes of reconciliation of cybersecurity, privacy and data protection (the triad)

		Reconciliation		
None	**Weak**		**Strong**	**Complete**
<-->				
	Clash	*Indifference* (non-interference)	*Complementarity*	
Zero-sum	Balancing		Convergence	Overlap

To the far right is strong reconciliation underscored by complementarity. 'Overlap' expresses the idea that cybersecurity, privacy and data protection are different facets of the same thing, thereby enjoying complete reconciliation. 'Convergence' points to the triad's shared goals and therefore underscores synergy and complementarity. To the far

---

[5] Cybersecurity is often looked at as a 'wicked problem'. CW Churchman, 'Wicked problems' 14 Management Science Guest Editorial; EF Malone and MJ Malone, 'The "wicked problem" of Cybersecurity Policy: Analysis of United States and Canadian Policy Response' (2013) 19 *Canadian Foreign Policy Journal* 158–177.

left is weak reconciliation underscored by clashes. 'Zero-sum' expresses the irreconcilability of the triad, while 'balancing' refers to the method of adjudication incorporated in the permissible limitations test characterising a mode of co-existence in which something has to give. An in-between state classed as 'indifference' points to reciprocal non-interference.

Throughout the book, I formulate an analytical framework to explore such modes of reconciliation, investigate whether one prevails over the others, and how desired forms of reconciliation can be achieved in EU law. The analytical framework is premised on the argument that cybersecurity, privacy and data protection are situated techno-legal objects. 'Techno-legal' reflects the reality of cybersecurity, privacy and data protection as being more than legal objects: the triad shares a common technological denominator comprising signals, data and information – and the infrastructure holding them – conjuring up cyberspace. Different technological designs have a bearing on the values expressed by the triad and thus their legal configuration. 'Situated' means within a jurisdiction, which for this book is the EU.

Thus, through a situated techno-legal analysis I explore: (i) cybersecurity, privacy and data protection as techno-legal objects within the EU constitutional architecture or *ordre public* underpinned by the rule of law (RoL) and the EU multilevel system of protection of human rights; (ii) the values the triad expresses; and (iii) the concrete substantiation of the triad across the Digital Single Market (DSM), the Area of Freedom, Security and Justice (AFSJ) and External Action (EA), mindful of the logics that govern these areas of EU law.

To analyse the concrete substantiation of the triad means to look at it along three axes: policy, law and technology. The analysis of EU law is carried out on a doctrinal plane and at two levels of abstraction: the applicable laws (higher level) and their implementation (lower level), which creates a bridge with technology. Here technology is looked at through the eyes of the jurist, as a regulatory object.

To evaluate the significance of each mode of reconciliation, I make use of different interpretive prisms. Zero-sum clashes will be examined through the lense of trade-off models developed in defence of the war on terror; the rule of law (RoL) will provide a framework rejecting zero-sum outcomes and supporting instead weak and strong reconciliation; and a techno-legal analysis will help investigating overlaps. In a techno-legal analysis, the architecture of rights, including the concept of the essence, can and should be used to understand whether the values imbued in technology and in rights are commensurable, as well as to expose areas of interdependence and of tension.

By bridging separate bodies of research, I produce key analytical mechanisms to gauge the theoretical relevance and weigh the practical feasibility of each mode of reconciliation. Thus, the disappearance or better the 'effacement of technology' from technology law effected by the regulatory ecosystem helps explain the hiatus between the mode of reconciliation of the triad drawn from the applicable law and from its technological implementation. Distinguishing between the letter of the law and its technological implementation also brings to the fore the limitations of the examination of technology as a regulatory object. The hiatus cannot be bridged at present because of the 'indeterminacy loop', whereby decisions by supranational courts reinforce the effacement of technology, and thus the hiatus.

The relevance of these findings cuts across the DSM, AFSJ and EA because of the 'functional interconnection' of relevant legislation as to substance (substantive interconnection) and procedure (procedural interconnection), which vindicate the choice of a non-sectoral analysis. In each area of decision-making, the effacement of technology takes on a different shape, reaching a climax in the EA, where it calls into question the reach of the EU's normative power.

My analysis shows that no mode of reconciliation is actively precluded, although some modes are more likely than others. Overlaps are possible in theory but highly difficult to achieve in practice: we cannot have it all. Indifference is a rare occurrence in light of the legislative frameworks selected for analysis, although the inclusion of peripheral legislation could possibly change this outcome. In some areas of interaction in the DSM and AFSJ, strong reconciliation seems possible. However, this outcome is frustrated in practice by technology effacement and procedural interconnection. The most likely outcome is weak reconciliation. Although this may not come as a surprise, what the analysis shows is that, by systematically removing technology from the law, zero-sum outcomes that are repugnant to EU law also become a possibility.

In conclusion, the book is a cry for policymakers and society to take technology law seriously and undertake corrective actions in support of human flourishing, autonomy and democracy. The book does not offer immediate solutions to the problem: there are no silver bullets that will strongly reconcile the triad. The doctoral thesis on which this book is based proposed a procedure for selecting permissible technologies that could maximise reconciliation on foot of a techno-legal analysis.[6] Such a procedure exposes conflicting values forcing decision-makers to prioritise some values over others. Thus, any method aiming to achieve high levels of reconciliation will only work if and when the role of technology will be made explicit in the applicable law and in court. As such, the book hopes to point to areas where solutions may be found.

Before proceeding to illustrate the contents of the book, I must spell out its limitations. Although I did my best to understand and engage with the work of engineers and computer scientists, a one-sided analysis is fraught with dangers and carries obvious limitations. The silver lining is that any inaccuracies this work may contain reinforce the overall message of the research: we can no longer ignore the role of technology in shaping the law and swaying it towards goals often far removed from those intended.

A second limitation is that, for methodological reasons, the main legislative frameworks analysed in this book are those that came into force no later than the end of 2021. In the interim, additional relevant legislation has been proposed[7] or adopted[8] as part of

---

[6] MG Porcedda, Cybersecurity and Privacy Rights in EU law. Moving Beyond the Trade-off Model to Appraise the Role of Technology (European University Institute, 2017), ch 8 and conclusions.

[7] See, eg, European Commission, 'Proposal for a Directive of the European Parliament and of the Council on the resilience of critical entities' (Communication) COM (2020) 829 final; European Commission, 'Proposal for a Regulation of the European Parliament and of the Council laying down harmonised rules on Artificial Intelligence (AI Act) and amending certain Union legislative acts' (Communication) COM (2021) 206 final; European Commission, 'Proposal for a Regulation on horizontal cybersecurity requirements for products with digital elements and amending Regulation (EU) 2019/1020 (Cyber Resilience Act)' (Communication) COM (2022) 454 final.

[8] See, eg, Regulation (EU) 2022/1925 of the European Parliament and of the Council on contestable and fair markets in the digital sector and amending Directives (EU) 2019/1937 and (EU) 2020/1828 (Digital Markets Act) OJ L 265; Regulation (EU) 2022/868 of the European Parliament and of the Council on European Data Governance and amending Regulation (EU) 2018/1724 (Data Governance Act) OJ L 152/1.

the EU strategies for cybersecurity, for data and of the digital agendas[9] and it will be for future research to appraise whether the outcomes of this analysis hold true in light of the resulting rules. The same is true for proving the conclusions of the analysis, which would necessitate empirical research.

Finally, and due to the scope of the study, a number of relevant paradigms and literatures could only be mentioned in passing; I tried to forge the path ahead in the conclusions. Ultimately, the investigation of the 'how' of reconciliation raises pressing questions as to the 'why' of actual outcomes. Only by understanding why some outcomes take precedence over the others and whether such mechanisms are a given, will it become possible to gauge the options available for change.

II. Plan of the Book

The book is divided into two parts. Part one includes the analytical framework and the analysis of the policy and law of cybersecurity, privacy and data protection taken individually. Chapter one introduces cybersecurity, privacy and data protection and explains why the triad can simultaneously both clash and converge. It develops the analytical framework for the analysis of the triad and, after showing that zero-sum outcomes are repugnant to EU law, identifies the elements of the EU *ordre public* relevant for the analysis, with a special focus on fundamental rights endowed with the essence and proportionality. Chapter two appraises the evolution of the EU's cybersecurity policy and examines the main dimensions of cybersecurity as they unfold in the DSM, the AFSJ and the EA, thereby identifying legal frameworks to be analysed in the second part of the book.

Chapters three and four address privacy and data protection separately. Each chapter analyses the scope of the right in EU law with a view to identifying the essential components of the rights, as well as reflecting on their essence. The findings, presented in analytical tables, are preliminary to the techno-legal analysis carried out in chapter five.

Part two of the book addresses the role of technology and includes the analysis of the triad in the DSM, AFSJ and EA. Chapter five contains a techno-legal analysis of the triad, founded on technical threat modelling and the understanding of rights as endowed with essential components and essence, to investigate interconnections and overlaps. Although theoretically possible, overlaps cannot be demonstrated in practice on account of the characteristics of the regulatory ecosystem. By reasoning on the concepts of 'technology neutrality', 'by design', 'state of the art' and standards I develop the analytical devices of the 'effacement of technology' and the 'indeterminacy loop'.

Chapters six to eight address the interplay of the triad in the DSM, AFSJ and EA respectively. Each investigates the mode of reconciliation of the triad effected by

---

[9] European Commission and High Representative of the European Union for Foreign Affairs and Security Policy, 'The EU's Cybersecurity Strategy for the Digital Decade' (Joint Communication) JOIN (2020) 18 final; European Commission, 'A European Strategy for Data' (Communication) COM (2020) 66 final; European Commission, 'A Europe fit for digital age. Shaping Europe's digital future' (Communication) COM (2020) 67 final; European Commission, '2030 Digital Compass: the European way for the Digital Decade' (Communication) COM (2021) 118 final.

policy, key legislative instruments and their implementation (high level and low level of abstraction) and technology. Although it is only possible to properly compare and contrast instruments in the DSM, for the sake of consistency legislative instruments across the three EU areas of decision-making are analysed along the following lines: definitions and scope, notion of security, presence of information security properties, explicit cross-references to other instruments, logics as well as legal devices put in place to achieve the instrument's goals. In the three chapters, technology is analysed as being at once part and parcel of the implementation of the applicable law as well as a regulatory target. The analysis of packet inspection techniques, relevant across the three areas of EU decision-making, helps to show both the limits of a techno-legal analysis in an ecosystem of technology effacement, as well as the perverse effects of such a disappearance, which could effect zero-sum games between cybersecurity, privacy and data protection. The conclusions sum up the arguments of the book and contain the seeds for future research. The law is correct as stated as of 30 June 2022.

PART 1

Introducing Cybersecurity, Privacy and Data Protection Law and their Interplay

1

Cybersecurity, Privacy and Data Protection: An Analytical Framework

This chapter introduces the analytical framework for the relationship between cybersecurity, privacy and data protection (the triad) in EU law, which I use and develop in forthcoming chapters. I begin by introducing the genesis and salient features of cybersecurity, privacy and data protection (I.A).

I then reflect on the ambivalent relationship of the triad (I.B). Revelations of mass-scale surveillance illustrate the triad's simultaneous clash and complementarity (I.B.i). I situate such an ambivalent relationship by drawing attention to the triad's shared technological environment of cyberspace, where information flows in the shape of data and signals (I.B.ii). Such an environment is open-ended, in that it equally caters to legitimate and illegitimate activities, thus bearing business and evidential significance. The unclear conceptual boundary between data, information and signals is reflected in legislation, thresholds for evidential (and business) access to data are not clearly delineated, making it possible, de facto and de jure, for data protection and privacy to be both pitted against security through cyberspace, while also being complementary to the security of cyberspace.

To study the relationship of the triad, I develop a conceptual framework placing clash and complementarity along a continuum ranging from none to complete reconciliation, through the guise of 'zero-sum' relation and overlap (I.C). Starting from zero-sum outcomes, I critique a theoretical model born out of the 'war on terror' to question the desirability of zero-sum outcomes and establish elements for an analytical framework to study the triad's relationship in EU law. Accordingly, I reconstruct cybersecurity, privacy and data protection as legally situated objects constrained by the EU *ordre public*, using the analysis of concrete policies cognisant of the role of technology.

I then trace the contours of the EU *ordre public* (II.A) and argue that the constitutional architecture of the EU, informed by the rule of law (RoL) and general principles stands against a zero-sum relation between security and rights, including cybersecurity, privacy and data protection. Rather, the constitutional architecture strives for reconciliation informed by proportionality and a desire for coherence. However, this constitutional architecture falls short of defining how to articulate the relationship between security and rights, which is instead left to hierarchically lower legal sources.

Turning to these lower sources to identify modes of reconciliation between cybersecurity, privacy and data protection as situated techno-legal objects of enquiry, I study the triad through EU policy, law and technology, where the latter is understood as a regulatory object (II.B). Interactions are conceptualised in particular in the Digital Single

Market (DSM), Area of Freedom, Security and Justice (AFSJ) and External Action (EA). By so doing, I argue that we must take into account the features and limitations of such areas of EU decision-making as they result from the Union's historical developments, hence contemplating the possibility that the triad may be reconcilable in theory but not in practice.

I. Studying the Relationship between Cybersecurity, Privacy and Data Protection

This section provides an introduction to cybersecurity, privacy and data protection, preliminary to separate analyses in chapters two–four (I.A). To illustrate the triad's ambivalent relationship (I.B), I look back at the lessons learnt from the revelations of Edward Snowden. Although surveillance per se is not the focus of this work, and Snowden's revelations are neither the first nor the last of their kind,[1] they help illustrate the triad's ambivalent relationship by showing how 'cyber' security can clash with privacy and data protection, whereas responses to the revelations demonstrate how the triad can be complementary (I.B.i). I then explain such an ambivalent relationship through the triad's common building blocks – cyberspace, information and data – which bring to surface the importance to the relationship of both techno-legal constructs and competing notions of security (I.B.ii). I conclude by developing a framework to conceptualise the relationship of the triad along an axis ranging from strong reconciliation to weak, which at one extreme takes the form of a zero-sum clash (I.C). Reflecting on a trade-off theory that enables zero-sum outcomes, I identify elements for an analytical framework to study the triad.

A. Introducing Cybersecurity, Privacy and Data Protection (the Triad)

Cybersecurity builds on computer security, comprised of systems and information security,[2] but has come to acquire a much broader meaning. Although computer security is a narrower concept, a short excursus can help grasping the main features of cybersecurity. Yost explains that in the early days of bulky mainframes housed in secure compounds, computer security was a branch of physical security reflecting the 'bodily'

---

[1] Eg, ECHELON, a global system for intercepting communications, now called FORNSAT. European Parliament, LIBE Secretariat, *Background Note. The European Parliament's temporary committee on the ECHELON interception system* (2014). Currently see 'The Pegasus project' *The Guardian* (2022) www.theguardian.com/news/series/pegasus-project; Decision (EU) 2022/480 of the European Parliament setting up a committee of inquiry to investigate the use of the Pegasus and equivalent surveillance spyware, and defining the subject of the inquiry, as well as the responsibilities, numerical strength and term of office of the committee [2022] OJ L98/72.

[2] D Herrmann and H Pridöhl, 'Basic Concepts and Models of Cybersecurity', in M Christen *The Ethics of Cybersecurity* (Cham, Springer, 2020) 12.

nature of threats – trespassing, sabotage and interception of emissions. The introduction of time-sharing, viz. pooling computing resources among multiple users, enabled new threats to information security that led US governmental authorities to enlist researchers in the search for computer security standards, including encryption, as well as techniques to certify such standards.[3]

Computer security experts understood security as 'techniques that control who may use or modify the computer or the information contained in it',[4] where 'control' could serve different purposes. For the military, the goal was securing the confidentiality of information according to military classifications of secrecy, while for businesses the aim was to secure the integrity of company-related information;[5] such different understanding of 'control' would be at the heart of clashes over encryption.[6] Research and practice led to the identification and loose codification of principles of information protection, such as 'confidentiality, integrity and availability' (CIA), followed by authentication, authenticity and non-repudiation, principles[7] which will be discussed at length in this book.

Early expert reports warned that abstaining from using unsecure environments would preclude the learning necessary to secure devices.[8] In interpreting such an approach, we must be cognisant of historical factors. Of special importance was the awareness that risk-aversion could undermine the competition for leadership over 'high-tech' products at a time when the Soviet Union, Europe and especially Japan threatened US dominance,[9] an awareness informing what McDermott called '*laissez innover*' approaches.[10] Member States of the then European Economic Community quickly lost terrain owing to their inability, or unwillingness, to pool the resources necessary to close the 'tech gap', understood as a state of 'falling behind' the technological progress of competitors and therefore being subject to the extraction of 'tributes'.[11]

The decision not to hamper unsecure environments arguably paved the way to the development of affordable computing and to networking thanks to the parallel development of computer networks through packet switching delivered with the TCP/IP protocols. Among others, DeNardis recalls that 'reliability, availability and performance were the primary concerns for [internet protocols], not security'.[12] The Internet's early security was rather a by-product of the lack of interoperability between networks.

---

[3] JR Yost, 'A History of Computer Security Standards', in KMM de Leeuwet et al. (eds), *The History of Information Security* (Oxford, Elsevier Science, 2007).
[4] JH Saltzer and MD Schroeder, 'The Protection of Information in Computer Systems' 63 *Proceedings of the IEEE* 1278–1308, 1280.
[5] Yost (n 3).
[6] See chs 2 and 7.
[7] Saltzer and Schroeder (n 4); RE Smith, 'A Contemporary Look at Saltzer and Schroeder's 1975 Design Principles' 10 *IEEE Security & Privacy* 20–25.
[8] Yost (n 3).
[9] OECD, *Gaps in Technology, Analytical Report* (1970); M Borrus and J Zysman, 'Industrial Competitiveness and American National Security', in Sandholtz et al. (eds), *The Highest Stakes. The Economic Foundations of the Next Security System* (Oxford, Oxford University Press, 1992) 9.
[10] J McDermott, 'A Special Supplement: Technology – the opiate of the intellectuals', *The New York Review*.
[11] Borrus and Zysman (n 9) 9.
[12] L DeNardis, 'A History of Internet Security', in KMM de Leeuwet et al. (eds), *The History of Information Security* (Oxford, Elsevier Science, 2007) 682.

12 *Cybersecurity, Privacy and Data Protection: An Analytical Framework*

Greater uptake of technology also offered opportunities for international collaboration for the development of governmental standards[13] under the aegis of the International Standardisation Organisation (ISO) and the International Telecommunication Union (ITU). Both provide definitions for CIA principles and elements of cybersecurity. However, governments were soon side lined, with standards increasingly developed autonomously by the marketplace.[14] Leading security products created 'some degree of standardisation', while also fostering the realisation that 'no product or system is impenetrable'.[15] Again, in interpreting such an approach we must be aware of historical trends and I would argue that here computer security met the rampant new trend of (multi-stakeholder) 'governance'.[16]

With this premise, inter-networking could hardly be secure at its inception, let alone after the exponential growth of networks[17] following the privatisation of the Internet at the end of the Cold War, the creation of the HTTP protocol and the World Wide Web (3W) in the early 1990s and extant escalating data flows. It was the 3W that gave depth to cyberspace, the security of which is the aim of cybersecurity. With high profile cyber incidents drawing headlines in the media since 'Black Thursday' in 1988,[18] resilience – ie quickly recovering from the aftershocks of attacks – would become the realistic governing motto of cybersecurity.

The increasing importance of networked information technologies, known as Critical Information Infrastructure (CII) to the services necessary for the functioning of society, aka Critical Infrastructure (CI), pushed computer security from the periphery to the centre of security concerns. A notable body of scholarship has studied whether cybersecurity is securitised, that is, presented as essential to the survival of the nation state.[19]

Against this background, cybersecurity goes beyond computer security's 'access control' to reflect the complexity of cyberspace as the intersection between critical (information) infrastructure and human activity,[20] enabling data flows that play a strategic role in a multipolar global order underpinned by a long-lasting trend of *laissez innover*. ITU members have agreed on the following definition

> Cybersecurity is the collection of tools, policies, security concepts, security safeguards, guidelines, risk management approaches, actions, training, best practices, assurance and

---

[13] Yost (n 3).
[14] ibid.
[15] ibid 619.
[16] S Borrás and J Edler (eds), *The Governance of Socio-Technical Systems. Explaining Change* (Cheltenham, Edward Elgar, 2014).
[17] BM Leiner, VG Cerf et al., 'A Brief History of the Internet version 3.2' (*Arxiv.org*, 1997) arxiv.org/html/cs/9901011. www.internetsociety.org/internet/history-internet/brief-history-internet/.
[18] Ie the Morris Worm, L DeNardis, 'The Internet Design Tension between Surveillance and Security' 37 *IEEE Annals of the History of Computing* 72–83, 683; S Landau, *Listening In. Cybersecurity in an Insecure Age* (Yale University Press 2017).
[19] B Buzan and O Weaver et al, *Security: a New Framework for Analysis* (Boulder, CO, Lynne Rienner, 1998); H Nissenbaum and L Hansen, 'Digital Disaster, Cyber Security, and the Copenhagen School' (2009) 53 *International Studies Quarterly* 1155; M Dunn Cavelty, 'From Cyber-Bombs to Political Fallout: Threat Representations with an Impact in the Cyber-Security Discourse' 15 *International Studies Review* 105.
[20] Dunn Cavelty (19); R Ottis and P Lorents, 'Cyberspace: Definitions and Implications' (Proceedings of the 5th International Conference on Information Warfare and Security, ICIW). R Mattioli, 'The 'State(s)' of cybersecurity' in G Giacomello (ed), *Security in Cyberspace* (London, Bloomsbury, 2014).

technologies that can be used to protect the cyber environment and organization and user's assets. Organization and user's assets include connected computing devices, personnel, infrastructure, applications, services, telecommunications systems, and the totality of transmitted and/or stored information in the cyber environment. Cybersecurity strives to ensure the attainment and maintenance of the security properties of the organization and user's assets against relevant security risks in the cyber environment.[21]

The breadth of this definition points to the ability of cybersecurity to accommodate many understandings of security within 'the cyber environment', beyond the original military and business objectives and for 'organisation and user's assets' to reflect political and economic preferences, to the detriment of international consensus on minimum security standards.[22]

A question remains as to whether cybersecurity is a right and, if so, whence it derives. A seminal German Federal Constitutional Court judgment acknowledged the existence of a right to integrity and confidentiality drawn from the right to dignity.[23] Shackelford suggests a right to cybersecurity may be elaborated building on corporate social responsibility and due diligence movements.[24] However, there is no consensus on this point.

In sum, cybersecurity's historically situated military and business origins have crystallised in a number of features: a favouring towards innovation over security, which is only applied ex post; consequently, preference for resilience premised on a risk-based approach; the provision of security standards within a logic of private or multi-stakeholder governance; and open-ended understanding of 'controls' and security serving multiple uses of the cyber environment.

'Privacy' is an umbrella term,[25] as is data protection. Both exist morally as enablers of the development and preservation of one's personality and identity in autonomy; in a legal sense, they are facets of dignity highly prized in a democracy to which autonomous individuals contribute. As Westin[26] noted, it is when rights' main features are both enhanced and threatened that they become cherished values requiring legal protection. Elsewhere I have built on Taylor and Arendt's work on late modernity and Westin and Arendt's work on intimacy to develop a law and society approach to privacy and data protection, following in the steps of Bobbio and Pugliese, aimed at unearthing the societal, cultural and technological factors that enhanced and threatened both privacy and personal data, thereby paving the way to the legal formulation of both rights.[27]

---

[21] ITU-T, *Recommendation X.1205. Overview of Cybersecurity* (2008).
[22] See chs 7–8.
[23] BVerfG, Judgment of the First Senate of 27 February 2008, 1 BvR 370/07, DE:BVerfG:2008:rs20080227. 1bvr037007 (German Bundesverfassungsgericht (Federal Constitutional Court)) paras 164–287.
[24] SJ Shackelford, 'Should Cybersecurity Be a Human Right? Exploring the 'Shared Responsibility' of Cyber Peace' (2017) 55 *Stanford Journal of International Law* 155–184.
[25] D Solove, "I've Got Nothing to Hide' and Other Misunderstandings of Privacy' (2007) 44 *San Diego Law Review* 745. Arguing 'personal identity' should be the umbrella term: N Andrade, 'The Right to Personal Identity in the Information Age. A reappraisal of a lost right' (PhD thesis, European University Institute, 2011).
[26] A Westin, *Privacy and Freedom* (Atheneum Press 1967).
[27] MG Porcedda, 'The Recrudescence of 'Security v. Privacy' after the 2015 Terrorist Attacks, and the Value of 'Privacy Rights' in the European Union', in E Orrù et al. (eds), *Rethinking Surveillance and Control Beyond the "security versus privacy" Debate* (Baden-Baden, Nomos, 2017). Building on: C Taylor, *Sources of the Self. The Making of the Modern Identity* (Cambridge, Cambridge University Press, 1989); *The Ethics of Authenticity* (Cambridge, MA, Harvard University Press, 1992); H Arendt, 'Freedom and Politics: a Lecture' (1960) 14

Privacy embraces an intermix of personality, reserve, intimacy and sociality – even societal surveillance as a mechanism to enforce norms.[28] Patterns of such intermix are expressed in different forms in all cultures of the world at individual, household and community level.[29] Actually, intimacy is a quintessentially animal need, a distance-setting mechanism to reproduce, breed, play and learn used in a dialectic manner with sociality,[30] understood as the desire for stimulation by fellows. Reserve and intimacy enable the development of one's personality by making sense of the different roles played by the individual in a community[31] and the safeguarding of one's social status. Intimacy and reserve enjoyed in private help maintain consistency among the roles played in the face of change, giving sense to one's biography.[32]

Societal appreciation of privacy predates contemporary ICTs as illustrated by Samuel Warren and Louis Brandeis' famous article,[33] inspired by the relentless intrusion into Warren's family life by the paparazzi of the time.[34] As the nascent technology of photography was sparking legal recognition of the right to one's image, Warren and Brandeis proposed that written accounts, as detailed and revealing as a picture, should similarly benefit from the protection of the law. Under the surface of 'the right to be let alone' subsumed under tort law,[35] Warren and Brandeis looked at privacy as 'a right to personality' or identity: the expression of one's life, such as emotions, sentiments, facts of life, happenings, actions, sexual life and relationships with others. It took the horrors of World War II (WWII) to consolidate national and develop international instruments protecting privacy as we know it today: an ensemble of private life, family life, home and communications.

As for data protection, scholarship typically points to the consolidation of nation states and population censuses as the first challenges to the protection of personal data, even though it was only the expansion of computing and early networking that sparked legal conversations on the need to protect data at rest and data flows. One wonders the extent to which memories of WWII influenced legislators.[36] In this respect, data protection concerns developed in parallel to cybersecurity and were affected by the same imperatives to *laissez innover* fuelled by tech gaps. This led to the adoption of

---

Chicago Review 28–46; *The Human Condition*, 2nd edn (Chicago, The University of Chicago Press, 1998); Westin, (1967); N Bobbio, *L'Età dei Diritti* (Einaudi 1997); G Pugliese, 'Appunti per una Storia della Protezione dei Diritti Umani' (1989) 43 *Rivista Trimestrale di Diritto e Procedura Civile* 619–659.

[28] Westin (n 26).
[29] ibid.
[30] ibid.
[31] RF Murphy, 'Social Distance and the Veil' (1964) 66 *American Anthropologist* 1257–1274. See also JH Reiman, 'Privacy, Intimacy and Personhood', in FD Schoeman (ed), *Philosophical Dimensions of Privacy: an Anthology* (Cambridge, Cambridge University Press, 1984); 310; J Cannataci (ed), *The Individual and Privacy: volume I* (London, Routledge, 2015).
[32] A Bagnasco, M Barbagli et al., *Sociologia, Cultura e Società. I concetti di base* (Il Mulino, 2001) 167.
[33] SD Warren and LD Brandeis, 'The Right to Privacy' (1980) 4 *Harvard Law Review*.
[34] A Gajda, *What If Samuel D. Warren Hadn't Married A Senator's Daughter?: Uncovering The Press Coverage That Led to the Right to Privacy* (Illinois Public Law and Legal Theory Research Papers Series, Research Paper No 07-06, 2007).
[35] W Prosser, 'Privacy' (1960) 48 *California Law Review* 383–423. In Germany: S Simitis, 'Privacy – An Endless Debate' (2010) 98 *California Law Review*.
[36] E Black, *IBM and the Holocaust: The Strategic Alliance between Nazi Germany and America's Most Powerful Corporation* (Dialog Press, 2012).

frameworks encapsulating principles governing the fair use of data either to enable their unencumbered flow, developed in parallel to principles of information security, as discussed in chapter 5, or to protect the rights of individuals to whom the data relate. Remarkably, EU Member States were aware of the relevance of data since the 1960s,[37] without, however, being able to jointly legislate until the creation of the Single Market.

The identity and personality of persons is often flattened and constrained by the categories developed by the entities using such data, entities who wield ultimate power over the relevant features of a human (and the profile group to which they are assigned), as those categories trace the boundaries of human action in society – from denial of access to services to outright manipulation of consumer and electoral behaviour. The full scale of the relevance of data to humans has only become clear with cyberspace and the creation of digital personae, or data doubles, increasingly decoupled from the human being.[38]

In sum, privacy and data protection foster the development of personhood and identity, which underly self-determination and lead to autonomy, and are thereby crucial for democracy. Privacy and data protection both achieved national and international human right status[39] well before they appeared in EU law, and the circumstances under which they developed greatly influences conceptual and legal approaches to them. First, privacy is seen as passive, while data protection is active.[40] Second, the EU did not legislate on privacy and data protection before the Single Market, deferring instead to the work of the Council of Europe (CoE). Third, the favouring of innovation fuelled by the tech gap influenced the approach to data protection, which became crystallised in principles of data handling.

B. The Ambivalent Relationship of the Triad

i. Snowden Revelations: Clash and Complementarity of the Triad

In June 2013, shortly after the publication of the EU's first Cybersecurity strategy, a global consortium of newspapers reported revelations by Edward Snowden concerning mass-scale surveillance programmes,[41] led by the US National Security Agency (NSA) in cooperation with the UK Government Communications Head Quarters (GCHQ) and many EU Member States. The revelations' substance was the object of much reporting

---

[37] Council of the European Union, Ministers of the Common Market, 'Resolution of the Science Ministers of the Common Market calling Maréchal group to investigate EU cooperation in 7 fields, including data processing and telecommunications – Luxembourg Resolution (October 1967)'; Commission of the European Communities, 'European Society Faced with the Challenge of Information Technologies: a Community Response', COM (79) 650 final.
[38] R Clarke, 'The Digital Persona and its Application to Surveillance' (1994) 10 *The Information Society*.
[39] See chs 3–4.
[40] S Rodotà, 'Data Protection as a Fundamental Right', in S Gutwirth et al. (eds), *In Reinventing Data Protection?* (Cham, Springer, 2009).
[41] B Gellman and L Poitras, 'Documents: U.S. Mining Data from 9 Leading Internet Firms; Companies Deny Knowledge' *Washington Post* (6 June 2013); G Greenwald and E MacAskill, 'NSA Taps in to Systems of Google, Facebook, Apple and Others, Secret Files Reveal' *The Guardian* (7 June 2013).

and study.[42] Mass surveillance drew on 'far-reaching, complex and highly technologically advanced systems designed by … intelligence services to collect, store and analyse … content data … and metadata of all citizens around the world, on an unprecedented scale and in an indiscriminate and non-suspicion-based manner'.[43]

The revelations showed how, under the cloak of national security concerns,[44] a huge proportion of global communications was submitted to the listening and retaining powers of intelligence services. Intelligence agencies disposed of wide instruments to collect communications-related information pursuant to poorly written legal bases, dubious warrants and barely passable oversight.[45] The revelations thus spurred a fresh discussion on the relevance of privacy and data protection to democracy after a 'long decade' of detrimental counterterrorism measures.[46] Resolutions adopted in the aftermath of the revelations demanded the stringent protection of rights,[47] exemplified by the European Parliament's (EP) stance that 'information flows and data, which today dominate everyday life and are part of any person's integrity, need to be as secure from intrusion as private homes'.[48] The revelations exposed the complex relationship between 'cyber' security, privacy and data protection, which can simultaneously both clash and complement each other.

The revelations pointed to a clash between cybersecurity, privacy and data protection. Cayford explains that information was acquired through a mix[49] of traditional methods, eg, bugging embassies and tapping political leaders' phones and newer methods, such as gathering phone metadata, tapping fibre-optic cables, circumventing encryption, launching cyber-attacks[50] and through 'zero-day' exploits – crucial vulnerabilities in

---

[42] 'The NSA files' *The Guardian* (2013) www.theguardian.com/us-news/the-nsa-files; M Cayford, *Paper on Mass Surveillance by the National Security Agency (NSA) of the United States of America. Extract from SURVEILLE Project Deliverable D2.8* (2014).

[43] European Parliament, *Resolution on the US NSA Surveillance Programme, Surveillance Bodies in Various Member States and their Impact on EU Citizens' Fundamental Rights and on Transatlantic Cooperation in Justice and Home Affairs* (2013/2188 (INI) [2014 OJ C378/104], § 1 and I.

[44] ibid, recital G; N Muižnieks, 'Human Rights at Risk When Secret Surveillance Spreads' (*The Council of Europe Commissioner's Human Rights Comment*, 2013) www.coe.int/en/web/commissioner/-/human-rights-at-risk-when-secret-surveillance-sprea-1 (accessed 16 August 2016).

[45] Article 29 Data Protection Working Party, *Opinion 04/2014 on Surveillance of Electronic Communications for Intelligence and National Security Purposes* (819/14/EN WP 215, 2014); Fundamental Rights Agency, *Surveillance by intelligence services: fundamental rights safeguards and remedies in the EU. Mapping Member States' legal frameworks* (Publications Office of the European Union, 2015). For the UK, *Big Brother Watch and Others v UK*, no. 58170/13, 62322/14 and 24960/15, CE:ECHR:2018:0913JUD005817013.

[46] European Parliament, LIBE Committee, *Statement by Professor Martin Scheinin* (Hearing within the Inquiry on Electronic Mass Surveillance of EU Citizens, 2013); LK Donohue, 'NSA Surveillance May Be Legal – but it's Unconstitutional' *The Washington Post* (21 June 2013); European Digital Rights (EDRI), *US Agencies Have Unlimited Access to Internet Data* (EDRI-gram newsletter, n. 11.12 2013); D Jenkins, 'Introduction. The Long Decade' in D Jenkins et al. (eds), *The Long Decade: How 9/11 Changed the Law* (Oxford, Oxford University Press, 2014).

[47] See generally United Nations, General Assembly *Resolution the right to Privacy in the Digital Age*, A/RES/68/167 (2013); Committee of Ministers of the Council of Europe, *Reply of the Committee of Ministers to Parliamentary Assembly Recommendation 2067 (2015) on Mass Surveillance* (CM/AS(2015)Rec2067-final, 2015).

[48] European Parliament (n 43), rec B.

[49] Cayford (n 42) 30. For a list, see: www.lawfareblog.com/snowden-revelations.

[50] Eg circumvention by intercepting data retained by major US cloud providers in transit unencrypted from their EU data centres to the US and cyber-attacks against Belgacom, the telco contracted by Union

software, unknown by vendors and users, which expose machines to the risk of serious attacks.

An EP resolution[51] denounced the NSA's purchasing campaign of zero-days; it then became apparent the NSA was also involved in the creation of zero-day exploits.[52] Such activities were rumoured in expert circles for years and were corroborated by the information security community,[53] alongside their heavy implications for privacy, data protection and network and information security – notably their ability to backfire by enabling cybercrime.[54] An example was the WannaCry ransomware that affected hospitals, car manufacturing plants and businesses around the world in 2017. The code underpinning the exploit was part of the arsenal developed by the NSA and released into the wild by a rogue group of purchasers.[55]

If the revelations laid bare the clashes between privacy, data protection and cyberspace security, responses to the revelations stressed their convergence. Of note are the reports by the CoE Parliamentary Assembly and the EP.

According to the CoE Parliamentary Assembly, Member States should ensure 'protection of privacy in the digital age and internet safety'[56] and the Assembly expressed deep worries 'about threats to Internet security by the practices of certain intelligence agencies … of seeking out systematically, using and even creating "back doors" and other weaknesses in security standards and implementation that could easily be exploited by terrorists and cyberterrorists or other criminals'.[57] To this effect the Assembly recalled the EP's urge to resist attempts to weaken Internet safety standards, both to protect privacy but also national security against threats 'posed by rogue States, terrorists, cyberterrorists and ordinary criminals'[58] and consequently proposed to develop 'user-friendly (automatic) data protection techniques'[59] to secure the Internet.

The EP noted 'there is no guarantee, either for EU public institutions or for citizens, that their IT security or privacy can be protected from attacks by well-equipped intruders ("no 100 % IT security")' and that 'to achieve maximum IT security, Europeans need to be willing to dedicate sufficient resources, both human and financial, to preserving Europe's independence and self-reliance in the field of IT'.[60] The EP clarified that state-sponsored surveillance on grounds of national security imperils the security of

---

institutions. European Parliament, *LIBE Committee Inquiry on the Electronic Mass Surveillance of EU Citizens: Protecting Fundamental Rights in a Digital Age. Proceedings, Outcome and Background Documents* (2014), § 90.

[51] European Parliament (n 43), § BS.

[52] J Ball and J Borger et al., 'Revealed: How US and UK Spy Agencies Defeat Internet Privacy and Security' *The Guardian* (6 Sep 2013).

[53] L Edwards and I Brown et al., 'Information Security and Cybercrime' in L Edwards et al. (eds), *Law and the Internet*, 3rd edn (Oxford, Hart, 2009); B Schneier, 'The NSA is Hoarding Vulnerabilities' (*CRYPTO-GRAM* 15 September 2016) www.schneier.com/crypto-gram/archives/2016/0915.htm (accessed 15 September 2016).

[54] Zero-days can be hacked and auctioned, see A Greenberg, 'The Shadow Broker Mess is What Happens When the NSA Hoards Zero-days' *Wired* (17 August 2016).

[55] C Frediani, *Cybercrime. Attacchi Globali, Conseguenze Locali* (Milan, Hoepli, 2017).

[56] Council of Europe, *Recommendation 2067 (2015) on Mass Surveillance* (2015), §§ 2.1 and 2.2; *Resolution 2045 (2015) on Mass Surveillance* (2015).

[57] Council of Europe (n 56), Resolution 2045, § 5.

[58] ibid § 17.12.

[59] ibid § 19.15.

[60] European Parliament (n 43), § 15.

cyberspace, ie cybersecurity,[61] and proposed the adoption of complementary actions for cybersecurity and privacy[62] and against surveillance.[63] Parliamentary reactions show that weakening cybersecurity undermines the paradigm elaborated by the European Court of Human Rights (ECtHR), whereby security should serve the enjoyment of rights, rather than subverting democracy in the name of defending it.

ii. The Triad's Ambivalent Relationship Explained Through Cyberspace, Data and Information

The triad's ambivalent relationship becomes clearer when looked at through the prism of data and information flows in cyberspace and their centrality to communications, the economy, CI and national security. As cybersecurity concerns the security of cyberspace, understanding the meaning of cyberspace as a techno-human endeavour optimised for information and data flows and exerting regulatory power is crucial. The ability of data and information to express personal information and communications with evidentiary relevance attracts the attention of law enforcement, thereby creating the opportunity for a clash, as does the historical business relevance of insecure systems. The triad's relationship is complicated by the ambiguity inherent in information and data – as well as signals – whereby the object of legal protection is open-ended. Thus, competing notions of security through and of cyberspace make it possible for the triad to exist in ambivalence.

Dunn Cavelty describes cybersecurity as 'a type of security that unfolds in and through cyberspace; the making and practice of cyber-security is both constrained and enabled by this environment'.[64] Despite its literary origins, 'cyberspace' is normally referred to in policy and widely defined as the interaction between technology and the human relations occurring thanks to such technology.[65] An example is Ottis and Lorents' definition of cyberspace as 'a time-dependent set of interconnected information systems and the human users that interact with these systems'.[66] The Tallin Manual further divides "technology" into two, so that cyberspace is comprised of a physical, 'logical' and social layer.[67] Both its human and technological components make of 'cyberspace' an inherently politico-legal notion capable of exerting regulatory influence.

---

[61] W Diffie and S Landau, 'Internet Eavesdropping: A Brave New World of Wiretapping' (2008) 299 *Scientific American Magazine* 4; S Landau, *Surveillance or Security? The Risk Posed by New Wiretapping Technologies* (Cambridge, MIT Press, 2010).
[62] European Parliament (43), §§ 90–110.
[63] Predicated on protection goals, see ch 5.
[64] Dunn Cavelty (n 19) 107.
[65] Coined by novelist William Gibson in 'Neuromancer'; 'cyber' comes from Norbert Wiener's cybernetics, which derives from the Greek 'kubernētēs', meaning 'steerman' (the word linked to 'govern*'). Mattioli (n 20). Policy examples: European Commission and High Representative of the European Union for Foreign Affairs and Security Policy, 'Cyber Security Strategy: An Open, Safe and Secure Cyberspace' (Joint Communication) JOIN (2013) 01 final; White House, *International Strategy for Cyberspace. Prosperity, Security, and Openness in a Networked World* (2011).
[66] Ottis and Lorents (20) 5, cited in Mattioli (n 20) 25.
[67] MN Schmitt (ed), *The Tallin Manual 2.0 on the International Law Applicable to International Jurisdictions* (Cambridge, Cambridge University Press, 2017) 12.

Studying the Relationship between Cybersecurity, Privacy and Data Protection 19

Indeed, following Leenes, technology is never 'neutral', because of its 'affordances', its ability to intentionally or unintentionally enable or inhibit behaviour,[68] expressed through notions such as 'code is law' or techno-regulation.[69] Technology's regulatory influence is particularly prominent in cyberspace; there, ICTs serve diverse human purposes, the conflicting values they express and different constitutional architectures.

Cyberspace's human element is woven into notions of space, either because those notions correspond to conceptualisations of the individual,[70] or because of the connection of space to dominance and control. Configurations of human-space relate to different regulatory possibilities.[71] Human activity in 'space' is free from constraints; when 'space' becomes a place, it becomes amenable to jurisdictional constructs and its extant pre-existing rules. Electronic Frontier Foundation's founder John Perry Barlow greatly contributed to the early politicisation of discourses on cyberspace[72] by presenting it as 'space', a terrain independent from state bureaucracy, where likeminded people could pursue an egalitarian, peaceful utopia.[73] Such an understanding of cyberspace has co-existed alongside alternative conceptions and modes of governance expressed by different epistemic communities and state actions, leading to clashes of values which have turned cyberspace into an arena of sovereign disputes.[74]

The technology of cyberspace is the Internet, which is a network of networks. A network comes into being with at least two computers connected by a single technology, whereby connection means the ability to exchange information.[75] Information in computing is part of a system and is expressed in bits and bytes as data. The exchange of information on the Internet happens thanks to a layered architecture and packet switching, whereby information is divided into data packets, each containing a portion of the information to be delivered.

Data represent the link between information – at the logical layer – and the network – at the physical layer: data are the vector transporting information, in the shape of bits and bytes, via networks. The networks or physical layer[76] is made of the communication channels and hardware that enable the material delivery of information just like depots, trucks, ships and airplanes within a postal system. At the physical layer, the Internet's communication channels are, unlike conventional telecoms, not supposed to be optimised for the applications using them, which led Isenberg to describe the

---

[68] R Leenes, 'Framing Techno-regulation: an Exploration of State and Non-state Regulation by Technology' (2011) 5 *Legisprudence*.

[69] ibid; L Lessig, *Code: And Other Laws of Cyberspace. Version 2.0* (New York, Basic Books, 2006); DK Mulligan and KA Bamberger, 'Saving Governance-by-Design' (2018) 106 *California Law Review* 697–784.

[70] M Wertheim, *The Pearly Gates of Cybersapce. A History of Space from Dante to the Internet* (New York, WW Norton & Company Inc. 1999).

[71] Dunn Cavelty (n 64).

[72] ibid 107.

[73] Wertheim (n 71).

[74] See Dunn Cavelty (n 19); H Nissenbaum, 'When Computer Security Meets National Security', in JM Balkin (ed), *Cybercrime, Digital Cops in a Networked Environment* (New York, New York University Press, 2007); G Christou, *Cybersecurity in the European Union. Resilience and Adaptability in Governance and Policy* (Basingstoke, Palgrave Macmillan, 2015); J Griffiths, 'Chinese President Xi Jinping: Hands off our Internet' *CNN* (16 December 2015).

[75] AS Tanenbaum and DJ Wetherall, *Reti di Calcolatori (Quinta Edizione)* (Milan, Pearson Italia, 2011).

[76] ibid, chs 1 and 2.

Internet as a 'stupid network'.[77] In a 'stupid' network, the intelligence is situated in the machines that originate the data flow, the centre of the network is based on infrastructure, and transport follows the need of data rather than network constraints. Data are transported in accordance with the end-to-end argument, whose broad version generates 'net neutrality', whereby delivery should follow best efforts regardless of the content carried.[78]

Data at rest or in transit can *express* anything; Andrade notes information is both an intellectual cosmos, ie a system helping us to make sense of reality, and *the* cosmos, in the sense of constituting the 'bricks' of the universe.[79] Thus, data *carry* anything, irrespective of meaning, in the form of signals. Since data flow from equipment ultimately operated by people, the information carried by networks in the form of content or metadata[80] can (in)directly identify individuals, be sensitive, reveal details about one's private life, or else flow from personal communications, falling into the remit of the right to respect for private and family life (privacy) and the right to data protection.[81] Data transmitted can also subvert the security of network and information systems and cyberspace. Data carrying information that for some needs to be secured, for others should best remain insecure.

The growing convergence of methods for the production and exchange of information, alongside the architecture of the Internet, has turned computer systems and networks into a field of innovation and growth[82] for both licit and illicit human activity. As our lives increasingly rely on cyberspace, so does crime: a global repository of information and a popular avenue for exchange, the Internet offers offenders seemingly boundless opportunities. For instance, would-be terrorists can find propaganda, information on how to manufacture explosive devices, how to affiliate with the extremist group of choice, interact with like-minded people and arrange terrorist acts.[83] Cyberspace enables fraud of all kinds and clandestine online markets where illicit goods, such as guns, drugs and cyberweapons are traded.[84] A third of all crimes reported in EU Member States in 2018 were computer-related crimes,[85] cybercrimes for short. Cyberspace can also be a platform for and target of military attacks. Zero-days are prominent in hybrid, state-sponsored attacks, starting from Stuxnet, the US-Israeli

---

[77] D Isenberg, 'The Dawn of the "Stupid Network"' 2 netWorker 24. Quoted in B Van Schewick, *Internet Architecture and Innovation* (Cambridge, MIT Press, 2010) 108.

[78] Van Schewick (n 77). T Wu, 'Network Neutrality, Broadband Discrimination' (2003) 2 *Journal on Telecommunications and High Tech Law*.

[79] Information always concerns the physical world, and we make sense of the world through information thanks to Shannon's work to describing anything through yes/no questions and bits, where 1 means 'no' and 0 means 'yes'. Andrade (n 25).

[80] Traffic and location data within the meaning of the Directive 2002/58/EC of the European Parliament and of the Council of 12 July 2002 Concerning the Processing of Personal Data and the Protection of Privacy in the Electronic Communications Sector, [2002] OJ L201/37 (e-Privacy Directive or EPD). See ch 3.

[81] See chs 3–4.

[82] For the interaction between architecture, economics and innovation, see Van Schewick (n 77).

[83] United Nations, Office on Drug and Crime (UNODC), *The Use of Internet for Terrorist Purposes* (2012).

[84] A Hutchings and JT Holt, 'The online stolen data market: Disruption and intervention approaches' (2017) 18 Global Crime 11–30.

[85] Europol, 'Internet Organised Crime Threat Assessment (IOCTA) 2019'.

Studying the Relationship between Cybersecurity, Privacy and Data Protection 21

malware that undermined the Iranian nuclear development programme.[86] ICTs and cyberspace naturally hold the evidence necessary to apprehend offenders, whether they are terrorists and their aiders, petty criminals or Advanced Persistent Threats (APTs)[87] carrying out hybrid attacks as state proxies.

Data and information are thus open-ended in a way that matters for the relationship of the triad. Such open-endedness is augmented by the semantic ambiguity between information and data.[88] The dictionary definition of *datum*, which stems from the Latin 'something given',[89] is 'a piece of information'. The plural 'data', meaning 'facts and statistics collected together for reference or analysis', is supplemented by two additional definitions relating to the fields of computers and philosophy.[90] Such a 'definitional gap' breeds debates[91] with applied relevance, because data and information[92] are often conflated in the applicable law.[93] As seen, a network exists when at least two computers are connected and thus able to exchange information parcelled out in data. This opens the door to uncertainty as to the object that deserves protection: is a single data packet delivered through Internet protocols as worthy as the ensemble of data packets reconstructed by computers, and is the ensemble of data packets as worthy as the content (information) intelligible to humans? Should any of these deserve protection vis-à-vis victims of crime, states challenged by organised crime and the collectivities challenged by terrorists?

The question goes to the heart of the triad's relationship. Mass surveillance revelations showed that privacy and data protection are a major obstacle to 'security' *through* cyberspace, as a venue for collecting intelligence, launching state-sponsored attacks and countering (cyber)crime. Accordingly, curbing surveillance capabilities in the name of privacy and data protection would hinder security gains; by extension, it would also hinder data-driven innovation, which thrives on unboundedness. Reactions to mass surveillance highlighted instead how surveillance activities put at risk the security *of* cyberspace as well as privacy and data protection. Cyberspace, information and related rights that unfold therein appear as objects of protection, because of our reliance on networks and information systems for CI, including private, official and business

---

[86] E Markatos and D Balzarotti (eds), *The Red Book. A Roadmap for Systems Security Research* (The SysSec Consortium: A European Network of Excellence in Managing Threats and Vulnerabilities in the Future Internet: Europe for the World 2013).
[87] See: csrc.nist.gov/glossary/term/advanced_persistent_threat.
[88] But see J Olster, 'Code is Code and Law is Law – the Law of Digitalization and the Digitalization of Law' (2021) 29 *International Journal of Law and Information Technology* 101–117, 103: data has evolved from 'given thing' into the syntactic representation of information in a sign; information has evolved from 'the impression that an object leaves with its observer' to something that forms the recipient's knowledge.
[89] Oxford Dictionary of English (2022), digital resource.
[90] ibid. In philosophy, 'things known or assumed as facts, making the basis of reasoning or calculation'.
[91] See N Purtova, 'The Law of Everything. Broad Concept of Personal Data and Future of EU Data Protection Law' (2018) 10 *Law, Innovation and Technology* 40–81. Citing L Floridi, 'Is Information Meaningful Data?' (2005) 70(2) *Philosophy and Phenomenological Research* 351 and L Bygrave, 'Information Concepts in Law: Generic Dreams and Definitional Daylight' (2015) 35(1) *Oxford Journal of Legal Studies* 91–120; Olster (88), citing M Hildebrandt, 'Law as Information in the Era of Data-Driven Agency' (2016) 79 *Modern Law Review* 1–30; R Gellert, 'Comparing Definitions of Data and Information in Data Protection Law and Machine Learning. A Useful Way Forward to Meaningfully Regulate Algorithms?' (2022) 16(1) *Regulation & Governance* 156–176.
[92] To which we can add signals, see chs 4, 6.
[93] See further chs 3, 4.

communications and activities. Attitudes towards data, information and their shared technology, as objects to either protect or monitor and seize, seem to vary according to notions of security, and with it the configuration of the relationship between cybersecurity, privacy and data protection.

C. Towards an Analytical Framework to Study the Reconciliation of the Triad

Having established that cybersecurity, privacy and data protection can both clash and be complementary, it is therefore crucial to explore the nature of 'clash' and 'complementarity' to understand whether and how the triad can be reconciled. I conceptualise these opposing states along a continuum, shown in Figure 1, enriched by three intermediate states.

Complementarity effects strong reconciliation and can be conceptualised as one of two options. First and to the far right, cybersecurity, privacy and data protection overlap, that is they express different facets of the same object, leading to complete reconciliation. Second, the triad converges towards the same goals and is therefore synergic, leading to strong reconciliation. Clashes effect weak reconciliation and can also be divided into two states, the first expressing the irreconcilability of the triad, which would stand in a zero-sum game, shown at the far left. Second, the triad could co-exist, but only through a balancing exercise. An in-between state is classed as indifference or non-interference, for want of a better expression.

Figure 1 Modes of reconciliation of cybersecurity, privacy and data protection (the triad)

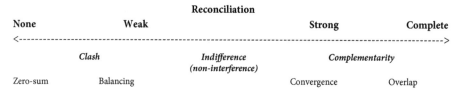

This book will explore such modes of reconciliation to identify whether one prevails and how desired forms of reconciliation can be achieved in EU law. Zero-sum clashes can be explained through the lens of trade-off theses; as will be shown, the rule of law provides a framework rejecting zero-sum outcomes and supporting instead weak and strong reconciliation; techno-legal analysis helps investigate overlaps.

Reasoning on the undesirability and limitations of zero-sum outcomes helps bring to the surface elements for an analytical framework to study the other modes of reconcilability of the triad. To ascertain the configuration of reconciliation within EU law, it is necessary to consider the role of cybersecurity, privacy and data protection as situated techno-legal objects within the EU constitutional architecture, the values they express and their concrete policy substantiation.

Thus, the first part of this book will outline the EU constitutional background and illustrate cybersecurity, privacy and data protection as separate legal objects. Common values emerging from part one of the book will then inform a techno-legal analysis to investigate the feasibility of complete reconciliation.

i. Elements for an Analytical Framework to Study the Reconcilability of the Triad

Reasoning on the limitations of zero-sum outcomes provides the opportunity to identify the constitutive elements of an analytical framework to investigate the mode of reconcilability of the triad. Zero-sum outcomes can be conceptualised as the extreme consequence of a trade-off between security and liberties and such occurrence is among the reasons why trade-off models have been met with strong critiques.[94] One example of a strongly critiqued trade-off model is Posner and Vermeule's where security and liberty are comparable items represented as two perpendicular axes delimiting an area of policy choices and limited by a frontier 'where security cannot be increased without corresponding decreases in liberty, and vice versa'.[95] The problematic argument is that, where policymakers are at the frontier: (i) the executive should reduce civil liberties at times of emergency (because); (ii) civil liberties hinder an effective response to a security threat, thus not excluding zero-sum outcomes. I review each argument in turn.

The argument supporting the efficient reduction of civil liberties in favour of security presupposes a benevolent ('not dysfunctional') choice between scarce resources,[96] an intrinsically political statement that warrants the discussion of a general theory of politics and judicial review. The following definition of politics aptly accommodates law as the mechanism for resolution of controversies over resources: 'A complex process hinging on a progression of intertwined events and actions, whereby, within any organized community, a multiplicity of actors reaches binding collective decisions aimed at settling controversies coming up within the community or in its external relations.'[97] Accordingly, politics is made up of three elements intertwined with the law: a scope – the organised community; an aim – resolution of conflict; and the means towards the aim – binding collective decisions.

---

[94] D Dyzenhaus, 'States of Emergency', in M Rosenfeld et al. (eds), *The Oxford Handbook of Comparative Constitutional Law* (Oxford, Oxford Handbooks Online, 2012) 460; P Herron, 'Beyond Balance: Targeted Sanctions, Security and Republican Freedom', in E Orrù et al. (eds), *Rethinking Surveillance and Control Beyond the Security versus Privacy Debate* (Baden-Baden, Nomos, 2017).
[95] E Posner and A Vermeule, *Terror in the Balance. Security, Liberty and the Courts* (Oxford, Oxford University Press 2007); A Vermeule, 'Critiques of the Trade-off Thesis' in D Jenkins et al. (eds), *The Long Decade: How 9/11 Changed the Law* (Oxford, Oxford University Press, 2014) 32.
[96] Posner and Vermeule (2007) 21–26. Posner and Vermeule refer to the idea that the executive should trump the judiciary as the 'deference thesis'; see section II.A.i below.
[97] V Mura, *Categorie della Politica. Elementi per una teoria generale* (Giappichelli Editore, 2004) 115. 'Un processo complesso, imperniato su successioni concatenate di eventi ed azioni, attraverso il quale, nell'ambito di una qualsiasi convivenza organizzata, una pluralità di attori perviene a prendere le decisioni collettive vincolanti finalizzate a dirimere i conflitti che insorgono nel proprio interno e/o nei rapporti esterni.' Translation mine.

Reference to an organised community calls for jurisdiction-specific analyses and is the first element of the analytical framework. Thus, the EU is a *sui generis*,[98] open-ended community made of institutions and Member States – the latter playing a prominent role[99] – and organised chiefly in accordance with its 'constitution', the Treaties.[100] The Treaties' approach to security and rights is informed by the moral and political foundations of Europe built on the legacy of dysfunctional governments that led to the catastrophe of WWII.[101] The idea that democratically elected governments could adopt wicked measures against liberties is woven into the fabric of Member States' law, as are the corresponding attempts to create a multilevel system of check and balances, of which the EU is part, pivoting around the rule of law and constraining executives also at time of emergency.

The conflict to be resolved in the case at hand is between security and rights, seen as scarce resources, ie assets such as commodities that are or can be made excludable, rivalrous, or both.[102] Non-rivalrous and non-excludable resources are usually conceptualised as public goods, to which cybersecurity and rights[103] are more amenable. Liberty and security are *understood* as being for all, so that they are non-excludable; rivalry paving to antinomies is intellectually generated by normative clashes between values.[104] It is precisely the controversy caused by the plurality of values that is quintessential to politics and is resolved through the law.[105] Values as assets are axioms containing worth per se, all meriting equal respect and thus existing before and beyond the law,[106] they can also be encapsulated in rules of behaviour bearing prescriptive content, such that they become principles bearing legal force.[107] For instance, for Alexy, constitutional rights can have the character of values and principles, which tend to collide. He claims

---

[98] *Avis 2/13 Opinion of the Court* EU:C:2014:2454, paras 157 and 158.

[99] A Milward, *European Rescue of the Nation State* (London, Taylor and Francis, 1999).

[100] See especially Case C-294/83 *Les Verts v Parliament* EU:C:1986:166, para 23. Consolidated versions of the Treaty on European Union (TEU) and the Treaty on the Functioning of the European Union (TFEU), OJ C 83/01 (Lisbon Treaty).The TEU and the TFEU must be read together: M Cremona, 'The Two (or Three) Treaty Solution: The New Treaty Structure of the EU', in A Biondi et al. (eds), *European Union Law After the Treaty of Lisbon* (Oxford, Oxford University Press, 2012).

[101] F Romero, 'Antifascismo e Ordine Internazionale' in A De Bernardi et al. (eds), *Antifascismo e Identità Europea* (Carocci 2004).

[102] Excludability refers to limiting enjoyment of goods by imposing a price, rivalry to a good's inability to be simultaneously enjoyed by multiple users. G Mankiw, *Principles of Economics*, 7th edn (Mason, OH, Cengage Learning 2013).

[103] Note that information and data are usually seen as non-scarce and non-rivalrous, A Murray, *Information Technology Law. Law and Society*, 4th edn (Oxford, Oxford University Press, 2019). Amenable does not mean actualised: M Dunn Cavelty, 'Breaking the Cyber-Security Dilemma: Aligning Security Needs and Removing Vulnerabilities' (2014) 20 *Science and Engineering Ethics* 701–715, 707.

[104] Note they can be made excludable and become prerogatives. See J Waldron, *Torture, Terrore and Trade-offs. Philosophy for the White House* (Oxford, Oxford University Press, 2010) ch 5; Bobbio, (1997).

[105] M Weber, *La Scienza come Professione. La Politica come Professione* (Einaudi 2004).

[106] Coinciding in the German doctrine of *Drittwirkung*, F Angelini, *Ordine pubblico e integrazione costituzionale europea. I principi fondamentali nelle relazioni interordinamentali* (Cedam, 2007). M Cremona, 'Values in EU Foreign Policy' in P Koutrakos et al. (eds), *Beyond the Established Orders Policy Interconnections between the EU and the Rest of the World* (Oxford, Hart Publishing, 2011). On principles and values, see A von Bogdandy, 'Founding Principles of EU Law: A Theoretical and Doctrinal Sketch' (2010) 16 *European Law Journal* 95.

[107] R Alexy, Theorie der Grundrechte (Suhrkamp Verlag; Auflage, 1986); 'Constitutional Rights and Legal Systems', in J Nergelius (ed), *Constitutionalism – New Challenges: European Law from a Nordic Perspective* (Boston, Brill, 2008). See section II below.

such collisions are resolvable, because principles are commensurable and because of the availability of scales, through the application of the fundamental technique of balancing, composed of a series of steps to assess suitability, necessity and proportionality.

The specific subset of values chosen by a community in a controversy contributes to the formation of the community's political identity and constitutes its legal ideal *ordre public*, understood as public policy or constitutional architecture, as against *law and order* or *material ordre public*, such as policing. Principles underly the choice of means of resolution of a controversy, informing in turn binding collective decisions, imposed through different types of power. In legal terms, the resolution of controversies can take many forms and ultimately entails 'the reaffirmation of sovereignty'[108] and of a particular *ordre public* understood in terms of constitutional architecture, such as Article 4 TEU's 'the territorial integrity of the State ... law and order and ... national security'.

The constitutional architecture feeds into and is nurtured by specific ways of addressing controversies. Such reaffirmation is strongly linked to the abstraction of what *the good life* means within a community, that is, the ideal of life or *vouloir-vivre* to which members of a community aspire.[109] Security can serve the interest of *vouloir vivre* either understood as Hobbesian survival, or as a communal life devoted to certain goals, such as the enjoyment of rights. One nation's *vouloir vivre* includes the scope of criminal liability – of goods and wrongs – and the disposition of the monopoly on the use of force.[110] The reconcilability of the triad must thus be assessed vis-à-vis the EU constitutional architecture and ideal of good life.

The argument that liberties hinder an effective response to a security threat rests on the comparability of security and liberties, represented as discrete and monolithic objects in a way that overlooks or misunderstands the meaning and values they embody.[111] Such misunderstanding can be explained with Solove's[112] pendulum argument: a trade-off descending into a zero-sum game can happen when the value of security swings towards its maximum level, becoming prized above liberties, which as a hindrance to security should be 'temporarily' compressed (and vice versa). The prioritisation of security over rights is often supported by securitising discourse, whereby a particular threat acquires existential value and thus justifies the adoption of any measure.[113] Undervaluing rights flattens their value and hinders an evaluation of the effects of a regulatory framework and policies limiting them; securitising discourse similarly frustrates an open-minded reflection on the diverse factors surrounding security issues, including the role of exogenous constraints such as technology.[114]

---

[108] In the sense of control over a territory, population and jurisdiction. A Cassese, *International Law*, 2nd edn (Oxford, Oxford University Press, 2005).

[109] Arendt (n 27); Taylor (n 27); Angelini (n 106) 217.

[110] Both 'particularly sensitive for the ability of a constitutional state to democratically shape itself', BVerfG, 2 BvE 2/08, DE:BVerfG:2009:es20090630.2bve000208, paras 252–260. Seeing the judgment as a 'cri de Coeur': J-C Piris, *The Lisbon Treaty. A Legal and Political Analysis* (Cambridge, Cambridge University Press, 2010).

[111] See especially D Solove, *Nothing to Hide: the False Tradeoff Between Privacy and Security* (New Haven, Yale University Press, 2011); JE Cohen, 'What Privacy is For' (2013) 126 Harvard Law Review 1094.Waldron (104).

[112] Solove (n 111).

[113] Buzan et al. (n 19).

[114] J Huysman, *The Politics of Insecurity* (London, Routledge, 2006).

Thus, an analytical framework for the study of the triad must treat 'cybersecurity', 'privacy' and 'data protection' as legally situated objects, whose meaning is appraised and given full normative depth in jurisdictional context. A contextual analysis of 'security' and 'rights' and related policies can give justice to exogenous constraints, such as technology, which embodies value-laden choices[115] affecting the relationship between security and rights. The following section examines the features of constitutional architecture of relevance to investigate the relationship of the triad.

II. The Triad within the EU Constitutional Architecture: A Policy, Law and Technology Analysis

In this section I give substance to the analytical framework to investigate the relationship between cybersecurity, privacy and data protection as legally situated objects in the EU constitutional order. I first illustrate how the EU *ordre public* acts as a backdrop and constraint for the relationship of the triad, by focussing in particular on the requirements found in Articles 2, 3 and 6 of the Treaty on the European Union (TEU) (II.A). Focussing on tenets of the Rule of Law (RoL) that incorporate general principles of EU law, I explain why the EU *ordre public* strives for the coherent reconciliation of the triad, including at times of emergency. The idea that democratically elected governments could descend into authoritarianism and adopt wicked measures against liberties is weaved into the fabric of EU law, as are the corresponding attempts to create a multi-level system of protection pivoting around the RoL.

Of particular importance is the RoL tenet of respect for human rights, which overlaps with fundamental rights as general principles of EU law, such as the respect for private and family life and the protection of personal data enshrined in the Charter of Fundamental Rights of the European Union[116] (Charter or CFR) (II.A.ii). The Charter embodies a test for permissible limitations for the resolution of controversies, viz. clashes, involving rights; the test includes a reinforced mechanism of proportionality whereby measures crushing the essence of rights are automatically invalid.

Foundational as they may be, primary law mechanisms for resolving controversies only point to the impermissibility of zero-sum outcomes; criteria of proportionality and coherence do not allow for the identification of the desired mode of reconciliation upfront. The mode of reconciliation must thus be distilled from the interpretation of hierarchically inferior sources. Thus, I outline how I will study the interplay of cybersecurity, privacy and data protection as legally situated objects in EU policy, law and technology (II.B).

---

[115] Leenes (n 68).
[116] Charter of Fundamental Rights of the European Union [2012] OJ C326/391 (CFR).

A. The EU Constitutional Architecture as a Constraint on the Relationship between Cybersecurity, Privacy and Data Protection

The public policy created by the Lisbon Treaty strives to reconcile potentially clashing objectives of public interest; coherence and consistency are inherent aims of any legal unity.[117] There are four objectives of public interest aiming to fulfil the EU's overarching goal of promoting 'peace, the preservation of its traditions and citizens' well-being' pursuant to Article 3(1) TEU. First, the AFSJ includes the protection of privacy and data protection and incorporates, among others, the fight against cybercrime. Second, technological advances in cyberspace foster the Digital Single Market (DSM), which thrives on the confidentiality of communications, the security of e-transactions and data flows. Third, the economic and monetary Union relies on institutions that represent critical infrastructure (CI) needing protection against cyberattacks. Finally, External Relations based on the EU's own internal values include digital diplomacy, the prevention of cyberwar and protection of digital rights.[118] The relationship between cybersecurity, privacy and data protection cuts across all four objectives.

Within EU law, the relationship between cybersecurity, privacy and data protection is fully bound by Article 2 TEU on Common Provisions, which acts as the normative springboard for pursuing the objectives of general interest listed in Article 3 TEU. Article 2 TEU is 'super primary law'[119] defining 'the very identity of the European Union as a common legal order'[120] and producing concrete legal effects.

The foundations of the EU *ordre public* enshrined in Article 2 TEU must be read together, as each requires the other in order to acquire meaning. Here I pick the RoL as a value-principle[121] binding all founding elements of the EU *ordre public* together. This is because the RoL has, at least in its thin understanding, 'progressively become a dominant organisational model of modern constitutional law and international organisations',[122] including the EU. Indeed, after *Les Verts* the value-principle of the RoL has gradually acquired constitutional weight and the character of 'dominant organizational paradigm'[123] exemplified, at the time of writing, by a line of cases involving Poland,

---

[117] TEU Art 13(1), TFEU Art 7. D Curtin and IF Dekker, 'The European Union from Maastricht to Lisbon', in P Craig et al (eds), *The Evolution of EU Law* (Oxford, Oxford University Press, 2011) 157–158 and 171.
[118] TEU Arts 3(2)–3(5).
[119] A Rosas and L Armati, *EU Constitutional Law – An Introduction* (Oxford, Hart Publishing, 2010) 43. Also 'constitutional' Von Bogdandy (107).
[120] *Poland v Parliament and Council*, C-157/21, EU:C:2022:98, para 145. European Commission, 'A New EU Framework to Strengthen the Rule of Law' (Communication) COM (2014) 158 final.
[121] Here I agree with those who see values and principles as strictly related. See fns 105 and 107.
[122] COM (2014) 158 final (n 120) 3.
[123] *Les Verts v Parliament*, C-294/83, para 23; D Curtin, *Executive Power in the European Union* (Oxford, Oxford University Press, 2009) 199. L Pech, *The Rule of Law as a Constitutional Principle of the European Union* (Jean Monnet Working Paper Series, New York University School of Law, 2009) 50. Further discussing TEU Arts 7 and 49 and conditionality, L Pech, *Rule of Law as a Guiding Principle of the European Union's External Action* (CLEER Working Papers, Centre for the Law of EU External Relations, TMC Asser Instituut Inter-university Research Centre, 2013).

including on conditionality for the protection of the Union budget.[124] The CJEU, whose jurisdiction is defined by the RoL, confirmed that the RoL has an 'umbrella' nature bearing interpretive value and encompassing sub-principles actionable before a court,[125] viz. the general principles of EU law.[126]

Due to the wide endorsement of the RoL, including at United Nations (UN) level,[127] there exist multiple definitions that reflect the objectives of the institutions that adopt it. Thus, the tenets of the RoL are open-ended and acquire meaning only in context. The EC's own list features six tenets: legality; legal certainty; prohibition of arbitrariness of the executive powers; independent and impartial courts; effective judicial review including respect for fundamental rights; and equality before the law.[128] These tenets widely correspond to the list developed by the CoE's Venice Commission taking into account ECtHR case law.[129] Such convergence is unsurprising, since the EC looks at the CoE as the general 'benchmark for human rights, the rule of law and democracy in Europe'.[130]

The tenets of the RoL have a double purpose. First, they are defining elements of the Union's *ordre public*, which aims to reconcile potentially diverging objectives such as those relating to the interplay of the triad. Second, the tenets act as the emergency break constraining available policy choices. Although different RoL tenets will surface in different parts of the book, the current analysis focusses on legality and fundamental rights as umbrella concepts in themselves. Legality has progressively incorporated other RoL tenets,[131] such as legal certainty. Premised on the complementarity between substantive (thin) and procedural (thick) RoL tenets expounded for instance by Kilpatrick,[132] the RoL incorporates the imperative that security serves the European composite *ordre public*, including at times of emergency. The 'human rights' tenet similarly subsumes RoL tenets such as proportionality and legal certainty and is of obvious relevance as privacy and data protection are fundamental rights in EU law.

---

[124] Eg, *Poland v Parliament and Council*, C-157/21; see euruleoflaw.eu/rule-of-law/rule-of-law-dashboard-overview/polish-cases-cjeu-ecthr/.
[125] TFEU Art 263. See ibid, Annex.
[126] See especially, T Tridimas, *The General Principles of EU Law* (Oxford, Oxford University Press, 2006).
[127] See United Nations, Secretary General, *The Rule of Law and Transitional Justice in Conflict and Post-conflict Societies. Report of the Secretary-General to the Security Council* (S/2004/616, 2004); United Nations, General Assembly, *Declaration on Principles of International Law Friendly Relations and Co-Operation Among States in Accordance with the Charter of the United Nations* (1970). See Pech, Rule of Law as a Guiding Principle of the EU's EA (2012) CLEER Working Paper 2012/3 (The Hague, T.M.C. Asser Instituut).
[128] COM (2014) 158 final (n 120) 4; European Commission, 'Annexes to the Communication A new EU Framework to strengthen the Rule of Law' (Communication) COM (2014) 158 final.
[129] The EC participates in the works of the Venice Commission as an observer. Council of Europe, European Commission for Democracy through Law (Venice Commission), *Report on the Rule of Law* (Study No 512/2009, 2011). Venice Commission, Rule of Law Checklist (Study No 711 / 2013, 2016).
[130] Art 10, Council of Europe, *Memorandum of Understanding between the Council of Europe and the European Union CM(2007)74 1* (117th Session of the Committee of Ministers, 2007). Angelini (106) 165. Negotiations for the Accession to the ECHR pursuant to TEU Art 6 are underway. See ch 3.
[131] P De Hert and S Gutwirth, 'Data Protection in the Case Law of Strasbourg and Luxembourg: Constitutionalism in Action', in S Gutwirth et al. (eds), *Reinventing Data Protection?* (New York, Springer, 2009). RoL and legality are often used interchangeably. J Waldron, 'The Concept and the Rule of Law' (2008) 43 *Georgia Law Review* 1. C Reed and A Murray, *Rethinking the Jurisprudence of Cyberspace* (Cheltenham, Edward Elgar, 2018).
[132] C Kilpatrick, 'On the Rule of Law and Economic Emergency: the Degradation of Basic Legal Values in Europe's Bailouts' (2015) 35 *Oxford Journal of Legal Studies*.

i. Legality as a Cornerstone of the RoL and the Composite EU ordre public, also at Times of Emergency

Institution and MS actions are first of all informed by legality, 'which implies a transparent, accountable, democratic and pluralistic process for enacting laws (supremacy of the law)'.[133] It is an overarching tenet and fundamental principle[134] that expresses the connection between the RoL and the other values-principles listed in Article 2 TEU, such as the principle of democracy, which constitutes 'one of the foundations of the European Union'.[135] Legality has both a 'thin' meaning, ie supremacy of the law, and a 'thick' one, which consists in the procedures that the law must follow in order to be considered supreme.

In this latter sense, legality expresses the principles governing the ideal *ordre public* as opposed to material *ordre public*, ie law and order and the pursuit of 'security' objectives, including in cyberspace. Within such a framework, 'security' serves legality; this approach has found substance in the AFSJ, which presupposes the reconciliation of security and rights.[136] The subordinate nature of security within the *ordre public* is further demonstrated by the fact that 'security' lacks autonomous significance. The Treaties embody different conceptions of security[137] and the few instances in which 'security' appears alone[138] in the Treaties do not allow for carving out a univocal meaning. Consequently, cybersecurity only acquires meaning in the context of specific policy objectives expressed by the applicable law.

Legality means that the conduct of EU institutions and Member States is constrained by the powers conferred by the Treaties and the Treaties' relationship with international law. Since the latter 'is part of the European Union legal order and is binding on the institutions', therefore 'EU law must be interpreted in the light of relevant rules of international law',[139] rules which apply to cyberspace.[140] The EU is fully subject to rules of customary (or peremptory) law.[141] Treaties to which the EU is not (yet) a party, and which do not express rules of customary law, do not supersede written primary law such as the Charter,[142] but instead supply guidelines of relevance when interpreting EU law.[143] This is particularly the case when EU law contains *renvois* to international

---

[133] European Commission (120) 4.
[134] *P Commission v CAS Succhi di Frutta*, C-496/99, EU:C:2004:236, para 63.
[135] *European Commission v Federal Republic of Germany*, C-518/07, EU:C:2010:125, para 41.
[136] European Commission, 'The European Agenda on Security' (Communication) COM (2015) 185 final, 3.
[137] N Grief, 'EU Law and Security' (2007) 32 *European Law Review* 752–765.
[138] In TEU Art 3(5) and (international order) 21, (own security) and TFEU 346 (Member States' essential interests to their security).
[139] *Hungary v Slovakia*, C-364/10 EU:C:2012:630, para 44.
[140] United Nations, General Assembly, *Report of the Group of Governmental Experts (GGE) on Developments in the Field of Information and Telecommunications in the Context of International Security*, A/70/174 (2015); J Kulesza, *International Internet Law* (London, Routledge, 2012); F Delrue and J Kulesza et al., *The Application of International Law in Cyberspace: is There a European Way?* (Policy in Focus, 2019). See ch 8. But on the effects doctrine compare Reed and Murray (n 131), 103–138.
[141] M Cremona, *External Relations of the EU and the Member States: Competence, Mixed Agreements, International Responsibility, and Effects of International Law* (European University Institute Working Paper LAW 2006/22, 2006).
[142] Rosas and Armati (n 120).
[143] *Wachauf V Bundesamt Für Ernährung Und Forstwirtschaft*, C-5/88, EU:C:1989:321, para 17.

treaties, such as the ECHR, Convention 108 and the Budapest Convention, all relevant for the triad.[144]

The reach of legality extends to emergencies, such as cyberattacks affecting national security and to an extent to other grounds justifying derogations from EU law, with consequences for fundamental rights and the applicability of the Charter. High levels of legality are preserved through a European composite or multilevel *ordre public*.

Emergencies constitute grounds allowing Member States to derogate from EU law[145] and are of different types: they can relate to public policy as ideal *ordre public*; public security as law and order and national security; or public health determinations. Cyberattacks affecting national security can trigger the solidarity clause laid down in Article 222 TFEU.[146] While actions taken pursuant to Article 222(1) fall on the shoulders of Member States, actions can and do overlap with AFSJ measures of shared competence within the clear remit of EU law. When emergencies warrant initiatives toward objectives other than public security, viz. law and order and national security, Member States' actions are likely to be firmly grounded in Union law, and thus must conform to the elements of its *ordre public*, including legality.

Member States also derogate from EU law in pursuit of 'their essential state functions', meaning the territorial integrity of the state, maintaining law and order such as when pursuing cybercriminals, and safeguarding national security, eg by means of cyber-intelligence operations.[147] In this case, the supremacy of EU law still applies to an extent. 'Although it is for Member States to take the appropriate measures to ensure their internal and external security, the mere fact that a decision concerns State security cannot result in European Union law being inapplicable.'[148] Indeed, the national security exemption cannot encroach on areas of EU law competence, including fundamental rights.[149] Furthermore, national actions in conflict with an act of EU law are still open to scrutiny by the CJEU, provided such acts do not entail a 'fundamental policy choice',[150] in keeping with the principle of conferral.

The Charter binds institutions, bodies, offices and agencies of the Union and Member States when they 'implement' EU law. Over time, scholarly opinion[151] and case

---

[144] M Cremona, 'A Triple Braid: Interactions between International Law, EU Law and Private Law', in M Cremona et al. (eds), *Private Law in the External Relation of the EU* (Oxford, Oxford University Press, 2016). See chs 3–4 (including the accession of the EU to the ECHR), 7–8.

[145] See TFEU Arts 36, 45(3), 52 and 65; similarly to 'emergency', grounds are undefined, so as to embrace different understandings of public policy across Member States. See *Van Duyn v Home Office*, C-41/74, EU:C:1974:133; *Ilonka Sayn-Wittgenstein v Landeshauptmann von Wien*, C-208/09, EU:C:2010:806. At times of emergency the Treaties give powers to the European Council to be exercised within the full remit of legality (Arts 15 and 22 TEU, 68 and 196 TFEU).

[146] European Commission and High Representative of the European Union for Foreign Affairs and Security Policy, 'Resilience, Deterrence and Defence: Building Strong Cybersecurity for the EU' (Joint Communication) JOIN (2017) 450 final, 8. See ch 8.

[147] Arts 4(2) TEU, 72 TFEU referring to 'internal security'.

[148] ZZ, C-300/11, EU:C:2013:363, para 38.

[149] Eg, EU citizens' privacy and the security and reliability of EU communication networks. European Parliament (n 43) §§ 16, 37.

[150] A Hinarejos, 'Law and Order and Internal Security Provisions in the Area of Freedom, Security and Justice: Before and After Lisbon', in C Eckes et al. (eds), *Crime within the Area of Freedom, Security and Justice: a European Public Order* (Cambridge, Cambridge University Press, 2011).

[151] Arguing for 'falling' or 'acting within the scope of EU law', see Hinarejos (151); P Craig, *The Lisbon Treaty, Revised Edition: Law, Politics, and Treaty Reform* (Oxford, Oxford University Press 2013) 211–213.

law have clarified the meaning of 'implementing' to include situations where Member States derogate from EU law. In *Åkerberg Fransson* the Court stated that applicability of EU law entails automatic application of the Charter.[152] The Court developed a test for when Member States are implementing EU law in *Hernández*, though case law is far from settled.[153] As for situations where Member States' action 'is not entirely determined by Union law', 'national courts are free to apply national standards of protection of fundamental rights', so long as such standards do not compromise the level of protection afforded by the Charter, as well as the primacy, unity and effectiveness of EU law.[154]

Thus, when Member States act partly or entirely outside the remit of Union law, they do not operate in a legal void. First, they are constrained by their constitutions, which guarantee rights forming the traditions common to the Member States and informing the general principles of Union law.[155] Furthermore, situations that are not covered by Union law are covered by the ECHR,[156] as exemplified by *Big Brother Watch and Others v UK* addressing ECHR 'compliance of an intelligence sharing regime'.[157] Such constraints define what Angelini calls a composite European *ordre public*[158] hinging on Article 6 TEU, which connects EU law, the constitutional traditions of Member States and the ECHR, thereby fostering homogeneity among these systems.

Incidentally, a composite European *ordre public* can foster greater cooperation between the CJEU and national courts, cooperation that for Hinarejos[159] prevents deference to the executive at times of emergency.[160] In this sense, the national security exception relied upon in emergency decision-making could engender a cooperative[161] form of deference of the CJEU to both national courts – since the latter are the day-to-day executor of national and EU law[162] – and to the ECtHR as a court of last resort, which has progressively defined the margin of manoeuvre of contracting parties to the ECHR in cases of national security exceptions.[163] Thus, deference of courts to the executive, eg at times of a cyber-attack, could be avoided by means of the macro European *ordre public* enshrined in Article 6 TEU, which defines the *vouloir vivre* of EU Members. Such a *vouloir vivre* allows to make exceptions at times of emergency by constraining

---

[152] *Åkerberg Fransson*, C-617/10, EU:C:2013:105, para 21.
[153] In C-198/13, the Court set three parameters relevant to the determination of 'implementing' EU law; see especially D Chalmers and G Davies et al, *European Union Law*, 4th edn (Cambridge, Cambridge University Press 2019) 277–281; Court of Justice of the European Union, Field of Application of the Charter of Fundamental Rights of the European Union (2021), 3–20. See ch. 3.
[154] *Åkerberg Fransson*, C-617/10, para 29.
[155] TEU Art 6(3).
[156] '[if] that situation is not covered by European Union law, [the referring court] must undertake that examination in the light of Article 8(1) of the ECHR.' *Dereci and others v Bundesministerium für Inneres*, C-256/11, EU:C:2011:734, para 72.
[157] *Big Brother Watch and Others v UK* nos. 58170/13, 62322/14 and 24960/15, CE:ECHR:2018:0913 JUD005817013, para 416.
[158] Angelini (n 106).
[159] Hinarejos (n 150).
[160] On deference, see generally Curtin (n 123).
[161] K Lenaerts, 'The Contribution of the European Court of Justice to the Area of Freedom, Security and Justice' (2019) 59 *International and Comparative Law Quarterly* 255.
[162] See also TEU Art 19(1).
[163] Council of Europe, Division de la Recherche de la Cour Européenne des Droits de l'Homme, *Sécurité nationale et Jurisprudence de la Cour Européenne des Droits de l'Homme* (Council of Europe, 2013).

the exercise rather than the guarantees of rights, thereby leaving access to impartial courts –another RoL tenet – unaffected.[164]

Before turning to fundamental rights, it is important to stress that the action of the EU Institutions and Member States must also conform to legal certainty or lawfulness, which corresponds to the general principle of legal certainty and protection of legitimate expectations.[165] The rationale of lawfulness is to 'respect the ordinary citizen as active centers of intelligence',[166] who interact with and can challenge the legal process. The existence of a legal basis permitting the actions of a state and its organs is a necessary but insufficient step to fulfil legal certainty.[167] The (domestic) law must also respect parameters of quality guaranteeing foreseeability and the protection of legitimate expectations.

The pacing problem faced by cyberspace regulation – ie keeping up with innovation in cyberspace[168] – often leads to legal grey areas that undermine legal certainty. As a corollary of the quality of law the legislator should resolve conflicts of laws in the shape of a clash either between rights or rights and objectives of general interest. With respect to the triad, conflict of laws can result from the piecemeal evolution of legislation in the DSM, AFSJ and EA, so that clashing objectives should be avoided when implementing regulatory packages.[169] Since rights-holders must enjoy 'legal protection against any arbitrary interference' by public authorities,[170] legal certainty should extend to all steps of the regulatory process, including quasi-legislative acts and soft law. Coherence stands to benefit from legal certainty.

ii. Fundamental Rights: Test for Permissible Limitations, Proportionality and the Essence as a Fail-Safe against Zero-Sum Outcomes[171]

Fundamental rights are a RoL tenet, general principles of EU law whereof the court ensures observance[172] and primary law: thanks to Article 6(1) TEU, the Charter enjoys a status analogous to that of a constitutional Bill of Rights within a nation state.[173] The Charter protects the right to privacy and the protection of personal data found in Articles 7 and 8 of Title II on Freedom, together with other first generation qualified rights, that is rights that 'are not absolute … but must be considered in relation to their function in society'.[174]

---

[164] See the data retention saga, ch 7.
[165] Tridimas (n 126).
[166] Waldron (n 131) 4.
[167] *Big Brother Watch and Others v UK*, 58170/13, para 305.
[168] On pacing issues, L Bennett Moses, 'How to Think about Law, Regulation and Technology: Problems with 'Technology' as a Regulatory Target' (2013) 5 *Law, Innovation and Technology* 7. On legal uncertainty, Reed and Murray (n 131).
[169] See C Reed, *Making Laws for Cyberspace* (Oxford, Oxford University Press, 2012).
[170] *WebMindLicenses*, C-419/14, EC:C:2015:832, para 81.
[171] This section partly develops work published in MG Porcedda, *On Boundaries. In Search for the Essence of the Right to the Protection of Personal Data* (Oxford, Hart Publishing, 2018).
[172] TEU, Art 6(3); *Nold KG v European Commission*, C-4/73, EU:C:1974:51, para 13; T Tridimas, 'Primacy, Fundamental Rights and the Search for Legitimacy', in P Maduro et al. (eds), *The Past and Future of EU Law. The Classics of EU Law Revisited on the 50th Anniversary of the Rome Treaty* (Oxford, Hart Publishing, 2010).
[173] S Rodotà, *Il Diritto ad Avere Diritti* Bari (Editori Laterza, 2012).
[174] *Schwarz*, C-291/12, EU:C:2013:670, para 33.

The meaning and scope of such rights is disciplined by Title VII on horizontal provisions and particularly by Article 52, which deals both with permissible limitations and rules on the interpretation of the rights' substance. Accordingly, the meaning and subsequent practical enjoyment of Charter rights results from a constant dialogue between the interpretation of their substance and limitations. The latter are disciplined by Article 52 (1), whereby

> Any limitation on the exercise of the rights and freedoms recognised by this Charter must be provided for by law and respect the essence of those rights and freedoms. Subject to the principle of proportionality, limitations may be made only if they are necessary and genuinely meet objectives of general interest recognised by the Union or the need to protect the rights and freedoms of others.

Objectives of general interest are those listed in Article 3 TEU, including material *ordre public*. Accordingly, Article 52 embodies a test for permissible limitations that encompasses several RoL tenets, including legality, lawfulness, non-arbitrariness and proportionality.[175] Thus, the enjoyment of fundamental rights must be as complete as possible and any limitations pertain to the exercise of rights, not to their guarantees. The Explanations[176] to the Charter clarify that limitations must be interpreted restrictively. Following settled case law, interferences cannot 'constitute, with regard to the aim pursued, disproportionate and unreasonable interference undermining the very substance of those rights'.[177]

The Explanations appear to equate the notion of 'very substance' used by the CJEU as early as *Hauer*[178] with the essence, which acts as a bridge between substance, exercise and limitations of rights. While Article 52(1) allows for the application of a margin of appreciation, respect for the essence is deemed to be stringent,[179] in that a violation of the essence of the right would be impermissible.

The notion of essence contained in the Charter originates from German law, where it is tied to dignity.[180] Brkan suggests that it was codified in EU law as a general principle

---

[175] On the role of the ECHR, see chs 3, 4. Before the Charter acquired Treaty-like status, the ECJ lacked its own test for permissible limitations (Craig (n 151) 221–2) and either avoided expressing itself on the proportionality of a measure vis-à-vis rights recognised in the Charter or relied entirely on ECHR rights, eg, as in *Parliament v Council*, C-317/04 and C-318/04, EU:C:2006:346 *(PNR cases)*; *Schmidberger*, C-112/00, EU:C:2003:333. The entry into force of the Lisbon Treaty marked a change, with the test being relied on in data retention cases. As for the EU fundamental rights doctrine, CFR Art 52 refers to the inviolability of the essence of fundamental rights: one of the questions of the test or 'checklist' elaborated by the Commission to assess the compliance of legislation with the Charter reads: 'would any limitation preserve the essence of the fundamental rights concerned?' European Commission, Better Regulation Toolbox, (2021) 244.

[176] *Explanations Relating to the Charter of Fundamental Rights* [2007] OJ C 303/02 (Explanations to the Charter).

[177] *Karlsson and Others*, C-292/97, EU:C:2000:202, para 45.

[178] *Hauer v Land Rheinland-Pfalz*, C-44/79, EU:C:1979:290, para 23.

[179] Craig (n 151) 224–226.

[180] ibid 223–224; M Brkan, *In search of the concept of essence of EU fundamental rights through the prism of data privacy* (Maastricht Working Papers, Faculty of Law 2017-01, 2017) 14; 'The concept of essence of fundamental rights in the EU legal order: Peeling the onion to its core' (2018) 14 *European Constitutional Law Review*. The essence may not be unique to the Charter. The HRC declared in the context of General Comments 27, 31, 32 and 34 that restrictions on rights must not intrude upon the 'essence' of a human right. MG Porcedda and M Vermeulen et al., *Report on Regulatory Frameworks Concerning Privacy and the Evolution of the Norm of the Right to Privacy. Deliverable 3.2, SurPRISE Project* (European University Institute 2013)

stemming from the constitutional traditions of at least eight Member States, and as a concept rooted in Article 17 ECHR and the case law of the Strasbourg Court, which was echoed by the early case law of the CJEU.[181]

According to a part of scholarship, the essence is a relative concept bearing declaratory nature, and can therefore be subjected to a proportionality test.[182] For instance, in Alexy's theory of rights, the idea of 'essence' or 'cores' corrects the stalemate that may derive from a pure application of balancing (proportionality) by supplying additional layers of analysis.[183] Other scholars see the essence as an absolute boundary.[184] Scheinin[185] argues that a violation of the core, or essence, entails the impermissibility of a limitation and therefore precludes the further application of the test for permissible limitations. According to him, the essence is to be seen as a metaphor, in that fundamental rights may hold multiple cores 'defined through a multitude of factors' and 'not preventing contextual assessment'.[186] This approach was lent weight by *État Luxembourgeois v B and Others* on the right to an effective remedy, where the CJEU stated there can be multiple aspects to the essence, of which the Court identifies a few.[187]

The CJEU has pronounced itself, both directly and indirectly, on the essence of Articles 7 and 8 CFR in *Coty, McB, Digital Rights Ireland, Schrems* and *Opinion 1/15*. When broaching the subject directly, the Court has identified the essence in substantive facet[s] of the rights expressed in a provision of secondary law. However, in a few cases the CJEU remained open to the idea that the essence may correspond to the ultimate protection of the guarantee of the right, thereby conflating it with the right to defence. This was the case of *Coty*[188] and *Schrems*,[189] where the Court relied on the essence to draw conclusions that could have been equally reached by using the RoL and the general principles of EU law.

Thus far the Court has neither committed to a single understanding of the essence, nor offered a methodology enabling to ascertain the contents of the essence. The literature challenges the feasibility of finding the essence at all,[190] or once and for all. I agree that the essence cannot be carved in stone; to say the opposite would challenge the

---

surprise-project.eu/wp-content/uploads/2013/06/SurPRISE_D3.2_Report-on-regulatory-frameworks-concerning-privacy-for-final-formatting_v094.pdf.

[181] Brkan (n 180) (2017) 16–12.

[182] Brkan (n 180) (2018) 225. See generally, M Dawson et al. (ed) 'Special issue: Interrogating the Essence of EU Fundamental Rights' 20 (2019) 6 *German Law Journal*.

[183] Alexy, Constitutional Rights (n 105). See United Nations, International Human Rights Instruments, *Report on Indicators for Monitoring Compliance with International Human Rights Instruments* (HRI/MC/2006/7, 2006) 3.

[184] Brkan (n 180) (2018).

[185] M Scheinin, *Terrorism and the Pull of 'Balancing' in the Name of Security. Law and Security, Facing the Dilemmas* (European University Institute Law Working Paper 11, 2009).

[186] Scheinin in Porcedda et al (n 180) 43–44.

[187] The essence 'includes, among other aspects', *État luxembourgeois*, C-245/19 and C-246/19, EU:C:2020:795, para 66.

[188] *Coty Germany*, C-580/13, EU:C:2015:485.

[189] *Schrems*, C-362/14, EU:C:2015:650.

[190] S Gutwirth and R Gellert, 'The Legal Construction of Privacy and Data Protection' 29 *Computer Law and Security Review* 522–530; O Lynskey, *The Foundations of EU Data Protection Law* (Oxford, Oxford University Press, 2015); M Tzanou, *The Fundamental Right to Data Protection. Normative Value in the Context of Counter-Terrorism Surveillance* (Oxford, Hart Publishing, 2017); Brkan (n 180) (2018).

evolutive approach to human rights so needed in the face of fast-paced technological developments. Yet, even if the essence cannot be static, engaging with its meaning is instrumental to: (i) exploring the relationship between the two rights and cybersecurity at a granular level, to ascertain overlap; and (ii) correcting 'the pacing problem', whereby the law tries to keep up pace with technological developments. Knowing in advance which technological features could violate the essence could help ruling out the use of specific technologies; knowing which features constitute the essence could inform the creation of compliant technologies. I will address this in chapter 5.

Looking for the essence, or core areas, of the right, forces one to answer the question as to what constitutes the peripheries of the right – ie tracing its boundaries. Elsewhere I proposed to look at boundaries of rights as attributes, a term borrowed from the UN Office of the High Commissioner for Human Rights' (OHCHR) work on indicators,[191] which refers to the intrinsic and distinctive substantive dimensions of a right. In EU law, attributes could coincide with the notion of 'essential component', understood as an element contained in the wording of a Charter right but also subsumed under such a wording.[192] The essence should be seen as the core of an essential component and stem from a purposive interpretation of the right, expressing those core elements that aim to fulfil the ultimate ends or values of a right.

Lynskey notes that the notion of the essence traces a distinction between elements of secondary law which express essential components/essence of the right, and those which do not. This statement could be supplemented (and corrected insofar as Lynskey conflates the essence with essential components) by the fact that the notion of the essence triggers a three-tiered system of protection in secondary law, which includes elements expressing the essence, those which express essential components, and those which express peripheral elements of the right. The grounds for permissible limitations found in both the Charter and the ECHR can affect the peripheral and essential components, but prohibit public authorities pursuing cybersecurity from limiting the essence.

In sum, EU primary law features mechanisms for resolving controversies that point to the impermissibility of zero-sum outcomes, so that only four of the five modes of reconciliation of the triad identified above apply in EU law. Such mechanisms establish criteria of proportionality requiring that limitations on the exercise – but not the guarantees – and derogations from fundamental freedoms be interpreted restrictively[193] and stress the importance of coherence. The essence, which can be seen as a fail-safe mechanism against zero-sum outcomes, embodies a type of granularity that will be used in chapter 5 to investigate whether the triad overlaps. However, primary sources do not allow to identify the desired mode of reconciliation upfront, which is instead left to hierarchically lower sources, as illustrated next.

---

[191] Porcedda (n 171); United Nations (n 183) 3.
[192] See Opinion 1/15, paras 94, 229; *Schrems*, C-362/14, para 41. The CJEU has not used 'essential component' as an autonomous term and has also referred to it as elements pertaining to the matter under analysis beyond the Charter, eg, 'the seriousness of the infringement of the data subject's rights and freedoms is an essential component of the weighing or balancing exercise on a case-by-case basis, required by Article 7(f) of Directive 95/46' *Asociaţia de Proprietari bloc M5A-ScaraA*, C-708/18, EU:C:2019:1064, para 56. See also *Schrems*, C-362/14, ECLI:EU:C:2015:627, Opinion of AG Bot; *W. Ż. and des affaires publiques de la Cour suprême*, C-487/19, EU:C:2021:289, Opinion of AG Tanchev. See chs 2, 4.
[193] *Sayn-Wittgenstein*, C-208/09, paras 86–91.

B. Cybersecurity, Privacy and Data Protection as Situated Objects: Law, Policy and Technology

As seen, privacy and data protection achieved national and international human rights status well before they appeared in EU law as general principles in *National Panasonic* and *Fisher*[194] and, for privacy, as a right common to Member States' constitutional traditions.[195] Cybersecurity, privacy and data protection acquired real weight first as objects of policy in a post-Maastricht environment and the nascent 'digital' policy of the 1990s. Cybersecurity as information and computer security was a concern of early 'digital' policies and became a more nuanced, self-standing policy objective substantiated in discrete legal instruments only in 2013. Both privacy and data protection became self-standing policy objectives earlier due to their instrumental character in the pursuit of the four freedoms.[196] Data protection informed legislation at once limiting and enabling the free flow of data and the services processing such data; privacy was incorporated in legislation on the liberalisation of telecommunications and on restrictions on the freedom of movement and family reunification.[197]

The triad now spans across all areas of EU policy: the DSM, the AFSJ and EA (including the CFSP and CSDP). Inevitably, the interplay of the triad is affected by the tensions that exist within and across different policy areas, tensions due to the legacy of the institutional development of EU policymaking, the epistemic communities that animate those policy areas and the values they pursue. An example of legacy institutional features is the sectoral policy approach, due to Member States' slow and progressive relinquishment of exclusive competence in areas such as telecoms or energy monopolies and law and order. Values expressed by different epistemic communities include the imperative to innovate in the DSM and the 'particularly serious' crime rhetoric in the AFSJ and are reflected in different meanings of cybersecurity across policy areas. To this must be added the external dimension of each policy area, which plays a significant role given the international nature of cyberspace and data flows. Thus, it is possible that the triad could be reconcilable in principle but not in practice in light of policy idiosyncrasies. To this effect, at various points this work will highlight tensions inherent in policy.

To produce results, policy must be translated into law, of which exist different types ranging from general to specific application,[198] but all working within the constraints of the EU constitutional order discussed earlier. Thus, laws vary in levels of abstraction and force, with the constitutional *ordre public* at the top and targeted or technical regulation at the bottom. The triad is the object of the full range of EU law, from primary to

---

[194] *National Panasonic v Commission*, C-136/79, EU:C:1980:169, para 17, in J Kokott and C Sobotta, 'The Distinction between Privacy and Data Protection in the Jurisprudence of the CJEU and the ECtHR' (2013) 3 *International Data Privacy Law* 222–228; *Fisher*, C-369/98, EU:C:2000:443, para 34.
[195] ibid.
[196] For privacy, *Runevič-Vardyn and Wardyn*, C-391/09, EU:C:2011:291, para 90. See also G González Fuster, *The Emergence of Personal Data Protection as a Fundamental Right in Europe* (Cham, Springer, 2014).
[197] See chs 4, 3; See I Walden (ed), *Telecommunications Law and Regulation*, 5th edn (Oxford, Oxford University Press, 2018); L Edwards and C Waelde, *Law and the Internet* (Oxford, Hart Publishing, 2009).
[198] European Commission (n 175) 120–131.

delegated instruments and across the main areas of EU law making: DSM, AFSJ and EA. Human rights are at once elements of the RoL, general principles, objectives of general interest and primary law enshrined in the Charter. The inclusion of privacy and data protection in the Charter marked the end of the secondary, instrumental character of both rights, especially after the Lisbon Treaty elevated the CFR to constitutional status, reinforced for data protection by Article 16 TFEU and for privacy by Article 8 ECHR. Both rights are implemented and substantiated by secondary law.[199] Cybersecurity does not have primary law 'anchoring' but gives significance to references to security found in primary law, either as a self-standing objective or as a limitation of EU primary law.[200]

EU instruments in each area of law-making reflect the same idiosyncrasies of policy. For instance, sectoral policy leads to sectoral legislation liable to produce fragmentation and to undermine coherence. Sometimes connections or synergies result from a spillover of successful regulatory solutions across instruments and sectors and from one legislative area into another.[201] As noted with respect to policy, I will also account for the possibility that the triad could be reconcilable in principle but not in practice, either: (i) in light of regulatory idiosyncrasies; or (ii) as we move from hierarchically higher to lower instruments.

With respect to (ii), the EU *ordre public* is fine-tuned for high level reconciliation but does not command how the triad is to be reconciled. That determination is left to a synthesis of values achieved through lawmaking and, in court, on a case-by-case basis, by weighing the proportionality of measures and their possible encroachment on the essence of rights. To identify fragmentation or synergies relevant to the triad, I will select comparators to study legislation across sectors. The research will investigate to what extent various levels of lawmaking can guide the reconciliation of the triad in light of (i) select regulatory techniques, especially technology neutrality for futureproofing[202] and design-based legislation aiming to infuse values in technology-related measures.

It should not be forgotten that the triad shares a common technological denominator: cyberspace. There, information, data and signals all relate to one another with data often acting as a regulatory proxy; the way how technology ('code'[203]) affects data flows and the processing of data plays a crucial but often hidden or invisible role. Just like policy and law, technology embodies inherent tensions in a way that affects, bottom-up, the area to which it is applied. Thus, different technological designs are capable of either easing or exacerbating tensions between select values. It is only by looking at the technologically-mediated application of laws that we can make sense of the relationship

---

[199] Included thanks to the modernising influence of several 'personal data protection' activists among the members of the Convention: Piris (n 110); González Fuster (n 196). See chs 3, 4.
[200] In agreement with scholars stating that cybersecurity is a facet of security among six found in EU law alongside CFSP, AFSJ, limitation of EU primary law, ground to restrict free movement and confidentiality of information. (G González Fuster, S Gutwirth et al, *Discussion Paper on Legal Approaches to Security, Privacy and Personal Data Protection, PRISMS Project, Deliverable 5.1* (2013).
[201] On sectoral influences, conflicts and mainstreaming: S Smismans and R Minto, 'Are integrated impact assessments the way forward for mainstreaming in the European Union?' (2017) 11 *Regulation & Governance* 231–251. See chs 6–8 on 'functional interconnection'.
[202] European Commission (n 175) 174.
[203] Lessig (n 70).

of the triad and how they can be reconciled. In this guise, the architecture of rights, including the concept of the essence, can and should be used to understand whether the values imbued in technology and in rights are commensurable as well as to expose areas of interdependence and of tension.

The assessment as to the reconcilability of the triad requires comparing the design of technology implementing the applicable law with the layered configuration of the rights in EU law – but there is a catch. The analysis of technological implementation is both a sizeable collaborative and interdisciplinary exercise and is easily frustrated by the proprietary nature of technology and its underlying code. Thus, in this research we can only meaningfully look at technology as a regulatory 'target',[204] addressed both by secondary legislation and technical standards. Such an exercise has limitations as will become apparent in chapters six to eight through the example of deep packet inspection, a technological application no longer considered relevant by some, but mentioned in law as recently as 2021 and still marketed.[205] The doubts emerging from that analysis will illustrate how the shortcomings of technology law, chiefly the invisibility or 'effacement' of technology from the law, ultimately make it impossible to determine how the triad can be reconciled, with adverse consequences for the enjoyment of cybersecurity, privacy and data protection.

III. Conclusion: An Analytical Framework to Study the Relationship of the Triad

This chapter offered a concise introduction to the concepts of cybersecurity, privacy and data protection (the triad) and their tangled or ambivalent relationship. A retrospective reflection of revelations of mass-scale surveillance in the mid-2010s showed that the triad can at once clash, ie data protection and privacy can be pitted against security through cyberspace, while also being complementary with the security of cyberspace. The ambivalent relationship can be explained by considering the shared technological environment: the triad interacts in the shared, open-ended environment of cyberspace where information – good and bad – flows in the shape of data and signals, concepts that can in some respect be seen as tautologies.

The ambivalent relationship between cybersecurity, data protection and privacy was conceptualised along an axis ranging from no to complete reconciliation. At one end of the spectrum, no reconciliation takes the form of a zero-sum clash, in which one element annihilated the other. Next to the right comes weak reconciliation, in the form of a clash that can be resolved through balancing. Somewhere in between stands indifference, in which the elements of the triad do not affect each other. At the other end of the spectrum lies strong reconciliation in the form of convergence and overlap leading to complete reconciliation.

---

[204] Mindful of Bennett Moses' urge to privilege the evolving socio-technical landscape than single technologies (n 163).
[205] Chs 6–8.

Conclusion: An Analytical Framework to Study the Relationship of the Triad

Starting with the rejection of zero-sum outcomes, this chapter identified elements for an analytical framework to investigate weak, strong and complete reconciliation. Accordingly, to analyse the reconcilability of the triad we must study cybersecurity, privacy and data protection as legally situated referents constrained by the EU *ordre public*, through the analysis of concrete policies cognisant of the role of technology.

The analysis identified the substance of the EU *ordre public*, where the rule of law provides a framework in support for weak and strong reconciliation. The test for permissible limitations enriched by the essence precludes zero-sum games between security, including cybersecurity, and rights, such as privacy and data protection. However, the constitutional architecture falls short of defining how to articulate the relationship between security and rights, which is instead left to hierarchically lower legal sources.

To treat cybersecurity, privacy and data protection as situated techno-legal objects of enquiry one must look at each separately and as they interact in the DSM, AFSJ and EA through policy, law and technology, bearing in mind the features and limitations of such areas of EU decision-making. This research will first address cybersecurity, privacy and data protection as self-standing regulatory objectives, but with an eye to their commonalities (Part 1 of the book). Thereafter, the focus will be on the interaction of the triad in the DSM, AFSJ and External Action (Part 2 of the book) through law, policy and technology.

2
The EU Cybersecurity Policy

The EU cybersecurity policy came of age in 2013. Originally addressed together with privacy and data protection, cybersecurity morphed into an independent policy objective at the end of the gradual expansion of the Union's competences beyond the Internal Market effected by the Maastricht, Amsterdam and Lisbon Treaties.

In section I, I examine the evolution of the Union's approach to cybersecurity before (I.A) and after 2013 (I.B) vis-à-vis legal, technological and political developments. Legally, the tensions inherent in the implementation of successive Treaties have led to policy fragmentation. The cybersecurity policy has also been influenced by geopolitically significant technological change. Finally, the cybersecurity policy has been influenced by the international socio-political landscape, from the 'long decade' of the war on terror[1] to shifting geopolitics, which have spurred a growing string of surveillance-related scandals as well as cyber-attacks. I subsequently appraise the state of the art of the cybersecurity policy to reveal the interactions and tensions between the different dimensions of the policy and the interplay of those dimensions with privacy and data protection.

In section II, I examine the Union's current cybersecurity policy across the three main areas of EU law making. I provide a synthetic overview of the main instruments and policy initiatives, both in force and in the making, within each area as well as the actors responsible for them. I also identify the tensions existing within each area and between initiatives and actors. Such tensions affect the coherence of EU cybersecurity law as well as the interplay between privacy, data protection and cybersecurity.

I. The Development of the EU Cybersecurity Policy

A. The EU's Approach to the Security of Cyberspace before 2013

The Union's policy on security in cyberspace has evolved in line with the expansion of the Union's competences within and beyond the Internal Market.[2] At first, the Union

---

[1] D Jenkins, 'Introduction. The Long Decade', in D Jenkins, A Jacobsen and A Henrikens (eds), *The Long Decade: How 9/11 Changed the Law* (Oxford, Oxford University Press, 2014).
[2] For analyses pre-dating the 2013 policy: MG Porcedda, *Data Protection and the Prevention of Cybercrime: the EU as an Area of Security?* (European University Institute Working Paper, Law 2012/25, 2012). From a

dealt with the 'Single Market' side of the information society, because Justice and Home Affairs (JHA), the so-called 'third pillar', was an area of intergovernmental decision-making subject to the principle of unanimity and outside the oversight of the Luxembourg courts.[3] The EU first addressed the challenges and opportunities of Web 1.0[4] in its White Paper and the so-called *Bangemann Report*,[5] and subsequently the Action Plan to Combat Cybercrime.[6] Web 1.0 is shorthand for the early World Wide Web created by hyperlinked information outlets and made possible by Tim Berners Lee's development of the HTTP protocol. At that time, although access to the Internet was limited, power was fairly distributed and data exchanges happened point-to-point and based on contracts,[7] which were more conducive to high levels of trust and therefore helped preserve the historical prioritisation of usability over security.[8]

Cycles of boom and bust moulded the Internet into its current form. The dot-com boom broadened the user base of the Internet, followed by the dot-com crash, which momentarily halted digital progress. Web 2.0 and cloud computing heralded a new era of the information society.[9] Web 2.0 enabled the production of information alongside its consumption, thanks to the nascent paradigm of cloud computing, which allowed the rationalisation of computing resources, whether in terms of storage capacity or power, to enable on-demand and simultaneous usage of Internet resources.[10] Such a process also enabled datafication and the monetisation of surplus personal data.[11] Such changes brought to an end point-to-point data exchanges, and laid the foundations for the increasing control of the Internet by

---

political science perspective: G Christou, *Cybersecurity in the European Union. Resilience and Adaptability in Governance and Policy* (Basingstoke, Palgrave Macmillan, 2015). A summary from an external relations' perspective: P Pawlak, *Operational Guidance for the EU's international cooperation on cyber capacity building* (European Union Institute for Security Studies 2018).

[3] It is disputed the EU had autonomous competence to adopt and enact measures of a criminal nature. P Craig and G de Búrca, *European Union Law: Text, Cases and Materials* (Press ed, 2015) 979.

[4] A Murray, *Information Technology Law. Law and Society*, 4th edn (Oxford, Oxford University Press, 2019) 111–116.

[5] European Commission, 'White Paper on Growth, Competitiveness, Employment. The Challenges and Ways forward into the 21st Century' (Communication) COM (93) 700; M Bangemann et al., The 'Recommendations to the European Council. Europe and the Global Information Society'. *The Bangemann Report* (1994).

[6] H Carrapico and A Barrinha, 'The EU as a Coherent (Cyber)Security Actor?' (2017) 55 *Journal of Common Market Studies* 1254, 1272.

[7] PE Hustinx, *Data Protection and Cloud Computing under EU Law* (2010).

[8] AS Tanenbaum and DJ Wetherall, *Reti di Calcolatori (Quinta Edizione)* (Pearson Italia, 2011) 727; S Landau, *Surveillance or Security? The Risk Posed by New Wiretapping Technologies* (Cambridge, MIT Press 2010) 38, 55–57. See ch. 1, section I.A.

[9] S Zuboff, 'Surveillance Capitalism and the Challenge of Collective Action' (2019) 28 *New Labor Forum* 10–29, 12.

[10] International Telecommunication Union (ITU) and International Organization for Standarization (ISO), *International Standard ISO/IEC 17788, Information Technology – Cloud computing – Overview and vocabulary, Recommendation ITU/T Y.3500* (International Telecommunications Union, 2014).

[11] S Zuboff, 'Big Other: Surveillance Capitalism and the Prospects of an Information Civilization' (2015) 30 *Journal of Information Technology* 75–89; Zuboff (n 9).

a handful of powerful corporations, which followed the libertarian, blitzkrieg-style motto 'move fast and break things'.[12] Two consequences are that legal grey areas were interpreted as the 'Wild West'[13] and that, since the old preference for usability over information security had not been challenged, the road was eased for the spread of cybercrime.

Against this background, EU institutions, and primarily the European Commission (Commission or EC), adopted a series of documents which would later fall under the umbrella of cybersecurity. In 2000, the Commission published its first Communication on cybercrime and the security of information infrastructure, called network and information security and critical information infrastructure protection (CIIP).[14] There, the Commission urged the adoption of a 'security by design' approach toward the information infrastructure, and acknowledged that 'the implementation of security obligations following in particular from the EU Data Protection Directives contributes to enhancing security of the networks and of data processing'.[15] As for cybercrime, the Commission encouraged investing and using 'effective prevention measures' 'so as to reduce the need to' follow a traditional criminal law stance based on reaction.[16] The communication also described encryption as 'an essential tool to facilitate the implementation and adoption of new services, including' e-commerce and capable of making 'a substantial contribution to the prevention of crime on the Internet'.[17]

A year later, the Commission adopted a Communication on network and information security (NIS).[18] NIS was understood as 'the ability of a network or an information system to resist, at a given level of confidence, accidental events or malicious actions [which] could compromise the availability, authenticity, integrity and confidentiality of stored or transmitted data as well as related services offered via these networks and systems'.[19] Therein, the Commission proposed its 'three-pronged approach', shown in Figure 1:

> The proposed policy measures with regard to network and information security have to be seen in the context of the existing telecommunications, data protection, and cyber-crime policies. A network and information security policy will provide the missing link in this policy framework.[20]

---

[12] One of the guiding mottos of Meta's founder Mark Zuckenberg; see A McCollum, 'The Unavoidable Truth of Moving Fast and Breaking Things' *TechCrunch* (New York, 10 March 2015).

[13] In spite of *opinio juris* to the effect that 'new technologies are subject to pre-existing international law absent a legal exclusion therefrom', MN Schmitt (ed), *The Tallin Manual 2.0 on the International Law Applicable to International Jurisdictions* (Cambridge, Cambridge University Press, 2017), 31; Landau (n 8) 37–63.

[14] European Commission, 'Creating a Safer Information Society by Improving the Security of Information Infrastructures and Combating Computer-Related Crime' (Communication) COM (2000) 890 final.

[15] ibid 11.

[16] ibid 14.

[17] ibid 24.

[18] European Commission, 'Network and Information Security: Proposal for a European Policy Approach' (Communication) COM (2001) 298.

[19] ibid 3.

[20] COM (2001) 298 final (n 18) 2.

Figure 1 The three-pronged approach, COM (2001) 298, 3

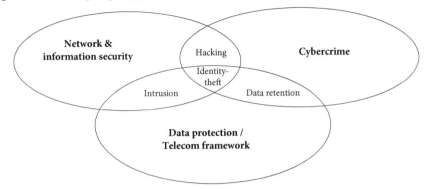

Accordingly, the protection of personal data, NIS and the prevention of cybercrime are seen as complementary strategies converging toward the same goal: ensuring a safe development of the information society. Therefore, not only was it acknowledged that the 'protection of privacy is a key policy objective in the European Union',[21] but also that privacy and data protection are not at odds with cybercrime prevention and the pursuit of cybersecurity. The provisions contained in the data protection legal regime[22] were explicitly linked to the prevention of certain types of cybercrimes, and the safeguarding of NIS. Furthermore, whereas the Commission acknowledged the need to criminally investigate cybercrime, it warned against creating 'solutions where legal requirements lead to weakening the security of communication and information systems'[23] – that is encryption.

Thanks to the new JHA powers conferred by the Treaty of Amsterdam,[24] in 2002 the Commission proposed Council Framework Decision 2005/222/JHA on attacks against information systems.[25] At that time, the data protection community criticised the Commission's approach as being too focussed on repression and security, and warned that, in adopting offences, 'there had to be perfect coherence with the existing rules on data protection'.[26] Despite the clear connection clauses of Decision 2005/222/JHA[27] to the Council of Europe (CoE) Budapest Convention on Cybercrime,[28] which covers a broad spectrum of cybercrimes and rules for the collection of e-evidence, the Decision solely addressed substantive rules on offences against NIS or 'cyber-dependent'

---

[21] ibid 24.
[22] Ie, Arts 17 Directive 95/46/EC and 4–5 Directive 97/66/EC, both repealed.
[23] COM (2001) 298 final (n 18) 25.
[24] S Peers, *EU Justice and Home Affairs Law* (Oxford, Oxford University Press, 2011) 17–41.
[25] Council Framework Decision 2005/222/JHA of 24 February 2005 on attacks against information systems [2005] OJ L69/67.
[26] Article 29 Data Protection Working Party, Opinion 9/2001 on the Commission Communication on 'Creating a safer information society by improving the security of information infrastructures and combating computer-related crime' (2001), respectively 3 and 5.
[27] Recital 15. See M Cremona, 'A Triple Braid: Interactions between International Law, EU Law and Private Law', in Cremona et al. (eds), *Private Law in the External Relation of the EU* (Oxford, Oxford University Press, 2016) 49–54.
[28] Convention on Cybercrime, Council of Europe, CETS n. 105, 23 November 2001.

crimes (below), the prevention of which was supported by data protection and privacy measures.

By the time the Decision was adopted, the political and technological climate had dramatically changed. After 2005, the Commission and the Council seemed to endorse a 'national security' approach towards cyber-attacks and cybercrimes, presented as existential threats to the Member States (MSs) and the Union.[29] According to the Report on the Implementation of the European Security Strategy, which first mentioned cybersecurity

> The EU Strategy for a Secure Information Society, adopted in 2006 addresses internet-based crime. However, attacks against private or government IT systems in EU Member States have given this a new dimension, as a potential new economic, political and military weapon.[30]

Arguably this reflected the 'war on terror' climate that followed 9/11, and the beginning of cyber-attacks against states. Indeed, after the attack against the World Trade Centre, politicians made, often successfully, the case for obtaining as unfettered as possible investigatory powers. The US led the way under the doctrine of the unitary executive, followed by the EU and its Member States, especially after the London and Madrid bombings. Policy responses, which have been amply commented upon in the literature,[31] have targeted critical infrastructure (CI), particularly airports or points of entry, stiffened criminal law provisions and even led to military action. At the same time, data became increasingly available thanks to the accumulation of surplus data or 'data exhaust'[32] – that is, personal data generated by users in the course of their online activities. Measures included demanding telcos retain data concerning the use of ICTs by their customers, which in the Union led to the invalidated Data Retention Directive.[33] Governments also vouched for sweeping powers of interception not matched by adequate safeguards, as was the case of the Budapest Convention.[34]

---

[29] European Council, Report on the Implementation of the European Security Strategy – Providing Security in a Changing World ((European Security Strategy) S407/08, 2008); Council, *The Stockholm Programme. An Open and Secure Europe Serving and Protecting Citizens* [2010] OJ C115. This shift is also noted by Carrapico and Barrinha (n 6) 1260.

[30] European Council (n 29) 7.

[31] For the US, see generally B Schneier, *Beyond Fear: Thinking Sensibly about Security in an Uncertain World* (New York, Springer, 2003); LK Donohue, *The Cost of Counterterrorism. Power, Politics and Liberty* (Cambridge, Cambridge University Press, 2008). For the EU, see generally M Levi and DS Wall, 'Technology, Security and Privacy in Post-9/11 European Information Society' (2004) 31 *Journal of Law and Society*; K Moss, *Balancing Liberty and Security. Human Rights, Human Wrongs* (Basingstoke, Palgrave Macmillan, 2011); F Galli and A Weyembergh (eds), *EU Counter-terrorism Offences. What Impact on National Legislation and Case Law?* (Editions de l'Université de Bruxelles 2012). At UN level, see M Scheinin, *Report of the Special Rapporteur on the Promotion and Protection of Human Rights and Fundamental Freedoms while Countering Terrorism*, A/HRC/13/37 (2009).

[32] Zuboff (n 11).

[33] Directive 2006/24/EC of the European Parliament and of the Council of 15 March 2006 on the Retention of Data Generated or Processed in Connection with the Provision of Publicly Available Electronic Communications Services or of Public Communications Networks and Amending Directive 2002/58/EC [2006] OJ L105/54 (Data Retention Directive).

[34] D Dragicevic and H Kaspersen et al., *Conditions and Safeguards under the Budapest Convention on Cybercrime*, Discussion Paper, EU/COE Joint Project on Regional Cooperation against Cybercrime (Council of Europe 2012); Article 29 Data Protection Working Party, (n 26); Opinion 4/2001 [on] the Council of Europe's Draft Convention on Cyber-crime (WP 41), (2001). See ch 7.

The beginning of the twenty-first century was also marked by the first cyber-attacks against nation states. Stuxnet, the US and Israeli-made malware that undermined the Iranian nuclear development programme, is an obvious example, but the first known attack was against an EU Member State, Estonia.[35] The Baltic country, which heavily relied on networked technologies, suffered a paralysis of its critical infrastructure, which revealed the disastrous effects of cyber-attacks.

As a result of these events, threats in cyberspace were increasingly cast as fundamental to the survival of the nation.[36] Subsequent EU policy documents, such as the Stockholm Programme,[37] demanded full respect for fundamental rights but no longer cast data as an important means of transaction and object of protection;[38] rather, data were dangerous vectors of attack and coveted sources of evidence and intelligence.

B. The Adoption of the EU Cybersecurity Policy

The policy developments implementing the Stockholm Programme and subsequent documents took place in the aftermath of the entry into force of the Lisbon Treaty, which had a seismic impact on cybersecurity. First, JHA-related matters became fully 'communitarised': the EU acquired specific competence in criminal law, an area which became subject to the ordinary legislative procedure based on a majority vote, and subject to the scrutiny of the Luxembourg Court. Second, Article 83 TFEU replacing Article 31 TEU came to include computer crime among measures with a cross-border dimension calling for common action. This offered a clear legal basis for the approximation of legislation on the fight against cybercrime. Third, the Charter of Fundamental Rights of the European Union (Charter and CFR), containing a self-standing right to data protection, became legally binding.[39] These steady but patchy developments mean that the cybersecurity policy could only evolve in a piecemeal and fragmented fashion. The policy has also been exposed to and affected by the tensions inherent in the implementation of those treaties: an example is the 'communitarisation' of the JHA 'pillar' which, following Carrera and Guild,[40] was not frictionless. Entrenched practices, in fact, are hard to erase; the 'pillars', and the logics informing them, may have indeed survived in the 2013 Cyber Security Policy, discussed next.

---

[35] S Brenner, *Cyberthreats and the Decline of the Nation-state* (London, Routledge, 2014) Stuxnet: 79–81, Estonia: 18–21, 75–87.

[36] On securitisation, see ch 1, ss I.A–I.C.

[37] European Commission, 'Delivering an Area of Freedom, Security and Justice for Europe's Citizens – Action Plan Implementing the Stockholm Programme' (Communication) COM (2010) 171 final, 5.

[38] Porcedda (n 2).

[39] Charter [2012] OJ C326/391 (CFR).

[40] S Carrera and E Guild, *The European Council's Guidelines for the Area of Freedom, Security and Justice 2020: Subverting the 'Lisbonisation' of Justice and Home Affairs?* (CEPS Essay n° 13/14, 2014). They show how the different JHA programmes sponsored by the institutions are at odds with one another.

i. The 2013 Cyber Security Policy

In February 2013 the Commission, jointly with the High Representative for Foreign Affairs and Security Policy (High Representative) adopted the first Cyber Security Policy.[41] The policy does not define cybersecurity, but a note clarifies that the term refers to

> The safeguards and actions that can be used to protect the cyber domain, both in the civilian and military fields, from those threats that are associated with or that may harm its interdependent networks and information infrastructure. Cyber-security strives to preserve the availability and integrity of the networks and infrastructure and the confidentiality of the information contained therein.[42]

Such a definition embodies a narrow version of cybersecurity and cyberspace. It refers to threats to networks and information infrastructure as in the now-repealed 2002 OECD security guidelines, rather than addressing human conduct in cyberspace or crime related to content.[43] This definition is not free from criticism[44] nor is the policy itself for being built on shaky ground. For instance, Fahey critiques the policy's overstretched risk-management approach unmatched by guidance on what constitutes risk in cyberspace, whereas Bendiek et al. deprecate the fuzziness of its key terms, such as resilience, which is inherently ambiguous.[45]

Cybersecurity is informed by five principles. First, EU laws concerning the physical world also apply to cyberspace. This means, second, that cybersecurity actions must respect the rights enshrined in the Charter, and particularly privacy and data protection, which are seen as benefitting from NIS. In this respect, the policy refers to personal data as a right to be safeguarded and states that the regulatory framework overseeing data protection has import for NIS, without however stressing any further connections, such as the positive preventative role played by the implementation of data protection rules noted in early documents.[46] A third principle is that the Internet and information flows should be available to everyone. Fourth, the governance of cyberspace should involve all relevant stakeholders and be democratic. Lastly, ensuring cybersecurity is a transversal responsibility concerning all actors.

---

[41] European Commission and High Representative of the European Union for Foreign Affairs and Security Policy, 'Cyber Security Strategy: An Open, Safe and Secure Cyberspace' (Joint Communication) JOIN (2013) 01 final.

[42] ibid 3.

[43] OECD, *Recommendation on Guidelines for the Security of Information and Networks. Towards a Culture of Security* (2002). For a distinction between cybersecurity and cybersafety, S Adams and M Brokx et al., *The Governance of Cybersecurity: A comparative quick scan of approaches in Canada, Estonia, Germany, the Netherlands and the UK* (Tilburg, Tilburg University, 2015) 26. See ch 6.

[44] R Mattioli, 'The 'State(s)' of Cybersecurity' in G Giacomello (ed), *Security in Cyberspace* (London, Bloomsbury, 2014); KE Silva, 'Europe's Fragmented Approach Towards Cyber Security' 2 *Internet Policy Review Journal on Internet Regulation* 4.

[45] E Fahey, 'The EU's Cybercrime and Cyber-Security Rulemaking: Mapping the Internal and External Dimension of EU Security' (2014) 5 *European Journal of Risk and Regulation* 46–60; A Bendiek, R Bossong et al., *The EU's Revised Cybersecurity Strategy. Half-Hearted Progress on Far-Reaching Challenges* (SWP Comments, 2017). Christou (n 2) notes that resilience has at least three meanings.

[46] Porcedda (n 2).

The five principles support five objectives, namely: i) achieving resilience; ii) reducing cybercrime; iii) developing cyber defence policy and capabilities; iv) developing industrial and technological resources; and v) adopting a coherent international cyber policy aligned with EU values. Each objective leads on to a set of actions shown in Figure 2.

Figure 2 Overview of the objectives of the Cybersecurity Strategy[47]

I. Achieving cyber resilience	increasing member states' and private sector capabilities
	improving information sharing
	step up cyber security awareness
II. Reducing cybercrime	transposing swiftly existing laws
	improving operational capabilities against cybercrime
	better coordination at EU level
III. Developing cyber defence policy and capabilities	assessing needs for EU operational cyber defence; fostering uptake of EU operational capabilities and tech
	Adopting a policy framework to protect networks used within CSDP missions and operations
	promoting dialogue and coordination between civilian and military actors in the EU
IV. Developing industrial and technological resources	promoting a single market for cyber security products
	fostering R&D investments and innovation
V. Coherent international cyber policy aligned with EU values	including cyberspace issues into EU external relations and CFSP
	supporting creation of norms of behaviour and confidence building in cyber security
	supporting promotion & protection of fundamental rights, including access to information and freedom of expression
	supporting global cyber security capacity building

The proposed objectives and actions, described by Carrapico and Barrinha as an attempt to pursue coherence in the field,[48] are streamlined into three pillars, corresponding to different actors operating under different legal frameworks. The first pillar is NIS, overseen by the Directorate General Connect and the European Union Network and Information Security Agency (ENISA) aka European Union Agency for Cybersecurity. The second is law enforcement to tackle cybercrime, which is within the remit of DG Home and Europol's Cybercrime Centre. The last pillar is defence, which is administered by the European External Action Service and the European Defence Agency. Each pillar is specified by dedicated legal measures.

---

[47] Figure 2 draws from Figure 1 of European Commission, Assessment of the EU 2013 Cybersecurity Strategy (Staff Working Document) SWD(2017) 295 final, (2017), 5.
[48] Carrapico and Barrinha (n 6) 1260.

Figure 3 The integration between NIS, LEAs and defence[49]

	Network and Information security	Law enforcement	Defence	
EU	• Commission/ENISA • CERT-EU • Network of competent authorities • EP3R	• EC3/Europol • CEPOL • Eurojust	• EEAS • European Defence Agency	Industry Academia
NATIONAL	• National CERTs • NIS competent authorities	• National Cybercrime Units	• National defence and security authorities	

When comparing the three pillars of the cybersecurity policy shown in Figure 3 with the three-pronged approach, one has the impression that the 'defence' pillar in today's policy has replaced the old data protection/telecom prong. Looking at 'cyberspace' as a 'domain' evokes militarisation, which for Fahey is actually a premise of the adopted definition of cybersecurity.[50] Moreover, the three pillars described in the policy stand in contrast with the definition of cybersecurity given above. The definition describes cybercrime as NIS, which does not square with the second pillar, whereby 'cybercrime' seems to embrace all misconduct in cyberspace – well beyond the ambiguity which Klimburg and Tiirmaa-Klaar claim for cyberspace.[51] This seems to suggest, at the very least, that the policy gives voice to competing and possibly conflicting interests, a conclusion also drawn by Carrapico and Barrinha, though based on a different analysis.[52]

Some of the policy's objectives fall neatly within a single pillar, whereas other objectives are cross-cutting. Achieving cyber resilience corresponds to NIS,[53] reducing cybercrime corresponds to law enforcement, and developing cyber defence policy and capabilities fits within defence. The objective of developing industrial and technological resources mostly concerns NIS but has a bearing on the other two pillars. Likewise, the objective 'international cyber policy' can concern any pillar and is therefore transversal to all.

C. The 2017 'Update' to the Cybersecurity Policy

The 2013 cybersecurity policy preceded by a few months the Snowden revelations,[54] whose far-reaching consequences impacted on the development of the EU cybersecurity

---

[49] JOIN (2013) 01 final (n 41) 17.
[50] Fahey (n 45) 49.
[51] A Klimburg and H Tiirmaa-Klaar, *Cybersecurity and Cyberpower: Concepts, Conditions and Capabilities for Cooperation for Action within the EU* (Think Tank, European Parliament, 2011).
[52] Carrapico and Barrinha (n 6).
[53] *cf* Ghernaouti, stating that resilience covers several dimensions translating into operational measures including the fight against cybercrime, cyber defence and the creation of adequate skills. S Ghernaouti, 'The Cyber Security Continuum to Enhance Cyber Resilience' in International Telecommunication Union (ed), *The Quest for Cyber Confidence* (International Telecommunications Union 2014) 76–83.
[54] See ch 1, s 1.2.

policy. Snowden's revelations, and the subsequent Cambridge Analytica scandal,[55] revealed the extent to which the information society relied on corporations that are engaged in the monopolistic control of data flows, a resource which the security apparatuses of Member States seem to have made ample use of. In the intervening years the Commission adopted the Digital Single Market (DSM) Strategy.[56] The expansion of data flows thanks to the Internet of Things (IoT) endowed with Artificial Intelligence (AI), such as autonomous cars and personal assistants, the Web 3.0 and data science, has both spurred the data economy[57] and broadened the 'attack surface', whereby offenders can target any devices connected to the Internet[58] and the databases making sense of the data such devices produce.

It is therefore unsurprising that the Commission found in 2017 that the five objectives identified in the 2013 Cyber Strategy were still valid, but that the Strategy was insufficiently equipped to address intervening challenges. Challenges include the impact of the IoT and the apportioning of responsibility between users and providers of products and services featuring digital or connected components. Other challenges are to guarantee the cybersecurity of sectors outside the scope of the NIS Directive (NISD) and managing crises in case of large-scale attacks.[59] The Commission also touches on the 'evolving cybercrime business models' dominated by the 'the efficiency of cybercrime monetization'[60] heralding the emergence of new actors. Cyber-attacks are in fact booming because 'the ever-increasing connectivity of poorly secured devices (reaching today the key systems that control citizens' cars, factories, homes, farms, hospitals and all critical infrastructures) have substantially increased the surface of possible cyber-attacks, eagerly used by cybercriminals'.[61] Some Member States reported that over half of all crimes are cybercrimes.[62]

To address 'the challenges caused by the new threat landscape and technological developments', the Commission released a cybersecurity package in 2017, backed by

---

[55] J Westby, "The Great Hack': Cambridge Analytica is Just the Tip of the Iceberg' (*Amensty International*, 2019) www.amnesty.org/en/latest/news/2019/07/the-great-hack-facebook-cambridge-analytica/.

[56] European Commission, 'A Digital Single Market Strategy for Europe' (Communication) COM (2015) 192 final.

[57] *Liability for Emerging Digital Technologies* (Staff Working Document) SWD (2018) 137 final. The Web 3.0, a.k.a. Web of Data, refers to online contents accompanied by metadata that are machine readable and therefore can be automatically processed. Data science relates to the techniques for analysing large datasets: A Berlee, V Mak et al., *Research Handbook on Data Science and Law* (Cheltenham, Edward Elgar, 2018). AI: European Commission, 'Artificial intelligence for Europe' (Communication) COM (2018) 237 final; 'Building a European Data Economy' (Communication) COM (2017) 9 final.

[58] See L Urquhart and D McAuley, 'Avoiding the Internet of Insecure Industrial Things' (2018) 34 *Computer Law & Security Review* 450–466.

[59] SWD(2017) 295 final (n 47) 57. Directive (EU) 2016/1148 of the European Parliament and of the Council of 6 July 2016 Concerning Measures for a High Common Level of Security of Network and Information Systems across the Union [2016] OJ L194/1 (NISD).

[60] ibid 57, 60. See generally, A Hutchings and TJ Holt, 'A Crime Script Analysis of the Online Stolen Data Market' (2015) 55 *British Journal of Criminology* 596–614; R Leukfeldt and A Lavorgna et al, 'Organised Cybercrime or Cybercrime that is Organised? An Assessment of the Conceptualisation of Financial Cybercrime as Organised Crime' (2017) 23 *European Journal on Criminal Policy and Research* 287–300.

[61] SWD(2017) 295 final (n 47) 60.

[62] European Commission, 'State of the Union 2017. Cyber Security Fact Sheet' (2017) www.consilium.europa.eu/media/21480/cybersecurityfactsheet.pdf; European Commission and High Representative of the European Union for Foreign Affairs and Security Policy, 'Resilience, Deterrence and Defence: Building Strong cybersecurity for the EU' (Joint Communication) JOIN (2017) 450 final.

the State of the Union.[63] A Joint Communication of the Commission and the High Representative proposes actions to successfully implement the 2013 Cybersecurity Policy. Although the Communication drops the reference to 'pillars', resilience, deterrence and international cooperation are broadly aligned with the NIS, law enforcement/defence and defence/diplomacy pillars and the transversal objectives thereof.

First, resilience against cyber-attacks aims to reinforce NIS in the DSM. The Commission proposes a suite of actions ranging from soft to hard law to fully implement existing measures, such as the NISD. In addition, the Communication urged that public authorities be adequately resourced, cyber-awareness information campaigns be undertaken, that cybersecurity be embedded in both curricula and trainings and to invest in research and development (R&D). The text touches upon issues of data protection, namely encryption, notification of data breaches and GDPR certification, but similarly to 2013, the Communication does not delve into ways how the implementation of the GDPR can be in synergy with the achievement of NIS.

Second, to effectively deter cybercrime the Communication proposes to rely on cybersecurity public-private partnership (PPP), where data exchanges are regulated by the GDPR. Another way is facilitating cross-border access to e-evidence, which however would also benefit the fight against other forms of crime deemed serious.[64] The Communication further addresses measures to strengthen defence.

Finally, to strengthen international cooperation the Communication suggests developing capacity building, external action initiatives typically sitting between the TFEU and the TEU, and cyber development projects based on 'permanent structured cooperation' (PESCO) as well as the European Defence Fund.[65] In this area, privacy and data protection are presented as EU core values and fundamental rights.

Shortly after the Communication was released, the EP issued a Resolution on cybercrime stressing that 'cyber-resilience is key in preventing cybercrime and should therefore be given the highest priority'.[66] The Council also stressed the importance of cybersecurity and implementing planned actions, particularly after the cyber-attacks against the Organisation for the Prohibition of Chemical Weapons (OPCW) in The Hague.[67]

D. The 2020 Cybersecurity Policy

The revised strategy 'leaves open a number of questions as to how its objective of an "open, safe and secure cyberspace" will be credibly defended, both internally

---

[63] European Commission, State of the Union 2017. Cybersecurity: Commission Scales up EU's Response to Cyber-Attacks (2017) europa.eu/rapid/press-release_IP-17-3193_en.htm.

[64] European Commission, Commission Decision of 5 July 2016 on the Signing of a Contractual Arrangement on a Public-private Partnership for Cybersecurity Industrial Research and Innovation between the European Union, Represented by the Commission, and the Stakeholder Organisation, C(2016) 4400 final. See ch 7.

[65] 'European Defence Fund – factsheet' (2019) ec.europa.eu/docsroom/documents/34509 (accessed 25 July).

[66] European Parliament, *Resolution of 3 October 2017 on the Fight against Cybercrime* (2017/2068(INI), [2017] OJ C346/04, 29).

[67] European Council, *Meeting Conclusions, 18 October 2018. Draft Council Conclusions on Cybersecurity Capability and Cyber Capacity Building in the EU*, 15244/1/18 (2019).

and externally'.[68] Such questions acquired renewed urgency in light of increased global economic competition via technological innovation, the extant broken consensus on how to achieve security in cyberspace and maintain 'cyberpeace' and the Covid-19 pandemic, which highlighted the importance and vulnerability of critical information infrastructure (CII).[69] China's leadership in 5G and the race to hegemony in AI and quantum technologies accompanies claims of 'cyber sovereignty', the meaning of which remains elusive.[70] Indeed, the international community has thus far found little agreement beyond the statement of principle that sovereignty applies in cyberspace as testified by the proliferation of venues to discuss similar issues.[71]

The Commission and High Representative's third cybersecurity policy[72] reflects such dynamics. Although the policy partly stands in continuity with the choices made in 2013 and 2017, it is permeated by the newfound importance of cybersecurity. Cybersecurity is cast as an essential international concern underpinning crucial national economic and security interests at a time of geopolitical shifts and eroding mechanisms of international collaboration. Such an essential role unveils the interconnection between values, economic and security concerns.

Cybersecurity's essential nature means it is instrumental to digital connectivity resting on resilient and green grids, as well as international stability and the safeguarding of rights, chiefly privacy, data protection and freedom of expression. Thus, rights depend on cybersecurity, not the opposite. Threats no longer come solely from rogue cyber offenders, but also from political shifts undermining multilateralism and the concentration of CII in the hands of foreign entities. Gone is the desire to foster innovation irrespective of ownership. Technological sovereignty – EU-grown technology – is presented as a response to insecurity born from the dependence on non-EU technology developed according to politically-motivated standards. At the same time, the policy advocates for greater involvement and leadership of Standards Setting Organisations (SSOs) and Standards Developing Organisations (SDOs). Thus, the policy does not appear to question the foundations of technology law-making, foundations which will be discussed later in the book.

To address these concerns, the policy proposes to rely on three tools – regulation, investment and policies – to adopt measures leveraging incentives, obligations and benchmarks in three areas affecting four communities: NIS authorities, law enforcement and judicial authorities, cyber diplomats and cyber defence. Note the absence of

---

[68] Bendiek et al (n 45), 1.
[69] On consensus in cyberspace, see United Nations, General Assembly, *Group of Governmental Experts on Developments in the Field of Information and Telecommunications in the Context of International Security A/72/327* (2017); SJ Shackelford, 'Should Cybersecurity Be a Human Right? Exploring the 'Shared Responsibility' of Cyber Peace' (2017) 55 *Stanford Journal of International Law* 155–184. On Covid-19: OECD, *Digital Economy Outlook* (2020), ch 7.
[70] J Griffiths, 'Chinese President Xi Jinping: Hands off our Internet' *CNN* (16 December 2015).
[71] See Schmitt (n 13), Rule 1; United Nations, General Assembly, *Report of the Group of Governmental Experts (GGE) on Developments in the Field of Information and Telecommunications in the Context of International Security A/68/98* (2013); Open-ended Working Group on Developments in the Field of Information and Telecommunications in the Context of International Security. Final Substantive Report. A/AC.290/2021/CRP.2 (2021).
[72] European Commission and High Representative of the European Union for Foreign Affairs and Security Policy, 'The EU's Cybersecurity Strategy for the Digital Decade' (Joint Communication) JOIN (2020) 18 final.

the market from the list of communities. Similar to the 2017 policy, the term 'pillars' is gone, but the three areas addressed by the 2020 policy largely overlap with the pillars of the 2013 policy. These are: (i) research, investment and policies; (ii) capacity building to prevent, deter and respond; and (iii) advance a global and open cyberspace. These areas roughly correspond to the three main areas of EU law making – the Internal Market and especially the DSM, the Area of Freedom, Security and Justice (AFSJ) and External Action (EA) – but the solutions proposed display concomitant internal and external dimensions that cut across the DSM, AFSJ and EA.

With respect to research, investment and policies, the 2020 policy aims to introduce product safety rules, revise the NISD and increase the resilience of connectivity in the EU, both with respect to the Internet and the Web, by developing an EU Domain Name System resolver called DNS4EU and a greater uptake of IPv6. Initiatives in the DSM refer to values and explicitly to privacy.

As for capacity building to prevent, deter and respond, the 2020 policy lays out the EU's commitment to enhance measures for cross-border access to e-evidence, including through supporting the Second Additional Protocol to the Cybercrime Convention. Here the Commission and High Representative validated the EU joint cyber unit and cyber diplomacy toolbox and proposed to introduce a cyber defence policy framework and a military CERT network. Initiatives in the external area of the AFSJ are oblivious to privacy and data protection.[73]

As for a global and open cyberspace, the 2020 policy tries to tackle insecurity generated by technology dependency by incentivising R&D initiatives to spur the EU supply-chain, leveraging the Cyber Industry, Technology and Research Competence Centre (CCCN). Moreover, the EU is to engage with, increase representation within and ultimately lead SSOs and SDOs to counter the fact that international standards are used to advance political and ideological agendas that 'often do not correspond with values of the EU'.[74] Greater involvement should aim for developing technology that is human-centric, 'privacy-focussed',[75] lawful, safe and ethical. The policy calls for a Standardisation Strategy to define objectives for international standardisation and greater outreach. The policy supports voluntary norms of state behaviour that uphold, among others, 'data privacy'[76] and reject mass surveillance.

The relationship between cybersecurity, privacy and data protection unfolds against the background of measures of questionable compatibility, which the next section introduces. Since writing about cyberlaw is like trying to pin down a moving target,[77] the following analysis should be taken as a snapshot of a highly fluid policy field.

II. The EU Cybersecurity Policy and Law Landscape

This section introduces the EU cybersecurity policy and law landscape, which will form the object of the analysis in chapters six to eight. As noted, recent policy documents

[73] See chs 7–8.
[74] JOIN(2020) 18 final (n 72), 20.
[75] ibid.
[76] ibid 21.
[77] Murray (n 4).

abandon the pillars of the 2013 policy in favour of three objectives that cut across the three main areas of EU law making (Internal Market, AFSJ, External Action). Such an approach better reflects reality, but for illustrative purposes this section is structured around the original 2013 pillars, as they better align with the three main areas of EU law-making. Thus, NIS relates to the DSM, cybercrime and the collection of e-evidence to the AFSJ and cyber defence, diplomacy and trade to the EA.

For each area I provide a non-exhaustive overview of the relevant legal and policy initiatives, synthetically illustrated in tables, as well as the actors taking them forward. I also identify the tensions existing within each area and between initiatives and actors. Such tensions affect the coherence of EU law as well as the interplay between privacy, data protection and cybersecurity.

A. Network and Information Security (NIS) and the DSM

The NIS dimension embraces the legal and operational initiatives in place to secure network and information systems as CII, and the services supporting such a goal. The 2016 NISD is the first instrument explicitly devoted to NIS, though it is not comprehensive, as the Commission itself noted in the revision of the 2013 cybersecurity policy. The NIS Directive is also not the first, nor the only instrument pursuing NIS, understood as the protection of the availability, authenticity, integrity and confidentiality of the data stored, transmitted, or processed on systems and the services offered by or accessible via those systems.[78] Since NIS was always seen as a precondition for the development of the information society, the instruments adopted over time to support the information society and its infrastructure – e-communication networks – also contained NIS objectives.

The long-standing incorporation of NIS objectives in Internal Market legislation carries two consequences. The first consequence is that NIS is intimately related to the development of the Internal Market: most instruments containing provisions on NIS are based on Article 114 TFEU[79] on approximation of laws, which serves the purpose of spurring the development of the Internal Market;[80] other instruments are based on Articles supporting the Internal Market, with the responsible DG in the area of NIS being DG Connect. The second consequence is that, since the development of the information society was regulated in a sectorial manner, NIS objectives are dispersed across sector-specific instruments. Nowadays, the NIS dimension of the cybersecurity policy is a jigsaw puzzle of provisions contained in instruments relating to the DSM and other areas of the Internal Market with a digital dimension.[81] Roughly, it is possible to identify four categories of instruments falling within NIS, some of which will be the focus of chapter six.

---

[78] NISD Art 4. See ch 6.
[79] Former TEC Art 95.
[80] A Savin, *EU Internet Law* (Cheltenham, Edward Elgar, 2013).
[81] COM (2015) 192 final (n 56); See MG Porcedda, 'Patching the Patchwork: Appraising the EU Regulatory Framework on Cyber Security Breaches' (2018) 34 *Computer Law & Security Review*.

In line with the historical regulatory divide between telecommunication infrastructure and content, the first category concerns rules on the ICT infrastructure to be secured, made of networks and related transmission components of all sorts, from satellites to Wi-Fi hotspots, as well as information systems, ie equipment enabling the flow of information within networks and possibly platforms for sharing information. Rules addressing network and information systems, which ought to be protected as CII,[82] are overseen by the Body of European Regulators for Electronic Communications (BEREC). The infrastructure relies on support services including the architecture of domains, that is the toponyms of the Web.[83] Within this group also fall rules establishing the boundaries of what constitutes infrastructure.

The second category of instruments falling within the NIS dimension is made of hard and soft measures devoted to NIS. Besides the NISD, under revision at the time of writing, there is the Union blueprint for responding to large-scale cybersecurity incidents and crises and the updated ENISA Regulation, better known as the 'Cybersecurity Act', which transforms ENISA into the 'EU Cybersecurity Agency'. Another measure, founded on Articles 173(3) and 188 TFEU, is the European Cybersecurity Industrial, Technology and Research Competence Centre and the Network of National Coordination Centres tasked with overseeing the cybersecurity part of the proposed Digital Europe Programme. The Centre is hoped to benefit from the work of the High-Performance Computing infrastructure and should improve the rate of EU companies delivering cybersecurity products and services worldwide (which accounted for 27 per cent of the global companies in 2017), thereby competing with US, Israeli, Chinese (the leader exporting €14,287 million of services), South-Korean, Japanese and Russian counterparts.[84] Primary actors are ENISA, the CSIRTs network, the Emergency Response Coordination Centre in the Commission and CERT-EU, as well as the Cybersecurity Competence Centre (3C).

A third category is made of instruments predating the NISD and addressing facets of NIS, including responses to data breaches,[85] in a sectorial manner. These are rules on the confidentiality of e-communication systems and of trade secrets,[86] instruments on the confidentiality, integrity and availability (CIA) of personal data and services processing them, as well as of transactions of data relating to payment services, e-government and assurance services. Soft law includes provisions to fund research in trust and cybersecurity. Relevant agencies and national networks are the European Data Protection Supervisor (EDPS), the European Data Protection Board (EDPB) and the European Banking Authority.

The fourth group encompasses instruments which are peripheral to NIS but bear relevance for it. For instance, instruments 'opening data' up to spur the development

---

[82] Council Directive 2008/114/EC of 8 December 2008 on the identification and designation of European Critical Infrastructures and the assessment of the need to improve their protection [2008] OJ L345/75.
[83] R Bendrath and J Hofmann et al., 'Governing the Internet: The Quest for Legitimate and Effective Rules', in A Hurrelmann et al. (eds), *Transforming the Golden-Age Nation State* (Basingstoke, Palgrave, 2007).
[84] SWD(2017) 295 final (n 47) 52. This is based on Highlights from the EU Cybersecurity Market size and Fragmentation, conducted by LSEC and PwC (Final report in October 2017).
[85] Porcedda (n 81).
[86] However, the relevance to NIS of rules protecting intellectual property rights with regard to databases and computer programs is debatable.

of the data economy may create risks of aggregation attacks,[87] which affect the confidentiality and availability of data, by revealing information that was meant to remain undisclosed, such as de-anonymising personal data.

The NIS-related objectives 'cyber resilience' and 'developing industrial and technological resources' should benefit from further plans to complement the NISD in relation to information flows, create a cybersecurity response fund, an EU-wide, one-stop-shop to help victims of cyber-attacks and actions to improve cybersecurity skills, both at Member State and industry level. NIS-relevant legislation is likely to come from FinTech, that is 'technology-enabled innovation in financial services'.[88] Furthermore, the Commission is studying options to address liability related to digital technologies,[89] and a joint initiative with industry to define a 'duty of care' principle for reducing product/software vulnerabilities and promoting 'security by design', with particular attention to high risk applications.[90] This initiative should include the screening of foreign direct investment in the EU.[91]

i. Tensions within the NIS Dimension

The breadth of instruments addressing NIS carries inherent challenges. Some have to do with the fact that, due to subsidiarity, many initiatives remain in the hands of Member States, which display differing levels of capability.[92] The law is an important instrument to improve capabilities: the NISD was proposed at a time when only 12 Member States had a cybersecurity policy, the first being Germany in 2005. Yet, the law is no panacea, due to existing gaps or the voluntary nature of provisions.

The problem is compounded by the piecemeal development of legislation in NIS, which comes with the downside of the proliferation of agencies, a point noted in the literature.[93] These include the CERT-EU, the CSIRT network, ENISA, the EDPB, the EDPS, BEREC, the European Banking Authority, the 3C and the cyber-security PPP, multiplied by 27 for each Union Member State.[94] Each agency addresses different facets of the same problem without a protocol for communications or an overarching structure of governance. The question is acutely visible in relation to the issue of standards.

---

[87] R Anderson, *Security Engineering. A Guide to Building Dependable Distributed Systems*, 3rd edn (New York, Wiley, 2020) 297.
[88] European Commission, 'FinTech Action plan: For a more competitive and innovative European financial sector' (Commission) COM (2018) 0109 final.
[89] COM (2018) 237 final (n 57); SWD (2018)137 final (n 57); 'Mid-Term Review on the implementation of the Digital Single Market Strategy. A Connected Digital Single Market for All' (Communication) COM (2017) 228 final (Staff Working Document) SWD (2017) 155 final (2017). European Commission, 'Proposal for a Directive on liability for Defective Products' (Communication) COM (2022) 495 final, published as this book went to press.
[90] European Commission, 'ICT Standardisation Priorities for the Digital Single Market' (Communication) COM (2016) 0176 final. See also: M Schaake and L Pupillo et al., *Software Vulnerability Disclosure in EuropeTechnology, Policies and Legal Challenges. Report of a CEPS Task Force* (Centre for European Policy Studies (CEPS) 2018).
[91] European Commission, 'Report on the evaluation of the European Union Agency for Network and Information Security (ENISA)' (Communication) COM (2017) 0478 final.
[92] See Cybersecurity Index & Cyber-wellness Profiles 2017 in European Commission (n 47), 72. Klimburg and Tiirmaa-Klaar (n 51).
[93] Bendiek (n 45) 1.
[94] Each Member State also follows different modes of coordination, see Christou (2).

Table 1 NIS-related instruments

ICT infrastructure to be secured	Measures on NIS	Measures addressing facets of NIS	Peripheral measures relevant to NIS
Infrastructure • European Electronic Communications Code (Directive (EU) 2018/1972) • Galileo Project – civilian (Regulation 1285/2013/EU) • Galileo project – military (Decision 1104/2011/EU) • Wi-fi4EU (Regulation (EU) 2017/1953) • INSPIRE (Directive 2007/2/EC) • Radio Equipment Directive (2014/53/EU) • Open Internet Regulation (2015/2120/EU) • Identification of Critical Infrastructure (Council Directive 2008/114/EC) • Regulation (EU) 2021/1153 establishing the Connecting Europe Facility • Regulation (EU) 2021/694 establishing the Digital Europe programme – Specific Objective 3 cybersecurity and trust • European DNS Resolver (DNS4EU) tender *Supporting/limiting infrastructure* • EU Top-level Domain (Regulation (EU) 2019/517) • Information Society Services (Directive 2015/1535/EU) • Audio-visual services (Directive (EU) 2018/1808)	• Network and Information Systems Directive ((EU) 2018/1808), under reform • Union Blueprint on Large-scale Cybersecurity Incidents (Recommendation 2017/1584) • Cybersecurity Act ((EU) 2019/881) • Public-private Partnership for Cybersecurity -CPPP (C(2016) 4400 final)) – soft law • Regulation (EU) 2021/887 Establishing the European Cybersecurity Industrial, Technology and Research Competence Centre and the Network of National Coordination Centres • Proposed Directive on the Resilience of Critical Entities (COM (2020) 829) • Cyber Resilience Act (COM (2022) 454 final)	• E-Privacy Directive (2002/58/EC and 2009/136/EC) • Regulation (EU) 2021/132 derogating from the e-Privacy Directive • E-Privacy Regulation (COM (2017) 10 final) • Trade Secrets Directive ((EU) 2016/943) • General Data Protection Regulation ((EU) 2016/679) • Payment Services 2 Directive ((EU) 2015/2366/EU) • E-Identification and Trust Services Regulation (910/2014/EU) • Databases Directive (96/9/EC) Legal Protection of Computer Programmes (Directive 2009/24/EC) • Copyright Directive ((EU) 2019/790) • Data Governance Act (Regulation (EU) • E-Commerce Directive (2000/31/EC) and Digital Services Act (Regulation (EU) 2022/2065)	• Free flow of Non-personal Data Regulation ((EU) 2018/1807) • Portability of Online Content Services Regulation ((EU) 2017/1128) • Enforcement of Consumer Protection Laws (Regulation (EU) 2017/2394) • Geo-blocking Regulation ((EU) 2018/302)

The Commission reports that a 'Memorandum of Understanding has been signed between the European Committee for Standardization (CEN), the European Committee for Electrotechnical Standardization (CENELEC) and the European Telecommunication Standards Institute (ETSI) to facilitate cooperation in defining standards.'[95] However, an EU common approach is still lacking, and the situation may be exacerbated by the development of national certification schemes.

A further issue to do with the piecemeal development of legislation in NIS is that different laws express different legitimate interests or rights protected by the Charter. The implementation of such freedoms, such as of expression and information, of research, to conduct a business, and rights such as that to property including intellectual property can clash with one another,[96] or with the security objective inherent in NIS. The list of rights and freedoms potentially clashing obviously includes privacy and data protection.

B. Cybercrime, e-Evidence and the AFSJ

In EU cybersecurity policies, cybercrime is seen as

> A broad range of different criminal activities where computers and information systems are involved either as a primary tool or as a primary target. Cybercrime comprises traditional offences (e.g. fraud, forgery, and identity theft), content-related offences (e.g. on-line distribution of child pornography or incitement to racial hatred) and offences unique to computers and information systems (e.g. attacks against information systems, denial of service and malware).[97]

The only instrument explicitly addressing 'cybercrime' is the Directive on attacks against information systems (Cybercrime Directive),[98] whereas Article 83 TFEU refers to 'computer crime'. The policy definition seems to follow in the steps of the Budapest Convention. The CoE's instrument lays down substantive rules on computer-related offences (eg fraud), content-related offences (eg child pornography), as well as offences against the CIA of computer data and systems (eg hacking). According to Gercke, the first category focuses on the method – the computer – used to commit traditional crimes, whereas the other two focus on the object of legal protection.[99] A fourth category, also focused on the object of legal protection, is that of copyright-related offences.[100] These offences can be clustered according to alternative taxonomies emphasising the role of technology or the modus operandi of cyber offenders.[101] Thus, CIA offences are also

---

[95] SWD (2017) 295 final (n 47) 17.
[96] CFR Arts 11, 13, 16–17.
[97] JOIN (2013) 01 final (n 41) 3.
[98] Directive 2013/40/EU of the European Parliament and the Council of 12 August 2013 on attacks against information systems and replacing Council Framework Decision 2005/222/JHA [2013] OJ L218/8 (AISD).
[99] M Gercke, *Understanding Cybercrime: Phenomena, Challenges and Legal Response* (International Telecommunication Union, Geneva, 2012), 12.
[100] But see ch 7, explaining the exclusion of copyright from the analysis.
[101] See generally DS Wall, *Cybercrime: The Transformation of Crime in the Information Age* (Oxford, Polity, 2007) 11–12, 30–69; J Clough, *Principles of Cybercrime* (Cambridge, Cambridge University Press, 2010); Gercke (2012); United Nations, Office on Drugs and Crime (UNODC), *Comprehensive Study on Cybercrime* (UNODC/CCPCJ/EG4/2013/3, 2013); M Yar and KFS Steinmetz, *Cybercrime and Society*, 3rd edn (London, Sage Publishing, 2020); AA Gillespie, *Cybercrime: Key Issues and Debates* (London, Routledge, 2019).

known as cyber-dependent, crime against the machine, true or narrow cybercrime, which would cease to exist without cyberspace; computer-related offences are also referred to as cyber-enabled cybercrimes; and content-related offences are also known as cyber-assisted or 'broad' cybercrimes. The latter two would exist irrespective of the technological environment.

The Budapest Convention was spurred by the increased difficulty in investigating and apprehending criminals due to the inherent cross-jurisdictional character of cybercrimes.[102] As a result, in addition to substantive definitions, the Convention addresses dual criminality, as well as the preservation, gathering and international exchange of e-evidence necessary for investigations. Although the EU is not party to the Budapest Convention, in keeping with the definition contained in the 2013 cybersecurity policy, the Union's legal approach to 'cybercrime' broadly reflects that of the Convention. Thus, the EU has legislated on all offences defined in the Budapest Convention as well as procedural measures to deal with cybercrime and the preservation and exchange of e-evidence. Consequently, this objective of the cybersecurity strategy appears, similarly to NIS, to be piecemeal (and, to some, ineffective[103]) and embraces five broad categories of measures shown synthetically in Table 2; chapter seven will address a selection of measures.

The first category concerns substantive offences against the CIA of data and systems, which is the remit of the Cybercrime Directive. The second category of measures addresses the computer-related or cyber-enabled offences of fraud and forgery, which is the remit of one instrument on fraud and counterfeiting of non-cash means of payment (FCD). The third category of rules concerns content-related or cyber-assisted crimes, which comprise a fast-growing list of crimes. Instruments include[104] Directives based in the AFSJ addressing child sexual abuse material (CSADir) and terrorism including terrorist-motivated cyber-attacks (CTD), as well as Regulations based in the DSM enabling the adoption of measures to deal with CSAM and addressing the dissemination of terrorist content online. Legislation on election interference falls into this category.

Cybercrimes need, like all offences, investigating and prosecuting, and this is the role of the fourth category of rules. In the EU, such rules take the form of instruments establishing agencies for cross-border police and judicial cooperation, such as Europol's European Cybercrime Centre (EC3), whose members of staff provide strategic, forensic and operational support to Member States in the fight against all forms of cybercrime.[105] The EC3 manages the Joint Cybercrime Action Taskforce, which gathers EC3 staff members, liaison officers from a number of EU Member States[106]

---

[102] Council of Europe, Explanatory Memorandum to the Cybercrime Convention, (2001); S Brenner, 'The Council of Europe's Convention', in JM Balkin et al. (ed), *Cybercrime, Digital Cops in a Networked Environment* (New York, New York University Press, 2007); A Flanagan, 'The Law and Computer Crime: Reading the Script of Reform' (2005) 13 *International Journal of Law and Information Technology* 98.

[103] F Calderoni, 'The European Legal Framework on Cybercrime: Striving for an Effective Implementation' (2010) 54 *Crime, Law and Social Change* 339–357.

[104] Rules on racism and xenophobia are neither conceptualised as cybercrime nor connected to the Additional Protocol to the Convention on Cybercrime Concerning the Criminalisation of Acts of a Racist and Xenophobic Nature Committed through Computer Systems, Council of Europe, ETS n. 189. Thus, Council Framework Decision 2008/913/JHA is not included in this analysis; Fundamental Rights Agency, *Ensuring Justice for Hate Crime Victims: Professional Perspectives* (2016).

[105] These were 80 in 2020, expected to grow to cope with workload, SWD(2017) 295 final (n 47) 39.

[106] Austria, France, Germany, Italy, the Netherlands, Spain and Sweden.

and non-EU law enforcement partners[107] posted at Europol headquarters. The EU's judicial cooperation agency Eurojust[108] has posted personnel at EC3 and contributes to Europol's investigations. The European Council Conclusions of 2016 created the European Judicial Cybercrime Network (EJCN), which gathers judicial prosecutors and practitioners at European level thereby helping cross-national investigations.[109] This category can house transnational public-private partnerships, whereby law enforcement agencies cooperate with non-governmental entities to carry out operations.[110] An example is the cPPP, under the H2020 programme, with the European Cyber Security Organization, which gathers representatives of industry and academia.[111] Finally, the group includes rules to confiscate and recover the illegal assets yielded by cybercrime throughout the EU and apprehend wanted cybercriminals on the run.

The last group of measures concerns the collection, preservation and exchange of e-evidence, which relate to both cybercrime and other crimes, as acknowledged by the Budapest Convention and its Second Additional Protocol, in the drafting of which participated the Commission. The group includes rules for mutual assistance in collecting cross-border evidence and draft measures to order a service provider offering services in the Union to produce or preserve e-evidence in criminal matters, regardless of the location of data and legal representatives of service providers. Other relevant measures for the collection of e-evidence relating to offences other than cybercrimes are found in the CSADir, CTDir and a Directive on combating trafficking in human beings. To prevent offenders from hiding behind anonymity and encryption, thereby improving accountability, the Commission is pressing for the uptake of IPv6. The new Internet Protocol, which will allow the reduction of the number of people sharing the same IP address down to six, is to be used in EU procurement, research and project funding, and at Member State level.[112] This group features the EU-level forum, which also deals with the use of encryption,[113] and the European Forensic Area,[114] created to harmonise approaches concerning the quality of evidence and enhance its admissibility.[115]

Finally, there are measures that have a bearing on cybercrime investigations, such as a framework regulating the collection of personal data for law enforcement purposes (LED) and establishing minimum standards on the rights, support and protection of victims of crime.

---

[107] Australia, Canada, Colombia, Norway, Switzerland and the US jointly represented by the Federal Bureau of Investigation and Secret Service.

[108] Eurojust, 'European Judicial Cybercrime Network' www.eurojust.europa.eu/Practitioners/Pages/EJCN.aspx (accessed 20 June 2019).

[109] SWD(2017) 295 final (n 47).

[110] Eg, V Dodd and D Gayle, 'Police to Hire Law Firms to Tackle Cyber Criminals in Radical Pilot Project' *The Guardian* (14 August 2016). On legal issues raised by PPs, see Council of Europe, Venice Commission, *Update of the 2007 Report on the Democratic Oversight of the Security Services and Report on Democratic Oversight of Signals Intelligence Agencies* (CDL-AD(2015)006, Study N 719/2013, 2015); Council of Europe, *Guidelines for the Cooperation between Law Enforcement and Internet Service Providers against Cybercrime, Adopted by the Global Conference Cooperation against Cybercrime* (2008).

[111] European Commission, Contractual Arrangement on a Public-private Partnership for Cybersecurity, C (2016) 4400 final.

[112] ibid 70.

[113] European Digital Rights (EDRI), *What Digital Rights Are at Imminent Risk? All of Them* (EDRi-gram newsletter 14.17 2016).

[114] ENoFS Institutes, enfsi.eu/ (accessed 20 June).

[115] European Commission, 'The European Agenda on Security' (Communication) COM (2015) 185 final.

Table 2 Cybercrime-related Instruments

Substantive Cybercrime	Cross-border judicial and police cooperation, PPPs	E-evidence	Rights
1. *Cyber-dependent* • Directive on attacks against information systems (2013/40/EU) 2. *Cyber-enabled* • Directive on Fraud and Counterfeiting ((EU) 2019/713) 3. *Cyber-assisted (content)* • Directive Combating the Sexual Abuse and Sexual Exploitation of Children and Child Pornography (2011/93/EU), to be reviewed • Regulation Derogating from the E-privacy Regulation (EU) 2021/1232 • Directive on Combating Terrorism ((EU) 2017/54) • Regulation on Addressing the Dissemination of Terrorist Content Online (EU) 2021/784 4. *Miscellanea* • On the European democracy action plan (COM (2020) 790 final)	• European Cybercrime centre (E3C), Regulation on the European Union Agency for Law Enforcement Cooperation (Europol) (2016/794/EU) • European Judicial Cybercrime Network (EJCN) • cPPP (Commission C (2016) 4400 final) • Decision on the European arrest warrant and the surrender procedures between Member States (2002/584/JHA) • Directive on the Freezing and Confiscation of Instrumentalities and Proceeds of Crime (2014/42/EU)	• European Investigation Order (2014/41/EU) • Proposal for a Regulation on European Production and Preservation Orders for Electronic Evidence in Criminal Matters (COM (2018) 225 final) • Proposal for a Directive laying down Harmonised Rules on the Appointment of Legal Representatives for the Purpose of Gathering Evidence in Criminal Proceedings (COM/2018/226 final) *Single articles* • Directive Combating the Sexual Abuse and Sexual Exploitation of Children and Child Pornography (2011/93/EU), and Directive on combating terrorism ((EU) 2017/54) • Directive on Preventing and Combating Trafficking in Human Beings and Protecting its Victims (2011/36/EU)	• Law Enforcement Directive ((EU) 2016/680) • Council Framework Directive on the Rights, Support and Protection of Victims of Crime (2012/29/EU)

Not directly applicable: Cybercrime Convention and its Additional Protocols

i. Tensions within the Cybercrime and e-Evidence Dimension

The only legal instrument containing a *renvoi*, or connection clause,[116] to the Budapest Convention is the Cybercrime Directive, which introduces substantive offences that constitute 'cybercrime'.[117] Accordingly, the legal meaning of 'cybercrime' in the Union should be restricted to cyber-dependent, true or narrow cybercrime. Yet, the cybersecurity policy addresses other forms of cybercrime that are not univocally defined. Indeed, the EP encouraged reaching shared definitions across EU institutions and EU Member States.[118]

The terminological problem masks the even deeper incongruence between responses to different forms of cybercrime.[119] Whereas the prevention of CIA offences is primarily rooted in technical measures and cyber hygiene, the prevention of CSAM production and consumption rests primarily on societal interventions. Finding clear definitions is very desirable from the perspective of legal certainty and the prevention of abuses of surveillance power,[120] but is not going to address the underlying contradiction of EU responses within the cybersecurity policy.

The response to cybercrime commands measures both for effectively responding to and deterring cybercrime, thus contributing to its prevention, and for collecting e-evidence in relation to other crimes. Following Nissenbaum, such a situation engenders a tension between two security requirements.[121] The need to avert CIA offences underpins pre-emption, based on strengthening computer security measures such as encryption. However, the need to collect evidence to investigate crimes calls for weakening computer security measures such as encryption. Landau and DeNardis aptly describe this contradiction as surveillance versus security.[122] Furthermore, similarly to the NIS pillar, there may be issues of coordination between the different agencies and even turf wars among the different communities embodying 'surveillance versus security'.

At its heart, law and order inherently harbours a tension between potentially clashing objectives synthesised as 'security versus liberty':[123] on the one hand, the preference for an efficient and effective state intervention against security threats, on the other, for protecting human rights of bystanders and also offenders. What is more, all offences subsumed under cybercrime violate one or more rights; several rights can also be interfered with by responses against cybercrimes. CIA offences affect the integrity of data and the confidentiality of communications, which are embedded in the rights to data protection and privacy. CSAM interferes with the rights of the child, including children's rights to data protection and their image. Hate speech challenges non-discrimination.

---

[116] See Cremona (n 27) and ch 7.
[117] Cybercrime Directive Recs 2, 14, 15, 24 (also mentioning NIS), 25–26 (also mentioning resilience of CI) and 28, Art 17.
[118] European Parliament (66) point 2. On definitional ambiguity: MG Porcedda, 'Lessons from PRISM and Tempora: the Self-contradictory Nature of the Fight against Cyberspace Crimes. Deep Packet Inspection as a Case Study' (2013) 25 *Neue Kriminalpolitik* 305–409. Fahey (n 45).
[119] European Parliament (n 66).
[120] ibid §65.
[121] H Nissenbaum, 'When Computer Security meets National Security', in JM Balkin (ed), *Cybercrime, Digital Cops in a Networked Environment* (New York, New York University Press, 2007).
[122] Landau (n 8); L DeNardis, 'The Internet Design Tension between Surveillance and Security' (2015) 37 IEEE *Annals of the History of Computing* 72–83.
[123] See E Posner and A Vermeule, *Terror in the Balance. Security, Liberty and the Courts* (Oxford, Oxford University Press, 2007). See ch 1, section I.C.

Fighting these forms of cybercrime may interfere with the freedom to conduct a business, copyright-related rights and the right to free speech and almost always with privacy and data protection.[124]

Finally, as noted earlier, different Member States allocate cyber responsibility to different ministries which could be in competition with one another. Whereas the creation of EU fora of cooperation on specific issues is likely to ease tensions, there is again a risk of proliferation of overlapping, even conflicting agencies. Tensions could also arise as a result of shared power between Member States and the EU and the constitutional framing of law and order.[125]

C. Cyber Defence, Diplomacy, Trade and the EA

All iterations of the EU cybersecurity policies stressed the need to develop capabilities in cyber defence and diplomacy and the 2020 policy has placed renewed emphasis on international supply chains. Cybersecurity was a priority of the Global Strategy on the EU Foreign and Security Policy[126] and is pursued by mainstreaming cyber issues into EU external relations, CFSP, international trade and Member States' diplomacy.[127] In practice, this means creating a 'convergence of Member States' positions on different cyber diplomacy and Internet governance topics' to 'present a coherent approach in major global cyber debates'[128] in line with EU values.

Activities are transversal to EU Treaties[129] and command a holistic approach to a wide range of themes.[130] In essence, measures relate to the TEU-based Common Foreign and Security Policy (CFSP) and Common Security and Defence Policy (CSDP) and the TFEU-based External Action. Initiatives are overseen by the European Defence Agency (EDA) and the European External Action Service (EEAS) in participation with the Council and the Commission; the latter can also take the lead depending on the area. Measures tend to be of a varied nature; they are divided into four groups and shown synthetically in Table 3 below. Chapter eight will focus on a subset of the rules listed here.

The first group concerns cyber defence initiatives undertaken within the updated Cyber Defence Policy Framework (CDPF). The state of implementation and guidance over the CDPF's six objectives rests on the Political-Military Working Group in the

---

[124] See chs 3, 4 and 7.
[125] Ch 1, section I.C discussing BVerfG, 2 BvE 2/08, DE:BVerfG:2009:es20090630.2bve000208.
[126] Council of the European Union, *Council Conclusions on implementing the EU global strategy in the area of security and defence*, 14 November 2016, 14149/16 (2016).
[127] See SWD (2017) 295 final (n 47). Council of the European Union, *Council Conclusions on Cyber Diplomacy*, 11 February 2015, 6122/15.
[128] SWD (2017) 295 final (n 47) 54. See also Carrapico and Barrinha (n 6).
[129] Eg, the 2017 Cybersecurity Policy action point on R&D supports Member States 'in identifying areas where common cybersecurity projects could be considered for support by the European Defence Fund'; Council of the European Union, *EU Cyber Defence Policy Framework* (2018 update) 14413/18 (2018).
[130] Klimburg and Tiirmaa-Klaar (n 51). See ch 8.

Council.[131] The CDPF aims at developing the cyber defence capabilities of Member States and the EU as a whole. First, this includes coordination activities performed by the EDA and its Project Team, such as the Cyber Defence Joint Program developed with interested Member States,[132] but also Permanent Structured Cooperation (PESCO). Capabilities include educational measures to close the skills gap in cybersecurity;[133] the European Security and Defence College is to oversee the cybersecurity-related education platform that was launched in 2018.[134] A third component are exercises, such as the CFSP Multi-Layer exercise, CSDP crisis management and the dedicated EU CSDP cyber defence exercise.[135] The European Defence Fund will support collaborative projects fostering innovation in defence-related research and in the industrial development of capabilities.

The second group of measures relates to cyber diplomacy under the umbrella of the 'Joint EU Diplomatic Response on Malicious Cyber Activities' or 'Cyber Diplomatic Toolbox', which deal with potential aggressors in cyberspace and joint response to malicious cyber activities, such as the adoption of restrictive measures. The toolbox includes 'cyber dialogues', that is annual, formal talks on technical and market-related issues in the form of bilateral relations with strategic players, eg, the US, Japan, India, South Korea and China. Cyber dialogues also help 'promoting the application of existing international law and voluntary norms of responsible state behaviour',[136] to the development of which the EU contributes by engaging in multi-stakeholder governance[137] in various international fora.[138] Examples are the UN Group of Governmental Experts (UN GGE) for voluntary norms[139] and the Organization for Security Co-operation for the adoption of confidence building measures on cooperation and transparency.[140] The EU position is expressed through Council Conclusions, eg, on Internet Governance, on Cyber Diplomacy and on EU priorities in UN human rights fora,[141] and Human

---

[131] SWD (2017) 295 final (n 47) 46.
[132] European Defence Agency, *Cyber Ranges: EDA's First Ever Cyber Defence Pooling & Sharing Project Launched By 11 Member States* (2017) www.eda.europa.eu/info-hub/press-centre/latest-news/2017/05/12/cyber-ranges-eda-s-first-ever-cyber-defence-pooling-sharing-project-launched-by-11-member-states.
[133] SWD (2017) 295 final (n 47).
[134] European Union External Action Service, *ESDC/Cyber platform: Inauguration Ceremony: ('Cybersecurity will shape the pace and nature of our lives, work and consumption habits')* (2018) eeas.europa.eu/headquarters/headquarters-homepage/55253/esdccyber-platform-inauguration-ceremony-cybersecurity-will-shape-pace-and-nature-our-lives_tm.
[135] See www.eeas.europa.eu/eeas/eu-military-exercise-%E2%80%93-milex-21_es; see also eda.europa.eu/news-and-events/news/2021/02/19/cyber-defence-exercise-brings-together-military-certs.
[136] SWD (2017) 295 final (n 47) 55.
[137] Council of the European Union, *Council Conclusions on Internet Governance*, 27 November 2014, 16200/14 (2014).
[138] As made possible by resources. SWD(2017) 295 final (n 47) 54.
[139] ibid.
[140] Permanent Council Decision No 1106 on the initial set of OSCE confidence-building measures to reduce the risks of conflict stemming from the use of information and communication technologies of 3 December 2013.
[141] Council of the European Union, *Council Conclusions on EU Priorities in UN Human Rights Fora in 2019*, 18 February 2019, 6339/19.

Rights Guidelines, eg, on freedom of expression online and offline[142] and on the defence of human rights.[143] Finally, action includes participation in relevant PPPs.

The third group concerns trade-related measures rooted in the TFEU. Instruments include measures to regulate the export of dual-use technology, for instance NIS-relevant tools for 'vulnerability disclosure'.

A final group encompasses mixed measures cutting across areas of law-making, such as provisions relating to the external areas of NIS (eg, data protection adequacy mechanisms) and the AFSJ (eg, information sharing with third countries), and the intersection of defence and diplomacy.[144] The creation of synergies between the market and military[145] on technological development, threat assessment and information sharing rely on making use of initiatives and institutions within the NIS and the EEAS. The EU Hybrid Fusion Cell, set up by the European Union Intelligence and Situation Centre (INTCEN), contributes to the early identification of hybrid threats, an area requiring progress due to 'insufficient level of strategic guidance and different maturity levels of Member States'.[146] Defence and diplomacy also converge in the PESCOs 'Cyber Rapid Response Teams and Mutual Assistance in Cyber Security' and 'Cyber Threats and Incident Response Information Sharing Platform', the governance and secretariat of which is shared between the Council, the EEAS and the EDA. The protection of the CIA of CSDP communication and information networks is coordinated by the EEAS Cyber Governance Board under the EEAS Secretary General.[147] Finally, international cooperation in defence matters, which is 'indispensable' given 'the borderless nature of the internet',[148] is also shared between the EEAS and CSDP bodies, in connection with NATO.[149] The European Centre of Excellence for Countering Hybrid Threats acts as the forum of interaction between the EU and NATO members.[150] International cooperation for capacity building displays a defence position.[151] The EU External Cyber Capacity Building Operational Guidelines, developed by the Commission and the European Union Institute for Security Studies,[152] supports the development of capabilities in selected third countries, in collaboration, among others, with the Global Forum on Cyber Expertise.

---

[142] *EU Human Rights Guidelines on Freedom of Expression Online and Offline*, Foreign Affairs Council Meeting, 12 May 2014.

[143] 'Ensuring Protection-EU Human Rights Guidelines on Human Rights Defenders, 2008' (2008) eeas.europa.eu/sites/eeas/files/eu_guidelines_hrd_en.pdf. See at eeas.europa.eu/topics/eu-enlargement/8441/human-rights-guidelines_en.

[144] European Union External Action Service, *Towards a Stronger EU on Security and Defence* (2018) eeas.europa.eu/headquarters/headquarters-homepage/35285/eu-strengthens-cooperation-security-and-defence_en.

[145] A Klimburg and C Callanan et al., *Synergies Between the Civilian and the Defence Cybersecurity Markets. Study for the European Commission's DG Communications Networks, Content and Technology* (Publications Office of the EU, 2016). It showed that most civilian cyber tools were used in military operations.

[146] SWD(2017) 295 final (n 47) 44.

[147] By the European Union Military Staff, the Crisis Management and Planning Directorate and the Civilian Planning and Conduct Capability.

[148] SWD(2017) 295 final (n 47) 57.

[149] See the Warsaw 2016 Joint Declaration, Ibid.

[150] 'Hybrid CoE' (2019) www.hybridcoe.fi/what-is-hybridcoe/.

[151] P Pawlak and P-N Barmpaliou, 'Politics of Cybersecurity Capacity Building: Conundrum and Opportunity' (2017) 2 *Journal of Cyber Policy* 123–144.

[152] Pawlak, (2018); *Operational Guidance for the EU's International Cooperation on Cyber Capacity Building. A Playbook (Task Force for Cyber Capacity Building)* (European Union Institute for Security Studies, 2018).

Table 3 Cyber defence, diplomacy and trade-related instruments

CFSP	Mixed initiatives, including on capacity building	CSDP	External Action (trade)

• Cyber Diplomacy Toolbox, 9916/17, including:
  • Restrictive Measures (Regulation (EU) 2019/796; Decision (EU) 2019/797)
  • Cyber dialogues
  • Multi-stakeholder governance (eg, UN GGE, IGF, UN Open Ended Working Group etc.)
	• EU Hybrid Fusion Cell, set up by the European Union Intelligence and Situation Centre (INTCEN) (Council Decision 2010/427/EU)
	• CFSP exercise Multi-Layer (ML16)
	• EU External Cyber Capacity Building Guidelines, 10496/18 (2018)
	• EU-NATO Cooperation – Warsaw 2016 Joint Declaration
	• European Centre of Excellence for Countering Hybrid Threats
	• PESCO Cyber Rapid Response Teams and Mutual Assistance in Cyber Security
	• PESCO Cyber Threats and Incident Response Information Sharing Platform
		• Cyber Defence Policy Framework (CDPF)14413/18 (2018)
		• Cyber Defence Joint Program
		• MILEX exercises
		• Cyber Defence Exercise
		• Regulation establishing the European Defence Fund ((EU) 2021/697) (Internal market BASIS)
			• Dual-use Export Controls (Regulation (EU) 2021/821)

i. Tensions within the Cyber Defence, Diplomacy and Trade Dimensions

Owing to the sensitivity of defence, diplomacy and trade to Member States and the composite rules which dominate the EA, this is an area where potential tension between Member States and EU institutions can reach the highest peak. Tensions tend to translate into inadequate funding and unclear mandates for EU institutions, which may hamper consistent action in the EA. For instance, the Commission found that a 'lack of mechanisms to mobilise Member States' collective expertise to assist efforts to build national cyber resilience in third countries'[153] undermines the effectiveness of capacity building initiatives. However, Carrapico and Barrinha note that the approach to this area could be self-defeating, in that the de-centralised strategy adopted by the EU means that cybersecurity governance stays with Member States.[154]

Similarly to the NIS and cybercrime areas, cyber external relations are the remit of multiple actors, namely the Council, the EEAS with its inner divisions, eg, INTCEN, the political-military group, the European Union Military Staff, the EDA, the European Union Institute for Security Studies and the European Security and ESDC, some of which are mirrored by similar structures at Member State level. Furthermore, these institutions, agencies and networks interact with counterparts in other areas covered by the cybersecurity policy. This engenders a cacophony of voices and initiatives which may bring about turf wars and hamper policy objectives.

Cyber external relations also suffer from intrinsic sources of tension: capacity building is a means to export norms and values, up until a tipping point where the recipient country develops cyber capabilities that could threaten the security of the capacity builder. Capacity building in itself harbours all the existing tensions within pillars (eg, reconciling law enforcement with human rights) that are worsened if the capacity builder has not resolved these tensions at home. Finally, the creation of capabilities for reconnaissance in the form of cyber intelligence, which rests in the hands of Member States, leads to an 'arms race' which inherently challenges civilian cybersecurity.

III. Conclusion: Tensions within Cybersecurity and the Way Forward

The analysis in this chapter has shown the plasticity of the concept of cybersecurity, which is in a constant dialogue with privacy and data protection. Such plasticity is reflected in successive EU cybersecurity policies, with the 2020 Policy placing special emphasis on convergence and overlaps across dimensions. Yet, this analysis has also shown the existence of clashes within dimensions and corresponding areas of law making and all the more so across dimensions and legislative areas.

Cyber defence exemplifies the overlap between areas. The CDPF recalls that 'several EU policies contribute to the objectives of cyber defence policy … and this framework also takes into account relevant regulation, policy and technology support in the civilian domain'.[155] Cyber defence initiatives support law enforcement, by contributing to the development of forensic techniques, and NIS with the protection of own network and

---

[153] SWD (2017) 295 final (n 47) 56.
[154] Carrapico and Barrinha (n 6), 1266.
[155] European Council, *EU Cyber Defence Policy Framework*, 15585/14 (2014), 4.

Conclusion: Tensions within Cybersecurity and the Way Forward 67

industrial cyber capabilities, from hybrid threats.[156] Given the dual-use nature of information technology, the CDPF encourages civil-military cooperation to develop 'strong technological capacities in Europe to mitigate threats and vulnerabilities'.[157]

All dimensions of the cybersecurity policy converge and overlap, to the extent that treating them separately is an artificial exercise. NIS covers measures to protect the CIA of civilian networks, failing which cybercrime measures come into effect.[158] Cybercrime legislation aims to protect *any* information system and data against offences in the form of unauthorised access, interference, or interception and ideally prevent such offences. Measures pursuing NIS and cybercrime rely on the same notion of network and information systems. Parallels can be drawn between the rules on securing e-government and assurance services contained in NIS measures, and the prosecution of forgery. Intelligence-led policing in the cybercrime pillar enhances capabilities in defence, and vice versa. Diplomacy is a way of attempting to export EU rules, particularly in NIS and possibly also values – though rules and values can also be imported.

Dimensions of the cybersecurity policy also harbour inherent tensions and can clash with one another. The call by the European Parliament for common definitions on cybercrime, cyber warfare, cybersecurity, cyber harassment and cyberattacks across the EU institutions and EU Member States[159] betrays the cacophony of interests generated by epistemic communities populating each area.[160] Priorities depend on the notion of '(in)security' embraced by the communities active in different areas, which vary from technical and operational security (NIS), criminal offences (cybercrime), through to national security and war (defence). Attack-proof network and information systems within the NIS pillar clash with the interests of obtaining intelligence for law enforcement and defence purposes, engendering a state of security versus surveillance. Pursuing hate crimes endangers freedom of expression online protected by NIS instruments and diplomacy. The need for law enforcement to access e-evidence affects the confidentiality of personal communications and the security of the data protected by NIS-related measures.

Cyberspace and its security are the theatre of several battles among several communities[161] and possibly the EU and its Member States. Tensions are the result of internal institutional and external policy factors[162] and find muted expression in the cybersecurity policy, taking form within and across areas of policymaking, to the detriment of coherence. Tensions are also exacerbated by the newfound relevance of cybersecurity to ideas of economic, military and political sovereignty. Such battles, tensions and incoherence must be borne in mind when looking at the interplay between cybersecurity, privacy and data protection. But first, privacy and data protection need to be introduced.

---

[156] European Commission and High Representative of the European Union for Foreign Affairs and Security Policy, 'Countering Hybrid Threats' (Joint Communication) JOIN (2016) 18 final. Hybrid threats are acts below the threshold of declared warfare that exploit vulnerabilities to achieve strategic objectives.

[157] European Council (n 155) 4.

[158] MG Porcedda, 'Brexit, Cybercrime and Cyber Security. From en Masse opt-out to Creative Opt-in in the AFSJ and Beyond?', in H Carrapico et al. (eds), *Brexit and Internal Security. Political and Legal Concerns in the Context of the Future UK-EU Relationship* (Basingstoke, Palgrave Macmillan, 2019).

[159] European Parliament (n 66).

[160] As discussed by Nissenbaum (n 124) in the US context.

[161] The Council's Horizontal Working Party on Cyber Issues (HWP) aims to dissolve such tensions: www.consilium.europa.eu/it/council-eu/preparatory-bodies/horizontal-working-party-on-cyber-issues/. Carrapico and Barrinha (n 6).

[162] On conflicting agendas and the use of mainstreaming to resolve that: S Smismans and R Minto, 'Are Integrated Impact Assessments the Way Forward for Mainstreaming in the European Union?' (2017) 11 *Regulation & Governance* 231–251.

3

Privacy: The Right to Respect for Private and Family Life

Having examined cybersecurity, this chapter focusses on the right to private and family life ('privacy') as a situated legal object. The first section of the chapter discusses the sources of the right (I.A) with a view to delimiting its scope, and focusses on the relationship between Article 7 of the Charter and Article 8 of the Council of Europe (CoE) European Convention on Human Rights[1] (ECHR) (I.B). This exercise enables us to identify the constitutive elements of the right, ie its attributes, essential components or limbs (I.B.i) and discuss the specificity of permissible limitations in the Charter (I.B.ii). On such a basis, I argue that potential conflicts between privacy and cybersecurity should not be resolved by automatically reaching for the case law of the European Court of Human Rights (ECtHR).

The second section of the chapter explores the contents of the essential components of Article 7 through case law and authoritative interpretations and the essence as identified by the Court of Justice of the European Union (CJEU). The findings are synthesised in Table 1 in the conclusions, which also speculates about the existence of core areas in addition to those found by the CJEU. Such an analysis will bring to the fore elements that will inform the techno-legal analysis contained in chapter five and the subsequent analysis of cybersecurity, privacy and data protection (the triad), in the main areas of EU law making.

I. Sources and Scope of Article 7 CFR

In EU law, the right to respect for private and family life is protected both as a general principle[2] and as a right enshrined in Article 7 of the Charter (CFR). As a right, privacy is also an element of the Rule of Law (RoL) and contributes to objectives of general interest of the EU. As seen,[3] the Charter binds institutions, bodies, offices and agencies of the Union and EU Member States when they 'implement' EU law, though case law is far from settled.

---

[1] Charter OJ C326 [2012] (CFR); Convention for the Protection of Human Rights and Fundamental Freedoms (as amended by Protocol Nos 11 and 14), Council of Europe, ETS n Åã 005, 4 November 1950.
[2] Fundamental rights recognised by the ECHR constitute general principles of Union law. *Åkerberg Fransson*, C-617/10, EU:C:2013:105, para 44.
[3] Ch 1, section II.A.ii.

For instance, in *Privacy International*, the Court declared that national legislation enabling a state authority to require e-communications service providers (ECSs) to forward metadata 'to the security and intelligence agencies for the purpose of safeguarding national security falls within the scope of' the e-privacy Directive (EPD), currently under revision[4] and thus EU Law.[5] The Court added that a directly implemented national measure that derogates from the requirement of the EPD that e-communications are to be confidential, without imposing processing obligations on ECSs is 'covered by national law only, subject to the application of the'[6] Law Enforcement Directive (LED),[7] without clarifying the role played by the Charter.

As more activities come within the scope of EU law, the reach of the Charter and Article 7 expand. In *Tele2Sverige*, the Court clarified that the interpretation of EU secondary law 'must be undertaken solely in the light of the fundamental rights guaranteed by the Charter'.[8] However, being part of a multilevel system of protection of human rights,[9] the Charter benefits from interpretive traditions drawn from a variety of instruments, illustrated in section I.A, including the ECHR, whose complex role vis-à-vis Article 7 CFR is discussed in section I.B.

A. Determination of the Relevant Sources to Interpret Article 7 CFR

Sources with interpretive value can be derived by complementing the source of the right explicitly listed in the Explanations to the Charter (Explanations),[10] ie the ECHR,[11] with interdependent instruments and sources acknowledged by EU law but having varying legal force in the jurisdiction. The sources of Article 7 CFR can be distinguished between instruments that are binding on the Member States including as contracting parties to international treaties, such as the ICCPR and the ECHR, and instruments of EU law,

---

[4] Directive 2002/58/EC [2002] OJ L201/37 (EPD) European Commission, 'Proposal for a Regulation of the European Parliament and of the Council concerning the respect for private life and the protection of personal data in electronic communications and repealing Directive 2002/58/EC (Regulation on Privacy and Electronic Communications)' COM (2017) 10 final, 2017/0003(COD).

[5] *Privacy International*, C-623/17, EU:C:2020:790.

[6] ibid, para 48.

[7] Directive (EU) 2016/680 of the European Parliament and of the Council of 27 April 2016 on the protection of natural persons with regard to the processing of personal data by competent authorities for the purposes of the prevention, investigation, detection or prosecution of criminal offences or the execution of criminal penalties, and on the free movement of such data, and repealing Council Framework Decision 2008/977/JHA, [2016] OJ L119/89 (Law Enforcement Directive or LED).

[8] *Tele2 Sverige and Watson and others*, C-203/15 and C-698/15, EU:C:2016:970, paras 127–128.

[9] See ch. 1 (2.1.1).

[10] Explanations [2007] OJ C303/02 (Explanations to the Charter); The Explanations have interpretive value (CFR Arts 52(7) and TEU 6(1)) and must be taken into account, alongside other provisions of the Treaty and the Charter, to interpret CFR, Art 51; see especially *Åkerberg Fransson*, C-617/10, para 20. Thus, the Court has not used the Explanations as a decisive interpretive criterion: D Chalmers, G Davies et al., *European Union Law*, 4th edn (Cambridge, Cambridge University Press, 2019) 264.

[11] The CJEU stated that ECHR Arts 8 and CFR 7 are sources of the right to private life in *Chakroun*, C-578/08, EU:C:2010:117, para 44.

binding on the institutions and on the Member States *qua* associates of the Union, such as the Charter, the Treaty, and related secondary law.

In practice, the sources of the right to respect for private and family life are an *ensemble* of the following, in order of increasing interpretive importance. First are international instruments of soft law adopted by consensus. Second, international law instruments supply guidelines for the interpretation of rights recognised within EU law,[12] chiefly Article 12 of the Universal Declaration of Human Rights (UDHR) and case law on Article 17 of the International Covenant on Civil and Political Rights (ICCPR).[13] Article 12 UDHR is the root of Article 8 ECHR;[14] according to Rehof, the relationship between the two provisions is bidirectional, in that the copious case law relating to Article 8 ECHR represents a legally binding elaboration of the principles enshrined in Article 12 UDHR for parties to the ECHR.[15] Article 12 UDHR laid the basis for Article 17 ICCPR,[16] which is to date the geographically most widely endorsed provision on 'privacy'[17] and is legally binding for the Member States. Although the Committee of Experts on Human Rights paid attention to works at United Nations' (UN) level, Article 17 ICCPR was only introduced in 1953 under the impulse of the Philippines' delegation,[18] so there is no direct cross-reference between Article 8 ECHR and Article 17 ICCPR.

Third, the case law of the ECtHR is, pursuant to Article 52(3) CFR, to be followed insofar as Article 7 CFR corresponds to Article 8 ECHR. However, the determination of 'accordance' flowing from Article 52(3) CFR is not immediate. Notwithstanding Article 6(3) TEU, the ECHR does not constitute, as long as the EU 'has not acceded to it, a legal instrument which has been formally incorporated into' EU law.[19] The same should apply, a fortiori, to the ICCPR. Fourth, on a par with the ECHR are the common constitutional traditions of Member States.[20]

The fifth and most important interpretive source is CJEU case law on general principles, primary and secondary law.[21] Relatedly, instruments of EU secondary law

---

[12] See ch 1 (II.A).

[13] Universal Declaration of Human Rights (UDHR). General Assembly of the United Nations, Resolution 217, 10 December 1948; International Covenant on Civil and Political Rights, I-14668, UNTS n° 999 (ICCPR).

[14] According to its preamble, the Convention is a first step 'for the collective enforcement of certain of the rights stated in the' UDHR. The first version of Art 8 proposed by M Rolin (Belgium) and M Teitgen (France) voted by the Committee on Legal and Administrative Questions included the reference 'as laid down in article 12' UDHR. Council of Europe, European Commission of Human Rights, 'Preparatory Work on Article 8 of the European Convention on Human Rights' www.echr.coe.int/library/COLFRTravauxprep.html.

[15] LA Rehof, 'Universal Declaration of Human Rights – Common Standard of Achievement', in A Eide and G Alfredsson (eds), (Zuidpoolsingel, Kluwer Law International, 1999).

[16] The *travaux préparatoires* of ICCPR, Art 17 stress the connection with UDHR, Art 12.

[17] M Scheinin, *Report of the Special Rapporteur on the Promotion and Protection of Human Rights and Fundamental Freedoms while Countering Terrorism*, A/HRC/13/37 (2009). 167 states are parties to the Convention, available at: treaties.un.org/Pages/ViewDetails.aspx?src=TREATY&mtdsg_no=IV-4&chapter=4&lang=en.

[18] Council of Europe (n 14).

[19] *Åkerberg Fransson*, C-617/10, para 44. Moreover, 'Union law does not govern the relations between the ECHR and the legal systems of the Member States, nor does it determine the conclusions to be drawn by a national court in the event of conflict between the rights guaranteed by that convention and a rule of national law'. It remains to be seen if resumed negotiations towards accession of the EU to the ECHR will be successful. See www.coe.int/en/web/human-rights-intergovernmental-cooperation/accession-of-the-european-union-to-the-european-convention-on-human-rights#.

[20] Although these are not used in practice: Chalmers et al. (n 10) 266.

[21] General principles infuse the Charter but go beyond it, theoretically broadening the scope of fundamental rights in EU law. ibid 260–263.

represent an implementation of the right[22] which determines its current understanding, but which can be overridden at any time by the courts.

In this chapter I focus on the analysis of the interpretation of the CJEU (ECJ and General Court) on the right to privacy as an 'Article 7' right following the acquisition of primacy by the Charter with the entry into force of the Lisbon Treaty on 1 December 2009. The analysis is supplemented by ECtHR judgments on Article 8 ECHR and case law of the Human Rights Committee on Article 17 ICCPR (HRC) discussed in the literature *to the extent they are relevant*; the next section clarifies the complex relationship between Article 7 CFR and Article 8 ECHR.

B. The Correspondence between Articles 8 ECHR and 7 CFR

The wording of the limbs protected by Article 7 CFR are the same as those protected by Article 8 ECHR, except for the term 'communications', which is used instead of 'correspondence',[23] to reflect the technological evolution occurred in the past 60 years. Pursuant to Article 52(3) CFR, the Articles therein that derive from the ECHR should be interpreted in light of the case law of the ECtHR. The Explanations clarify that Article 7 is a right derived from Article 8 ECHR. In *La Quadrature du Net*, the Grand Chamber reasserted that Article 52(3) CFR 'is intended to ensure the necessary consistency between the rights contained in the Charter and the corresponding rights guaranteed in the ECHR, without adversely affecting the autonomy of EU law and … the [CJEU]'.[24] The Court then stated that 'the corresponding rights of the ECHR for the purpose of interpreting the Charter' must be taken into account 'as the minimum threshold of protection'.[25]

That the ECHR constitutes a minimum threshold of protection does not settle the question of whether Article 7 CFR has the same scope of Article 8 ECHR. The CJEU declined to answer the question posed by the referring national court in *Tele2Sverige* of whether the decision in *Digital Rights Ireland* 'extended the scope of Article 7 and/or Article 8 of the Charter beyond that of Article 8 of the ECHR, as interpreted by the ECtHR'. The Grand Chamber followed the AG's Opinion, rejecting the question as inadmissible;[26] in motivating its decision, the Court simply stressed that 'the first sentence of Article 52(3) does not preclude Union law from providing protection that is more extensive than the ECHR'.[27] Such an approach is consistent with the autonomy of the EU legal order.[28]

The case of *Dereci*, concerning the impact on the right to respect for private and family life of the refusal of the applicants' right of residence,[29] provides useful

---

[22] *Mircom*, C-597/19, EU:C:2021:492.
[23] See especially *PPU McB*, C-400/10, EU:C:2010:582, para 53.
[24] *La Quadrature du Net and Others*, C-511/18, EU:C:2020:791, para 124.
[25] ibid.
[26] *Tele2 Sverige and Watson and Others*, C-203/15 and C-698/15, EU:C:2016:572, Opinion of AG Saugmandsgaard Øe, para 73.
[27] *Tele2 Sverige*, C-203/15 and C-698/15, para 129.
[28] See ch 8, section II.
[29] *Dereci and others v Bundesministerium für Inneres*, C-256/11, EU:C:2011:734.

guidance when conceptualising the relationship between the scope of Articles 7 CFR and 8 ECHR. There, the Grand Chamber held that, '*in so far as Article 7 [CFR] ... contains rights which correspond to rights guaranteed by Article 8(1) [ECHR], the meaning and scope of Article 7 of the Charter are to be the same as those laid down by Article 8(1) of the ECHR, as interpreted by the case-law of the*'[30] ECtHR (emphasis added). The Court then gave a valuable indication of the relevant applicable instrument depending on whether the situation of the applicants in the main proceedings is covered by EU law or not. If it is, the referring court should review the situation in light of Article 7 CFR; conversely, 'it must undertake that examination in the light of Article 8(1)' ECHR.[31] And yet, in *Privacy International* the CJEU added that a directly implemented national measure subject to the application of the LED – a EU law instrument – 'must comply with, inter alia, national constitutional law and the requirements of the ECHR,'[32] without clarifying the role of the Charter in such a situation.

The cases suggest two potential situations of mismatch between Articles 7 CFR and 8 ECHR. First, following *Dereci*, the two provisions could embody different bundles of rights[33] or cover different objects (divergence as to breadth). Second, following *Privacy International*, when the two Articles cover the same bundle of rights, the ECHR constitutes the benchmark of interpretation or minimum threshold of protection. However, following *La Quadrature du Net*, the EU can depart from the interpretation of the ECtHR with a view to granting higher protection, by either extending the scope of the right[34] or interpreting permissible limitations differently (divergence as to depth). I review these in greater detail in the following.

i. Divergence as to the Breadth of Protection: Article 7 CFR Deals with a Narrower 'Bundle of Rights' than Article 8 ECHR

The 6,000 plus cases on Article 8 ECHR dealt with by the ECtHR dwarf the CJEU's sporadic case law on Article 7 CFREU; consequently, Strasbourg's case law is more detailed than Luxembourg's. The ECtHR case law is also broader in that, unlike the Charter whose scope of application is limited to the scope of application of EU law, the scope of application of the ECHR is not tied to a *sui generis* legal order governed by the Treaty of London. Furthermore, the ECtHR has been using Article 8 in an expansive way, to offer protection to situations that the ECHR would not have otherwise covered on account of the social circumstances in which it was adopted, such as collective health protection, the processing of personal data and the protection of the environment.[35]

---

[30] ibid, para 70. This revisits the Court's approach in *McB*, C-400/10 PPU, para 53.
[31] *Dereci and others*, C-256/11, para 72.
[32] *Privacy International*, C-623/17, para 48.
[33] On privacy and data protection as bundle of rights: S Rodotà, 'Data Protection as a Fundamental Right', in S Gutwirth (ed), *In Reinventing Data Protection?* (New York, Springer, 2009).
[34] See especially Opinion of AG Saugmandsgaard Øe, C-203/15 and C-698/15, Para 78.
[35] See generally Rehof (n 15); V Zeno-Zencovich, 'Articolo 8. Diritto al Rispetto della Vita Privata e Familiare', in S Bartole (ed), *Commentario alla Convenzione Europea per la Tutela dei Diritti dell'Uomo e delle Libertà Fondamentali* (Cedam, 2001). P van Dijk, 'Article 8', in P van Dijk (ed), *Theory and Practice of the European Convention on Human Rights*, 4th edn (Cambridge, Intersentia, 2006).

One only need look at the summary of the Guide on Article 8 ECHR prepared by the Jurisconsult to grasp the reach of the right.[36] The limb of private life encompasses cases relating to spheres of private life, physical, psychological or moral integrity including environmental issues, privacy per se, identity and autonomy (including gender identity). Cases concerning the family life limb touch on all family members and possible family relationships, immigration, expulsion and testimonial privilege. Home cases cover housing, commercial premises, law firms, journalists' homes and the home environment including noise and pollutants. Finally, the case law on correspondence deals with prisoners, lawyers' and professionals' correspondence, surveillance of telecommunications in a criminal context and special secret surveillance. Thus far, the CJEU has either provided an autonomous interpretation, or referred to the case law of the ECHR by analogy.[37]

The most accurate way of analysing the respective reach of Articles 8 ECHR and 7 CFR would be to engage in a case-by-case comparison, a task beyond the scope of this work. A way of comparing in a synthetical manner the reach of the two provisions is offered by work on indicators. Human rights organisations such as the UN Office of the High Commissioner for Human Rights (OHCHR) and the EU Fundamental Rights Agency use indicators as a way of measuring, monitoring and ultimately improving the implementation of human rights.[38] To enable measurements, indicators cluster the variety of situations protected by a given right into synthetic categories called 'attributes'.[39] Attributes for Article 8 ECHR were proposed by the Equality and Human Rights Commission's Human Rights Measurement Framework (HRMF),[40] which is 'conceptually anchored'[41] in the OHCHR work on indicators. The HRMF indicators relating to the right to respect for private and family life[42] aim to measure results on six attributes: (I) private life including, (i) physical and psychological integrity, (ii) personal social and sexual identity, and (iii) personal development, autonomy and participation; (II) personal information and surveillance; (III) correspondence; (IV) family life; (V) home; and (VI) environmental rights. In the following I use HRMF's attributes to compare the scope of Articles 8 ECHR and 7 CFR.

First, elements of 'physical and psychological integrity' covered by Article 8 ECHR[43] pertain to Article 3 CFR, whereby 'everyone has the right to respect for his or her

---

[36] Jurisconsult of the ECtHR, Guide on Article 8 of the European Convention on Human Rights. Right to respect for private and family life (last updated 31 December 2020).

[37] See, eg, Chalmers et al (n 10) ch 6.

[38] Fundamental Rights Agency, *Using Indicators to Measure Fundamental Rights in the EU: Challenges and Solutions* (2nd Annual FRA Symposium Report, 2011); United Nations, International Human Rights Instruments, *Report on Indicators for Monitoring Compliance with International Human Rights Instruments* (HRI/MC/2006/7, 2006); United Nations, High Commissioner for Human Rights (OHCHR), *Human Rights Indicators. A Guide to Measurement and Implementation* (HR/PUB/12/5, 2012).

[39] United Nations (n 38) 3. Attributes are the intrinsic and distinctive substantive dimensions of a right; see ch 1, section II.A.ii.

[40] The HRMF borrows from the OHCHR study the concepts of attributes and structural, process and outcome indicators, measuring respectively the commitment to rights in principle, the efforts made to implement rights and the practical results of such efforts.

[41] J Candler and H Holder et al, *Human Rights Measurement Framework: Prototype Panels, Indicator Set and Evidence Base* (Equality and Human Rights Commission, 2011) 16.

[42] The 2011 study (ibid) contained a dashboard of 10 indicators (41–50) on 'The Right to Respect for Private and Family Life' derived from ECHR, Art 8.

[43] Eg, *Glass v UK* no 61827/00, CE:ECHR:2004:0309JUD006182700, mentioned in Candler and Holder et al. (n 41).

physical and mental integrity'. Such principles are, according to the Explanations, 'already included in the Convention on Human Rights and Biomedicine, adopted by the Council of Europe (ETS 164 and additional protocol ETS 168)'. The CJEU case of *A, B, and C*[44] could provide some guidance on where to draw the line between Articles 3 and 7 CFR.[45] AG Sharpston found the asking of explicit questions concerning an applicant's sexual activities and proclivities to be violating both Articles 3 and 7 of the Charter, the first because of their content of a medical nature (while noting that homosexuality is not a medical or psychological condition), the second because of its intrusiveness.[46] Article 3 could thus cover the performance of medical activities, whereas Article 7 could deal with the consequence of such activities for the mind, body and life of individuals.[47]

Second, with respect to 'personal information and surveillance', given that the protection of personal data is overseen by Article 8 CFR as clearly stated in *Tele2 Sverige*, 'personal information' should not fall within the scope of Article 7.[48] Left on its own, surveillance is one of the forms by which the right can be limited and is therefore to be treated in the context of the analysis of permissible limitations.

Third, 'environmental protection' does also not fall within the scope of Article 7 but rather Article 37 CFR, which states that a high level of environmental protection and the improvement of the quality of the environment must be integrated into the policies of the Union and ensured in accordance with the principle of sustainable development. Such interpretation is supported by the case of *Commission v Austria*,[49] concerning the failure of the Republic of Austria to fulfil its obligations under Articles 28 EC and 29 EC as a consequence of prohibiting lorries of over 7.5 tonnes carrying certain goods from using a section of the A 12 motorway in the Inn valley (Austria). One of the arguments adduced by Austria to justify its decision was the 'protection of health and the environment and … the need to ensure respect for private and family life enshrined in Article 7 [CFR] and Article 8(2)' ECHR.[50] In appraising the argument of the Republic of Austria, the ECJ recalled that the 'protection of health and the protection of the environment are essential objectives of the European Union' overseen by '[Articles 2, 3(1)(p) and 174(1) EC] and reaffirmed in Articles 37 and 35 of the Charter'.[51] In other words, the Court did not refer to Article 7 CFR (nor 8 ECHR), but rather to the dedicated Articles of the Charter, which it is subsequently necessary to treat as separate rights.

In sum, Article 7 deals with a narrower bundle of rights than Article 8 ECHR. As for the principles or attributes they both cover, the question as to whether the Charter offers greater protection to individuals than the ECHR can only be fully answered on a case-by-case basis, which I will do to an extent in chapter seven. In the interim, the test

---

[44] *A, B, and C*, C-148/13 to C-150/13, EU:C:2014:2406.
[45] *A, B, and C*, C-148/13 to C-150/13, EU:C:2014:2111, Opinion of AG Sharpston.
[46] ibid, paras 60–63 and 67. While the Grand Chamber followed the reasoning of the AG, the Court did so by relying on CFR, Arts 1 and 7 instead of 3 and 7, as AG Sharpston had done.
[47] But compare T Lock, 'Article 7 CFR', in M Kellerbauer (ed), *The EU Treaties and the Charter of Fundamental Rights: a Commentary* (Oxford, Oxford University Press, 2019) 2116. He refers to the Explanations to Art 52(3) to state that, by virtue of Art 8 ECHR rights provided in Art 7 CFR also find expression in other rights of the Charter.
[48] On the relationship between CFR, Arts 7 and 8, see below, section II.C and ch 4.
[49] *Commission v Austria*, C-28/09, EU:C:2011:854.
[50] ibid, para 118.
[51] ibid, paras 120–122.

for permissible limitations applicable to each right offers building blocks for an answer, to which I now turn.

ii. Divergence as to the Depth of Protection: The Test for Permissible Limitations Applicable to Art 8 ECHR Differs from that Applicable to Art 7 CFR

As a qualified right,[52] privacy is subject to permissible limitations, but interferences or attacks must comply with criteria laid down in primary law. Pursuant to Article 8(2) ECHR, interferences must be: (i) 'in accordance with the law'; (ii) 'necessary in a democratic society'; and (iii) 'in the interests of national security, public safety or the economic well-being of the country, for the prevention of disorder or crime, for the protection of health or morals, or for the protection of the rights and freedoms of others'. Over time, the ECtHR morphed the Convention's wording into a stepped procedure geared at assessing the legality and lawfulness of measures, including the quality of the law to minimise the occurrence of arbitrariness,[53] their necessity and proportionality in a democratic society and whether they pursue legitimate aims, questions triggering political issues that can entail the application of a margin of appreciation.

The Court does not always follow the same steps and in the same order.[54] The assessment of the criterion of necessity entails at least two steps but de Hert and Gutwirth identify four steps, exemplified by *Niemietz v Germany*.[55] The first step consists in evaluating whether the measure responds to a pressing social need, which, according to De Hert and Gutwirth, appears to be rarely applied with regards to Article 8 ECHR.[56] The second is whether the interference responds to a legitimate aim[57] and the third step is the proportionality test. Furthermore, the Court has developed standards that vary according to the matter at hand. For instance, measures of secret surveillance are reviewed according to standards different from those concerning ordinary law enforcement.[58]

Insofar as Article 7 CFR corresponds to Article 8 ECHR, the permissibility of an interference should be assessed against the existence of an adequate legal basis, the legitimacy of the aim pursued by the interference (in a democracy) and the degree of intensity of the interference vis-à-vis the aim pursued and the factual circumstances.[59] However,

---

[52] Judgment in *Schwarz*, C-291/12, EU:C:2013:670, para 33.
[53] *P.G. and J.H. v the United Kingdom* no. 44787/98 CE:ECHR:2001:0925JUD004478798, paras 37–38, 46, 63.
[54] See also Art 29 Data Protection Working Party, *Opinion 01/2014 on the Application of Necessity and Proportionality Concepts and Data Protection within the Law Enforcement Sector* (536/14/EN WP 211, 2014).
[55] *Niemietz v Germany* no. 13710/88 CE:ECHR:1992:1216JUD001371088, para 37. P De Hert and S Gutwirth, 'Data Protection in the Law of Strasbourg and Luxembourg: Constitutionalism in Action', in S Gutwirth (ed), *Reinventing Data Protection?* (New York, Springer, 2009).
[56] ibid; eg, *Leander v Sweden* no. 9248/81 CE:ECHR:1987:0326JUD000924881, para 58. See also *Handyside v UK*, no. 5493/72, in MG Porcedda, M Vermeulen et al., *Report on Regulatory Frameworks Concerning Privacy and the Evolution of the Norm of the Right to Privacy. Deliverable 3.2, SurPRISE Project* (European University Institute, 2013) surprise-project.eu/wp-content/uploads/2013/06/SurPRISE_D3.2_Report-on-regulatory-frameworks-concerning-privacy-for-final-formatting_v094.pdf.
[57] *Klass and Others v Germany* no. 5029/71 CE:ECHR:1978:0906JUD000502971, para 48.
[58] *Iordachi and Others v Moldova* no. 25198/02, CE:ECHR:2009:0210JUD002519802, para 39; *Big Brother Watch and Others v UK* nos. 58170/13, 62322/14 and 24960/15 CE:ECHR:2021:0525JUD005817013.
[59] "The Court's task is not to review the relevant law or practice in the abstract but rather to confine itself, without overlooking the general context, to examining the issues raised by case before it', *Peck v the United*

the correspondence of Articles 7 CFR and 8 ECHR has been questioned by Gonzáles Fuster[60] on account of the respective clauses on permissible limitations. It is worth recalling the wording of Article 52(1), the Charter's horizontal clause on permissible limitations of Charter rights, whereby 'Any limitation on the exercise of the rights and freedoms recognised by this Charter must be provided for by law and respect the essence of those rights and freedoms.' Furthermore, 'subject to the principle of proportionality, limitations may be made only if they are necessary and genuinely meet objectives of general interest recognised by the Union or the need to protect the rights and freedoms of others'. The Explanations clarify that limitations must be interpreted restrictively and cannot 'constitute, with regard to the aim pursued, disproportionate and unreasonable interference undermining the very substance of those rights'.[61] The formulation of the Article would also allow for the application of a margin of appreciation.

Gonzáles Fuster expresses three doubts. The first is in relation to the correspondence between the tests of 'in accordance with the law' versus 'provided for by law', 'necessary in a democratic society' versus the 'proportionality principle' and the 'legitimate aims' versus the 'objectives of general interest'. The latter may harbour the greatest divisions, as the Union's objectives of general interests are those contained in Articles 3 and 4(1) TEU, and 35(3), 36 and 346 TFEU.[62] Two further reasons for mismatch Gonzáles Fuster indicates are the obligations, set out in Article 52(1) CFR, to respect the essence of the right, and the possibility for Union law to grant additional protection to the fundamental rights pursuant to Article 52(3) CFR. These two points may create a permanent mismatch between the protection afforded by the two courts and could pave the way to an independent interpretation of the right.

As for the essence, Vermeulen points out 'the ECtHR has not used the doctrine of the "essence" of a right in cases relating to article 8, which would act as the ultimate limit of a restriction on article 8 [as] explained by Judge Matscher's dissenting opinion on the scope of Article 5(1)'.[63] Craig states that the reference to the essence is stringent in EU law, and should be interpreted in accordance with the legal tradition it originates from.[64]

As for the greater protection the Charter can afford, the question is to what extent the CJEU departs from the approach of the ECtHR, taking into account the distinct powers and remits the two courts have. The question is beyond the scope of this work, though in chapter seven I will discuss differences in the approach of the two Courts in *La Quadrature du Net* and *Big Brother and Others v UK*. Article 7 could also enjoy greater protection thanks to the following EU law remedies highlighted by Craig:

Kingdom, no. 44647/98, CE:ECHR:2003:0128JUD004464798, para 102. *P.G. and J.H. v. the United Kingdom*, no. 44787/98, para 62. *Perry v the United Kingdom* no. 3737/00 CE:ECHR:2003:0717JUD006373700, para 45 and following. *P.G. and J.H. v the United Kingdom*, no. 44787/98, para 44.

[60] G González Fuster, *The Emergence of Personal Data Protection as a Fundamental Right in Europe* (Cham, Springer, 2014).

[61] *Karlsson and Others*, C-292/97, EU:C:2000:202, para 45. See also *Satakunnan and Satamedia*, C-73/07, EU:C:2008:727; *Schecke and Eifert*, C-92/09 and C-93/09, EU:C:2010:662.

[62] See generally P Craig, *The Lisbon Treaty, Revised Edition: Law, Politics, and Treaty Reform* (Oxford, Oxford University Press, 2013) 223–226.

[63] Vermeulen (n 56) 28.

[64] Craig (n 62) 223–225; see ch 1, section II.A.

legality leading to annulment and damages liability,[65] where the criteria for standing have been broadened.

Another factor leading to a mismatch between Articles 7 CFR and 8 ECHR is that Union secondary law[66] to an extent defines permissible limitation.[67] The crucial point is that the potential mismatch between Articles 7 CFR and 8 ECHR needs to be accounted for when appraising the interplay between the triad: potential conflicts between privacy and cybersecurity should not be resolved by automatically reaching for the case law of the ECtHR.

II. Essential Components of Article 7 of the Charter

Article 7 CFR reads 'Everyone has the right to respect for his or her private and family life, home and communications.' In what follows, I expound the legal meaning of the right through its formulation. The analysis covers first the meaning of 'everyone has the right to' and 'respect for' and then systematises the right's limbs or essential components (as opposed to the essence[68]) as follows: private life, comprising of: (i) physical and psychological integrity; (ii) personal social and sexual identity; and (iii) personal development, autonomy and participation – this follows the systematisation of the HRMF; family life; home; and correspondence. I review the interpretation of Article 7 in light of human rights treaties that supply interpretive guidelines – chiefly the ECHR followed by the ICCPR. I then sketch how the right is implemented by secondary law relevant to the relationship between cybersecurity, privacy and data protection.

A. 'Everyone has the Right to'

Article 7 CFR follows the positive formulation of Article 8 ECHR, viz 'having a right to'. The *travaux préparatoires* of Article 8 ECHR leave unexplained the reason for preferring a positive formulation, as against the 'negative' formulation found in Articles 12 UDHR and 17 ICCPR,[69] viz forbidding interferences with the right. Perhaps this is because the formulation of Article 12 UDHR, which for Morsink derives from the Fourth Amendment to the US Constitution, is itself an anomaly, given that other provisions of the UDHR are construed positively.[70] In the Charter, 'everyone' refers to persons who are affected by the application of EU law. The addressees of the Charter are therefore a subset of ECHR rights holders.

---

[65] Respectively TFEU Arts 263 and 340, ibid.
[66] Eg, EPD, Art 15 and GDPR, Art 23, to the extent they apply to privacy.
[67] The requirement in *WebMindLicenses* (§81) whereby 'the exercise of fundamental rights must be provided for by law implies that the legal basis which permits the interference with those rights must itself define the scope of the limitation on the exercise of the right concerned', Opinion of AG Saugmandsgaard Øe, C-203/15 and C-698/15, para 136. This was confirmed in Opinion 1/15, Opinion 1/15 of 26 July 2017 pursuant to Article 218(11) TFEU EU:C:2017:592, para 139.
[68] See ch 1, section II.A.ii.
[69] Scheinin (n 17).
[70] Among the countries that were active proponents of the right, Latin American constitutions construe it in terms of inviolability: J Morsink, *The Universal Declaration of Human Rights: Origins, Drafting and Intent*

The applicable law, particularly the EPD, gives substance to the right to respect for private life and communications of users and subscribers of publicly available ECSs.[71] Recipients of such rights have grown in parallel to mobile and Internet connectivity, to the point that the proposed e-privacy Regulation (EPR) acknowledges that 'Basic broadband internet access and voice communications services are to be considered as essential services for individuals to be able to communicate and participate to the benefits of the digital economy.'[72] To the extent that the protection of personal data is instrumental to the right to privacy, the GDPR offers protection to a wider range of individuals than the EPD.

B. 'Respect for': Vertical and Horizontal Obligations

The notion of 'respect for' in Article 7 CFR embodies both positive and negative obligations, drawn from the minimum threshold of protection offered by the ECHR as supplemented by other international instruments, and the effects produced by the Charter, including through its implementation by means of secondary law.

The ECtHR has focussed on the notion of 'interference' in the second paragraph of Article 8 ECHR to interpret the provision *a contrario*.[73] Far from only embodying negative obligations to 'refrain from' infringing, Article 8 ECHR entails positive state obligations[74] (actions), first acknowledged in *Marckx v Belgium*. There, the ECtHR stated that, 'by guaranteeing the right to respect for family life, Article 8 presupposes the existence of a family';[75] in this guise, 'respect' could simply be a reminder for the competent authorities that private and family life are a fait accompli that predates the state. Articles 12 UDHR and 17 ICCPR corroborate such a minimum threshold of protection. The former includes both negative state obligations and positive ones,[76] implicit in the formulation of the second paragraph.[77] The Human Rights Committee (HRC)[78] interprets Article 17 ICCPR in a similar vein, as attacks upon privacy can come from disparate sources.[79] According to Scheinin, Article 17 ICCPR distinguishes between 'plain (and presumably permissible) "*interference*" and actual *violations* of the right'

(Pennsylvania, University of Pennsylvania Press, 1999). The International Bill of Rights Documented Outline contains a list of the national constitutions containing a right to privacy, some predating Warren and Brandeis' paper (United Nations, Economic and Social Council, *Commission on Human Rights Drafting Committee. International Bill of Rights* (E/CN4/AC1/3/ADD1 Part 1, 1947).

[71] EPD, Art 1.

[72] Draft Art 18, European Council, Regulation on Privacy and Electronic Communications 2017/0003(COD). Mandate for negotiations with EP, 6087/21, (2021). The draft EPR applies to legal persons, though Lock finds that the personal scope of the right to private life can extend to legal persons (n 47) 2117.

[73] See generally Zeno-Zencovich (n 35).

[74] ibid. For Lock, positive obligations under Art 7 CFR are due 'where formulated by the ECtHR' (n 47), 2116.

[75] *Marckx v Belgium* no. 6833/74 CE:ECHR:1979:0613JUD000683374, para 31.

[76] Rehof (n 15).

[77] Morsink (n 70).

[78] Human Rights Committee (CCPR), *General Comment no. 16. Article 17 (The right to Respect of Privacy, Family, Home and Correspondence, and Protection of Honour and Reputation)* (1988).

[79] M Nowak, 'Chapter on Article 17', in M Nowaket et al. (eds), *UN Covenant on Civil and Political Rights, CCPR Commentary, 4th edn* (N.P. Engel, 2005).

and creates a positive obligation to ensure that the prohibition of such interferences is enforced and thus to legislate, whenever state parties have effective control over the territory.[80]

Articles 12 UDHR and 17 ICCPR also address interferences that are horizontal, ie committed by natural and legal persons. However, most claims brought under Article 17 ICCPR are directed against the state, which is nevertheless under no obligation to reinstate a condition of private life that has been impaired.[81] Article 8 ECHR, by contrast, works only vertically, but is capable of producing some sort of horizontal indirect effects. States may face 'positive obligations … [that] involve the adoption of measures designed to secure respect for private life even in the sphere of the relations of individuals between themselves',[82] and the case law of the ECtHR can be cited in national cases.[83]

What about horizontal and vertical obligations in EU law? According to Craig the provisions of the Charter are likely to trigger, at a minimum, horizontal indirect effects.[84] The Charter has the same legal values of the Treaties[85] and, as such, its provisions should be capable of producing direct effects insofar as they meet the criteria identified by the case law of the Court.[86] An inherent limitation is embodied in Article 52(5) CFR: unlike provisions that contain rights, provisions that contain principles 'may be implemented by legislative and executive acts' and are 'judicially cognisable only in the interpretation of such acts'. Unhelpfully, the Explanations only provide illustrative examples of principles that are to be 'observed'. That rights must be 'respected' includes the possibility that they can be invoked between individuals when formulated in a peremptory and unconditional manner and do not require to be given concrete expression by provisions of EU or national law,[87] as is the case for Article 31(2) on a right to annual paid leave.

The Explanations are silent about the difference between rights and freedoms, under which Article 7 is clustered. Furthermore, Article 7 CFR is not reinforced by a Treaty provision akin to Article 16 TFEU.[88] Since the protection of the right is ensured by EU secondary law,[89] the extent to which the limbs of Article 7 enjoy vertical and horizontal direct effect depends on the instrument of secondary EU law at hand. At the same time, an instrument such as the EPD lays down measures designed to secure respect for private life in the sphere of the relations of individuals between themselves,[90] especially

---

[80] Characterised as '*arbitrary* interference, *unlawful* interference or *unlawful* attacks': M Scheinin, *Written testimony related to the surveillance program conducted under Section 702 of the FISA Amendments Act* (2014) 2.
[81] Nowak (n 79).
[82] *X and Y v the Netherlands* no. 8978/80 CE:ECHR:1985:0326JUD000897880, para 23. This includes the adoption of criminal law provisions, *Lopez Ribalda v Spain* nos. 1874/13 and 8567/13 CE:ECHR:2019:1017 JUD000187413, para 113.
[83] De Hert and Gutwirth (n 55).
[84] Craig (n 62) 208–211.
[85] TEU Art 6(1).
[86] Chalmers et al. (n 10) 308–325.
[87] *Bauer and Willemorth*, C-569/16 and C-570/16, EU:C:2018:871 para 85. *Max-Planck-Gesellschaft zur Förderung der Wissenschaften e.V.* restates the lack of horizontal direct effect of Directives, eg, Court of Justice of the European Union, *Field of Application of the Charter of Fundamental Rights of the European Union* (2021), 14–16. See also Chalmers et al. (n 10) 308–325.
[88] Insofar as the right to data protection is instrumental to protecting the right to privacy, the positive obligations stemming from Art 16 TFEU will also benefit the right to privacy.
[89] *Mircom*, C-597/19, para 114.
[90] The effect of provisions will change with the adoption of the proposed EPR.

between providers of ECSs on publicly available e-communication networks and users of such services, between Information Society Services (ISS) and its user, and between service providers and law enforcement agencies.

C. 'His or Her Private ... Life'

Similarly to Article 8 ECHR, Article 7 CFR does not explicitly protect honour and reputation. The *travaux préparatoires* of Article 8 ECHR point to an intentional exclusion of attacks against honour and reputation, which were instead connected to freedom of expression enshrined in Article 10.[91] This might have been a consequence of the discussions which occurred around Article 12 UDHR and are codified in Article 17 ICCPR.[92]

As for specific elements falling within the notion of private life, the General Court mentioned one's personal financial situation, including pension contributions[93] and *a contrario* the availability of one's funds.[94] Information about one's life is part and parcel of private life[95] and is a clear area of overlap with data protection.[96] Making such information freely available to third parties endangers the right. In Opinion 1/15, the Grand Chamber made an *a contrario* remark about the essence of Article 7, whereby

> even if PNR data may, in some circumstances, reveal very specific information concerning the private life of a person, the nature of that information is limited to certain aspects of that private life, in particular, relating to air travel.[97]

Thus, the revelation of very specific information concerning the private life of a person, not limited to certain aspects of that private life, could be seen to be part of the essence of private life. The finding, which is reminiscent of the mosaic theory in the US,[98] begs the question of whether there exists a threshold for determining when information is no longer limited to certain aspects of private life and therefore the essence is violated.

---

[91] Council of Europe (n 14); Zeno-Zencovich (n 35).

[92] The Drafting Assembly expressed concern that protecting 'honour' could have an impact on free speech and the press; as an adjustment, the adjective 'inviolable' was expunged from Art 12 UDHR. See generally, Morsink (n 70); Rehof (n 15). Art 17 ICCPR offers lower protection to honour and reputation, as demonstrated by the wording 'unlawful attacks', Nowak (n 79); Council of Europe (n 14). To safeguard the potentially competing right of freedom of expression, the burden of proof of the unlawfulness of attacks against honour and reputation is on the plaintiff (*Simons v Panama* 460/91 and *I.P. v Finland* 450/91 in J Blair, *The International Covenant on Civil and Political Rights and its (First) Optional Protocol. A short Commentary based on Views, General Comments and Concluding Observations by the Human Rights Committee* (Frankfurt, Peter Lang, 2005).

[93] *Dennekamp v Parliament*, T-115/13, EU:T:2015:497, para 44.

[94] *Al Assad v Council*, T-202/12, EU:T:2014:113, para 115.

[95] *European Commission v Federal Republic of Germany*, C-518/07, EU:C:2010:125, para 21. *Digital Rights Ireland and Seitlinger and Others*, C-293/12 and C-594/12, EU:C:2014:238, paras 34–35.

[96] The finding in *YS and Others* that the notion of private life 'means, *inter alia*, that that person may be certain that the personal data concerning him are correct and that they are processed in a lawful manner' could be *per incuriam* (see ch 4). *YS and others*, C-141/12 and C-372/12, EU:C:2014:2081, para 44.

[97] Opinion 1/15, para 150.

[98] I Škorvánek, B-J Koops et al., '"My Computer Is My Castle": New Privacy Frameworks to Regulate Police Hacking' [2020] *Brigham Young University Law Review* 997–1082, 1073–1079. Discussing the mosaic theory is beyond the scope of this work.

Activities of a professional nature also fall within the remit of private life,[99] following the ECtHR in *Niemietz*, as

> it is, after all, in the course of their working lives that the majority of people have a significant, if not the greatest, opportunity of developing relationships with the outside world. This view is supported by the fact that ... it is not always possible to distinguish clearly which of an individual's activities form part of his professional or business life and which do not.[100]

The CJEU has not developed an autonomous definition of private life, but relies instead on the case law of the ECtHR,[101] which has found the concept to cover 'the physical and psychological integrity of a person ... aspects of an individual's physical and social identity ... gender identification, name and sexual orientation and sexual life ... personal development ... relationships with other human beings and the outside world ... personal autonomy.'[102]

Such a broad conceptualisation, which is taken to be more encompassing than 'privacy',[103] is coupled with the settled view that it is not 'possible [n]or necessary to attempt an exhaustive definition of the notion'. Such a stance, which has made of Article 8 ECHR 'one of the most frequently contested rights in case law pursuant to the Convention',[104] has left open the possibility to extend the scope of the application of the right vis-à-vis societal changes under the 'living instrument' doctrine. As there are no circumstances falling a priori within the scope of the four limbs of the right,[105] the ECtHR has adopted an evolutive interpretation of privacy in line with present-day conditions including social, technological and cultural developments.[106]

As I discuss elsewhere, the evolutive approach to privacy is instrumental to the development of identity and personality, whose full expression evolves with time(s).[107] Respecting one's identity and personality is a way of acknowledging one's dignity and ability of autonomous action. For Chalmers and Trotter, the Charter embodies three notions of autonomy: individual control, relational autonomy and individual flourishing.[108] Such notions overlap to an extent with the three clusters chosen here that synthesise the meaning of 'private life' in Article 7 CFR: physical and psychological

---

[99] Citing the ECtHR cases of *Amann v Switzerland* and *Rotaru v Romania*, *Schecke and Eifert*, C-92/09 and C-93/09, para 59.

[100] *Niemietz v Germany*, no. 13710/88, para 29.

[101] The notions of private life, family life and home are autonomous concepts, whose 'protection does not depend on their classification under domestic law, but on the factual circumstances of the case', *Chiragov and Others v Armenia* no. 13216/05 CE:ECHR:2015:0616JUD001321605, para 206.

[102] *Pretty v the United Kingdom* no. 2346/02 CE:ECHR:2002:0429JUD00234602, para 61.

[103] The ECHR toolkit points to 'privacy' being mainly about rights to confidentiality and seclusion and thus narrower: www.coe.int/en/web/echr-toolkit/le-droit-au-respect-de-la-vie-privee-et-familiale.

[104] LA Bygrave, *Data Privacy Law. An International Perspective* (Oxford, Oxford University Press, 2014) 6.

[105] Zeno-Zencovich (n 35). Similarly, Art 17 ICCPR embraces wide definitions of the limbs, though not as comprehensive as those subsumed under Art 8 ECHR: HRC (n 78); Nowak (n 79); Blair (n 70).

[106] In the context of family life: *X and Y v the Netherlands*, no. 8978/80, para 139.

[107] MG Porcedda, 'The Recrudescence of 'Security v. Privacy' after the 2015 Terrorist Attacks, and the Value of 'Privacy Rights' in the European Union', in E Orrù et al. (eds), *Rethinking Surveillance and Control Beyond the "Security versus Privacy" Debate* (Baden-Baden, Nomos, 2017). For identity in Art 17 ICCPR, see a discussion of *A.R. Coeriel et al. v the Netherlands* by Blair (n 70) and *Monaco v Argentina* by Nowak (n 79).

[108] D Chalmers and S Trotter, 'Fundamental Rights and Legal Wrongs: the Two Sides of the Same EU Coin' (2016) 22 *European Law Journal* 9, cited in D Chalmers, G Davies and G Monti, *European Union Law*, 4th edn (Cambridge, Cambridge University Press, 2019) 267–271.

integrity (excluding in the context of medicine and biology); personal social and sexual identity; and personal development, autonomy and participation, discussed next.

i. Physical and Psychological Integrity

At a minimum, the right to private life 'covers the physical and psychological integrity of the person', as the ECtHR stated in *Pretty v UK*;[109] the ECJ referred to 'privacy or the integrity of the individual' in passing in *Bavarian Lager*.[110] Physical and psychological integrity – excluding medicine and biology – result from the combination of the *forum internum* of the mind and the *forum internum* and *externum* of the body.

The mind's *forum internum* concerns unspoken thoughts, feelings and emotions, as discussed by scholarship, from Warren and Brandeis' 1890 article to our days.[111] Once considered the most inaccessible part of the individual, advances in neuroscience and brain imaging could soon be challenging this assumption,[112] as shown by the emergence of neuroprivacy as a sub-discipline.[113] The CJEU's emphasis on how undisclosed retention and use of telecommunications data is 'likely to generate in the minds of the persons concerned the feeling that their private lives are the subject of constant surveillance'[114] highlights the effects of surveillance on the mind's *forum internum*. The backdrop to this warning is the memory of Europe's dictatorial experiences; advances in psychology and scanning technology showing how fear affects the brain[115] will soon offer tools to observe the effects of old, new and fused[116] forms of surveillance on the brain.

The body's *forum internum* concerns genetic characteristics and unique physical traits, or biometric features, that cannot be forgone or altered by the individual.[117] In *S and Marper v UK*, the ECtHR stressed the need to protect DNA samples and profiles on account of their ability to reveal relationships between individuals and their unpredictable future uses.[118] Although fingerprints are not as revealing as cellular samples and DNA profiles, the Court found fingerprints to 'objectively contain unique information

---

[109] *Pretty v the United Kingdom*, no. 2346/02, para 61.

[110] *Bavarian Lager Ltd*, C-28/08 P, EU:C:2010:378, para 58.

[111] Eg, RL Finn and D Wright et al., 'Seven Types of Privacy', in S Gutwirth (ed), *European Data Protection: Coming of Age* (Dordrecht, Springer, 2013). See ch 1, section I.A.

[112] Although the 'technology to … reconstruct something like a stream of consciousness is not yet here', 'techniques … are being refined at pace' S Rainey and S Martin et al., 'Brain Recording, Mind-Reading, and Neurotechnology: Ethical Issues from Consumer Devices to Brain-Based Speech Decoding' (2020) 26 *Science and Engineering Ethics* 2295–2311.

[113] D Hallinan and P Schütz et al., 'Neurodata and Neuroprivacy: Data Protection Outdated?' (2014) 12 *Surveillance & Society* 55–72.

[114] *Digital Rights Ireland*, C-293/12 and C-594/12, para 37.

[115] On the use of MRIs to study trauma and fear, see B Van der Kolk, *The Body Keeps the Score. Mind, Brain and Body in the Transformation of Trauma* (London, Penguin Books, 2014). R Poldrack, 'Neuroscience: The Risks of Reading the Brain' (2017) 541 *Nature*. There, he reviews BJ Sahakian and J Gottwald, *Sex, Lies, and Brain Scans: How fMRI Reveals What Really Goes on in our Minds* (Oxford, Oxford University Press, 2017).

[116] On fusion technology, AH Michel, *There Are Spying Eyes Everywhere – and Now They Share a Brain* (*Wired.com* 2021) www.wired.com/story/there-are-spying-eyes-everywhere-and-now-they-share-a-brain/.

[117] On genetic privacy, see generally D Hallinan, *Protecting Genetic Privacy in Biobanking through Data Protection Law* (Oxford, Oxford University Press, 2021).

[118] *S. and Marper v the United Kingdom* nos. 30562/04 and 30566/04 CE:ECHR:2008:1204JUD003056204, paras 39, 71.

about the individual concerned allowing his or her identification with precision in a wide range of circumstances and (...) thus capable of affecting his or her private life'.[119] *Marper* was later cited by the CJEU in *Schwarz*, but only in passing, as the Court held that '... taking two fingerprints is not an operation of an intimate nature ... nor does it cause any particular physical or mental discomfort' and 'the combination of two operations designed to identify persons may not *a priori* be regarded as giving rise in itself to a *greater* threat to the right(s)'[120] to private life. Neither there, nor in the subsequent case of *Willems*,[121] did the Court elaborate on how the exposure of bodily parts affects physical integrity.

The body's *forum externum* concerns 'the right to own one's body, which also comprises a right to act in a manner injurious to one's health, including committing suicide'.[122] It also means control of and resistance to undesired or forced access to one's body, as is the case of intrusive body searches,[123] body scanning, corporal sanctions[124] and sexual violence including rape,[125] among the 'gravest acts'[126] where 'fundamental values and essential aspects of private life are at stake'.[127]

The internal and external *fora* of the mind and body are challenged by legislation such as instruments authorising the creation of biometric databases.[128] The *fora* are safeguarded, by proxy, through data protection-related rules on profiling, genetic data and biometric data.[129]

ii. Personal Social and Sexual Identity

The notion of identity is composite and relates to the way in which individuals portray themselves, and are portrayed, to the external world. The need to display a unified and dignified identity and personality, so crucial in life in society,[130] corresponds to the

---

[119] ibid, paras 78 and 84.
[120] *Schwarz*, C-291/12, paras 48–49.
[121] *Willems*, C-446/12 to C-449/12, EU:C:2015:238.
[122] Nowak (n 79) 389. However, such autonomy can be contrary to the common good and has paved the way to decisions such as that imposing the wearing of safety belts, no 208/1986, CCPR/C/37/D/208/1986.
[123] Personal body searches must respect the dignity of the searched, and be performed by a person of the same sex, Human Rights Committee (CCPR), (1988). Strip-searching was deemed arbitrary in the presence of alternative, less intrusive methods (United Nations, Human Rights Committee, *Comments of the Human Rights Committee: United Kingdom of Great Britain and Northern Ireland* (CCPR/C/79/Add 55, 1979). Blair (n 70).
[124] Discussing ECtHR *Costello-Roberts v United Kingdom*, Zeno-Zencovich (n 35).
[125] Eg, abuse of a mentally ill woman in *X and Y v the Netherlands*, no. 8978/80.; abuse of a minor girl in *M. C. v Bulgaria* no. 39272/98 CE:ECHR:2003:1204JUD003927298.
[126] *Lopez Ribalda v Spain*, nos. 1874/13 and 8567/1, para 113.
[127] *M. C. v Bulgaria*, no. 39272/98, para 150.
[128] Such as the Prüm regime. V Toom, *Cross-Border Exchange and Comparison of Forensic DNA Data in the Context of the Prüm Decision. Study for the European Parliament's Committe on Civil Liberties, Justice and Home Affairs* (2018). See also European Council, Council of the European Union Working Party on Information Exchange and Data Protection (DAPIX), 'Preview Towards the Next Generation Prüm on DNA Data Exchange in the EU' 13511/19 (2020).
[129] Defined in Arts 4 (4), (13) and (14) of Reg (EU) 2016/679 [2016] OJ L119/1 (GDPR), read in light of Recital 75. See ch 4.
[130] See ch 1, section I.A and Porcedda (n 107).

forum externum of the mind. In keeping with a broad approach to private life, courts do not define the meaning of identity.

In *A, B, and C* the CJEU makes a small, yet significant reference to the unique nature of identities and their need for legal protection. While acknowledging the usefulness of standardised tools of assessment, the ECJ stated that relying solely on stereotyped notions of homosexuality is not sufficient to grant the status of refugee, since it is necessary to 'take account of the individual situation and personal circumstances of the applicant',[131] and decided in fact that reliance on stereotyped notions is precluded by EU law. Another useful indication of the relevance of identity comes from the ECtHR, whereby

> private life requires that everyone should be able to establish details of their identity as individual human beings and that an individual's entitlement to such information is of importance because of its formative implications for his or her personality.[132]

Cases on identity/personality typically concern several issues,[133] three of which have been tackled by the Luxembourg Court, namely one's name as the first identifier, one's reputation and one's sexual orientation. I discuss each in turn.

First, on names, the CJEU stated that a person's name,[134] forename and surname[135] are 'a constituent element' of one's identity and private life, 'the protection of which is enshrined in Article 7 [CFR] … and in Article 8 [ECHR]. Even though Article 8 [ECHR] does not refer to it explicitly, a person's name, as a means of personal identification and a link to a family, none the less concerns his or her private and family life'.[136] Hence, individuals have a right 'to protection of … identity and private life' and '… the way in which [States decide to structure the name requirements in an official document] must observe that individual's right to protection of his private life'. For the Court, it is apparent that

> where the name of a person appears incorrectly or ambiguously in documents issued by a State in order to prove his identity, this is liable to cause serious inconvenience for that person … in so far as it may give rise to doubts as to his real identity, the authenticity of the passport or the veracity of the information contained in it.[137]

Such inconvenience is liable to cause reputational damage. The ECtHR recognises the particularly sensitive nature of the name in the case of transsexual and transgender individuals.[138] Likewise, Article 17 ICCPR protects one's choice of a surname.[139]

Second, the social reflection of one's identity is fundamental for life in a community, and its deterioration can have dire effects on participation in society and one's wellbeing. Although honour and reputation do not fall within the scope of Articles 8 ECHR

---

[131] *A, B, and C*, C-148/13 to C-150/13, para 62.
[132] *Mikulić v Croatia* no. 53176/99 CE:ECHR:2002:0207JUD005317699, para 54.
[133] See generally Jurisconsult (n 36) 54–63.
[134] *Ilonka Sayn-Wittgenstein v Landeshauptmann von Wien*, C-208/09, EU:C:2010:806, para 52.
[135] *Runevič-Vardyn and Wardyn*, C-391/09, EU:C:2011:291, para 66.
[136] *Sayn-Wittgenstein*, C-208/09, para 52.
[137] *U*, C-101/13, EU:C:2014:2249, paras 48–50.
[138] Discussing *Res v United Kingdom, Cossey v United Kingdom* and *B. v France*, Zeno-Zencovich (n 35).
[139] In *A. R. Coeriel et al v The Netherlands* (543/91), discussed in Blair (n 70).

and 7 CFR, social identity is a matter of reputation, one often surfacing in relation to private life. In cases relating to names such as *Sayn-Wittgenstein* and *Runevič*, the Court said that the lack of recognition of one's name may entail 'having to dispel suspicion of false declaration caused by the divergence'[140] between different versions of the same name. In *Schecke and Eifert*, the publication of data on a website naming applicants as recipients of public funds and reporting the precise amount received affected their private lives[141] because it impacted on their social identity, since anyone can access that information and draw conclusions on the matter. Similarly, in *Google Spain*, the wide availability on the Web of information on the applicant's past insolvency was likely to stain his social identity, and hence affected his private life.[142] The importance of 'being forgotten' or 'de-referenced' for one's reputation is testified by the lively case law on the matter.[143]

A stain to social identity can be intolerable in the case of restrictive measures in the context of terrorism, due to 'the opprobrium and suspicion that accompany the public designation of the persons covered as being associated with a terrorist organisation'.[144] In this case, public recognition of the illegality of the association with terrorism was fundamental for rehabilitating Mr Ayadi 'or constituting a form of reparation for the non-material harm which he has suffered by reason of that illegality'.[145] Along similar lines, the HRC deemed that the dissemination of the UN Security Council's terrorist list containing full contact details about the applicants constituted an attack on their honour and reputation,[146] in view of the negative association that some persons could make between the applicants' names and the title of the sanctions list.[147]

Third, sexual orientation has been the object of evolving case law in recent decades. As AG Sharpston noted, within the EU 'homosexuality is no longer considered to be a medical or psychological condition'.[148] For the ECJ, 'it is common ground that a person's sexual orientation is a characteristic *so fundamental* to his identity that he should not be forced to renounce it'[149] or to conceal it, whether alone or in a group.[150] Respect for sexual orientation means being free from the threat of imprisonment for one's homosexuality,[151] not being submitted to detailed questioning as to sexual practices, due to their sensitive nature and importance to identity,[152] and forbidding the use of a psychologist's expert report to assess said orientation.[153] In the case law, the absence of

---

[140] Judgment in *Sayn-Wittgenstein*, C-208/09, para 68. See also *Runevič-Vardyn*, C-391/09, para 78. The Court upheld the choice of Austria to remove the noble appellative from Ms Sayn-Wittgenstein's surname on grounds of public policy, namely equality and non-discrimination as understood in Austria.
[141] *Schecke and Eifert*, C-92/09 and C-93/09, para 58.
[142] *Google Spain and Google*, C-131/12, EU:C:2014:317, para 98.
[143] Eg, *Google (Territorial scope of de-referencing)*, C-507/17, EU:C:2019:772.
[144] *P Ayadi v Commission*, C-183/12, EU:C:2013:369, para 68.
[145] ibid, para 70.
[146] *Sayadi and Vinck v Belgium*, no. 1472/2006, CCPR/C/94/D/1472/2006.
[147] One's social identity can also be affected by constantly being referred to as insane when medical reports prove the opposite, HRC, *Birhashwirwa et al. v Zaire* no. 242/87, discussed in Blair (n 70).
[148] Opinion of AG Sharpston, C-148/13 to C-150/13, para 60.
[149] Emphasis added, *X and Others*, C-199/12 to C-201/12, EU:C:2013:720, para 46.
[150] ibid, para 70.
[151] ibid, para 57.
[152] *A, B, and C*, C-148/13 to C-150/13.
[153] *F*, C-473/16, EU:2018:36, para 62.

a law criminalising homosexuality in extra-EU countries has not been deemed to be a necessary condition for the enjoyment of one's sexual identity; conversely, the ECtHR has stated that the mere existence of a norm criminalising certain sexual behaviour, even if not enforced, constitutes an interference with private life,[154] as did the HRC.[155]

To the extent that the protection of personal data is instrumental to privacy, Articles 9–10 on sensitive data and 17 GDPR on a right to erasure help to ensure the protection of one's reputation. The protection of one's reputation and sexual identity can also be ensured by protecting e-communications enshrined in the EPD, as I discuss below.

iii. Personal Development, Autonomy and Participation ('The Outer Circle')

This sub-attribute of 'private life' clusters together personal development, autonomy and participation, facets that are often presented together and not easily distinguished in case law. For instance, according to the ECtHR, 'although no previous case has established as such any right to self-determination as being contained in Article 8 [ECHR], the Court considers that the notion of personal autonomy is an important principle underlying the interpretation of its guarantees' including 'a right to personal development'.[156] The reason why the facets are often joined is that this sub-attribute of private life stems from and integrates the two just analysed.

The respect of one's uniqueness and identity is a precondition to free personal development, autonomy and participation in a democratic society.[157] Vice versa, the enjoyment of this attribute requires the absence of regimentation, constriction or monitoring by other parties, eg, the state and its agents. The protection of diversity and autonomous participation effected by placing checks on state surveillance stems from the crushing experience of dictatorial regimes, experience which is alluded to in the case law of the CJEU and openly discussed in that of the ECtHR.

As for the CJEU, since *Digital Rights Ireland*, the Court has stated that the information collected through the now invalidated Data Retention Directive,

> taken as a whole, may allow very precise conclusions to be drawn concerning the private lives of the persons whose data has been retained, such as the habits of everyday life, permanent or temporary places of residence, daily or other movements, the activities carried out, the social relationships of those persons and the social environments frequented by them.[158]

This, and the fact that individuals have no control over the way such information is and can be subsequently used can engender 'the feeling that their private lives are the subject of constant surveillance'.[159] The ECJ does not draw conclusions from the acknowledgment of the impact of surveillance on people's feelings (the mind's *forum internum*), but

---

[154] *Dudgeon v United Kingdom*, *Norris v Ireland* and *Modinos v Cyprus* discussed in Blair (n 70).
[155] In *Toonen v Australia* 488/92, Art 17 ICCPR also protects adults' consensual sexual activity in private (Concluding Comments on United Republic of Tanzania 1999 UN doc. CCPR/C/79/Add. 97), in ibid.
[156] *Pretty v the United Kingdom*, no. 2346/02, para 61.
[157] See ch 1 and Porcedda (107).
[158] *Digital Rights Ireland*, C-293/12 and C-594/12, para 27. Copied in *La Quadrature du Net and Others*, C-511/18, para 117.
[159] *Digital Rights Ireland*, C-293/12 and C-594/12, para 37. Copied in *Privacy International*, C-623/17, para 71.

refers widely to the ECtHR case law on interception and measures of secret surveillance that began with *Klass v Germany*.

In *Klass v Germany*, the ECtHR stated that the existence of secret surveillance unknown to the public, and hence unchallengeable, could reduce Article 8 'to a nullity'.[160] Moreover, measures of secret surveillance 'characterise the police state', a threat that could become true for ECHR contracting states 'on the ground of defending democracy'.[161] In *Malone v UK*, Judge Pettiti posited that 'the mission of the [CoE] and of its organs is to prevent the establishment of systems and methods that would allow "Big Brother" to become master of the citizen's private life'.[162] In *Big Brother and Others v UK*,[163] Judge Pinto de Albuquerque warns that 'society built upon [treating everyone as a suspect] is more akin to a police state than to a democratic society. This would be the opposite of what the founding fathers wanted for Europe when they signed the Convention in 1950.'[164]

Such case law, taken together, points to how the feeling of being surveilled can interfere with people's mastery of their own lives and the flourishing of democracy, thereby linking psychological integrity, personal development and identity, autonomy and participation. Psychological research into the impact of fear on behaviour,[165] including when generated by surveillance, helps explaining how interference with personal development can crush autonomy and participation. Hence, the attribute under analysis is instrumental to the nexus between democracy and private life. Enjoying private life in a democratic society is substantiated in the freedom to be autonomous and to participate without the constant control of the state[166] and, it should be added, Cohen's 'informational' or Zuboff's 'surveillance'[167] capitalism.

Participation is not only limited to individual, atomised interventions. The ECtHR has found Article 8 to entail, to a certain degree, 'the right to establish and develop relationships with other human beings' as 'it would be too restrictive to limit the notion to an "inner circle" in which the individual may live his own personal life as he chooses and to exclude therefrom entirely the outside world not encompassed within that circle'.[168] In this guise, the development of social relations represents the 'outer circle', and is a precondition for participation in social life. Such a 'zone of interaction of a person with others' attracts the protection of Article 8 ECHR 'even in a public context';[169] 'the right

---

[160] *Klass and others v Germany*, no 5029/71, para 36.
[161] ibid, paras 42, 49.
[162] *Malone v the United Kingdom* no. 8691/79 CE:ECHR:1985:0426JUD000869179, concurring opinion of Judge Pettiti.
[163] *Big Brother Watch v UK* – no 58170/13. In allowing automated data gathering and analysis, the case represents a step back from previous cases and is reminiscent of *Klass v Germany*. See ch 7.
[164] *Big Brother and Watch v UK*, no. 58170/13, partly Concurring, partly dissenting Opinion of Judge Pinto de Albuquerque, para 22, 181.
[165] S Peters, *The Chimp Paradox. The mind management programme for confidence, success and happiness* (Vermilion 2012).
[166] The object of the Article is 'essentially' that of protecting the individual against arbitrary interference by public authorities, *Marckx v Belgium*, no. 6833/74, para 31.
[167] Building on Castell's theories, see JE Cohen, *Between Truth and Power* (Oxford, Oxford University Press, 2019); S Zuboff, *The Age of Surveillance Capitalism* (London, Profile Books, 2019).
[168] *Niemietz v Germany*, no. 13710/88, para 29.
[169] *Peck v the United Kingdom*, no. 44647/98, para 57. For video surveillance guidelines, see *Lopez Ribalda v Spain*, nos. 1874/13 and 8567/1.

to lead a 'private social life' can extend to 'activities taking place in a public context' so that 'a zone of interaction of a person with others, even in a public context ... may fall within the scope of "private life".[170] This extends to communications.

In the applicable law, personal development, autonomy and participation are ensured by both limiting interferences and enhancing opportunities for expression. Thus, limitations on the repurposing of information collected in the course of communications[171] enable the creation of a space for individuals to participate in the information society in as an unmonitored manner as possible. At the same time, provisions on informed consent[172] are meant to enable the expression of autonomy[173] or 'data subject's wishes'.[174] The extent to which this is the case is open to debate, as varieties of wrap contracts 'tricking' users into giving consent without having been properly informed, such as pre-ticked boxes, are capable of providing a false sense of autonomy while emptying consent of its meaning.[175] The extent to which fights over the exact definition and interpretation of consent, eg, in *Planet49*,[176] are capable of restoring autonomy is also open to debate. Reforms of the EPD contained in the e-Privacy Regulation (EPR) could be read as both an expression of autonomy in that a 'direct choice' supersedes the browser settings adjusted by a user, but also as an attempt to negate the choice expressed through browser settings by creating choice fatigue.[177] Insofar as the protection of personal data benefits privacy, the extra safeguards afforded to special categories of personal data, such a political party affiliation or trade union membership,[178] help to ensure personal development, autonomy and participation.

D. Family Life (The 'Inner Circle')

In family life cases, such as *McB*, the ECJ stated that 'it is clear that Article 7 [CFR] contains rights corresponding to those guaranteed by Article 8(1) [ECHR] ... [and] must therefore be given the same meaning and the same scope as Article 8(1) of the ECHR, as interpreted by the case-law of the'[179] ECtHR. In such case law, family life, a term with autonomous meaning,[180] represents the 'inner circle' of the individual, a group which predates the existence of the state and is to be respected and protected

---

[170] ibid, para 88.
[171] EPD, Arts 5, 6, 9 for service providers and EPD, Art 15 for the state.
[172] EPD, Arts 2, 5–6, 9–10 and 13.
[173] Eg, Chalmers and Trotter (n 108) in Chalmers et al. (n 10) 267.
[174] *Planet 49*, C-673/17 EU:C:2019:801, para 58.
[175] On wrap contracts and consent: NS Kim, 'Online Contracting: Causes and Cures' in J Rothchild (ed), *Research Handbook on Electronic Commerce Law* (Cheltenham, Edward Elgar Publishing, 2016); E Kosta, 'Peeking into the Cookie Jar: The European Approach towards the Regulation of Cookies' (2013) 21 *International Journal of Law and Information Technology* 380–406.
[176] *Planet 49* (n 174).
[177] Draft Art 4a, read with Rec 20a EPR, which reads 'consent may be expressed by using ... appropriate technical settings of a software application enabling access to the internet ... Consent directly expressed by an end-user in [such a manner] shall prevail over software settings. Any consent requested and given by an end-user to a service shall be directly implemented ... by the applications of the end user's terminal.'
[178] Art 9 GDPR.
[179] Emphasis added. *McB*, C-400/10 PPU, para 53.
[180] See *Chiragov v Armenia*, para 206, fn 101 above.

regardless of 'the circumstances in, and time at which, family is constituted'.[181] Similarly to cases concerning sexual orientation, ECtHR judgments on family evolved in line with 'developments in society and changes in the perception of social, civil-status and relational issues'.[182]

In the EU, protection of the family has been instrumental in eliminating 'obstacles to the exercise of the fundamental freedoms guaranteed by the Treaty'.[183] The CJEU noted the negative impact of certain policies on family life, for instance the freezing of funds[184] and also adjudicated on family issues in the context of cooperation in civil matters. There, it has ruled that the determination of what constitutes 'family environment' can be linked with the concept of habitual residence.[185] The ECJ has also ruled on the family rights of the natural mother and father, stating that there can be a difference between their entitlements. In *McB*, the Court expressed itself on the essence of family life. In particular, the fact that, 'unlike the mother,[186] the natural father is not a person who automatically possesses rights of custody in respect of his child ... does not affect the essence of his right to private and family life'.[187] For the Court, the right of the natural father substantiates in being entitled to 'apply to the national court with jurisdiction, before the removal, in order to request that rights of custody in respect of his child be awarded to him, which, in such a context, *constitutes the very essence of the right* of a natural father to a private and family life'.[188]

This framework is enriched by the case law of the ECtHR, for which a family and each of its members have equal value irrespective of the degree of legitimacy binding its members.[189] Such a distinction 'would not be consonant with the word "everyone", and this is confirmed by Article 14 [ECHR] with its prohibition, in the enjoyment of the rights and freedoms enshrined in the Convention, of discrimination grounded on "birth"'.[190] In the case of parent-child relationships, family life results more from the element of continuous care,[191] and it is the duty of the state to 'allow those concerned to lead a normal family life',[192] particularly to enable 'as from the moment of birth the child's integration in his family'.[193] Cohabitation is not a determining factor in assessing the existence of family life, as stated in cases of expulsions and immigration;[194] matters

---

[181] *Chakroun*, C-578/08, para 63.
[182] *X and Others v Austria* no. 19010/07 CE:ECHR:2013:0219JUD001901007, para 139. The ICCPR is unlikely to supply guidelines, as family life does not protect the consequences of cohabiting outside of marriage (*Hoofdman v the Netherlands* 602/94), nor the prohibition of gay marriage (*Joslin et al. v New Zealand* 902/99) Zeno-Zencovich (n 35).
[183] *Runevič-Vardyn*, C-391/09, para 90.
[184] *Ayadi*, C-183/12 P, para 68.
[185] *PPU Mercredi*, C-497/10, EU:C:2010:829, para 56.
[186] Art 17 ICCPR protects the right of a parent to visit his or her minor children (*HRC Fei v Colombia* 514/92 and *L.P. Czech Republic* 946/00), Blair (n 70).
[187] *McB*, C-400/10 PPU, para 57.
[188] ibid, para 55. Emphasis added.
[189] The Court either considered the factual situation (*Abdulaziz et al. v United Kingdom*, no. 9214/80 9473/81 9474/81) or the prospective chance of founding a family (ECtHR, *Boughanemi v France*, no. 22070/93), in Nowak (n 79).
[190] *Marckx v Belgium*, no. 6833/74, para 31.
[191] ibid.
[192] ibid.
[193] ibid.
[194] *C. v Belgium* no. 21794/93 CE:ECHR:1996:0807JUD002179493, para 25. See also *Berrehab v The Netherlands* no. 10730/84 CE:ECHR:1988:0621JUD001073084, para 21. Forcing a 13-year-old to choose

of transfers of custody, especially outside the family of origin, have to be carefully assessed.[195] Family life also requires the continuity of one's living environment, as in *Moustaquim v Belgium*,[196] on the deportation of a young man who had lived in Belgium since the age of two.

Instruments addressing family rights are beyond the scope of this research, although the exploration of 'group privacy' grounded in family rights arguments,[197] as well as the possible regulation of home or personal assistants by the EPR[198] could ensure the protection of private life and generate relevant case law on the matter.

E. Home

Thus far, the CJEU has not delivered an interpretation of the right to a home in EU law in the context of Article 7 CFR,[199] as opposed to the case law of the ECHR, where 'home' has an autonomous meaning.[200] The protection currently afforded to the home is in keeping with the adage that one's home is one's castle, in the light of the social role played by the home. In a case concerning eviction, *Stolyarova v Russia*, the ECtHR reaffirmed that

> the margin of appreciation in housing matters is narrower when it comes to the rights guaranteed by Article 8 ..., because Article 8 concerns rights of central importance to the individual's identity, self-determination, physical and moral integrity, maintenance of relationships with others and a settled and secure place in the community.[201]

What is being protected is a broad notion of one's private space 'covering residential premises' and extending 'also to certain professional or business premises [which] includes not only the registered office of a company owned and run by a private individual ... but also that of a legal person and its branches and other business premises ...'.[202] The protection of the workplace was first established in *Niemietz v Germany* through a broad interpretation of the word 'home'.[203]

If someone lost his or her house, the notion of home could protect a tent (but not a car).[204] The right to a home, however, does neither embody a right to a house or

---

whether to stay in one country alone or to follow the parents when they have been expelled amounts to arbitrary interference (HRC, *Bakhtiyari et al. v Australia* 1069/02), see especially Zeno-Zencovich (n 35).

[195] *Olsson v Sweden* no. 13441/87 CE:ECHR:1992:1127JUD001344187; *Eriksson v Sweden* no. 11373/85 CE:ECHR:1989:0622JUD001137385.

[196] *Moustaquim v Belgium* no. 12313/86 CE:ECHR:1991:0218JUD001231386, paras 45–46.

[197] L Taylor and L Floridi et al. (eds), *Group Privacy: New Challenges of Data Technologies* (Cham, Springer, 2017).,

[198] EPR Draft Recs 13a and 16.

[199] The Court referred to the risk for 'the consumer, and possibly his family ... of losing his dwelling in a forced sale' and to 'the right to respect for the home, guaranteed under Article 7' CFR without further comments about the relationship between the two. *Sánchez Morcillo and Abril García*, C-539/14, EU:C:2015:508 (Order), paras 41, 46.

[200] *Chiragov v Armenia*, para 206, nns 101, 138 above; contextually also Nowak (n 79); Zeno-Zencovich (n 35).

[201] *Stolyarova v Russia* no. 15711/13 CE:ECHR:2015:0129JUD001571113, para 59.

[202] *Bernh Larsen Holding As and Others v Norway* no. 24117/08 CE:ECHR:2013:0314JUD002411708, para 104.

[203] Premised on the French 'domicile', *Niemietz v Germany*, no. 13710/88, para 30.

[204] Nowak (n 79); Rehof (n 15).

property, nor to certain lifestyles.[205] Rather, respect for the home protects dwellers from unlawful, discriminatory or harassing searches and arrests.[206] The violation of the home is often coupled with that of communications.

European courts and legislators have not likened users' computer equipment to 'home', thereby not succumbing to the seduction of space-based analogies in cyberspace.[207] However, in a comparative study of police hacking in Italy, Germany and the Netherlands cleverly entitled 'my home is my castle', Škorvánek et al. found that the protection of the home is being extended to computers as a container, almost an extension of private life.[208] Such an approach could influence European courts in the future. Moreover, if confirmed references to home or personal assistants in the draft EPR[209] could help ensuring the protection of this limb of the right.

F. (Confidential) Communications

This limb entitles individuals to choose with whom and how to share information under the understanding that information shared privately will remain confidential, whichever the means of communication chosen. The reasons for keeping information confidential in a democratic society are akin to those that justify the shielding of private life from surveillance. The monitoring of communications, through interception and retention, can engender a police state that undermines the aim and objectives of human rights and democracy.

In *WebMindLicenses*[210] concerning the interception of communications, the ECJ acknowledged the potential for abuse and arbitrariness of such interceptions,[211] quoting relevant ECtHR judgments. Disputes concerning data retention legislation provided the opportunity to interpret the confidentiality requirements enshrined in the EPD, which the CJEU did in light of Article 7 CFR. The Court found that the EPD gives 'concrete expression to the rights enshrined in Articles 7'[212] and entitles users of ECSs to the anonymity, in principle, of their communications and related metadata, unless they have either agreed otherwise or the derogations exhaustively listed in Article 15(1) EPD apply.[213] Metadata stands for traffic and location data produced through the use of ECSs.[214]

---

[205] See *Velosa Barreto v Portugal, Akdivar v Turkey, Buckley v United Kingdom*, respectively, in LA Rehof, 'The Universal Declaration of Human Rights: A Commentary' in A Eide (ed), (Scandinavian University Press, 1992).
[206] See HRC *Aumeeruddy Cziffra et al. v Mauritius* 35/78, *Coronel et al. v Colombia* 778/97, and *García v Colombia* 687/1996, in Zeno-Zencovich (n 35).
[207] D Hunter, 'Cyberspace as Place and the Tragedy of the Digital Anticommons' (2003) 91 *California Law Review*. See generally M Aiken, *The Cyber Effect* (London, John Murray, 2016).
[208] Škorvánek et al (n 98) 1070–72.
[209] Eg, draft recs 13a and 16.
[210] *WebMindLicenses*, C-419/14, EC:C:2015:832, para 71.
[211] ibid, paras 77–78.
[212] Together with Art 8, *Privacy International*, C-623/17, para 57.
[213] ibid, paras 57–58.
[214] Art 2 EPD.

92 Privacy: The Right to Respect for Private and Family Life

It is in its data retention cases that the ECJ identified the essence in 'the content of the electronic communications as such',[215] whose respect requires the absence of 'legislation permitting the public authorities to have access on a generalised basis'[216] to such content. However, the Court has subsequently emphasised that metadata is 'no less sensitive than the actual content of communications', on account of the 'sensitive nature of the information which that data may provide and the possibility of establishing a profile of the persons concerned on the basis of that data' as well as its likelihood 'to generate a feeling ... of constant surveillance'.[217] For this reason, the transfer of such data to security and intelligence agencies constitutes a particularly serious interference with Article 7 CFR. I will come back to this in chapters six and seven.

The Court's identification of the essence is problematic. First, 'access to the contents of e-communications as such' is the objective of interception, which can be a permissible derogation from the principle of confidentiality. Second, the finding whereby metadata are as sensitive as content data contributes to weakening the essence. This may reflect the reality that, in the Internet's layered architecture, Transmission Control Protocol (TCP) packets can be seen as both contents and metadata,[218] which highlights the imprecision of notions such as 'contents' and 'metadata' vis-à-vis the layered architecture of 'e-communications'. Such contradictions are reflected in the wording of draft EPR Articles stating that the essence of the right to private life can be limited.[219]

In the vaster case law of the ECtHR, protecting correspondence means first of all enabling such correspondence to take place[220] and ensuring confidentiality no matter the means of communications: letters, phone calls,[221] telephone numbers, computers and emails,[222] use of the internet,[223] voice recording[224] and CCTV,[225] whether at home, in the context of business activities, or in a state of deprivation of liberty.[226] In assessing the degree to which confidentiality of communications applies, the ECtHR has made use of the concept of 'a person's reasonable expectations as to privacy [as a] significant, yet not conclusive, factor'.[227]

The Strasbourg Court attaches lower protection to communications when individuals have willingly or knowingly made activities and information public, unless such

---

[215] *Digital Rights Ireland*, C-293/12 and C-594/12, para 39.
[216] *Schrems*, C-362/14, EU:C:2015:650, para 94.
[217] *Privacy International*, C-623/17, para 71.
[218] '[T]raffic data is constituted by IP layer header information (network layer) and transport layer (TCP/UDP) header; domain names and URLs cannot be considered "traffic data"'. Transport layer payload is content; European Data Protection Board, Letter to BEREC. Data protection Issues in the Context of Regulation (EU) 2015/2120, OUT2019-0055, 3 December, (2019), 2, 6. See ch 6.
[219] EPR Draft Recital 16a, see ch 7.
[220] *Golder v the United Kingdom* no. 4451/70 CE:ECHR:1975:0221JUD000445170, para 43.
[221] See *Halford v the United Kingdom* no. 20605/92 CE:ECHR:1997:0625JUD002060592, para 44.
[222] *Copland v the United Kingdom* no. 62617/00 CE:ECHR:2007:0403JUD006261700, para 43.
[223] *K.U. v Finland* no. 2872/02 CE:ECHR:2008:1202JUD000287202, para 49.
[224] *P.G. and J.H. v the United Kingdom*, no. 44787/98, paras 59–60.
[225] *Peck v the United Kingdom*, no. 44647/98, paras 57–63.
[226] *Herczegfalvy v Austria* no. 10533/83 CE:ECHR:1992:0924JUD001053383, para 91. When deprived of liberty, confidentiality applies in particular to the relationship with one's lawyer: *Golder v the United Kingdom*, no. 4451/70, para 43. For the HRC, respecting prisoners' communications means applying only non-arbitrary censorship and control (*Pinkney v Canada* 27/77) and permitting to get in touch with families and friends (*Estrella v Uruguay* 74/80). See Blair (n 70); Nowak (n 79).
[227] Eg, *P.G. and J.H. v the United Kingdom*, no. 44787/98, para 57.

information becomes part of a permanent or systematic record,[228] which in the EU is a matter dealt with under data protection law.

The EPD gives concrete expression to the qualified right to confidentiality of communications, alongside the 'right to privacy', for users of e-communications.[229] Thus, 'users' enjoy confidential communications, including protection against access by ISSs to users' computer equipment for retrieving and storing information.[230] The latter limits tracking practices by adtech that are the increasing object of litigation.[231] Confidentiality extends to traffic and location data originally collected by ECSs to provide connectivity and for billing purposes, and users are protected against unsolicited communications for direct marketing.[232]

The EPD allows individuals to willingly consent to practices that undermine the enjoyment of confidentiality – though this may better serve service providers' interests than protect users' autonomy. Significantly, the drafters of the Budapest Convention on Cybercrime stated that the application of cookies can amount to the cybercrime of 'illegal access', which is a violation of the principle of confidentiality, yet the application of cookies is lawful if users do not actively remove or reject them.[233]

Finally, confidentiality is protected by obliging service providers to adopt duty of care measures, ie using technical and organisational measures (TOMs) to safeguard the security of its services, and to adopt remedial measures when such security is compromised through data breaches.[234] Objectives that justify limitations to confidentiality include the prevention, investigation, detection and prosecution of criminal offences such as cybercrimes, and the unauthorised use of the e-communication systems. Elements of cybersecurity are thus weaved into the fabric of the EPD, both as factors that can enhance or limit confidentiality.

The draft EPR incorporates the Court's data retention case law by giving equal status to communications in data and metadata[235] while acknowledging a greater number of circumstances that enable a limitation of confidentiality with respect to such data. The EPR's provisions on security[236] – whether of communications or terminal equipment is unclear – are more extensive and seem to emphasise the limiting role security objectives can have on confidentiality. The EPR incudes far more grounds for limiting the private life and confidentiality of individuals' communications and metadata, including for instance for purposes of managing epidemics.[237]

---

[228] ibid, para 58.
[229] EPD Art 1, Recs 3 (acknowledging the ECHR and constitutional traditions) and 21. ECSs are defined in the European Electronic Communications Code (EECC), see ch 6.
[230] EDP Art 5, Kosta (n 175); L Edwards (ed), *Law, Policy and the Internet* (Oxford, Hart Publishing, 2018) chs 3, 5.
[231] Information Commissioner's Office, 'Update Report into Adtech and Real Time Bidding'; L Mc Gowran, 'DPC sued for 'failure to act' on complaint made against Google' (15 March 2022).
[232] EPR Arts 6, 9 and 13. Protection should also extend to the use of systems 'without human intervention', eg, robo-callers and spam botnets.
[233] Council of Europe, Explanatory Memorandum to the Cybercrime Convention, (2001), § 47. On Confidentiality, see chs 1, 5–7.
[234] EPD Art 4.
[235] EPR Draft Arts 5, 6, 6a and Recs 21–24.
[236] EPR Draft Arts (2e) (Recs 8aa and 13), 6(a), 6(b) and 6(c) (Recs 16 and 16a), 13 (Rec 27).
[237] This may include the use of automated systems. EPR Draft Art 11.

III. Conclusion: Essential Components of Article 7 CFR, Essence

In this chapter I examined the meaning of private life in EU law with a view to identifying elements for an analysis of its interplay with cybersecurity and data protection. The Charter's and ECHR's open-ended provisions enable the Luxembourg and Strasbourg Courts to avoid defining the contents of rights once and for all, thereby accommodating changing social and legal norms in the interpretation of rights.

The Courts' open-endedness benefits an evolutive understanding of rights at the expense of the identification of a clear content of the essence. By means of example, although *X and Others* seems to suggest that one's sexual orientation is a core area of the right to private life, the Court both questions the possibility of identifying core areas of the expression of sexual orientation and stresses the futility of such an exercise. Thus, it is '… unnecessary to distinguish acts that interfere with the core areas of the expression of sexual orientation … from acts which do not affect those purported core areas …'.[238] In the short term, vagueness as to the essence of the right weakens the possibility to understand whether measures, including technologies, are proportionate and impose clear and strict permissible limitations stemming from the application of *leges generales* and *speciales*.

Table 1 summarises the attributes, limbs or essential components of Article 7 CFR. The first column to the left lists attributes/essential components. The next column to the right summarises its content. The last columns lists the essence as identified by the CJEU.

Table 1 Summary of essential components of the right to respect for private and family life

Attribute	Description	Essence (CJEU)
Private life	Private life concerns those elements that are relevant to develop and maintain one's personality and identity, understood as unique and worthy of equal respect.	[the revelation of] very specific information concerning the private life of a person, not limited to certain aspects of that private life.
i. Physical and psychological integrity	Integrity includes: The *forum internum* of the mind, ie one's thoughts, feelings and emotions. The *forum internum* of the body: genetic characteristics and unique physical traits. The *forum externum* of the body: the right to own one's body and protect it from undesired or forced access to it.	

(continued)

---

[238] *X and Others*, C-199/12 to C-201/12, para 78.

Table 1 *(Continued)*

Attribute	Description	Essence (CJEU)
ii. Personal social and sexual identity	It concerns the '*forum externum*' of mental integrity, which substantiates in the coherent portrayal of one's personality and identity to the external world. It includes control over one's name, the upkeep of one's reputation, the expression of one's sexual orientation, but also the manifestation of one's beliefs and personality in the form of attitudes, behaviours and clothing.	(Potentially the expression of one's sexual identity, but the identification of core areas may be impossible in practice).
iii. Personal development, autonomy and participation ('outer circle')	Concerns the partaking of individuals in the democratic society. The development of one's personality in the spirit of self-determination. Autonomy of one's movements and actions. Participation in social and political life as one sees fit. All the above require a minimum degree of control, even if conducted in public. The possibility to develop social relations of an amicable or professional nature. In this sense, this component concerns the 'outer circle' of one's life and links with the 'inner circle' of one's family.	
Family	The 'inner circle', one's kin by blood and election, which represents the first mode of existence in society and comes before the state. It includes horizontal and vertical relationships regardless of their seal of legitimacy, and is substantiated in emotional and material ties with individuals and surroundings.	For a father, the possibility to apply for the right to custody.
Communications	The ability of individuals to choose with whom and how to share information, and the presumption that information shared privately should remain confidential, regardless its content and the mode of communication. This includes the expectation that information shared privately will not be used against the individual.	The content of communications.
Home	One's settled and secure place in the community, where individuals can develop ties of an intimate nature and nurture self-determination, far away from the public gaze and undesired intrusion.	

Based on the Court's interpretation delivered in *État Luxembourgeois v B and Others*,[239] other attributes or essential components could feature an essence. Since it is for the Court to identify core elements, it is only possible to speculate on potential candidates by drawing from a purposive interpretation of the right.[240]

For physical and psychological integrity, one such candidate could be the *forum internum* of the mind and body, representing the seat of one's personality and one's unique traits. With time, the Court may also find it necessary to identify core areas of expression of one's sexual identity. As for personal identity more widely, a core area could be the recognition of one's original or acquired name, so long as it does not conflict with imperative needs of *ordre public*. In cases concerning the social reflection of one's identity, the essence could be defined as the absence of offensive misrepresentations of the person, ie, a faithful representation of one's persona. Personal development, autonomy and participation are crushed by unlawful surveillance and any form of regimentation. In light of case law on secret measures of surveillance, a candidate for the essence could be the absence of secret external constraints and regimentation. The core of family life may be to be able to carry out continuous care for its members without interruption, and to have such care recognised by third parties or society. In light of the social and individual function of the (broadly understood) home, the essence may be identified in a minimum zone of physical intimacy, eg, the bathroom or the bedroom. The essential components and essence will be further elaborated in chapter five, before which, however, I must analyse the right to data protection.

---

[239] C-245/19 and C-246/19, para 66; see ch 1, s 2.1.2.
[240] See ch 1, s 2.1.2 and Porcedda (n 107).

4
The Right to the Protection of Personal Data

Chapters two and three examined cybersecurity and privacy in EU law. Here[1] I examine the right to the protection of personal data (data protection), which is safeguarded as a general principle and as a right enshrined in Article 8 of the Charter of Fundamental Rights of the European Union[2] (Charter or CFR). I begin by introducing and examining the sources of the right. Data protection, similarly to privacy, benefits from interpretive traditions drawn from a variety of instruments identified in the Explanations to the Charter (Explanations) and the European multilevel system of protection of human rights.[3] I focus on EU (I.B) and Council of Europe (CoE) (I.C) sources, including Article 8 of the European Convention on Human Rights (ECHR),[4] in relation to which I address the question of data protection's independence as a right (I.C.i).

After discussing the sources, I examine the right's scope, meaning and limitations (II.A–II.C). The analysis aims not so much at delivering a comprehensive account of data protection in EU law, for which exist several dedicated works,[5] but at conceptualising the architecture of the right instrumental to the analysis of the reconcilability of the triad. Finally (III), I outline the essential components and essence of the right, synthetically shown in Table 1(3), which will inform the techno-legal analysis in chapter five.

I. Sources of Article 8 CFR

The right to data protection has a complex architecture resulting from the four sources of Article 8 CFR identified by the Explanations, sources which will assist in defining the scope, meaning and limitations of the right. Two sources stem from EU law and two

---

[1] Sections II and III develop work that appeared in ss 5 and 6 of MG Porcedda, *On Boundaries. In Search for the Essence of the Right to the Protection of Personal Data* (Oxford, Hart Publishing 2018).
[2] Charter [2012] OJ C326/391 (CFR). It binds institutions, bodies, offices and agencies of the Union and Member States when they 'implement' EU law; see ch 1, section II.A; ch 3, section I.
[3] Explanations [2007] OJ C303/02; on their interpretive value, see ch 3, section I.A, n 10.
[4] Council of Europe [1950] ETS no 005 (ECHR).
[5] See generally: LA Bygrave, *Data Privacy Law. An International Perspective* (Oxford, Oxford University Press, 2014); G González Fuster, *The Emergence of Personal Data Protection as a Fundamental Right in Europe* (Cham, Springer, 2014); O Lynskey, *The Foundations of EU Data Protection Law* (Oxford, Oxford University Press, 2015); M Tzanou, *The Fundamental Right to Data Protection. Normative Value in the Context of Counter-Terrorism Surveillance* (Oxford, Hart, 2017); H Hijmans, *European Union as Guardian of Internet Privacy: the Story of Art 16 TFEU* (Cham, Springer, 2016).

from CoE instruments. EU sources are Articles 16 TFEU and 39 TEU, which replace Article 286 TEC, as well as EU secondary law. CoE sources are Article 8 ECHR and Convention 108.[6] I review each in turn, starting with the foremost sources, which I argue are the EU Treaties and secondary law (I.A); there I contextualise and explain the importance and unusual emphasis assigned to secondary law. I then discuss CoE sources (I.B), where I address the debate concerning the separation between privacy and data protection. I conclude by discussing the sources, of varying legal force in the EU legal system, that supply guidelines for the interpretation of the right.

A. EU Sources

The first sources of the right listed in the Explanations are Articles 16 TFEU[7] and 39 TEU. Such sources perform a dual role, in that they sanction the status and independence of the right to data protection and delegate to secondary law the role of providing additional meaning to the right. As such, EU primary and secondary sources pertaining to Article 8 CFR must be read together.

i. Articles 16 TFEU and 39 TEU

Articles 16 TFEU and 39 TEU frame the protection of one's personal data as a right,[8] rather than as an economic freedom. Article 39 TFEU is formulated by way of derogation of Article 16(2) TFEU. It is therefore appropriate to start the analysis from Article 16 TFEU, which reads

> 1. Everyone has the right to the protection of personal data concerning them. 2. The European Parliament and the Council ... shall lay down the rules relating to the protection of individuals with regard to the processing of personal data by Union institutions ... and by the Member States when carrying out activities which fall within the scope of Union law, and the rules relating to the free movement of such data. Compliance with these rules shall be subject to the control of independent authorities. The rules adopted on the basis of this Article shall be without prejudice to the specific rules laid down in Article 39 TEU.

Paragraph one, which enunciates the right and is identical to Article 8 CFR but for 'them' instead of 'his or her', is formulated in a way capable of producing direct effects.[9] The reference to the 'free movement of personal data' in paragraph two is seen by some as reinforcing the qualified nature of the right, a point I discuss later in this chapter. Article 16 TFEU must be read in combination with Declarations no 20 and 21 to the

---

[6] Convention for the Protection of Individuals with regard to Automatic Processing of Personal Data, Council of Europe, CETS n. 108, 28 January 1981.

[7] See especially Hijmans (n 5).

[8] See ch 1, sections I.A, II.A and II.B. See generally Y Poullet and A Rouvroy, 'The Right to Informational Self-determination and the Value of Self-development. Reassessing the Importance of Privacy for Democracy', in S Gutwirth et al. (eds), *Reinventing Data Protection?* (New York, Springer-Verlag, 2009). González Fuster (n 5); Lynskey (n 5).

[9] H Hijmans and A Scirocco, 'Shortcomings in EU Data Protection in the Third and the Second Pillars. Can the Lisbon Treaty be Expected to Help?' (2009) 46 *Common Market Law Review* 1485–1525, 1517–1518. See also Hijmans (5), 36–38. See ch 3, section II.B and ch 8.

Treaty. Declaration no 20 clarifies that rules adopted pursuant to Article 16 TFEU shall provide for specific derogations when directly affecting national security, which is outside of the scope of EU law. Declaration no 21 to the Treaty encourages the adoption of specific rules on data processing in the fields of judicial cooperation in criminal matters and police cooperation.[10] The second indent of paragraph two connects the provision to Article 39 TEU, which reads

> 2. ... In accordance with Article 16 [TFEU] and by way of derogation from paragraph 2 thereof, the Council shall adopt a decision laying down the rules relating to the protection of individuals with regard to the processing of personal data by the Member States when carrying out activities which fall within the scope of this Chapter [the common foreign and security policy (CFSP)], and the rules relating to the free movement of such data. Compliance with these rules shall be subject to the control of independent authorities.

The external area of the Area of Freedom, Security and Justice (AFSJ)[11] is the overlapping policy sector of the AFSJ and CFSP that resulted from the internationalisation of domestic security threats. This area has acquired special prominence on account of international intelligence-led policing and the tendency to regulate data exchanges by means of international agreements.[12]

Both Articles 16 TFEU and 39 TEU lay down a positive obligation for the legislator to adopt new rules pertaining to the 'protection of individuals with regard to the processing of personal data' and the free movement of such data. The legislator includes both EU institutions, bodies, offices and agencies, and the Member States when they operate within the scope of EU law. It is in this light that secondary law acquires interpretive value, as I discuss next.

ii. EU Secondary Law

Secondary law plays a triple role with respect to Article 8 CFR. First, instruments adopted prior to the Charter, the Data Protection Directive (DPD) and European Data Protection Supervisor (EDPS) Regulation (EDPSR)[13] are sources of inspiration of the right. Second, the Explanations also state that the DPD and EDPSR 'contain

---

[10] Hijmans and Scirocco (n 9).

[11] See generally M Cremona and J Monar et al. (eds), *The External Dimension of the European Union's Area of Freedom, Security and Justice* (London, Peter Lang, 2011).

[12] See ch 8. The original data protection strategy encompassed a draft resolution extending the application of the general directive to those areas that were then falling outside the scope of Community law, eventually leading to Council Framework Decision 2008/977/JHA. European Commission, 'Proposal for a Directive concerning the protection of individuals in relation to the processing of personal data; Recommendation for a Council Decision on the opening of negotiations with a view to the accession of the European Communities to the Council of Europe Convention for the Protection of Individuals with Regard to the Automatic Processing of Personal Data; Commission Communication on the Protection of Individuals in Relation to the Processing of Personal Data in the Community and Information Security' (Communication) COM (90) 314 final.

[13] Regulation 45/2001/EC of the European Parliament and of the Council of 18 December 2000 on the protection of individuals with regard to the processing of personal data by the Community institutions and bodies and on the free movement of such data [2001] OJ L 8/1 (EDPSR); Directive 95/46/EC of the European Parliament and of the Council of 24 October 1995 on the protection of individuals with regard to the processing of personal data and on the free movement of such data [1995] OJ L281/31 (Data Protection Directive or DPD).

conditions and limitations for the exercise of the right to the protection of personal data'. The CJEU found Article 8 CFR to be (retrospectively) 'implemented inter alia by Articles'[14] of the DPD, as well as the e-Privacy Directive (EPD), the DPD's *lex specialis* clarifying and complementing 'the DPD in the telecommunications sector'.[15] Provisions of the EDPSR should be similarly able to implement Article 8 CFR, given that the EDPSR was found to have 'in essence, the same objectives'[16] of the DPD. Third, instruments repealing the DPD and EDPSR adopted pursuant to Articles 16 TFEU and 39 TEU both embody the positive obligation therein and, as the laws they replace, implement the right.

Secondary law's apparent ability to exert force over primary law has puzzled scholars such as Lynskey and led Van der Sloot, the latter to the point of refuting the fundamental right nature of data protection.[17] References to secondary law must, however, be read in light of Article 52(2) CFR, whereby 'Rights recognised by this Charter for which provision is made in the Treaties shall be exercised under the conditions and within the limits defined by those Treaties.' Although the Explanations do not mention that Article 52(2) applies to Article 8 CFR, the right to data protection is manifestly 'a right for which provision is made in the Treaties' by virtue of Article 286 TEC as replaced by Articles 16 TFEU and 39 TEU.[18] As a result, the interpretive and limiting force exerted by secondary law exists only by virtue of, and to the extent to which, primary law has bestowed such a force.

Following Craig, reading Charter rights through the lens of Article 52(2) CFR means that the CJEU should take into sufficient account secondary law that has extensively refined the purview of the right. In such a way, secondary legislation cannot be used to unduly limit primary law and can be challenged on fundamental rights grounds.[19] Indeed, secondary laws enjoy a presumption of lawfulness 'and accordingly produce legal effects until such time as they are withdrawn'.[20] Thus, the regime contained in instruments of secondary law implementing Articles 8 CFR and 16 TFEU should inform the interpretation of both the purview and limitation of the right to data protection. This is essentially what the CJEU does when it finds Article 8 CFR to be implemented by certain provisions drawn from secondary law, without however being constrained by it in future interpretations of the right.

---

[14] *Google Spain and Google*, C-131/12, EU:C:2014:317, para 69.

[15] E-Privacy Directive 2002/58/EC [2002] OJ L201/37 (EPD); see *Deutsche Telekom*, Case C-543/09, EU:C:2011:279, para 50.

[16] *YS and others*, C-141/12 and C-372/12, EU:C:2014:2081, para 46.

[17] Lynskey (n 5) due to the market objective of the DPD. But *cf* Poullet and Rouvroy (n 8). Supporting the latter 'In the mind of the Union legislature, the Union legislation ... serves to protect fundamental rights and freedoms'. *Bavarian Lager Ltd*, C-28/08 P, EU:C:2010:378, para 51. See section II below. B Van der Sloot, 'Legal Fundamentalism: is Data Protection Really a Fundamental Right?', in R Leenes et al. (eds), *Data Protection and Privacy: (In)visibilities and Infrastructures* (Cham, Springer, 2017).

[18] *Google (Territorial scope of de-referencing)*, C-507/17, EU:C:2019:772, para 54. It follows the Opinion of AG Szpunar.

[19] P Craig, *The Lisbon Treaty, Revised Edition: Law, Politics, and Treaty Reform* (Oxford, Oxford University Press, 2013) 228–230.

[20] *Schrems*, C-362/14, EU:C:2015:650, para 52.

There are four instruments of secondary law that bear interpretive significance. The first is the GDPR, which updated[21] and uniformed[22] the provisions of the DPD as the *lex generalis* disciplining most processing of personal data. Similarly to the DPD, the GDPR lays down both general principles and detailed provisions aiming to enforce such principles. Such principles, in keeping with the DPD's approach of modernising pre-existing data protection instruments, represent the latest edition of fair information practice principles (FIPs), first elaborated in the US under the guidance of chairperson Willy Ware – who also oversaw the development of information security principles – and later incorporated in the OECD Guidelines and Convention 108.[23] Consequently, the principles act as the bridge between Article 8 CFR and the GDPR.

The second relevant instrument is the Regulation (EDPSR2)[24] repealing the first EDPSR. The third and fourth instruments are *leges speciales* complementing and particularising the GDPR: the EPD, which could soon be replaced by the EPR and the Law Enforcement Directive (LED).[25] The LED is meant to apply to the prevention, investigation, detection and prosecution of criminal offences,[26] but not to national security. The latter is the sole responsibility of Member States under Articles 72 TFEU and 4(2) TEU, although is a limited concept that 'cannot be extended to other sectors of public life that are, to varying degrees, related to it'.[27]

In this work, Article 8 is read in light of Article 52(2) CFR and secondary law is used to supplement the interpretation of the limbs of the right to data protection. Reading Article 8 in light of Article 52(2) CFR also bears consequences for the interpretive role of Article 8 ECHR and Convention 108, which I discuss next.

---

[21] Article 29 Data Protection Working Party and Working Party on Police and Justice, *The Future of Privacy: Joint Contribution to the Consultation of the European Commission on the Legal Framework for the Fundamental Right to Protection of Personal Data* (WP 168, 2009); V Reding, *The Review of the EU Data Protection Framework*, SPEECH/11/183 (2011); G Buttarelli, 'Latest Developments in Data Protection' (Presentation at the meeting of the Heads of Agencies, Stockholm, 19 October 2012).

[22] Vis-à-vis the DPD's general and flexible character, *IPI*, C-473/12 EU:C:2013:715, para 31.

[23] See W Ware (chair), Records, Computers and the Rights of Citizens. Report of the Secretary's Advisory Committee on Automated Personal Data Systems (1973); C Bennett and C Raab, *The Governance of Privacy. Policy Instruments in a Global Perspective* (Cambridge, The MIT Press, 2006); R Gellman, 'Fair Information Practices: A Basic History (Version 1.89)' (2012) Constantly updated at: bobgellman.com/rg-docs/rg-FIPShistory.pdf. See further at n 29.

[24] Regulation (EU) 2018/1725 of the European Parliament and of the Council of 23 October 2018 on the protection of natural persons with regard to the processing of personal data by the Union institutions, bodies, offices and agencies and on the free movement of such data, and repealing Regulation (EC) No 45/2001 and Decision No 1247/2002/EC [2018] OJ L 295/39 (EDPSR2).

[25] Law Enforcement Directive (EU) 2016/680 [2016] OJ L119/89 (LED); European Commission, '*Regulation on Privacy and Electronic Communications*' (Communication) COM (2017) 10 final, 2017/0003 (COD). The LED repeals the much-criticised Council Framework Decision 977/2008/JHA. See generally F Dumortier et al., 'La Protection des Données dans l'Espace Européen de Liberté, de Sécurité et de Justice' (2009) 166 *Journal de Droit Européen* 23; European Commission, 'A Comprehensive Approach on Personal Data Protection in the European Union' (Communication) COM (2010) 609 final.

[26] But compare *Privacy International*, C-623/17, which has somewhat reduced the scope of the LED.

[27] Subject to the 'pre-emption' clause, Arts 2(2) TFEU and 72 TFEU. *Privacy International*, C-623/17, EU:C:2020:5, Opinion of AG Sanchez-Bordona, para 80.

B. Council of Europe Instruments: The ECHR and Convention 108

That Article 8 ECHR and Convention 108 are sources of Article 8 CFR is in keeping with the history of data protection.[28] The adoption of CoE Convention 108 in 1981 – and the related OECD Guidelines[29] – offered asylum to the need of data protection, or 'data privacy', that had been in search of international legal protection since the 1960s.[30] The ECtHR gave data protection concrete recognition, in the absence of a dedicated provision,[31] by subsuming the right recognised by Convention 108 under Article 8 ECHR. Convention 108 was seen as initially offering sufficient protection; the creation of the Single Market and the data flows resulting from the commercialisation of the Internet paved the way for the adoption of the DPD, which contained connection clauses to both the ECHR and Convention 108.[32]

By contrast, Article 16 TFEU and the GDPR contain no references to the ECHR. Furthermore, Convention 108 plays an important but limited part in the current architecture of EU data protection. Such disconnection underpins the autonomy of the system for the protection of personal data offered within the Union vis-à-vis CoE conceptions of privacy and bears immediate consequences for the interpretation of Article 8 CFR, to which I turn next.

i. The ECHR and the Independence of Data Protection from Privacy

Reading the right to data protection in light of Article 52(2) CFR affects the role played by the European Court of Human Rights (ECtHR) case law on Article 8 ECHR – and especially Convention 108 – in the interpretation of Article 8 CFR. First, judgments of the ECtHR do not hold primary interpretive value, but rather special significance in the interpretation of the scope, meaning and limitations of Article 8 CFR and its implementation by secondary law. Second, such judgments cannot supersede Union law in case of conflict, leaving the CJEU free to make independent findings. Such an interpretation, which is supported by a systematic reading of the Charter, is necessary to safeguard the EU data protection architecture and is arguably underpinned by the principle of autonomy.[33]

---

[28] See generally Bennett and Raab (n 21); González Fuster (n 5); S Simitis, 'Privacy – An Endless Debate' (2010) 98 *California Law Review*.

[29] Organization for the Economic Cooperation and Development, Recommendation of the Council Concerning Guidelines Governing the Protection of Privacy and Transborder Flows of Personal Data, C(80)58/FINAL, as amended on 11 July 2013 by C(2013)79.

[30] See generally A Westin, *Privacy and Freedom* (New York, Atheneum Press, 1967); S Rodotà, *Elaboratori Elettronici e Controllo Sociale* (Mulino 1973).

[31] 'There is no equivalent provision … in the ECHR', *Sergejs Buivids*, C-345/17, Opinion of AG Sharpstone, para 61.

[32] See Rec 10 DPD, whereby the Directive was to ensure a high level of protection of the right to privacy expressed by Art 8 ECHR and general principles and Rec 11 DPD whereby the 'principles of the protection of the … right to privacy … contained in this Directive, give substance to and amplify those contained in' Convention 108.

[33] 'Any action by the bodies given decision-making powers by the ECHR … must not have the effect of binding the EU and its institutions, in the exercise of their internal powers, to a particular interpretation of the rules of EU law' *Avis* 2/13 Opinion of the Court EU:C:2014:2454, para 184. See ch 8.

The combined reading of Articles 8 and 52 CFR supports the disconnection of Article 8 CFR from 8 ECHR. As established, data protection is a right for which provision is manifestly made in Articles 16 TFEU and 39 TEU. Furthermore, and *a contrario*, data protection is not one of the rights covered by the rule of interpretation contained in Article 52(3) CFR discussed in chapter three. As articulated by AG Saugmandsgaard Øe in *Tele2Sverige* and endorsed obiter by the CJEU, Article 8 CFR

> establishes a right that does not correspond to any right guaranteed by the [ECHR], namely the right to the protection of personal data, as is confirmed, moreover, by the explanations relating to Article 52 [CFR]. Thus, the rule of interpretation laid down in the first sentence of Article 52(3) [CFR] does not, in any event, apply to the interpretation of Article 8 [CFR].[34]

The independence of Article 8 CFR from Article 8 ECHR guarantees the integrity of the 'architecture', or 'complete system of personal data protection'[35] in the EU, as criticisable as such an architecture may be, as I discuss below. The point can be illustrated by reference to Kranenborg's classification of the ECtHR case law. Kranenborg found that, in interpreting cases concerning personal data, the ECtHR

> excludes from the scope of the protection of privacy under Article 8 ECHR the processing ... of personal data: i) which is (*sic*) not private in itself; ii) which are not systematically stored with a focus on the data subject; and iii) if the data subject could reasonably expect the processing (disclosure).[36]

Kranenborg's point (ii), whereby data not systematically stored with a focus on the data subject are outside the scope of Article 8 ECHR, may need to be revisited in light of recent cases addressing measures of secret surveillance that I discuss in chapter seven, but generally still applies. An example can be found in the criteria determining the applicability of Article 8 ECHR in *Lopez Ribalda*, concerning the use of video-surveillance systems in the workplace, which validates the findings in *Herbeq*, whereby the monitoring in a public place using a camera that does 'not record the visual data' is not in itself a 'form of interference with private life'.[37]

Adopting the approach of the ECtHR distilled by Kranenborg would undermine the independence of the EU data protection architecture. As to point (i), individuals 'are not deprived of their right to de-referencing', one of data subjects' rights enshrined in Article 17(3) GDPR, even when they 'make their sensitive data manifestly public'.[38]

---

[34] *Tele2 Sverige and Watson and others*, C-203/15 and C-698/15, EU:C:2016:572, Opinion of AG Saugmandsgaard Øe para 79; *Tele2 Sverige and Watson and others*, C-203/15 and C-698/15, EU:C:2016:970, para 129.
[35] *Google (Territorial scope of de-referencing)*, C-507/17, EU:C:2019:15, Opinion of AG Szpunar, para 44.
[36] H Kranenborg, 'Access to Documents and Data Protection in European Union: on the Public Nature of Personal Data' (2008) 45 *Common Market Law Review* 1079–1114, 1093. See generally P De Hert and S Gutwirth, 'Data Protection in the Case Law of Strasbourg and Luxembourg: Constitutionalism in Action' in Serge Gutwirth (ed), *Reinventing Data Protection?* (Springer 2009); S Gutwirth and R Gellert, 'The Legal Construction of Privacy and Data Protection' 29 *Computer Law & Security Review* 522–530. G González Fuster and S Gutwirth, 'Opening up Personal Data Protection: A Conceptual Controversy' (2013) 29 *Computer Law & Security Review* 531–539.
[37] See *Lopez Ribalda v Spain* nos. 1874/13 and 8567/13 CE:ECHR:2019:1017JUD000187413, paras 87–89; *Herbecq and the Association 'Ligue Des Droits De L'homme' v Belgium* nos. 32200/96 and 32201/96 CE:ECHR: 1998:0114DEC003220096.
[38] *GC and Others (De-referencing of sensitive data)*, C-136/17, EU:C:2019:773, paras 63–65. Although in such a case the processing is presumed to be lawful, it still attracts balancing.

As to point (ii), the Court has found video surveillance to fall, in principle, within the scope of data protection law 'in so far as it constitutes automatic processing', and 'covers, even partially, a public space'.[39] Following *M5A-Scara A*, a video surveillance system using a camera constitutes 'automatic processing of personal data ... where the device installed enables personal data, such as images allowing natural persons to be identified, to be recorded and stored'.[40] 'The specific methods of installing and operating that device' inform the proportionality assessment of 'the data processing by a video surveillance device'.[41] As for point (iii), the generic expectations of processing by data subjects have limited bearing on whether such processing is legitimate or not, which is generally determined by virtue of adherence to provisions regulating the lawfulness of processing.[42]

The combined reading of Articles 8 and 52(2) CFR and the extant disconnection of Article 8 CFR from 8 ECHR will arguably persist if the EU acceded to the ECHR.[43] Indeed, interference with the right to data protection, whatever its purpose[44] 'must always be examined and assessed in conformity with the legislation of the Union concerning the protection of personal data'.[45]

The formal independence of the EU from the CoE does not prevent the CJEU from relying on the case law of the ECtHR, and the CJEU has done so aplenty. What is problematic is that the CJEU has de facto followed in the steps of the ECtHR, which treats data protection matters as subsidiary to privacy matters, by conflating Articles 7 and 8 CFR in different lines of cases.[46] Such an approach sits uncomfortably with the design of the Charter and fuels debates on the need for a right to data protection conceived independently from privacy.

In defence of an autonomous right to data protection, the combination of primary and secondary law as interpreted by the CJEU[47] sets Article 8 CFR apart from Articles 8 ECHR and 7 CFR. What is more, the CJEU generally treats the processing of *any personal data* as an interference with Article 8 CFR,[48] the permissibility of which

---

[39] *Ryneš*, C-212/13, EU:C:2014:2428, paras 24, 33. If the video surveillance system enables the monitoring of identifiable individuals in a public place, the finding should stand irrespective of whether the system records data (eg, Art 35(3)a GDPR).

[40] *Asociaţia de Proprietari bloc M5A-ScaraA*, C-708/18, EU:C:2019:1064, para 35.

[41] ibid, paras 49–50.

[42] Reasonable expectations matter with respect to further processing (*Deutsche Telekom*, C-543/09, para 66) and the legitimate interest basis, European Data Protection Board, *Guidelines 3/2019 on processing of personal data through video devices* (2020) 12–13.

[43] Negotiations addressing the caveats set by *Opinion 2/13* are currently ongoing: see www.coe.int/en/web/human-rights-intergovernmental-cooperation/accession-of-the-european-union-to-the-european-convention-on-human-rights#.

[44] As the 'any undermining of privacy and the integrity of the individual' (*Bavarian Lager*, para 59) or as the 'rights and freedoms?'

[45] *Bavarian Lager Ltd*, C-28/08 P, para 59.

[46] The 'reasoning of the Court is permeated by a "privacy thinking"'. G González Fuster and R Gellert, 'The Fundamental Right of Data Protection in the European Union: in Search of an Uncharted Right' (2012) 26 *International Review of Law, Computers & Technology* 73–82, 79.

[47] *Promusicae*, C-275/06, EU:C:2008:54. By contrast, and possibly *per incuriam*, 'the limitations which may lawfully be imposed on the right [to data protection] correspond to those tolerated in relation to article 8' ECHR, *Schecke and Eifert*, C-92/09 and C-93/09, EU:C:2010:662, para 52.

[48] *Digital Rights Ireland and Seitlinger and Others*, C-293/12 and C-594/12, EU:C:2014:238. Emphasis added.

must be examined in conformity with EU law. The CJEU has also stated that, 'in order to find [a right to erasure]' it is not 'necessary that the inclusion of the information [that the data subject wishes to erase] causes prejudice to the data subject'.[49] And yet, the Court does not always analyse the right to data protection independently from the right to private life, with cases falling on a continuum characterised, at each extreme, by the denial of the right to data protection and a full recognition of the right examined in its own right.

At one extreme of the spectrum are old cases where data protection is seen under the lens of both Article 8 ECHR, as in *Österreichischer Rundfunk and Others*[50] and private life, such as *Lindqvist, Schecke and Eifert* and even *Google Spain and Google (Google Spain)*.[51] At the other end of the spectrum lie cases analysed solely in light of an independent right to data protection. Examples include *Deutsche Telekom, Scarlet Extended, Sabam* and *Belgium v Facebook*.[52]

In between each extreme lies a rich array of cases where the Court establishes the existence of separate rights under Articles 8 and 7 CFR, but instead of carrying out separate analyses of the interference of a given measure with each right, it carries out a joint analysis. For instance, *ASNEF and FECEDEM* refers to 'the significance of the *data subject's rights* arising from Articles 7 and 8'[53] [CFR]. In *YS and others*[54] and *X*, the Court states that to protect '*privacy* ... enshrined in Article 8 [CFR], the fees which may be levied under Article 12(a) [DPD] may not ... constitute an obstacle to the exercise of the right of access'.[55] In *Ryneš*, '... according to settled case-law, the protection of the fundamental right to private life guaranteed under Article 7 ... requires that derogations and limitations in relation to the *protection of personal data* must apply only in so far as is strictly necessary'.[56] In *Digital Rights Ireland*, the CJEU found the DPD and EPD to create a 'system of protection of the right to privacy ... with regard to the processing of personal data' and that 'to establish the existence of an interference with [privacy] it does not matter whether the information on the *private lives* concerned is sensitive or whether the persons concerned have been inconvenienced in any way'.[57] The passage, which casts the DPD as an implementation of Article 7 CFR, is further taken up in the first *Schrems* case.[58]

---

[49] *Google*, C-507/17, para 45.
[50] *Österreichischer Rundfunk and Others*, C-465/00, C-138/01 and C-139/01, EU:C:2003:294.
[51] *Bodil Lindqvist*, C-101/01, ECLI: EU:C:2003:596; *Schecke and Eifert*, C-92/09 and C-93/09. The 'right to privacy with respect to the processing of personal data' paras 58, 66 and 74 in *Google Spain and Google*, C-131/12. See González Fuster and Gellert (n 46); M Tzanou, 'Data Protection as a Fundamental Right Next to Privacy? 'Reconstructing' a not so New Right' (2013) 3 *International Data Privacy Law* 88–99.
[52] *Deutsche Telekom*, C-543/09; *Scarlet Extended*, C-70/10, EU:C:2011:771; *Sabam*, C-360/10, EU:C:2012:85; *Belgium v Facebook*, C-645/19, EU:C:2021:483.
[53] *ASNEF and FECEDM*, C-468/10 and C-469/10, EU:C:2011:777, paras 40–41. Emphasis added.
[54] 'The protection of the fundamental right to respect for private life means, inter alia, that that person may be certain that the personal data concerning him are correct and that they are processed in a lawful manner.' *YS and others*, C-141/12 and C-372/12, para 44.
[55] Citing *Rijkeboer*, para 47, *X*, C-486/12, EU:C:2013:836, para 29. Emphasis added.
[56] *Ryneš*, C-212/13, para 28.
[57] *Digital Rights Ireland*, C-293/12 and C-594/12, para 29, quoting para 47 from *Schecke and Eifert*, C-92/09-C-93/09. Then *Digital Rights Ireland* paras 32 and 33, taken from ground 75 of *Österreichischer Rundfunk and Others*, C-465/00, C-138/01 and C-139/01.
[58] *Schrems*, C-362/14, para 87.

The 'middle' cases just listed are a direct product of old formulations contained in the DPD and EPD that refer to the 'right to privacy with respect to the processing of personal data', which solders data protection with privacy. Such an approach is not unique to the CJEU. A study I conducted before the entry into force of the GDPR shows that national DPAs relied on any combinations of Articles 7 and 8 CFR, 8 ECHR and national constitutions to enforce the applicable data protection law.[59] However, such an approach applies even with respect to cases solely based on the interpretation of the GDPR, such as *Latvijas Republikas Saeima*, which AG Szpunar described as 'arguably the first case on data protection *au sens large*', where the CJEU read the GDPR in light of privacy and even the DPD.[60]

The fact that private life remains relevant to interpret the GDPR underpins a longstanding difficulty to conceptualise the value of data protection as independent from privacy. For instance, in *ASNEF and FECEDEM*,[61] the Court found Article 8(1) to be 'closely connected with the right to respect for private life expressed in Article 7' CFR. In *Digital Rights Ireland*, the Court states that 'the protection of personal data resulting from the explicit obligation laid down in article 8(1) [CFR] is especially important for … article 7'[62] CFR; the infringement of data protection may suffice to determine the infringement of privacy, but not vice versa. In *Latvijas Republikas Saeima*, the processing of data on convictions, a 'behaviour that gives rise to social disapproval', 'is liable to stigmatise the data subject, thereby constituting a serious interference with … private or professional life'.[63]

The hesitance of the Court to acknowledge a self-standing right to data protection both reflects and informs scholarship that questions the independence of Article 8 vis-à-vis Article 7 CFR.[64] Van der Sloot suggests treating data protection as a consumer right and de Hert claims it is an 'inherently hollow' procedural right.[65] On a more moderate note, Poullet and Rouvroy, Tzanou, and Lynskey support the independence of Article 8 CFR, but see its value as being instrumental to privacy.[66] Others acknowledge that data protection captures dimensions not protected by private life, with Gellert, Gutwirth and von Grafenstein claiming that the value of the right rests in it being

---

[59] MG Porcedda, *Use of the Charter of Fundamental Rights by National Data Protection Authorities and the EDPS* (Robert Schuman Centre for Advanced Studies Working Paper 2017) hdl.handle.net/1814/47004.

[60] *Latvijas Republikas Saeima (Points de pénalité)*, C-439/19, EU:C:2021:504, paras 75, 77; *Latvijas Republikas Saeima (Points de pénalité)*, C-439/19, EU:C:2020:1054, Opinion of AG Szpunar, para 3.

[61] 'The significance of the data subject's rights arising from Articles 7 and Article 8(1) … is closely connected with the right to respect for private life expressed in Article 7'. *ASNEF and FECEDM*, C-468/10 and C-469/10, paras 40–41.

[62] *Digital Rights Ireland*, C-293/12 and C-594/12, para 53.

[63] *Latvijas Republikas Saeima*, C-439/19 para 75.

[64] Similarly González Fuster and Gellert (n 46).

[65] P De Hert and D Wright, *Privacy Impact Assessment*, vol 6 (Dordrecht, Springer, 2012) 179; P De Hert, 'Data Protection as Bundles of Principles, General Rights, Concrete Substantive Rights and Rules. Piercing the Veil of Stability Surrounding the Principles of Data Protection (Foreword)' (2017) 2(3) *European Data Protection Law Review* 160–179. Van der Sloot (n 17).

[66] Poullet and Rouvroy (n 8); Lynseky (n 5); Tzanou (n 5). Reviewing older contributions: González Fuster and Gutwirth (n 36); Looking at EU law but conflating Arts 7 and 8: V Boehme-Neßler, 'Privacy: a Matter of Democracy. Why Democracy Needs Privacy and Data Protection' (2016) 6 *International Data Privacy Law* 222–229.

instrumental to many rights.[67] Some appreciate the intersection between privacy and data protection, but either refrain from asserting its instrumentality to privacy, such as González Fuster or treat the latter as a self-standing right with its own autonomous goals, as did the late Rodotà.[68]

Although all positions have merit, the debate could be solved in light of human rights' classic characteristics of interdependence, interrelatedness and indivisibility,[69] whereby reciprocal instrumentality does not cause the loss of each right's independent value. For instance, the Maastricht Guidelines point to all rights being instrumental to dignity[70] and the right to privacy is arguably itself instrumental to a bundle of family entitlements, such as Article 9 CFR. The fact that data protection may be instrumental to several civil and political rights, including privacy, does not invalidate its autonomous value.

Elsewhere I conducted a historical investigation into the social purposes of Articles 7 and 8 CFR to show that both rights help protecting and nurturing identity, personality and autonomy.[71] However, the two Articles pursue their common purposes differently on account of their scope but also approach.

In agreement with Rodotà, Gellert and von Grafenstein,[72] data protection is dynamic, precautionary and future-orientated. Data protection not only helps prevent known interferences with established rights, but also harms that are tangible and not ascribable to other rights, as well as future harms. Processing operations that make an individual identifiable deserve protection, on account of the harms that such a processing may pose to the rights and freedoms of individuals in the present but also the future. As AG Sanchez-Bordona stated with reference to identifiability, 'the possibility that advances in technical means will, in the ... future, significantly facilitate access to increasingly sophisticated instruments for collecting and processing data justifies the safeguards put in place'.[73] What is more, similarly to other human rights, privacy and data protection can also clash, as will be discussed in chapter five.

---

[67] Recognising situations where the processing of personal data is: (i) outside the scope of privacy; (ii) within the scope of privacy; and (iii) within the scope of privacy and data are 'sensitive', where 'the interest of the data subject increases gradually' Kranenborg (n 36) 1094. Gutwirth and Gellert (n 36); J Kokott and C Sobotta, 'The Distinction between Privacy and Data Protection in the Jurisprudence of the CJEU and the ECtHR' (2013) 3 *International Data Privacy Law* 222–228; M von Grafenstein, 'Refining the Concept of the Right to Data Protection in Article 8 ECFR' (2020) 7 *Europeand Data Protection Law Review* 190–205.

[68] González Fuster (n 5); S Rodotà, 'Data Protection as a Fundamental Right', in S Gutwirth (ed), *In Reinventing Data Protection?* (New York, Springer, 2009).

[69] United Nations, 'Vienna Declaration and Programme of Action adopted by World Conference on Human Rights in Vienna', § 5.

[70] 'It is now undisputed that all human rights are indivisible, interdependent, interrelated and of equal importance for human dignity.' The Maastricht Guidelines on Violations of Economic, Social and Cultural Rights. Background paper submitted by the International Commission of Jurists. E/C.12/2000/13, § I.4.

[71] MG Porcedda, 'The Recrudescence of 'Security v. Privacy' after the 2015 Terrorist Attacks, and the Value of 'Privacy Rights' in the European Union', in E Orrù et al. (eds), *Rethinking Surveillance and Control Beyond the 'Security versus Privacy' Debate* (Baden-Baden, Nomos, 2017). Reaching similar conclusions: Boehme-Neßler (n 66). Privacy and data protection as contributing to identity: N Andrade, 'The Right to Personal Identity in the Information Age. A Reappraisal of a Lost Right' (PhD thesis, European University Institute 2011).

[72] Rodotà (n 68); R Gellert, 'Data Protection: a Risk Regulation? Between the Risk Management of Everything and the Precautionary Alternative' (2015) 5 *International Data Privacy Law* 3–19; von Grafenstein, (2021).

[73] *Breyer*, C-582/14, EU:C:2016:339, Opinion of AG Sanchez-Bordona, para 66.

Neither human rights doctrine, the formulation of Article 8 CFR, nor the applicable law stand in the way of interpreting data protection as an autonomous right. Treating Article 8 CFR as an independent right has the advantage of offering individuals greater protection than that offered by the ECHR, on account of the breadth of EU secondary law and, as Lynseky notes,[74] the understanding, developed by the CJEU, that exceptions and limitations to fundamental rights must be construed narrowly. Such arguments do not detract from the fact that, whenever data protection and privacy overlap, the ECtHR can supply guidelines of special significance on account of its sizable case law on personal data processing developed since the adoption of Convention 108, to which I turn now.

ii. *Convention 108 and Convention 108+*

Convention 108[75] is the first international Treaty on data protection, laying down rules on the processing of personal data relied on by the ECtHR in its Article 8 case law since *Z. v Finland* and *Rotaru v Romania*.[76] The Convention's Explanatory Memorandum highlights the influence played by the OECD Privacy Guidelines in the drafting process.[77] Both texts elaborated FIPs, ie the rules of thumb for processing personal data so as to, for the OECD, remove the obstacles to the free flowing of personal data and for the CoE, support the formulation of a right to data protection. The Convention incorporated all FIPs included in the OECD Guidelines, namely collection limitation, data quality, purpose specification, use limitation, security safeguards, openness and individual participation,[78] with the exception of accountability. The latter is incorporated in Convention 108+, which will succeed Convention 108 once Protocol 223 enters into force.[79] Convention 108 went however beyond the OECD Guidelines, for instance by prohibiting the automatic processing of special categories of personal data, such as those revealing racial origin, health or criminal convictions, unless domestic laws provide appropriate safeguards.[80] The innovation, solidly anchored in the DPD and the GDPR, displays the influence played by Convention 108 in EU data protection law.

---

[74] Lynskey (n 5).

[75] Convention 108. (1083) Additional Protocol to the Convention for the Protection of Individuals with regard to Automatic Processing of Personal Data, regarding supervisory authorities and trans-border data flows, Council of Europe, CETS n.181, 8 November 2001.

[76] *Rotaru v Romania* no. 28341/95 CE:ECHR:2000:0504JUD002834195; *Z v Finland* no. 22009/93 CE:ECHR:1997:0225JUD002200993.

[77] Explanatory Memorandum of Convention for the Protection of Individuals with regard to Automatic Processing of Personal Data, Council of Europe. See especially 'Co-operation with OECD and the EEC'.

[78] Art 5 on quality encompasses the principles of collection limitation, data quality, purpose specification and use limitation. Art 7 embodies the security safeguards principle. Art 8 incorporates the principles of individual participation and openness.

[79] When either all CoE contracting states ratify the Protocol (Art 37(1)), or by 2023 if 38 signatories will have ratified it (Art 37(2)). In the interim, ratifying states can apply the Protocol on a provisional basis (Art 37(3)), as Bulgaria, Cyprus, Estonia, Lithuania and Norway did. See Council of Europe Treaty office's website: www.coe.int/en/web/conventions/full-list?module=treaty-detail&treatynum=223. Protocol amending the Convention for the Protection of Individuals with regard to Automatic Processing of Personal Data (Convention 108+), CETS n. 223, 10 October 2018.

[80] Convention 108, Art 6. which creates interdependence with other rights (eg the prohibition of discrimination).

Not only was Convention 108 a harmonising factor in the field for the Member States of the then European Communities (ECs), but also very influential in the adoption of the DPD, which reproduced its structure and drew heavily from its content,[81] as exemplified by the *renvoi* or connection clause therein.[82] The formulation of FIPs in Convention 108 still forms the bedrock of Union secondary data protection law and an indirect, yet particularly important source of Article 8 CFR. Convention 108 is an indirect source because the Union (and the ECs before) have yet to take the opportunity, created by an amendment to the Convention in 1999,[83] to accede to the Treaty and its successor. Should the Union sign and ratify Convention 108+, as a mixed agreement it would become an integral part of EU law with greater force than secondary law and binding upon the Union and its Member States.[84] Convention 108 is important because, as explained by the amendment's Memorandum, the change was informed by 'the wish to develop co-operation' with the CoE, a wish which has grown stronger and informed cross-contamination[85] with a view to fostering 'a stronger international forum on data protection, particularly vis-à-vis third countries'.

In the GDPR, Convention 108 is only mentioned in Recital 105, as a factor that 'should be taken into account' in assessing the adequacy of the data protection legislation of third countries and organisations, with a view to allowing the transfer of personal data.[86] Such a marked change from the DPD reinforces the separation of the Union's legal framework, which would enable greater protection than the CoE's legal framework as interpretated by the ECtHR. In addition, Convention 108 and especially 108+, which is similar in spirit to the GDPR,[87] may become the minimum standard for establishing the adequacy of a third country, ie 'a level of protection … that is essentially equivalent to that guaranteed within … Union legislation … read in light of the Charter'.[88] Such a role, which would be in keeping with the rationale that sparked the amendment enabling the EU to accede to Convention 108, is auspicated by a number of authors, such as Bygrave, Greenleaf and Pauletto,[89] to ensure the broadest possible adoption of European standards of data protection.

---

[81] European Union Network of Independent Experts on Fundamental Rights, *Commentary of the Charter of Fundamental Rights of The European Union* (2006) 91.

[82] See n 32 above.

[83] Amendments to Convention 108 approved by the Committee of Ministers, in Strasbourg, on 15 June 1999.

[84] Following *Haegenam*, C-181/73 (an integral part of EU law) and *Commission v Germany*, C-61/94 (above secondary law), discussed in M Cremona, 'Who Can Make Treaties? The European Union', in D Hollis (ed), *The Oxford Guide to Treaties*, 2nd edn (Oxford, Oxford University Press, 2020). See ch 8.

[85] See especially G Buttarelli, *Convention 108: from a European reality to a global treaty* (2016); LA Bygrave, 'The 'Strasbourg Effect' on Data Protection in Light of the 'Brussels Effect': Logic, Mechanics and Prospects' (2021) 40 *Computer Law & Security Review*.

[86] Pursuant to the GDPR and the LED, European Data Protection Board (EDPB), *Recommendations 01/2021 on the adequacy referential under the Law Enforcement Directive* (2021), point 31.

[87] See Council of Europe, *The modernised Convention 108: novelties in a nutshell* (2018).

[88] On DPD, Art 25(6), the ECJ stated 'The word "adequate" … admittedly signifies that a third country cannot be required to ensure a level of protection identical to that guaranteed in the EU legal order', following the view formulated by the AG in point 141 of his Opinion. *Schrems*, C-362/14, para 71.

[89] Bygrave (n 85) 10–11, citing G Greenleaf 'How Far can Convention 108+ "Globalise"? Prospects for Asian Accessions' [2020] *University of New South Wales Faculty of Law Research Series* 55 and C Pauletto, the Protection of Individuals with Regard to the Processing of Personal Data', *Computer Law and Security Review* (40).

In sum, Convention 108(+) supplies guidelines for the interpretation of Article 8 CFR, guidelines that acquire special significance when stemming from the case law of the ECtHR that is within remit of EU data protection law. If the EU signed either Convention 108 or its modernised version, the Treaty would become a source of conform interpretation. In light of the participation of the EU in the negotiations, the absence of disconnection clauses in the modernised Convention and the possibility for the modernised Convention to represent the minimum standard for the protection of personal data in Union law, Convention 108+ deserves attention when interpreting Article 8 CFR. Convention 108 remains a binding source in areas that fall outside the scope of EU law and hence of the Charter, as I will discuss in chapter eight.

C. Other Relevant Sources

There are several international treaties and soft laws incorporating FIPs that exert influence, via policy, legislation and judgments, on the Union's understanding of data protection. Bygrave rightly notes that Union data protection law now incorporates innovations originating outside of Europe, such as data breach notification, privacy by design, certification and impact assessments,[90] innovations that influence the interpretation of the right. Keeping such sources in mind is relevant both historically and prospectively, in light of the 'internationalisation' of data protection.[91] According to Zalnieriute, a non-orthodox approach to customary international law formation could support the view that 'there is a general fundamental right to [so-called] data privacy under customary international law', whose 'international constitutional moment'[92] would go back to legal reactions (*opinio juris*) to Edward Snowden's revelations of mass surveillance.

The European Data Protection Board (EDPB) interacts with a list of international organisations and supervisory authorities outside the EU within international cooperation frameworks on privacy and data protection matters.[93] Second in the EDPB list is the OECD, a traditional forum of discussion for cross-border issues such as the enforcement of 'data privacy' laws and the adoption of standards to ensure the security of (personal) data within a wider cybersecurity strategy.[94] The OECD acts as an arena for post-WWII economic leaders, chiefly the EU, Japan, Korea, UK and US, to confront, understand and possibly reconcile opposing views. For instance, Bennett and Raab argue that the OECD Guidelines were an attempt to justify self-regulatory approaches.[95] Although the list prepared by the EDPB is non-exhaustive, notably

---

[90] Bygrave (n 85) 5–6.
[91] Such instruments are not *strictu sensu* sources of Art 8, but become relevant when making the case for the international application of personal data protection, including with a view to agreeing on universal attributes.
[92] M Zalnieriute, 'Towards International Data Privacy Cooperation: Strategies and Alternatives' (PhD thesis, European University Institute 2014), 114.
[93] See edpb.europa.eu/our-work-tools/support-cooperation-and-enforcement/international-cooperation-cooperation-other_en.
[94] Eg, the abrogated OECD, *Recommendation on Guidelines for the Security of Information and Networks. Towards a Culture of Security* (2002).
[95] Bennett and Raab (n 21).

absent are the United Nations (UN), possibly for want of a dedicated data protection forum. The interpretation of the International Covenant on Civil and Political Rights (ICCPR), the update of soft law instruments such as the UN Guidelines and the work of the Special Rapporteur on Privacy[96] offer a laboratory for *opinio juris* in this area that could feed back into EU data protection law.

II. Essential Components of Article 8 CFR

Article 8 CFR contains three paragraphs. This section brings into focus the architecture of the right to data protection, the main features of its limbs or essential components and its essence (II.A, II.B and II.C).[97] I offer an interpretation in light of case law, secondary law relevant to the relationship between cybersecurity, privacy and data protection as interpreted by the EDPB and EDPS, as well as, where relevant, Convention 108+.

A. Paragraph One: An Inclusive Right to Data Protection

Article 8(1) enunciates the general rule whereby individuals enjoy the right to having their personal data protected, which is reproduced in Article 16(1) TFEU: 'Everyone has the right to the protection of personal data concerning him or her'. Each part of the enunciation is reviewed in turn.

i. 'Everyone has the Right To'

This wording stresses the omnibus nature of the provision, which applies to whom Charter rights apply: anybody falling under the ever-expanding jurisdiction of EU law, irrespective of nationality or residence.[98] The practical enjoyment of the right lies in the combined reading of this limb with the scope of secondary law disciplining the processing[99] of personal data, ie the GDPR, EDPSR2, EPD and LED, as interpreted by the Court.

With reference to the GDPR, the *lex generalis*, the protection of Article 8 CFR does not apply inter alia to the processing of data rendered permanently anonymous, unstructured files or sets of files and data processed in the course of household activities.[100]

---

[96] Art 17 ICCPR-related Human Rights Committee cases could provide guidelines for interpreting Art 8 CFR in light of General Comment n. 16, but the Court has not availed itself of such cases. General Assembly of the United Nations, 'Resolution 45/95. Guidelines for the regulation of computerized personal data files', (1990). J Cannataci, 'Right to privacy. Report of the Special Rapporteur on the right to privacy'. A/HRC/40/63, (2019).
[97] On attributes, essential components and limbs, see ch 1, section II.A.ii and iii.
[98] Buttarelli, Convention 108: from a European reality to a global treaty, (2016). European Data Protection Board, *Guidelines 3/2018 on the territorial scope of the GDPR (Article 3)*, v 2.1 (2019), 14. See Recs 14 and 16 GDPR and discussion of national security, section I.A.ii.
[99] 'Processing' is explained in section III.B below.
[100] Art 11 and Rec 26, GDPR, *Breyer*, C-582/14, EU:C:2016:779; Article 29 Data Protection Working Party, *Opinion 05/2014 on Anonymisation Techniques* (0829/14/EN WP216, 2014). Art 2(1) and Rec 15, Art 2(2)(c) and Rec 18, GDPR, as in *Bodil Lindqvist*, C-101/01; *Ryneš*, C-212/13; *Sergejs Buivids*, C-345/17, EU:C:2019:122, para 43. See generally R Leenes, 'Who Controls the Cloud?' 11 *Revista de Internet, Derecho y Politica*.

Individuals enjoy the protection of Article 8 CFR when processing activities fall within the 'establishment' and 'targeting' criterion found in Article 3 GDPR as interpreted by the EDPB.[101] The targeting criterion is met when controllers 'offer goods and services to data subjects in the Union', including Information Society Services (ISSs) and irrespective of payment, and 'monitor the behaviour' of data subjects in the Union, when this behaviour takes place in the Union.[102] If an establishment is located outside the Union, Union law applies where Member State law applies by virtues of international law.[103] Note that Convention 108 and 108+ are also omnibus.[104]

ii. [The Protection of] 'Personal Data Concerning Him or Her'

The Explanations do not provide interpretive elements for defining 'personal data'. In the absence of a test developed by the Court, WP29 Opinion 4/2007 on Article 2(a) DPD provides guidance in principle, pending the adoption of guidelines by the EDPB on Article 4(1) GDPR.[105] The definition in the applicable law contains four cumulative elements: (i) 'any information'; (ii) 'relating to' (concerning) an; (iii) 'identified or identifiable'; (iv) 'natural person', each reviewed in turn.

The applicable law defines data as 'any information' (i), regardless of its degree of sensitivity, format (paper, electronic, audio) and truthfulness. The conflation between data and information creates a 'definitional gap', which is not unique to data protection law.[106] Case law has clarified when certain information falls within the definition of personal data without unpacking the meaning of 'data'.[107] The definitional gap stems not only from semantic ambiguity[108] but also from the syncretic genesis of 'personal data protection' and could also be an explicit legislative choice.

As for the syncretic genesis, 'personal data protection' was heavily influenced by traditions such as the German *datenschutz* and FIPs, described by González Fuster and Gutwirth to be respectively proscriptive and permissive in nature.[109] Crucially, FIPs place an emphasis on information, whereas the German *Datenschutzgesetz*, the

---

[101] Art 3(1), Rec 22 GDPR. *Google Spain and Google*, C-131/12, para 52; EDPB (n 98) 5–13.
[102] Art 3(2), Rec 24 GDPR; EDPB (n 98) 13–22. On ISSs, European Data Protection Board, *Guidelines 2/2019 on the processing of personal data under Article 6(1)(b) GDPR in the context of the provision of online services to data subjects Version 2.0* (2019).
[103] GDPR Art 3(3) and Rec 25 on diplomatic missions and consular posts.
[104] Buttarelli (n 98).
[105] Article 29 Data Protection Working Party, *Opinion 4/2007 on the Concept of Personal Data* (01248/07/EN WP 136, 2007). The CJEU found its own case law on the DPD to apply, in principle, to the GDPR, on account of the identical scope of relevant provisions in the two instruments, *Mircom*, C-597/19, EU:C:2021:492, para 107. Also using Opinion 2/4007: N Purtova, 'The Law of Everything. Broad Concept of Personal Data and Future of EU Data Protection Law' (2018) 10 *Law, Innovation and Technology* 40–81.
[106] It concerns concepts such as signals and communications, see chs 1 and 6. See also J Olster, 'Code is Code and Law is Law – the Law of Digitalization and the Digitalization of Law' (2021) 29 *International Journal of Law and Information Technology* 101–117.
[107] Eg, 'most of those websites store information on all access operations in logfiles' and 'IP addresses are series of digits assigned to networked computers to facilitate their communication over the internet' *Breyer*, C-582/14, paras 14–15. 'Thus, whether data are processed and transmitted by conventional, even old fashioned means … or whether the processing is by a more modern method … is not determinative', *Sergejs Buivids*, C-345/17, Opinion of AG Sharpstone, para 48.
[108] Ch 1, section I.B.
[109] González Fuster and Gutwirth (n 36) 533–35.

regulation of the automated processing of information stored in files,[110] emphasises the 'computer' acceptation of data. In the English Oxford Dictionary, such an acceptation means 'the quantities, characters, or symbols on which operations are performed by a computer, which may be stored and transmitted in the form of electrical signals and recorded on magnetic, optical, or mechanical recording media'.

As for an explicit legislative choice, the applicable law protects personal data used with two types of 'means'. The first are automated means, to which the format of computerised, binary data easily apply.[111] The second are means other than automated, namely manual means when the intention is to create a filing system, which is 'any structured set of personal data which are accessible according to specific criteria'.[112] The understanding of data as pieces of information and facts is more fitting to this second understanding. Following Recital 15 GDPR, 'the protection of natural persons should be technologically neutral and should not depend on the techniques used' to prevent the 'serious risk of circumvention'. Here the paradigm of technology neutrality, which I discuss in chapter five, applies to the techniques, or means, of data processing, but this affects, by extension, our understanding of data and information. If the definitional gap is capable of accommodating the broad material scope of data protection, it is also of difficult resolution and fuels what Purtova describes as the overreach of the definition of personal data, whereby 'everything is data and all data has meaning; hence, everything is or contains information' that could identify an individual.[113]

As for the other three cumulative elements, Article 8 CFR grants protection to a datum not as a generic unit of digitalisation, but as (ii) relating to an (iii) identified or identifiable (iv) natural person. This is because the datum's relation to an identified or identifiable natural person is, following *Breyer* and *M.I.C.M* (*Mircom*),[114] relative to the individual interpreting a datum, eg, the controller or processor.

In principle, data satisfy the 'relate to' (ii) element of the definition when they do one of three things. First, when they relate, directly or indirectly, to an individual. Second, data are personal when used for the purpose of affecting an individual. Third, they are personal when they result in affecting an individual. Know-how is excluded from the notion of personal data.

---

[110] ibid; González Fuster (n 5).
[111] Also 'automatic' in the GDPR. Eg, a video recording of persons stored on a continuous recording device, *Ryneš*, C-212/13, paras 23, 25. In *Google*, C-507/17 the meaning of automatic is assumed. In *Mircom*, C-597/19, para 33 the CJEU seems to follow the referring court, which states that the uploading of the pieces of a file is automatic 'as that characteristic can be eliminated only by certain programs'. 'Digitalisation' is to be understood as the conversion of analogue information into a digital' and mainly binary 'format in order to store it on a physical carrier', Olster (n 106) 104.
[112] GDPR, Rec 15, Art 4(6), whether centralised, decentralised or dispersed on a functional or geographical basis; it includes 'a set of personal data' 'consisting of the names and addresses and other information concerning the persons contacted, if those data are structured according to specific criteria which, in practice, enable them to be easily retrieved for subsequent use; it is unnecessary that they include data sheets, specific lists or other search methods.' *Jehovan Todistajat*, C-25/17 EU:C:2018:551, para 52.
[113] Olster relies on semantics to argue that 'data' can never be personal and proposes to talk instead of the protection of personal information (n 106) 104. Conversely, using information theory to state that information should be ultimately understood as data: R Gellert, 'Comparing Definitions of Data and Information in Data Protection Law and Machine Learning. A Useful Way Forward to Meaningfully Regulate Algorithms?' (2022) 16(1) *Regulation & Governance*. I share Gellert's conclusion in that data are the closest proxy for information and other concepts (ch 6). Purtova (n 105) 53.
[114] *Breyer*, C-582/14, paras 45–49; *Mircom*, C-597/19, para 102.

In addition, the person must be 'identified'[115] or identifiable'[116] (iii) through so-called 'identifiers', such as online identifiers, location data and factors relating to mental identity. To 'identify' means it must be possible to distinguish a person from all other members of the group through means that are reasonably likely to be used. Such means are conceived of in evolutionary terms: the assessment of the potential capability of a technology to 'identify' individuals in Recital 57 GDPR should rely on a dynamic test applied to technological developments, test tempered by a systematic interpretation of the law. In *Breyer*[117] the court found 'reasonable' means to be those within the framework of the law, provided they are lawful and include the transfer of data from third parties in possession of additional information enabling identification. Since the formulation of the GDPR is very close to that contained in the DPD interpreted in *Breyer*,[118] the Court's interpretation is arguably still relevant, as exemplified by *Mircom* and the EDPB's reference to a 'reasonability test' to determine whether data relate or not to a person based on objective and contextual aspects.[119]

Fourth, the individual must be a 'natural person', that is a living human[120] being, irrespective of residence and nationality. Such a natural person is called a data subject.

The applicable law provides examples of identifiers to distinguish data subjects, such as online identifiers, ie IP addresses, cookie identifiers and radio frequency identification tags, which are provided by the 'devices, applications, tools and protocols' of natural persons, and leave traces which are capable of identifying an individual, particularly when 'combined with unique identifiers and other information received by the servers' that allow building profiles of such individuals.[121] The array of potential identifiers supports Purtova and Olster's assertions as to the overreach of data protection law. However, the interpretive reliance on relative, objective and contextual criteria of identifiability creates a potential Achille's heel. Data that no longer identify a natural person can be considered anonymous and fall outside the scope of data protection law and therefore the right. Anonymisation has been denounced not only for its lack of robustness, which for the EDPB can be measured with the criteria of singling-out, linkability and inference, but also for its ability to enable to circumvent data protection law.[122]

---

[115] *Latvijas Republikas Saeima*, C-439/19 para 60.

[116] 'Whether the data subjects are difficult to identify is not a criterion set out in Directive 95/46', *Sergejs Buivids*, C-345/17 Opinion of AG Sharpstone, para 36.

[117] *Breyer*, C-582/14. Following the systematic interpretation of the AG (n 73).

[118] GDPR, Rec 26 contains a formulation similar to DPD, Rec 26, but places 'likely' before 'reasonably'. But *cf* D Bogdanov and T Siil, *Anonymisation 2.0: Sharemind as a Tool for De-Identifying Personal Data – Part 1: Definitions* (2018) sharemind.cyber.ee/anonymisation-2_0-part-1-definitions/.

[119] European Data Protection Board, Guidelines 04/2020 on the use of location data and contact tracing tools in the context of the COVID-19 outbreak (2020) 5.

[120] GDPR. Rec 27. Unlike the DPD, the GDPR does not protect the data of legal persons (Art 1(2), Rec 14). European Commission, 'Proposal for a Regulation of the European Parliament and of the Council on the Protection of Individuals with Regard to the Processing of Personal Data and on the Free Movement of such Data (General Data Protection Regulation)' COM (2012) 11 final. See M Viola de Azevedo Cunha, 'The Concept of Personal Data in the Post Lisbon Era: is there Need (and room) for Change?' in S Gutwirth (ed), *Data Protection in Good Health?* (Dordrecht, Springer, 2012). Personal data of legal persons are protected within the limits of Arts 12 and 13 EPD on unsolicited communications: *Schecke and Eifert*, C-92/09 and C-93/09, paras 53,87. This was relied on in *Latvijas Republikas Saeima*, C-439/19.

[121] GDPR Rec 30, Art 4(1).

[122] P Ohm, *The Rise and Fall of Invasive ISP Surveillance*, Working Paper no. 8-22 (University of Colorado Law School 2008) papers.ssrn.com/sol3/papers.cfm?abstract_id=1261344. EDPB (n 119) 5. Incidentally, this would neutralise the overreach of data protection law.

The applicable law identifies 'special categories of personal data', aka 'sensitive data', meriting reinforced protection. These are data relating to criminal convictions and offences or related security measures, 'data revealing racial or ethnic origin, political opinions, religious or philosophical beliefs, or trade union membership and concerning a natural person's sex life or sexual orientation' and, starting with the GDPR, genetic data, biometric data for the purpose of uniquely identifying a natural person and data concerning health.[123] Article 6 of Convention 108+ contains a similarly updated list of sensitive data.

Since sensitive data are, pursuant to Recital 51 GDPR 'by their nature, particularly sensitive in relation to fundamental rights and freedoms', the Court found their processing 'liable to constitute a particularly serious interference' in *GC and Others* and *Latvijas Republikas Saeima*.[124] Sensitive data are not a core principle of data protection law,[125] but rather express the instrumentality of data protection to other rights, because the processing of such data entails the potential simultaneous interference of multiple rights.[126] Following Simitis, since the normally applicable law cannot ensure adequate protection,[127] sensitive data require heightened safeguards and trigger a higher threshold for permissible interferences. The meaning of 'heightened' safeguards requires to discuss the notion of protection, discussed next.

iii. 'The Protection of': Architecture and Essence of Article 8

The meaning of 'protection' enshrined in Article 8 CFR is multi-layered. 'Protection' is both part of the name of the right and draws its meaning from a combination of human rights theory, the traditions on which the right rests and the applicable law. From a human rights perspective, protection engenders both a negative duty to refrain from interfering with the right and a positive duty of ensuring the right, which is expressed by Articles 16 TFEU and 39 TEU. Those provisions also bring into sharp focus that the object of protection is not data as such, but rather *individuals* with regard to the processing of their personal data. Duties enshrined in the notion of protection are both vertical and horizontal and may also trigger an obligation to fulfil.

'Protection' embodies and reflects the traditions informing the right to data protection, traditions helpfully synthesised by González Fuster and Gutwirth[128] as 'proscriptive' and 'permissive'. The German, proscriptive notion 'not to process' data is translated into the idea that an instrument that 'provides for the processing of personal data' 'constitutes an interference with' Article 8 CFR.[129] However, the permissibility of the interference is assessed by appraising the compliance of the safeguards enabling the

---

[123] Art 10 GDPR, protected for their ability to give rise to social disapproval and result in stigmatisation of the data subject, eg, *Latvijas Republikas Saeima*, C-439/19 para 112. GDPR, Art 9(1) defined at Arts 4(13), 4(14) and 4(15), as supplemented by Recs 34–35.
[124] *GC and Others*, C-136/17, para 44; *Latvijas Republikas Saeima*, C-439/19, para 74.
[125] But *cf* Bygrave (n 5) 145–67. Rather, they can be seen as a specification of the rule of law (proportionality) enshrined in the test for permissible limitations as I discuss in Porcedda (n 1).
[126] The context of their processing 'could create *significant risks* to the *fundamental rights and freedoms*', Rec 51 GDPR).
[127] Simitis (n 28).
[128] González Fuster and Gutwirth (n 36).
[129] *Digital Rights Ireland*, C-293/12 and C-594/12, para 36.

processing of personal data articulated by the permissive tradition (FIPs) with the test contained in Article 52 CFR. The combination of proscriptive and prescriptive traditions suffuses both case law, eg, the data retention legal saga sparked by *Digital Rights Ireland* and the Court's pronouncements on the essence of the right, and legislation via data protection principles.

Given both the prominent position of 'protection' in Article 8 and the Explanation's silence on its meaning, 'protection' must be taken to mean the 'system' or 'architecture' for safeguarding personal data expressed by the article and its sources. Recital 11 GDPR lays down three criteria for 'effective protection', which consist in the setting out in detail of: (i) the rights of data subjects; (ii) the obligations of those who process and determine the processing of personal data; and (iii) powers for monitoring, ensuring compliance with the rules and sanctions for infringements. Criteria (i) and (iii) reflect Articles 8(2) and (3) CFR and criterion (ii) is the flipside to Article 8(2) CFR. The three criteria provide the framework for the architecture of the EU applicable data protection law and the safeguards enabling the use of personal data. The architecture's structure draws from the ensemble of the provisions contained in Articles 8 CFR and 16 TFEU, as implemented by the applicable law and as interpreted by the EDPS, EDPB and courts.

Data protection principles enshrined in Articles 5(1) and (2) GDPR offer a condensed version of safeguards and particularly criteria (i) and (ii), acting as the bridge between the right and the applicable law. These are 'lawfulness, fairness and transparency', 'purpose limitation', 'data minimisation', 'accuracy', 'storage limitation', 'integrity and confidentiality' and 'accountability'. The principles 'lawfulness, fairness and transparency' and 'purpose limitation' and 'accuracy' are found in Article 8(2) CFR and I will analyse them in that context. Here I focus on the principles that are implicitly amenable to Article 8(1) CFR, 'integrity and confidentiality' and possibly 'data minimisation', to introduce which I illustrate the principle of 'accountability'.

Accountability relates to the second criterion listed in Article 11 GDPR for the 'effective protection' of data subjects: it embodies actionable protection as the architrave of the applicable data protection law. Accountability means that the entity that decides the purposes and means of processing of personal data, aka the controller,[130] is responsible for compliance with data protection principles and, by extension, the provisions of the GDPR that express such principles. Accountability thus embodies 'horizontal' protection duties incumbent upon data controllers, who are the beneficiaries of processing and act as the gatekeepers of data subject rights. Those duties are further specified in chapter IV of the GDPR and particularly by Article 24 (and 19 LED). The controller must implement appropriate technical and organisational measures (TOMs), including policies, to ensure and to be able to demonstrate that processing is performed in accordance with the GDPR. In abidance to the principle of technology neutrality (chapter five), the law rarely provides examples of TOMs, but Recital 77 clarifies that they can be identified by means of approved codes of conduct and certifications, EDPB guidelines and indications provided by a Data Protection Officer (DPO). Such obligations are

---

[130] GDPR Art 4(7). See generally, EDPB, Guidelines 07/2020 on the concepts of controller and processor in the GDPR, 7 July 2021. This begs the question whether the controller is an implicit essential component of the right; see n 141 below.

complemented by Articles 25 and 32 GDPR (as well as 20 and 29 LED and 4 EPD) that specify other principles fundamental to the notion of protection: 'data minimisation', 'accuracy', 'storage limitation', and 'integrity and confidentiality'.

The importance of 'data minimisation', 'accuracy' and 'storage limitation' to protection is exemplified by Article 25 GDPR on data protection by design and by default.[131] In detail, controllers must adopt appropriate TOMs *designed* to implement all data protection principles in an effective manner throughout the personal data life cycle (when determining the means for processing and at the time of the processing itself). Article 25(1) places a special emphasis on data minimisation, whereby the data processed must be those that are 'adequate, relevant and limited to what is necessary in relation to the purposes for which they are processed'.[132] This can be explained with the fact that, the fewer the categories of data disclosed by the data subject, the lesser the risks of breaches of security or otherwise within a single processing operation. Thus, the controller must also adopt TOMs for ensuring the principle of data minimisation *by default* (Article 25(2)). Data minimisation also links to accuracy and purpose limitation, in that a suitably carved identification of purposes leads to a more targeted collection of personal data and also good data cleansing practices.[133] Indeed, the controller must adopt TOMs to ensure that purpose limitation, accuracy and storage are respected *by default* (Article 25(2)).

The principle of 'integrity and confidentiality'[134] requires that data be processed 'in a manner that ensures appropriate security of the personal data, including protection against unauthorised or unlawful processing and against accidental loss, destruction or damage', using appropriate TOMs. Article 32 GDPR, which creates obligations for both controllers and processors, lists four TOMs: (a) pseudonymising and encrypting personal data; (b) ensuring the ongoing confidentiality, integrity, availability (aka CIA) and *resilience* of processing systems and services; (c) in case of an accident, swiftly restoring the availability and access to personal data; and (d) regularly testing, assessing and evaluating the effectiveness of the TOMs implemented. As for other duties, adherence to an approved code of conduct or certification mechanism are elements that can contribute to demonstrating compliance. Article 29 LED lists ten security-related 'controls' and TOMs.

The security and confidentiality principle is of crucial importance. In *Digital Rights Ireland*[135] the Court ruled that adherence to minimum safeguards of data security precludes an endangerment to the essence of personal data. Such a view was confirmed in *Opinion 1/15*, with a slightly different wording:

> As for the essence of the right to the protection of personal data ... the envisaged agreement ... lays down ... rules intended to ensure, inter alia, the security, confidentiality and integrity of that data, and to protect it against unlawful access and processing.[136]

---

[131] European Data Protection Board, Guidelines 4/2019 on Article 25. Data Protection by Design and by Default, v 2.0, (2020).
[132] GDPR Art 5(c); *Latvijas Republikas Saeima*, C-439/19; Art 5(4)(c), Convention 108+.
[133] 'Initially lawful processing of accurate data may, in the course of time, become incompatible with the Directive', *Google Spain and Google*, C-131/12, para 93.
[134] GDPR Art 5 (f); Convention 108+, Art 7. Art 7(j) LED refers to integrity as lack of corruption.
[135] *Digital Rights Ireland*, C-293/12 and C-594/12, para 40.
[136] *Opinion 1/15* of 26 July 2017 pursuant to Article 218(11) TFEU EU:C:2017:592, para 150.

A contrario, the essence lies in the presence of rules intended to ensure the CIA of data. Although the Court relies on secondary law, such a notion of the essence can be distilled directly from Article 8 (1). Security, confidentiality and integrity are facets of protection and there is a semantic overlap between to 'protect' and 'secure'; the Court's comments about the essence can also stem from a holistic reading of the right.[137] The 'security and confidentiality' requirement embodies a minimum threshold, in keeping with the qualified nature of the right to data protection, which tempers the application of TOMs in general.

The adoption of TOMs by the controller and, with respect to security and confidentiality, also the processor, is conditional on the nature, scope, context and purposes of processing as well as the risks of varying likelihood and severity for the rights and freedoms of natural persons. The state of the art and the cost of implementation are relevant in evaluating the use of TOMs *designed* to implement data protection principles and to ensure security pursuant to Articles 25 and 32 GDPR. The contemporary understanding reflected in the applicable law is that to protect data means to shield them against risks stemming from processing operations,[138] risks which could lead to detrimental consequences for the rights and freedoms of data subjects. Risks include discrimination, damage to the reputation, loss of rights and freedoms and may concern sensitive information of children, or effect profiling; risks also arise from the processing of large amounts of personal data and affect a large number of data subjects.[139] Loss of security engenders specific risks, such as unauthorised or unlawful processing and accidental loss, destruction or damage, as well as identity theft or fraud, financial loss, loss of confidentiality of personal data protected by professional secrecy, unauthorised reversal of pseudonymisation, accidental or unlawful alteration of data, which 'may in particular lead to physical, material or non-material damage'.[140]

There are no shortage of open-ended questions. Protection relies on the good faith of the data controller, who performs a risk assessment based on the state of the art and therefore the (cyber)security market. The 'minimum safeguards of data security' are not carved in law and indeed the supply failure by the market has prompted the intervention of the regulator (see chapter six). This casts a long shadow on the ability of Article 8(1) CFR, Articles 5(1)(f) and 32 GDPR to produce direct effects. Other questions are whether the notions of 'controller' and 'risk' are as central to the right as they are to the applicable law; I believe they are not,[141] but demonstrating these points is beyond the scope of this work.

---

[137] See Porcedda (n 1) discussing Lynseky's (n 5) holistic and Tzanou's (n 5) purposive approach.

[138] See Article 29 Data Protection Working Party, 'Statement on the Role of a Risk-Based Approach in Data Protection Legal Frameworks', in *14/EN WP 218* (2014). R Gellert, *The Risk-based Approach to Data Protection* (Oxford, Oxford Universitty Press, 2020). Risk is tied to understanding security as protection against threats, which is operationalised through risk-assessment (ch 5, section I). If and when risk-based approaches will be out of regulatory fashion, the right is formulated in a manner capable of reflecting other understandings of 'securing'.

[139] GDPR, Rec 75.

[140] GDPR, Art 5(f), Rec 83.

[141] Controllership is pivotal to secondary law but may need to be rethought in light of the ability of data pods to turn data subjects into controllers, thus torpedoing the right. Risks operationalise the provision of security as protection against threats, by providing a quantifiable approach; their prevalence reflects a regulatory fashion that may wane; the right is formulated in a manner capable of reflecting other understandings of 'securing'.

B. Paragraph Two: Obligation to Process Data Fairly, Purpose Limitation as Essence and Data Subjects' Rights

The second paragraph of Article 8 spells out the conditions under which personal data can be processed and endows data subjects with a 'bundle of subjective rights'.[142]

> Such data must be processed fairly for specified purposes and on the basis of the consent of the person concerned or some other legitimate basis laid down by law. Everyone has the right of access to data which has been collected concerning him or her, and the right to have it rectified.

i. 'Such Data must be Processed': A Double Limitation?

The expression 'such data must be processed' specifies the conditions under which personal data of individuals can be used. Processing covers

> any operation or set of operations which is performed on personal data or on sets of personal data, whether or not by automated means, such as collection, recording, organisation, structuring, storage, adaptation or alteration, retrieval, consultation, use, disclosure by transmission, dissemination or otherwise making available, alignment or combination, restriction, erasure or destruction.[143]

Processing includes 'profiling' and pseudonymisation,[144] as well as, among others: loading personal data on an internet page (by an individual); a search engine finding information published or placed on the Internet by third parties, indexing it automatically, storing it temporarily and, finally, making it available to Internet users according to a particular order of preference; making data available in association with names, even if already published; and the record of one's daily work and rest periods.[145]

In light of the ambiguous approach of the Court to the right, the wording of paragraph 2 appears to lend itself to different interpretations, including acting as a limitation supplementary to the general clause contained in Article 52 CFR.[146] For Van der Sloot, the right is 'in itself already a compromise'[147] between the legitimate interests of data subjects and market stakeholders, as expressed in the DPD. The fact that the right expresses a historical compromise does not mean the market has (retained) the upper hand, although there is a difference between interpretation and implementation.

As for interpretation, AG Szpunar stated that the GDPR 'transcends the internal-market approach of' the DPD and 'is designed to ensure a complete system of personal data protection in the'[148] EU. The Court supports the latter statement in that

---

[142] González Fuster and Gellert (n 46) 80.
[143] GDPR, Art 4(2). This definition follows DPD, Art 2(b) save for the substitution of 'blocking' by 'restriction'.
[144] Arts 4(4) and 4(5) GDPR respectively.
[145] Respectively: *Bodil Lindqvist*, C-101/01, para 25; *Weltimmo*, C-230/14, EU:C:2015:639, para 37. *Google Spain and Google*, C-131/12, para 41. *Schecke and Eifert*, C-92/09 and C-93/09, para 58 *Satakunnan and Satamedia*, C-73/07, EU:C:2008:727, paras 48–49. *Worten*, C-342/12, EU:C:2013:355, para 19.
[146] See González Fuster and Gutwirth (n 46) 532–535.
[147] Van der Sloot (n 17) s 5.
[148] *Google*, C-507/17, Opinion, para 44. Although the GDPR has many souls, it responds to the positive obligations set out in Art 16(2) TFEU in a way that appears to privilege the protection, rather than the flow, of personal data.

the GDPR aims 'to guarantee a high level of protection of personal data throughout the' EU[149] on account of its Recitals 11, 13 and Article 16 TFEU. The market imperative presents a challenge at the level of implementation, due to the centrality of data to innovation, which in turn has become instrumental to global competition. If in the 1960s McDermott could suggest that laissez faire had become '*laissez innover*',[150] today we can talk of '*laissez processer*'. Discussions around new forms of data governance may further define the interpretation of the right and its enforcement, which is addressed by Article 8(3).

The fact that Article 8(2) expresses the syncretic nature of data protection and the unavoidability of 'data processing … in modern societies'[151] does not necessarily mean it embodies a double limitation, as shown by the constraints placed on the legitimate interest legal basis.[152] By comparison, although the compromises embedded in Articles 8 ECHR and 7 CFR are not spelled out, they are nonetheless embedded and visible on a daily basis: one has a 'private' life only because one also has a public life; similarly, family life is a counterpart to life lived alone or in society. In sum, Article 8(2) of the Charter 'authorises the processing of personal data if certain conditions are satisfied',[153] conditions analysed next.

ii. [Processed] 'Fairly for Specified Purposes and on the Basis of the Consent of the Person Concerned or Some Other Legitimate Basis Laid Down by Law'

Taken as a whole, the first limb of Article 8(2) refers to the expectation that the processing must be legitimate in three ways: in relation to data protection law as a whole (fairness), the interests of the controller in pursuing the processing (purpose specification/limitation) and the legal system/*ordre public* as a whole (lawfulness). The three principles are not mutually exclusive, but rather cumulative. This is due to their common roots in the rule of law, which effects functional interconnections: fairness stems from legal certainty (and lawfulness), purpose specification from proportionality and non-arbitrariness and lawful processing stems from legality.

Such interconnections are reflected in secondary law. We begin with lawfulness and end with purpose limitation, which, similarly to security and confidentiality, play a very important role in data protection. Lawfulness and fairness are mirrored in the first data protection principle, which includes transparency. Article 5(1)(a) of the GDPR reads that personal data must be 'processed lawfully, fairly and in a transparent manner'. The conditions of lawfulness clearly refer to purpose specification and fairness.[154] The requirement whereby processing operations other than those for which the personal

---

[149] *Google*, C-507/17, para 54.
[150] J McDermott, 'A Special Supplement: Technology – the opiate of the intellectuals', *The New York Review* (1969).
[151] González Fuster and Gellert (n 46) 80.
[152] *Rīgas Satiksme*, C-13/16, ECLI:EU:C:2017:336.
[153] *Deutsche Telekom*, C-543/09, para 52.
[154] Art 6 GDPR; see also Art 8 LED. In connection to the legitimate aim of the controller, see *Google Spain and Google*, C-131/12, para 74; *Worten*, C-342/12, para 45.

data have been collected are compatible with the original purpose clearly connects with specification, fairness, consent and also lawfulness, as found in *Deutsche Telekom*.[155]

The provisions on consent[156] also link to fairness and purpose limitation. Consent has to be assessed in light of the whole GDPR, in that 'consent given in the context of a written declaration ... which constitutes an infringement ... shall not be binding'.[157] The explicit reference to consent in Article 8 CFR begs the question of its centrality to the data protection architecture as against criticisms that the concept is unable to adequately protect data subjects. Although it is useful to note that debates on consent go hand in hand with critiques of data protection as a right, it will be for future work to take sides.

Purpose limitation is also a self-standing data protection principle listed in GDPR, Article 5(1)(b), whereby data must be 'collected for specified, explicit and legitimate purposes and not further processed in a manner that is incompatible with those purposes ...'. The Article 29 Data Protection Working Party (WP29) noted that this principle is 'preliminary to several other data protection tenets and contributes to "transparency, legal certainty and predictability", which in turn enable control by the data subject'.[158] Furthermore, for the WP29 the purpose must be legitimate, specific and explicit to both controller and data subjects, thus encapsulating fairness. In *Digital Rights Ireland* the use of data for several purposes for which the data subject is not informed was seen as likely to generate a feeling of 'constant surveillance'.[159]

On such bases, the functional interconnection of the three principles can be easily explained. If a processing is not fair, then there is no guarantee of purpose limitation, which would void consent or challenge lawfulness. If the purposes of the processing are indeterminate, then the processing cannot be fair, paving the way to uninformed consent and a general disrespect for lawfulness. If the processing is carried out without consent or pursuant to the wrong legal basis, then it is unfair, and there is no guarantee that the purpose is specified and limited as expected.

Of these, purpose specification or limitation takes pride of place. The Court found in *Digital Rights Ireland* that 'EU legislation ... must lay down clear and precise rules ... so that the [concerned] persons ... have sufficient guarantees to effectively protect their personal data against the risk of abuse ...'.[160] Purpose limitation was subsequently found to relate to the essence of data protection, alongside integrity and confidentiality. In *Opinion 1/15* the Court stated that 'as for the essence of the right to the protection of personal data, enshrined in Article 8 of the Charter, the envisaged agreement limits ... the purposes for which PNR data may be processed'[161] which led to a finding of non-encroachment of the essence.

---

[155] *Deutsche Telekom*, C-543/09, para 66; Before the GDPR: Article 29 Data Protection Working Party, 'Opinion 03/2013 on Purpose Limitation', in *00569/13/EN WP 203* (2013). See also *ASNEF and FECEDM*, C-468/10 and C-469/10. GDPR, Art 6(4), Rec 50; LED Art 9(1).
[156] GDPR, Art 4(11), Rec 32. See *Bavarian Lager Ltd*, C-28/08 P, para 77.
[157] Arts 7(1)-(2) GDPR.
[158] Article 29 Data Protection Working Party (n 155), 11.
[159] *Digital Rights Ireland and Seitlinger and Others*, C-293/12 and C-594/12, para 37.
[160] ibid, para 54.
[161] *Opinion 1/15*, para 150.

C. Everyone has the Right of Access to Data which has been Collected Concerning Him or Her, and the Right to have it Rectified

The second limb of Article 8(2) lists two rights evocative of the 'participation' FIP and instrumental to at least one data protection principle. First, data subjects enjoy the right of access, ie to obtain from the controller confirmation as to whether or not personal data concerning them are being processed, to obtain a free copy of personal data being processed, if possible via electronic means and additional information about the processing.[162] Such a right includes notification of the appropriate safeguards that attach to data transferred outside of the Union. It finds its limits in the potential negative effects it may have on the rights or freedoms of others, including trade secrets or intellectual property, and in particular copyright protecting software, and law enforcement.[163]

Second, data subjects have the right to obtain from the controller without undue delay the rectification of inaccurate personal data concerning him or her. Rectification is thus antecedent to and instrumental in realising the principle of accuracy, whereby the data must be

> accurate and, where necessary, kept up to date; every reasonable step must be taken to ensure that personal data which are inaccurate, having regard to the purposes for which they are processed, are erased or rectified without delay.[164]

The importance of rectification and accuracy can be best understood in relation to the 'personal' criterion of data protection, which links it with a person and their identity. To maintain accuracy means to respect and reflect the individual's uniqueness, giving relevance to the individual behind the piece of information.[165] Data which are inaccurate become inadequate and hence, 'every reasonable step should be taken to ensure' that they are rectified,[166] whereas data which are outdated become irrelevant, and hence must be erased.[167]

In line with the interpretation given by the Court in *Google Spain* whereby the requirements of Article 8(2) were 'implemented inter alia by' several Articles of the DPD, the corresponding provisions of the GDPR – and arguably Article 16 LED – implement and further specify the content of this attribute. Sometimes the GDPR veers from the DPD and case law. For instance, Article 16 GDPR differs from the DPD, *Google Spain* and Convention 108+,[168] in that rectification is limited to the incorrectness of the data, whereas

---

[162] GDPR, Art 1, superseding *X*, C-486/12, para 25. Access can include a summary of the data held in an intellegible form, as in *YS and others*, C-141/12 and C-372/12. See also Art 9(1)(b) Convention 108+. European Data Protection Board, Guidelines 01/2022 on data subject rights – Right of access v. 1.0 (2022).
[163] GDPR Rec 63; LED Art 15.
[164] GDPR, Art 5(d). Also Convention 108+, Art 5(4)(d). Accuracy corresponds to data quality.
[165] The importance of accurate data transcends the field of personal data protection; see *U*, C-101/13, EU:C:2014:2249, paras 44, 47.
[166] GDPR, Rec 39. See *Google Spain and Google*, C-131/12, para 93.
[167] For which 'prejudice to the data subject' is not a precondition, *Google*, C-507/17, para 45. Individuals are 'not deprived of their right to de-referencing' even when they 'make their sensitive data manifestly public', although in such a case the processing is lawful. *GC and Others*, C-136/17, paras 63–65.
[168] Convention 108+, Art 9(1)(e).

the rectification becomes optional if the stored data infringes the GDPR, EU or Member State law 'to which the controller is subject'.[169] However, in cases in which the processing is unlawful, then the data subject can claim a stronger entitlement, that of erasure.

In sum, the second limb of Article 8(2) CFR takes substance in the control exercised by natural persons on their own personal data, which translate into at least six entitlements, subject to the restrictions foreseen by the GDPR.[170] Such entitlements vary in the degree of intensity and relate to each other as complementary[171] or alternative steps of a strategy geared at controlling one's data and averting the harms that may result from processing operations. In detail, individuals could demand access, resort to restriction with a view to either demand rectification or object to the processing; they could request the portability of their personal data and, as a more drastic measure, their erasure. No case law has, thus far, given indication of the essence.

D. Paragraph Three: Control by an Independent Authority Ensuring Compliance

Paragraph 3 of Article 8 reads 'compliance with these rules shall be subject to control by an independent authority'. It presupposes the existence of a supervisory authority, which is 'an essential component of the protection of individuals with regard to the processing of personal data'[172] because it is enshrined in 'primary law of the European Union', namely Articles 8(3) CFR and 16(2) TFEU.[173] The provision adds layers to the meaning of 'protection' by expressing obligations to protect and fulfil.[174] Such an independent authority is the guardian of the right[175] monitoring compliance with data protection laws.

i. 'Compliance'

'Compliance' serves the purpose of ensuring a high level of protection of 'the fundamental rights of natural persons as regards the processing of their personal data'.[176] In light of case law 'these rules' must be seen as referring to the entire system of data protection rules as opposed to the rules explicitly mentioned in Article 8 itself.

ii. 'Control'

'Control' must engender, following *Facebook*, 'effective protection from infringements of data subjects' fundamental rights', including to avoid the practice of 'forum shopping designed to circumvent' those rights and the practical application of provisions 'that

---

[169] GDPR, Rec 65.
[170] At Art 23. Convention 108+ recognises most entitlements, except for portability.
[171] Access is not a condition for exercising other rights: EDPB (n 162) 2.
[172] *Schrems*, C-362/14, para 41.
[173] ibid, para 40.
[174] Drawn from Art 16 TFEU and benefitting from its effects and those produced by the GDPR.
[175] Seen as the 'right to privacy' in *Commission v Austria*, C-614/10, EU:C:2012:631, para 52.
[176] *Facebook Ireland and Others*, C-645/19, EU:C:2021:483, para 67.

give effect to those rights'.[177] The investigation of infringements of provisions giving effect to those rights according to a risk-based approach[178] is not in keeping with obligations incumbent on authorities.[179]

Control goes hand in hand with independence, which is an expression of agency typically ascribed to humans. As such, this limb contains the seeds for acknowledging the need for the presence of human control in data processing. Secondary law provisions prohibiting or limiting the adoption of automated individual decisions go in such a direction. Bygrave suggests that human control could be a data protection principle;[180] here I argue that the requirement of human control could be derived from the combined reading of Article 8(2), second limb and Article 8(3) and thus take the form of an implicit essential component of the right.

iii. 'By an Independent Authority'

The provision for independent control has a strong basis in the rule of law, particularly in the availability of independent tribunals and an effective remedy enshrined in Article 47 CFR. Such an overlap, also noted by De Hert,[181] should not be seen as implying the redundancy of personal data protection, but rather as a demonstration of the interdependency and interrelatedness of fundamental rights.

The GDPR defines a supervisory authority as an independent public authority that is established by a Member State.[182] Whereas Member States are free to choose the most appropriate institutional model for the authority,[183] such a model must ensure 'independence'. In the context of the DPD the Court said that the wording 'with complete independence' engendered 'an autonomous interpretation, independent of Article 267 TFEU, based on the 'actual wording of that provision and on the aims and scheme' of the DPD.[184]

The essential criteria for independence are found in Articles 51 and 52 GDPR, which codify the Court's case law on the absence of directions and instructions, as well as of political influence, including the threat of early termination, which could lead to 'prior compliance' or partiality.[185] Following *Schrems*, independence, which is intended to ensure the 'effectiveness and reliability of … the protection of individuals',[186] should be also exercised vis-à-vis the Commission. An authority 'must be able to examine' the adequacy of a transfer of data in the context of hearing a claim lodged by a person with reference to such transfer, even if the Commission has already issued a decision. To do otherwise would mean depriving individuals of their right to a claim.[187] The provisions on independence serve the ultimate task of supervisory authorities, namely to ensure

---

[177] ibid, para 68.
[178] Proposed in response to accusations of underperformance by the DP Commission, Regulatory Strategy 2021–2026, (2021).
[179] *Facebook Ireland*, C-645/19, para 67.
[180] As I discuss in (n 1) elaborating on Bygrave (n 5).
[181] De Hert (n 65).
[182] GDPR, Art 4(21).
[183] *Commission v Hungary*, C-288/12, EU:C:2014:237, para 68.
[184] *Commission v Austria*, C-614/10, para 40.
[185] *Commission v Hungary*, C-288/12, paras 51–54. See also Arts 41-2 LED.
[186] *Schrems*, C-362/14, para 41.
[187] ibid, para 53.

the appropriate application of data protection rules in order to safeguard data subjects' rights and enable the free flow of personal data.[188] In order to carry out their tasks, authorities are endowed with harmonised powers[189] and are required to cooperate in an effective and sincere manner, as interpreted by the Court in *Facebook*.[190]

III. Conclusion: Essential Components of Article 8 CFR, Essence

As seen in chapter three, the Charter's open-ended provisions enable the Court to avoid defining the contents of rights once and for all, thereby interpreting rights in light of the evolution of social and legal norms. Table 1 summarises the attributes, essential components or limbs of Article 8 CFR. The first column to the left lists essential components. The next column to the right summarises its content. The last column lists the essence openly identified by the CJEU.

Table 1 Summary of essential components and essence of the right to respect for data protection

Essential component	Description	Essence (CJEU)
Protection	In the broad sense, the system or architecture of personal data protection comprising principles, rights and duties. In a more restrictive sense, the principles and related technical and organisational measures to protect individuals against harms that may derive from data processing operations. Examples are data minimisation and integrity and confidentiality.	(a contrario) The provision of security safeguards in the legal basis.
Fairness, lawfulness and purpose limitation (legitimate processing)	The expectation for data subjects that the processing must be legitimate, which refers to three interrelated principles stemming from the rule of law: • Fairness (includes transparency); • Purpose limitation (could include storage limitation); • Lawful legal basis.	The provision of purpose limitation in the legal basis.

(continued)

---

[188] For monitoring to be ensured, data should possibly be stored in the European Union: *Digital Rights Ireland*, joined case C-293/12 and C-594/12, para 68.
[189] Codified in Art 58 GDPR, unlike the DPD (*Weltimmo*, C-230/14, paras 48–49.)
[190] *Facebook Ireland*, C-645/19.

Table 1 *(Continued)*

Essential component	Description	Essence (CJEU)
Data subject rights	Data subjects' control over their personal data, enabling them to intervene in the processing. It includes: (i) accessing the data and obtaining a copy; and (ii) rectifying inaccurate data. It supports a range of options available to the data subject specified in the applicable law. Currently this includes objecting to processing, including profiling; restricting the processing of one's personal data; erasing data; and transferring one's data.	
Independent control (human oversight)	The availability of oversight concerning data processing and the respect of the principles relating to the processing of personal data. Expresses the rule of law principle of access to justice, entitling individuals to claim without hindrance the intervention of an authority for the protection of his or her right. It can implicitly command human involvement in the processing and that a human being must be involved in the process (also drawn from data subject rights).	
Sensitive data: affect the threshold of permissible interferences.		

The elements of the essence identified by the Court appear to be strongly connected to the traditions that gave rise to data protection: data security is reminiscent of the proscriptive tradition, whereas purpose limitation embodies the permissive tradition. I will elaborate these in further work. Other essential components could include an essence, which should however only be identified on the basis of broad scholarly consensus;[191] a purposive reading of the right supports the inclusion of *access* and *human oversight* in the essence. The evolution of data protection from principles, to legal requirements, to right endowed with an essence generates a complex architecture whereby some requirements are more stringent than others and call for reinforced duties on the parts of the beneficiaries of the processing vis-à-vis data subjects. This point will be taken up in the next chapter, to which I turn.

---

[191] See ch 1 and method in Porcedda (n 1).

PART 2

Technology and the Triad in the DSM, the AFSJ and the EA

5

Cybersecurity, Privacy and Data Protection as Techno-Legal Objects: Investigating the Role of Technology

Chapters two to four analysed cybersecurity as a policy object and privacy and data protection as fundamental rights in EU law. This chapter builds on such analysis to investigate the mode of interaction between cybersecurity, data protection and privacy (the triad). In chapter one I proposed five relational modes, of which four are viable in EU law: weak reconciliation through balancing, indifference, strong reconciliation through complementarity and overlap (complete reconciliation).

I begin by examining whether the common goals of integrity and confidentiality create overlaps (I). To examine the role of integrity and confidentiality I look at the triad as techno-legal objects; I compare and contrast the engineering/computer science and legal approaches to the triad, which are not fully amenable to one another. Such an analysis brings to the fore the role of technology understood in scientific terms and as a 'regulatory target'.[1]

The techno-legal analysis shows the triad could overlap, but not spontaneously; the analysis also reveals hidden tensions, including between privacy and data protection. Strong reconciliation could still be achieved if clashes were resolved, but only as a result of explicit design choices mandated by legislation. However, the available technology law techniques are not up to the task.

The remainder of the chapter analyses such technology law techniques with a focus on technology neutrality and 'by design', which are inherently imperfect and prone to collision (II). I show that the use of such techniques within co-decision delegatory frameworks gives rise to the disappearance or more properly the 'effacement of technology'. Thus, technology becomes invisible and feeds an indeterminacy loop that hinders the resolution of clashes inherent in the technological underpinnings of the triad.

The indeterminacy loop creates problems in the courts and the resulting legislation falls short of redressing market failures to the detriment of cybersecurity, privacy

---

[1] Borrowing the expression used by LB Moses, 'How to Think about Law, Regulation and Technology: Problems with 'Technology' as a Regulatory Target' (2013) 5 *Law, Innovation and Technology* 5, and in keeping with her invitation to privilege the evolving socio-technical landscape.

and data protection taken alone and within the triad (III). The analysis sets the ground for chapters six to eight, which investigate the mode of relationship of the triad in the Digital Single Market (DSM), Area of Freedom, Security and Justice (AFSJ) and External Action (EA).

I. Leveraging Technology to Appraise the Reconciliation of the Triad

Cybersecurity, privacy and data protection all aim to preserve confidentiality; integrity is explicitly important to cybersecurity and data protection and implicitly to some facets of privacy. If confidentiality and integrity coincided across the triad, there could be a strong case for the triad to overlap and therefore be completely reconcilable. Treating the elements of the triad as techno-legal objects allows for the investigation of such a possibility. In practice, this means to marry work on security properties, protection goals and design strategies stemming from threat modelling with the categorisation of privacy and data protection as rights endowed with essential components and essence.

I begin with 'technological' conceptualisations to explain threat modelling, security properties, protection goals and design strategies, which are synthetically illustrated in Table 1. I then add the 'legal' conceptualisation of rights I discussed in chapters three and four, the results of which are shown in Tables 2 and 3. I finally question whether integrity and confidentiality as well as other relevant protection goals bear the same meanings and scope, from both an engineering/computer science (technologists') and legal perspective.

A. Technology: Security Properties, Threat Modelling, Protection Goals and Design Strategies

Herrmann and Pridöhl explain that cybersecurity builds on the identification of assets[2] to protect against threats, understood as undesired events or attacks of a safety or security origin to which assets are exposed, such as exploits stemming from weaknesses.[3] The impact of an attack on an asset multiplied by the likelihood that an attack takes place – which depends on exposure, exploitability and potential for success – provides the

---

[2] As 'any circumstance or event with the potential to adversely impact an asset through unauthorized access, destruction, disclosure, modification of data, and/or denial of service.' Following ISO/IEC PDTR 13335, assets are 'anything that has value to' an entity. European Network and Information Security Agency (ENISA), 'Glossary' (*ENISA*) www.enisa.europa.eu/topics/threat-risk-management/risk-management/current-risk/risk-management-inventory/glossary.

[3] D Herrmann and H Pridöhl, 'Basic Concepts and Models of Cybersecurity', in M Christen (ed), *The Ethics of Cybersecurity* (Cham, Springer, 2020) 16. A weakness is a generic type of mistakes that occurs frequently and vulnerabilities are the concrete realisation of a weakness.

calculation of risk.[4] Cybersecurity entails continuous risk assessment and management exercises premised on threat modelling. The identification of threats is conceptually tied to security canons, principles or properties (security properties (SPs)).

SPs have evolved over time and grown in number: they include both the original *confidentiality, integrity* and *availability* (CIA) and authentication, authorisation or control, reliability and utility. Such properties have acquired stable definitions through the work of Standards Setting Organisations (SSOs), such as the International Standardisation Organisation (ISO) and the International Telecommunication Union (ITU). Table 1 shows the definitions of all SPs contained in ISO 27000 and ITU-T X.800. Smith notes that 'attempts to codify information security principles for general practice have ... failed to thrive'.[5]

Threat modelling consists of analysing the system to be protected through the lens of an attacker. There exist several forms of threat modelling, such as OWASP's Threat Modelling Cheat Sheet and PASTA, and the very successful Cyber Kill Chain® and ATT&CK™, standing for Adversarial Tactics, Techniques, and Common Knowledge.[6] A good reference for explanatory purposes is the now-deprecated Microsoft STRIDE model.[7] STRIDE is the acronym of threats that are the negation of information SPs: Spoofing negates authentication, Tampering challenges integrity, Repudiation negates non-repudiation, Information disclosure challenges confidentiality, Denial of service hinders availability and Elevation of privilege challenges authentication.

Protection goals (PGs) are the privacy and data protection counterpart to SPs and have been identified through work that took inspiration from threat modelling. Examples include the LINDDUN project containing a fully-fledged privacy threat modelling premised on Microsoft STRIDE, the ENISA study on engineering privacy by design (PbD) and the Internet Engineering Task Force (IETF) Request for Comments (RFC) 6973.[8] The first two studies identify a different set of protection goals[9] that show strong similarities, so that in this analysis they are clustered together, with definitions provided in Table 1. A word of caution is that both the ENISA and LINDDUN studies

---

[4] ibid.

[5] RE Smith, 'A Contemporary Look at Saltzer and Schroeder's 1975 Design Principles' (2012) 10 *IEEE Security & Privacy* 20.

[6] PASTA at www.owasp.org/images/a/aa/AppSecEU2012_PASTA.pdf (16–61); E Hutchins, M Cloppert and R Amin, *Intelligence-driven computer network defense informed by analysis of adversary campaigns and intrusion kill chains* (Lockheed Martin, 2011); MITRE: attack.mitre.org/.

[7] Microsoft, 'The STRIDE Threat Model' (*Microsoft*, 2005) msdn.microsoft.com/en-us/library/ee823878 (v=cs.10).aspx; Microsoft, 'Applying STRIDE' (*Microsoft*, 2005) msdn.microsoft.com/en-us/library/ee798544%28v=cs.20%29.aspx

[8] G Danezis et al., *Privacy and Data Protection by Design – from Policy to Engineering* (ENISA 2014); K Wuyts, *LINDDUN: a privacy threat analysis framework*; Internet Engineering Task Force (IETF), *Privacy Considerations for Internet Protocols. Request for Comments (RFC) 6973* (2022).

[9] Eg, LINNDUN features unlinkability, anonymity and pseudonymity, undetectability and undefinability, plausible deniability, confidentiality, content awareness, policy and consent compliance. The ENISA study includes unlinkability, plausible deniability, CIA, transparency and intervenability. See MG Porcedda, *Privacy by Design in EU law. Matching Privacy Protection Goals with the Essence of the Rights to Private Life and Data Protection* (Lecture Notes in Computer Science, 2018), which this chapter develops.

conflate privacy with data protection, the former because it draws from the repealed Data Protection Directive (DPD), the latter because it builds on the understanding of privacy elaborated by US scholar Solove.

To safeguard protection goals, some authors, including those involved in the ENISA study, propose design strategies (DSs), understood as tools to 'translate vague legal norms in concrete design requirement'.[10] Accordingly, a system of data processing should *minimise* the amount of data, *hide* it from view, *store* data in separate batches and *aggregate* data whenever possible. A system of data processing should enable its controllers to *inform* individuals whose data are being collected, *enforce* the rules, and *demonstrate* their enforcement; moreover, it should enable both controllers and individuals to *control* how the system works and to question the data.[11] DSs correspond directly or indirectly to PGs and thus to threats, as shown synthetically in Table 1.

Table 1 maps the relationship between SPs and PGs (first column), their definitions (second column), corresponding threats (third column) and DSs (forth column). The symbol (*) shows an overlap between protection goals and security properties at least in some models. Authentication is a specification of availability and integrity, marked by the symbol (❖) to highlight that this property could be strongly connected to protection goals corresponding to those two security properties. The symbol (✚) highlights a clash between the protection goals and security property plausible deniability and non-repudiation. Sources are shown in square brackets: [E] for Enisa, [L] for LINDDUN, [M] for Microsoft STRIDE, [ITU] for X.800/811 and [ISO] for 27000. Where relevant, footnotes point to a different source. Entries with no source are my own additions.

B. Linking Technological and Legal Notions of Cybersecurity, Privacy and Data Protection

The previous section analysed cybersecurity, privacy and data protection as 'technological' objects endowed with SPs, PGs and DSs. To this is added the analysis of privacy and data protection as 'legal' objects, ie, rights endowed with essential components and an essence, with a view to assessing the reconcilability of the triad. I begin with privacy, continue with data protection and then discuss the findings.

Table 2 illustrates the connection between privacy and cybersecurity as techno-legal objects. Reading the table from left to right, the columns list the paragraphs of Article 7 CFR, the corresponding essential components, the essence as identified by the CJEU, PGs and SPs and finally DSs.

---

[10] J-H Hoepman, *Privacy by Design Strategies (The Little Blue Book)* (2022) 2.
[11] Danezis et al (n 8).

Table 1 Definitions of security properties, protection goals and design strategies

Protection goals/ Security properties	Definition	Threats	Design strategy
Availability* ✥	The property of being accessible and useable upon demand by an authorised entity [ISO][ITU]; data is accessible and services are operational [E]	Denial of Service [M]	
Confidentiality*	The property that information is not made available or disclosed to unauthorised individuals, entities, or processes [ISO][ITU]; protection of communications or stored data against interception and reading by unauthorised persons [E]; hiding the data content or controlled release of data content [L]	Disclosure of information [M] [L]	Aggregate, minimise, separate
Integrity* ✥	The property that data has not been altered or destroyed in an unauthorised manner [ITU]; Property of accuracy and completeness [ISO]; data which has been sent, received, or stored are complete and unchanged [E]	Tampering [M]	Control?
Intervenability	Intervention is possible concerning all ongoing or planned privacy-relevant data processing, in particular by those persons whose data are processed [E]	Non-intervenability	Hide
Plausible deniability ✥	The ability to deny having performed an action that other parties can neither confirm nor contradict (eg a whistleblowers can deny action) [L]	Non-repudiation [L] ✥	
Transparency	Privacy-relevant data processing, including the legal, technical and organisational setting, can be understood and reconstructed at any time [E]. Amenable to content awareness: users are aware of their personal data and only the minimum necessary information is sought and used for the performance of the function to which it relates + policy and consent compliance: the whole system informs data subjects about the system policy, or allow to specify consent before access the system [L].	Content unawareness – Policy and consent non-compliance [L]	

(continued)

Table 1 *(Continued)*

Protection goals/ Security properties	Definition	Threats	Design strategy
Unlinkability – Anonymity and Pseudonymity – Undetectability and unobservability	Privacy-relevant data cannot be linked across domains that are constituted by a common purpose and context: processes have to be operated in such a way that the privacy-relevant data are unlinkable to any other set of privacy relevant data outside of the domain. [L][E]. Includes Anonymity and Pseudonymity – Undetectability and unobservability [L]	Linkability – Indentifiability – Detectability [L]	Inform Minimise?

Security properties	Definition	Threat	
Authentication	The process of corroborating an identity [ISO][ITU]	Spoofing [M]	
Authorisation ✤	The granting of rights, including the granting of access based on access rights [ITU]	✤ Elevation of privilege [M]	
Non-repudiation ✤	The ability to prevent a sender from denying later that he or she sent a message or performed an action.	Repudiation [M]	
Reliability	Property of consistent intended behaviour and results [ISO]	Unreliability	
Utility	The information is relevant and useful for the purpose for which it is needed [ITU][12]	Uselessness	

[12] See International Telecommunications Union, XSTR-SEC-MANUAL, Security in telecommunications and information technology, 7th edn, ITU-T Technical Report (09/2020).

Table 2 Technical and legal understandings of the right to privacy (Article 7 CFR)

	Essential component	Essence (CJEU)	Protection goal (PG) & security property (SP)	Design strategy (DSs)
Private life		Revelation of very specific information concerning the private life of a person (not limited to certain aspects)	Confidentiality (PG/SP) Authorisation (SP) Authentication (SP) Unlinkability (PG)	Hide Aggregate, minimise, separate
	i. Physical & psychological integrity			
	ii. Personal social & sexual identity	The expression of one's sexual identity	/	/
	iii. Personal development, autonomy & participation ('outer circle')		/	/
Family	Family	For a father, the possibility to apply for the right to custody	/	/
Communications	Communications	The content of one's communications	Confidentiality (PG/SP) Plausible deniability (PG) Authentication/ authorisation (SP)	Hide
Home	Home		Unlinkability (PG) Confidentiality (PG/SP)	Separate Hide

The essential component 'family' does not give rise to PGs and SPs that are independent from private life, communications and home. Private life concerns those elements that are relevant to develop and maintain one's personality and identity, understood as unique and worthy of equal respect. For the CJEU, the revelation of very specific information concerning the private life of a person, not limited to certain aspects thereof, affects the essence of the right. In this guise, the PG/SP confidentiality and related design strategy 'hide' are instrumental to preserving the essence. The SPs authorisation and authentication could also be used as mechanisms to limit access to information that may impinge on the essence, to check with certainty the identification of a party (the intended sender or recipient of communications) and subsequently gain access to a service or device if one has the permission to access it. Keeping very specific information private could be achieved with the PG unlinkability and related DSs aggregate, minimise and separate.

'Communications' concerns the ability to share information with other individuals, under the presumption that information shared privately should remain confidential, regardless of its content and the mode of communication and with the expectation that any information shared privately will not be used against the individual. The content of communications represents, for the CJEU, an element of the essence. The SPs confidentiality, authentication and authorisation could help protect this essential component and the essence for the same reasons expounded for private life. The PG of plausible deniability could also matter in the case of a whistle-blower wishing to deny their actions. The relevant DS is 'hide'.

The essential component 'home' refers to one's settled and secure place in the community, where individuals can develop ties of an intimate nature and nurture self-determination, far away from the public gaze and undesired intrusion. This essential component is also enhanced by the SP confidentiality against measures of surveillance (eg listening devices, cameras etc) and the PG unlinkability. The latter calls for the DSs 'hide' in relation to a minimum zone of physical intimacy and the DS 'separate', which enables to discard information capable of violating the essence.

Should other facets of the essence come to surface, other PGs, SPs and DSs could acquire protective significance. Future research will enrich the table with references to provisions in the applicable law to highlight gaps and areas of intervention.

Table 3 illustrates the relationship between the right to data protection and cybersecurity as techno-legal objects. Reading the table from left to right, the columns list the paragraphs of Article 8 CFR, the corresponding essential components, the essence as identified by the CJEU, the corresponding principles in the GDPR and FIPs, protection goals (PGs), DSs and SPs.

All essential components of data protection benefit from a combination of PGs, SPs and DSs. I focus on the essential component 'legitimate processing' to help illustrate Table 3. The component embodies the expectation for data subjects that the processing must be legitimate, which refers to three interconnected principles stemming from the rule of law: fairness, purpose limitation and lawful legal basis. Transparency is subsumed under fairness. Fairness and transparency are served by the PG transparency, particularly in the LINDDUN sense of policy and consent compliance, in a self-explanatory manner. Purpose limitation, which also expresses a core area of the right, relates to the PG/SP confidentiality and the DSs 'hide', in that data which are not disclosed to unauthorised parties are less likely to be processed unlawfully. It also calls for the PG unlinkability, in that personal data kept in separate batches, aggregated, or minimised are also less likely to be processed without authorisation. Confidentiality and unlinkability appear important PGs/SPs to protect the essence.

The analysis in Tables 2-3 shows that PGs leverage the CIA SPs to protect and fulfil the right to data protection and especially the essence identified by the CJEU. Many more SPs and PGs are useful for data protection than they are for privacy. This is not surprising when considering that PGs were developed to pursue 'data privacy'. Furthermore, there is a strong relationship between SPs and FIPs: Willy Ware, who as Yost explains was involved in early discussions on information security standards, chaired the Records, Computers and the Rights of Citizens' panel that elaborated Fair Information Practices Principles (FIPs).[13] SPs and PGs appear to work in a mostly

---

[13] JR Yost, 'A History of Computer Security Standards', in K de Leeuw and J Bergstra (eds), *The History of Information Security* (Oxford, Elsevier Science, 2007); W Ware, (chair), *Records, Computers and the Rights of Citizens. Report of the Secretary's Advisory Committee on Automated Personal Data Systems* (1973). See ch 4, section I.

Table 3 Technical and legal understandings of the right to data protection (article 8 CFR)

Art 8		Essential component	Essence (CJEU)	GDPR Principle (& FIP)	Protection goals (PGs)	Design strategy	Security property (SPs)
Paragraph 1	Protection	The whole architecture of data protection ToMs: Security Subsumed ToM minimisation	confidentiality & integrity	Integrity and confidentiality FIP security	**Confidentiality Availability, Integrity** Intervenability	Hide Control Minimise	**Availability** Authentication and non-repudiation (organisational measures) **Confidentiality Integrity**
				Data minimisation FIP collecting limitation	Unlinkability Transparency		Integrity Utility
Paragraph 2	Legitimate processing	Lawful legal basis Fairness Subsumed: transparency		Lawfulness, fairness and transparency FIP openness	**Transparency** (policy & consent compliance)	/ Inform	Authorisation
		Purpose specification	Purpose limitation	Purpose limitation FIPs purpose specification, use limitation	Confidentiality Unlinkability *Intervenability*	Hide Separate (minimise, aggregate) *Demonstrate*	Confidentiality
	Individual rights[14]	Access Rectify		Accuracy FIPs individual participation, data quality	**Availability Non-repudiation Integrity** Intervenability Transparency	Control Inform Delete	**Availability** Authentication **Integrity Non-repudiation**
Paragraph 3	Oversight	Supervisory authority*		FIP Independent Control	Intervenability[15]	Control	Non-repudiation
		Implied: Human intervention (also from data subjects' rights)		Accountability FIP accountability	ditto	ditto	Ditto
Sensitive data: makes interferences automatically severe (It affects the threshold of permissible limitations and can help exercising other rights freely)					Unlinkability, confidentiality *[Plausible deniability]*	Separate	Confidentiality

---

[14] This essential component implies other rights laid down in the GDPR.
[15] It presupposes non-repudiation.

complementary manner, with some limitations. By reflecting on complementarity and limitations of the techno-legal understandings of cybersecurity, privacy and data protection it becomes possible to draw some conclusions as to the reconcilability of the triad.

C. Mode of Reconciliation of the Triad: From Overlap to Indeterminacy

The triad's common properties could potentially lead to an overlap, whereby the triad is fully reconciled, in that cybersecurity, privacy and data protection coincide. However, to assess whether the triad overlaps or is otherwise strongly reconciled it is necessary to address three observations and related questions raised by the analysis of cybersecurity, privacy and data protection as techno-legal objects.

First of all, 'CIA' express both SPs and PGs. The same could apply to authentication as a by-product of integrity and availability. Insofar as these dimensions fulfil cybersecurity, data protection and privacy, one could say that the triad overlaps. Although it is beyond this research to investigate which causes the other, the matter would be secondary in light of the triad's coincidence. But does strong reconciliation in the guise of overlap hold in practice? We must consider whether technologists and lawyers share a common vocabulary.[16]

Second, and by contrast to the first point, intervenability, non-repudiation and plausible deniability seem to be at odds with one another.[17] Intervenability presupposes the SP non-repudiation, which means the ability to prevent senders from denying later that they sent a message or performed an action, so that liability can be attributed. While this is very important for personal data protection, namely to ensure the accountability of data controllers, it undermines plausible deniability as instrumental to confidential communications and thus privacy. Intervenability can also both enhance and undermine sensitive data. Tensions across PGs and SPs pit privacy against data protection and point to areas of potential tension within both; further research could show similar tension within cybersecurity. How can such tensions be eased?

Third, the analysis performed in these pages was unrelated to the practice of risk management and the courts' protection of fundamental rights based on the proportionality test. Both exercises have points in common but are fundamentally different in nature. How do the overlaps and tensions highlighted pan out when compared to the reality of risk management and proportional assessment?

The three questions posed are interrelated and warrant a joint answer. Let us begin with the joint vocabulary, to then consider the third and second questions. For technologists, CIA, authentication, etc, are SPs, loosely defined by standards such as ISO 27000 and ITU-T X.800. Technologists acknowledge the legal significance of privacy and data protection but are not bound by it. Anderson sees privacy as 'the ability and/or right to protect your personal information and … to prevent invasions of your personal space',

---

[16] A discussion of ontologies is beyond the scope of this work and will be tackled in further research.
[17] Which reinforces arguments about 'by design' approaches not being easy fixes to privacy and data protection. See section II.B below.

whereas confidentiality 'involves an obligation to protect some other person's or organisation's secrets if you know them'.[18]

The IETF recognises that 'privacy is a complicated concept with a rich history that spans many disciplines ... often ... applied to personal data'[19] but traditionally only dealt with 'data confidentiality and integrity' narrowly understood.[20] Rachovitsa notes that the IETF broadened its approach after Edward Snowden's revelations[21] and started working on privacy by design (PbD), as exemplified by RFC 6973's consideration of PGs including data minimisation, anonymity and confidentiality (but not integrity).[22] PGs are to privacy and data protection what SPs are to cybersecurity.

In law, confidentiality and integrity do not have settled meaning; availability and other properties rarely surface in legal documents. General Comment 16, interpreting the International Covenant on Civil and Political Rights' right to privacy, states that 'the integrity and confidentiality of correspondence should be guaranteed de jure and de facto'.[23] A search of UN-related case law using the keywords 'integrity' and 'confidentiality' does not yield any results.[24] If this is unsurprising, given that rights acquire greater significance in smaller jurisdictions, case law on the European Convention on Human Rights and Charter[25] do not fare better.

There are as many nuances of the meaning of confidentiality as there are situations protected by both Articles 7 CFR and 8 ECHR. ECtHR case law on e-communications, interception and secret measures of surveillance[26] rarely unpacks the meaning of 'confidentiality' and 'integrity' vis-à-vis data or e-communications.[27] The CJEU, whose case law explicitly addresses integrity and confidentiality in cyberspace,[28] similarly does not offer exhaustive definitions. While the reasons and consequences of such an approach are discussed later, for the time being the point is that there is little by way of supranational case law that can create a bridge bewtween the legal and technological understanding of confidentiality and integrity.

The applicable law differs slightly from case law, as both the e-Privacy Directive (EPD) and the General Data Protection Regulation (GDPR)[29] refer to confidentiality,

---

[18] R Anderson, *Security Engineering. A Guide to Building Dependable Distributed Systems*, 2nd edn (New York, Wiley, 2011) 29. In addition, secrecy is 'an engineering term that refers to the effect of the mechanisms used to limit the number of principals who can access information'. (ibid).

[19] IETF (n 8).

[20] Internet Engineering Task Force (IETF), *Internet Security Glossary, v.2. Request for Comments (RFC) 4949* (2007).

[21] A Rachovitsa, 'Engineering and Lawyering Privacy by Design: Understanding Online Privacy both as a Technical and an International Human Right Issues' (2016) 24 *International Journal of Law and Information Technology* 374.

[22] IETF (n 8).

[23] Human Rights Committee (CCPR), *General Comment n. 16. Article 17 (The right to Respect of Privacy, Family, Home and Correspondence, and Protection of Honour and Reputation)* (1988).

[24] See juris.ohchr.org/search/documents.

[25] Council of Europe [1950] ETS n. 005; Charter [2012] OJ C326/391 (CFR).

[26] Jurisconsult of the ECtHR, *Guide on Article 8 of the European Convention on Human Rights. Right to respect for private and family life* (last updated 31 December 2020).

[27] Eg, *S. and Marper v the United Kingdom*, case nos. 30562/04 and 30566/04 CE:ECHR:2008:1204JUD 003056204 para 99.

[28] Such as *Digital Rights Ireland* and *Opinion 1/15* on the essence of data protection and privacy, see chs 3–4.

[29] E-privacy Directive 2002/58/EC [2002] OJ L201/37 (EPD); General Data Protection Regulation (EU) 2016/679 [2016] OJ L119/1 (GDPR).

and to a more limited extent integrity. Examples can be found in Regulations detailing the EPD[30] and, in the GDPR, Recitals 39, 49, 75 and 83, Articles 32 and obviously 5(1)(f) on integrity and confidentiality. Such provisions fall short of explicitly referring to ITU and ISO standards or definitions, but their language is close to the technological understanding of confidentiality and integrity, especially on account of the provisions' spirit informed by a risk-management logic understood as the containment of threats.

What is more, technologists and legislators do not always deal with the same object of protection: often the former are concerned with the assets of an organisation, typically legal people, while the latter deal with individual right bearers, typically natural people. Technologists and legislators do not share by default a common vocabulary, so that the overlap between the triad is not a guaranteed outcome.

What about technologists' and legislators' practice being amenable to one another? The court's language when reviewing interferences with fundamental rights, including interferences caused by technology, is the test for permissible limitations. Technologists' focus on risk management as the containment of threats resembles the courts' focus on limiting interferences and state obligations to respect and protect rights.[31] Taking into account due differences between risk management and proportionality assessments, the alignment between threats, SPs, PGs, DSs, essential components and the essence, offers a template for observing the overlap of the triad and potentially effecting its reconciliation.

Such an approach is, however, hindered in practice by features that risk management and proportionality assessment have in common. Although the proportionality assessment within judgments of the CJEU and ECtHR have binding interpretive force, unlike risk assessments which are performed by and for discrete entities, both proportionality and risk assessments are sensitive to technological change. The outcome of both types of assessment could warrant re-examination when measures are implemented by new technological solutions that create new circumstances. Furthermore, risk assessments and judgments are contingent, if in a different manner, as risk assessments are performed on a case-by-case basis.[32] The test for permissible limitations follows a loose template, which in the EU includes a core-periphery addition that adds a new threshold of intrusions, to avoid a reductionist approach to fundamental rights.[33] The test is however not set in stone, which is compounded with the absence of an exhaustive definition of the rights to privacy and data protection.

Born from the evolutive interpretation of human rights,[34] the absence of an exhaustive definition of the scope, contents and essence of privacy and data protection turns them into open-ended legal objects. Such open-endedness hinders the establishment of an a priori threshold of intrusion for legislative as well as technological measures and ushers in the need to resort to case-by-case litigation to establish the permissibility

---

[30] Commission Regulation 611/2013/EU of 24 June 2013 on the measures applicable to the notification of personal data breaches under Directive 2002/58/EC of the European Parliament and of the Council on privacy and electronic communications (Commission Regulation on Data Breaches) [2013] OJ L172/2.

[31] Arguing risk management and balancing both serve proportionality: R Gellert, *The Risk-based Approach to Data Protection* (Oxford, Oxford University Press, 2020) 240.

[32] ibid 241.

[33] See ch 1, section II.A.ii.

[34] Eg, 'living instrument' and 'practicality and effectiveness' doctrines. P De Hert, 'A Human Rights Perspective on Privacy and Data Protection Impact Assessments' in P De Hert and D Wright (eds), *Privacy Impact Assessment*, vol 6 (Dorcrecht, Springer, 2012). See chs 3–4.

of limitations. Such a process may take years, during which the technology being challenged becomes prevalent and difficult to eradicate due to vested interests, as argued by Tribe and Collingridge: making 'any regulatory effort will be expensive, dramatic and resisted'.[35]

Courts do not supply guidelines to choose between conflicting PGs, SPs and DSs that play out across or within single technologies and systems. Easing such clashes[36] can only be the product of a conscious decision of prioritising one value over the other. However, secondary law also fails to provide guidance on how to choose between conflicting properties and goals, as discussed shortly.

In sum, the techno-legal analysis aligning threats, SPs, PGs, DS, essential components and the essence offers a framework for observing the overlap of the triad and a possible template for informing the choice of permissible technologies that effect maximum reconciliation. Such a template is currently unstable due to the combined: (i) lack of a common vocabulary between technologists and legislators; (ii) inherent tensions in PGs/SPs; (iii) the open-ended interpretation of the essential components and essence of privacy and data protection; (iv) the nature of secondary law. This leads not only to uncertainty as to the overlap of the triad, but also to the potential indeterminacy of reconciliation. Such indeterminacy is so engrained in the law that the assessment of reconciliation can only be performed on a case-by-case basis, by delving into the technologies used to implement a given measure. The remainder of this chapter aims to demonstrate why the law leads to indeterminacy and with what consequences.

II. Technology as a Regulatory Target: The Effacement of Technology from the Law and its Consequences

EU technology law draws from a variety of techniques, a compendium of which is the Better Regulation toolbox.[37] The following analysis focusses on technology neutrality (TN), 'by design' and the related concepts of technical and organisational measures (TOMs) and state of the art (SoA), as well as standards. The choice of principles and techniques is dictated by intellectual parsimony. Other relevant concepts, such as risk, contribute to the 'effacement of technology' and extant indeterminacy but arguably do not cause them;[38] for techniques and concepts more widely, I defer to the regulation literature,[39] which informs part of this analysis without however being its main focus.

---

[35] D Collingridge, *The Social Control of Technology* (Pinter 1980); L Tribe, *Channeling Technology Through Law* (Bracton Press Ltd, 1973) cited by JA Chandler, 'The Autonomy of Technology: Do Courts Control Technology or Do They Just Legitimize its Social Acceptance?' (2007) 27 *Bulletin of Science, Technology and Society* 339.

[36] As exemplified by 'the processing of personal data to the extent strictly necessary and proportionate for the purposes of ensuring network and information security ... by [entities] constitutes a legitimate interest of the data controller concerned.' Rec 49 Regulation 2016/679/EU, [2016] OJ L119/1 (GDPR).

[37] European Commission, Better Regulation Toolbox (2021).

[38] See especially, H-W Micklitz and T Tridimas (eds), *Risk and EU Law* (Cheltenham, Edward Elgar Publishing, 2015); building on the work of Julia Black, Gellert (n 31) stresses that regulation and risk assessment both aim to prevent harms, 18, 46–47. For Impact Assessments, De Hert and Wright (n 34).

[39] See especially, J Black, 'Critical Reflections on Regulation' (2002) 27 *Australian Journal of Legal Philosophy*; R Baldwin, M Cave and M Lodge, *Understanding Regulation. Theory, Strategy and Practice*, 2nd edn (Oxford, Oxford University Press. 2011). M Goodwin, B-J Koops and R Leenes, *Dimensions of Technology Regulation* (Nymegen, Wolf Legal Publishers (WLP), 2010).

After reviewing the pros and cons of TN and 'by design' and their potential collision (III.A–III.B), I observe how they operate in practice, by leveraging TOMs and SoA as well as standards, thus connecting with co-decision delegatory forms of regulation (III.C). In so doing, I highlight how such regulatory techniques and frameworks initially helped depoliticising technology,[40] so that it could be regulated within what is now the Single Market. However, taking inspiration from Chandler's suggestion that technology becomes invisible in court,[41] I conclude (III.D) by showing how the interplay of such techniques and regulatory frameworks make technology disappear from the law and creates an indeterminacy that prevents one from identifying a priori a mode of reconciliation of the triad.

A. The Principle of Technology Neutrality

The principle of technology neutrality (TN) relates to debates as to whether technology is ever 'neutral';[42] in law, it requires that legislation does neither favour ('force') nor discriminate against a specific technology. TN is inherently ambiguous and changes meaning according to its use in practice.

In the literature, TN can have one of six meanings: (i) performance standards clarifying the desired output and limiting negative externalities, but not the technology to achieve it, as in Better Regulation frameworks and the NIS Directive; (ii) the desired principle to apply across the board, as in the now repealed Framework Directives; (iii) an approach that abstains from picking technological winners, and pushes the market in that direction, as found in the OECD principles for Internet Regulation;[43,44] (iv) a way to future-proof the law;[45] (iv) frameworks that apply online as they do offline, that is that are functionally equivalent;[46] (vi) neutrality as to the implementation of a type of technology.[47]

---

[40] J Kronlund, *Integration through Depoliticization: how a Common Technology Policy was Established in the EU* (CORE (Copenhagen Research Project on European Integration) Working Paper, 1995).
[41] Chandler (n 35).
[42] A Carr-Chellman and D Carr-Chellman, 'Special Issue: Technology Neutrality, Ethics, Values, and Human Social Systems' (2012) 52 *Educational Technology*; M Hildebrandt and L Tielemans, 'Data Protection by Design and Technology Neutral Law' (2013) 29 *Computer Law & Security Review* 509.
[43] OECD, *OECD Council Recommendation on Principles for Internet Policy Making* (2011).
[44] W Maxwell and M Bourreau, *Technology neutrality in Internet, telecoms and data protection regulation* (Global Media and Communications Quarterly, 2014); M Cave and T Shortall, 'How Incumbents can Shape Technological Choice and Market Structure – the Case of Fixed Broadband in Europe' (2016) 18(2) *Info* 1–16. For goal (iii), Hildebrandt and Tielemans (n 42), C Reed, 'Taking Sides on Technology Neutrality' (2007) 4 *Script-ed*.
[45] B-J Koops, 'Should ICT Regulation be Technology Neutral?', in B-J Koops et al. (eds), *Starting Points for ICT Regulation* (The Hague, TMC Asser Press, 2005); C Reed, *Making Laws for Cyberspace* (Oxford, Oxford University Press, 2012); LB Moses, 'Regulating in the Face of Socio-Technical Change', in R Brownsword, E Scotford and K Yeung (eds), *The Oxford Handbook of the Law and Regulation of Technology* (Oxford, Oxford University Press, 2017); BA Greenberg, 'Rethinking Technology Neutrality' (2016) 100 *Minnesota Law Review* 1495; Hildebrandt and Tielemans (n 42).
[46] Koops (n 45); Hildebrandt and Tielemans (n 42). Also Reed (n 45), suggesting further differentiations among forms of TN based on the prism of legislative techniques such as technology indifference between online and offline actions.
[47] Eg, e-signatures, Reed (n 45).

The variety of meanings of TN shows that the principle serves as many purposes as does its antonym, specificity; in turn, different purposes call for different regulatory strategies[48] decided at different levels of decision-making.[49] Typically, the determination of technological specifications is left to instruments such as standards.

With such a variety of definitions, the origins of TN remain uncertain. Wylly suggests the principle could have first been relied upon by the England's seventeenth century Board of Longitude.[50] Maxwell and Bourreau find that TN – understood as performance standards clarifying the desired output but not the technology to achieve it and limiting negative externalities – is rooted in the US 1980s 'better regulation' movement to enhance safety,[51] eg, for automobiles, as told by Mashaw and Harsft, though the latter do not refer to technology neutrality but rather to 'forcing'.[52] For Reed, the concept entered EU technology law via the US and was cemented by the 1997 Framework on Global e-Commerce.[53] In technology law, TN found a fully-fledged application in legislation liberalising the market of telcos and it is in this context that TN is often discussed.[54]

Building on Maxwell and Bourreau, I find that the origin of the use of TN in the EU can be traced back to the New Approach/New Legislative Framework (NLF),[55] whereby legislators set political goals and leave the details of regulation to specialised bodies.[56] Resulting from a failure of Command and Control strategies[57] that followed the *Cassis de Dijon* judgment, the New Approach/NLF aimed at depoliticising technical products in the EU and overcome protectionist attitudes hindering what is now the Single Market.[58] TN could thus be strongly linked to regulatory approaches based on co-decision and delegation of standardisation.

The principle of TN finds as many supporters as it has detractors. Reed critiques the inherent ambiguity of the constructs underlying TN, such as functional equivalence.[59]

---

[48] Maxwell and Bourreau (n 44).
[49] Bennett Moses (n 45).
[50] P Wylly, 'Evaluating the Costs of Technology Neutrality in Light of the Importance of Social Network Influences and Bandwagon Effects for Innovation Diffusion' (2015) 23 *NYU Environmental Law Journal* 298.
[51] Maxwell and Bourreau (n 44).
[52] J Mashaw and DL Harfst, 'From Command and Control to Collaboration and Deference: The Transformation of Auto Safety Regulation' (2017) 34 *Yale Journal on Regulation* 167.
[53] Reed (n 45). W Clinton, 'A Framework for Global Electronic Commerce', in B Fitzgerald (ed), *Cyberlaw* (Farnham, Ashgate, 2006) clintonwhitehouse4.archives.gov/WH/New/Commerce/read.html or www.w3.org/TR/NOTE-framework-970706; General Assembly, 'UNCITRAL Model Law on Electronic Commerce. Resolution A/51/628'.
[54] Reed (n 44); Cave and Shortall (n 44); M Bourreau et al., *The Future of Broadband Policy, Part 2: Technological Neutrality, Path Dependency and Public Financing* (Robert Schuman Centre for Advanced Studies (RSCAS) 2017).
[55] Better Regulation Toolbox (n 37), TN at 174, NLF at 124. The NLF is now disciplined by Regulation (EU) No 1025/2012 of 25 October 2012 on European standardisation [2012] OJ L316/12.
[56] Kronlund (n 40); P Craig and G de Búrca, *European Union Law: Text, Cases and Materials* (Oxford, Oxford University Press, 2015).
[57] Baldwin et al (n 39).
[58] Kronlund (n 41); Craig and de Búrca (n 56); D Chalmers, G Davies and G Monti, *European Union Law*, 4th edn (Cambridge, Cambridge University Press, 2019) 644.
[59] Reed (n 44, 45).

Scholars also find fault with the ability of TN to do one, several or all of the following:[60] favour the incumbent technology and producers, thereby undermining innovation; reduce investment; cause competition among standards; make technology invisible;[61] exacerbate information asymmetries, pre-empt consumers from choosing between substitutes; give false impression of future-proofing while 'passing the buck' to law and administrative bodies over questions arising from new technologies; hide technology from debate; mistake 'equal application' for 'equivalence'. What is more, these shortcomings impact on the work of courts.[62]

The point is that TN may fail all its purported goals.[63] Koops rightly observes that drafting technology neutral legislation is only feasible if the legislator fully understands the technology and its implications,[64] also for the future, as well as what objective(s) it wants to achieve.[65] As a result, some concede that technology specificity may be preferable in some circumstances. Hildebrandt and Tielemans suggest that specificity may be needed to fulfil the goals of TN, particularly with respect to the paradigm of 'by design', to which I now turn.[66]

B. The Principle of 'By Design'

'By design' was first used with reference to *privacy by design* (PbD), whereby 'privacy' is embedded into system design.[67] The brainchild of Ann Cavoukian, then Information and Privacy Commissioner of Ontario, Canada, PbD stems from Privacy Enhancing Technologies (PETs), another concept coined by Cavoukian together with the Netherlands Data Protection Authority.[68] PbD has since evolved into the idea of embedding 'privacy' in technology, business practices, including processes, and physical design; it has been keenly embraced by computer scientists, legal scholars and ethicists, also as a multidisciplinary effort.[69]

---

[60] See Bennett Moses (n 45); Greenberg (n 45); Koops (n 45); Reed (n 45); Hildebrandt and Tielemans (n 42); Maxwell and Bourreau (n 45); Cave and Shortfall (n 44); Wylly (n 50); Chandler (n 35); M Grabowski, 'Are Technical Difficulties at the Supreme Court Causing a "Disregard of Duty"?' [2011] *Journal of Law, Technology & Internet* 93; Bourreau et al (n 49).
[61] See especially Chandler (n 35).
[62] See section III below.
[63] Reed (n 44).
[64] ibid.
[65] Koops (n 45).
[66] Hildebrandt and Tielemans (n 42).
[67] A Cavoukian, *Privacy by Design ... Take the Challenge* (2009).
[68] ibid, R Clarke, 'Introducing PITs and PETs: Technologies Affecting Privacy' *Privacy Law & Policy Reporter* www.rogerclarke.com/DV/PITsPETs.html. PbD has been so successful that it has almost completely supplanted PETs. See B-J Koops and R Leenes, 'Privacy Regulation Cannot be Hardcoded. A Critical Comment on the 'Privacy by Design' Provision in Data-protection Law' (2014) 28 *International Review of Law, Computers & Technology* 151; Cavoukian's (67) PETs Plus has not had a similar success.
[69] Cavoukian (n 67) 3. DW Schartum, 'Making Privacy by Design Operative' (2016) 24 *International Journal of Law and Information Technology* 151; E Orrù, 'Minimum Harm by Design: Reworking Privacy by Design to Mitigate the Risks of Surveillance', in R Leenes et al. (eds), *Data Protection and Privacy: (In)visibilities and Infrastructures* (Cham, Springer, 2017); Koops and Leenes (n 68); Rachovitsa (n 21); P Tsormpatzoudi, B Berendt and F Coudert, *Privacy by Design: From Research and Policy to Practice - the Challenge of Multi-disciplinarity* (Cham, Springer, 2015).

First endorsed by the Madrid Resolution,[70] the GDPR gave statutory footing to 'by design' approaches: Article 25 lays down the obligation, for the controller, to implement *data protection by design* (DPbD) and by default.[71] 'By default' expresses the principle of necessity (data minimisation) and addresses default settings resulting from design.[72]

Another member of the 'by design' family is *security by design* (SbD), a contemporary reformulation of Saltzer and Schroeder's Security Design Principles for building secure systems.[73] There exist various versions of SbD, such as OWASP's SbD Principles and Smith's reformulation of the original principles: continuous improvement, least privilege, defence in depth, open design, chain of control, deny by default, transitive trust, trust by verify, separation of duty and the principle of least astonishment.[74] Similarly to DPbD, SbD has found its way into legislation.[75] The concept of defaults is as relevant for SbD as it is for PbD/DpBD, though it is difficult to operationalise.[76]

'By design' approaches are an expression of design-based legislation, which attempts to mould reality through the creation of boundaries in technology, on the understanding that design has an ordering power.[77] Design-based legislation is perhaps the object of the best-known debates in cyberspace and IT law.[78] Such debates revolve around the feasibility and desirability of embedding public law values in design,[79] and enhancing co-[80] and private regulation.[81] Indeed, design-based approaches leverage the private sector: companies are regulators either de facto, by virtue of designing and controlling technology, or de jure, as a result of delegation and through standardisation.[82]

---

[70] International Conference of Data Protection and Privacy Commissioners, *Joint Proposal for a Draft of International Standards on the Protection of Privacy with regard to the processing of Personal Data (The Madrid Resolution)* (30th International Conference of Data Protection and Privacy Commissioners, 2009)).

[71] The gap between PbD and DPbD could be narrow. First, in its original formulation, Cavoukian (n 67) argued that PbD can be achieved by building FIPs into technologies and systems (see also Schartum (n 69)); 'privacy' in PbD means information privacy as defined by FIPs, thus similar to data protection. Second, although legislation specifying Art 7 CFR does not contain rules on PbD, the proposed EPR will be a *lex specialis* of the GDPR and therefore controllers should be similarly required to implement by design principles.

[72] A Bourka et al., *Recommendations on Shaping Technology According to GDPR Provisions. Exploring the Notion of Data Protection by Default* (ENISA, 2019) 11. European Data Protection Board, *Guidelines 4/2019 on Article 25. Data Protection by Design and by Default, v 2.0* (2020), see ch 4, section II.A.iii.

[73] Herrmann and Pridöhl (n 4); JH Saltzer and MD Schroeder, 'The Protection of Information in Computer Systems' (1975) 63 *Proceedings of the IEEE* 1278.

[74] See wiki.owasp.org/index.php/Security_by_Design_Principles; Smith (n 5).

[75] See Rec 97 Dir 2018/1972 [2018] OJ L321/37 and Art 51(1) Reg 2019/881 [2019] OJ L151/15, ch 6.

[76] Bourka et al. (n 72) 20–21.

[77] L Lessig, *Code: And Other Laws of Cyberspace. Version 2.0* (New York, Basic Books, 2006); R Leenes, 'Framing techno-regulation: an Exploration of State and Non-state Regulation by Technology' (2011) 5 *Legisprudence*; Baldwin et al. (n 39).

[78] A Murray, 'Internet Regulation', in D Levi-Faur (ed), *Handbook on the Politics of Regulation* (Cheltenham, Edward Elgar, 2013).

[79] Koops and Leenes (n 68); B-J Koops and others, *Starting Points for ICT Regulation* (The Hague, TMC Asser Press, 2005); DK Mulligan and KA Bamberger, 'Saving Governance-by-Design' (2018) 106 *California Law Review* 697.

[80] I Kamara, 'Co-regulation in EU personal data protection: the case of technical standards and the privacy by design standardisation 'mandate'' (2017) 8 *European Journal of Law and Technology*.

[81] NA Sales, 'Privatizing Cybersecurity' (2018) 65 *UCLA Law Review* 620; I Kilovati, 'Privatized Cybersecurity Law' (2020) 10 *UC Irvine Law Review*; KE Eichensehr, 'Public-Private Cybersecurity' (2017) 95 *Texas Law Review* 467.

[82] Lessig (n 77); Kamara (n 80); MG Porcedda, 'Regulation of Data Breaches in the European Union: Private Companies in the Driver's Seat of Cybersecurity?', in C Helena and O Bures (eds), *Security Privatization. How Non-security-related Private Businesses Shape Security Governance* (Cham, Springer, 2018).

Technologists have focused on developing technical 'protection goals' that embed legal requirements into software and hardware development. Legal scholars have highlighted the limitations of PbD requirements stemming from the applicable law. Pagallo, Leenes and Koops, as well as Schartum, argue that it is not possible to hard-wire legal rules in computer systems, notably because legal rules require flexible application.[83] Another inherent constraint in the implementation of PbD/DPbD principles lies in the fact that 'privacy' and 'data protection' are qualified rights subject to permissible limitations.[84]

i. 'TN' and 'By Design': Colliding Paradigms?

Technology neutrality and by design sit in a complex relationship. Baldwin, Cave and Lodge report known tensions between principle-based legislation, such as technology neutral legislation, and design-based legislation,[85] as acknowledged by Koops and Leenes. Maxwell and Bourreau also recognise that there is tension between performance standards clarifying the desired output and design standards; although their view on 'by design' is unclear, they claim that standards for the NIS Directive and DPbD are best served by performance standards.[86] An example of the collision of paradigms could be found in Art 4(e)(i) of Annex II of Regulation 1025/2012 disciplining the NLF.

Hildebrandt and Tielemans find that DPbD can potentially fulfil all the goals that technology neutral legislation pursues, especially if technology producers became subject to the same rules as end-users.[87] However, provisions mandating adherence to PbD, DPbD and SbD have historically been addressed to the users, not the producers, of technology. It is therefore impossible to make sense of such a complex relationship without considering how the two principles operate in practice. Explaining how TN and by design principles operate in EU technology law is instrumental to demonstrating why it is difficult to determine an a priori mode of reconciliation of the triad.

C. TN and By Design in Practice: TOMs, SoA, Standards and the New Legislative Framework

The TN and 'by design' principles are given effect by and operate within an ecosystem of regulatory techniques and frameworks. TN and 'by design' are closely related to technical and organisational measures (TOMs), 'state of the art' (SoA) and standards, the New

---

[83] See U Pagallo, 'On the Principle of Privacy by Design and its Limits', in S Gutwirth et al. (eds), *European Data Protection: in Good Health?* (Cham, Springer, 2012) Koops and Leenes (n 69); Kamara (n 80); Schartum (n 69).

[84] Kamara (n 80); Rachovitsa (n 22) F Bieker et al., *A Process for Data Protection Impact Assessment under the European General Data Protection Regulation* (Cham, Springer, 2016).

[85] Baldwin, Cave and Lodge (n 39); Koops and Leenes (n 68).

[86] Maxwell and Burreau (n 44).

[87] Hildebrandt and Tielemans (n 42).

Approach/Legislative Framework and similar co-decision delegatory frameworks. This section discusses the workings of such a regulatory ecosystem, with a view to drawing findings that are relevant for the relationship of the triad.

Within secondary law instruments concerning cybersecurity, privacy and data protection, the principles of TN and by design find expression in the obligation, for the addressees of those instruments, to adopt TOMs to fulfil the objectives of the instruments or inhibit the use of undesired 'tools'.[88] Pending the analysis of concrete statutory examples in chapters six to eight, here it is enough to stress that instruments lack both examples of TOMs and tools and abstain from specifying how TOMs can meet the statutory objectives.

The selection of TOMs, and how measures will meet the objectives of the instrument, is left to practitioners, who are given limited guidance: the only requirement is that measures conform to the SoA. The SoA embodies TN, especially its future proofing meaning. The fact that technology neutral obligations are specified by technology neutral requirements creates high levels of indeterminacy and uncertainty. TeleTrust and ENISA draw from the 1978 Federal Constitutional Court '*Kalkar*' decision to define 'the "state of the art" technology level as being situated between 'the innovative and dynamic '"existing scientific knowledge and research" technology level and the more established "generally accepted rules of technology" level'. Technical measures ... pass into the 'state of the art' stage when they reach market maturity (or at least are launched on the market).[89] Thus, either way the SoA is a dynamic concept determined by markets[90] and is tied to standardisation[91] and often synonymous with industry standards.[92]

Standards can be international, national, or European harmonised.[93] In the first case, they are adopted by international SSOs such as the ITU and ISO, in the second by national standardisation bodies, in the third by three Standards Developing Organisations (SDOs) officially listed in the Standardisation Regulation:[94] CEN, CENELEC and ETSI.

CEN, CENELEC and ETSI supervise the adoption of technical standards under a mandate (delegation) by the European Commission, which also establishes the essential

---

[88] TOMs is DSM parlance, while 'tools' is AFSJ parlance: 'tools ... in order to commit [cybercrime] offences', Rec 16, Directive 2013/40/EU [2013] OJ L218/8.

[89] IT Security Association of Germany (TeleTrust) and European Agency for Cybersecurity (ENISA), *IT Security Act (Germany) and EU Data Protection Regulation: Guidelines on 'State of the Art'. Technical and Organisational Measures* (2021) 11.

[90] Eg, 'in line with the state of the art in the industry': European Commission, 'Protecting Fundamental Rights in the Digital Age' (Communication) COM (2021) 819 final, 13. EDPB (n 72) 8.

[91] 'The dynamics dwindle there, e.g due to process standardisation' Teletrust and ENISA (n 89) 16. A candidate cybersecurity certification scheme to serve as a successor to the existing SOG-IS (www.sogis.eu/) 'as defined by the supporting documents of the EUCC scheme' ENISA, EUCC 278.

[92] See European Data Protection Supervisor (EDPS), 'Opinion 5/2018. Preliminary Opinion on privacy by design'. There, an example of the state of the art is Danezis (n 8). European Cyber Security Organisation, *State of the Art Syllabus, Overview of existing Cybersecurity standards and certification schemes v2* (2017).

[93] ES Bremer, 'Government Use of Standards in the United States and Abroad', in JL Contreras (ed), *The Cambridge Handbook of Technical Standardisation Law* (Cambridge, Cambridge University Press, 2019) 35.

[94] Regulation (EU) No 1025/2012 (n 55).

requirements standards must meet.[95] Such a '*sui generis* intertwined procedure'[96] is the New Approach, now called New Legislative Framework (NLF). Lundqvist adds that once drawn up, standards can become European Harmonised Standards (EHS) by virtue of their 'referencing', ie publication, in the Official Journal 'C' series. Thanks to such a process, products developed in adherence to a EHS receive a presumption of conformity to the essential requirements laid down in union harmonising legislation.[97]

Although in principle EHSs remain voluntary, due to the standstill principle and the practical difficulties of demonstrating conformity by means of alternative standards,[98] EHSs have legal bearing. In *James Elliot*, the CJEU acknowledged that EHSs form part of EU law,[99] and that the Court can interpret them, even if they have no binding effects, by virtue of the need to provide uniform interpretation to all parts of EU law in light of Article 267 TFEU.[100] Volpato and Eliantonio suggest that the subsequent unprecedented referencing of a standard in the 'L' series in 2019,[101] instead of the 'C' series, was a by-product of the judgment.

Insofar as an instrument requires its addressee(s) to adopt 'TOMs' that need to conform to essential requirements, without however listing the measures and articulating the requirements, the instrument conforms in principle to TN. When such an instrument also mandates that privacy, data protection or security requirements must be adhered to 'by design', the instrument also conforms to PbD, DPbD and SbD principles. Insofar as TN aims to establish performance standards or the desired principle to apply across the board, and PbD, DPbD and SbD aim to express design standards, they aim to convey an impression of conformity with essential requirements, if not a presumption as in the New Approach/NLF. Thus, a technology neutral instrument mandating TOMs to be 'designed' in accordance with standards tied to the SoA adheres to the spirit of the framework created by the New Approach/NLF, if not its exact procedures and legal outcomes. Chapter six will offer an overview of DSM instruments inspired by the logics of the New Approach/NLF and chapter seven will discuss whether the New Approach/NLF exerts any influence in the AFSJ.

In light of the relevance for the triad of such a regulatory approach, it is important to scrutinise the workings of frameworks paving the way to standards drafted under controlled delegation of legislative power.[102] This is not a critique of standardisation per se. Standardisation helped to remove protectionist measures by lessening belligerence between states and de-politicising technology as parliaments delegated to experts

---

[95] See Bremer (n 93); PWJ Verbruggen, 'Tort Liability for Standards Development in the United States and European Union', in JL Contreras (ed), *The Cambridge Handbook of Technical Standardisation Law* (Cambridge, Cambridge University Press, 2019); B Lundqvist, 'Public Law, European Constitutionalism and Copyright in Standards', in Contreras ibid.

[96] Lundqvist (n 95) 125.

[97] ibid 125–126.

[98] Bremer (n 93) 35–40.

[99] *James Elliot*, C-613/14, EU:C:2016:821, para 40.

[100] But compare the AG, who equates EHS to acts within the meaning of Art 267 TFEU, discussed in Lundqvist (n 92) 129–132. *James Elliot*, C-613/14, EU:C:2016:63, Opinion of AG Sanchez-Bordona.

[101] A Volpato and M Eliantonio, *The Butterfly Effect of Publishing References to Harmonised Standards in the L series* (European Law Blog, 2019). But compare *Stichting Rookpreventie Jeugd and Others*, C-160/20, EU:C:2022:101.

[102] See *James Elliot*, C-613/14, Opinion para 55.

in the interest of 'objective' decision-making and is at the origin of the Internet and the information technology revolution.[103] However, the regulatory reliance on standardisation permeating legislation on the triad – and EU IT law in general – suffers from three self-reinforcing pitfalls.

The first pitfall is a potential democratic deficit. Lundqvist refers to the New Approach as 'a regulatory technique and strategy for de-regulation'.[104] For him, the 1985 Council Resolution that ushered in the New Approach 'was the starting point of "outsourcing" the creation of product requirements to the industry on a EU level through self-regulation under'[105] SSOs. Although Lundqvist does not expressly criticise the framework, the fact that 'it is the composition of the technical bodies that creates de facto self-regulation by industry'[106] adds to claims that the New Approach/NLF favours a democratic deficit.[107]

SDOs and SSOs have long been criticised in light of their composition, which taints the presumption of objectivity and enables their members to pursue vested interests.[108] As Smismans shows, expertise and interests can and do clash.[109] SDOs and SSOs are populated by industry representatives[110] and multinational corporations are known to have made strategic use of SDOs and SSOs, thereby threatening the ability of delegating institutions to control them, not least because regional SDOs tend to align themselves with international bodies.[111] Although in *Stichting Rookpreventie Jeugd* the CJEU did not take issue with the participation of industry in the elaboration of ISO standards, the Standardisation Regulation is notably under revision to foster better representation of non-industry stakeholders.[112]

The democratic deficit is particularly important when standards affect the realm of fundamental rights. Lundqvist notes that the position of the CJEU in *James Elliot* leaves open the question of whether EHS should conform to the founding principles found in Regulation 1025/2012, the European Commission's documentation and the principle of good governance,[113] as well as rule of law (RoL) principles in general. Standards adopted beyond the abovementioned principles could breach the RoL both from a thin and a thick perspective. The second pitfall is the suitability of standards to

---

[103] L DeNardis, 'A History of Internet Security', in K de Leeuw and J Bergstra (eds), *The History of Information Security* (Oxford, Elsevier Science, 2007) 682.
[104] Lundqvist (n 95) 126.
[105] ibid 127.
[106] Lundqvist (n 95) 126.
[107] Kronlund (n 41); S Smismans, 'Democratic Participation and the Search for an Institutional Architecture that Accommodates Interests and Expertise', in S Piattoni (ed), *The European Union Democratic Principles and Institutional Architectures in Times of Crisis* (Oxford, Oxford University Press, 2015).
[108] M Rosario and S Schimdt, 'Standardisation in the European Community', in C Freeman, M Sharp and W Walker (eds), *Technology and the Future of Europe Global Competition and the Environment in the 1980s* (London, Cengage Learning, 1992).
[109] S Smismans, 'Constitutionalising Expertise in the EU: Anchoring Knowledge in Democracy', in J Priban (ed), *The Self-Constitution of Europe* (Leiden, Brill, 2016).
[110] Baldwin et al (n 39).
[111] J Lembke, *Competition for Technological Leadership* (Cheltenham, Edward Elgar, 2002); Baldwin et al (n 39).
[112] *Stichting Rookpreventie Jeugds*, C-160/20. See Rec 4, Art 1, European Commission, 'Proposal for a Regulation amending Regulation (EU) No 1025/2012 as regards the decisions of European standardisation organisations concerning European standards and European standardisation deliverables' (Communication) COM (2022) 32 final, published as Regulation (EU) 2022/2480, OJ L323/1 as this book went to press.
[113] Lundqvist (n 95), mentioning Hettne (2008) 129–132.

lay down requirements implementing rights enshrined in Articles 7 to 8 CFR and 16 TFEU. The European Commission adopted mandate M/530[114] to produce a PbD and DPbD standard in 2014, taking into account the prospective adoption of the GDPR. That similar standards are meant to create a market compliant with the EU notion of data protection and privacy raises the question of what constitutes the 'essential requirements' to be met. The answer should be informed by a techno-legal analysis akin to the one performed at the start of this chapter and account for the collision between TN and 'by design'. Further questions are how delegates of companies that were criticised for lobbying hard to water down fundamental rights protections in the GDPR would draft such standards,[115] and whether the involvement of consultants through the HAS Consultants Framework introduced in 2018[116] can counterbalance Big Tech.[117] Mandate M/530 led to a voluntary standard to be published (or endorsed) at national level, behind a paywall, rather than in the Official Journal and not leading to a presumption of conformity.[118]

The third pitfall is that the NLF was developed for products and services. 'Measures', technical and organisational, applying to cybersecurity, privacy and data protection often rely on software; although some claim that software could be classed as a product,[119] there is no consensus on this point. For the Commission, 'items containing intangible elements or presenting connectivity features qualify as "products" and defects in these products are covered by the Product Liability Directive'. However, the complexity of items may undermine legal certainty: 'updates would usually close safety holes through patches, but new codes also add or remove features in ways that change the risk profile of these technologies'.[120] Traditional categories of goods and services are ill-suited to adequately capture the interconnections between software and hardware and the admixture of products and services, coupled with the presence of a complex supply-chain that creates dependency.[121]

---

[114] European Commission, 'Commission implementing decision C(2015) 102 final of 20.1.2015 on a standardisation request to the European standardisation organisations as regards European standards and European standardisation deliverables for privacy and personal data protection management pursuant to Article 10(1) of Regulation (EU) No 1025/2012 of the European Parliament and of the Council in support of Directive 95/46/EC of the European Parliament and of the Council and in support of Union's security industrial policy. Mandate M/530.' For a discussion of the development of the standard, see Kamara (n 80).

[115] G Riekeles, 'I Saw First-hand How US Tech Giants Seduced the EU - and Undermined Democracy' The Guardian (28 June 2022) www.theguardian.com/commentisfree/2022/jun/28/i-saw-first-hand-tech-giants-seduced-eu-google-meta.

[116] G Maes and G Ascensao, Presentation 'Drafting standards for citation in OJEU (CEN and CENELEC, 2019).

[117] Verbruggen (n 95) notes the paucity of case law on liability for standards developments by SSOs and SDOs.

[118] Standard EN 17529:2022 became available as this book went to press; shop.standards.ie/en-ie/standards/i-s-en-17529-2022-1299700_saig_nsai_nsai_3142494/. As the CJEU suggests in Stichting Rookpreventie, C-160/20, (paras 36–37), access could be achieved by submitting a request pursuant to Reg 1049/2002.

[119] K Alheit, 'The Applicability of the EU Product Liability Directive to Software' (2001) 34(2) *Comparative and International Law Journal of Southern Africa* 194. Cited in Lina Jasmontaite et al., CANVAS – Constructing an Alliance for Value-driven Cybersecurity, White paper (2020).

[120] European Commission, 'Liability of defective products accompanying the document Communication Artificial intelligence for Europe COM (2018) 237 final' (Staff Working Document) SWD (2018) 137 final, 9.

[121] Interdependency can relate to 'i) the tangible parts/devices (sensors, actuators, hardware), ii) the different software components and applications, to iii) the data itself, iv) the data services (i.e. collection, processing, curating, analysing), and v) the connectivity features'. ibid, 9. See ch 6, section II.B.iii.

The Effacement of Technology from the Law 151

Due to the unclear regime applying to software and ICT products, instruments regulating the triad have long unequally addressed: (i) developers of standards to which TOMs must adhere[122] (EU law only addresses national standards if they manifestly hinder competition);[123] (ii) producers of TOMs; and (iii) the addressees of legislation mandating the adoption of suitable measures, ie the end-users. Producers of TOMs, often software developers, are bound by rules on product liability read in the light of *James Elliot* but are rarely captured by obligations contained in instruments mandating the use of TOMs.[124] In turn, the addressees of such legislation bear the brunt of the choice of suitable TOMs. Thus, instruments mandating the adoption of suitable TOMs binding for the end-users in charge of choosing TOMs exert weak force on SSO/SDOs developing standards, and have not been binding for developers of measures that are intended to adhere to standards. Thus, frameworks that delegate the adoption of standards *de facto* favour TOM's developers as opposed to end-users that are bound by, and liable for them. Furthermore, software developers are unlikely to be bound by such standards to the extent that 'product' developers are.

Legislative reform ongoing at the time of writing is trying to remove such imbalance and reinforce mechanisms of liability and redress. The extent to which recently introduced definitions of digital content and services[125] are capable of capturing the complexity of ICTs and redress imbalance between stakeholders remains to be seen in light of the scope of application of the Directives and national transposition. The European Parliament called on the Commission 'to redefine the terms "product" and "safe product" as part of its revision of the [General Product Safety Directive], in coordination with the possible revision of… the Product Liability Directive' so as to reflect 'the complexity of emerging technologies' and 'new market realities'.[126] The Commission is in the process of amending rules for the 'complementary legal frameworks' of product safety[127] and liability[128] and is exploring solutions to oblige developers and vendors to secure the infrastructure on which network and information systems rest.[129] Although it will be for future research to analyse such reforms, their impact will still be constrained by a regulatory ecosystem that effaces technology from the law, as I discuss below.

---

[122] Verbruggen's (n 95) analysis reviews tort liability for standards development at national level.
[123] See Fra.bo discussed in Verbruggen (n 95).
[124] Hildebrandt and Tielemans (n 42); EDPS (n 92). See ch 6, section III.
[125] Digital Content Directive (EU) 2019/770 [2019] OJ L136/1 dealing with the conformity of digital content or a digital service with the contract; Sale of Goods Directive (EU) 2019/771 [2019] OJ L136/28 dealing with conformity of goods with contract.
[126] European Parliament, European Parliament Resolution of 25 November 2020 on addressing product safety in the single market (2019/2190(INI)) [2021] C 425/04, points 4 and 1.
[127] European Commission (n 118), 4. European Commission, 'Proposal for a Regulation on general product safety' (Communication) COM (2021) 346 final; European Commission, 'Evaluation of Council Directive 85/374/EEC of 25 July 1985 on the approximation of the laws, regulations and administrative provisions of the Member States concerning liability for defective products' (Staff Working Document) SWD (2018) 157 final (2018).
[128] European Commission, 'Proposal for a Directive on liability for Defective Products' (Communication) COM (2022) 495 final, published as this book went to press.
[129] European Commission, 'Proposal for a Regulation on horizontal cybersecurity requirements for products with digital elements and amending Regulation (EU) 2019/1020 (Cyber Resilience Act)' (Communication) COM (2022) 454 final, published as this book went to press.

D. Interim Conclusions: Technology Effacement and Indeterminacy

TN and 'by design' principles serve a regulatory framework that has pegged the implementation of 'technical and organisational measures' to the SoA and therefore standards, which are produced in line with the New Approach/NLF. Frameworks that follow similar patterns of delegation to SSOs/SDOs and ultimately industry suffer from the same issues as frameworks that adhere to the New Approach/NLF.

The regulatory combination of TN, by design and NLF-inspired frameworks generate a state of technological indeterminacy, whereby the desired design requirements of TOMs are couched in TN terms and pegged to a SoA defined by private actors via non-binding standardisation procedures. Technology disappears from the applicable law and reappears as TOMs created by unaccountable developers – the market – thus breaking the link between the applicable laws and TOMs as ways to implement such laws. EU law hitherto lacks the mechanisms to coax SSOs/SDOs and developers – the market – into conforming to, and being liable for, cybersecurity, privacy and data protection as defined in the applicable law and, for the latter two, primary law.

The technology indeterminacy characterising EU technology law challenges the ability to establish whether the triad overlaps or is strongly reconciled on account of common features or goals, given that the meaning of those features and goals is not contained in the law itself. Although the meaning of such a statement will become clearer with reference to specific DSM, AFSJ and EA instruments, before moving to such instruments it is necessary to discuss how the effacement of technology affects courts and creates an indeterminacy loop.

III. Courts, the Effacement of Technology and the Indeterminacy Loop

Courts interpret the application of the law within the boundaries of the law. If the law overlooks technology because TOMs, the SoA and standards are not incorporated in legislation, courts may be precluded from scrutinising technology expressed in terms of TOMs, the SoA and standards. Similarly, if the law does not lay down rules about the specifics of technology, it is unlikely that courts will interpret the law in a manner that brings technology and its specifics to surface. This potential shortcoming is inherent in technology neutral legislation. For Greenberg,[130] technology neutral law suffers from a problem of penumbra, ie it lacks certainty, and one of perspective, ie it can be interpreted from several angles, eg, the technological output or design. The problem can be further compounded by technologies that are too complex.

Noting that tackling technological innovations in case law requires considerable technical expertise, Chandler and Grabowski even argue that courts may have an

---

[130] Greenberg (n 45). Two additional problems are that of prediction (promise to anticipate known unknowns), and pretence (assumed irrelevance of the socio-political context).

aversion to delving into technology irrespective of the characteristics of law, primarily because of a lack of technical knowledge. Irrespective of its reasons, such an aversion carries serious risks.[131] Grabowski described such risks in terms of: (i) undermining the effectiveness and relevance of the role of courts; (ii) potentially discouraging affected parties from submitting important cases for judicial review; (iii) the disregard of important cases by courts, despite the relevant social questions they raise; (iv) and even worse, a disregard of duty by the court.[132] Chandler further warns that courts' avoidance is 'helping to make the technology an invisible part of the cultural "wallpaper," such that rejection of the technology is irrational'.[133] Thus, the effacement of technology at regulatory level is difficult to resolve at judicial level and could compounded any courts' aversion to delve into technology caused by technological complexity.

At EU level, AG Villalón poignantly notes that 'it is not for the [CJEU], but only for the national court, if necessary, to examine the technical aspects of [a] matter'.[134] CJEU case law offers several examples of judgments that do not scrutinise technologies used to implement legislation, which is felt to be outside the remit of the Court. Examples include *Schwarz* and *Willems* on biometric passports[135] and several cases on monitoring that will be the object of analysis in the coming chapters. One is the *Digital Rights Ireland* case, which was acclaimed for its invalidation of the much debated and litigated Data Retention Directive (DRD).[136] However, at para 49 the CJEU seems to find data retention 'to be appropriate for attaining the objective pursued by [the DRD]. … several methods of electronic communication … limit the ability of the data retention measure to attain the objective pursued … [without] however [making] that measure inappropriate'. The DRD was technology neutral.

The *Scarlet* and *SABAM* judgments, discussed in chapter six, were similarly acclaimed for their protection of fundamental rights vis-à-vis the enforcement of technology-neutral digital rights management. Yet, even if the Court was pronouncing itself on the use of Deep Packet Inspection (DPI), it never mentioned it explicitly and referred instead to a 'filtering system', stating 'it is common ground that [the] implementation of that filtering system would require … active observation of all electronic

---

[131] Chandler (n 35); Grabowski (n 60). B Fung, 'The Aereo Case is Being Decided by People who Call iCloud 'the iCloud.' Yes, Really', *The Washington Post* (13 April 2014) www.washingtonpost.com/news/the-switch/wp/2014/04/23/the-aereo-case-is-being-decided-by-people-who-call-icloud-the-icloud-yes-really/.

[132] Grabwoski (n 60); for (i) quoting Judge Shelton and for (iv) quoting the Concurring Opinion of Judge Scalia in the case of City Of Ontario, *California, et al. v Quon et al.* (Court Of Appeals For The Ninth Circuit, No. 08-1332.

[133] Chandler (n 35). Such a warning has inspired the broader claim of this work that technology has become invisible in technology law.

[134] *Scarlet Extended*, C-70/10, EU:C:2011:255, Opinion of AG Villalón, para 50.

[135] 'Nothing in the case file submitted to the Court suggests that (an iris scan) would interfere less' and 'the court has not been made aware of any (alternative) measures'. *Schwarz*, C-291/12, EU:C:2013:670, paras 41–52. The Court may be indirectly inviting the submission of better evidence, an interpretation which is frustrated by the subsequent *Willems*, C-446/12 to C-449/12, EU:C:2015:238.

[136] *Ireland v Parliament and Council*, C-301/06, EU:C:2009:68 (Data Retention I); *Digital Rights Ireland and Seitlinger and Others*, C-293/12 and C-594/12, EU:C:2014:238. See generally T Ojanen, 'Privacy is More than Just a Seven-Letter Word: The Court of Justice of the European Union Sets Constitutional Limits on Mass Surveillance. Case Note on Court of Justice of the European Union, Decision of 8 April 2014 in Joined Cases C-293/12 and C-594/12, Digital Rights Ireland and Seitlinger and Others' (2014) 10 *European Constitutional Law Review* 528.

communications conducted on the network of the ISP'.[137] The Court did not take the opportunity to elaborate on AG Villalón's Opinion. AG Villalón stresses that the 'nature of the filtering to be carried out' has legal significance, but that 'that neither the national court nor SABAM makes the slightest reference to the specific rules according to which that monitoring' is conducted, forcing him to engage in a cautious analysis in the footnotes.[138] The lack of technical information is per se an indication of the inconsequentiality of technology for the proceedings. The CJEU similarly chose to overlook DPI in *La Quadrature du Net*, discussed in chapter seven.

Such issues are exacerbated by the fact that the specifics of technology are the object of standards. It will be interesting to see whether the publication of standards in the 'L' series of the Official Journal following *James Elliot* will lead the CJEU to scrutinise information technologies. However, only instruments whose 'measures' were adopted on the basis of the New Approach/NLF procedures and are published in the Official Journal will create EHSs that form part of EU law and can be interpreted by the CJEU.[139] Conversely, actors will conform to standards that do not form part of EU law and that cannot be interpreted by the CJEU. This state of affairs exacerbates problems related to the New Approach/NLF.

In sum, the effacement of technology from the law is augmented at judicial level and could be made worse by technologies that are too complex. The interplay between: (i) the test for permissible limitations, which is tech-agnostic; (ii) open-ended rights as discussed earlier and in chapters three and four; (iii) and the lack of scrutinisation of technology or their specifics by courts hides the complexity entailed by different technological choices, the impact that such technological choices have on the law and the values underpinning different technological choices or tech specifications.

The outcome is an indeterminacy loop, whereby the effects of technologies on the implementation of measures and of rights elude the applicable law and its interpretation, and which balancing formulas devised for the digital age are unable to redress.[140] This challenges the identification of a set mode of co-existence for the triad. Far from invalidating the importance of judicial decisions, which set the criteria to identify interference, or the respect, protection and fulfilment of rights in concrete circumstances, these conclusions point to the need to appreciate the limitations of existing judgments in providing sufficient answers for the object of this enquiry and the need to explore alternative solutions, such as technological courts or the publication of expert opinion.

---

[137] *Scarlet Extended*, C-70/10, EU:C:2011:771, paras 39–40.
[138] *Scarlet Extended*, C-70/10, Opinion paras 49–50. In the notes, the AG also makes comments on technology neutrality.
[139] For Lundqvist (n 95) 129–132, the Court's departure from the interpretation suggested by the AG, insofar as EHS should be equated to acts within the meaning of Art 267 TFEU, precludes judicial review and thus invalidation of the EHS. On the effects of standards adopted by SSOs and referenced by EU secondary law, see *Stichting Rookpreventie Jeugd*, C-160/20, paras 42–52; the Grand Chamber's consideration as to the lack of necessity, for a legislative measure, to provide details of a technical measure (para 43), reinforces the findings of the regulatory ecosystem discussed in these pages.
[140] M Susi, 'The Internet Balancing Formula' (2019) 25 *European Law Journal* 198–212; R Alexy, 'Mart Susi's Internet Balancing Formula', ibid 213–220.

IV. Conclusion

This chapter analysed cybersecurity, privacy and data protection as techno-legal objects, through the lenses of technologists and lawmakers. Accordingly, a techno-legal analysis blended security properties (SPs), protection goals (PGs) and design strategies (DSs) of the triad with the essential components of privacy and data protection to explore the potential for overlap and thus complete reconciliation. Overlap as a theoretical possibility proved difficult to demonstrate in practice on account of: (i) the lack of a common vocabulary between technologists and legislators; (ii) inherent tensions in PGs/SPs; (iii) the open-ended interpretation of the essential components and essence of privacy and data protection; (iv) the nature of secondary law. Strong reconciliation is not ruled out but could only be achieved through laws that mandate the most protective design choices or technologies.

The examination of EU technology law points to the law's inability to mandate such design choices and the extant impossibility to establish an a priori mode of reconciliation of the triad. The combination of technology neutrality, by design, technical and organisational measures (TOMs), the state of the art (SoA) and standards, which operate in a co-decision delegatory environment pioneered by the New Approach and developed by the New Legal Framework (NLF), efface technology from binding law[141] and judicial decisions, triggering an indeterminacy loop. The elements that would be necessary to determine whether the triad are reconciled are left out of the law and case law, making it difficult to draw conclusions.

Chapters six to eight provide a contextual analysis of the triad in the DSM, AFSJ and EA in search for such conclusions. Before turning to the DSM, it makes sense to add two observations, to which I will return in the book conclusions.

The first observation is that, although this research does not aim to appraise the impact of the full spectrum of regulatory techniques on the triad, the analysis just conducted brings to the fore the need to weigh whether such techniques are working as intended and especially to scrutinise such techniques' unintended effects.

The second observation is that such a research endeavour should help identify the best regulatory options and adopt corrective measures where needed. For instance, it seems urgent to analyse whether frameworks adopted to 'depoliticise' technology and build the Single Market are still beneficial. As Flear notes in the context of health,[142] EU law originally prioritised the bringing of goods to the market over alternative objectives, so that the improvement of health or the goods themselves was not a primary concern. The current EU fundamental rights mandate requires a change of emphasis, so that the priority should no longer be the opening of new markets but rather to maximise reconciliation between market and fundamental right objectives. Such an outcome could be pursued by using the techno-legal analysis discussed in (I), which connects the essential components of rights with technological principles,[143] to operationalise values to embed

---

[141] Bearing in mind that technology was unlikely to feature prominently in cyberlaw since cyberspace became a regulatory target after the strategy of depoliticization of technology discussed in section II.

[142] M Flear, 'Regulating New Technologies: EU Internal Market Law, Risk and Socio-technical Order', in M Cremona (ed) *New Technologies and EU Law* (Oxford, Oxford University Press, 2017).

[143] Porcedda (n 9) and Cybersecurity and Privacy Rights in EU Law. Moving Beyond the Trade-off Model to Appraise the Role of Technology (European University Institute, 2017), ch 8, with the caveats discussed in section I.

in technology, to supplement fundamental rights impact assessments and to inform tests for permissible limitations that favour the most protective technologies. Another example of corrective measures is that TN is not desirable under all circumstances and specificity may bring advantages; Reed cites inter alia increased legal certainty, reduced costs of compliance, avoidance of spill-over of legislation to other unforeseen areas and keeping up with the 'pacing issue', whereby legislation can be quickly outpaced by new technologies.[144] Additional corrective measures could include the creation of specialised technology courts.

This matters because, as Leenes explains, 'techno-regulation' as the 'deliberate employment of technology to regulate human behaviour'[145] either enables or inhibits conduct. Chandler goes further and argues that individuals mould their behaviour so as to adapt to novel technologies, which become endowed with seemingly autonomous lives. She convincingly argues that law and, relatedly, judgments, may end up justifying the existence and rationale of technologies, eventually rubber-stamping societal approval and acceptance.[146]

Techno-regulation could be the unintended result of collective conduct but also orchestrated by actors with strong vested interests, threatening to lead to what Cohen calls a modulated democracy, whereby surveillance infrastructures organise the world for us, force us to look at the world through their lens, and are ultimately exploited by powerful commercial and political interests.[147] As Brownsword put it, 'a fully techno-regulated community is no longer an operative moral community'.[148]

Techno-regulation impacts on the *voulouir vivre* of a nation and ultimately the *ordre public* of societies and has inspired the search for new constitutional ways to deal with the digital from debates over 'code' to digital constitutionalism.[149] The regulation of human conduct by means of technology cannot be left to chance: it is the job of law and politics to re-appropriate decision-making as to which values technology should pursue. However, for such a re-appropriation to happen, the 'effaced' technology must be made visible in the technology law ecosystem again. I now turn to such an ecosystem in the DSM, AFSJ and the EA in chapters six to eight.

---

[144] See generally Koops (n 45); for criminal law, A Flanagan, 'The Law and Computer Crime: Reading the Script of Reform' (2005) 13 *International Journal of Law and Information Technology* 98. Reed (n 44), discussing how the automotive industry kept up with technological change. On the pacing problem, see Reed (n 44) 282; Bennett Moses (1).
[145] Leenes (n 77) 149.
[146] Chandler (n 35).
[147] JE Cohen, 'What Privacy is For' (2013) 126 *Harvard Law Review* 1094.
[148] R Brownsword, 'Code, Control and Choice: Why East is East and West is West' (2005) (25)(1) *Legal Studies* 1, 14, quoted in Leenes (n 77) 159.
[149] Lessig (n 77); E Celeste, 'Digital Constitutionalism. A New Systematic Theorisation' (2018) 33 *International Review of Law, Computers & Technology* 76–99.

6

The DSM: Network and Information Security (NIS), Privacy and Data Protection

Chapter five showed the potential for a theoretical overlap of cybersecurity, privacy and data protection (the triad) and thus complete reconciliation. There I also showed, however, how the regulatory ecosystem could invalidate such a finding in practice. This chapter is the first of three that deals with the practice of reconciliation in the three main areas of EU law. The Digital Single Market (DSM) is the obvious point to start. It is the oldest and most established area of EU law making, where Network and Information Security (NIS), privacy and data protection legislation were first developed. Here I reflect on the relationship between the triad in the DSM along the three areas of analysis of this book: policy, law and technology.

I begin by observing how the changing technological and political landscape, characterised by increased privatisation and the convergence of previously separated technologies, informed successive DSM policies expressing different stances on the relationship between NIS, privacy and data protection (I). The analysis of policy documents does not lead to firm conclusions on the configuration of the relationship between NIS, privacy and data protection.

I then undertake a comparative analysis of a selection of NIS-related instruments in force at the time of writing: the European Electronic Communications Code (EECC), the NIS Directive (NISD), the Cybersecurity Act (CSA), the e-Identity and Assurance Services Regulation (eIDAS Reg), the General Data Protection Regulation (GDPR), the e-privacy Directive (EPD) and, insofar as data breaches and security incidents are concerned, the second Payment Services Directive (PSD2) (II). The analysis shows that, at a high level of abstraction, measures tend to be complementary or effect such synergies that none of the elements of the triad appears to require limitation for the sake of fulfilling the other.[1] I call this strong reconciliation, as opposed to weak reconciliation, which refers to the outcome of the application of a balancing formula in a proportionality test arising from conflict between the elements of the triad.

Finally, I analyse whether the strong reconciliation found at a high level of abstraction holds true at a lower level of abstraction, by looking at the implementation of the law through technical and organisational measures (TOMs) or 'technology' (III). The example of Deep Packet Inspection (DPI), a measure that was highly contested in

---

[1] This work does not attempt to investigate causation.

the 2010s but appears to have gone mainstream, enables me to show how NIS-related technologies can seriously interfere with the right to privacy and data protection, thereby unsettling claims about the strong reconcilability of the triad. The analysis of DPI raises important questions for how to manage current and new TOMs that affect the triad.

I. Reconciliation of Network and Information Security, Privacy and Data Protection: Policy

Successive DSM policies have taken different stances on the relationship between NIS, privacy and data protection on account of the changing technological and political landscape, characterised by increased privatisation and the convergence of previously separated technologies. In the early days of the liberalisation of telecommunications,[2] public networks and connectivity, services tended to be offered by traditional telcos and were regulated separately from services available online. The latter, such as Information Society Services (ISS), e-commerce and audio-visual services, constituted a separate fraction of the market subjected to a dedicated regulatory regime. Electronic privacy was only disciplined in relation to traditional telcos. EU law did not target providers of non-public networks, nor economic actors enabling connectivity but not owning the network; no specific legislation existed for actors offering ICT-specific security and software was addressed from a copyright perspective only. Against this background, the regulation of NIS matters was seen as helping to create a level-playing field and to protect (consumer) rights.[3]

At the turn of the millennium the newly developed three-pronged approach[4] placed greater emphasis on the complementarity between measures adopted to secure network and information systems and privacy, through which data protection was protected. However, by then the convergence of infrastructure and services[5] had begun muddling neatly defined sectors and breeding a panoply of partly overlapping, yet disjointed instruments. As a result, the relationship between NIS, privacy and data protection has also become blurred and appears to be differently couched in policy documents that focus on the confidentiality, integrity and availability (CIA) of network and information systems, as opposed to cybersecurity policies at large.

Policy documents that focus on the CIA of network and information systems appear to have assimilated the three-pronged approach and assert the complementarity between

---

[2] See generally I Walden (ed), *Telecommunications Law and Regulation*, 5th edn (Oxford, Oxford University Press, 2018); L Edwards and C Waelde, *Law and the Internet* (Oxford, Hart Publishing, 2009); A Savin, *EU Telecommunications Law* (Cheltenham, Edward Elgar, 2018).

[3] M Bangemann et al., *The 'Recommendations to the European Council. Europe and the Global Information Society'. The Bangemann Report* (European Commission, 1994); European Commission, 'White Paper on Growth, Competitiveness, Employment. The Challenges and Ways forward into the 21st Century' (Communication) COM (93) 700. A retrospective critique: G Giacomello, *National Governments and Control of the Internet. A Digital Challenge* (London, Routledge, 2005).

[4] See ch 2, section II.A.

[5] A Renda, 'Quali Nuove Regole per la 'Information Superhighway' Europea?', in F Passarelli (ed), *Unione europea: Governance e Regolamentazione* (Il Mulino, 2006); A Gravosto, 'Le Telecomunicazioni in Europa: Governance e Regulation' in Passarelli ibid.

NIS and the two rights, as exemplified by a speech by then DG Justice Commissioner Reding to the NATO Parliamentary Assembly in May 2013.[6] There, Ms Reding depicted data protection rules and cybersecurity as two sides of the same coin. After stressing that they serve the same purposes, she noted they are mutually reinforcing; data minimisation[7] reduces the damage of a successful cyber-attack, whereas better rules on personal data and 'cyber'-related issues increase trust in e-services. Reconciliatory policies include the DSM Strategy, where privacy and data protection are an integral component of trust and security.[8] Another example is the 2016 Communication on cyber resilience, whereby data security, including personal data, is described as essential for the EU to be a leading player in the field. There, the plan was to create a single cyber market based on certification, enabling the multi-stakeholder approach of the c-PPP (PPP in cybersecurity) to reach 'common digital security, privacy and data protection requirements'.[9] The EU Security Union Agenda contains the acknowledgment that cooperation between ENISA and the EDPB is of 'key importance'[10] for cybersecurity, and that encrypted information are essential to cyberspace, cybersecurity and to protect fundamental rights, including privacy and data protection.[11]

By contrast, the 2013 and 2017 cybersecurity strategies, where NIS is a dimension of cybersecurity, do without the three-pronged approach and cast privacy and data protection as one of many elements of the policy. The 2020 policy avoids any language that may suggest complementarity but rather states that cybersecurity is 'essential ... for safeguarding fundamental rights and freedoms, including the rights to privacy and to the protection of personal data'.[12] Data protection and privacy are also mentioned in the context of international efforts to build voluntary norms of responsible state behaviour. 'The EU should make sustained efforts to protect human rights defenders, civil society and academia working on issues such as cybersecurity, data privacy, surveillance and online censorship.'[13] After all, privacy and especially data protection are EU regulatory exports[14] and their protection fits in a cybersecurity policy conscious of EU values.[15] More of this in chapter eight.

In sum, policy documents do not allow the drawing of clear conclusions on the configuration of the relationship between NIS, privacy and data protection. I therefore turn to analysing their interplay in the applicable law.

---

[6] V Reding, *The EU's data protection rules and cyber security strategy: two sides of the same coin*. Speech before the NATO Parliamentary Assembly/Luxembourg, SPEECH/13/436 (2013).

[7] Meaning the collection of those personal data that are strictly necessary to achieve the purposes of data processing. See further in ch 4.

[8] European Commission, 'A Digital Single Market Strategy for Europe' (Communication) COM (2015) 192 final; European Commission, 'A Europe fit for digital age. Shaping Europe's digital future' (Communication) COM (2020) 67 final; '2030 Digital Compass: the European way for the Digital Decade' (Communication) COM (2021)118 final.

[9] European Commission, 'Strengthening Europe's Cyber Resilience System' (Communication) COM (2016) 640 final, 12.

[10] European Commission, 'EU Security Union Strategy' (Communication) COM (2020) 605 final, 8.

[11] ibid, 13. See ch 7.

[12] European Commission and High Representative of the European Union for Foreign Affairs and Security Policy, 'The EU's Cybersecurity Strategy for the Digital Decade' (Joint Communication) JOIN (2020) 18 final, 5.

[13] ibid, 22.

[14] A Bradford, 'The Brussels Effect' 107 *Northwestern University Law Review*.

[15] P Pawlak, *Operational Guidance for the EU's International Cooperation on Cyber Capacity Building* (European Union Institute for Security Studies, 2018).

II. Reconciliation of NIS, Privacy and Data Protection: Law[16]

Even if the analysis of policy documents proved inconclusive, an analysis of the applicable law adopted in the DSM could help cast light on the relationship between the NIS cybersecurity dimension, privacy and data protection. As seen in chapter two, the NIS dimension embraces the legal and operational initiatives to secure network and information systems as Critical Information Infrastructure (CII). Currently the regulatory landscape is characterised by a high degree of fragmentation, and relevant instruments can be divided into four categories. The first is made of instruments, or provisions within them, to secure the ICT infrastructure within the telco framework overseen by the Body of European Regulators for Electronic Communications (BEREC). The second category encompasses NIS laws planned for by the EU cybersecurity policy. A third category includes sector-specific instruments, some predating the 2013 cybersecurity policy and addressing facets of NIS, such as responding to data breaches and security incidents. The fourth category encompasses instruments which are peripheral to NIS but bear relevance for it.

At the time of writing a number of NIS-relevant rules are being overhauled. This includes the e-privacy Regulation[17] (EPR) repealing the EPD, the NIS2 repealing the NISD[18] and an amendment to the eIDAS Reg,[19] which are due to streamline the field and partly redress the fragmentation that characterises this regulatory area. Although an analysis of draft legislation is beyond the scope of this research, I will illustrate if and how proposals could change the outcome of the analysis.

I begin by introducing the EECC,[20] the NISD,[21] the CSA,[22] the eIDAS Reg,[23] the GDPR,[24] the EPD[25] and, insofar as data breaches and security incidents are concerned, the PSD2[26] (III.A). I then compare these instruments from several angles: their definitions

---

[16] This section develops works in MG Porcedda, 'Patching the Patchwork: Appraising the EU Regulatory Framework on Cyber Security Breaches' (2018) 34 *Computer Law & Security Review*.

[17] European Commission, 'Proposal for a Regulation on Privacy and Electronic Communications', (Communication) COM (2017) 10 final, 2017/0003 (COD) (EPR).

[18] European Commission, 'Proposal for a Directive of the European Parliament and of the Council on measures for a high common level of cybersecurity across the Union, repealing Directive (EU) 2016/1148', COM(2020) 823 final, adopted as Directive (EU) 2022/2555, OJ L333/80 as this book went to press.

[19] European Commission, Proposal for a Regulation amending Regulation (EU) No 910/2014 as regards establishing a framework for a European Digital Identity, COM (2021)281.

[20] Directive (EU) 2018/1972 of the European Parliament and of the Council of 11 December 2018 establishing the European Electronic Communications Code (Recast) [2018] OJ L321/36 (EECC).

[21] Directive (EU) 2016/1148 of the European Parliament and of the Council of 6 July 2016 concerning measures for a high common level of security of network and Information systems across the Union [2016] OJ L194/1 (NISD).

[22] Regulation (EU) 2019/881 of the European Parliament and of the Council of 17 April 2019 on ENISA (the European Union Agency for Cybersecurity) and on information and communications technology cybersecurity certification and repealing Regulation (EU) No 526/2013 (Cybersecurity Act or CSA) [2019] OJ L151/15.

[23] Regulation (EU) 910/2014 of 23 July 2014 on electronic identification and trust services for electronic transactions in the internal market and repealing Directive 1999/93/EC [2014] OJ L257/73 (eIDAS Regulation).The website of DG Connect has a list of the qualified trust service providers (webgate.ec.europa.eu/tl-browser/#/) and the free e-signature package (ec.europa.eu/cefdigital/wiki/display/CEFDIGITAL/DSS).

[24] General Data Protection Regulation (EU) 2016/679 [2016] OJ L119/1 (GDPR).

[25] E-privacy Directive 2002/58/EC [2002] OJ L201/37 (EPD).

[26] Directive (EU) 2015/2366 of the European Parliament and of the Council of 25 November 2015 on Payment Services in the Internal Market, amending Directives 2002/65/EC, 2009/110/EC and 2013/36/EU and Regulation (EU) No 1093/2010, and repealing Directive 2007/64/EC [2015] OJ L337/35.

and scope, notion of security, presence of explicit cross-references, common logics as well as structures put in place to achieve their goals (III.B). The outcome will enable me to show that the applicable law engenders 'strong reconciliation' between NIS, privacy and data protection at a high level of abstraction (III.C), with some caveats (III.E). The revisions of the NISD, eIDAS Reg and EPD, underway at the time of writing, does not call into question the main findings (III.D).

A. Overview of Legal Instruments Relevant to NIS

The EECC, NISD, CSA, eIDAS Reg, GDPR and EPD pursue different aims and bear different scopes.[27] Whereas NIS is the primary aim of the NISD, and cybersecurity of the CSA, 'security' is one among many objectives of the EECC, eIDAS Reg, GDPR and EPD. Moreover, all instruments lay down requirements for EU institutions, Member States and National Regulatory Authorities.

Taken together, these instruments apply to a seemingly vast array of addressees: personal data controllers and processors (GDPR and EPD[28]), providers of electronic communications networks and associated facilities (to the public EECC, otherwise NISD, CSA, defined below), electronic communications services and associated services (EECC, NISD, CSA, possibly eIDAS Regulation), ICT services (CSA), electronic registered delivery services[29] and trust services[30] (eIDAS Reg), operators of essential services (OESs)[31] as well as digital service providers (DSPs)[32] (NISD, CSA) and entities accessing terminal equipment[33] (to an extent EECC, EPD, GDPR).

Sometimes different labels apply to the same entity, as stressed by the Court of Justice of the European Union (CJEU) in *Skype Communications* with regard to Information Society Services (ISSs) and Electronic Communications Services (ECSs).[34] Such a reality exemplifies the fragmentary approach to law making[35] in the DSM, whereby actors are simultaneously bound by an overarching framework (*lex generalis*) as well as rules specific to sectors of activity (*lex specialis*). The role of *lex generalis* is played by the

---

[27] EECC, Art 1, NISD, Art 1, CSA, Art 1, eIDAS Reg, Art 1, GDPR, Arts 1–3 and EPD, Art 1.
[28] See ch 4.
[29] eIDAS Reg, Arts 3(36)–(37).
[30] eIDAS Reg, Arts 3(16), (19). Trust services can be qualified and a list of providers of such services is offered on the website of DG Connect (webgate.ec.europa.eu/tl-browser/#/), alongside the free e-signature package (ec.europa.eu/cefdigital/wiki/display/CEFDIGITAL/DSS).
[31] OESs are public or private entities providing services dependent on network and information systems that are essential for the maintenance of critical activities that would be highly disrupted by an incident (Arts 4(4), 5(1) NIDS). OESs operate in energy, transport, banking, financial market infrastructures, health, the drinking water supply and distribution, as well as digital infrastructure, ie Internet exchange points (IXPs), domain name system (DNS) service providers and Top Level Domain (TLD) name registries (Annex II NISD).
[32] Three ISSs offered in the EU: search engines, online marketplaces (ie ECSs) and cloud computing (NISD Art 4(5)). But see section II.D below.
[33] Art 1, Commission Directive 2008/63/EC of 20 June 2008 on competition in the markets in telecommunications terminal equipment [2008] OJ L162, 20–26. '(a) Equipment ... connected to the interface of a public telecommunications network to send, process or receive information; ... the connection may be made by wire, optical fibre or electromagnetically; ... (b) satellite earth station equipment.'
[34] *Skype Communications*, C-142/18, EU:C:2019:460, paras 47–48.
[35] These labels also exemplify technology neutrality, see ch 5 and section III below.

EECC and the GDPR, with the EPD, eIDAS Reg, NISD and CSA being the *lex specialis* of one, the other, or both. The EECC is *lex specialis* in relation to the security of publicly available e-communication networks and services.

The overlapping nature of differently labelled entities also reveals the overlapping scope of the instruments under analysis. In essence, in addition to similar entities these instruments also deal with the same basic units: networks and data. Networks enable cyberspace, while data flows give cyberspace meaning and purpose. Demonstrating how the instruments under analysis similarly address networks and data is crucial for understanding the relationship between NIS, privacy and data protection and is what I turn to next.

B. Comparative Analysis of Selected Instruments

In this section I compare and contrast the EECC, eIDAS Reg,[36] the NISD, CSA, GDPR, EPD and PSD2 on the following grounds: definitions and scope of the basic units (II.B.i), notion of security and reference to information security properties (II.B.ii); presence and nature of explicit cross-references between the texts (II.B.iii); the logics informing the instruments (II.B.iv) and the 'recipes' they adopt to pursue their goals, which rest on a mixture of TOMs (II.B.v).

i. Definitions of Basic Units: Networks, Signals, Communications, Information and Data

The analysis of definitions adopted by each instrument is a pre-condition for examining the notions of security they espouse and pursue. I start with networks, followed by signals, communications, information and then data. Electronic communication networks are

> transmission systems ... which permit the *conveyance of signals* by wire, radio, optical or other electromagnetic means, including satellite networks, fixed (circuit- and packet-switched, including internet) and mobile networks, electricity cable systems, to the extent that they are used for the purpose of *transmitting signals*, networks used for radio and television broadcasting, and cable television networks, irrespective of the type of *information* conveyed.[37]

This definition of networks is adopted by the EPD, the NISD and, by extension, the CSA.[38] Networks enable the provision of ECSs, which are

> a service normally provided for remuneration via electronic communications networks, which encompasses ...: (a) 'internet access service';[39] (b) interpersonal communications service; and

---

[36] NB the overhaul of the NISD repeals Arts 19 eIDAS Reg and 40–41 EECC by the end of the transposition period (21 months after the date of entry into force of the Directive repealing the NISD). See section II.D below.
[37] They include switching or routing; EECC, Art 2(1) (emphasis added); see further EECC, Art 2(2) and (8).
[38] EPD, Art 2, NISD, Art 4(1)(a), CSA, Art 2(2).
[39] Defined in Art 2(2), second paragraph of Regulation (EU) 2015/2120 [2015] OJ L310/1. See Body of European Regulators for Electronic Communications (BEREC), *BEREC Report on OTT services*, BoR (16) 35 (2016).

(c) services consisting wholly or mainly in the conveyance of signals such as transmission services used for the provision of machine-to-machine services and for broadcasting.[40]

ECSs now include number-based and number-independent interpersonal communications services, that is Over-The-Top (OTT) services[41] such as voice telephony, messaging services and electronic mail services, which previously were solely classed as ISSs.[42] Whenever ECSs are publicly available, they fall within the remit of the EPD, whose scope has therefore broadened (with consequences for the fight against 'cybercrime' discussed in chapter seven). If the services are not publicly available, and/or are DSPs, they fall within the remit of the NIS Directive.

The main purpose of e-communications networks and services is to 'convey' or 'transmit' signals. Although the concept of signals is beyond immediate grasp, surprisingly it is defined neither in the EECC, nor in the other instruments analysed here. The EECC states that conveyance of signals 'remains an important parameter for determining the services falling into the scope of this Directive' but that 'the definition should cover also other services that enable communication' and 'from an end-user's perspective it is not relevant whether a provider conveys signals itself or whether the communication is delivered via an internet access service'.[43] Case law is no more enlightening.[44] Savin notes that 'signals consist of *information* – words, messages, images, sounds or any combination thereof'.[45]

Communications is a term of common use and easier to relate to but, similarly to signals, it is not defined in the EECC. A definition is instead contained in the EPD, as 'any *information* exchanged or conveyed between a finite number of parties' by means of a publicly available ECS.[46] To complicate matters further, 'communications' is an essential component of the right to respect for private and family life, called 'correspondence' in Article 8 ECHR.[47] The European Court of Human Rights (ECtHR), followed by the CJEU, has consistently stressed that any communication deserves protection irrespective of the technological medium for its delivery;[48] both courts have come to acknowledge the importance of bulk, raw data for the right to private life and therefore subsume it under the scope of communications to be kept confidential.[49] But what are signals and communications for, if not to convey and exchange information?

---

[40] EECC, Art 2(4). It excludes services providing, or exercising editorial control over, content.
[41] EECC, Art 2 (6), (7). See BEREC (n 39).
[42] See Art 1(b) Directive (EU) 2015/1535 of the European Parliament and of the Council of 9 September 2015 laying down a procedure for the provision of information in the field of technical regulations and of rules on information society services (codification), [2015] OJ L241. 'Any service normally provided for remuneration, at a distance, by electronic means and at the individual request of a recipient of services.'
[43] Rec 15 EECC.
[44] *UPC DTH*, C-475/12, EU:C:2014:285, para 44. The meaning of signals is assumed. Skype Communications, C-142/18, upholds *UPC DTH*.
[45] Savin (n 2) 5.
[46] Art 2(d) EPD. Broadcast communications (eg, TV or radio) do not fall within this definition, unless 'the information can be related to the identifiable subscriber or user receiving the information'.
[47] Council of Europe [1950] ETS n. 005. See ch 3.
[48] Extending to emails: *Copland v the United Kingdom* no. 62617/00 CE:ECHR:2007:0403JUD006261700, para 41.
[49] *Big Brother Watch and Others v UK* nos. 58170/13, 62322/14 and 24960/15 CE:ECHR:2018:0913JUD005817013; *Digital Rights Ireland and Seitlinger and Others*, C-293/12 and C-594/12, EU:C:2014:238.

Similarly to signals, the legal instruments under analysis make ample use of 'information' without defining it. For instance, 'ICT service' is a service 'consisting fully or mainly in the transmission, storing, retrieving or processing of *information* by means of network and information systems'.[50] In the NISD, information system are: '(a) an electronic communications network within the meaning of *point (a) of Article 2 of Directive 2002/21/EC*' (now Article 2(1) EECC); (b) 'any device or group of interconnected or related devices, one or more of which, pursuant to a program, perform automatic processing of *digital data*'; and '(c) *digital data* stored, processed, retrieved or transmitted by elements covered under points (a) and (b) for the purposes of their operation, use, protection and maintenance'.[51] This definition shows how network and information systems are interrelated, actually indivisible, and that information is substituted with a 'proxy': data.

All instruments under analysis postulate a link between data, information and signals.[52] Furthermore, both the EECC and the EPD conceptualise communications in terms of information, as seen above. Information should ultimately be understood as data, not least because, to be transmitted, it must ultimately be expressed in the form of digital signals, hence digital/computer data. In the GDPR, personal data is 'any *information* relating to an identified or identifiable natural person ("data subject")'.[53] In the eIDAS Reg, 'person identification data' are 'a set of data enabling the identity of a natural or legal person, or a natural person representing a legal person to be established'.[54] There, identity is information expressed in the form of data (which begs the question as to why the legislator did not opt for the existing notion of personal data). Gellert reaches a similar conclusion based on information theory.[55]

The use of different terms may reflect the fact that signals, data and information relate to the physical, logical and content layers respectively, which are part of separate regulatory frameworks, eg, 'the carrier – the wires covering the signal' and 'the content – the substance running on the wires'.[56] At the physical layer, electromagnetic signals are raw data, which are capable of encompassing all existing information.[57] Such data can be both non-personal, ie, carrying information on the state of a network or collected from environmental sensors and personal, ie, concerning an individual.

In sum, the five instruments deal with various applications of network and information systems and signals/information, exemplified through the notion of data, which these systems are meant to store, transmit and process. These findings lay the foundations for the analysis of the concept of 'security' and its bearing on the possibility of reconciling data protection, privacy and cybersecurity in its 'NIS' configuration.

---

[50] CSA, Art 2(13) (emphasis added).
[51] NISD, Art 4 (emphasis added).
[52] In the EECC, even if signals are analogue at the source, circulation over electronic networks requires their transformation into digital signals, which are conceptualised as data.
[53] GDPR, Art 4 (1); I articulated the conflation as a 'definitional gap' in chs 1 and 4.
[54] eIDAS Reg, Art 3(3).
[55] R Gellert, 'Comparing Definitions of Data and Information in Data Protection Law and Machine Learning. A Useful Way Forward to Meaningfully Regulate Algorithms?' (2022) 16(1) *Regulation & Governance* 156–176.
[56] Savin (n 2) 3.
[57] According to Andrade, 'information' not only helps make sense of complexity, but is also a foundational element of the world we live in. N Andrade, 'The Right to Personal Identity in the Information Age. A reappraisal of a lost right' (PhD thesis, European University Institute 2011).

ii. Notions of 'Security'

Here I focus on notions of 'security' other than public security contained in the instruments under analysis.[58] The CSA contains the first legal definition of 'cybersecurity' in EU law as 'the *activities* necessary *to protect* network and information *systems*, the *users* of such systems, and *other persons* affected by cyber threats'.[59] The definition uses 'to protect' instead of 'to secure' (or 'prevent'), but does not constrain itself to a class of protective activities.[60] Thus, 'activities necessary to protect' can be taken to include initiatives that go beyond the remit of the 'NIS' prong of cybersecurity. Either way,[61] the security of NIS as defined in the NISD and, by extension, the EECC, is part and parcel of cybersecurity.

Building on the findings of the previous section, in the context of services regulated by the instruments under analysis, protecting network and information systems means safeguarding e-communication networks and data processed therein. For instance, e-identification and trust services are means of securing information systems in the sense of the NISD, 'i.e. digital data stored, processed, retrieved or transmitted by elements covered under points (a) and (b) for the purposes of their operation, use, protection and maintenance'[62] in that they oversee the authenticity and integrity 'of stored or transmitted or processed data'.[63] Even hazards prima facie unrelated to cybersecurity fit the argument. The transposition by Member States of the Framework Directive – now repealed by the EECC – placed great emphasis on 'integrity', ie, continuity of service that could be undermined by causes other than cyber-attacks,[64] such as physical hazards. Physical security is now subsumed under the 'all-hazard risk-based approach' in the context of the NISD (and to an extent the EECC).[65] The fact that 'integrity' is expressed in the context of confidentiality, availability and authenticity clearly anchors 'integrity' to information security properties.[66] However, continuity of service appears to be the ultimate goal of duty of care obligations enshrined in Articles 14 and 16 NISD,[67] in keeping with the overall policy objective of resilience.

Because of the link between data, information and signals, the definition of cybersecurity embraces all five instruments under analysis: protection should benefit not only

---

[58] EECC, Art 2(21), also 'harmful interference', at 2(20); ENISA, Art 2(1); NISD, Art 4 (2); eIDAS Reg, Recs 20, 28, 44, 48 and 72, also Arts 7, 11; GDPR, Arts 5(f), 24, 25; EPD, Rec 20, Art 4.

[59] CSA, Art 2(1) (emphasis added).

[60] As did the repealed Regulation (EU) 526/2013 of the European Parliament and of the Council of 21 May 2013 concerning the European Union Agency for Network and Information Security (ENISA) and repealing Regulation (EC) No 460/2004 [2013] OJ L165/41.

[61] Also noting the mismatch, G González Fuster and L Jasmontaite, 'Cybersecurity Regulation in the European Union: The Digital, the Critical and Fundamental Rights' in *The Ethics of Cybersecurity* (2020).

[62] NISD, Art 4(1)(c).

[63] NISD, Art 4(2).

[64] European Network and Information Security Agency (ENISA), *Annual Incident Reports 2016. Analysis of Article 13a Annual Incident Reports in the Telecom Sector* (2017).

[65] Art 2(b) Commission Implementing Regulation 2018/151 of 30 January 2018 laying down rules for the application of Directive (EU) 2016/1148 of the European Parliament and of the Council as regards further specification of the elements to be taken into account by digital service providers for managing the risks posed to the security of network and information systems and of the parameters for determining whether an incident has a substantial impact. [2018] OJ L26/48.

[66] See ch 5, section I.A and below.

[67] See section III below.

systems, but also the *users* of such systems and *other persons*. The CSA is silent as to the meaning of 'users'; it is unlikely that users would be confined to 'a natural or legal person using or requesting a publicly available electronic communications service'.[68] 'Other persons' means the beneficiaries of secure networks and information systems beyond the users of such systems. Such a wording acknowledges that anybody could suffer as a result of threats to network and information systems, due to the role of CII in contemporary societies. Examples include high-profile cyber-attacks to power plants, such as in Germany and the US, many hospitals and even an entire healthcare system during the Covid-19 global pandemic, which calls into question the security of personal data.[69] The GDPR, which applies to the EPD and, arguably, the eIDAS Reg insofar as 'person identification data' are concerned, defines security as 'integrity and confidentiality': these are a subset of information security properties featuring in the definition of 'cyber' 'security' found in the CSA and the EECC.

Clearly, there are differences between instruments concerning the scope of application of 'security', both in terms of services and types of data, information and signals. Although the nature of such instruments as *lex specialis* can create variable zones of cybersecurity,[70] this does not detract from the fact that all instruments aim to secure the same 'ecosystem' made of infrastructure, the various services it enables, the stored, transmitted and processed data/information/signals and the people that, directly or indirectly, operate in such an ecosystem.

Notwithstanding the differences, the understandings of security harboured by the instruments come together through security properties. Network and information security in the NISD and EECC is explicitly bound to the CIA triad plus authenticity, which can be understood as a variation of authentication.[71] The CIA triad plus authenticity are also features of the European Cybersecurity Certification framework introduced by the CSA. The framework's purpose 'should be to ensure that' certified ICT products, services and processes 'comply with specified requirements that aim to protect the availability, authenticity, integrity and confidentiality of stored, transmitted or processed data or of the related functions of or services offered by, or accessible via those products'.[72] Insofar as the eIDAS Reg pursues NIS objectives, security is understood as CIA canons.[73] Furthermore, integrity and confidentiality are one of the data protection principles.[74] Keeping in mind the caveats discussed in chapter five, integrity and confidentiality are part of the essence of the right and confidentiality is the essence of the right to privacy.[75] Since the pursuit of privacy and data protection by design

---

[68] As in EECC, Art 2(13).
[69] K Zetter, 'A Cyberattack Has Caused Confirmed Physical Damage for the Second Time Ever' *Wired* (1 August 2015); W Ralston, 'The Untold Story of a Cyberattack, a Hospital and a Dying Woman' ibid (11 November 2020); S Sharwood, 'US Declares Emergency after Ransomware Shuts Oil Pipeline that Pumps 100 Million Gallons a Day' *The Register* (10 May); PricewaterhouseCoopers, 'Conti Cyber-attack on the HSE. Independent Post Incident Review'.
[70] See section III below.
[71] See ch 5, section I.A.
[72] CSA, Rec 75.
[73] See section II.B.iii below.
[74] GDPR Art 5(f).
[75] See ch 5, section II, ch 4, section III and ch 3, section III; such finding does not exclude the possibility that national courts may have identified other core areas of the rights.

Law 167

requires reliance on the additional security properties of availability and authenticity,[76] as a result the five instruments engender the same notion of security. In other words, the instruments partly overlap and broadly converge insofar as the security of network and information systems and related services are concerned.

The overlapping notions of NIS contained in the instruments just reviewed is clear in light of the techno-legal analysis done in chapter five setting aside for the time being the misalignment between legal and engineering concepts. The values of 'integrity' and 'confidentiality' pursued by instruments implementing the right to data protection converge toward those protected by measures that preserve the 'availability/authenticity, integrity/confidentiality of stored/transmitted/processed *data* or *services*'.[77] The same applies to confidentiality vis-à-vis privacy. The overlapping values suggest the absence of conflict between instruments and warrant a prima facie strong reconciliation (and by extension a high degree of coherence) at a high level of abstraction.[78]

The complementarity is reinforced by cross-references to cybersecurity, privacy and data protection appearing in the provisions and recitals of the instruments. Cross-references are of three types: (i) no prejudice across instruments; (ii) cooperation; (iii) complementarity of goals. Such cross-references express different strengths of reconciliation.

First of all, the instruments not only include formulaic Recitals listing the potentially affected fundamental rights,[79] but also provisions recalling the need to respect the applicable law related to such rights. For instance, international agreements concluded by the Union with third countries or international organisations pursuant to the NISD, allowing such countries or organisations to participate in the Cooperation Group, must take into account the need to ensure adequate protection of data.[80] In the eIDAS Reg, 'the use of pseudonyms in electronic transactions shall not be prohibited'[81] can be seen as a privacy rights-enhancing feature; then,

> authentication for an online service should concern processing of only those identification data that are adequate, relevant and not excessive to grant access to that service online. Furthermore, requirements under [the GDPR] concerning confidentiality and security of processing should be respected by trust service providers and supervisory bodies.[82]

Trust service providers should employ staff who have received appropriate training regarding *security* and *personal data protection* rules.[83] These provisions serve a logic of

---

[76] Ch 5, section I.A.
[77] In the instruments analysed, these include communication services offered by, or accessible via network and information systems, and the network and information systems themselves; essential/digital services offered by, or accessible via network and information systems; and e-identification schemes and trust services, accessible via network and information systems.
[78] Ch 5, section II showed that overlaps are theoretical and must be demonstrated at a lower level of abstraction, taking into account TOMs. Section IV below will address whether strong reconciliation holds true at a low level of abstraction.
[79] Eg, NISD, Rec 75.
[80] NISD, Arts 2, 113, Rec 72.
[81] eIDAS Reg, Rec 11, Art 5(2).
[82] eIDAS Reg, Rec 4; reference was to the GDPR was originally to the DPD (Directive 95/46/EC). Art 67(2)(f) embodies a measure of data minimisation.
[83] eIDAS Reg, Art 24(2)(b).

non-interference, whereby the implementation of one instrument should not prejudice the application of other instruments.

Second, authorities created under the various instruments are expected to act jointly whenever security incidents affect personal data.[84] In addition to this, ENISA must cooperate 'at the operational level and *establish synergies*' with 'supervisory authorities dealing with (…) the protection of privacy and personal data' 'with a view to addressing issues of common concern'.[85] Likewise, the NISD obliges competent authorities and a single point of contact to consult and cooperate with national data protection authorities.[86] These provisions highlight that authorities overseeing NIS share 'common concerns' that require collaboration, which takes reconciliation a step further.

Finally and crucially, the CSA features Articles spelling out the complementarity between the protection goals of privacy, data protection and NIS instruments. The Act underlines how the GDPR and the EPD 'contribute to a high level of cybersecurity' in the DSM.[87] The legislator entrusted ENISA with the task of supporting the development and implementation of 'Union policy in the field of electronic identity and trust services', 'the promotion of an enhanced level of security of electronic communications' as well as Member States, upon request, 'in the implementation of specific cybersecurity aspects of Union policy and law relating to data protection and privacy, including by providing advice to the EDPB'.[88]

In sum, insofar as the instruments pursue different facets of NIS, they complement one another. This analysis seems to confirm that the law strongly reconciles the NIS side of cybersecurity with privacy and data protection. This finding is reinforced by the fact that the instruments are predicated on the same preventative paradigm, which hinges on 'technical and organisation measures' and is presented as instrumental to the achievement of the DSM, as I discuss next.

iii. Risk, Prevention and 'Technical and Organisational Measures': Averting Incidents and Personal Data Breaches

The instruments studied are predicated on the same risk paradigm and security logic, which they pursue with similar strategies, including for dealing with security incidents and data breaches. I review the paradigms of risk assessment and management and the logic of prevention in turn, followed by a focus on 'technical and organisation measures' (TOMs) and for responding to incidents and breaches.

All instruments are predicated on the paradigm of risk assessment and management, that is, they aim to identify potential risks, understood as vulnerabilities to threats.[89] By means of example, the CSA assumes that 'increased digitisation and connectivity increase cybersecurity risks, thus making society as a whole more vulnerable to cyber threats and exacerbating the dangers faced by individuals'.[90] Against this background,

---

[84] See section II.B.iii below.
[85] CSA, Art 7.
[86] NISD, Art 8(6).
[87] CSA, Rec 15 (and EECC).
[88] CSA, Art 5.
[89] See ch 5.
[90] CSA, Rec 3.

the CSA encourages the basing of 'efficient cybersecurity policies' 'on well-developed *risk assessment* methods, in both the public and private sectors ... and ... interoperable risk management solutions', which 'will increase the level of cybersecurity in the Union'.[91] Risk also informs the EPD on the security of processing and data breaches,[92] as well as the GDPR, which features different shades and types of risks, including security risks.[93] The purpose of assessing risks is to manage them, so as to pursue aims, such as building trust, protecting individuals and supporting the continuity of services within the DSM.

The logic embodied in all instruments is to prevent as many risks as possible from materialising.[94] An example is the EPD, whereby 'measures should be taken to *prevent* unauthorised access to communications in order to protect the confidentiality of communications, including both the contents and any data related to such communications'.[95] Likewise in the GDPR, which aims to *prevent* 'unauthorised access to or use of personal data and the equipment used for the processing', 'maintaining security' and '*preventing* infringements'.[96] Prevention is also at the heart of ENISA's tasks. The Union Cybersecurity Agency must support Member States in their efforts to improve the *prevention*, detection and analysis of cyber threats, and their actions in *preventing* and responding to cyber threats.[97] In this latter example, prevention is coupled with detection and response, because no ICT product or service 'is wholly cyber-secure'.[98]

Perennial insecurity is caused, among many, by 'dependency', whereby 'modern ICT products and systems often integrate and rely on one or more third-party technologies and components such as software modules, libraries or application programming interfaces'.[99] In other words, although prevention is better than cure, 'the occurrence of cyberattacks is presumed'[100] so that risks cannot be completely removed and, by extension, the presence of vulnerabilities accepted. Detection could happen too late across the supply-chain and force organisations to respond to minimise harms. Several recent incidents were caused by exploiting vulnerable intermediary services, such as shopping cart platforms or third-party services used by e-commerce websites. The Magecart

---

[91] CSA, Recital 49

[92] EPD, Art 4, Rec 20. Article 29 Data Protection Working Party, *Statement on the Role of a Risk-based Approach in Data Protection Legal Frameworks* (14/EN WP 218, 2014); European Network and Information Security Agency (ENISA), *Risk Management: Implementation Principles and Inventories for Risk Management/Risk Assessment methods and tools* (2006).

[93] See Porcedda (n 16); R Gellert, 'Data Protection: a Risk Regulation? Between the Risk Management of Everything and the Precautionary Alternative' (2015) 5 *International Data Privacy Law* 3–19.

[94] The approach is to accept risks and manage them, as opposed to the precautionary principle, which requires a degree of certainty before action is taken. R Baldwin and M Cave et al., *Understanding Regulation. Theory, Strategy and Practice*, 2nd edn (Oxford, Oxford University Press, 2011); D Wright and R Gellert et al., 'Minimizing Technology Risks with PIAs, Precaution, and Participation' (2011) 30 IEEE *Technology and Society Magazine* 47. Gellert (n 93). However, for the EDPS, some measures in the GDPR express the precautionary approach: European Data Protection Supervisor (EDPS), 'Opinion 5/2018. Preliminary Opinion on privacy by design', para 61.

[95] EPD, Rec 21.

[96] GDPR, Recs 39, 83 (emphasis added).

[97] CSA, Arts (5)(1), 4(5).

[98] ibid, Rec 10.

[99] ibid, Rec 11.

[100] ibid, Rec 7.

group exploited almost 17,000 e-commerce sites up until 2019, including the site of British Airways, for which the company was fined over £200 million.[101]

Finally, in order to deal with risks, all instruments rely on a similar recipe based on TOMs appropriate to the seriousness of the threat and the likelihood of the risk incurred. Four out of the five instruments discussed here feature an explicit reference to TOMs that embody duty of care requirements[102] suitable to the risk(s) faced by each instrument's addressee. These are found in Articles 14(1) and 16(1) NISD for essential and digital services respectively, 19 eIDAS Regulation, 40 EECC, 5, 24, 25 and 32 GDPR and 4 EPD. The outlier is the CSA which does not mention TOMs anywhere in the text,[103] though its long Title III is devoted to the establishment of a cybersecurity certification framework, which is 'a comprehensive set of rules, technical requirements, standards and procedures that are established at Union level and that apply to the certification or conformity assessment of specific ICT products, services or processes'.[104] Certification is an organisational measure aimed at creating parameters for technical measures based on the concept of assurance.[105] For instance, the certificate or the EU statement of conformity shall refer to technical specifications, standards and procedures related thereto, including technical controls, the purpose of which is to decrease the risk of, or to prevent cybersecurity incidents.[106] Furthermore, ENISA has a central role in the identification of TOMs suitable to achieve cybersecurity across the board.

All instruments aim to embed their security objective(s) in the design of technology, a desire stemming from a longstanding trend and recently streamlined in legislation. 'Data protection by design' (DPbD) and 'security by design' (SbD) are explicitly pursued by Articles 25 GDPR,[107] 51(i) CSA, 12(3)(c) eIDAS Reg and appear in Recital 97 EECC. The CSA describes SbD as a strategy to 'implement measures at the earliest stages of design and development to protect the security of those products, services and processes to the highest possible degree, in such a way that the occurrence of cyberattacks is presumed and their impact is anticipated and minimised'.[108]

Although some instruments specify the nature of organisational measures to be adopted – the GDPR is, basically, a compendium of organisational measures – they only provide rare examples of technical measures. This approach is, I argue, an embodiment of technology neutrality, whose tension with 'by design' objectives I discussed in chapter five. Instead, examples of technical measures are usually found in delegated legislation and Recitals.[109] An instance of the former is Commission Regulation 611/2013/EU,[110]

---

[101] Europol, 'Internet Organised Crime Threat Assessment (IOCTA) 2019', 19, 36, 60.

[102] PWJ Verbruggen and P Wolters et al., *Towards Harmonised Duties of Care and Diligence in Cybersecurity* (Tilburg University, 2016) research.tilburguniversity.edu/en/publications/towards-harmonised-duties-of-care-and-diligence-in-cybersecurity. González Fuster and Jasmontaite (n 61).

[103] Unlike the 2013 Regulation, see n 60 above.

[104] CSA, Art 2(9).

[105] Section III.A.ii below.

[106] CSA, Art 52(4).

[107] And by extension the EPD, see ch 5, section II.A.ii and MG Porcedda, *Privacy by Design in EU law. Matching Privacy Protection Goals with the Essence of the Rights to Private Life and Data Protection* (Lecture Notes in Computer Science 2018).

[108] CSA, Rec 7, second indent.

[109] Following Reed, the eIDAS Reg and the EECC should be more properly classed as aiming at implementation neutrality, as the instruments are about specific 'technologies'. C Reed, *Making Laws for Cyberspace* (Oxford, Oxford University Press, 2012) 189–204.

[110] Commission Regulation 611/2013/EU of 24 June 2013 on the Measures Applicable to the Notification of Personal Data Breaches under Directive 2002/58/EC of the European Parliament and of the Council on

which lists measures capable to render unintelligible personal data, such as 'encryption with standardised key, or replacement of data by its hashed value calculated with a standardised cryptographic keyed hash function'. An example of the latter is Recital 97 EECC, which promotes 'the use of encryption for example, end-to-end where appropriate', to safeguard the security of networks and services. I will discuss the possible impact on 'public security, and … the investigation, detection and prosecution of criminal offences' in chapter seven.

When strategies for prevention fail, the five instruments foresee additional TOMs to remedy the violation of security, which is called an 'incident' in the EECC, eIDAS, NIS and ENISA instruments, and a personal data breach in the EPD and GDPR. These notions acquired legal significance with the amendment of the EPD and the Framework Directive in 2009.[111] A decade ago there existed websites that kept a tally of the occurrence and scale of breaches, but these endeavours have now run out of steam, since breaches have become almost daily news. Owing to a variety of factors, incidents and breaches have increased both in scale, size and consequences. The US firm Equifax lost the records of about 150 million people[112] and following incidents some companies can go bankrupt.[113]

The GDPR defines data breaches as 'a breach of security leading to the accidental or unlawful destruction, loss, alteration, unauthorised disclosure of, or access to, personal data transmitted, stored or otherwise processed'.[114] An incident is an 'event having an actual adverse effect on the security of' network and information systems, electronic communications networks/services or e-identification and assurance services.[115] The breach is system-, or instrument-, specific; 'personal data are in many cases compromised as a result of incidents'.[116]

In previous work of mine[117] I compared relevant provisions within the five instruments plus the PSD2. Here I update the original analysis in light of legislative changes occurring since 2018 with the coming into force of the EECC and the CSA. First, however, I introduce the PSD2, which is a horizontal instrument devoted to regulating 'payment service providers' ranging from traditional credit institutions and electronic money institutions, through payment institutions to payment institution services.[118] Similarly

---

Privacy and Electronic Communications (Commission Regulation on Data Breaches) [2013] OJ L172/2, Art 4. The Regulation is likely to be overhauled with the revision of the EPD.

[111] Art 2(i), introduced by Directive 2009/136/EC of the European Parliament and of the Council of 25 November 2009 Amending Directive 2002/22/EC on Universal Service and Users' Rights relating to Electronic Communications Networks and Services, Directive 2002/58/EC Concerning the Processing of Personal Data and the Protection of Privacy in the Electronic Communications Sector and Regulation (EC) No 2006/2004 on Cooperation between National Authorities Responsible for the Enforcement of Consumer Protection Laws (Citizens' Rights Directive) [2009] OJ L337/11.

[112] G Corfield, 'US Govt Accuses Four Chinese Army Soldiers of Hacking Equifax and Siphoning 145m Americans' Personal Info' *The Register* (20 February 2020); FT Commission, 'Equifax Data Breach Settlement' (2020) www.ftc.gov/enforcement/cases-proceedings/refunds/equifax-data-breach-settlement.

[113] D Olenick, 'Data Breach Causes 10 Percent of Small Businesses to Shutter' *SC Magazine* (29 October 2019).

[114] GDPR, Art 4(12).

[115] Respectively NISD, Art 4(7), EECC, Art 2(42) and Rec 31, eIDAS Reg, Art 10.

[116] NISD, Rec 63.

[117] Porcedda (n 16).

[118] Money institutions deal with digital money. For examples of e-money providers: www.e-ma.org/our-members; money remittances and forex services: paymentinstitutions.eu/about-epif/the-payment-institutions-sector/about. D Baker, *New Payment Initiation Service Providers & The Card Networks* (The London Institute of Banking and Finance, 2017) www.libf.ac.uk/news-and-insights/news/detail/2017/04/04/new-payment-initiation-service-providers-the-card-networks. For account information services, see Art 4(3), Annex I PSD2.

to the EECC, the PSD2 features a combination of TOMs to prevent-detect-respond in adherence to the logic of risk assessment and management[119] just discussed. The PSD2 lays down preventative measures against fraud and counterfeiting perpetrated by subverting information security properties, notably integrity and confidentiality and can be more forthcoming than other instruments in asserting the complementarity between security and data protection. For instance,[120] the security policy document should include 'a description of security control and mitigation measures taken to adequately protect payment service users against the risks identified, including fraud and illegal use of sensitive and personal data'.[121] This is hardly surprising given that personal data are traded in illegal data markets for their potential to enable financial fraud.[122] Ransomware has taken centre stage in the fight against cybercrime and is a great risk to personal data, as acknowledged by Europol and the EDPB.[123]

Notwithstanding the legislative changes occurring since 2018, the fundamentals of the instruments remain unvaried: data are a proxy for signals and information, and the notion of security as NIS is shared by the six instruments. Although called by different names, incidents and personal data breaches share a substantive core, which is then adapted to the context of each instrument. In the following, the text identifies the shared core, while the words in square brackets are those that are instrument-specific:

> an[y] event leading to the [accidental or] unlawful destruction, loss, alteration, unauthorised disclosure of, or access to [personal] data transmitted, stored or otherwise processed [in connection with the provision of a given service offered by, or accessible via, network and information systems]; [or that compromises the availability, authenticity and authentication thereof]; [or the security of electronic communications networks or services].

The six instruments adopt a common blueprint for the response to incidents and breaches, made of a combination of ToMs to minimise harm and damage: (technical) mitigation, assessment of gravity and scale of incident/breach, notification to responsible authorities, information to individuals and the public, cooperation between responsible authorities, creation of inventories, responsibility, liability and sanctions. However, despite a shared blueprint of strategies, the practice varies widely. Moreover, the use of these strategies depends, in part, on the gravity of the incident, the type of service affected and the degree of control Member States have over the victim entity.

---

[119] Measures are called 'technical regulatory standards' (Arts 95, 98) or 'technical security and data protection' (Art 5 last indent). Risk assessment and management appear in Art 95 and Recs 91, 92 and 96.

[120] See Arts 97(3) (authentication) and 98(2) (technical standards on authentication and communication) whereby the safety of payment service users' funds and personal data must be ensured.

[121] PSD2, Art 5. Services must 'ensure a high level of technical security and data protection' (Art 5(1)(j)(a), Rec 93), by embedding DPbD and by default (Rec 89). The European Banking Authority should 'systematically assess and take into account the privacy dimension, in order to identify the risks associated with each of the technical ... to minimise threats to data protection' when 'developing regulatory technical standards on authentication and communication' (Rec 94).

[122] A Hutchings and TJ Holt, 'A Crime Script Analysis of the Online Stolen Data Market' (2015) 55 *British Journal of Criminology* 596–614; Europol, (2019).

[123] 'Internet Organised Crime Threat Assessment (IOCTA) 2020'; European Data Protection Board, *Guidelines 1/21 on Examples regarding Data Breaches, v1.0* (2021). See generally L Connolly and DS Wall, 'The Rise of Crypto-ransomware in a Changing Cybercrime Landscape: Taxonomising Countermeasures' (2019) 87 *Computers and Security*.

The adoption of preventative measures is one of the ways in which the gravity of an incident can be contained, yet, as discussed above, technical mitigation is rarely covered directly by the law. An exception is delegated legislation tied to Articles 4(a) and (b) EPD[124] with reference to encryption with standardised key. Each instrument adopts self-standing criteria to assess the gravity of incidents. For instance, delegated legislation lays down parameters to distinguish between substantial and significant incidents within the meaning of the NISD[125] and EDPB guidance establishes the criteria for harm stemming from personal data breaches.[126]

The gravity of an incident, understood in terms of the likelihood of harm to individuals or services, determines whether breaches must be notified to the responsible supervisory authority at national level, to affected services in case of incidents, to affected individuals in case of personal data breaches and to the general public.[127] Obligations vary also in respect of the importance of the service, and the expected degree of control Member States have over service providers.[128] Notification fulfils many purposes, such as awareness and mutual learning, and lays the foundations for self-improvement. In this latter sense, notification to the general public[129] can be seen as a reputational disincentive against ignoring security requirements.

A cornerstone of mutual learning is the compilation of inventories on incidents. In this respect, the CSA brings much-needed order to data collection and analysis, in that ENISA is now the recipient of information concerning incidents within the NISD, summaries of breaches of security or loss of integrity in the context of trust services within the eIDAS Reg and notifications of security incidents within Article 40 EECC. This is with the aim of 'supporting the regular review of Union policy and activities by preparing an annual report on the state of the implementation of the respective legal framework'.[130] National supervisory authorities are, pursuant to Article 33 GDPR, the counterpart for personal data breaches.

Cooperation between bodies responsible for incidents and personal data breaches is widely featured in the instruments. This is the case whenever incidents are likely to compromise personal data, such as Article 15(4) and Recital 63 NISD, and Article 20 (2) eIDAS Reg.

The last strategy adopted by the six instruments in response to incidents and breaches is the responsibility and liability of service providers affected by breaches, as well as sanctions. Here there is the widest variation across instruments, with the exclusion of the CSA, which is not directly concerned with service providers. Only the GDPR,

---

[124] Commission Regulation (EU) 611/2013 (n 1110).
[125] Commission Implementing Regulation (EU) 2018/151 (n 65).
[126] EDPB (n 123); Article 29 Data Protection Working Party, *Guidelines on Personal Data Breach Notification under Regulation 2016/679* (*WP 250 rev.01* 2018).
[127] There is the additional problem of how to exchange information enabling to take action, or actionable information: see European Union Agency for Cybersecurity (ENISA), *Actionable information for security incident response* (2015); *ENISA 2014 Standards and tools for exchange and processing of actionable information* (2015).
[128] See eIDAS Reg, Rec 38, Arts 10(1) in the context of e-identification and 19(1) first indent for qualified and non-qualified trust service providers; NISD, Arts 14(3) for OESs and Art 16(5) for operators of digital services that supply OES, and 16(3)–(4) for other incidents.
[129] Eg, NISD, Art 19(6), eIDAS Reg, Art 19(2) second indent.
[130] CSA, Art 5(6).

PSD2 and eIDAS Reg explicitly address liability,[131] which, in any case, is for Member States to discipline in detail. Two instruments, the GDPR and PSD2, adopt inversion of the burden of proof 'to prove fraud or gross negligence on part of the payment service user'.[132] Only the GDPR foresees a clear and homogeneous system of administrative fines, proportional to the degree of intention, negligence, and gravity of the omission.[133] The EECC only mentions responsibility in conditional terms ('should'). In keeping with its 'minimal harmonisation' approach, the NISD is silent about liability.

This overview of measures taken in response to incidents and breaches highlights the limitation of similarities between instruments pursuing similar goals. These limitations carry serious consequences[134] and point to the fragmentation of legislation in the DSM.

iv. Legislative Reforms of the NIS Directive, E-Privacy Directive and eIDAS Regulation

The regulatory landscape is set to change with the repeal of the EPD by the EPR and the amendment of the NISD and the eIDAS Reg. Such reforms could affect the analysis contained in these pages, but a firm conclusion will only be possible after the publication of final drafts.

The proposed EPR, for which the Council adopted a mandate for negotiations with the European Parliament in February 2021,[135] contains a number of novelties, including definitions, a marked differentiation between content and metadata as well as explicit reference to NIS and 'security measures'. As expected, the EPR defers to the GDPR for what concerns the prevention, mitigation and management of data breaches. The EPR is more forthcoming in relation to NIS-related threats. Proposed Article 6 affords providers of electronic communications networks and services ample leeway to process data in order to maintain or restore the security of networks and services and, relatedly, detect or prevent any attacks. Proposed Article 8 enables the use of processing and storage capabilities of terminal equipment and the collection of information from end-users' terminal equipment to maintain or restore the security of ISS and the terminal equipment itself, included in the context of software updates. The current draft does not affect the analysis in terms of definitions, notions of security, risk assessment and management paradigm, including the logic of prevention 'by design' through TOMs. However, the text frames NIS objectives as limitations to the rights to privacy and data protection, including to their essence,[136] in a way capable of jeopardising the findings of strong reconciliation.

---

[131] Respectively GDPR, Arts 4(7)–(8) and 5(2); PSD2, Arts 92, 72–74; eIDAS Reg, Art 11 insofar as e-identification services are concerned, for liability of trust service providers see Recs 37, 67.
[132] PSD2, Art 72(2).
[133] GDPR, Arts 83–84.
[134] See section III.A below.
[135] Council, Regulation on Privacy and Electronic Communications 2017/0003(COD. Mandate for negotiations with EP, 6087/21, (2021).
[136] See ch 3, section III.

A Directive repealing the NISD, called NIS2 and containing significant changes was proposed in December 2020.[137] The political agreement repeals Articles 19 eIDAS Reg and 40–41 EECC[138] with effect from the date of transposition of the Directive but enables the survival of sectoral approaches[139] and thus residual fragmentation. As for addressees, the NIS2 replaces existing definitions with essential entities incorporating DSPs – in what is a welcome and much-needed innovation[140] – and important entities encompassing broader sectors of the economy relying on CII, both defined in an Annex. Although it is a Directive fitting within a minimum harmonisation framework,[141] the NIS2 pursues a stronger Command and Control logic, for instance by introducing supervision for essential entities.[142] By providing a definition of both NIS and cybersecurity,[143] the NIS2 clarifies that the two do not mean the same thing. The analysis I proposed in these pages, in terms of definitions, notions of security, risk assessment and management paradigm, including the logic of prevention 'by design' through TOMs, or better 'technical, operational and organisational measures' (TOOMs) linked to the 'state of the Art' (SoA), remains valid in light of NIS2;[144] furthermore, standardisation is now included at Article 22. The NIS2 regards 'security and privacy by default and by design' as crucial in the context of the adoption of appropriate and proportionate TOMs to 'manage the risks posed to the security of network and information systems'.[145]

Finally, the Commission proposed an amendment to the eIDAS Regulation in June 2021. Upon evaluation, the eIDAS was found to have 'contributed positively to the further development of the Single Market' but was in need of 'improvements in terms of effectiveness, efficiency, coherence and relevance to deliver' remote identification and verification, where security plays a role in increasing trust.[146] The evaluation points to the ineffectiveness of current tools for eID security breaches and the fragmentation of the regulation of eID incident management, which I had stressed in the original analysis of cybersecurity breaches. The draft aims to offer 'a common technical architecture and reference framework and common standards to be developed in collaboration with the Member States'.[147] It introduces the requirements for European Digital Identity Wallets

---

[137] European Commission, 'Proposal for a Directive of the European Parliament and of the Council on measures for a high common level of cybersecurity across the Union, repealing Directive (EU) 2016/1148', COM (2020) 823 final, (2020). Analysis based on European Parliament and Council, 'Political Agreement on the NIS 2 Directive, 10193/22 (17 June 2022)'. Adopted as this book went to press, see n 18 above.
[138] NIS2 draft Arts 39–40.
[139] ibid, draft Art 2b on sector-specific Union acts.
[140] See critique of DSPs in Porcedda (n 16). NIS2 draft Art 2a.
[141] ibid, draft Art 3.
[142] ibid, draft Arts 28–29; important entities are subject to ex post supervisory regime (draft Art 30).
[143] ibid, draft Art 4(2)–(3).
[144] ibid, draft Art 18.
[145] ibid, draft Rec 54. Also, 'DPbD ... should be fully exploited' Rec 26c. See further European Data Protection Supervisor (EDPS), 'Opinion 5/2021 on the Cybersecurity Strategy and the NIS 2.0 Directive 6722/21'.
[146] European Commission, Report from the Commission on the evaluation of Regulation (EU) No 910/2014 on electronic identification and trust services for electronic transactions in the internal market (eIDAS) (Staff Working Document) SWD(2021)130 final, (2021), 77. The provision of identity is based on a principle of certification, where Member States 'could become authoritative sources for a series of legal identity attributes, while private sectors stakeholders could also become attribute providers for additional attributes for specific use cases' (ibid, 78), presupposing the development of a commercial model for private identity providers.
[147] European Commission 'Proposal for a Regulation amending Regulation (EU) No 910/2014 as regards establishing a framework for a European Digital Identity, COM(2021) 281 final, 2021/0136 (COD)', 2.

to be certified by accredited public or private sector bodies and relying on certification schemes adopted under the CSA.[148] The proposed document also establishes clear links with the NIS2[149] and can be expected to include a repeal of Article 19. The draft does not challenge prima facie the analysis I proposed in these pages, in terms of definitions, notions of security, risk assessment and management paradigm, including the logic of prevention 'by design' through TOMs.

C. Interim Conclusion: Strong Reconciliation of NIS with Privacy and Data Protection in the Law

I can now turn to drawing interim conclusions. The six instruments deal with various applications of network and information systems, and the information/signals, exemplified through the proxy of data, that these systems are meant to transmit, store and process. Notwithstanding the differences between instruments concerning the scope of application of 'security', which makes the strategy to pursue NIS look like leopard spots, all instruments lay down measures to secure the same 'ecosystem' made of infrastructure, the various services it enables, the stored, transmitted and processed data/information/signals, and the people that, directly or indirectly, operate in such an ecosystem. The understandings of security harboured by the instruments converge, and a comparison shows that there is no tension between instruments, which pursue either the same or complementary values. This complementarity is reinforced by cross-references to cybersecurity, privacy and data protection appearing in the instruments' provisions and recitals. Furthermore, it is reinforced by the fact that the instruments are predicated on the same paradigm, which hinges on risk management, and a preventative security logic pursued with similar strategies, based on the adoption of TOMs linked to the SoA. When these strategies fail, as is presumed by the risk management paradigm, the instruments engender similar approaches to minimise the consequences of security incidents and data breaches.

In sum, insofar as the instruments pursue facets of NIS, the law does not seem to harbour conflicts requiring the application of a proportionality test. Rather, instruments seem to complement one another, effecting what I call strong reconciliation between the NIS side of cybersecurity with privacy and data protection. Reconciliation is strong, rather than complete, because overlap is currently hampered by the mismatch between technical and legal understandings of security properties, as they are expounded in chapter five.[150] There is a caveat, however: privacy and data protection instruments pursue rights, while NIS instruments pursue continuity of service, which evidences a tension between rights and DSM objectives, where 'human security' is just one of the objectives.[151]

---

[148] Draft Arts 6a, 6b, 6c and 6d and Rec 10, draft Art 12.
[149] Draft Recs 22 and 23.
[150] See ch 5, section I.C.
[151] See generally MD Cavelty, 'Breaking the Cyber-Security Dilemma: Aligning Security Needs and Removing Vulnerabilities' (2014) 20 *Science and Engineering Ethics* 701–715. Auspicating a clear objective for NIS legislation: González Fuster and Jasmontaite (n 61).

The conclusions drawn here harbour further limitations. First, I analyse a subset of instruments in force at the time of writing, so that inclusion of newer instruments could bring about a different outcome.[152] Second, I do not address how NIS can be reconciled with the investigation of offences,[153] including of illicit acts laid down by Member States in the transposition of the instruments under analysis, which I will discuss in chapter seven. Finally, the analysis is conducted at a high level of abstraction: it does not include the analysis of implementing instruments, also at national level, and their practical effects, which would require an empirical analysis. Instead, in section III I look at the instruments at a lower level of abstraction, by considering how technology as a regulatory target affects the implementation of the instruments.

III. Reconciliation of NIS, Privacy and Data Protection: Technology

The analysis of DSM instruments shows complementarity between NIS, privacy and data protection and the presence of overlaps in some areas, but the discrepancy between the application of some rules creating a 'variable geometry security' leads to a finding of strong reconcilability. Does strong reconcilability hold true at implementation level, when we factor in technology?

This is difficult territory, because technology is both the target of legislation, due to its role as the foundation of NIS, as well as the means to implement legislation in the guise of technical measures. With the exception of the EPD and GDPR, there are no CJEU rulings directly concerned with the interplay of the instruments under analysis and NIS-relevant case law is generally scant. Pertinent but limited interpretations are contained in a line of cases dealing with monitoring – originating from the connected but differently regulated fields of copyright, data protection, intermediary liability and network neutrality – and the data retention saga.[154] However, case law cannot offer guidance to confirm whether the complementarity of NIS, privacy and data protection holds true due to the 'indeterminacy loop' introduced in chapter five.

The analysis of instruments carried out in section II shows that the regulatory ecosystem of the triad in the DSM is conducive to 'the effacement of technology'. The missing definition of the basics – communications, data, information and signals[155] – fits within a broader strategy of technology neutrality (TN) that leaves ICT products, services and processes, to use the language of the CSA, in a conceptual limbo. Instruments rely on 'technical and organisational measures' (TOMs) adhering 'by design' to goals tied to the 'state of the art' (SoA) and standards drawn up in co-decision delegatory frameworks that conjure up the disappearance of technology from technology law. Such a reality frustrates the opportunity of defining the relationship between NIS, privacy and data

---

[152] Eg the European Data Governance Act: eur-lex.europa.eu/legal-content/EN/TXT/?uri=CELEX%3A32022 R0868&qid=1656182979333 (cybsec & DP).

[153] Eg, PSD2, Art 94 (1), GDPR, Rec 49, Art 23.

[154] On monitoring, see section III.B.iii below. A line of cases beginning with *Digital Rights Ireland*, C-293/12 and C-594/12.

[155] Section III.B above.

protection in the abstract. The quest for answers forces one to go further than specific TOMs, and explore vendor-specific technological solutions, with extant implications not only for the research question of this book, but also the regulation of NIS, privacy and data protection at large.

In section III.A I begin with the analysis of organisational measures relied on to deal with data breaches and security incidents[156] and progressively broaden the focus to technical measures and standards. The goal is to show how 'the effacement of technology' from technology law challenges the finding of complementarity of the triad and forces us to explore technical measures in practice. Section III.B is dedicated to the analysis of one technical measure, deep packet inspection (DPI), which finds application both in NIS and the fight against cybercrime and will therefore also be analysed in chapter seven. In section III.C I present interim conclusions that cast a doubt as to the strong reconcilability of NIS with privacy and data protection.

A. State-of-the-Art ToMs and the Regulation of ICT Products, Services and Processes: Strong Reconciliation (Im)possible?

Data breaches and security incidents command a number of 'organisational measures', such as the criteria used to assess the scale of incidents/breaches, the threshold for the notification of incidents/breaches and cooperation between responsible authorities, or the creation of inventories. Although such measures are inspired by similar principles across the board, they are construed differently in each of the six instruments.[157] The discrepant application of otherwise similar measures stems partly from the fact that the applicable law pursues multiple and, at times conflicting, objectives.[158]

Misaligned measures create a 'variable geometry security' that runs counter the achievement of cybersecurity and contributes to the preclusion of the overlap of NIS, privacy and data protection at DSM level. By streamlining practices contained in different instruments, the NIS2 Directive is likely to resolve the most egregious differences, before the adoption of further sectoral legislation.[159]

The analysis can, at this point, become quite abstract, in the sense that there is no exhaustive compendium of 'organisational measures'. All the law requires is that the entities responsible for adopting organisational measures conform to the SoA, a market-driven dynamic[160] term found in both the GDPR in relation to TOMs and the CSA in relation to security practice and offenders' attacks. For instance, compliance with the DPbD can be demonstrated by adhering to an approved certification mechanism, the criteria and requirements for which are to be laid out in delegated acts of the Commission and developed by standardisation organisations. Due to the law's

---

[156] Section III.B.iii above.
[157] See Porcedda (n 16).
[158] The law tries to safeguard personal data and therefore avert harms to data subjects while also minimising the bureaucratic burden for businesses: M Burdon and B Lane et al., 'Data Breach Notification Law in the EU and Australia – Where to Now?' (2012) 28 *Computer Law & Security Review* 296–307.
[159] European Commission, 'Proposal for a Directive of the European Parliament and of the Council on the resilience of critical entities' (Communication) COM (2020) 829 final.
[160] See ch 5, section II.C.

open-endedness, ENISA and TeleTrust argue that 'because IT infrastructures depend greatly on application and sector, it is not possible to fully list the individual components' and that 'compliance with the state of the art must ... be based on all relevant components of data processing'.[161]

Among others, the SoA in NIS includes patching known vulnerabilities and keeping systems updated to avoid exposure to potential exploits; ENISA and Teletrust define this organisational measure as 'vulnerability and patch management'.[162] In general, software (security) updates straddle the organisational-technical measures divide and open a window into the complex world of network and information systems and related 'ICT products' discussed in chapter five. A case in point was *Consumentenbond/SamsungR* in the Netherlands, which concerned liability for failure to release software updates of the operating systems of smartphones.[163] Commenting on the case, Wolters points out there are limited circumstances under which EU law imposes an obligation to update smartphone software, and shows the prominent role played by national law and litigation in light of the case.[164]

The legal uncertainty around responsibility for vulnerabilities is undermining NIS and contributing to the failure of market-based solutions.[165] Initiatives such as the Digital Content and Sale of Goods Directives mentioned in chapter five aim to create limited duties to patch vulnerabilities and mitigate insecurity in ICTs.[166] The Digital Content Directive does not apply to internet access providers; the proposed EPR enables data controllers to process data for the sake of maintaining security on networks and in the terminal equipment of users, including to run software updates, but does not oblige controllers to do so. It remains to be seen whether the applicable instruments, alongside more recent proposals addressing additional sectors and liability, will work as intended in light of the interplay between EU and national private law.[167]

---

[161] IT Security Association of Germany (TeleTrust) and European Agency for Cybersecurity (ENISA), *IT Security Act (Germany) and EU Data Protection Regulation: Guidelines on 'State of the Art'. Technical and Organisational Measures* (2021), 16.

[162] ibid, 84–86. See also T Moore, 'The Economics of Cybersecurity: Principles and Policy Options' (2010) 3 *International Journal of Critical Infrastructure Protection* 103–117; I van de Poel, 'Core Values and Value Conflicts in Cybersecurity: Beyond Privacy Versus Security', in M Christen et al. (eds), *The Ethics of Cybersecurity* (Cham, Springer, 2020).

[163] Verbruggen (n 102).

[164] PTJ Wolters, 'The Obligation to Update Insecure Software in the Light of Consumentenbond/SamsungR' (2019) 35 *Computer Law & Security Review* 295–395. A software provider's contractual liability depends on its contractual obligations and avenues for extra-contractual liability claims depend on national law. See also European Commission, 'Liability of defective products accompanying the document Communication Artificial intelligence for Europe COM (2018) 237 final' (Staff Working Document) SWD (2018) 137 final, 6–11.

[165] M Schaake, L Pupillo et al., *Software Vulnerability Disclosure in Europe. Technology, Policies and Legal Challenges. Report of a CEPS Task Force* (Centre for European Policy Studies (CEPS) 2018).

[166] Ch 5, section II.C; Arts 7–9 Digital Content Directive (EU) 2019/770 [2019] OJ L136/1 dealing with the conformity of digital content or a digital service with the contract; Sale of Goods Directive (EU) 2019/771 [2019] OJ L136/28 dealing with conformity of goods with contract. See O' Doherty M, *Internet Law* (Dublin, Bloomsbury 2020).

[167] On the interplay between EU and national private law, see the recently-proposed Regulation on general product safety, Directive on liability for Defective Products and Cyber Resilience Act mentioned in ch 5, section II.C; H-W Micklitz, *La Mano Visibile del Diritto Privato Europeo in Materia Normativa – La Trasformazione del Diritto Privato Europeo dall'autonomia al Funzionalismo nella Concorrenza e nella Regolamentazione* (European University Institute, 2010). On private regulatory law, see ch 8.

Thus, there is no compendium of TOMs to reflect an ever-changing SoA informed by standards; technology neutrality becomes a necessary device to facilitate the dynamism of standards that also give meaning to 'by design' approaches. Standardisation and certification[168] are the regulatory means for developing and selecting TOMs adhering *prima facie* with the principles identified by each instrument. Delegation to standardisation is part of co-regulatory approaches[169] ushered in by the 'New Approach to Harmonisation and Standardisation', developed into the Better Regulation agenda and the White Paper on European Governance,[170] and perfected in the New Legislative Framework (NLF),[171] which was discussed in chapter five.

The introduction of NLF-inspired standardisation in the law applicable to the triad is predicated on the 'recent convergence of technologies and the digitisation of society, businesses and public services' that 'are blurring the traditional separation between general and ICT standardisation' following which 'ICT standardisation should be part of a European digital strategy'.[172] The GDPR contains several examples, notably Articles 25 on DPbD and by default, 42 on certification (seals and marks) and 43 on certification bodies. In the NLF, binding laws lay down principles which standards need to observe, and standards are laid down by alternative instruments adopted by standardisation bodies, which are private or not-for-profit organisations populated by 'stakeholders' predominantly made of industry representatives, as discussed in chapters one, two and five. The NISD acknowledges this state of affairs when it states that 'Standardisation of security requirements is a market-driven process' and calls for the desirability of 'draft harmonised standards'.[173] The promotion of convergent implementation of Articles 14(1)(2) and 16(1)(2) is best achieved by encouraging the use of European standards[174] 'or internationally accepted standards and specifications relevant to the security of network and information systems'.[175] The latter is explained by the 'global nature of security' requiring 'closer international cooperation to improve security standards'.[176] The NISD entrusts ENISA, in collaboration with Member States, to 'draw up advice and guidelines regarding the technical areas to be considered (…) as well as regarding already existing standards'.[177]

---

[168] For reference see JL Contreras (ed), *The Cambridge Handbook of Technical Standardisation Law* (Cambridge, Cambridge University Press, 2019).

[169] I Kamara, 'Co-regulation in EU Personal Data Protection: the Case of Technical Standards and the Privacy by Design Standardisation 'Mandate'' (2017) 8 *European Journal of Law and Technology*.

[170] P Craig and G de Búrca, *European Union Law: Text, Cases and Materials* (Oxford, Oxford University Press, 2015) 171–179.

[171] ibid 166–167 and 620–627. Regulation (EU) No 1025/2012, [2012] OJ L316/12.

[172] European Parliament, *European Parliament Resolution of 4 July 2017 on European Standards for the 21st Century* (2016/2274(INI)) [2017] OJ C334/2, points 21–22; European Commission, 'ICT Standardisation Priorities for the Digital Single Market' (Communication) COM (2016) 0176 final.

[173] NIDS, Rec 66.

[174] NISD, Art 19, Rec 66 in accordance with Regulation (EU) No 1025/2012 (n 171).

[175] NISD, Art 19(1).

[176] ibid, Rec 43. See ch 8.

[177] ibid, Art 19(2).

A clear example of legislation following the logics of the NLF is Title III of the CSA which lays down the European cybersecurity certification schemes for ICT products, services and processes.[178] The CSA defines a 'European cybersecurity certificate' as

> 'a document issued by a relevant body, attesting that a given ICT product, ICT service or ICT process has been evaluated for compliance with specific security requirements laid down in a European cybersecurity certification scheme'.[179]

The latter is 'a comprehensive set of rules, technical requirements, standards and procedures that are established at Union level and that apply to the certification or conformity assessment of specific ICT products, ICT services or ICT processes'.[180] Importantly, ENISA adopts the definition of 'standard' of Regulation (EU) No 1025/2012, which disciplines the NLF.[181]

Although the CSA focusses mostly on European certification, it encourages 'closer international cooperation to improve cybersecurity standards, including the need for definitions of common norms of behaviour'.[182] The suggestion that 'certification schemes should be non-discriminatory'[183] evokes the language of TN. That schemes should be 'based on European or international standards', unless international standards 'are ineffective or inappropriate to fulfil the Union's legitimate objectives in that regard', appears to be a fail-safe mechanism in case the international standard contradicts the Union's objectives, objectives left unspecified. An international standard based on an equally international notion of 'privacy' is very likely to fall foul of meeting the expectations of EU data protection law.[184]

Certification is to set 'assurance levels', that is 'a basis for confidence that an ICT product, ICT service or ICT process meets the security requirements of a specific European cybersecurity certification scheme … but as such does not measure the security of the … product … concerned'.[185] Assurance levels can be basic, substantial or high and depend on the risk associated with the envisioned use of the technology.[186] The European Cybersecurity Certification Group (ECCG) is tasked with adopting a rolling work programme containing priorities for certification.[187]

The ECCG's first certification scheme is the Common Criteria based European candidate cybersecurity certification scheme,[188] which includes rules related to handling vulnerabilities. The ECCG then issued a candidate cybersecurity certification scheme

---

[178] CSA, Arts 46–65.
[179] ibid, Art 2(11).
[180] ibid, Art 2(9), with Art 2(10) defining national schemes.
[181] Art 2(1) Regulation (EU) No 1025/2012 (n 174); CSA, Art 2(19). Further reference to standards are in CSA, Recs 46, 49, 50, 54, 53, 59, 62, 66, 69, 75, 77, 84, 86, 98, 99; and Arts 8, 21, 22, 52, 54, 59.
[182] ibid, Rec 54.
[183] ibid, Rec 69.
[184] See ch 5, section II and 8, section III.
[185] CSA, Art 2(21).
[186] ibid, Art 52.
[187] ibid, Arts 62, 47. See Rolling plan for ICT standardisation: digital-strategy.ec.europa.eu/en/policies/rolling-plan-ict-standardisation; and joinup.ec.europa.eu/collection/rolling-plan-ict-standardisation/cybersecurity-network-and-information-security.
[188] ENISA May 2021: www.enisa.europa.eu/publications/cybersecurity-certification-eucc-candidate-scheme-v1-1.1

for cloud services.[189] Following the mandate by the European Commission, CEN also adopted standard 17529:2022 for PbD and DPbD, which will not be cited in the Official Journal.[190] These endeavours exemplify how 'technical (and organisational) measures' relevant for NIS are those adopted by practitioners based on a dynamic SoA. As a result, it is impossible to determine whether the implementation of the legal instruments effects strong reconciliation of the triad because the factors necessary for the determination fall outside of the remit of the applicable law and are found, at best, within forms of delegated governance that are not directly accessible to the public.

The only way of assessing the extent to which NIS, privacy and data protection are reconciled is to explore the SoA. I now turn to the analysis of one such SoA measure in the context of NIS-relevant instruments which featured – implicitly – in preliminary rulings relating to monitoring adopted by the CJEU.

B. State of the Art Technical Measures: The Example of Deep Packet Inspection (DPI)

In this section I appraise deep packet inspection (DPI), which has attracted the attention of standard setting organisations (SSOs)[191] and of global media for its controversial applications.[192] DPI can be used for both preserving NIS and fighting against all forms of cybercrime, and I will therefore also discuss this in chapter seven. After describing the nature of DPI, its usage and pros and cons (III.B.i), I review its impact on the relationship between cybersecurity, privacy and data protection (III.B.ii), following which I will draw interim conclusions.

i. DPI: Nature, Usage, Pros and Cons

DPI is a technique placed in network internal nodes[193] empowering Internet Service Providers (ISPs)[194] to actively perform additional functions by screening the application

---

[189] ENISA, European Cybersecurity Certification Scheme for Cloud Services: www.enisa.europa.eu/topics/publications/eucs-cloud-service-scheme.
[190] CEN: standards.cencenelec.eu/dyn/www/f?p=205:110:0::::FSP_PROJECT,FSP_LANG_ID:63633,25&cs=1C8CD445079952A8B5B3C613E79FCD16F. See Ch 5.II.C.
[191] International Telecommunication Union (ITU-T), *Requirements for deep packet inspection in next generation networks, Recommendation ITU-T Y.2770* (2012).
[192] This includes my own first reflections, on which s III.B partly draws: MG Porcedda, 'Lessons from PRISM and Tempora: the Self-contradictory Nature of the Fight against Cyberspace Crimes. Deep Packet Inspection as a Case Study' (2013) 25 *Neue Kriminalpolitik* 305–409. For the use of DPI by the NSA, see M Cayford, *Paper on Mass Surveillance by the National Security Agency (NSA) of the United States of America. Extract from SURVEILLE Project Deliverable D2.8* (2014) 16–18. See also P Ohm, *The Rise and Fall of Invasive ISP Surveillance*, Working Paper n. 8-22 (University of Colorado Law School, 2008) papers.ssrn.com/sol3/papers.cfm?abstract_id=1261344; S Stalla-Bourdillon and E Papadaki et al., 'From Porn to Cybersecurity Passing by Copyright: How Mass Surveillance Technologies are Gaining Legitimacy … The Case of Deep Packet Inspection Technologies' (2014) 30(6) *Computer Law & Security Review* 670–686. See ch 7, with respect to XKeyscore.
[193] Body of European Regulators for Electronic Communications (BEREC), *A Framework for Quality of Service in the scope of Net Neutrality* (BoR (11) 53, 2011) 18–20.
[194] Used as a shorthand for relevant electronic communication services and information society services a previously defined.

layer of packets and even their payload – viz. content, hence the term 'deep' – sent over the networks. The ITU-T defines DPI as 'analysis, according to the layered protocol architecture OSI, of payload and/or packet properties deeper than transport layer header information, and other packet properties in order to identify the application unambiguously'.[195] DPI is an 'enabling technology',[196] in that its function depends on the applications or modules installed in the DPI engine (its central part): recognition, notification and manipulation.

Recognition uses data mining and 'artificial intelligence' algorithms 'to analyse, on- and offline, any parts of the packets, at any layer of the Internet architecture, against specific patterns or features – keywords or 'signatures' contained in a predefined library'.[197] Recognition compares the obtained data on the basis of such patterns. According to ITU-T requirements, the signature can be used for approximate identification, such as behavioural elements or heuristics, and exact matching. 'Notification consists in sending alerts in relation to the patterns and keywords identified and is usually conducted offline. DPI engines combining recognition and notification functions are called "passive". Manipulation, or "active" DPI, affects the destination of the packets and can be performed both on- and offline'.[198]

DPI engines can also be looked at from the angle of the hierarchical level at which they apply and whether they are used in situ or remotely. Packet path level actions include: accepting the packet and forwarding it to the packet forwarding function; discarding the packet (silently or otherwise); redirecting the packet to other output interfaces; replicating/mirroring the packet to other output interfaces; classifying traffic, local measurements, and reporting of measurement data; and prioritisation, blocking, shaping and scheduling methods of individual packets. Node level actions include: dynamic building of new DPI policy rules and/or modification of existing rules; generating of logging/tracing data and reporting to policy management; detecting and reporting of unidentifiable applications; notifying intrusion detection systems (eg, by reporting traffic samples, suspicious packets). Network level actions include resource management, admission control and high-level filtering (at the level of network subsystems) as well as content charging based on subscribers' application types.[199] The latest evolution of DPI, which is deep content inspection, performs its analysis on the reconstructed packet.[200]

---

[195] ITU-T (n 191) 5; ITU-T's technical characteristics refer to New Generation Networks; DPI can also be used in other layered applications.
[196] M Mueller, *DPI Technology from the Standpoint of Internet Governance Studies: an Introduction (v1.1). The Network is Aware* (Syracuse University School of Information Studies, 2011) 2; R Bendrath and M Mueller, 'The End of the Net as We Know it? Deep Packet Inspection and Internet Governance' (2011) 13 *New Media and Society* 1142. RW Del Sesto, Jr., and J Frankel, 'How Deep Packet Inspection Changed the Privacy Debate': dpi.priv.gc.ca>; T Berners-Lee, 'No Snooping': www.w3.org/DesignIssues/NoSnooping.html; R Bendrath, 'Global Technology Trends and National Regulation: Explaining Variation in the Governance of Deep Packet Inspection' (International Studies Annual Convention, New York City, 15–18 February 2009); A Daly, 'The Legality of Deep Packet Inspection' (First Interdisciplinary Workshop on Communications Policy and Regulation 'Communications and Competition Law and Policy – Challenges of the New Decade'); Ohm (n 192).
[197] See W Song and M Beshley et al., 'A Software Deep Packet Inspection System for Network Traffic Analysis and Anomaly Detection' (2020) 20 *Sensors*; LF Pikos, 'Packet Analysis for Network Forensics: A Comprehensive Survey' (2020) 32 *Forensic Science International* 1–12. Porcedda (n 192), 378.
[198] ITU-T (n 191) 10; Porcedda (n 192), 378.
[199] ibid 12.
[200] Eg, www.clearswift.com/blog/what-is-a-deep-content-inspection-engine.

In general, DPI is likely to challenge 'network neutrality' or the broad version of the end-to-end argument, because the lower layers involved in the core function of the Internet should be unaware of the data they carry and unable to control them.[201] Thus, 'well behaved'[202] intermediary nodes in the core of the Internet should use their router software solely to look into the IP header of the packet, ie the outer envelope which contains the addressing information of the message to be sent, and either deliver the message or pass it to another node that can deliver it. Because of these modules or applications, DPI can serve many purposes,[203] to the advantage or detriment of end-users.

DPI can be performed to their detriment of *end users* and without their knowledge, with Clarke[204] suggesting the header and payload can be screened for: email addresses to build mailing lists for spam, or to detect credit card details; changing the content of the message and forwarding it;[205] pretending to be the recipient of the message and forging a response; or for surveillance. DPI's surveillance capabilities may have contributed to making it so attractive to private actors and law enforcement. For instance, it has been argued that DPI was suitable to fulfil the legal requirements of the United States Communications Assistance for Law Enforcement Act, whereby all ISPs must install any available technologies enabling lawful wiretapping.[206] Thereafter, companies began using DPI for lucrative services either with a view to recover the investment, or to perform ad-injection and traffic prioritisation in the guise of 'network management'.[207] In turn, organisations interested in the protection of digital property rights lobbied for its use, and it was soon apparent that DPI could be used for policing the networks from all sorts of content deemed unlawful.[208] DPI appears to be at the heart of the 'sovereign RUnet', a moniker given to Russian legislation aimed at controlling the Russian net to ensure 'cyber sovereignty'.[209]

DPI can be used in favour of end-users to act as a gateway between the Internet and other networks or for caching popular web pages. For Clarke, DPI enables ISPs to scan the application header/payload to act as a proxy-server at the request of *end users* to filter

---

[201] Ohm (n 192); B Van Schewick, *Internet Architecture and Innovation* (Cambridge, MIT press, 2010). 'It is … possible to automatically analyse network traffic in real time (i.e. Deep Packet Inspection), even on a core network level'. Body of European Regulators for Electronic Communications (BEREC), 'Response to the eprivacy Directive questionnaire, BoR(16) 133', 5.
[202] R Clarke, *Deep Packet Inspection: its nature and implications* (www.rogerclarke.com 2009).
[203] BEREC (n 201) 5.
[204] Clarke (n 202).
[205] This is what Comcast did in 2007 to block peer-to-peer networks: it 'sent 'reset' TCP packets in the place of end users'. Body of European Regulators for Electronic Communications (BEREC), Quality of Service, BoR (11) 53 (2011), 29.
[206] ibid 28; Ohm (n 192).
[207] S Landau, *Surveillance or Security? The Risk Posed by New Wiretapping Technologies* (Cambridge, MIT Press, 2010). However, Google's ad injection does not come easily: J Mullin, 'Privacy Lawsuit over Gmail Will Move Forward' (16 August 2016). Traffic prioritisation is part of network management, ie all actions (and tools) to administrate, operate and maintain networked systems. Bendrath (n 196). Traffic management can have legitimate objectives, ie avoiding congestion, but it can be performed according to less intrusive means than DPI, such as application-agnostic measures: Ohm (n 192) 51.
[208] B Marczak, J Dalek et al., *Bad Traffic. Sandvine's PacketLogic Devices Used to Deploy Government Spyware in Turkey and Redirect Egyptian Users to Affiliate Ads?* (Tspace, 2018). See ch 7.
[209] I Stadnik, *Sovereign RUnet all the way down* (2019) www.internetgovernance.org/2019/04/03/sovereign-runet-all-the-way-down/.

spam or webpages, provide firewalls or anonymous remailers or else reverse-proxy.[210] Indeed, DPI evolved from shallow and meso-packet inspection tools, which looked solely into IP for the destination address and TCP, eg, for port numbers suggesting the application used, and started being distributed at the turn of the millennium to detect and prevent malware.[211] DPI combines functionality from intrusion detection/prevention systems and stateful firewalls to detect and block attacks; it does so by checking each packet against known signatures. DPI is embedded in widely available off-the-shelf solutions that can be installed or even run remotely through cloud computing.[212]

Although DPI can be used to the benefit of NIS, the ITU-T warns that DPI 'may not be applicable to the international correspondence in order to ensure the secrecy and sovereign national legal requirements placed upon telecommunications'.[213] DPI can severely interfere with the exercise of communications, as when it silently discards a packet, or the confidentiality of communication, as when it replicates/mirrors packets. Herrmann and Pridöhl rightly note that the acceptability of DPI is open to debate and comes under pressure when one compares packets to letters.[214] How does packet analysis affect the relationship between NIS, privacy and data protection?

ii. *Permissibility of DPI vis-à-vis the Triad: Compliance with a Legal Obligation and Preserving the Integrity and Security of the Network*

'The packets screened by DPI carry data produced in the course of "personal Internet usage" and communications',[215] eg e-mails, Voice over Internet Protocol (VOIP), etc. The monitoring of information produced in the course of communications, including traffic and location data (metadata),[216] constitutes an interference with the right to private life irrespective of whether the correspondence is private.[217] Furthermore, individuals have a reasonable expectation of privacy if there is no warning about the monitoring of 'correspondence'.[218] Article 5 EPD gives concrete expression to these rights by enshrining the principle of confidentiality of communications and related traffic data.[219] The CJEU said the essence of Article 7 CFR includes the 'content of a communication'[220] and the revelation of 'very specific information concerning the private life of a person ... [not] limited to certain aspects of that private life'.[221]

---

[210] Clarke (n 202); M Mueller, *The Narrative (March 16, 2021)* (Internet Governance, 2021). www.internetgovernance.org/2021/03/16/the-narrative-march-16-2021/.
[211] Bendrath (n 196); BEREC (n 193).
[212] See Pikos (n 197).
[213] ITU-T (n 191) 1.
[214] D Herrmann and H Pridöhl, 'Basic Concepts and Models of Cybersecurity' in M Christen (ed), *The Ethics of Cybersecurity* (Cham, Springer, 2020) 37.
[215] *Copland v the United Kingdom*, no. 62617/00, para 41; Porcedda (n 192), 378.
[216] Metadata 'can give rise to an issue under Article 8 as such information constitutes an 'integral element of the communications made by telephone. The mere fact that these data may have been ... in the form of telephone bills, is no bar to finding an interference with' Art 8 ECHR. *Copland*, para 43.
[217] *Niemietz v Germany*, no. 13710/88 CE:ECHR:1992:1216JUD001371088, para 32.
[218] See *Copland v the United Kingdom*, no. 62617/00, para 42.
[219] *La Quadrature du Net and Others*, C-511/18, EU:C:2020:791, paras 107 and 109. EPD, Arts 5, 6 and 9, Rec 24.
[220] *Digital Rights Ireland*, C-293/12 and C-594/12, para 39. Ch 3, section III.F.
[221] *Opinion 1/15* of 26 July 2017 pursuant to Article 218(11) TFEU EU:C:2017:592, para 150.

DPI also interferes with the right to data protection,[222] because data produced in the course of 'personal Internet usage'[223] and communications contain information susceptible to identify an individual (eg the IP address[224] in a packet). Furthermore, the monitoring of behaviours online of individuals located in the EU gives rise to the application of the GDPR.[225]

Since DPI is susceptible of interfering with both rights, it should only be allowed for NIS purposes if it can withstand a test for permissible limitations. Accordingly, the first requirement pursuant to Article 52(1) CFR is that the intrusion must be provided for by the law (or in accordance with the law).[226] Articles 40 EECC, 14 and 16 NISD could constitute a legal basis for the use of DPI to filter spam and prevent malware.[227] These legal bases have to be read in light of the provisions on monitoring contained in the EPD and the GDPR, taking into account the Court's interpretation of the essence, as well the potential applicability of other provisions on monitoring.

Several DSM instruments prohibit generic monitoring, while sometimes enabling specific monitoring.[228] One such instrument is the long-standing prohibition of generic monitoring laid down in the e-Commerce Directive (ECD),[229] whereby Member States cannot oblige ISPs 'to monitor the information which they transmit or store, nor a general obligation actively to seek facts or circumstances indicating illegal activity'. As the CJEU clarified in *La Quadrature du Net*, when the monitoring interferes with Articles 7 and 8 CFR, GDPR and EPD rules take precedence over the ECD, whose prohibition of monitoring cannot be taken to undermine the requirements of privacy and data protection rules.[230] This finding extends to exceptions pursuant to

---

[222] *Sabam*, C-360/10, EU:C:2012:85, para 45.

[223] *Copland v the United Kingdom*, no. 62617/00, para 41.

[224] *Scarlet Extended*, C-70/10, EU:C:2011:771, para 51. Dynamic addresses can be personal data: *Breyer*, C-582/14, EU:C:2016:779. IP addresses are both personal data and traffic data: *Mircom*, C-597/19, EU:C:2021:492, para 113.

[225] Art 3(2) GDPR.

[226] Such a law should respect parameters of quality specified by the courts. With respect to ECHR, Art 8(2), the law must be accessible and respect the rule of law (*Shimovolos v Russia*, no. 30194/09 CE:ECHR:2011: 0621JUD003019409, para 67). When they do not establish secret measures of surveillance, laws must enable individuals to foresee (*Rotaru v Romania*, no. 28341/95 CE:ECHR:2000:0504JUD002834195, para 59), if need be with appropriate advice, with sufficient precision the consequences produced upon them and thus regulate their conduct. As for the Charter, the CJEU set parameters of quality in *Digital Rights Ireland* and subsequent case law.

[227] European Data Protection Board, Letter to BEREC. Data protection issues in the context of Regulation (EU) 2015/2120, OUT2019-0055, 3 December, (2019).

[228] Namely laws on privacy, data protection, e-commerce, net neutrality and copyright. All such instruments contain clauses to the effect of not prejudicing each other. 'Specific monitoring' has been found to be permissible in a copyright context (*Telekabel*, in L Edwards, "With Great Power Comes Great Responsibility?': The Rise of Platform Liability', in Edwards (ed), *Law, Policy and the Internet* (Oxford, Hart Publishing, 2018)) and is now enshrined in the revised legislative framework. Since this work does not address copyright, see especially C Geiger and BJ Jütte, 'Platform Liability Under Art. 17 of the Copyright in the Digital Single Market Directive, Automated Filtering and Fundamental Rights: An Impossible Match' (2021)70 *GRUR International Journal of European and International IP Law* 517–543. See also *Poland v Parliament and Council*, C-401/19, EU:C:2022:297. However, the overhaul of these frameworks has created tensions, as discussed with respect to the GDPR and the ECD by G Sartor, 'Liabilities of Internet users and providers', in M Cremona (ed), *New Technologies and EU Law* (Oxford, Oxford University Press, 2017).

[229] Art 15 Directive 2000/31/EC of the European Parliament and of the Council of 8 June 2000 on certain legal aspects of information society services, in particular electronic commerce, in the Internal Market (Directive on Electronic Commerce) [2002] OJ L178/1.

[230] *La Quadrature du Net and Others*, C-511/18, paras 199–201.

Articles 15 EPD and 23 GDPR respectively, which cannot be interpreted as being capable of conferring on Member States the power to undermine rights.[231]

Another relevant provision is the prohibition of monitoring of 'specific content' laid down by the Open Internet Access Regulation[232] (OIR). The latter, as interpreted by BEREC,[233] obliges providers of e-communications to the public to treat all traffic equally (excluding interconnecting traffic and terminal equipment practices). Providers of e-communications to the public include providers of e-communications services (ECSs) or networks in the sense of the EECC and exclude services that are not publicly available (as in the NISD). Reasonable traffic management measures are allowed but they cannot, inter alia, be based on commercial considerations[234] and monitor 'specific content'.

The prohibition of monitoring 'specific content' enshrined in the OIR concerns content provided by end-users such as text, pictures and video; the EDPB considers domain names, unique resource identifiers (URLs) and Transport Layer payload to be content data.[235] Monitoring techniques that rely on traffic data (metadata), ie information contained in the IP packet header and in some – unspecified – cases transport protocol layer (eg TCP) header, are allowed; to be sure, metadata gives access to a wealth of information.[236] Unreasonable traffic management techniques include the following: 'blocking, slowing down, altering, restricting, interfering with, degrading or discriminating between specific content, applications or services, or specific categories'.[237]

However, there are three legitimate aims pursuant to which such traffic management techniques can be used, including specific monitoring, so long as the processing of personal data is lawful,[238] is 'necessary for the achievement of the respective exception ("except as necessary")' and applied 'only for as long as necessary'.[239] Here I review two exceptions.

The first, contained in Article 3(3)(a), is to comply with a legal obligation to which the provider of internet access services (IASs) is subject. Article 3(3)(a) OIR enables ISPs to perform monitoring of specific content as part of a legal obligation 'to which

---

[231] ibid, para 201 and 212. The CJEU refers to Art 7 CFR 'or any of the other guarantees enshrined therein'.

[232] Art 3(3), Reg (EU) 2015/2120 Regulation (EU) 2015/2120 of the European Parliament and of the Council of 25 November 2015 Laying down Measures Concerning Open Internet Access and Amending Directive 2002/22/EC on Universal Service and Users' Rights Relating to Electronic Communications Networks and Services and Regulation (EU) 531/2012 on Roaming on Public Mobile Communications Networks within the Union [2015] OJ L310/1.

[233] Body of European Regulators for Electronic Communications (BEREC), *BEREC Guidelines on the Implementation by National Regulators of European Net Neutrality Rules* (BoR (16) 127, 2016); 'Guidelines on the Implementation of the Open Internet Regulation, BoR (20) 112'.

[234] The CJEU decided that measures blocking or slowing down traffic based on commercial considerations are incompatible with Art 3(3) OIR in *Telenor Magyarország*, C-807/18, EU:C:2020:708. Hence, DPI could not be used for ad-injection and traffic prioritisation.

[235] EDPB (n 227).

[236] BoR (20) 112 (n 233) paras 69 and 70. These are traffic data in the EPD; domain names, URLs and transport layer payload are content data. See Pikos (n 197).

[237] OIR, Art 3(3), third subparagraph; 'rules against altering the content, applications or services refer to a *modification* of the content of the communication (OIR, Rec 11). See especially BoR (20) 112 (n 233).

[238] OIR, Art 3(4). Here I do not review the exception in accordance with letter (c) to prevent *impending* network congestion and mitigate the effects of *exceptional* or temporary network congestion; for a discussion, EDPB (n 227); BoR (20) 112 (n 233).

[239] BoR (20) 112 (n 233), para 79. This is in keeping with the principle of proportionality, which is prominent in the OIR, eg, Art 14.

the provider of [IAS] is subject ... including with orders by courts or public authorities vested with relevant powers'. Recital 13 OIR refers to criminal law requiring the blocking of specific content, applications and services, which I will elaborate upon in chapter seven.[240] Thus, this provision seems to enable IASs to resort to DPI engines that monitor TCP payload by means of exemption.

IAS can be both ISSs and e-communication services,[241] and are thus subject to the ECD. Article 15 ECD states they cannot be required to perform 'a general obligation to monitor the information which they transmit'. This begs the question of how to interpret other obligations to which IAS are bound. The evolution of copyright case law could offer some answers. The early cases of *Scarlet Extended*[242] and *Sabam*[243] both concerned the permissibility of injunctions obtained by SABAM, a company representing copyright holders, against Scarlet Extended (an IAS) and Netlog (an online social networking platform and ISS), to install a DPI system (Audible Magic[244]) for filtering e-communications with a view to preventing copyright-infringing file sharing. Both Scarlet and Netlog appealed, and the Court decided that the applicable law, construed in the light of fundamental rights, must be interpreted as precluding an injunction made against an ISP that requires it to install a preventative system for 'filtering', which applies indiscriminately to all individuals using those services, for an unlimited period of time (and at the expense of either Scarlet or Netlog).

The literature[245] finds these early cases to lie at one extreme of possible approaches to filtering. Edwards stressed that the sweeping nature of the injunctions obtained by SABAM was clearly repugnant to the exercise of several Charter rights. She also notes that the Court did not ban filtering altogether, leaving the door ajar to considering the permissibility of 'strictly targeted' injunctions,[246] as it did in *Telekabel*.[247] According to Geiger and Jütte the case of *Glawischnig-Piesczek* lies at the other end of the spectrum; the case concerned a hosting provider not subject to Article 3(3)(a) OIR, but it illustrates the Court's approach to Article 15 ECD, which permits an injunction targeting specific content uploaded by specific users.[248] Neither *Telekabel* nor *Glawischnig-Piesczek* feature an analysis of the implications of such injunctions for privacy and data protection. However, this is unlikely to be the end of the debate as developments pertaining to copyright are sparking new landmark cases.[249]

---

[240] 'National implementations of Art 110 of Directive (EU) 2018/1972 on Public Warning systems' could constitute such an exemption. BEREC (n 202) para 81.
[241] *La Quadrature du Net and Others*, C-511/18, para 204.
[242] *Scarlet Extended*, C-70/10.
[243] *Sabam*, C-360/10.
[244] (www.audiblemagic.com/). M Mueller and A Kuehn et al., 'Policing the Network: Using DPI for Copyright Enforcement' (2012) 9 *Surveillance & Society* 348; S Kulka and F Zuiderveen Borgesius, 'Filtering for Copyright Enforcement in Europe after the Sabam Cases' (2012) 11 *European Intellectual Property Review* 54.
[245] See especially Edwards (n 228); Geiger and Jütte (n 228).
[246] Edwards (n 228), 280.
[247] A court injunction prohibiting an IAS 'from allowing its customers access to a website placing protected subject-matter online without the agreement of the rightsholders' can comply with fundamental rights when that injunction does not specify the measures which the IAS must take and when that IAS 'can avoid incurring coercive penalties for breach of that injunction by showing that it has taken all reasonable measures', provided some parameters are complied with. *UPC Telekabel Wien*, C-314/12, EU:C:2014:192.
[248] A hosting provider is a CAP (content and application provider), which is an end-user in the OIR. BoR (20) 112 (n 233). *Glawischnig-Piesczek*, C-18/18 EU:C:2019:821. Geiger and Jütte (n 228) 536.
[249] Copyright is beyond the scope of this work. For a review of Art 17 Directive 2019/790 on copyright see Geiger and Jutte (n 228); *Poland v Parliament and Council*, C 401/19.

The second exception, pursuant to Article 3(3)(b) is to preserve the integrity and security of the network, of services provided via that network, and of the terminal equipment of end-users. The exception can justify the monitoring of specific content to preserve NIS and avert denial of service (DoS) attacks, spoofing IP addresses, hacking attacks and cyber-attacks occurring as a result of malware and identity theft of end users caused by spyware.[250] Article 3 goes hand in hand with Article 4(1) EPD and 40 EECC, whereby ECSs and public network access providers must employ suitable technical and procedural means to ensure the security of the network and related services.

The fact that malware-oriented DPI can detect and block threats means it both prevents crime, protects personal data and the principle of confidentiality of communications, a point recognised by the EDPS[251] and the predecessor of the EDPB in the context of email services.[252] BEREC states that, 'in order to identify attacks and activate security measures, the use of security monitoring systems ... is often justified ... Monitoring of traffic to detect security threats may be implemented in the background on a continuous basis'. Traffic management measures ... are only triggered when concrete security threats are detected'.[253] Such monitoring should be subject to strict interpretation and to proportionality requirements, and closely assessed by National Regulatory Authorities, because 'security is a broad concept'[254] and DPI could be sold as a malware solution but with additional purposes enabled,[255] so that network security could be an excuse to circumvent the prohibition of monitoring.[256]

This provision enshrines the paradox of undertaking the ongoing background monitoring of specific content (TCP payload), which clearly interferes with communications confidentiality and data security, to safeguard communications confidentiality and data security. From the perspective of permissible limitations, the interference enabled by Article 3(3)(b) OIR[257] may be prima facie justified. What is more, since the interference aims at better protecting the rights, it could be argued it is of a positive nature.

Given the interference is for the sake of preserving the integrity and confidentiality of communications and of personal data, it should therefore be in harmony with the reading of the essence of Articles 7 and 8 CFR by the CJEU in *Digital Rights Ireland* and *Opinion 1/15*. However, there is a problem in the analysis, as monitoring is liable to infringe the essence of privacy, viz. the content of communications and very specific information unlimited to a narrow domain of one's private life, depending on how such content is cast. The essence of data protection is not prima facie interfered with, although further analysis will question not only such non-interference, but also the significance of the essence of data protection as such.

In sum, copyright infringement cases show that DPI could be used to the extent it meets the parameters of 'specific monitoring' but does not amount to 'a general

---

[250] Recital 14 OIR, BoR (20) 112 (n 233), para 83–87.
[251] European Data Protection Supervisor (EDPS), *Opinion on Net Neutrality, Traffic Management and the Protection of Privacy and Personal Data* ([2011] OJ C34, 1–17).
[252] Article 29 Data Protection Working Party, *Opinion 2/2006* on Privacy Issues related to the Provision of Email Screening Services (00451/06/EN WP 118, 2006).
[253] Examples include blocking IP addresses, IAS and port numbers, and should be proportionate. BoR (20) 112 (n 233), para 85.
[254] ibid., para 87.
[255] Landau (n 207).
[256] BoR (20) 112 (n 233) para 87.
[257] *Niemietz v Germany*, no. 13710/88, para 36.

obligation to monitor the information which they transmit', a finding that may affect the use of DPI for NIS purposes by analogy. DPI can simultaneously enhance and interfere with privacy and data protection: its use for the sake of preserving the integrity and confidentiality of personal data and communications comes at the price of interfering with the essential components of the two rights and both 'permissible' uses of DPI sit uncomfortably with the essence of privacy. The outcome leaves several questions unanswered: where does an analysis of TCP payload stop being 'specific' and start instead encroaching on the essence of Article 7 CFR? And can a DPI system be configured in such a manner as to transparently meet these criteria? How to enforce purpose limitation of DPI? And what minimum security safeguards apply to its use? These questions are relevant not only in the DSM, but also in the AFSJ, in light of the rulings *Big Brother Watch and Others* and *La Quadrature du Net*.[258] However, here I reflect on the findings with a view to establishing the mode of reconcilability of the triad in the DSM.

iii. Implications of the Ambiguity of DPI for the Triad

We have seen that the use of DPI for the sake of NIS can simultaneously enhance and infringe privacy and data protection: DPI interferes with some of the features of Articles 7 and 8 CFR in order to safeguard them. DPI seems prima facie compatible with the essence of data protection. However, as discussed in chapter five, insofar as the SoA of security measures is drawn from the market, the significance of the essence of data protection remains elusive; more of this in chapter 8. Furthermore, the fact that DPI can be easily repurposed puts under pressure the practical implementation of purpose limitation arrangements that, reading a contrario the relevant CJEU judgments, form part of the essence of data protection. DPI is openly incompatible with the essence of privacy, because of its ability to reveal content and very specific information about individuals which may not be limited to narrow domains. However, the meaning of the essence of privacy also remains elusive. Consequently, the strong reconcilability of the triad found at a high level of abstraction may not hold true at a lower level of abstraction.

Figure 1 Meaning of 'content' of a packet (OSI and TCP/IP architecture) following interpretation by the EDPB

#	OSI model	TCP/IP model	Packet	EDPB
7	Application	Application	Payload (includes URLs, domain names)	Content OR Specific content
6	Session			
5	Presentation			
4	Transport	Transport	Header (IP address)	'Generic content' OR Traffic data/metadata
3	Network	Network		
2	Data link	Network access layer		
1	physical			

---

[258] *Big Brother Watch and Others v UK*, no 58170/13; *La Quadrature du Net and Others*, C-511/18.

Following BEREC and the EDPB, IP and TCP headers constitute generic content/traffic data, the monitoring of which is permissible under certain circumstances (see Figure 1). The TCP payload constitutes specific content, which can be permissible by means of exception so long as it does not amount to general monitoring. This is even though it has been found that 'metadata' can be as telling as intelligible content, as both the ECtHR and the CJEU have found and Pikos shows.[259] A joint reading of BEREC and EDPB guidance implies that content is what is produced by the end-user, eg, the actual text or sound at the application layer, but the point as to what 'permit[s] the acquisition of knowledge of the content of' e-communications has not been explicitly clarified by the Court. Thus far, the CJEU has shunned opportunities to define what 'content' is in relation to packets, what constitutes 'monitoring' when data protection and privacy are in the balance[260] and therefore what measures are permissible in relation to packet capture and analysis for DSM purposes.

Breyer, the first case to deal with the processing of personal data (dynamic IP addresses) for the sake of addressing cyber-attacks, provides limited guidance. Following the decision, Article 7(f) DPD precludes national legislation pursuant to which an online media services provider may collect and use personal data relating to a user of those services, without their consent, only in so far as the collection and use of that data are necessary to facilitate and charge for the specific use of those services by that user, even though the objective of aiming to ensure the general operability of those services may justify the use of those data after a consultation period of those websites. This judgment could thus be read as permitting the use of shallow packet analysis; however, the questions asked were not conducive to an analysis of the systems used.

In *Scarlet* and *SABAM*, the CJEU found that the systematic analysis of all content, plus the collection and identification of users' IP addresses as traffic and personal data would constitute an impermissible interference with Article 8 CFR.[261] Hence, the Court condemned both the analysis of the content – possibly the signatures used by Audible Magic to recognise digital rights-protected material – and the identification of individuals, which did not require vision of the full content, but IP header only. The Court did not perform an assessment of the interference of DPI with the right to private life but rather referred to filtering. The Court also did not take advantage of the analysis of technology by AG Villalón, who noted that the CJEU was given 'no information regarding either the intensity or the depth of the monitoring to be carried out' and that 'the nature of the filtering ... is clearly not without impact at a legal level'.[262] AG Villalón observed that the system used by Audible Magic is capable of detecting the content of the files exchanged on a peer-to-peer networks.

---

[259] Metadata are part of 'correspondence' and 'communications' in case law. *Big Brother Watch and Others v UK*, no. 58170/13, para 184; *La Quadrature du Net and Others*, C-511/18. Pikos (n 197).

[260] Case law repeatedly asserted the independence of the EPD and GDPR from the ECD, even in the face of tensions created by the overhaul of these frameworks; see Sartor (n 228). Although amendments had a detrimental effect on the practical non-encroachment across instruments, I submit that the predicament is anyway a legal fiction. Since the law overlooks TOMs, the predicament of non-encroachment is oblivious to the fact that all such instruments deal with the same technological environment; case law has thus far been unable to redress the matter. Although this section provides evidence in this respect, it will be for further research to elaborate on the predicament of non-encroachment across the board.

[261] *Scarlet Extended*, C-70/10, paras 51–53.

[262] *Scarlet Extended*, C-70/10, EU:C:2011:255, Opinion of AG Villalón, paras 49–50. See ch 5, section III.

Telekom Deutschland had the potential to shed much-needed light as the German *Verwaltungsgericht Köln* stayed proceedings to refer to the CJEU the crucial question of whether Article 3(3) OIR second subparagraph, third sentence is to be understood as meaning that identification of the traffic generated from video-streaming from IP addresses, protocols, URLs and SNIs and using pattern matching, during which certain header information is compared with typical video-streaming values, constitutes monitoring of the specific content of the traffic. The ruling does not answer the question.

The cases reviewed rely on the metadata/content divide without defining the threshold for 'content' and 'knowledge', and without engaging with the systems that perform the processing of such data. Court rulings consequently overlook the reality of systems capable of circumventing the prohibition of monitoring and by that token of interfering with the confidentiality of content and data, affecting the essence of privacy and de facto undermining the essence of data protection. BEREC[263] has warned that network security could be an excuse to circumvent the prohibition of monitoring and encourages national regulators to control and audit 'security monitoring systems'. ENISA released some guidance with respect to specific actions, but the guidance does not cover continuous monitoring and does not make any findings with respect to the permissibility of traffic management measures.[264] This leaves us with two conclusions.

One conclusion is that the answer to the question of the reconcilability of the triad can only be found by undertaking an exhaustive analysis of all commercially available DPI solutions to identify the combination of functions capable of integrating information security properties with the operationalised version of the essence, eg the techno-legal analysis I proposed in chapter five. As an effective analysis can only be done by inspecting the code and data flow diagrams, without the collaboration of vendors all an outside researcher can do is to offer educated guesses. Song et al. point out that 'algorithms of anomaly detection engines in commercial intrusion detection systems are in the vast majority of cases an object of commercial secret'.[265] Ironically, an analyst of legal permissibility shares the fate of information security researchers, in that only reverse-engineering and red teaming could help to access the information necessary to ascertain the permissibility of the technology.[266] Even such a risky analysis is likely to produce two outcomes.

First, the analysis of commercial DPI systems could show that a technical measure cannot reconcile at once all information security properties and all operationalised attributes and essence of the two rights. In other words, technical measures are likely to harbour compromises, whereby a given criterion can only be fulfilled at the expense of others. The second outcome is that the analysis could show that NIS, privacy and data protection are not complementary at the technological level. One outcome does not exclude the other, and both are equally likely. Only shallow packet inspection is likely

---

[263] Body of European Regulators for Electronic Communications (BEREC), *Guidelines on net neutrality*, BoR (16) 127, (2016), § 87.
[264] European Union Agency for Cybersecurity (ENISA), *Guideline on assessing security measures in the context of Article 3(3) of the Open Internet regulation* (2018). BoR (20) 112 (n 233) para 87.
[265] Song et al (n 202) 5.
[266] A Guinchard, 'The Computer Misuse Act 1990 to Support Vulnerability Research? Proposal for a Defence for Hacking as a Strategy in the Fight Against Cybercrime' (2017) 2 *Journal of Information Rights, Policy and Practice*.

compatible with the confidentiality of communications, but as Pikos shows, metadata on its own can be extremely revealing. As a result, the triad could only be weakly reconciled through balancing as part of a proportionality assessment.

An alternative conclusion stems from the open-ended nature of the rules overseeing the technological implementation of NIS-related legislation. In discussing the measures available to end-users to monitor copyright infringement, Geiger and Jütte argue that leaving too much choice to such end-users can undermine legal certainty.[267] Such an argument applies to all monitoring measures. The point is that the law does not deal with the potential contradictions of technology, not even at the last and highest level of legal recourse, making it impossible to determine the permissibility of different options, with some options potentially violating the essence of rights. As the obligation to adopt appropriate TOMs applies to technology users and not its designers,[268] the reconcilability between NIS, privacy and data protection will remain unresolved so long as the question of which technology is permissible remains unaddressed.

IV. Conclusion: Strong Reconciliation of NIS with Privacy and Data Protection Challenged by Technology

The chapter explored the mode of reconciliation of the triad in the DSM through an analysis of policy, relevant law in force at the time of writing and technology. While policy documents are inconclusive, the EU applicable law points to areas of overlap and effects strong reconciliation, although for different end goals: network and information systems are protected by NIS legislation to guarantee the continuity of service and by privacy and data protection legislation to protect fundamental rights. The two can meet in the concept of human security but are not exactly overlapping.

The analysis of TOMs yields results that seemingly back the findings from the analysis of policy documents and challenge the findings from the comparative analysis of instruments. Measures that enable the pursuit of NIS and by extension privacy and data protection, such as DPI, would not pass the test for permissible limitations because they would affect the essence of at least Article 7 CFR. As for Article 8 CFR, the dynamicity of technical (and organisational) measures points to the elusiveness of the essence of data protection, which is to be respected with the provision of 'security safeguards' in the legal basis; I will return to this in chapter 8. The ambiguity of DPI results from the fact that the application of standard tests shuns the configuration of DPI engines: different objectives entail the use of different modules, which interfere with the two rights differently and hence have varying degrees of permissibility.

Such a finding can be explained in light of the 'effacement of technology' and indeterminacy loop developed in chapter five. The specifics of technology and possible usage are not subsumed under technology-neutral concepts such as SoA, TOMs, content and monitoring; judges have not filled in the vacuum and thus the test for permissible

---

[267] Geiger and Jütte (n 228).
[268] EDPS (n 94). See ch 5, section II. NISD provisions applicable to cloud computing service providers are partly addressing developers, whose security obligations are lower than those of cloud service users, as I note in (n 16). Under the NIS2, cloud computing providers will be subjected to more stringent security obligations.

limitations provides little guidance; and rights are open-ended. What is more, these trends are mutually reinforcing as part of the indeterminacy loop.

Indeed, against this background, the market has free rein to identify sub-standard solutions that suit the whims of different communities, whose interests may prevail over the respect of the two rights and NIS. As the cybersecurity market is notoriously characterised by a high degree of failure, it is unlikely that a solution will be found there, certainly not without remedial action. However, since this state of affairs is not the result of the law of physics, but rather is artificially created,[269] it can therefore be redressed. Re-building the broken bridge between law and technology is one such way to do so, and several actions can be undertaken internally and externally to do so. But first I must illustrate the relationship between the fight against cybercrime, privacy and data protection.

---

[269] L Lessig, The Law of the Horse: What Cyberlaw Might Teach (1999) 113 *Harvard Law Review* 501–549.

7
The AFSJ: The Fight against Cybercrime, e-Evidence, Privacy and Data Protection

Chapter six addressed the interplay between Network and Information Security (NIS), privacy and data protection within the Digital Single Market (DSM). This is the second of three chapters exploring the mode of reconciliation between cybersecurity, privacy and data protection in the main areas of EU law making. Here I focus on cybercrime and the collection of electronic evidence (e-evidence), which fall within the Area of Freedom, Security and Justice (AFSJ). The AFSJ is now governed by the TFEU, although the old 'third pillar' intergovernmental communities and logics of decision-making still play a role[1] and engender results different to those observed for the DSM. Similarly to chapter six, here I reflect on the relationship between the triad in the AFSJ with the three areas of analysis of this book: policy, law and technology.

In section I I observe how the changing security and political landscape, characterised by the emergence of cybercrime alongside other elusive threats such as terrorism, and the increasing relevance of e-evidence to most investigations, informed successive security policies that expressed different ideas about the relationship between cybercrime and the collection of e-evidence with privacy and data protection. AFSJ policies appear to cast the relationship between the triad according to the focus and the understanding of 'crime' harboured in specific documents. An analysis of sample AFSJ policy documents published between 2015 and 2021 reveals that reconciliation can be either strong, in the form of complementarity, or weak in the guise of balancing, depending on the issue at hand. As a result, policy documents express a degree of ambiguity which prevents us from drawing firm conclusions as to the mode of reconciliation of the triad in the AFSJ.

In section II I analyse select instruments that criminalise offences falling under the broad 'cybercrime' umbrella: attacks against information systems, frauds, child pornography – aka child sexual abuse material (CSAM) and exploitation – and 'cyber-terrorism'. I also refer to upcoming legislation for the collection of e-evidence and, where relevant, the Law Enforcement Directive (LED). The diversity of cybercrime legislation hinders a comparative analysis akin to that undertaken for NIS instruments. Instead, each instrument is reviewed separately, but following the same parameters used in chapter six. The analysis demonstrates the presence of a substantive functional interconnection between NIS,

---

[1] See S Peers, *EU Justice and Home Affairs Law* (Oxford, Oxford University Press, 2011).

attacks against information systems and frauds, which supports strong reconcilability of the triad, in the form of complementarity. In practice, however, the letter of the law does not support this finding for legislation on fraud, which adopts a balancing logic instead. Such a balancing logic also underpins legislation addressing CSAM and cyberterrorism, though the LED provides safeguards aimed to guarantee the legality of interferences. As for rules concerning the collection and use of e-evidence, which include pending reforms and the second additional protocol to the Budapest Convention, recent case law attempts to rein in the extremes pursued by intelligence-led policing, while also opening up new challenges. The area is, however, unsettled. The combined reading of substantive and procedural provisions highlights a 'procedural functional interconnection' between NIS, cybercrime and e-evidence instruments, which tilts the triad towards weak reconciliation. In sum, the law seemingly matches the ambiguity expressed by policy documents, partly because the effacement of technology and the indeterminacy loop first discussed in chapter five are also at play in the AFSJ.

Finally, in section III, I examine how *tools* and 'technology' affect the reconcilability of the triad. The example of deep packet inspection (DPI) enables me to draw a parallel with chapter six and show how technologies used to curb cybercrime can seriously interfere with the right to privacy and data protection, as well as with NIS, thereby exemplifying a tension between different notions of security. The analysis shows that such an outcome is the result, in part, of the law's disconnect from the very technology used to enforce it, technology determined by the enforcers of the law – law enforcement, intelligence agencies and private actors. In such a scenario, the effort to apply classic proportionality potentially engenders seriously distorting effects. Ever more sophisticated procedural safeguards to comply with the rule of law can do little against technologies capable of subverting rights and cybersecurity when left uncontrolled. Against this background, it becomes difficult to reconcile not only the fight against cybercrime with privacy and data protection, but also with the fight against cybercrime itself, NIS and the protection of Critical Information Infrastructure (CII). The analysis shows the need for the legislator to engage more profoundly with the law's underlying technological environment.

I. Reconciliation of the Fight against Cybercrime, e-Evidence, Privacy and Data Protection: Policy

Successive security strategies have taken different stances on the relationship between cybercrime, privacy and data protection,[2] on account of both the changing techno-geopolitical landscape and the evolving EU institutional framework that greatly affected policing-making in the AFSJ. This makes it difficult to point to clear trends as to the reconcilability between cybersecurity, privacy and data protection.

---

[2] For policy preceding 2012, see MG Porcedda, *Data Protection and the Prevention of Cybercrime: the EU as an Area of Security?* (European University Institute Working Paper, Law 2012/25, 2012).

At the turn of the millennium, the increased frequency and damage caused by cyber-exploits,[3] and difficulty in apprehending offenders often located in different jurisdictions,[4] firmly placed cybercrime on the policy agendas of industrialised countries. Despite the theoretical quandaries raised by legislating 'virtual' and often transborder crimes,[5] a group of industrialised countries, spearheaded by the US, began working towards a cybercrime treaty under the aegis of the Council of Europe (CoE).[6] Concurrent EU policy asserted the functional interconnection between NIS, data protection and cybercrime, under the 'three-pronged approach' lasting, to an extent, to this day.[7] The policy also acknowledged the minimum international standardisation effected by the CoE Cybercrime Convention (Convention),[8] viewed as the starting point for developing common EU rules on cybercrime. Such a choice was met with criticism by the Article 29 Data Protection Working Party (WP29), on account of three risks: the potential over-reach of substantive definitions of cybercrime, the extant expansion of investigatory powers,[9] and a 'light touch' approach to human rights protection enshrined in the Convention.[10]

Policy developments in the following decade proved the latter two risks to be well-founded, as AFSJ-related policymaking, still ruled by intergovernmental practices and unencumbered by the Charter of Fundamental Rights of the European Union (CFR),[11] developed against the background of the 'war on terror'. The latter was predicated on a trade-off between security and liberties as well as new forms of garnering intelligence.[12] Public-private partnerships[13] and the spread of portable electronic devices and cloud computing, enabled the seizing of metadata and content data, at rest and in transit, in ways not dissimilar to the substantive offences proscribed by the Convention. References to the three-pronged approach were dropped to make room for a logic of security

---

[3] S Landau, *Listening In. Cybersecurity in an Insecure Age* (New Haven, Yale University Press, 2017) ch 2.

[4] S Brenner and B-J Koops (eds), *Cybercrime and Jurisdiction. A Global Survey* (The Hague, TMC Asser Press, 2006).

[5] S Brenner, 'Is There Such a Thing as 'Virtual Crime'?' (2001) 4 *California Criminal Law Review*. Cybercrime raises issues both with the scope of crimes and investigations as well as the appearance of new forms of misconduct and dual criminality issues. A Flanagan, 'The Law and Computer Crime: Reading the Script of Reform' (2005) 13 *International Journal of Law and Information Technology* 98.

[6] Council of Europe, Explanatory Memorandum to the Cybercrime Convention, (2001); S Brenner, 'The Council of Europe's Convention', in JM Balkin (ed), *Cybercrime, Digital Cops in a Networked Environment* (New York, New York University Press, 2007); B Clough, 'A World of Difference: The Budapest Convention on Cybercrime and the Challenges of Harmonisation' (2014) 40 *Monash University Law Review*.

[7] Established in COM (2001) 298, see ch 1, section I.A; section II.A below.

[8] Convention on Cybercrime, Council of Europe, CETS n. 105, 23 November 2001.

[9] An open research question is whether the Convention was instrumental in establishing rules to ease investigations into terrorism following the 9/11 attacks. See G Hosein and J Eriksson, 'International Politics Dynamics and the regulation of dataflows. Bypassing domestic restrictions', in J Eriksson and G Giacomello (eds), *International Relations in the Digital Age* (London, Routledge, 2007).

[10] Convention, Art 15; Article 29 Data Protection Working Party, Opinion 4/2001 On the Council of Europe's Draft Convention on Cyber-crime (WP 41) (2001); Opinion 9/2001 on the Commission Communication on 'Creating a safer information society by improving the security of information infrastructures and combating computer-related crime' (2001).

[11] Charter [2012] OJ C326/391.

[12] D Jenkins and A Jacobsen et al. (eds), *The Long Decade: How 9/11 Changed the Law* (Oxford, Oxford University Press, 2014). See ch 1, section II.D and III below.

[13] MG Porcedda, 'Public-Private Partnerships: A 'Soft' Approach to Cybersecurity? Views from the European Union' in G Giacomello (ed), *Security in Cyberspace: Targeting Nations, Infrastructures, Individuals* (London, Continuum Books, Bloomsbury Publishing, 2014).

premised on the commonality between cybercrime and other forms of particularly serious crime with a cross-border dimension, such as terrorism, justifying investigative techniques based on the interception of private communications and retention of personal data.

The adoption of the Lisbon Treaty, the communitarisation of police and judicial cooperation in the AFSJ, the new status of the CFR and the waning of the terrorist threat inspired policies to move beyond the 'war on terror', search for a reconciliatory tone and fulfil Article 16 TFEU, particularly through the adoption of the LED.[14] Snowden's revelations sparked a renewed interest in the reconciliation of the triad, as evidenced by policy discourse and substantiated by the attempts to challenge the legality of mass surveillance techniques effected by the Data Retention Directive (DRD).[15]

The judicial saga sparked by the invalidation of the DRD and national initiatives to give mass surveillance techniques statutory footing has opened policy conundrums that are yet to settle, particularly in the wake of new waves of terrorist attacks in the mid-2010s, namely missing out on crucial e-evidence because of its volatile or encrypted nature, exemplified by the fear of 'going dark'.[16] According to the 2020 Security Union Strategy,[17] 85 per cent of investigations into serious crime require access to e-information and e-evidence; in 65 per cent of cases the evidence is located outside the jurisdiction.[18] The 'going dark' debate echoes the 'cryptowars' of the 1990s,[19] which centred around the US government ban on the export of products featuring strong encryption and the lifting of which, just before the start of the 'war on terror', supported the uptake of e-commerce, privacy-enhancing technologies (PETs) and data protection-friendly digital solutions. After the terrorist attacks of the mid-2010s, LEAs voiced the need for encrypted services to include a backdoor, giving them on-demand 'exceptional access' to information scattered across cloud-based services for the sake of facilitating investigations,[20] with potentially dire consequences for NIS, privacy and data protection.[21]

The risk of substantive overreach voiced by the WP29 in 2001 proved to be well-founded. In the 2013 EU cybersecurity policy, cybercrime was taken to mean 'different criminal activities where computers and information systems' are either 'a primary tool or ... target' and to comprise 'traditional offences (e.g. fraud ...), content-related offences

---

[14] Law Enforcement Directive (EU) 2016/680 [2016] OJ L119/89 (LED).

[15] See ch 1, section I.B. D Drewer and J Ellermann, 'Europol's Data Protection Framework as an Asset in the Fight against Cybercrime' (Joint ERA-Europol conference Making Europe Safer: Europol at the Heart of European Security, The Hague, 18–19 June 2012). Directive 2006/24/EC [2006] OJ L105/54 (DRD).

[16] Landau (n 3) xi; B-J Koops and E Kosta, 'Looking for Some Light Through the Lens of "Cryptowar" History: Policy Options for Law Enforcement Authorities against "going dark"' (2018) 34 *Computer Law & Security Review*; G Giacomello, *National Governments and Control of the Internet. A Digital Challenge* (London, Routledge, 2005); H Abelson and R Anderson et al., 'Keys Under Doormats: Mandating Insecurity by Requiring Government Access to all Data and Communications' [2015] *Journal of Cybersecurity* 1–11.

[17] European Commission, 'Security Union Strategy' (Communication) COM (2020) 605 final.

[18] Europol, Internet Organised Crime Threat Assessment (IOCTA) 2020 (2020).

[19] Giacomello (n 16); L DeNardis, 'A History of Internet Security' in K de Leeuw et al. (eds), *The History of Information Security* (Oxford, Elsevier Science, 2007).

[20] W Diffie and S Landau, 'Internet Eavesdropping: A Brave New World of Wiretapping' (2008) 299 *Scientific American Magazine* 4. Abelson et al. (n 16); Koops and Kosta (n 16).

[21] S Landau, *Surveillance or Security? The Risk Posed by New Wiretapping Technologies* (Cambridge, MA, MIT Press, 2010).

(e.g. on-line distribution of child pornography …) and offences unique to computers and information systems (e.g. … malware).'[22] This definition, which reflects the categorisation of the Convention and remains unchallenged, complicates the attempt to untangle the relationship between cybersecurity, privacy and data protection, as the many categories subsumed under cybercrime share few commonalities beyond the fact that they are all 'offences' for which 'cyberspace' plays a role. AFSJ policies adopt a mode of reconciliation between cybercrime, data protection and privacy dependent on the policy objective and the specific 'crime' under analysis, even though policies that tackle multiple objectives are no stranger to contradictory approaches. A look at sample policy documents in the years 2015–2021 exemplifies the point.

The Renewed European Internal Security Strategy[23] stressed the importance of garnering evidence, thereby portraying privacy and data protection as rights that must be safeguarded. The Renewed ISS calls for both better information sharing, accessibility and interoperability to prevent and fight cybercrime, as well as safer and more secure ICTs to increase cybersecurity, but looks at privacy and data protection as rights to be complied with.[24] The policy is silent as to the matter of exceptional access[25] as against the European Parliament's (EP) 2017 resolution on cybercrime, whereby the use of cryptography for interpersonal communications is defended. The EP saw data protection not only as a right, but also as a resource in the fight against cybercrime, eg, as embodied in the obligation to disclose security breaches and to share information on risks introduced by the GDPR.[26]

The 2020 Security Union Strategy,[27] which supersedes the Agenda on Security,[28] attempts to synthesise the competing interests it voices. The cybersecurity section, discussed in chapter six, looks at cybersecurity and data protection as complementary. The section on 'emerging threats' is split into cybercrime, modernising LEAs, and countering illegal content online. By stating that a 'resilient environment created by strong cybersecurity is the first defence'[29] against cybercrime, which encompasses real cybercrimes and frauds that affect business and personal data alike, the Strategy acknowledges the link between NIS and cybercrime. It also indirectly acknowledges the complementarity between data protection and the fight against cybercrime.

In the Strategy, illegal content online, including child pornography and terrorism, is not labelled as a cybercrime. The aim of 'maximising the use of tools available at EU level'[30] to counter illegal content online implicitly expresses the logic of balancing investigatory interests with privacy and data protection. Moreover, the Strategy states

---

[22] European Commission and High Representative of the European Union for Foreign Affairs and Security Policy, 'Cyber Security Strategy: An Open, Safe and Secure Cyberspace' (Joint Communication) JOIN (2013) 01 final, 3.
[23] Council, *Draft Annex Conclusions on the Renewed European Internal Security Strategy 2015–2020, 9797/15* (2015).
[24] ibid, 4.
[25] Abelson et al. (n 16).
[26] European Parliament, *Resolution of 3 October 2017 on the fight against cybercrime (2017/2068(INI))* [2018] OJ C346/04, points 3 and 5.
[27] COM (2020) 605 final (n 17).
[28] Referring to the Convention as the 'international standard for cooperation and a model for national and EU legislation', ibid, 20.
[29] ibid, 10.
[30] ibid, 14.

that modernised police forces must avail themselves of the latest techniques, embedded in draft EU law and the 2nd Additional Protocol to the Convention; encryption plays a crucial role in securing cyberspace, privacy and personal data, but it also hinders an effective response to crime and terrorism.[31] The search for 'balanced technical, operation and legal solutions' that preserve privacy, the security of communications and the efficacy of investigation is an attempt to square the circle of exceptional access. The same Strategy fosters an understanding of reconciliation in the sense of complementarity and balancing depending on the issue at hand.

In sum, policy documents prevent us from reaching firm conclusions as to the reconcilability of the triad. I therefore turn to the analysis of cybercrime legislation adopted in the AFSJ.

II. Reconciliation of the Fight against Cybercrime, e-Evidence, Privacy and Data Protection: Law

This section appraises the relationship between cybercrime, privacy and data protection stemming from the analysis of the applicable law. A preliminary observation is that the meaning of cybercrime is not easy to define, much like 'cyber' itself.[32] Yar and Steinmetz claim that cybercrime refers to 'a diverse range of illegal and illicit activities that share in common the unique electronic environment ("cyberspace") in which they take place'.[33] Existing taxonomies emphasise different traits common to cybercrimes.[34] The conceptual ambiguity of 'cybercrime' reflected in policy documents, international and EU law informs semantic choices as well as the scope of this analysis.

The Cybercrime Convention encompasses offences against the 'confidentiality, integrity and availability' (CIA) of computer data and systems (eg hacking), computer-related offences (eg fraud), content-related offences (eg child pornography), as well as copyright-related offences.[35] Article 83 TFEU empowers the EU to establish minimum rules concerning the definition of criminal offences and sanctions in the area of 'computer crime'. The only EU statutory reference to cybercrime is contained in the Directive on attacks against information systems[36] (Cybercrime Directive), an instrument that covers exclusively CIA offences against information systems and ancillary provisions.

---

[31] Council, Council Resolution on Encryption. Security through encryption and security despite encryption (2020).
[32] See ch 2, section III.B.
[33] M Yar and KFS Steinmetz, *Cybercrime and Society*, 3rd edn (London, Sage Publishing, 2020) 6.
[34] Ch 2, n 101.
[35] The infringement of copyright and IP rights are left out as they are not a criminal offence in EU law, although they represent an interesting case of lobbies pushing for quasi-criminalisation and greater monitoring. For the UK, see Flanagan (n 5); T Aplin, ' 'United Kingdom", in Lindner et al. (eds), *Copyright in the Information Society: A Guide to National Implementation of the EU Directive*, 2nd edn (Edward Elgar 2019).
[36] Directive 2013/40/EU of the European Parliament and the Council of 12 August 2013 on Attacks against Information Systems and Replacing Council Framework Decision 2005/222/JHA, [2013] OJ L218/8 (Cybercrime Directive). See Art 17 and Recs 2, 14, 15, 24 (mentioning NIS), Recs 25, 26 (mentioning resilience of critical infrastructures) and Rec 28.

Here cyber-dependent, crime against the machine, true and CIA offences are treated as coterminous as they would all cease to exist without cyberspace; cyber-enabled and computer-related offences (frauds) are also used interchangeably. Both should be seen as narrow cybercrime,[37] while cyber-assisted or content-related offences that would exist irrespective of the technological environment are broad[38] cybercrime. As far as legislation is concerned, limiting the analysis of the relationship between cybercrime, privacy and data protection to the Cybercrime Directive would produce partial results. Thus, this chapter embraces a wider selection of instruments, on account of the emphasis placed by EU law on the Budapest Convention and the composite nature of the policy response to cybercrimes.

The legal status of the Convention in EU law, and therefore its ability to produce legal effects, is at best unclear. The Cybercrime Directive contains a *renvoi*, or connection clause,[39] to the Convention: it is 'the legal framework of reference for combating cybercrime, including attacks against information systems' and hence the Cybercrime Directive 'builds on that Convention.'[40] Such a *renvoi*, especially when compared with more stringent examples,[41] may possibly acknowledge the Conventions' role as a 'reference for combating cybercrime' and therefore signal the wish to follow CoE's initiatives in the area, rather than a desire for the Convention, and by extension its meaning of cybercrime, to bind the Union, all the more as the Union is not party to the Convention. However, the legal status of the Convention may change as all Member States except Ireland have ratified the Convention, as more instruments citing the Convention are adopted and in light of references by the Court of Justice of the European Union (CJEU) to the Convention as a legal basis for the expedited preservation of data.[42]

The cybercrime dimension embraces five categories of measures that make it, similarly to NIS, piecemeal and potentially ineffective.[43] The first three categories relate to substantive offences against the CIA of data and systems, measures on fraud and forgery such as counterfeiting of means of payment and content-related or cyber-assisted crime or broad cybercrime, such as the 'sexual exploitation of children'. These will be the focus of section II.A. A fourth category of measure concerning provisions for investigating and prosecuting crime, including rules governing agencies created for cross-border

---

[37] Justified later as well as in MG Porcedda, 'Cybersecurity and Privacy Rights in EU Law. Moving beyond the Trade-off Model to Appraise the Role of Technology' (PhD Thesis, European University Institute, 2017).

[38] H Kaspersen, 'Jurisdiction in the Cybercrime Convention' in B-J Koops et al. (eds), *Cybercrime and Jurisdiction: a Global Survey* (The Hague, TMC Asser, 2006).

[39] M Cremona, 'A Triple Braid: Interactions between International Law, EU Law and Private Law', in M Cremona et al. (eds), *Private Law in the External Relation of the EU* (Oxford, Oxford University Press, 2016).

[40] Cybercrime Directive, Rec 15. On the limited ability of the Directive to do so, see S Summers, C Schwarzenegger et al., *The Emergence of EU Criminal Law. Cybercrime and the Regulation of the Information Society* (Oxford, Hart Publishing, 2014), 239–240.

[41] Such as the renvoi to Convention 108 contained in the GDPR, see ch 4.

[42] See Cybercrime Directive, Rec 15. European Commission, 'Report from the Commission assessing the extent to which the Member States have taken the necessary measures in order to comply with Directive 2013/40/EU on attacks against information systems and replacing Council Framework Decision 2005/222/JHA' (Communication) COM (2017) 0474 final; *La Quadrature du Net and Others*, case C-511/18, EU:C:2020:791, paras 164–165.

[43] See ch 2, section III.B; F Calderoni, 'The European Legal Framework on Cybercrime: Striving for an Effective Implementation' (2010) 54 *Crime, Law and Social Change* 339–357.

police and judicial cooperation, will not be covered here. The final category encompasses instruments governing the collection, preservation and exchange of e-evidence, which relate to both cybercrime and other crimes, which will be the focus of section II.B.

The analysis of this section will point to a substantive and procedural functional interconnection between NIS, the fight against cybercrime and the investigation thereof that affects the relationship between elements of the triad in antithetical ways. Since the law potentially introduces solutions that practically challenge reconcilability, the analysis leads to the need to investigate the 'tools' and technologies relied on by the law (section III).

A. Reconciling the Fight against Cybercrimes with Privacy and Data Protection

In this section I review examples from each of the three substantive legal categories of the cybercrime dimensions to exemplify the *intended* relationship between cybercrime, privacy and data protection. The instruments are the Cybercrime Directive, the Directive on Fraud and Counterfeiting,[44] the Directive on combating child sexual abuse, sexual exploitation and pornography,[45] better referred to as Child Sexual Abuse Material (CSAM) and, in passing, the Directive on Combating Terrorism.[46] On account of the conceptual variety characterising cybercrime, each instrument is analysed independently but following similar criteria, to enable loose comparisons between instruments and with the analysis carried out in chapter six. Criteria include the introduction of the instrument, scope and offences, direct references to privacy and data protection and other elements that can explain the relationship with privacy and data protection, such as the underlying logic and legislative principles relied upon. The analysis will show the limited role played by the LED and that only the Cybercrime Directive effects strong reconciliation with the triad on account of its substantive functional interconnection to NIS.

i. Directive 2013/40 on Attacks against Information Systems (Cybercrime Directive): Strong Reconciliation Through Substantive Functional Interconnection

The Cybercrime Directive is based on Article 83(1) TFEU and is thus solidly anchored in the AFSJ; it repeals Council Framework Decision 2005/222/JHA[47] while maintaining

---

[44] Directive (EU) 2019/713 of the European Parliament and of the Council of 17 April 2019 on combating fraud and counterfeiting of non-cash means of payment and replacing Council Framework Decision 2001/413/JHA [2019] OJ L123/18 (FCD).

[45] Directive (EU) 2011/93 of the European Parliament and of the Council of 13 December 2011 on combating the sexual abuse and sexual exploitation of children and child pornography, and replacing Council Framework Decision 2004/68/JHA [2011] OJ L335/1 (CSADir).

[46] Directive (EU) 2017/541 of the European Parliament and of the Council of 15 March 2017 on combating terrorism and replacing Council Framework Decision 2002/475/JHA and amending Council Decision 2005/671/JHA [2017] OJ L88/6 (CTDir).

[47] Council Framework Decision 2005/222/JHA of 24 February 2005 on attacks against information systems [2005] OJ L69/67.

the Decision's *renvoi* to the Convention. The text refers to 'cybercrime' in Article 17 and several recitals. The Cybercrime Directive establishes minimum rules concerning the definition of five criminal offences and sanctions in the area of attacks against information systems corresponding to CIA crimes in the Convention. Although an in-depth scrutiny of the definitions is beyond the scope of this research, it is worth noting that they are far from unproblematic. First, conduct such as access, interference, or interception, becomes an offence only when done intentionally and without right, ie 'not authorized by the owner or by another right holder of the system or of part of it, or not permitted under national law'.[48] Summers et al. note that the absence of definitions on basic criminal law concepts and principles in EU law undermines the intended harmonisation inherent in the 'intent' threshold and 'without right' defence.[49] Second, the adequacy of substantive definitions and their ability to apply to new conduct is highly debated.[50] Finally, precisely defining the remit of each offence can be difficult since one offence may involve 'several stages of a criminal act, where each stage alone could pose a serious risk to public interests'.[51]

The first offence is illegal access to information systems, which covers hacking, cracking and abuse of credentials. Examples of this offence, which is often the first stage or step in the cybercrime chain,[52] are many. During the Covid-19 pandemic, the European Medical Agency was the object of a series of attacks to garner information about the vaccine against the Covid-19 virus.[53] Access 'to the whole or to any part of an information system' is an offence where the *actus reus* is 'committed by infringing a security measure' and without defences.[54]

The second offence, illegal system interference, criminalises the creation of botnets, a portmanteau for robot networks, that is

> establishing remote control over a significant number of computers by infecting them with malicious software through targeted cyber-attacks. [...] the infected network of computers that constitute the botnet can be activated without the computer users' knowledge in order to launch a large-scale cyber-attack that could cause 'serious damage.[55]

Botnets can be used to distribute malicious content, but the large-scale attacks just described are typically (distributed) denial of service attacks ((D)DoS), whereby the enslaved computers, called zombies, send more access requests to a server than it can handle with the purpose of paralysing it. Estonia suffered such attacks in 2007,

---

[48] Cybercrime Directive, Art 2(d).
[49] Summers et al. (n 40), ch 7.
[50] Eg, for the UK, S McKay (ed) and A Guinchard et al., *Reforming the Computer Misuse Act 1990* (2020); A Guinchard, 'The Computer Misuse Act 1990 to Support Vulnerability Research? Proposal for a Defence for Hacking as a Strategy in the Fight against Cybercrime' (2017) 2 *Journal of Information Rights, Policy and Practice*.
[51] Cybercrime Directive, Rec 5.
[52] Although not of case law, because apprehending the offenders is hindered by obstacles in attributing attacks. On attribution, see S Brenner, *Cyberthreats and the Decline of the Nation-state* (London, Routledge, 2014) 9–17, 32–45, 60–70.
[53] D Sabbagh, 'Hackers accessed vaccine documents in cyber-attack on EMA' *The Guardian* (9 December 2020).
[54] Cybercrime Directive, Art 3.
[55] ibid, Rec 5.

which opened the eyes of policy-makers to the relevance of cybersecurity.[56] Ever since, (D)DoS attacks have become easier thanks to: (i) the availability of botnets for hire[57] or booter services; (ii) the spread of insecure connected devices, also known as the Internet of Things (IoT), which can be easily enslaved as shown by the Mirai botnet;[58] and (iii) fast-flux networks, where zombies change constantly and quickly, so that the take-down of some zombies does not affect the operation of the botnet.[59] It is a crime to seriously hinder or interrupt 'the functioning of an information system by inputting computer data, by transmitting, damaging, deleting, deteriorating, altering or suppressing such data, or by rendering such data inaccessible'.[60] If spamming has the objective of flooding an email account, it would be akin to a DDoS attack and qualify as illegal system interference.[61] Note that DDoS attacks affect availability and integrity without necessarily affecting confidentiality.[62]

The third prohibited conduct is illegal data interference, ie 'deleting, damaging, deteriorating, altering or suppressing computer data on an information system, or rendering such data inaccessible',[63] covering worms, viruses and malware such as Trojans, which are tools within the meaning of Article 7, as well as ransomware. Viruses are a string of code that self-propagates and needs a host environment; worms are self-contained programs that self-propagate; malware, portmanteau for malicious software, is a generic term for malicious code.[64] Known threats, tracked and categorised by information security companies, evolve constantly.[65]

The fourth offence is illegal interception, which includes, among others,

> the listening to, monitoring or surveillance of the content of communications and the procuring of the content of data either directly, through access and use of the information systems, or indirectly through the use of electronic eavesdropping or tapping devices by technical means.[66]

Forms of illegal interception are unlawful probes and spyware (ie spying software), various forms of sniffers, such as key-sniffing, as well as copying data, better known as

---

[56] Brenner (n 52) 18–21, 75–87.
[57] R Musotto and DS Wall, 'Are Booter Services (Stressers) Indicative of a New Form of Organised Crime Group Online?' (UNODC Linking Organized Crime and Cybercrime Conference).
[58] European Union Agency for Cybersecurity (ENISA), *Guideline on Assessing Security Measures in the Context of Article 3(3) of the Open Internet Regulation* (2018); L Urquhart, 'Exploring Cybersecurity and Cybercrime: Threats and Legal Responses' in Edwards (ed), *Law, Policy and the Internet* (Oxford, Hart Publishing, 2018).
[59] R Perdisci and I Corona et al., 'Early Detection of Malicious Flux Networks via Large-Scale Passive DNS Traffic Analysis' (2012) 9 *IEEE Transactions on Dependable and Secure Computing* 714–726.
[60] Cybercrime Directive, Art 4.
[61] Ie, sending SMTP traffic to port 25. See Cybercrime Convention Committee (T-CY), *T-CY Guidance Note #5 DDOS attacks. Adopted by the 9th Plenary of the T-CY (4–5 June 2013)* T-CY (2013) 10E Rev; *T-CY Guidance Note #2 botnets. Adopted by the 9th Plenary of the T-CY (4–5 June 2013)* T-CY (2013) 6E Rev.
[62] F Yamaguchi and F Liner et al., 'Vulnerability Extrapolation: Assisted Discovery of Vulnerabilities using Machine Learning' (5th USENIX Workshop on Offensive Technologies (WOOT)) [2011].
[63] Cybercrime Directive, Art 5.
[64] For definitions, see at: csrc.nist.gov/glossary/term/exfiltration; www.sans.org/security-resources/glossary-of-terms/.
[65] Through threat-modelling, see ch 5, section I.
[66] Cybercrime Directive, Rec 9

data exfiltration.[67] Many practices revealed by Edward Snowden are amenable to illegal interception,[68] defined as 'intercepting ... transmissions of computer data to, from, or within an information system, including electromagnetic emissions from an information system carrying such computer data'.[69] The *actus reus* must be committed by technical means and only concerns non-public transmission of data.

Lastly, the Cybercrime Directive covers tools used for committing offences, although without *wishing to carve them in stone* to factor in the diversity of attacks and the 'rapid developments in hardware and software'.[70] Tools are '(a) a computer programme, designed or adapted primarily for the purpose of committing cybercrimes; (b) a computer password, access code, or similar data by which the whole or any part of an information system is capable of being accessed'.[71] Prohibited conduct is 'the intentional production, sale, procurement for use, import, distribution or otherwise making available' of such tools. To prevent over-reach of the offence, such as criminalising legitimate uses of tools by pen-testers,[72] the intent element of the offence is specified: the conduct constitutes an offence only if the tool is for the perpetration of an offence defined in Articles 3–6. The idea is to hit those who trade these tools, given the proliferation of cybercrime-as-a-service, botnets for hire and 'dark' markets where tools are exchanged.[73]

Although identity theft[74] is not a self-standing offence, 'setting up effective measures against identity theft and other identity-related offences constitutes another important element of an integrated approach against cybercrime'.[75] Furthermore, Member States can consider the commission of illegal data and system interference 'by misusing the personal data of another person, with the aim of gaining the trust of a third party, thereby causing prejudice to the rightful identity owner'[76] as an aggravating circumstance.

Summers et al. note how legislation pursuant to the DSM does not refer to criminal law because of lack of competence of relevant institutions in this regard.[77] However, the Cybercrime Directive refers to instruments within the DSM and is substantively

---

[67] See at csrc.nist.gov/glossary/term/exfiltration; www.sans.org/security-resources/glossary-of-terms/.

[68] Honeypots – systems purposefully designed with flaws so as to attract cyber-offenders – could potentially fall within this category. See A Flanagan and I Walden, 'Honeypots: a Sticky Legal Landscape?' (2009) 29 *Rutgers Computer and Technology Law Journal* 317.

[69] Cybercrime Directive, Art 6.

[70] Cybercrime Directive, Rec 16; see section III below.

[71] ibid, Art 7.

[72] ibid, Rec 16. Guinchard (n 55); McKay et al. (n 55).

[73] See generally TJ Holt and O Smirnova et al., *Data Thieves in Action: Examining the International Market for Stolen Personal Information and Cybercrime* (Basingstoke, Palgrave MacMillan, 2016); A Hutchings and TJ Holt, 'The Online Stolen Data Market: Disruption and Intervention Approaches' (2017) 18 *Global Crime* 11–30; C Bradley and G Stringhini, *A Qualitative Evaluation of Two Different Law Enforcement Approaches on Dark Net Markets* (IEEE 2019); Europol (n 18).

[74] See generally Summers et al (n 40); Cybercrime Convention Committee (T-CY), *T-CY Guidance Note #4 Identity Theft and Phishing in relation to Fraud. Adopted by the 9th Plenary of the T-CY (4–5 June 2013)* T-CY (2013) 8E Rev.

[75] Cybercrime Directive, Rec 14.

[76] ibid, Art 9(5), 'unless those circumstances are already covered by another offence, punishable under national law'.

[77] Summers (n 40).

functionally interconnected with them.[78] Such a substantive functional interconnection between NIS and the Cybercrime Directive effects strong reconciliation between the fight against CIA crimes, privacy and data protection. To demonstrate both substantive functional interconnection and strong reconciliation, I analyse the Cybercrime Directive through the criteria used to compare NIS laws in chapter six: notion of security, mention of information security properties, presence of cross-references including to complementarity, logic of the instrument and devices relied on to pursue its goals.

As for the notion of security, the Cybercrime Directive aims to protect against, and if possible prevent, attacks against the same information systems and computer data, irrespective of the ownership and purpose of such systems, addressed by instruments pursuing NIS (chapter six). Similarly to the NIS Directive (NISD), information systems are a device or group of inter-connected or related devices that automatically process data, which can be personal.[79] Alternatively, the information system can also mean the data necessary for its own functioning.[80] Computer data are 'a representation of facts, information or concepts in a form suitable for processing in an information system, including a programme suitable for causing an information system to perform a function'.[81]

In terms of information security properties, the Cybercrime Directive criminalises conduct that undermines the security of information systems and computer data. The underlying purpose of criminalising such conduct is similar to that of legislation pursuing NIS. Such a claim is made manifest by observing the interaction between security properties[82] and CIA crimes. Illegal access entails a violation of authorisation/control and possibly authentication; illegal system interference is the consequence of the loss of availability; illegal data interference corresponds to loss of integrity; illegal interception corresponds to loss of confidentiality. Offences against CIA are understood as security incidents and personal data breaches in NIS. It is exactly because CIA crimes target the properties governing the security of information systems that they are referred to as 'narrow' or true cybercrimes.

In chapter six, the presence of provisions in NIS legislation encouraging cooperation among cybersecurity and data protection authorities acted as a litmus test to ascertain the degrees of reconciliation between NIS, data protection and privacy.[83] Those provisions can also be said to effect a functional interconnection between instruments. Therefore, the inclusion of provisions encouraging cooperation between LEAs and

---

[78] MG Porcedda, 'Brexit, Cybercrime and Cyber Security. From en Masse Opt-out to Creative Opt-in in the AFSJ and Beyond?' in Carrapico et al. (eds), *Brexit and Internal Security Political and Legal Concerns in the Context of the Future UK-EU Relationship* (Basingstoke, Palgrave Macmillan 2019).

[79] Device means a single computer, mobile phone, tablet, satellite etc, interconnected means networked, related means able to form part of a system, Cybercrime Directive, Art 2(a).

[80] Second limb of Art 2(a) Cybercrime Directive and Art 4(1)(c) NISD.

[81] Cybercrime Directive, Art 2 (b). Comparing the scope of application of computer data in the EU Directive and CoE Convention, see Summers (42) 237; European Commission, 'Report assessing the extent to which the Member States have taken the necessary measures in order to comply with Directive 2013/40/EU on attacks against information systems and replacing Council Framework Decision 2005/222/JHA' (Communication) COM (2017) 0474 final; MG Porcedda and DS Wall, 'Data Crime, Data Science and the Law' in Mak et al. (eds), *Research Handbook on Data Science & Law* (Cheltenham, Edward Elgar, 2018).

[82] See ch 5, section I and ch 6, section II.

[83] Beyond the formulaic provisions specifying the need to respect fundamental rights, which express weak reconciliation.

data protection authorities in the Cybercrime Directive exemplifies both degrees of reconciliation between cybersecurity, privacy and data protection and functional interconnection. The Cybercrime Directive encourages international cooperation relating to the security of information systems, computer networks and computer data, and give proper consideration of the security of data transfer and storage in case of international agreements involving data exchange.[84] Moreover, the Cybercrime Directive contains provisions that spell out its complementarity with the goals pursued by NIS legislation in force at the time it was adopted, chiefly the predecessors of the General Data Protection Regulation (GDPR) and the European Electronic Communications Code, covered in chapter six, but not of the LED. Ensuring 'an adequate level of protection and security of information systems by legal persons, for example in connection with the provision of publicly available' e-communications services (ECSs) 'in accordance with' the e-Privacy Directive (EPD) and GDPR 'forms an essential part of a comprehensive approach to effectively counteracting cybercrime'.[85]

The Cybercrime Directive acknowledges the link between large-scale cyber-attacks and 'the loss or alteration of commercially important confidential information or other data'[86] and allows Member States to frame the loss or compromising of personal data as an aggravating factor to cybercrimes, for instance in relation to damage caused by botnets.[87] The same applies in case of identity theft.

As for the logic, similarly to NIS instruments, the Cybercrime Directive is predicated on the paradigm of risk assessment and management, and therefore resilience. For instance, the 'identification and reporting of threats and risks posed by' cyber-attacks is 'a pertinent element of effective' prevention and response to cyber-attacks and of improvement of 'the security of information systems'.[88] Thus, supplying threat-related information is instrumental to 'threat assessments and strategic analyses of cybercrime'.[89] By aiming to 'facilitate the prevention of' cybercrime, the Cybercrime Directive embraces a logic of prevention.[90] Indeed, 'criminal law responses to cybercrime' should be complemented with an 'effective comprehensive framework of prevention measures' that includes 'an appropriate level of protection of information systems'.[91]

As for legislative 'devices' used to further the goals of legislation, NIS legislation pursues prevention 'by design', through technical and organisational measures appropriate to the seriousness of the threat and the likelihood of the risk incurred, measures which are rarely spelled out owing to the logic, or principle, of technology neutrality. Similarly, the Cybercrime Directive refers to 'Appropriate levels of protection … against reasonably identifiable threats and vulnerabilities in accordance with the *state of the art*'.[92] Provisions on 'tools' are also silent as to the measures to be criminalised,

---

[84] Cybercrime Directive, Rec 27.
[85] ibid, Rec 26.
[86] ibid, Rec 6. On confidential information, see T Aplin, 'Trading Data in the Digital Economy: Trade Secrets Perspective' in Lohsse et al. (eds), *Trading Data in the Digital Economy: Legal Concepts and Tools* (Oxford, Hart Publishing, 2017).
[87] Cybercrime Directive, Rec 5.
[88] ibid, Rec 12.
[89] ibid, Rec 24.
[90] ibid, Art 1.
[91] ibid, Rec 2.
[92] ibid 26 (emphasis added).

or conversely legitimately used. 'Security measures' to be broken by those committing illegal access are undefined. Similarly, any Commission's revisions of the Cybercrime Directive should be based, among others, 'on technological developments, for example those enabling more effective enforcement in the area of attacks against information systems or facilitating prevention or minimising the impact of such attacks'.[93]

The functional interconnection between laws on NIS and CIA crimes is an indicator of strong reconciliation between CIA crimes, privacy and data protection. The substantive provisions of the Cybercrime Directive concern values amenable to the goals pursued by privacy and data protection instruments, with the overlaps and limitations discussed in chapter five and the ones that will be discussed below vis-à-vis data processing for law enforcement purposes. The protection of the integrity of personal data processed by digital services converges with the prevention of illegal data interference, and the confidentiality of personal communications converges with the prevention of interception of computer data. On this basis the Cybercrime Directive appears to privilege a strong form of reconciliation between the triad.

ii. Directive 2019/713 on Fraud and Counterfeiting (FCD): Substantive Functional Interconnection Lost and Weak Reconciliation

The FCD repeals Council Framework Decision 2001/413/JHA[94] and is based on Article 83(1) TFEU, for its serious and cross-border dimensions; it explicitly complements and reinforces the Cybercrime Directive, whose definitions of 'information systems' and 'computer data' it adopts.[95] Similarly to its predecessor, the FCD contains neither a *renvoi* to the Convention,[96] nor a legally meaningful reference to "cybercrimes".[97]

The FCD has a broader scope than its predecessor, as the legislator took the opportunity to extend the criminalisation of frauds and counterfeiting to non-cash means of payments that are non-corporeal, ie digital, as well as to e-money and virtual currencies.[98] *Mens rea* requires intent but, unlike the Cybercrime Directive, defences only apply to Article 6.[99] In terms of *actus reus*, omissions should not be criminalised and there is no *de minimis* exception, owing to the fact that large-scale frauds often result from the combination of many individual frauds involving only small amounts.[100]

Fraudulent use of non-cash payment instruments, irrespective of their corporeal nature, is an offence when such instruments are: (a) stolen or otherwise unlawfully

---

[93] ibid, Rec 25.
[94] Council Framework Decision 2001/413/JHA of 28 May 2001 combating fraud and counterfeiting of non-cash means of payment [2001] OJ L149/1. Ireland opted out. FCD, Rec 38, Art 19.
[95] FCD, Rec 15, Arts 2(e), (f).
[96] The FCD covers forgery within the meaning of the Convention only indirectly.
[97] Except for FCD, Rec 28.
[98] ibid, Rec 15, Arts 2(a), 2(c)–(d).
[99] ibid, Rec 14.
[100] ibid, Recs 14, 30. See DS Wall, 'Crime, Security and Information Communication Technologies: The Changing Cybersecurity Threat Landscape and Implications for Regulation and Policing' in Brownsword et al. (eds), *The Oxford Handbook of the Law and Regulation of Technology* (Oxford, Oxford Univeristy Press, 2017).

appropriated or obtained; (b) counterfeit or falsified.[101] Article 4 FCD criminalises: (a) stealing or otherwise unlawfully appropriating; and (b) fraudulently counterfeiting or falsifying *corporeal* non-cash payment instruments; (c) *possession* of corporeal non-cash payment instruments acquired as in (a) and (b), as well as; (d) '*procurement* for oneself or another' for fraudulent use.

Non-corporeal, non-cash payment instruments are used fraudulently if they are unlawfully obtained following the commission of one of the offences laid down in Articles 3 to 6 of the Cybercrime Directive, or misappropriated (a).[102] Other offences include: (b) fraudulent counterfeiting or falsification; (c) the holding[103] of an unlawfully obtained, counterfeit or falsified non-corporeal, non-cash payment instrument for fraudulent use; and (d) the procurement for oneself or another, including the sale, transfer or distribution, or the making available, of an unlawfully obtained, counterfeit or falsified non-corporeal non-cash payment instrument for fraudulent use.

The 'collection and possession of payment instruments with the intention to commit fraud, through ... phishing, skimming or directing or redirecting payment service users to imitation websites, and their distribution, for example by selling credit card information on the internet' are also offences irrespective of actual commission of fraud.[104] Similarly offensive is hindering or interfering with the functioning of an information system or introducing, altering, deleting, transmitting or suppressing computer data without right.[105] Frauds must also cause an unlawful loss of property to make an unlawful gain for the perpetrator or a third party.[106]

Article 7 FCD mirrors Article 7 of the Cybercrime Directive and is similarly premised on the 'dual use' nature of tools, seeking to circumscribe criminalisation by targeting activities such as crimeware-as-a-service, carding and illicit data markets in general.[107] It proscribes the production, procurement or making available of '*tools*', ie devices or instruments, 'computer data or any other means primarily designed or specifically adapted for the purpose of committing' a selection of offences in the FCD.

Identity theft is understood to worsen the consequences of fraud 'because of reputational and professional damage, damage to an individual's credit rating and serious emotional harm', as reported in the literature, thereby requiring Member States to adopt adequate assistance, support and protection of victims.[108] However, identity theft is not conceptualised as a potential aggravating circumstance to fraud and counterfeiting.

Many frauds and counterfeiting (forgery in the language of the Convention) are intimately tied to CIA offences and consequently enjoy a strong connection with NIS, which potentially translates into strong reconcilability with privacy and data protection. Such an intimate connection is demonstrated by relying on the criteria used to illustrate

---

[101] FCD, Art 3, Recs 8–9.
[102] ibid, Art 5(a), Rec 15; "Misappropriation' should mean the action of a person entrusted with a non-corporeal non-cash payment instrument, to knowingly use the instrument without the right to do so, to his own benefit or to the benefit of another'.
[103] As opposed to 'possession'. The provision lays down a potential defence.
[104] FCD, Rec 13.
[105] ibid, Art 6(a)–(b).
[106] ibid, Art 6.
[107] See n 73 above.
[108] C Kopp and R Layton et al, 'The Role of Love Stories in Romance Scams: a Qualitative Analysis of Fraudulent Profiles' (2015) 9 *International Journal of Cyber Criminology* 205–217; M Aiken, *The Cyber Effect* (London, John Murray, 2016); Summers et al. (n 40) 244–247. FCD, Rec 31, Art 16.

the substantive functional interconnection between the prevention of and fight against CIA offences and NIS.

First of all, the Directive borrows its understanding of information systems and computer data from the Cybercrime Directive and is concerned with the 'security' of such systems and data. Second, even if fraud and forgery are classed as computer-related crimes where information systems are a means to a fraudulent end, perpetrating such crimes often presupposes the compromising of information security properties. To commit fraud, data integrity and confidentiality are often jeopardised; counterfeiting is a violation of data integrity. Frauds and counterfeiting are often the outcome, or directly benefit from, a series of CIA crimes.[109] The violation of integrity and confidentiality is often aggravated by the time lag between the offence, as such a time lag can allow for 'a spiral of interlinked crimes' to unravel.[110] These points make a strong case for subsuming fraud and counterfeiting under the category of narrow or true cybercrime.

As for cooperation between authorities, the FCD encourages cooperation between LEAs and authorities tasked with dealing with incidents under the second Payment Services Directive (PSD2) and the NISD,[111] which is an additional indicator of functional interconnection between this instrument and legislation on NIS/CIA offences. In terms of logics, although risk assessment/management and resilience are not predominant, Recital 6 suggests the FCD embraces technology neutrality.[112] As for devices to achieve its goals, the FCD encourages prevention by means of information and awareness-raising campaigns, research and education programmes and recognises the importance of monitoring and statistics.[113] This shows the marked affinity between NIS/CIA legislation and FCD. The same cannot be said for affinity with legislation on the two rights.

In sum, insofar as the FCD explicitly 'complements and reinforces' the Cybercrime Directive[114] and condemns the violation of integrity and confidentiality, it can be said to benefit from the Cybercrime Directive's substantive functional interconnection with NIS legislation, including in relation to data protection and privacy. The centrality of personal data to frauds and counterfeiting criminalised by the FCD, widely acknowledged in policy documents such as the 2020 Strategy, successive Europol's reports and the literature, cannot be overstated.[115] There are few instances of frauds and counterfeiting that do not thrive on the violation of confidentiality, especially of personal information.[116] However, such a factual overlap is not reflected in the letter of the law. The link between the FCD and Cybercrime Directive and thus NIS falls short of extending to privacy and data protection.

---

[109] As made explicit in FCD, Art 6. See MG Porcedda and D Wall, *The Chain and Cascade Effects in Cybercrime: Lessons from the TalkTalk Case Study* (IEEE 2019) ieeexplore.ieee.org/document/8802510.
[110] ibid. See FCD, Rec 32.
[111] FCD, Rec 25, 24, 36 and 38. Directive 2015/2366/EU [2015] OJ L337/35 (PSD2).
[112] FCD, Rec 35 in passing. See ch 5, section II.A.
[113] FCD, Arts 17–18.
[114] ibid, Rec 15.
[115] COM (2020) 605 final (n 17); Europol, 'Internet Organised Crime Threat Assessment (IOCTA) 2019'. Europol (n 18); P Hunton, 'Data Attack of the Cybercriminal: Investigating the Digital Currency of Cybercrime' (2012) 28 *Computer Law & Security Review* 201–207; MG Porcedda and D Wall, 'Modelling the Cybercrime Cascade Effect in Data Crime' (3rd Workshop on Attackers and Cyber-Crime Operations (WACCO), held Jointly with IEEE EuroS&P 2021).
[116] Eg, the use of spoof identities created with entirely fake data.

The FCD does not devote much attention to privacy and data protection in addition to the formulaic endeavour to respect fundamental rights.[117] Member States must ensure that investigative tools, such as those which are used in countering organised crime or in other serious crime cases, are effective, proportionate to the crime committed and available to the persons, units or services responsible for investigating or prosecuting FCD offences.[118] LEAs must respect the GDPR (NB not the LED), and particularly legitimate grounds of processing, in the context of investigations relating to offences in the FCD.[119] The FCD is silent on personal data breaches – as opposed to incidents under NIS and the PSD2 – and consequently does not encourage cooperation with data protection authorities, let alone acknowledge the complementarity of their action.

The only provision that acknowledges the link between frauds, counterfeiting and personal data concerns measures to protect victims whose personal data have been misused.[120] The FCD does not encourage the adoption of preventative measures against identity theft, which is, anyway, not an aggravating circumstance for fraud. Moreover, the fact that the procurement for fraudulent use of non-corporeal means of payments 'should be punishable without it being necessary to establish all the factual elements of the unlawful obtainment and without requiring a prior or simultaneous conviction for the predicate offence which led to the unlawful obtainment'[121] will make it difficult to establish links between frauds and the violation of data protection and privacy principles, including negligence on the part of data controllers.

The analysis of the FCD challenges the idea that substantive functional interconnection between frauds and NIS legislation extends to instruments protecting personal data and privacy. The explicit attitude of the FCD towards data protection and, to a lesser degree, privacy, appears closer to weak reconciliation understood as balancing, rather than complementarity facilitating strong reconciliation. Perhaps of the two possible logics harboured by Article 83(1) TFEU, the fight against serious crime and the related investigative investment prevails over the management of computer related crime premised on prevention and resilience. The objective of preventing fraud seems to be left to the Proposal amending the eIDAS Regulation and establishing a framework for a European Digital Identity.[122] Such an approach places the FCD at the intersection between narrow and broad cybercrimes, whose provisions focus on the investigation of cybercrime.

iii. Directive 2011/93 on Combating Child Sexual Abuse (CSADir) and Regulation 2021/1232 (CSAReg): Procedural Functional Interconnection and Uncertain Reconciliation

The CSADir was adopted pursuant to two legal bases in the AFSJ. One is Article 82(2) TFEU on minimum rules concerning criminal matters having a cross-border dimension,

---

[117] FCD, Rec 38.
[118] ibid, Art 13.
[119] ibid, Rec 27.
[120] ibid, Art 16.
[121] ibid, Rec 15.
[122] COM (2021) 281 final, see ch 6, section II.D.

aimed to facilitate mutual recognition of judgments and judicial decisions and police and judicial cooperation. The other is Article 83(1) TFEU on establishing minimum rules and sanctions in the area of sexual exploitation of children, as a serious crime with a cross-border dimension. As the CSADir contains no connection clauses to the Convention,[123] offences against children conducted by means of ICTs should not be classified as 'cybercrime' in the EU legal order.

The CSADir defines four categories of serious crime: offences concerning sexual abuse, offences concerning sexual exploitation, offences concerning child pornography and solicitation of children for sexual purposes.[124] Pornography, better referred to as child sexual abuse material (CSAM), is broadly defined and includes: any material, including realistic images visually depicting a child, or someone appearing to be a child, engaged in real or simulated explicit conduct, viz. pseudo child pornography; or any depiction, including realistic images, of the sexual organs of a child, or someone appearing to be a child, for primarily sexual purposes.[125] Children are persons below 18, though the CSADir enables a degree of flexibility by taking into account the age of sexual consent, which varies across Member States.

The CSADir recognises that the use of new technologies and the Internet is enabling the increase and spread of sexual abuse, exploitation and pornography of children, as well as the online *solicitation* of children for sexual purposes via social networking websites and chat rooms.[126] Accordingly, the CSADir defines cyber-enabled offences and identifies instruments to curb such offences. It is an offence to 'knowingly obtaining access, by means of information and communication technology, to child pornography'.[127] Solicitation of children for sexual purposes when conducted intentionally and by means of ICTs is also proscribed.[128] Hence, it is a crime if an adult proposes that a child who has not reached the age of sexual consent to meet for the purposes of engaging in sexual activities or for producing child pornography and 'that proposal was followed by material acts leading to such a meeting'.[129] Furthermore, an attempt, by means of ICTs, to acquire, possess, or knowingly obtain access to child pornography 'by an adult soliciting a child ... to provide child pornography depicting that child' is also punishable as a criminal offence.[130]

The CSADir clarifies that child pornography 'cannot be construed as the expression of an opinion', and measures to combat it include 'making it more difficult for offenders to upload such content onto the publicly accessible web' and 'seeking to secure the removal of such content from servers'.[131] Thus, pursuant to Article 25, Member States must adopt measures to ensure the prompt *removal* 'of web pages containing or disseminating child pornography hosted in their territory and to endeavour to obtain the

---

[123] Art 9 Convention.
[124] CSADir, Arts 3–6.
[125] See Flanagan (n 5); Y Akdeniz, 'Media Freedom on the Internet: an OSCE Guidebook' (OSCE, 2016) 42–47; AA Gillespie, *Cybercrime: Key Issues and Debates* (London, Routledge, 2019) chs 7, 9.
[126] CSADir, Recs 3, 12.
[127] ibid, Art 5(3).
[128] ibid, Art 6; sexual purposes refers to offences in Arts 3 and 5.
[129] CSADir, Arts 3(4), 5(6).
[130] ibid, Art 6(2).
[131] ibid, Rec 46; see Akdneiz (n 125) 42–47.

removal of such pages hosted outside of their territory'.[132] In light of the fact that third countries may be unwilling or unable to cooperate, Member States can take measures to *block* access to web pages containing or disseminating child pornography towards the Internet users *within their territory*.[133] Note that the CSADir is silent about how to *detect* offending material.

Article 25 CSADir is seen as 'one of a number of provisions in the Directive to facilitate prevention and mitigate secondary victimisation'.[134] The provision acknowledges that the removal of child pornography can be achieved by means of public action, such as legislative, non-legislative, judicial or other, so long as measures include adequate safeguards, respect the principles of necessity and proportionality, including the provision of information to interested parties, and enable judicial redress.[135] There are many initiatives to detect, block and remove child pornography involving a broad range of parties.[136] Such initiatives are grounded outside of the AFSJ and include voluntary measures, public-private partnerships and also measures based in the Digital Single Market (DSM).

Voluntary DSM-based measures range from 'established' blocking initiatives such as CleanFeed to solutions such as Apple's proposal of Client-Side Scanning (CSS).[137] An illustration of PPPs is 'We Protect Global Alliance to End Child Sexual Exploitation Online',[138] formed with the merger of 'We Protect' and the Global Alliance against child sexual abuse online. The Global Alliance's aim is to identify and remove 'known child pornography material' and increase 'as much as possible the volume of system data examined' and its work is based on memoranda of understanding drawn between police services and private actors, whose legal status and guarantees remain uncertain.[139]

Following the adoption of the European Electronic Communications Code, which broadens the scope of the e-privacy Directive (EPD) to messaging services and email providers,[140] Regulation (EU) 2021/1232 on a temporary derogation from certain provisions of the EPD[141] for the purpose of combating online child sexual abuse

---

[132] CSADir, Art 25(1).

[133] ibid, Rec 47, Art 25(2).

[134] European Commission, 'Report from the Commission to the European Parliament and the Council assessing the implementation of the measures referred to in Article 25 of Directive 2011/93/EU of 13 December 2011 on combating the sexual abuse and sexual exploitation of children and child pornography' (Communication) COM (2016) 872 final, 1.

[135] CSADir, Rec 47.

[136] Information society service providers (ISSs), internet users, dedicated hotlines usually run by an NGO or a consortium of NGOs, ISPs and private companies, LEAs and the judiciary. European Commission (n 134).

[137] TJ McIntyre, 'Child Abuse and Cleanfeeds: Assessing Internet Blocking Systems', in Brown (ed), *Research Handbook on Governance of the Internet* (Cheltenham, Edward Elgar, 2013); H Abelson and R Anderson et al., *Bugs in our Pockets: The Risks of Client-Side Scanning* (2021) arxiv.org/abs/2110.07450.

[138] Available at: ec.europa.eu/home-affairs/what-we-do/policies/cybercrime/child-sexual-abuse/global-alliance-against-child-abuse_en.

[139] Global Alliance Partners, *Guiding principles on the Global Alliance against child sexual abuse online. Annex to the Declaration on Launching the Global Alliance against child sexual abuse online* (2012) ec.europa.eu/dgs/home-affairs/what-is-new/news/news/2012/docs/20121205-declaration-anex_en.pdf as I discuss in Porcedda (n 13).

[140] Directive 2018/1972 [2018] OJ L321/36 (EECC), see ch 6, section II; European Commission, '2020 EU Strategy for a more effective fight against child sexual abuse' (Communication) COM (2020) 607 final.

[141] Regulation (EU) 2021/1232 of the European Parliament and of the Council of 14 July 2021 on a temporary derogation from certain provisions of Directive 2002/58/EC as regards the use of technologies by providers of number-independent interpersonal communications services for the processing of personal and other data for the purpose of combating online child sexual abuse [2021] OJ L274/41. Directive 2002/58/EC [2002] OJ L201/37 (EPD).

(CSAReg) was signed into law. The Regulation is based on both Articles 16(2) TFEU on data protection and 114(1) TFEU on approximation of provisions to pursue the establishment and functioning of the Internal Market.[142] The Regulation aims to enable the pursuit of measures against child pornography contained in the CSADir by number-independent interpersonal communications service providers up until 3 August 2024. Thus, the time-limited objective of the CSAReg is to restrict the confidentiality of communications on grounds of the seriousness of child sexual abuse online. It pursues such an objective by enabling providers to adopt undefined 'specific technologies' – excluding the 'scanning of audio communications' – for the 'processing of personal and other data to the extent strictly necessary to' detect online child sexual abuse on their services, report and remove it.[143] The remainder of the CSAReg is devoted to data protection standards, the collection of statistics and oversight by national data protection authorities.

As a DSM instrument addressing service providers, the Regulation addresses detection, thereby filling a gap created by the CSADir. Such an intervention straddles the DSM-AFSJ divide, thereby creating a form of functional interconnection different to that discussed in the context of narrow or CIA crimes, and common to all content crimes, that is based on procedure rather than substance, thus called 'procedural functional interconnection' or 'functional interconnection as to procedure'. In particular, CSAM challenges different notions of security, each commanding different solutions.

First, and at its heart, CSAM challenges the security, safety and integrity of children stemming from real-world, offline human conduct. Network and information systems assist in the perpetration of the offence, in that they facilitate the reaching of both victims through grooming and 'consumers' of CSAM in its many forms – live, recorded and depicted. As a broad cybercrime, CSAM subverts neither information security properties nor the physical infrastructure of the network. Thus, the prevention of CSAM does not rest *primarily* on technical measures, but rather on societal action, which could make use of network and information technologies as a medium. In this guise, EU law mandates Member States to undertake education and training to discourage any form of abuse against children, or else to organise awareness-raising campaigns – including online – and foster research and education programmes aimed at reducing the risk of children becoming victims of sexual abuse or exploitation.[144]

Second, from a human rights perspective, measures against CSAM can be seen as addressing positive state obligations to protect and fulfil all rights of the child, including privacy and data protection.[145] Thus, Member States should endeavour to 'protect the privacy, identity and image of child victims, and to prevent the public dissemination of any information that could lead to their identification'.[146] This second approach to

---

[142] In keeping with case law: *Ireland v Parliament and Council*, case C-301/06, EU:C:2009:68 (Data Retention I).
[143] CSAReg, Art 1.
[144] CSADir, Art 23.
[145] 'A child's physical and moral well-being', *La Quadrature du Net*, C-511/18, para 128; *Commissioner of the Garda Síochána e.a*, case C-140/20, EU:C:2022:258, para 49. See *X and Y v the Netherlands*, no. 8978/80 CE:ECHR:1985:0326JUD000897880; L-A Sicilianos, L Lazarus et al., *Respecting human rights and the rule of law when using automated technology to detect online child sexual exploitation and abuse. Independent experts report* (Council of Europe, 2021), 33–47.
[146] CSADir, Art 21(6).

CSAM affects security properties in two ways. Insofar as the offence concerns electronic forms of CSAM, mainly videos or images of abused children, then there can be said to be an underlying interest to protect the confidentiality of the data, ultimately to protect children. Yet, the objectives of making data and services unavailable is achieved by encroaching on the confidentiality of everybody's communications. Technical solutions can be used to detect, block and remove content, thereby both supporting and undermining security properties.[147]

Data protection is explicitly listed in the CSADir clause, mandatory for Union law, ensuring the respect for fundamental rights and observance of the principles recognised by the Charter and is also one of the principles to be observed when setting up sex offender registers.[148] Differently from the CSADir, as a *lex specialis* of the EPD, the CSAReg is squarely placed within the data protection legal framework: services scanning and filtering content and traffic data fall within the supervision of data protection authorities and must act within the strict parameters of data protection law. The CSADir lacks references to cooperation with cybercrime authorities, though the text is now dated and, following the 2020 Strategy, a proposal amending or repealing it is set to be published at the end of 2022 (see chapter two). The CSADir also lacks references to data protection authorities and the predecessor of the LED; Rec 97 LED contains a clause of non-encroachment with the CSADir.

The CSADIR and CSAReg converge on a common 'serious crime' logic, whereby personal communications and data harbour evidence that command the imposition of permissible limitations on the rights to privacy and data protection. Although neither the CSADir nor the CSAReg mention technology neutrality, language used in both instruments is largely in keeping with this paradigm. As an example, Member States shall 'ensure that *effective investigative tools*, such as those which are used in organised crime or other serious crime cases are available to persons ... responsible for investigating or prosecuting offences'.[149] Tools are also implicit in Article 25 CSADir concerning 'measures' to remove or block web pages depicting child pornography. As seen, the CSAReg refers to undefined 'specific technologies'. Those technologies are crucial in assessing the possibility of reconciling the fight against broad cybercrimes, privacy and data protection: it remains to be seen whether a rights-enhancing result – the detection of child pornography in private communications and the blocking or removal of web pages – could be achieved by measures that are overly intrusive, and therefore impermissible.

In sum, the modality of reconciliation between the triad gleaned from the CSADir and CSAReg remains open-ended and spuriously indifferent. On the one hand, CSAM infringes children's right to data protection and privacy. The effective removal of, or blocking access to, web pages containing or disseminating child pornography within the EU pursuant to the CSADir can protect psychological and bodily integrity, enshrined in 'private life', confidentiality and fulfil data subject rights.[150] On the other hand, unlike the discussion on NIS/narrow cybercrimes, the CSADir does not carve a special role

---

[147] See section III below.
[148] CSADir, Recs 50 and 43 respectively. Charter [2012] OJ C326/391 (CFR).
[149] CSADir, Art 15 (3).
[150] Chs 3–5.

for privacy and data protection and the CSAReg clearly limits confidentiality of data and communications. Both texts attempt to balance competing interests by relying on a proportionality test within the framework of the Rule of Law (RoL). Since the instruments embrace technology neutrality, measures of detection and enforcement remain unidentified. Consequently, a prima facie appraisal of the application of permissible limitations remains incomplete unless 'tools' are factored in the analysis. I will address this in section III.

iv. *The Proliferation of Cybercrimes: Cyber-Terrorism, Electoral Interference and Prospective Weak Reconciliation*

Many real-world offences have acquired a cyberspace dimension by virtue of the uptake of ICTs and connectivity. As a result, the family of cyber-assisted or broad cybercrimes is potentially as vast as the list of existing offences. The Cybercrime Convention Committee (T-CY)[151] published guidance discussing how substantive crimes defined in the Convention and Protocol could subsume offences that are not explicitly mentioned in either instrument. Two examples that are high on the political agenda are cyber-terrorism – a concern since 9/11[152] – and electoral interference, which acquired prominence more recently.

The CoE T-CY states that 'the substantive crimes in the Convention may be carried out to facilitate terrorism, to support terrorism, including financially, or as preparatory acts'.[153] Such are the objectives of the Directive on combating terrorism (CTDir), which is based on Article 83(1) TFEU. It is intended to proscribe cyber-attacks[154] as a form of terrorism, namely illegal system interference and illegal data interference when committed for specific listed purposes.[155] Since 'behaviour … should be punishable also if committed through the Internet, including social media',[156] the CTDir introduces measures against 'public provocation content online' and foresees safeguards[157] while restating the general prohibition of monitoring.[158] It is the only instrument referring to the LED, which applies to exchange of information for investigative purposes.[159] The CTDir is complemented by a Regulation laying down uniform rules to address the misuse of hosting services for the dissemination to the public of terrorist content online (CTReg)[160] and based on Article 114 TFEU. The relationship between the CTDir and CTReg effects the same

---

[151] Representing state parties pursuant to Art 46 Convention.
[152] See United Nations, Office on Drug and Crime (UNODC), *The Use of Internet for Terrorist Purposes* (2012); Brenner (n 52); Summers et al. (n 40) 168–177.
[153] Cybercrime Convention Committee (T-CY), Guidance note #11. Aspects of Terrorism covered by the Budapest Convention. Adopted by the 16th Plenary of the T-CY (14–15 November 2016) T-CY(2016)11.
[154] CTDir, Art 3(i). European Commission, 'Proposal for a Directive on combating terrorism and replacing Council Framework Decision 2002/475/JHA on combating terrorism' (Communication) COM (2015) 625 final.
[155] Where Cybercrime Directive (EU) 2013/40, Arts 9(3), 9(4)(b) or (c) and Art 9(4)(c) apply, for purposes in CTDir, Art 3(2).
[156] CTDir, Rec 6.
[157] ibid, Arts 21–23.
[158] ibid, Rec 23.
[159] ibid, Rec 25.
[160] Regulation (EU) 2021/784 of the European Parliament and of the Council of 29 April 2021 on addressing the dissemination of terrorist content online [2021] OJ L172/79 (CTReg).

procedural functional interconnection between the DSM and AFSJ observed for the CSADir and CSAReg.

The T-CY also acknowledges that cyber-borne interference with elections, exemplified by the exposure of Hilary Clinton's emails during the 2015 US presidential campaign and the Cambridge Analytica scandal, could be covered by the Convention's substantive provisions.[161] To curb election interference the Commission proposed a host of measures in 2018,[162] including the Network of Cybersecurity Competence Centres to better target and coordinate available funding for cybersecurity cooperation, research and innovation. Amendments to the e-Commerce Directive (ECD) contained in the Digital Services Act also aim to tackle electoral interference.[163]

Instruments criminalising broad/content-related/cyber-assisted cybercrimes such as cyber-terrorism and electoral interference acknowledge that prevention rests *primarily* on societal action, rather than technical measures, which is the responsibility of Member States. By means of example, awareness that radicalisation of terrorists takes place in prisons warrants preventative intervention aimed at penal institutions.[164] Thus, EU law instruments only deal with the manifestation of the conduct online, the 'firefighting' of which requires investigatory powers and cooperation with service providers. The consequence for the triad is weak reconciliation effected through the application of a test for permissible limitations within the framework of the RoL, which is reflected in mentions of privacy and data protection in mandatory provisions calling for the respect of fundamental rights.[165]

v. *The Shrinking Divide between Forms of Cybercrime: Procedural Functional Interconnection Effects Weak Reconciliation*

Instruments that lay down new cyber-assisted offences make provisions for the adoption of wide investigatory powers and measures. This is in keeping with the spirit of the Convention, Article 14 of which enables parties to apply the same procedural rules applicable to offences contained in the Convention for the collection of e-evidence relating to any criminal investigation. For instance, the CoE T-CY suggests that 'the

---

[161] RS Mueller, *Report on the Investigation into Russian Interference in the 2016 Presidential Election. Submitted Pursuant to 28 C.F.R. § 600.8(c)* (2019); Information Commissioner's Office, *Investigation into the Use of Data Analytics in Political Campaigns. A Report to Parliament* (2018). Cybercrime Convention Committee (T-CY), 'Aspects of election interference by means of computer systems covered by the Budapest Convention, T-CY(2019) 4, T-CY Guidance Note#9'. See generally: Landau (n 3) 158–170; Freedom House, *Freedom of the Net 2019. The Crisis of Social Media* (2019); C Marsden and T Meyer et al, 'Platform Values and Democratic Elections: How can the Law Regulate Digital Disinformation?' (2020) 36 *Computer Law & Security Review*.

[162] European Commission, State of the Union 2018: European Commission proposes measures for securing free and fair European elections (2018) ec.europa.eu/commission/presscorner/detail/en/IP_18_5681; European Commission, 'On the European democracy action plan' (Communication) COM (2020) 790 final.

[163] See the duty to assess against the risk of 'foreseeable negative effects on civic discourse and electoral processes' as per Art 34(1)(c) Regulation (EU) 2022/2065 of the European Parliament and of the Council on a Single Market For Digital Services (Digital Services Act), OJ L277/1, adopted as this book went to press.

[164] R Dati, (Rapporteur), *Draft Report on prevention of radicalisation and recruitment of European citizens by terrorist organisations (2015/2063(INI))* (European Parliament, Committee on Civil Liberties, Justice and Home Affairs, 2015). See JP-coops: jpcoopsproject.eu.

[165] Eg, CTDir, Rec 19.

procedural and mutual legal assistance tools in the Convention may be used to investigate terrorism.[166] Once available, investigative measures become normalised and their use is advocated for the investigation of any crimes. For instance, legislation combating the trafficking of human beings contains a recommendation to the effect that 'those responsible for investigating and prosecuting such offences' 'have access to the *investigative tools* used in organised crime or other serious crime cases' including 'the interception of communications, covert surveillance including *electronic surveillance*'.[167] The relevance of e-evidence to a growing variety of investigations puts under pressure the confidentiality of communications and data and seems to embolden those who call for exceptional access. Accordingly, the differences between narrow and broad cybercrime shrink, with consequences for the reconcilability of triad.

Investigations rest on the collection of information and the borderless nature of cybercrime often requires cross-border cooperation in the guise of joint investigations and exchange of information, typically through Europol.[168] Thus, the logics and measures of investigation of narrow and broad cybercrime tend to converge, including reliance on DSM-based procedures and related procedural functional interconnection. As offending content and e-evidence is hosted by intermediaries – what Kohl calls gatekeeping[169] – DSM legislation creates provisions aimed at onboarding intermediaries in the fight against crimes. Legislation traces the borders of the duty of care and liability of intermediaries, by introducing obligations to preserve data, prohibitions of general monitoring and safe harbours against liability.

In so doing, AFSJ instruments effect a functional interconnection with DSM measures that is procedural, rather than substantive: the first step for the investigation and prosecution of cyber-enabled offences is solidly anchored in the DSM. What is more, the open-ended, technology neutral approach of legislation allows the addressee of legislation to choose appropriate measures to counter not only content crimes, but also cybercrimes and even NIS-related incidents such as in the PSD2.[170] Poignantly in the

---

[166] Cybercrime Convention Committee (T-CY), *T-CY Guidance Note #11. Aspects of Terrorism covered by the Budapest Convention. Adopted by the 16th Plenary of the T-CY (14–15 November 2016)* T-CY (2016) 11.

[167] Rec 15 Directive 2011/36/EU of the European Parliament and of the Council of 5 April 2011 on Preventing and Combating Trafficking in Human Beings and Protecting its Victims, and Replacing Council Framework Decision 2002/629/JHA [2011] OJ L101/1.

[168] Eg, Council Framework Decision 2006/960/JHA of 18 December 2006 on simplifying the exchange of information and intelligence between law enforcement authorities of the Member States of the European Union [2006] OJ L386/89; Peers (n 1) 914–915; Regulation 2016/794/EU of the European Parliament and of the Council of 11 May 2016 on the European Union Agency for Law Enforcement Cooperation (Europol) and replacing and repealing Council Decisions 2009/371/JHA, 2009/934/JHA, 2009/935/JHA, 2009/936/JHA and 2009/968/JHA [2016] OJ L135/53.

[169] U Kohl, 'The Rise and Rise of Online Intermediaries in the Governance of the Internet and Beyond – Connectivity Intermediaries' (2012) 26 *International Review of Law, Computers & Technology*; 'Google: the Rise and Rise of Online Intermediaries in the Governance of the Internet and Beyond (Part 2)' (2013) 21 *International Journal of Law and Information Technology* 187–234. See also U Kohl and C Fox, 'Internet Governance and the Resilience of the Nation State', in U Kohl (ed), *The Net and the Nation State. Multidisciplinary Perspectives on Internet Governance* (Cambridge, Cambridge University Press, 2017); L Edwards, "With Great Power Comes Great Responsibility?": The Rise of Platform Liability' in L Edwards (ed), *Law, Policy and the Internet* (Oxford, Hart Publishing, 2018).

[170] Member States 'shall permit processing of personal data by payment systems and payment service providers when necessary to safeguard the prevention, investigation and detection of payment fraud', PSD2, Art 94 (1).

GDPR 'the processing of personal data to the extent strictly necessary and proportionate for the purposes of ensuring network and information security ... and the security of the related services offered by, or accessible via, those networks and systems' constitutes a legitimate interest of the data controller.[171]

In conclusion, when it comes to investigations, all forms of cybercrimes tend to converge because data are no longer the object of protection, but rather bear evidence; consequently, relevant instruments or parts thereof engender a classic (weak) reconciliation between rights and security, which commands the application of a balancing formula as part of a proportionality test. Otherwise said, the logic expressed in the letter of the law can conflict with its implementation, so that the same instrument can engender different, and not always consistent, logics. This is a fast-evolving area of law benefitting from wide debates in criminal substantive and procedural law, debates that go beyond the scope of this study. However, the finding of this analysis is that developments in the collection of e-evidence have the ultimate bearing on the relationship between the triad, developments to which I turn next.

B. How the Collection of e-Evidence Affects the Reconciliation of the Fight against Cybercrime with Privacy and Data Protection

Article 83 TFEU complements rules on police and judicial cooperation in criminal matters, of different scope of application, placing an emphasis on the collection of relevant information, the exchange of evidence and the adoption of common techniques to investigate offences.[172] The overhaul of the data protection legal framework pursuant to Article 16 TFEU, Snowden's Revelations, the invalidation of the Data Retention Directive (DRD) by *Digital Rights Ireland*[173] and waves of terrorist attacks have set in motion significant ongoing legal reform.

The European Commission is planning to revise the European Investigation Order Directive (EIOD) to bring it into line with the LED, at a minimum to correct its rules on purpose limitation.[174] The scope of application of the LED itself may come under pressure, with the CJEU stating that the LED will apply where Member States 'directly implement measures that derogate from the rule that electronic communications are

---

[171] GDPR, Rec 49.
[172] Eg, TFEU, Art 87(c) limits the scope of common investigative techniques to 'serious forms of organised crime', restrictions open to challenge given the broad interpretation adopted by Member States in this area; see Summers et al. (n 40) chs 1–2. Art 87(c) TFEU allows for a certain interpretive largesse of 'organised crime' capable of facilitating the extension of common investigative techniques to a broad range of serious crimes, as exemplified by Europol's IOCTA reports (n 18) 115. See further A Lavorgna and A Sergi, "Serious', Therefore Organised? A Critique of the Emerging "Cyber-Organised Crime" Rhetoric in the United Kingdom' (2016) 10 *International Journal of Cyber Criminology* 1–23.
[173] *Digital Rights Ireland and Seitlinger and Others*, C-293/12 and C-594/12, EU:C:2014:238.
[174] Directive 2014/41/EU of the European Parliament and of the Council of 3 April 2014 regarding the European Investigation Order in criminal matters [2014] OJ L130/1 (EIOD); European Commission, 'Way forward on aligning the former third pillar acquis with data protection rules' (Communication) COM (2020) 262 final.

to be confidential, without imposing processing obligations on providers of electronic communications services'.[175]

The invalidation of the DRD has sparked a judicial saga – centred around the interpretation of Articles 15(1) EPD, 23(1) GDPR, 7 and 8 CFR and 8 ECHR – which encapsulates the trends of evidentiary law-making: the negotiation for greater powers of investigations, as against the definition of stringent and precise safeguards for privacy and data protection. The outcome of the judicial saga is likely to be incorporated in pending legislative proposals, chiefly the draft EPR, the European Regulation on European Production and Preservation Orders for electronic evidence in criminal matters[176] (EPPOR) and others that may flow in response to international developments, such as the ratification of the Second Additional Protocol to the Cybercrime Convention.[177]

The objective of this section is not to revise each measure, for which I defer to existing literature,[178] but rather to show how the constant negotiation for greater powers and more stringent safeguards is affecting the reconcilability between the fight against cybercrime, privacy and data protection. I begin with the CJEU case of *La Quadrature du Net* and the ECtHR case of *Big Brother Watch and Others v UK* (*Big Brother Watch*), judgments that are tracing the contours of permissible evidentiary approaches. After discussing lessons that can be drawn from the combined analysis of the two cases, I briefly discuss the EPPOR and draw the overall conclusions of section II.

i. Case Law (I): La Quadrature du Net *(CJEU)*

La Quadrature du Net stems from three separate requests for a preliminary ruling[179] aimed to determine the compatibility with EU law of national measures on intelligence,[180]

---

[175] *La Quadrature du Net*, C-511/18, para 103.

[176] COM (2017) 10 final (EPR); European Commission, 'Proposal for a Regulation on European Production and Preservation Orders for electronic evidence in criminal matters' COM (2018) 225 final – 2018/0108 (COD), 3; European Commission, 'Proposal for a Directive laying down harmonised rules on the appointment of legal representatives for the purpose of gathering evidence in criminal proceedings' COM (2018) 226 final 2018/0107 (COD).

[177] Eg, United States CLOUD Act (Clarifying Lawful Overseas Use of Data) of 23 March 2018; See European Commission, 'Recommendation for a Council Decision authorising the participation in negotiations on a second Additional Protocol to the Council of Europe Convention on Cybercrime (CETS No. 185)' (Communication) COM (2019) 71 final.

[178] For EU Criminal Law, see Peers (n 1); Summers at al. (n 40). For data retention, see generally: N Ni Loideain, *EU Data Privacy Law and Serious Crime. Data Retention and Policymaking* (Oxford, Oxford University Press, 2021); M Zubik and J Podkowik et al. (eds), *European Constitutional Courts towards Data Retention Laws* (Cham, Springer 2021); M Tzanou, *The Fundamental Right to Data Protection. Normative Value in the Context of Counter-Terrorism Surveillance* (Oxford, Hart Publishing, 2017).

[179] Raised in proceedings between *La Quadrature du Net and others v the French Prime Minister and Others*, case C-520/11, the *French Data Network and Others v the Prime Minister and Others*, C-512/18 and the *Ordre des Barreaux francophones et germanophone, and Others v the Belgian Council of Ministers*, C-520/18, concerning the interpretation of Arts 15(1) EPD and 12–15 e-commerce Directive (ECD).

[180] One of the cases concerns the much-criticised French '*loi reinseignement*' stemming from amendments to the Code on Internal Security. Commission Nationale de l'Informatique et des Libertés (CNIL), 'Délibération 2015-078 du 5 mars 2015 portant avis sur un projet de la loi relatif au reinsegnement'; W Maxwell, *French Surveillance Law Permits Data Mining, Drawing Criticism from Privacy Advocates* (Hogan Lovells, 2015) www.hldataprotection.com/2015/08/articles/international-eu-privacy/french-surveillance-law-permits-data-mining-drawing-criticism-from-privacy-advocates/; B Dambrine, *The State of French Surveillance Law (White Paper)* (2015).

data retention, and the obligations imposed on network operators. Although not the last in the data retention saga, *La Quadrature du Net* is the landmark case establishing criteria for the compatibility of measures of e-evidence with the EPD and the GDPR broadly followed in the subsequent cases of *Prokuratuur*[181] and *Commissioner of the Garda Síochána e.a.*[182]

In line with settled case law, interferences compatible with Article 15(1) EPD are those proportionate to the objectives pursued. There are three categories of 'seriousness' of the interference, drawn from the detriment caused to private life and natural persons:[183] (i) interferences that cannot, in principle, be classified as serious; (ii) serious interferences; and (iii) particularly serious interferences. Four objectives of general interest potentially justify such interferences – provided there is a connection between the data processed and the objective pursued – shown here in reverse hierarchical order:[184] (a) the fight against criminal offences in general or ordinary crime; (b) the fight against serious crime, including particularly serious crime; (c) the prevention of threats to, and attacks on, public security; and (d) safeguarding national security. The Court occasionally exemplifies such categories by referring to specific offences: child pornography is subsumed under (b) and the prevention of terrorism is subsumed under (d).[185] If we combine interferences (i)–(iii) with objectives (a)–(d), we obtain a matrix of permissible measures for the collection of e-evidence; in the following, metadata means traffic and location data.

Particularly serious interferences (iii) include the general and indiscriminate retention of metadata, which however cannot be continuously used for preventative purposes on account of the detrimental effect such retention would have on a democratic society.[186] Such interferences also include the automated data analysis of, inter alia, metadata, ie 'a screening of all [metadata] retained by providers',[187] as well as the real-time collection of data that allows the terminal equipment of specific persons potentially linked to a terrorist threat to be located, which can be aggravated by the real-time collection of traffic data.[188] All such particularly serious interferences with Articles 7 and 8 (and 10) CFR, and *a fortiori* minor interferences, can only be justified to counter 'a serious threat to national security that is shown to be genuine and present or foreseeable', as exemplified by terrorism.[189] Such a condition is necessary but insufficient, in that the national measures must 'define the scope of the limitation on the exercise of the right concerned', 'lay down the substantive and procedural conditions governing that use'[190] and include additional safeguards, eg, an effective review by an independent authority whose decision is binding.

---

[181] *Prokuratuur*, C-746/18, EU:C:2021:152.
[182] *Commissioner of the Garda Síochána*, C-140/20.
[183] The CJEU subsumes privacy under data protection in *La Quadrature du Net*, C-511/18, paras 146–147, 155, 207
[184] *Commissioner of the Garda Síochána*, C-140/20, para 56.
[185] *La Quadrature du Net*, C-511/18, paras 154 and 179.
[186] ibid, para 177.
[187] ibid, paras 174, 172. On paras 170–174, see section IV.
[188] GPS tracking or other, ibid, para 187.
[189] ibid, paras 188–189.
[190] ibid, paras 175–176.

Serious interferences (ii) include the general and indiscriminate retention of IP addresses of the initiator of communications[191] for tracking the clickstream of a person and the instruction of providers of e-communication services (ECSs) to expeditiously preserve metadata for specified purposes, though never for ordinary crime.[192] Targeted retention of metadata can draw from 'objective and non-discriminatory factors' 'according to the categories of persons concerned or using a geographical criterion' for a period of time that is limited but extendable.[193] Only fighting against serious crime[194] – and *a fortiori* preventing serious threats to public security and safeguarding national security – can justify the adoption of such measures.

Interferences of a minor nature (i) that can be justified to tackle criminal offences include, following *Ministerio Fiscal*, the general and indiscriminate retention of data relating to the civil identity of individuals.[195] Note that the matrix is not flawless: the targeted retention of metadata is a particularly serious interference,[196] yet it is permissible not only for national security, but also in relation to serious crime and public security.

Member States are also allowed to make recourse to an instruction requiring providers of ECSs to: generally and indiscriminately retain metadata in given circumstances; expeditiously retain metadata upon request; automatedly analyse content data; collect metadata in real-time. In such cases, the EPD applies to processing by ECSs irrespective of the reasons of such processing, whereas the GDPR applies to subsequent processing operations on such data by LEAs pursuant to Article 23(1)(d) and (h). By contrast, the LED applies where the derogation from the rule that electronic communications are to be confidential does not impose 'processing obligations on' ECSs.[197]

The judgment restates[198] that the same entity can both be ECSs and Information Society Services (ISSs), with particular reference to Internet Access Services (IASs) and web-based email services.[199] The Court clarifies that the e-commerce Directive cannot undermine the requirements contained in the GDPR and the EPD[200] and Article 23(1) GDPR precludes legislation requiring ECSs to retain personal data generally and indiscriminately. Finally, the CJEU reiterates the prohibition of processing content data.[201] Before elaborating on the significance of these findings, let us move onto the ECtHR judgment in *Big Brother Watch*.

---

[191] ibid, para 153. Following para 152, IP addresses constitute traffic data, but are not considered to be as sensitive as other traffic data; see section III below.
[192] ibid, para 164–165.
[193] *Commissioner of the Garda Síochána*, C-140/20, para 101.
[194] ibid, para 166, *a contrario*. Such as offences relating to CSAM proscribed by Art 2(c) CSADir, ibid, para 73.
[195] *La Quadrature du Net*, C-511/18, para 157. Such that 'the purchase of pre-paid SIM card, is subject to a check of official documents establishing the purchaser's identity and the registration', *Commissioner of the Garda Síochána*, C-140/20, para 72.
[196] *La Quadrature du Net*, C-511/18, para 146–147.
[197] ibid, para 103.
[198] *Skype Communications*, C-142/18, EU:C:2019:460.
[199] *La Quadrature du Net*, C-511/18, paras 204–205.
[200] ibid, para 199.
[201] ibid.

ii. Case Law (II): Big Brother Watch and Others v UK (ECtHR)

The Grand Chamber of the ECtHR re-examined[202] the decision of the First Section on *Big Brother Watch and others*,[203] a case sparked by Snowden's Revelations concerning the compatibility of the United Kingdom's Regulation of Investigatory Power Act and related Codes of Practice with Article 8 ECHR. There, the Court reviews three questions, of which the first – the permissibility of bulk interception of cross-border communications by intelligence services – is the most important for this research.

In its analysis of the first question, the ECtHR posits that the compliance of a system of intelligence-gathering must be assessed as a whole in light of its 'end-to-end safeguards'.[204] The Court relies on two crucial interpretive keys. First, the ECtHR finds that the intrusion into the right to privacy varies according to the stages of intelligence gathering as the Court has taken them to be.[205] Second, on account of the peculiarity of legislation permitting secret surveillance, the ECtHR examines jointly two requirements of the test for permissible limitations that would otherwise be assessed separately: 'in accordance with the law' and 'necessary in a democratic society'.[206]

In relation to the first interpretive key, the ECtHR subdivides the intelligence gathering under analysis into four stages: (i) the interception and initial retention of communications and its metadata, or 'packets', which is deemed not to be particularly serious; (ii) the automated application of specific selectors, including 'strong selectors' such as email addresses, to the retained data; (iii) the examination of selected communications to the data by analysts; and (iv) the subsequent retention of data, its use (eg in the guise of an intelligence report) and exchange thereof. The Court states that the intensity of the intrusion into privacy, and therefore the need for safeguards, increases at each stage, reaching its peak when analysts examine the content or metadata of intercepted communications. To justify the need of safeguards for the automatic processing of data at stage (ii), even if in 'coded form' and requiring 'computer technology' or expertise, the ECtHR relies on *S. and Marper v UK*.[207]

In relation to the second interpretive key, the ECtHR premise is that Contracting States have a legitimate need for secrecy on account of the necessity for bulk intelligence gathering to protect national security or 'essential national interests', as shown by expert evidence and state practice.[208] Bulk interception of cross-border communications is described as 'a valuable technological capacity' to gather intelligence and identify new threats, such as global terrorism and the sexual exploitation of children.[209] The ECtHR emphasises that many such threats come from 'international networks of hostile actors

---

[202] *Big Brother Watch and Others v the United Kingdom*, nos. 58170/13, 62322/14 and 24960/15, CE:ECHR:2021:2505MAD005817013 (*Big Brother Watch 2*).
[203] *Big Brother Watch and Others v the United Kingdom*, nos. 58170/13, 62322/14 and 24960/15, CE:ECHR:2018:0913JUD005817013.
[204] *Big Brother Watch 2*, nos. 58170/13, 62322/14 and 24960/15, paras 360, 350.
[205] ibid, para 325.
[206] ibid, para 334.
[207] *S. and Marper v the United Kingdom*, nos. 30562/04 and 30566/04, CE:ECHR:2008:1204JUD003056204. However the Court does not cite para 99 listing measures for the protection of data, including 'procedures for preserving the integrity and confidentiality of data'. *Big Brother Watch 2*, no. 58170/13, paras 325–330.
[208] ibid, paras 323, 338.
[209] ibid, paras 322–233.

with access to increasingly sophisticated technology' enabling them to evade detection and 'disrupt digital infrastructure and even the proper functioning of democratic processes through the use of cyberattacks'.[210] Cyberattacks are characterised as 'a serious threat to national security which by definition exists only in the digital domain and as such can only be detected and investigated there'.[211] On such grounds, the ECtHR concedes a 'wide margin of appreciation' provided, as conventional, that strong safeguards are imposed to avoid that a system of secret surveillance set up to protect national security and 'other essential interests' ends up undermining or even destroying democratic processes under the cloak of defending them.[212] Note the reference to 'essential interests', which is not listed as a separate ground in Article 8(2) enabling the limitation of the right to privacy, though the reference is dropped in the formal assessment of the measures.

The Grand Chamber continues its analysis on two pragmatic premises that result from technological developments. One premise is that bulk data collection differs from targeted data collection, on which much of the Court's case law has focused hitherto, in three ways. Bulk interception targets international communications; it is used for foreign intelligence gathering, detection and investigation of cyber-attacks, counter-espionage and counter-terrorism, and is applied to data flows through 'packets', whereas targeted interception concerns individuals in the territory, the investigation of crime and is applied to devices.[213] As such, the ECtHR feels the need to update its approach and to reconsider the six safeguards it developed in its case law on targeted interception, to arrive at eight safeguards that reduce the contracting States' margin of appreciation in operating a bulk interception system.[214] The eight criteria are: (i) the grounds for authorising bulk interception; (ii) the circumstances enabling the interception of an individual's communications; (iii) the procedure for granting authorisation; (iv) the procedure for selecting, examining and using intercepted material; (v) the precautions taken when sharing material with third parties; (vi) limits on the interception and retention of related data; (vii) independence of supervision; (viii) procedures for ex post facto review.

The second premise is that the collection of metadata and content data can be equally intrusive,[215] but the different use made of these data in practice affects the appraisal of intrusiveness and the extant conditions for permissibility.[216] On such a basis, the ECtHR conducts separate assessments for the use of content and metadata. Ultimately, since under the section 8(4) RIPA regime both categories of data are processed similarly, the Court's findings apply to both metadata and content data.

The ECtHR found the bulk interception of cross-border communications not to contain sufficient 'end-to-end' safeguards against arbitrariness and abuse, on account of: 'the absence of independent authorization, the failure to include the categories of

---

[210] ibid, para 340.
[211] ibid, para 323.
[212] ibid, paras 338–39.
[213] ibid, paras 341, 344–46.
[214] ibid, paras 274, 335, 361.
[215] ibid, paras 342, 363.
[216] ibid, para 364.

selectors in the application for a warrant, and the failure to subject selectors linked to an individual to prior internal authorization'.[217] Therefore, section 8(4) RIPA does not meet the 'quality of the law' requirement and the interference does not keep to what is necessary in a democratic society, thus engendering a violation of Article 8 ECHR.

Insofar as the data retention regime is concerned, the ECtHR defers to the EU to confirm the findings of the First Section, whereby Part 4 of RIPA was not 'in accordance with the law' because data could be accessed to combat any crimes, not just serious ones and access to data does not require prior independent review.[218]

iii. Case Law (III): Lessons from La Quadrature du Net and Big Brother Watch

The judgments issued by the CJEU and the ECtHR 'concerns situations which, as was the prevailing view … are not comparable'.[219] Bearing in mind the difference between national/foreign intelligence-gathering, the internal-external security nexus as well as the different remit of the two Courts,[220] the two judgments offer misaligned interpretations of the permissibility of bulk collection and automated analysis of data. I outline four differences.

First, the ECtHR may be said to show more deference towards ECHR Contracting States than the CJEU does towards EU Member States.[221] The ECtHR does not outright ban bulk and untargeted intelligence gathering, which in CJEU parlance correspond to generic and indiscriminate collection and retention, for preventative purposes. The CoE Court also permits the use of bulk and untargeted intelligence gathering, including on a continuous basis, subject to checks on the selectors, for a broader range of objectives (eg, organised crime, cyber-attacks) than its EU counterpart. As a result, the CJEU may seem to adopt a more protective approach to fundamental rights.

Second, the ECtHR engages with the technology to a greater extent than the CJEU does,[222] in that it discusses expert evidence, the functioning of the Internet and conceptualises the stages of intelligence gathering. It is on this basis that the ECtHR concedes to a wider use of automated analysis, building on older cases such as *S. and Marper v the United Kingdom* on automated processing of biometric data. It is interesting, however, that the Court does also not reflect on the qualitative difference between compiling a

---

[217] ibid, para 425.
[218] *Big Brother Watch 2*, no 58170/13, third plea, para 467. See M Tzanou, *Big Brother Watch and Others v. the United Kingdom: A Victory of Human Rights over Modern Digital Surveillance?* (Verfassungsblog, 2018) verfassungsblog.de/big-brother-watch-and-others-v-the-united-kingdom-a-victory-of-human-rights-over-modern-digital-surveillance/.
[219] *Commissioner of the Garda Síochána e.a*, C-140/20, EU:C:2022:941, Opinion of AG Sánchez-Bordona, para 39.
[220] Not only do the judgments concern different situations and review different applicable laws, but they also arise from judicial proceedings that have different purviews and aims.
[221] But cf *Commissioner of the Garda Síochána*, C-140/20, paras 50, 56, 61. They seems to contain concessions to Member States on striking a balance between different rights and defining national security as hierarchically superior to other security-related objectives.
[222] But with limitations. See NN Loideain, *Not So Grand: The Big Brother Watch ECtHR Grand Chamber Judgment* (2021), infolawcentre.blogs.sas.ac.uk/2021/05/28/not-so-grand-the-big-brother-watch-ecthr-grand-chamber-judgment/.

database for biometrics, which is resource-intensive and cannot be done in bulk, as against automated bulk screening of all communications. Unlike *S and Marper v the United Kingdom*, the Court does not place much emphasis on the responsibility incumbent on states developing new technologies for automated analysis.

Third, the two Courts differ as to the permissibility of access to content. The ECtHR appears to permit access to the contents of communications, as against the CJEU, which restates the prohibition of accessing the content of communications, thereby leaving the distinction between content and metadata, and consequently the threshold for the violation of the essence of Article 7 CFR as discussed in chapters one, three and six, unresolved.

Finally, whereas the ECtHR creates a straightforward framework for the permissibility of direct, unmediated evidence gathering, the CJEU creates a patchwork of measures insofar as the collection of evidence mediated by the private sector is concerned. The judgment highlights areas of tension between the ECD, the EPD and the GDPR, which are left largely unresolved.[223] The two judgments are a product of the ongoing battle between two camps: those who seek wider investigatory powers, and those who seek greater human rights safeguards. The pronouncements of the two Courts is likely to have an impact on law making, to which I now turn.

iv. *Legislative Reforms: The European Production and Prosecution Order Regulation (EPPOR) and the Second Additional Protocol to the Cybercrime Convention*

Since the European Investigation Order Directive (EIOD) concerns access to e-evidence without containing 'any specific provisions on this type of evidence',[224] it is hoped to be complemented by the EPPOR. Work on the proposal, initially based on Article 82(1), have proceeded slowly, but at the time of writing trialogues are in progress.[225] The Regulation's purported objective is to remedy the volatility of e-evidence 'for criminal proceedings stored or held by service providers in another jurisdiction', easing the securing and gathering thereof. The EPPOR 'is also expected to foster trust in the digital single market by improving security and reducing the perception of impunity for crimes committed on or through networked devices'.[226] The proposal would affect investigations on cybercrimes set out in the Directives on Cybercrime,[227] Fraud and

---

[223] See section III below.
[224] COM (2018) 225 final (n 176), 4. See S Tosza, 'All Evidence is Equal, but Electronic Evidence is more Equal than any Other: The Relationship between the European Investigation Order and the European Production Order' (2020) 1 *New Journal of European Criminal Law*.
[225] Á Tinoco-Pastrana, 'The Proposal on Electronic Evidence in the European Union' (2020) 1 *Eurcrim* 46–50; T Wahl, *Progress on E-Evidence Package – Stakeholders Remain Critical* (Eurcrium, 2022). eucrim.eu/news/progress-on-e-evidence-package-stakeholders-remain-critical/. See progress at: www.europarl.europa.eu/legislative-train/theme-a-new-push-for-european-democracy/file-jd-cross-border-access-to-e-evidence-production-and-preservation-orders/03-2022
[226] COM (2018) 225 final (n 176), 10.
[227] Recital 23 Cybercrime Directive points to the need to cooperate with service providers to preserve potential evidence, provide elements helping to identify offenders and eventually shut down, completely or partially, information systems or functions that have been compromised or used for illegal purposes.

Counterfeiting (FCD), as well as offences laid down in the Directives against Child Sexual Abuse (CASDir) and on Combating Terrorism (CTDir).[228]

The proposal gives 'the judiciary and law enforcement *tools* to address the way criminals communicate today and to counter modern forms of criminality. Such *tools* are conditional on their being subject to strong protection mechanisms for fundamental rights.'[229] This statement encapsulates both the spirit and logic of the instrument.

As for the spirit, personal and communication data are regarded as evidence, the collection of which interferes with privacy and data protection and calls for limitations to be imposed within the boundaries set by the RoL. This follows a weak reconciliatory approach underpinned by the implementation of a test for permissible limitations on a case-by-case basis. Indeed, 'the European Preservation Order' is 'issued or validated by a judicial authority in a concrete criminal procedure after an individual evaluation of the proportionality and necessity in every single case'.[230] 'Given the different levels of intrusiveness of the measures imposed in relation to the data pursued, the proposal' sets out conditions and safeguards.[231] Against such a background, one cannot expect statements of complementarity between 'security' and rights. Judgment on the strength of the RoL approach taken[232] can only be passed on the final draft.

As for the underlying logic, the reference contained in the explanatory memorandum to 'tools' suggests, prima facie, that the instrument embraces technology neutrality. However, 'tools' is used both as a synonym for 'measures'[233] and as technology,[234] whereby the EPPOR should be reviewed if and when 'new forms of communication tools' arise.

Unlike the EIOD and the Budapest Convention,[235] the proposal does not prima facie deal with proactive, surveillance-orientated measures such as real-time interception, nor automated analysis. This could, on its own, offer greater guarantee of adherence to the RoL, and therefore reconciliation of the triad in the classic sense of proportionality, if the shortcomings identified by the EDPS and the EDPB are redressed.[236]

The EPPOR is meant to 'be complemented … by continued work towards an additional protocol to the Budapest Convention'.[237] The final draft of the Second Additional Protocol was adopted in November and opened for signature in May 2022.[238] Unlike

---

[228] COM (2018) 225 final (n 176), 18 relating to Art 5.
[229] ibid (emphasis added).
[230] ibid, 4.
[231] Encapsulated in proposed Arts 1(2) and Recs 12–14, Arts 5, 11 and Recs 51–52, 54–57 and ch 4 on remedies, ibid, 6.
[232] ibid, 6 and 11.
[233] ibid, Recs 4, 8, 61.
[234] ibid, Rec 62.
[235] See ch V EIOD on the interception of telecommunications and Art 31 Convention on interception of one participating state in the territory of another participating state.
[236] European Data Protection Board, 'Opinion 23/2018 of the EDPB on Commission proposals on European production and preservation orders for electronic evidence in criminal matters (Art. 70.1.b) (2018)'; European Data Protection Supervisor (EDPS), 'Opinion 7/2019 on Proposals regarding European Production and Preservation Orders for electronic evidence in criminal matters' (2019).
[237] COM (2018) 225 final (n 176), 10.
[238] Second Additional Protocol to the Convention on Cybercrime on enhanced co-operation and disclosure of electronic evidence CETS No. 224 12/05/2022.

the drafting of the Convention itself, greater multi-stakeholder involvement led to reinforced safeguards for human rights, as the Protocol adds a provision on personal data protection[239] that reflects the spirit of Convention 108+.

v. Modes of Reconciliation of Collection of e-Evidence, Privacy and Data Protection: The Danger of a Zero-Sum Game between Surveillance and Security

The need for 'effective investigative tools' mentioned in NIS instruments and laws tackling cybercrime at large creates a procedural functional interconnection between the investigation of NIS-related illicit behaviour, all cybercrimes and most offences, interconnection underpinned by the understanding of data as evidence. The collection of e-evidence is premised on an inextinguishable appetite for data extraction, partly facilitated by new forms of content and metadata unknowingly volunteered by individuals when using digital devices and social media, and partly challenged by the broader uptake of encryption.[240]

There are no one-size-fits-all investigative techniques into cybercrime and generic offences,[241] but all 'tools' are capable of breaching information security properties (SPs) and protection goals (PGs) in some way. Techniques leveraging interception, of which there are many as evidenced by Snowden's Revelations, subvert confidentiality, which is a PG/SP shared by cybersecurity, privacy and data protection.[242] Interception also interferes with the essence of privacy, viz. the contents of communication and potentially of data protection, viz. rules on confidentiality and integrity. Against this background, the presence of shared SPs/PGs is insufficient to determine the reconcilability of privacy, data protection and the investigation of all cybercrimes.

Confidentiality is enshrined in Article 7 CFR and the EPD, where it prohibits Member States from listening, tapping, storing, intercepting or surveilling communications and the related traffic data by persons other than users, without the consent of the users concerned (and Article 8 CFR, the GDPR and the LED).[243] The scope of confidentiality can be restricted to safeguard national security, defence, public security, and the prevention, investigation, detection and prosecution of criminal offences or of *unauthorised use of the electronic communication system*.[244] The limitation of confidentiality could degenerate into a zero-sum game between security and liberty[245] if pursued in contempt of the principles of necessity, appropriateness and proportionality within a

---

[239] ibid, Art 14.
[240] Landau (n 3) 117–124
[241] ibid, 125–152.
[242] M Cayford and C van Gulijk et al., *Consolidated Survey of Surveillance Technologies, SURVEILLE Project Deliverable D2.9* (2015); European Parliament, *Resolution on the US NSA Surveillance Programme, Surveillance Bodies in Various Member States and their Impact on EU Citizens' Fundamental Rights and on Transatlantic Cooperation in Justice and Home Affairs* (2013/2188 (INI) [2014] OJ C 378/104. See tools and techniques collated by Lawfare: www.lawfareblog.com/snowden-revelations. Ch 5, section I.
[243] EPD, Art 5(1); GDPR chiefly Art 5(1)(f), see ch 4. For the LED, see fn 246 below.
[244] ibid, Art 15(1) (emphasis added).
[245] See ch 1, section I.C.

democratic society, and the general principles enshrined in Article 2 TEU. The LED[246] provides a framework against zero-sum outcomes for the processing of personal data in the field of law enforcement, by mandating minimum safeguards protecting privacy and data protection – setting aside, for the time being, the question of the essence.

Recent judgments and proposed instruments applicable to the investigation of cybercrimes – both as cyber-exploits and cyber-attacks – develop and include stronger safeguards to reconcile the interests at stake, by leveraging permissible limitations within the framework of the RoL. This means that the reconcilability between investigations into cybercrime, privacy and data protection rests on the application of classic balancing. The assessment of reconcilability is necessarily done on a case-by-case basis, for each legal instrument, and focussing on the intended outcome, rather than the workings of tools and measures to investigate crime. Judicial interpretation typically targets the permissibility of the intended outcome, such as 'interception' and 'automated analysis', vis-à-vis the pursuit of particular objectives. The practicalities of such tools and measures are left to playbooks and manuals developed by ground operators, viz. LEAs, intelligence agencies and the private sector, sometimes working together in partnership, whether willingly or reluctantly as in the US PRISM programme.

To understand the reconcilability between the triad, it is necessary to investigate the possibility that the law lays down safeguards that are routinely undermined by the very tools used to pursue the law's objectives. Landau and De Nardis have discussed the problem as a trade-off not between security and liberties, but between (cyber) security and surveillance.[247] In its Resolution on mass surveillance,[248] the EP noted that the fight against crime can endanger critical information infrastructure (CII). To address this point, it is necessary to engage with the tools themselves, as I do next.

III. Reconciliation of the Fight against Cybercrime, E-evidence, Privacy and Data Protection: Technology

Since the same investigative goal can be achieved through a variety of intelligence techniques and applicable in a targeted or bulk manner, provisions often give generous leeway on how to achieve the investigative goal, leeway that affects the reconcilability of the triad. This section begins with a reflection on the role of 'tools' and technology neutrality (TN), followed by examples of tools and an analysis of deep packet inspection (DPI) to thwart and investigate cybercrimes, which helps creating a parallel with chapter six. Not least because the use of DPI is challenged by increasingly encrypted data flows, the chapter briefly reviews other tools to counter and investigate (cyber) crimes, before drawing conclusions.

---

[246] Arts 22, 25, 29 and 44 LED also contain rules reinforcing data security, integrity and confidentiality.
[247] Landau (n 3) 21; L DeNardis, 'The Internet Design Tension between Surveillance and Security' (2015) 37 *IEEE Annals of the History of Computing* 72–83.
[248] European Parliament (n 242).

A. 'Use of Tools' and Implicit Reference to Technology Neutrality (TN)

Of the instruments covered in this chapter, only the LED and the Fraud and Counterfeiting Directive (FCD) openly embrace TN. However, all instruments refer to 'tools', eg, to commit cyber-attacks[249] and frauds,[250] as well as to deal with content-related offences such as CSAM and terrorism.[251] Reference to 'tools' as opposed to a specific measure is a form of future proofing. Thus, whenever 'tools' can be taken to include technology,[252] then the relevant instrument adheres to the spirit if not the letter of TN, with the extant theoretical implications introduced in chapter five – the effacement of the technology and indeterminacy loop – and practical consequences seen for NIS.[253] The Regulation against Child Sexual Abuse (CSAReg) exemplifies the point.[254]

The CSAReg aims at supporting the reduction of online CSAM by permitting the use of 'specific technologies'. These are undefined or else loosely hinted at, eg, webmail and messaging services '*scanning* either the *content*, such as images and text, or the *traffic data* of communications using, in some instances, *historical data*' by deploying '*hashing technology* for images and videos and *classifiers* and *artificial intelligence* for analysing text or traffic data'.[255] 'Specific technologies' should be 'limited to *content* data and related *traffic data* … strictly necessary for' detecting and removing online child sexual abuse material and reporting it to LEAs and other organisations.[256] Specific technologies 'are in accordance with the state of the art in the industry and are the least privacy-intrusive', including with regard to Data Protection by Design and by default, and 'to the extent that they are used to *scan* text in communications, they are *not able to deduce the substance of the content of the communications but* are *solely* able to *detect patterns* which point to possible online child sexual abuse'.[257] The *systematic filtering* and *scanning* of text is seemingly allowed insofar as it is used to detect '*patterns* which point to possible concrete reasons for suspecting online child sexual abuse'.[258] This may be an attempt to incorporate the findings of *La Quadrature du Net*, as is the sunset clause of August 2024, although the extent to which this understanding of time-limitedness is in keeping with the CJEU's view is open to debate.[259] Until challenged in court, the presumption of legality characterising secondary Union law[260] applies to the CSAReg.

As seen, the CSAReg fills in the gap created by the Directive against Child Sexual Abuse (CSADir), which made provisions for blocking access to web pages and removing web pages containing offending content, without, however, first addressing the

---

[249] Cybercrime Directive, Art 7, Rec 16.
[250] Art 13, Recs 16 and 22 FCD.
[251] Respectively CSADir, Art 25 and CTDir, Art 21.
[252] The EPPOR (section III.B.iv) appears to be an exception, but this can only be assessed on the basis of the final draft.
[253] See chs 5, sections II–III and 6, section III.
[254] A similar analysis could be conducted for the Combating Terrorism Regulation (CTReg).
[255] CSAReg, Rec 7 (emphasis added).
[256] ibid, Art 3(a)(iii) (emphasis added).
[257] ibid, Art 3 (b).
[258] ibid, Rec 16.
[259] *La Quadrature du Net*, C-511/18, paras 177–182.
[260] *Schrems*, C-362/14,EU:C:2015:650, para 52.

problem of how to detect such a content. The removing or blocking of web pages can be achieved through different technological avenues, eg, TCP/IP header filtering, TCP/IP content filtering, HTTP proxy filtering, DNS tampering and keyword searching, as well as hybrid techniques that combine elements of each.[261] Indeed, the CSAReg enables the systematic filtering and scanning of content and traffic data, including historical data; scanning rests on hashing technology, classifiers and artificial intelligence.[262] Several 'specific technologies' could fulfil the CSAReg's aim, each potentially enabling different modalities of reconciliation of the triad – DPI engines are one such technology.

The disconnect between provisions laying down an investigative objective, and the concrete options for pursuing such objectives, is common across the board. The French *Loi Reinseignement*[263] lays down provisions endowing the French intelligence services with new techniques, two of which were discussed in *La Quadrature du Net*.[264] The first technique is the collection in real time, on the networks of the operators and persons, of relevant information or documents.[265] The second technique is the automated analysis of data to detect weak links or signals enabling the identification of terrorist activity.[266]

The law gave rise to much discussion, also drawing from existing examples, as to how such techniques could be implemented in practice. Real time collection of information requires either the cooperation of telcos (ECSs), which is labour-intensive and hence time-consuming and expensive – as in the US PRISM programme – or the use of specific hardware, eg, a probe to tap networks directly.[267] Tapping the network to perform automated analysis is at the heart of Tempora, which rests on Xkeyscore DPI software.[268] Many members of the French-speaking technical community came to the conclusion that if the private sector is not co-opted into surveillance, then intelligence agencies need to use DPI to tap the network to extract data flows[269] and subsequently

---

[261] See especially, C Marsden, 'Internet Service Providers. Content, Control and Neutrality', in I Walden (ed), *Telecommunications Law and Regulation*, 4th edn (Oxford, Oxford University Press, 2012); R Anderson and SJ Murdoch, 'Tools and Technology of Internet Filtering', in R Deibert (ed), *Access Denied: The Practice and Policy of Global Internet Filtering* (Cambridge, MA, MIT Press, 2008); I Brown, 'Internet Censorship: be Careful What You Ask For' (2008) /papers.ssrn.com/sol3/papers.cfm?abstract_id=1026597.

[262] Sicilianos et al (n 145); Abelson et at (n 137).

[263] Loi no. 2015-912 du 24 juillet 2015 relative au renseignement, as subseqently modified.

[264] The Loi also authorises the use of an IMSI catcher to intercept communications between a device and a phone mast.

[265] *La Quadrature du Net*, C-511/18, para 42.

[266] ibid, para 43. 'For the sole purpose of preventing terrorism, the operators and persons referred to in Article L. 851-1 may be required to implement on their networks automated data processing practices designed ... to detect links that might constitute a terrorist threat.' See CNIL (n 180), 9.

[267] CNIL (n 180), 8–9.

[268] E King, *Witness Statement to the Investigatory Power Tribunal in Privacy International and Bytes for All v. Secretary of State for Foreign and Commonwealth Affairs and Others*, Case No. IPT/13/92/CH (Privacy International, 2015) www.privacyinternational.org/sites/default/files/2019-08/2015.01.19%20Eric%20 King%20Witness%20statement.pdf; J von Appelbaum and A Gibson et al., 'NSA Targets the Privacy-conscious' *Panorama 60 Jare* (Germany); S Gallagher, 'NSA "Touches" More of Internet than Google. In Deep Packet Inspection, it's not the Size of the Data that Matters' *Arstechnica* (13 August 2013).

[269] See L Chemla, *Agent de Double-langage Reflets Info* (22 April 2015) reflets.info/articles/agent-de-double-langage; A Archambault, *Boites Noires: l'Utilisation de DPI Semble Inévitable* (2015) www.techniques-ingenieur. fr/actualite/articles/boites-noires-lutilisation-de-dpi-semble-inevitable-1696/; F Tréguer, *Surveillance: Petite Histoire de la Légalisation du Deep Packet Inspection Le Club de Mediapart* (16 November 2017) https://blogs. mediapart.fr/felix-treguer/blog/161117/surveillance-petite-histoire-de-la-legalisation-du-deep-packet-inspection-0; *Les Boites Noires, si ce n'est pas du DPI, qu'est-ce que ça Sera?* pixellibre.net/2015/04/les-boites-noires-si-ce-nest-pas-du-dpi-quest-ce-que-ca-sera/; R Karayan, 'Loi sur le Renseignement: ce que les Métadonnées Peuvent Dire de Vous' *L'express* (5 May 2015) lexpansion.lexpress.fr/high-tech/loi-sur-le-renseignement-tout-ce-que-les-metadonneespeuvent-dire-de-vous_1677322.html.

perform automated analysis. The fact that the technical community is left wondering about the significance of the measures exemplifies the ambiguity of technology neutral provisions. As for DSM legislation, the legal analyst has no other solution than exploring the lawfulness of a range of tools capable of implementing such provisions.

B. Deep Packet Inspection (DPI) in the Fight against Cybercrimes

In chapter six, DPI was presented as a versatile solution to monitor activities in cyberspace, including for the sake of NIS. DPI can not only support the prevention of CIA cybercrime, but also detect broad cybercrime and help collect e-evidence. Case law and instruments issued after 2020 seem to legitimise DPI, though I still maintain that[270] such developments are worrying at many levels, jeopardise the reconcilability of the triad and ultimately challenge cybersecurity.

i. DPI and the Prevention of CIA Crimes

The substantive functional interconnection between NIS and narrow cybercrime means that the use of DPI to maintain NIS also prevents cybercrime.[271] Such an objective can be achieved because DPI combines functionality from intrusion detection/prevention systems and stateful firewalls to detect and block attacks, by checking each packet against known signatures.[272]

In this guise, the use of DPI for NIS purposes allowed by the exceptions contained in the Open Internet Regulation (OIR)[273] can contribute to the 'comprehensive framework of prevention measures accompanying criminal law responses to cybercrime'.[274] The OIR explicitly refers to the threats of cyber-attacks occurring due to malware and identity theft of end users caused by spyware.[275] BEREC's list of threats to security discussed in chapter six corresponds to offences within the Cybercrime Directive: denial of service attacks to illegal system interference, spoofing IP addresses to illegal data interference [and forgery], and hacking attacks to illegal access. Whichever 'security monitoring

---

[270] MG Porcedda, 'Lessons from PRISM and Tempora: the Self-contradictory Nature of the Fight against Cyberspace Crimes. Deep packet Inspection as a Case Study' (2013) 25 *Neue Kriminalpolitik* 305–409.

[271] DPI can thwart malware attacks, ie illegal data interference (Cybercrime Directive, Art 5), affecting industrial secrets and obviously users' personal data and private life. DPI can also block DDOS, worms and spam, which amount to illegal system interference (Cybercrime Directive, Art 6) affecting the availability of systems, crucial for both operators and users; spam is also prohibited by EPD, Art 13 in the context of direct marketing spam.

[272] Under Einstein, DPI engines already analyse all traffic passing through US governmental networks for security purposes. See A Kuhen and M Mueller, 'Einstein on the Breach: Surveillance Technology, Cybersecurity and Organizational Change', in G Giacomello (ed), *Security in Cyberspace. Targeting Nations, Infrastructures, Individuals* (London, Bloomsbury, 2014). See also IBM: securityintelligence.com/evolving-threats-why-deep-packet-inspection-is-critical-for-intrusion-prevention/.

[273] Reg (EU) 2015/2120 [2015] OJ L310/1 (OIR) Arts 3(3) (b), (c).

[274] Cybercrime Directive, Rec 2.

[275] ibid, Art 9 and OIR, Rec 14.

systems' used for cybercrime prevention may be run continuously in the background,[276] although BEREC clarifies that specific actions should only be triggered vis-à-vis the detection of concrete threats, and provides examples including blocking of IP addresses, Internet Access Services and port numbers.[277]

The use of DPI for NIS translates into its de facto permissibility for the sake of narrow cybercrime prevention. Such a reality does not remove DPI's ambiguity and contradictions, which I will discuss with respect to the fight against all cybercrimes.

ii. DPI for the Fight against All (Cyber)Crimes

Recent legislation[278] and cases such as *La Quadrature du Net* and *Big Brother Watch* contribute to clarify the permissibility of DPI for the fight against all cybercrimes.[279] The CSAReg provides a legal basis for the use of active DPI for the detection of CSAM, which arguably exceeds the limits imposed by the CJEU in *La Quadrature du Net* as regards its interpretation of time-limitedness, given that such engines can be used for three and a half years. The presence of a legal basis does not, of its own, make a measure permissible; the law must include safeguards and the interference must be necessary and proportionate. Arguably only real child pornography is capable to satisfy both requirements and it is likely that the CSAReg will become the object of litigation.[280]

The findings of the ECtHR Grand Chamber in *Big Brother Watch* can be seen as allowing intelligence agencies to use DPI[281] on account of its usefulness in gathering intelligence and identifying new threats with respect to global terrorism, the sexual exploitation of children and cyber-attacks posed by 'international networks of hostile actors' capable of evading detection.[282] These findings chime with Brenner's concern that the inadequate criminal law response to soaring rates of cybercrime could contribute to bring about the decline of the nation-state.[283] All offences reviewed in these pages, with the exception of cybercrimes that are minor, could trigger the application of wide margins of appreciation, provided states respect the eight criteria identified by the ECtHR.

---

[276] Body of European Regulators for Electronic Communications (BEREC), 'Guidelines on the Implementation of the Open Internet Regulation, BoR (20) 112', § 85.
[277] This may suggest IP/TCP inspection only, but BEREC (ibid § 84) does not provide more details.
[278] In addition to Convention, Art 21, whereby states can enable 'service providers' to conduct real-time (confidential) interception ('collection or recording') of content data, relating to specified communications; EIOD, Arts 30 and 31, enabling the interception of telecommunications.
[279] C Parsons, 'Deep Packet Inspection and Law Enforcement', Technology, Thoughts and Trinkets (2 July 2009) christopher-parsons.com/deep-packet-inspection-and-law-enforcement/; Tréguer (n 269); 'Dutch-Russian Cyber Crime Case Reveals How the Police Taps the Internet' *Electrospaces.net* (26 August 2017). LF Pikos, 'Packet Analysis for Network Forensics: A Comprehensive Survey' (2020) 32 *Forensic Science International: Digital Investigation* 1–12.
[280] DPI could not prevent abuse, but solely block the circulation of pictures and support the identification of perpetrators (see Landau (n 3) 125–126). It is questionable whether detection should be pursued by an Internal Market instrument. The CSADir and CSAReg should be reviewed to comply with the LED's requirement of including the objectives and purposes of the processing and the personal data to be processed and human intervention to back up decisions stemming from automated processing (LED, Arts 8, 10).
[281] *La Quadrature du Net*, C-511/18, paras 346, 372–388, 417.
[282] ibid, paras 323 and 340.
[283] See Brenner (n 52).

The findings of the CJEU in *La Quadrature du Net* paint a more complex picture. The genuine and present threat of terrorism, including cyber-attacks in the Combating Terrorism Directive, justifies 'recourse to an instruction requiring' ECSs to perform generic passive – ie collection only – TCP/IP packet inspection for a limited period of time, without precluding active DPI, that is the scanning of content. The fight against all cybercrimes and other crimes, as forms of serious crime and threats to public security, can also benefit from passive TCP/IP packet inspection engines, based on objective and non-discriminatory selectors/signatures/keywords. IP addresses of the initiator of the communication can be captured generically, on account of their lower sensitivity, as they are 'generated independently of any particular communications'.[284] The CJEU states that the retention of IP addresses by ECSs

> beyond the period for which that data is assigned does not, in principle, appear to be necessary for the purpose of billing the services at issue, with the result that the detection of offences committed online may therefore prove impossible without recourse to a legislative measure under Article 15(1) EPD, with offences including cases of 'particularly serious child pornography'.[285]

By requiring ECSs to have recourse to the retention of metadata, automated analysis and real-time collection inter alia of metadata and the real-time collection of technical data concerning the location of the terminal equipment, the CJEU implicitly acknowledges the gatekeeping role of ECSs. What is more, the judgment presupposes that ECSs have the requisite infrastructure in place, infrastructure that is for them to determine, according to the state of the art (SoA). This is in keeping with Open Internet Regulation (OIR) rules empowering ISPs to perform monitoring of content 'to comply with Union legislative acts … to which the provider of internet access services is subject, or with measures … giving effect to such … legislative acts …, including with orders by courts or public authorities vested with relevant powers'.[286]

Examples includes criminal law requiring the blocking of specific content, applications and services.[287] The judgment leaves unresolved tensions discussed in chapter six as to the prohibition of continuous monitoring and the potential encroachment of the essence.

iii. *DPI: Unresolved Tensions and Significance for the Triad*

Not only does DPI risk engendering a feeling of constant surveillance,[288] it literally implements constant monitoring by ISPs/ECSs, which is problematic in light of EU rules prohibiting such monitoring discussed in chapter six. *La Quadrature du Net* does not address the problem: the CJEU deals with the relationship between Article 15(1)

---

[284] *La Quadrature du Net*, C-511/18, para 152.
[285] ibid, para 154. The Court includes acquisition in the list of such offences, however, it is unclear whether this is the Court's position or the position of the intervening governments.
[286] OIR, Art 3(3)(a).
[287] ibid, Rec 13, which does not mention detection.
[288] *Digital Rights Ireland*, C-293/12 and C-594/12, para 37.

ECD and the applicable privacy and data protection law from a narrow angle, in keeping with the question asked by the referring court, thus avoiding discussing the interplay between DSM instruments.

The CJEU states that automated analysis involves, for ECSs 'the undertaking on behalf of the competent authority of general and indiscriminate *processing*… covering all traffic and location data of all users of' e-communications systems, which derogates 'from the obligation of principle … to ensure the confidentiality of electronic communications and related data' and 'is likely to reveal the nature of the information consulted online'.[289] For this reason, automated analysis can only be permissible subject to strong adherence to proportionality. And yet, for service providers to expeditiously retain or monitor data in real time, they must be able to monitor, or even better, they must already be monitoring on a continuous basis. This lays bare the limits of the prohibition of monitoring enshrined in Article 15(1) of the e-commerce Directive, which applies to a number of ISSs that are also public ECSs,[290] and instead implicitly reinforces the ambiguity created by Article 3 OIR.

As discussed in chapter six, the stakes of intrusion are high and problematic due to the content/metadata (specific content) divide. The divide is porous: the EDPB does not explain the circumstances under which the TCP header can constitute traffic data.[291] The divide is also questionable: it is the Court's settled case law that metadata 'provides … information that is no less sensitive, from the perspective of the right to privacy, than the actual content of communications'.[292] Thus, the use of TCP filtering or full DPI for fighting against all cybercrimes interferes with the confidentiality of the content of communications of a potentially large number of users and of their personal data in a way which does not tangibly benefits such users. And yet, *La Quadrature du Net* implicitly suggests that signatures, or keywords, that enable us to draw precise conclusions, do not amount to 'the acquisition of knowledge of the content', which is the threshold the CJEU identified in *Digital Rights Ireland* for the encroachment upon the essence of Article 7 CFR. The Court does not delve into whether precise conclusions reveal 'very specific information about individuals which may not be limited to narrow domains', another facet of the essence identified in *Opinion 1/15*. It should be remembered that in *WebMindLicenses*, relating to proceedings concerning tax evasion[293] between a legal person, WebMindLicenses, and the Hungarian National Tax and Customs Authority, the Court stated that evidence stemming from criminal procedure, and used to make a decision in the context of administrative tax procedure, 'obtained and used in breach of the rights guaranteed by EU law and, especially, by the Charter … must be disregarded and the contested decision which is founded on that evidence must be annulled …'.[294]

---

[289] *La Quadrature du Net*, C-511/18, paras 172, 173 and 174.
[290] Both by virtue of the EECC and case law, such as *La Quadrature du Net* itself (para 205); *Google*, C-193/18, EU:C:2019:498; *Skype Communications*, C-142/18.
[291] European Data Protection Board, Letter to BEREC. Data protection issues in the context of Regulation (EU) 2015/2120, OUT 2019-0055, 3 December, (2019).
[292] *La Quadrature du Net*, C-511/18, para 184.
[293] The evidence against WebMindLicenses Kft. was obtained in the course of a parallel criminal investigation, not yet concluded at the time of the judgment, where WML's emails and communications were intercepted without a court order.
[294] *WebMindLicenses*, C-419/14, EC:C:2015:832, paras 87–89.

Two contradictory conclusions can be drawn. First, all forms of packet analysis are permissible, irrespective of the fact that keywords and signatures enable to draw precise conclusions on the individuals concerned, thereby emptying the meaning of the essence of privacy. Legislation would, in this case, nurture a misplaced understanding of proportionality that emphasises the correctness of the procedures surrounding the use of DPI engines – eg, the oversight of the choice of selectors – irrespective of whether the very use of DPI engines subverts the values that those procedures are purported to protect.

Second and conversely, keywords and signatures can potentially reach the threshold for 'the acquisition of knowledge of the content' or reveal 'very specific information about individuals which may not be limited to narrow domains'. Such an outcome requires a conversation as to when keywords and signatures are capable of encroaching upon the essence of privacy to determine what types of packet analysis are permissible and design engines accordingly. The same applies to devising mechanisms to ensure that purpose limitation requirements central to the essence of Article 8 CFR are enforceable. Legislation should, in this case, not just be concerned with procedural oversight, but with substantive proportionality criteria, too. This latter outcome acquires particular value when considering not just privacy and data protection, but also cybersecurity.

According to Landau, the security risks can dwarf the enormous privacy ones, as systems put in place could be exploited both by insiders – due to the appeal of big data – and malicious outsiders.[295] 'After the 2006 AT&T scandal, it emerged that the Narus DPI engine could be configured, once sold, as users saw fit.[296] Infamously, in the "Athens Affair", CALEA-compliant software sold by Ericsson to Vodafone Greece was used to intercept the government's communications for almost a year before the 2004 Olympic Games'.[297] In October 2016 Yahoo was placed under the spotlight as Reuters revealed it had installed a program, on behalf of the US Government, to scan incoming emails live for 'selectors' ie terms used by a terrorist group.[298] Some weeks before, the company had disclosed a severe breach affecting 500 million accounts.[299] Though the link between the two events has not been ascertained, the former chief security officer, who had quit after discovering that such a program was installed, said the scanning program used could have been exploited by hackers due to a programming flaw.[300]

In sum, the use of DPI to police cybercrimes undermines privacy, data protection and cybersecurity both taken individually and as a triad. Responses to Snowden's revelations, such as the incorporation of encryption in Internet protocols encouraged by IETF Request for Comments 7258, challenge the use of DPI, leading some to call it 'dead'.[301]

---

[295] Landau (n 21); on big data: J Lanier, *Who Owns the Future?* (London, Penguin Books, 2013).
[296] R Poe, 'The Ultimate Net Monitoring Tool' *Wired* (17 May 2006).
[297] Landau (n 21); Porcedda (n 270), 383.
[298] J Menn, 'Exclusive: Yahoo Secretly Scanned Customer Emails for U.S. Intelligence Sources' *Reuters* (4 November 2016) www.reuters.com/article/us-yahoo-nsa-exclusive-idUSKCN1241YT.
[299] O Solon, 'Yahoo Confirms 'state-sponsored' Hackers Stole Personal Data From 500m Accounts' *The Guardian* (23 September 2016) www.theguardian.com/technology/2016/sep/22/yahoo-hack-data-state-sponsored.
[300] Menn (n 298).
[301] Internet Engineering Task Force (IETF), 'Request for Comments: 7258, Pervasive Monitoring Is an Attack, 2014'; 'Ep', *Deep packet inspection is dead, and here's why* (Institute for Advanced Studies – Network Security 2017) security.ias.edu/deep-packet-inspection-dead-and-heres-why.

Although only empirical research can ascertain the extent of its use, the literature points to it still being used and sold; DPI is referred to in legislation adopted as recently as 2021.[302]

The point is not the survival of DPI, which can be complemented – or supplanted – by packet analysers exploiting weak signals,[303] data flow analytics, machine learning and other forms of bulk and targeted surveillance. Rather, the point is to exemplify the contradictions arising from the regulatory ecosystem where technology disappears from the law and neither the law nor courts give sufficient indication of the permissibility of such a technology. The next section contains observations about lawful hacking to draw conclusions on how technology affects the reconcilability of the triad.

C. Beyond DPI: Technical Measures to Fight Cybercrime and Visions of Reconciliation Through Technology

The disconnect between provisions laying down an investigative objective and the concrete options for pursuing such objectives makes it difficult to reach conclusions as to the mode of reconcilability of the triad and to operationalise ways of choosing between established options for bulk and targeted surveillance such as lawful hacking or solutions such as Client-Side Scanning (CSS).[304]

Lawful hacking formally endows law enforcement agencies with powers of conducting interceptions, including of computer data. It consists of infecting devices with malware, with as many modus operandi as those available to cyber-offenders.[305] When done under warrant, lawful hacking is an established investigatory technique used in democratic states, as exemplified by the 'Magic Lantern' in the US, the *Loi Reinseignement* in France and the *Bundestrojaner* in Germany.[306] The latter was at the heart of a German Federal judgment that reviewed the permissibility of section 5.2 no. 11 of the North Rhine-Westphalia Constitution Protection Act, which enabled secret monitoring and reconnaissance on the Internet as well as secret access to information technology systems.[307] In determining the unlawfulness of the provision, and the safeguards to be implemented,[308] the Federal Constitutional Court found that the 'general

---

[302] Pikos (n 279); B Marczak, J Dalek et al., *Bad Traffic. Sandvine's PacketLogic Devices Used to Deploy Government Spyware in Turkey and Redirect Egyptian Users to Affiliate Ads?* (Tspace, 2018). See also: cybersecurity.att.com/blogs/security-essentials/what-is-deep-packet-inspection; legislation on export controls, see ch 8. Furthermore, the technical community is working at versions of DPI capable of circumventing encryption: Pikos (n 279).
[303] V Rieß-Marchive, *Vectra Networks veut Détecter les Signaux Faibles sur le Réseau* (2015) www.lemagit.fr/actualites/4500249649/Vectra-Networks-veut-detecter-les-signaux-faibles-sur-le-reseau. See Pikos (n 279).
[304] Abelson et al (n 137).
[305] For the use of honeypots, see Flanagan and Walden (n 68).
[306] Landau (n 3) 139, (n 21); G Cluley, 'Government' Backdoor R2D2 Trojan Discovered by Chaos Computer Club' *NakedSecurity* (9 October 2011); European Digital Rights (EDRI), *The Spanish Police might use Spying Trojans on Individuals' Computers* (EDRI-gram newsletter, no. 11.12 2013).
[307] BVerfG, *Judgment of the First Senate of 27 February 2008*, 1 BvR 370/07, DE:BVerfG:2008:rs20080227.1bvr037007.
[308] Measures could be used to pursue paramount legal interests, eg, the life and freedom of persons or the survival of the state. The infiltration had to be authorised by a court.

right of personality' can manifest 'as a fundamental right to the guarantee of the confidentiality and integrity of information technology systems'.[309] The German Federal Court's strong assertion as to the interrelatedness of NIS, privacy and data protection has no equivalent in the European Courts, with the CJEU's findings as to the essence of privacy and data protection being a weak counterpart.

Legal hacking can be targeted or untargeted. The latter is based on aggressive cyber-weaponry, such as zero-day attacks and techniques exemplified by those developed by the CIA and publicised by Wikileaks' 'Vault 7'.[310] Notwithstanding the risks, targeted lawful hacking is seen as the way forward by leading cybersecurity experts such as Susan Landau.[311] Here the point is neither to endorse nor critique lawful hacking, but once more to illustrate the difficulties created by the effacement of technology in legislation authorising the use of information technologies.

Legal hacking undermines NIS and 'implies by default the processing of personal data and a possible intrusion of privacy'.[312] The interference with the two rights requires the identification of the presence of a violation of the essence, but the ambiguity of the concept makes this difficult to achieve. Since it seriously interferes with private life, the confidentiality of communications and the security and fairness of processing, lawful hacking must be done proportionately. Proportionality implies, among others, that the Trojan or other malware is de-installed or de-activated once it is of no more use. Failure to do so would expose the user(s), who can be many if the machine is a server, to attacks such as becoming a zombie within a botnet, or the victim of other cybercrimes. The contradiction of using malware to counter (cyber)crime is self-evident, when one takes the triad into account: an implementation of proportionality faithful to the RoL would need to be technology conscious. Such objective is currently hindered by technology-agnostic legislation and case law.

The array of techniques is vast – ranging from exceptional access to weakening encryption to CSS which is at once mass and targeted – and each is problematic in its own ways.[313] All techniques can undermine NIS at the expense of a few or many users and engender a clash between surveillance and security.

The collection of e-evidence, be it to investigate cybercrime or other offences, squarely places the relationship of the triad into the realm of classic proportionality and weak reconciliation. However, the principle of proportionality, applied without a prior analysis of the investigative technologies, risks focussing on procedures, while missing the potential subversive nature of such technologies for both fundamental rights and cybersecurity. DPI offered a relevant example in light of recent judgments and legislation, but the analysis of other techniques, such as 'lawful hacking', could produce similar outcomes.

---

[309] European Data Protection Supervisor (EDPS), Dissemination and use of intrusive surveillance technologies, Opinion 8/2015; BVerfGE 120, 274, para 166.
[310] Landau (n 3) 122. See: wikileaks.org/ciav7p1/.
[311] Landau (n 3).
[312] EDPS (n 309).
[313] Abelson et al (n 137).

IV. Conclusion: Weak Reconciliation of the Fight against Cybercrime, e-Evidence, Privacy and Data Protection Challenged by Technology

This chapter reviewed the reconcilability of cybersecurity, privacy and data protection in the AFSJ. Policy documents point to strong reconciliation for CIA crime and fraud and weak reconciliation for cyber-assisted, 'content' cybercrimes.

The approach to the reconciliation between cybercrime, data protection and privacy borne by the applicable law is also mixed. The Cybercrime Directive and Fraud and Counterfeiting Directive (FCD) are functionally interconnected to NIS as to their substance, which supports the complementarity and even the potential overlap between the fight against cybercrime, privacy and data protection. However, the complementarity between the triad found in the Cybercrime Directive is only partly visible in the FCD and absent in the Directive against Child Sexual Abuse. The latter espouses, much like all broad cybercrimes, a weak understanding of reconciliation enabling permissible limitations, a logic also followed by laws on the collection of e-evidence. Furthermore, when it comes to investigating the offences they create, the Cybercrime Directive and FCD rely on the same suite of solutions relied on for the fight against broad cybercrimes and even NIS instruments with respect to illicit behaviour. There appears to be a 'procedural' functional interconnection between NIS and the full gamut of cybercrimes that requires the reframing of the relationship of the triad as one of reconciliation between potentially contradictory objectives to be resolved on a case-by-case basis, under the Pole star of the principle of proportionality. And yet, even this conclusion could be thrown into disarray if the law were to favour solutions that practically challenge reconcilability.

An investigation of the concept of 'tools' in the legislation points to the relevance of concepts such as 'technology neutrality' and 'state of the art' in the AFSJ. Here the effacement of technology is caused by delegating the choice of 'tools' to agencies engaged in law enforcement and by onboarding the private sector in the fight against crimes through DSM legislation. In light of its gatekeeping role the private sector determines the infrastructure for the fight against crime based on the SoA, with the seal of approval of Courts, thus aggravating the technology indeterminacy loop.

The analysis of DPI as a relevant example in light of recent judgments and 'lawful hacking', shows that 'tools' to collect e-evidence squarely places the relationship of the triad into the realm of classic proportionality and weak reconciliation. However, reliance on proportionality tests carried out without a prior analysis of the investigative technologies,[314] risks focussing on procedures, while missing the potential subversive nature of such technologies for both fundamental rights and cybersecurity.

---

[314] The teams of the EU-funded projects that sponsored the doctoral research informing this monograph produced a range of assessments to determine how to select the least rights-infringing technologies. See especially: SurPRISE project, D3.4, Exploring the Challenges – Synthesis report, http://surprise-project.eu/wp-content/uploads/2013/06/SurPRISE-D3.4-Exploring-the-Challenges-Synthesis-Report.pdf, p. 24; SURVEILLE project, D2.9, Consolidated Survey of Surveillance Technologies https://surveille.eui.eu/wp-content/uploads/sites/19/2015/04/D2.9-Consolidated-survey-of-surveillance-technologies.pdf.

8
The EA: 'Cyber' External Action, Privacy and Data Protection

This chapter is the last of three that investigates the mode of reconciliation of cybersecurity, data protection and privacy ('the triad') in the three main areas of EU law. Chapter six examined the reconcilability of the triad within the Digital Single Market (DSM), while chapter seven examined the reconciliation of the triad in the Area of Freedom, Security and Justice (AFSJ) from a policy, law and technology perspective. The findings of a high-level analysis of legislation pointing to both strong and weak reconciliation were put into disarray by a close analysis of technical and organisational measures and tools that implement such legislation. Due to the specifics of the regulatory environment, technical and organisational measures and tools effect weak reconciliation and even open the door to zero-sum games against which the fail-safe of the 'essence' is powerless.

That analysis also showed that reconciling the triad becomes increasingly challenging as we move from older to newer EU policy areas, where integration is weaker and national variations are more entrenched.[1] Such a trajectory has a bearing on external relations since, following Cremona, the international role of the EU results from, and is in constant dialogue with, the internal role.[2]

The impact of internal policymaking on external relations means that tensions that have been left unresolved internally are likely to be replicated externally. By the same token, policy areas that have not been made consistent internally are likely to remain disjointed internationally. The tensions identified in the DSM and the AFSJ are already at work at the policy level in the External Action (EA), which comprises of matters straddling the Treaty on European Union (TEU) and Treaty on the Functioning of European Union (TFEU)[3] divide and the external dimension of the DSM and AFSJ. The EA includes the Common Commercial Policy, treaty-making, including for mutual

---

[1] 'Tension, between different interests and players within the Union polity, including Member States ... the Union's institutions and other non-State actors' were all factors against the creation of a coherent identity for Member States: M Cremona, 'The Union as a Global Actor: Roles, Models and Identity' (2004) 41 *Common Market Law Review* 553–573, 565.

[2] M Cremona, 'A Triple Braid: Interactions between International Law, EU Law and Private Law' in M Cremona et al. (eds), *Private Law in the External Relation of the EU* (Oxford, Oxford University Press, 2016).

[3] Consolidated versions of the Treaty on European Union (TEU) and the Treaty on the Functioning of the European Union (TFEU), OJ C83/01 (Lisbon Treaty).

legal assistance, humanitarian aid, the Common Foreign and Security Policy (CFSP) and the Common Security and Defence Policy (CSDP). This chapter builds on and buttresses the warning that the study of the EA is challenged by its configuration as an umbrella embracing many self-standing legal fields.[4]

Section I examines the approach of the three EU cybersecurity policies to the relationship between the triad in the EA. To this effect, I use the findings of previous chapters to examine how dynamics inherent to the development of the EA affect the relationship of the triad and to illustrate how external relations reproduce tensions observed in the DSM and AFSJ, tensions compounded by the geopolitical significance of cybersecurity. The section exposes the difficulty of addressing the 'EA' and shows how burgeoning policy initiatives and entrenched regulatory approaches make it nearly impossible to identify one mode of reconciliation of the triad in the EA.

Section II shows how the overarching framework within which the triad interacts in the EA and its umbrella nature, whereby different legal matters co-exist, precludes the identification of a clear relational mode for the triad. The diversity of the EA precludes the type of comparative cross-instrument analysis carried out in chapter six and requires instead to analyse the interplay of the triad on classes of instruments, as done in chapter seven. I exemplify the challenge of appraising the relationship of the triad in the EA through the Cyber Diplomacy Toolbox, with a focus on restrictive measures against cyber-attacks and a reference to the Dual-use Regulation. The analysis shows that restrictive measures effect weak reconciliation, but that it is not possible to draw firm conclusions on the relationship of the triad solely on the basis of EA legal acts.

Section III is devoted to technology as a regulatory target, an implementing measure and the lens through which one must explore the reconcilability of the triad. I begin by reflecting on the role of technical attribution for restrictive measures and deep packet inspection (DPI) therein. I then demonstrate how 'the effacement of technology' from EU law fosters the porousness of legislation enabling the circulation of values, regulatory techniques and implementing tools and bring to the fore the hiatus between the EU's aspiration to pursue values and its concrete ability to deliver such values caused by reliance on international standardisation. The consequences are such as to challenge not just the reconcilability of the triad, but also the delivery of cybersecurity, privacy and data protection individually taken.

I. Reconciliation of Cybersecurity, Privacy and Data Protection in the EA: Policy

Examining the relationship of the triad in the EA is a complex task on account of the constitutional configuration underpinning external action, the influence exercised by internal policymaking, and the piecemeal nature of policy initiatives. Cremona

---

[4] See especially M Cremona and H-W Micklitz (eds), *Private Law in the External Relation of the EU* (Oxford, Oxford University Press, 2016); M Cremona and J Scott (eds), *EU Law beyond EU Borders* (Oxford, Oxford University Press, 2019).

points to a development of the EA in stages reflecting the acquisition of competences by the EU and the progressive interaction between EU, international and private law.[5] Value-infused law-making with a global reach is at the heart of the EA[6] in abidance with Articles 3(5) and 21 TEU. Those provisions require the EU to engage in the difficult task of respecting and promoting fundamental rights while advancing the EU's own interests, interests embodying power dynamics.[7] The difficulty lies in the fact that values and interests can be at once interdependent, entangled and in tension.[8] Such is the challenge for cybersecurity, privacy and data protection: they implicate values and interests that can be both entangled and clashing.

Cremona predicted that 'an integrated identity' would 'emerge incrementally out of concrete policy initiatives'[9] which are 'strongly linked with the internal policy-making of the EU'. The relative infancy of the area – cybersecurity acquired EA relevance only in 2008, shortly after the cyber-attacks against Estonia[10] – means that such an integrated identity is still in the making. However, the dynamics influencing interventions in the DSM and AFSJ, described in chapters six and seven respectively, are also at play here in a way that challenges easy answers with respect to the triad. A dynamic specific to the EA is the progressive depiction of cybersecurity as an essential international concern underpinning crucial national economic and security interests at a time of geopolitical shifts and eroding mechanisms of international collaboration. This existential turn reflects the use of cyber-attacks as an instrument of interference[11] and their integration in warfare operations including as a precursor to kinetic conflict, as in Georgia in 2008 and Ukraine in 2022,[12] and informs the realisation that technology plays a role in supporting or eroding 'strategic autonomy' and 'sovereignty'.[13] Against this treacherous background, privacy and data protection seem to move increasingly backstage.[14]

The 2013 Cybersecurity Policy[15] posits that the EU's core values command respect in the digital as well as in the physical world. The 2013 Policy opens with a list of principles for cybersecurity, starting with the tenet that cybersecurity actions must respect the rights enshrined in the Charter.[16] It emphasises the importance of data protection for information sharing and of data subjects' rights in general. Achieving a high level of

---

[5] Cremona (n 2).
[6] Cremona and Scott (n 4), Introduction.
[7] M Cremona, 'Extending the Reach of EU Law: the EU as an International Legal Actor', in M Cremona et al. (eds), *EU Law beyond EU Borders* (Oxford, Oxford University Press, 2019).
[8] ibid.
[9] Cremona (n 1) 572.
[10] European Council, *Report on the Implementation of the European Security Strategy – Providing Security in a Changing World* ((European Security Strategy) S407/08, 2008) 7.
[11] MN Schmitt (ed), *The Tallin Manual 2.0 on the International Law Applicable to International Jurisdictions* (Cambridge, Cambridge University Press, 2017).
[12] Independent International Fact-Finding Mission on the Conflict in Georgia, 'Report – Volume II'; P Jakub, *Russia's war on Ukraine: Timeline of cyber-attacks* (European Parliament, 2022) www.europarl.europa.eu/RegData/etudes/BRIE/2022/733549/EPRS_BRI(2022)733549_EN.pdf.
[13] Respectively in European Commission and High Representative, JOIN 'Resilience, Deterrence and Defence: Building Strong Cybersecurity for the EU' (Joint Communication) (2017) 450 final, 18; European Commission and High Representative, JOIN 'The EU's Cybersecurity Strategy for the Digital Decade' (Joint Communication) (2020) 18 final.
[14] European Council, *Informal meeting of the Heads of State or Government. Versaille Declaration* (2022) www.consilium.europa.eu/media/54773/20220311-versailles-declaration-en.pdf.
[15] European Commission and High Representative, JOIN (2013) 01 final.
[16] Charter [2012] OJ L326/391 (CFR).

data protection is specifically a target for CFSP interventions. Privacy is listed among the rights to be protected online. The sentence 'Reciprocally, individuals' rights cannot be secured without safe networks and systems'[17] can be read as emphasising the interdependence between cybersecurity and rights, as are the post-Snowden declarations discussed in chapter one and six.

The 2017 Cybersecurity Policy[18] places less emphasis on specific values, perhaps understandably given its primary aims of consolidating achievements and keeping up with evolving challenges. Unsurprisingly, in relation to defence,[19] the 2017 Policy does not contain references to any rights. One of the central objectives of defence is to ensure the confidentiality, integrity and availability (CIA) of its communications systems, but confidentiality is not couched in terms of privacy. 'The right to privacy and protection of personal data (sic)' are specifically mentioned as EU core values and fundamental rights guiding 'the EU's international cybersecurity policy.'[20] The 2017 Policy emphasises the support of multi-stakeholder governance[21] in various international fora. One such forum is the United Nations Group of Governmental Experts (UN GGE), wherein participating Member States helped developing voluntary norms for responsible state behaviour, including the respect for internationally recognised international rights, without committing to new legal instruments at UN level,[22] a point reiterated in the 2020 policy.

The 2020 Cybersecurity Policy[23] represents a continuation insofar as it plans for evolving challenges. The 2020 Policy displays greater integration between the internal and external dimension, without however taking on the challenge of addressing consistency between potentially incompatible measures. Technological sovereignty – EU-grown technology – is presented as a response to insecurity born from the dependence on non-EU technology developed according to politically-motivated standards. At the same time, the policy advocates for greater involvement and leadership within Standards Setting Organisations (SSOs) and Standards Developing Organisations (SDOs) for the purposes of advancing non-descript EU values. The 2020 Policy plans to upskill cyber investigations to be capable of dealing with encryption and encourages the development of mutual legal assistance mechanisms. Simultaneously, it contains proposals for the development of strong encryption, eg, through quantum computing, including for defence purposes.[24] The 2020 Policy reiterates the support for voluntary norms of state behaviour that uphold, among others, 'data privacy'[25] and reject mass

---

[17] JOIN (2013) 01 final (n 15), 4
[18] JOIN (2017) 450 final (n 13).
[19] See generally J Rehrl, *Handbook on Cybersecurity. The Common Security and Defence Policy in the European Union* (Federal Ministry of Defence of the Republic of Austria, 2018) op.europa.eu/en/publication-detail/-/publication/63138617-f133-11e8-9982-01aa75ed71a1.
[20] JOIN(2017) 450 final, 18 (n 13).
[21] Council of the European Union, Council Conclusions on Internet Governance, 27 November 2014, 16200/14 (2014).
[22] European Commission, 'Assessment of the EU 2013 Cybersecurity Strategy' (Staff Working Document) SWD (2017) 295 final.
[23] European Commission and High Representative, JOIN (2020) 18 final.
[24] On 'striking the right balance' Council, Council Resolution on Encryption. Security through Encryption and Security despite Encryption, (2020).
[25] JOIN (2020) 18 final (n 22).

surveillance. Initiatives in the external area of the AFSJ are oblivious to privacy and data protection, whereas initiatives in the DSM with EA relevance refer to values and explicitly to privacy. The complete expunction of data protection and references to 'data privacy' – a term foreign to EU law – is a recurrent theme across EA documents and represents a deterioration compared to previous policies as well as vis-à-vis policy documents requiring to integrate fundamental rights into EU external policy.[26]

In sum, policy documents cannot enable us to draw firm conclusions as to the reconcilability between the triad in the EA. This is, however, in keeping with the findings from chapters six and seven. Next I turn to the illustration of a flagship EA policy and the analysis of related legal acts to show an example of a mode of reconciliation for the triad.

II. Reconciliation of Cybersecurity, Privacy and Data Protection in the EA: Law

Initiatives in CSDP and CFSP are overseen by the European Defence Agency (EDA) and the European External Action Service (EEAS) in participation with the Council; measures are heterogenous and pertain to defence, diplomacy and trade or cut across all of these groups.[27] A fully-fledged analysis of the interplay between the triad in the EA is inhibited by several factors. Such factors relate both to the overarching framework within which the triad interacts in the EA (II.A) and the umbrella nature of the EA, whereby different legal and otherwise independent matters co-exist.

First, the EA includes legislative acts formally adopted according to Article 289 TFEU[28] and legal acts adopted pursuant to the CFSP,[29] though a Decision pursuant to Article 39 TEU on data protection in the CFSP is still missing. Studying the interplay of the triad in the EA means studying the interplay between EU private regulatory law and external relations law, an endeavour characterised by unique methodological challenges. Following Micklitz,[30] one should first distil the international stance of each instrument and policy as situated in its own legal field responding to separate (market) logics and Treaty rules, then draw comparisons. Only some of the instruments covered in this research benefit from sufficient background research to this effect.

The extraterritorial effects of Article 8[31] CFR and the GDPR are widely studied,[32] but not as much can be said about the Network and Information Security Directive (NISD)

---

[26] On mainstreaming obligations, see European Commission and High Representative of the European Union for Foreign Affairs and Security Policy, 'EU Action Plan on Human Rights and Democracy 2020–2024' (Joint Communication) JOIN (2020)5 final, 4.
[27] See ch 2, section II.C.
[28] On the formalism of Art 289 TFEU, see P Craig and G de Búrca, *European Union Law: Text, Cases and Materials* (Oxford, Oxford University Press, 2015) 113–114.
[29] TEU, Arts 25, 31.
[30] H-W Micklitz, 'The Internal versus External Dimension of European Private Law: a Conceptual Design and a Research Agenda' in M Cremona et al. (eds), *Private Law in the External Relation of the EU* (Oxford, Oxford University Press, 2016) 14.
[31] Which has 'certain extraterritorial effects', by virtue of ch VI GDPR, *Schrems* and *Opinion 1/15*: T Lock, 'Article 8 CFR' in M Kellerbauer (ed), *The EU Treaties and the Charter of Fundamental Rights: a Commentary* (Oxford, Oxford University Press, 2019), 2126.
[32] PE Hustinx, 'EU Data Protection Law: the Review of Directive 95/46/EC and the General Data Protection Regulation' in M Cremona (ed), *New Technologies and EU Law* (Oxford, Oxford University Press, 2017);

or the Cybersecurity Act (CSA).[33] Research on autonomy, connection clauses and the EU-Council of Europe (CoE) relationship can help make claims with respect to the applicability of the European Convention on Human Rights (ECHR), Convention 108 and the Cybercrime Convention in EU law,[34] but work needs to be undertaken to ascertain the international significance of the Directive on Attacks against Information Systems (Cybercrime Directive) as a 'transposition' of the Cybercrime Convention and proposed e-evidence legislation 'transposing' the Second Additional Protocol to the Cybercrime Convention in EU law.[35] Further research is required before cross-examining the EA import of DSM and AFSJ cybersecurity instruments to attempt to draw conclusions – if at all possible – as to the reconcilability of the triad in the EA.

Such a state of affairs precludes the comparative and cross-instrument analysis carried out in chapter six and forces one to analyse the interplay of the triad on classes of instruments, as done in chapter seven. In the interest of consistency, I will analyse legal acts in line with the same criteria of chapters six and seven: definitions and scope, notion of security, presence of explicit cross-references, logics as well as structures put in place to achieve the instrument's goals. I will focus on legal acts connected to the Cyber Diplomacy Toolbox laying down restrictive measures (RMs), with particular emphasis on Council Decision 2019/797 and Council Regulation 2019/796 as flagship cybersecurity instruments[36] (II.B). The analysis will emphasise functional substantive and procedural interconnections with both NIS and cybercrime law and show weak reconciliation between RMs for cybersecurity purposes, privacy and data protection. The outcome is by no means representative of the EA, as the inclusion of other instruments, such as the Dual-use Regulation,[37] may instead effect strong reconciliation (II.C). In practice, the EA is destined to harbour the inherent contradictions of cybersecurity policymaking and the uneasy role of privacy and data protection within it, making it difficult to draw firm conclusions about the triad in the EA.

A. The Overarching Framework for the Relationship between the Triad in the EA

The EA develops under the auspices of TEU Articles 2 and 3(5) TEU on Common provisions[38] and 21 TEU on General provisions on the Union's External Action emphasising

---

C Kuner, 'The Internet and the Global Reach of EU Law' in M Cremona et al. (eds), *EU Law beyond EU Borders* (Oxford, Oxford University Press, 2019).

[33] Directive (EU) 2016/1148 [2016] OJ L194/1 (NISD); Reg (EU) 2019/881 [2019] OJ L151/15 (CSA).
[34] As conducted in chs 3, 4 and 7.
[35] Directive 2013/40/EU [2013] OJ L218/8 (Cybercrime Directive); European Commission, 'Proposal for a Regulation of the European Parliament and the Council on European Production and Preservation Orders for electronic evidence in criminal matters' COM (2018) 225 final; Second Additional Protocol to the Convention on Cybercrime on enhanced co-operation and disclosure of electronic evidence CETS No. 224 12/05/2022.
[36] Council Decision (EU) 2019/797 of 17 May 2019 concerning restrictive measures against cyber-attacks threatening the Union or its Member States [2019] OJ L1291/13 (RMDir); Council Regulation (EU) 2019/796 of 17 May 2019 concerning restrictive measures against cyber-attacks threatening the Union or its Member States [2019] OJ L1291/1 (RMReg).
[37] Regulation (EU) 2021/821 of the European Parliament and of the Council of 20 May 2021 setting up a Union regime for the control of exports, brokering, technical assistance, transit and transfer of dual-use items (recast) [2019] OJ L206/1 (Dual-use Regulation).
[38] See ch 1, section III.A.

values and principles underpinning the creation of the EU.[39] Cremona notes that the institutional framework pursues 'milieu goals'[40] shaping conditions beyond one's national boundaries: law and legality of the EU's actions are part and parcel of the EA and act as a substantive and procedural constraint. Thus, 'Union's action on the international scene' must fulfil and 'advance in the wider world' a series of principles that promote strong reconciliation of the triad.[41]

'Democracy, the rule of law, the universality and indivisibility of human rights and fundamental freedoms, respect for human dignity, the principles of equality and solidarity, and respect for the principles of the United Nations Charter and international law'[42] all figure highly in the various Cybersecurity Policies.[43] Examples include the explicit support for the work of the UN GGE and bilateral 'cyber dialogues' with strategic players[44] as vehicles for 'promoting the application of existing international law and voluntary norms of responsible state behaviour', including fundamental rights. In further help of a mutually beneficial relationship between cybersecurity, privacy and data protection comes the obligation to ensure consistency between the different areas of the Union's external action and between these and the EU's other policies. However, there can be a mismatch between intentions and practice.[45]

For what concerns TEU provisions on the CFSP, and within it the CSDP, the adoption of legislative acts is excluded by virtue of Article 24 TEU, so that CFSP measures take the shape of general guidelines, decisions and cooperation as established in Articles 25–29 and 39 TEU. Such a diffuse form of policymaking complicates the task of drawing conclusions on prevailing forms of reconciliation between cybersecurity, privacy and data protection in this area. Crucially, a decision pursuant to Article 39 TEU, which lays down special rules for the processing of data in the CFSP in derogation to Article 16 TFEU, has not been adopted yet.[46] Although this frustrates efforts to ascertain the relationship of the triad in the CFSP, a complete legal void is dodged for three reasons.

---

[39] On the difference between values in Art 2 and principles in Art 21 TEU see M Cremona, 'Values in EU Foreign Policy', in P Koutrakos and M Shaw (eds), *Beyond the Established Orders. Policy Interconnections between the EU and the Rest of the World* (Oxford, Hart Publishing, 2011); E Herlin-Karnell, 'EU Values and the Shaping of the International Legal Context', in F Amtenbrink and D Kochenov (eds), *European Union's Shaping of the International Legal Order* (Cambridge, Cambridge University Press, 2013).

[40] Cremona (n 7), Citing Wolfers, 69–70.

[41] ibid.

[42] See Cremona (n 39); L Pech, *Rule of Law as a Guiding Principle of the European Union's External Action* (CLEER Working Papers, Centre for the Law of EU External Relations, TMC Asser Instituut Inter-university Research Centre, 2013).

[43] On a principle-based approach: P Pawlak and P-N Barmpaliou, 'Politics of Cybersecurity Capacity Building: Conundrum and Opportunity' (2017) 2 *Journal of Cyber Policy* 123–144; P Pawlak, *Operational Guidance for the EU's International Cooperation on Cyber Capacity Building. A Playbook (Task Force for Cyber Capacity Building)* (European Union Institute for Security Studies, 2018).

[44] These are annual, formal talks with counterparts such as the US, Japan, India, South Korea and China on technical and market-related issues. SWD (2017) 295 final (2017) (n 22) 55. For examples prior to the cybersecurity policy, see MG Porcedda, 'Transatlantic Approaches to Cyber-security: the EU-US Working Group on Cyber-security and Cybercrime', in Pawlak (ed), *The EU-US Security and Justice Agenda in Action*, vol no. 127–30 December 2011 (European Union Institute of Security Studies, 2011).

[45] On (in)coherence: H Carrapico and A Barrinha, 'The EU as a Coherent (Cyber)Security Actor?' (2017) 55 *Journal of Common Market Studies* 1254, 1272, 1268.

[46] See ch 4, section I.A.

First, the distinction between rules adopted pursuant to Articles 16 TFEU and 39 TEU is not a clear one, and becomes blurred in the external area of the AFSJ.[47] The external area of the AFSJ is the overlapping policy sector of the AFSJ and CFSP (and CSDP) that resulted from the internationalisation of domestic security threats[48] and which has acquired special prominence due to the increase in international intelligence-led policing, the regulation of data exchanges by means of international agreements and restrictive measures. This area will play increasing importance in relation to cybersecurity,[49] as exemplified by the EU's participation in the negotiation of the Second Additional Protocol to the Cybercrime Convention,[50] the solidarity clause at Article 222 TFEU[51] and the adoption of CFSP legal acts on restrictive measures in the aftermath of cyber-attacks. Even if the Lisbon Treaty does not contain clear rules to select the appropriate legal basis[52] for data processing activities in the external area of the AFSJ, fundamental rights obligations stemming from the Charter apply irrespective of the legal basis chosen, although the Court may have limited jurisdiction.[53] The open matter is which instrument applies for implementing Articles 8 – and 7 to an extent – in a given area:[54] the GDPR, the Law Enforcement Directive or a Decision pursuant to Article 39 TEU.

Second, irrespective of the answer to such a question, all EU institutions and bodies must process personal data in accordance with the second EDPS Regulation (EDPSR2).[55] This includes the Council and the EEAS as well as other institutions and bodies that may be active in the field of the EA.

Third, Member States are still subject to the ECHR, Convention 108 and upcoming modernised Convention 108+, the latter two lacking a disconnection clause.[56] Should

---

[47] Council, *Draft Internal Security Strategy for the European Union: Towards a European Security Model*, 5842/2/10 (2010), 16.

[48] See, among others, M Cremona and J Monar et al. (eds), *The External Dimension of the European Union's Area of Freedom, Security and Justice* (Brussels, Presses Interuniversitaires Europeennee, 2011).

[49] See, to this effect, European Commission and High Representative JOIN (2016) 18 final.

[50] European Commission, 'Recommendation for a Council Decision authorising the participation in negotiations on a second Additional Protocol to the Council of Europe Convention on Cybercrime (CETS No. 185)' (Communication) COM (2019) 71 final (2019).

[51] The 2020 Cybersecurity Policy invites reflection on the relationship between the Cyber Diplomacy Toolbox and the solidarity clause, JOIN (2020) 18 final (n 22), 17. Actions taken pursuant to Art 222(1) can and do overlap with measures of shared competence taken in the AFSJ, and vice versa. M Cremona, 'The EU and Global Emergencies: Competence and Instruments', in Antoniadis et al. (eds), *The European Union and Global Emergencies: A Law and Policy Analysis* (Oxford, Hart Publishing, 2011).

[52] See *Parliament v Council*, C-130/10, EU:C:2012:472, para 42–45. On the choice of the appropriate legal basis, M Cremona, 'Who Can Make Treaties? The European Union', in Hollis (ed), *The Oxford Guide to Treaties*, 2nd edn (Oxford, Oxford University Press, 2020).

[53] C Hillion, 'Decentralised Integration? Fundamental Rights Protection in the EU Common Foreign and Security Policy' (2016) 1 *European Papers – A Journal on Law and Integration*; *European Parliament v Council*, C-658/11, EU:C:2014:41, Opinion of Advocate General Bot, para 119. See also Herlin-Karnell (n 39). On CFSP within the Treaties, see M Cremona, 'The Two (or Three) Treaty Solution: The New Treaty Structure of the EU', in Biondi et al. (eds), *European Union Law After the Treaty of Lisbon* (Oxford, Oxford University Press, 2012); 'The position of CFSP/CSDP in the EU's constitutional architecture', in Blockmans et al. (eds), *Research Handbook on the EU's Common Foreign and Security Policy* (Cheltenham, Edward Elgar, 2018).

[54] *Parliament v Council*, C-130/10, paras 83–84. *Parliament v Council*, C-263/14, EU:C:2016:435.

[55] Reg (EU) 2018/1725 [2018] OJ L 295/39 (EDPSR2).

[56] On disconnection clauses, Cremona (n 2); C Timmermans, 'The Specificity of Private Law in EU External Relations: The Area of Freedom, Security, and Justice', in Cremona et al. (eds), *Private Law in the External Relations of the EU* (Oxford, Oxford University Press, 2016).

the Union sign and ratify Convention 108+, it would become a mixed agreement[57] subject to the provisions of Articles 3(5) TEU and 216(2) TFEU and related settled case law. Hence, Convention 108+ would be binding upon the Union and its Member States, forming an integral part of EU law.[58] While Convention 108+ would not have primacy over primary law, including general principles and fundamental rights, it would enjoy greater force than secondary law, which should be interpreted in a manner consistent with it.[59] Following Cremona,[60] if the EU became a party it would be for the CJEU to interpret the provisions of Convention 108+ to determine their legal effect, including their capability to produce direct effect, and the need for consistency between the two texts. The EU accession to Convention 108+ is not straightforward.[61]

For what concerns provisions contained in the six EA Titles of the TFEU, to whom Article 21 TEU apply by virtue of Article 205 TFEU, legislative acts are not expressly excluded.[62] Yet, restrictive measures adopted on the basis of the procedure under Article 215 TFEU, which is linked to the CFSP and is thus not the legislative procedure, are not legislative acts.[63] Such measures are adopted following a Council Decision by the Council acting by a qualified majority on a joint proposal from the High Representative and the Commission. The varied legal nature of the EA affects the remit of the jurisdiction of the CJEU[64] as well as the applicability of instruments implementing Articles 7 and 8 CFR. For instance, the GDPR does not apply to Member States when they carry out activities falling within the scope of Title V, Chapter II TEU, which begs the question of which instrument applies to acts implementing CFSP Council Decisions.

Lessons from the data retention judicial saga[65] suggest that the GDPR should apply to processing activities carried out by entities – such as data controllers and processors in the private sectors – that can be solely subjected to the GDPR. The LED should apply to processing activities carried out by entities tasked with the enforcement of the law when carrying out functions in pursuance of internal security and law and order. A future Decision based on Article 39 TEU should apply to Member States' entities tasked with foreign policy duties in the course of activities falling solely within the CFSP.

B. The Cyber Diplomacy Toolbox with a Focus on Cyber-Related Restrictive Measures

In 2017 the Council adopted a Conclusion accompanying a Framework for a Joint EU Diplomatic Response to Malicious Cyber Activities, known as the 'Cyber Diplomacy

---

[57] On mixed agreements, Cremona (n 52).
[58] Following *Haegenam*, C-181/73, in ibid.
[59] After *Kadi* and *Commission v Germany*, C-61/94, discussed in ibid. See also A Rosas and L Armati, *EU Constitutional Law – An Introduction* (Oxford, Hart Publishing, 2010).
[60] Cremona (n 52).
[61] See ch 4.
[62] Eg, see Arts 207(2) on the commercial policy and 214(3) on Humanitarian aid.
[63] Decisions are based on Art 29 TEU (CFSP), and Art 215 for subsequent measures in the form of a regulation (which is not a legislative act).
[64] Erlbacher, 'Article 215 TFEU', in M Kellerbauer (ed), *The EU Treaties and the Charter of Fundamental Rights: a Commentary* (Oxford, Oxford University Press, 2019) 1641.
[65] Ch 6, section III.B, ch 2, section II.B, ch 7 s II.B.

Toolbox' (Toolbox).[66] The Conclusions outline the common approach to the response to malicious activities and establish principles that should guide the Framework.

In terms of the common approach, the Council builds on the Conclusions on the EU Cybersecurity strategy and on Cyber Diplomacy to reiterate the growing need to protect the integrity and security of the EU. The Council vows to engage in ongoing cyber diplomacy while aiming for coherence among the EU cyber initiatives, with emphasis on the NIS Directive (NISD) and criminalisation of malicious cyber activity. The Conclusions stress that the EU's cyber diplomatic efforts adhere to the peaceful settlement of international disputes in cyberspace and the 'commitment to actively support the development of voluntary, non-binding norms of responsible State behaviour' drawn from the 2010, 2013 and 2015 reports of the UN GGE.[67]

The Conclusions list six guiding principles pertaining to measures falling within the Framework,[68] three of which stand out for the relationship of the triad. Thus, measures must serve to 'protect the integrity and security of the EU, its Member States and their citizens', 'be proportionate' according to certain criteria 'to the impact of the cyber activity' and 'respect applicable international law', so as not to violate fundamental rights and freedoms.

The Conclusions are silent about the contents of the Framework,[69] which was left to the Implementing Guidelines.[70] The Guidelines list preventative and reactive measures, in the guise of 'diplomatic, political or economic actions that can be used to prevent or respond to a malicious cyber activity' including those amounting to 'unfriendly acts'. The first, preventive measures, are confidence-building measures (CBMs), awareness raising on EU policies and EU cyber capacity building in third countries.[71] The second group features cooperative measures through EU-led political and thematic dialogues or through démarches by the EU delegations. Third, stability measures are Statements by the High Representative and on behalf of the Council of the EU, EU Council Conclusions and Diplomatic démarches by the EU delegations and signalled through EU-led political and thematic dialogue. The fourth are restrictive measures (RMs), followed by the fifth and last group, viz possible EU support to Member States' lawful responses.

---

[66] Council, 'Draft Council Conclusions on a Framework for a Joint EU Diplomatic Response to Malicious Cyber Activities' ('Cyber Diplomacy Toolbox') – Adoption, 9916/17, 7 June 2017'.

[67] United Nations, General Assembly, *Report of the Group of Governmental Experts (GGE) on Developments in the Field of Information and Telecommunications in the Context of International Security*, A/70/174 (2015); *Report of the Group of Governmental Experts (GGE) on Developments in the Field of Information and Telecommunications in the Context of International Security* A/68/98 (2013).

[68] The other principles are taking into account the broader context of the EU external relations with the state concerned, providing for the attainment of the CFSP objectives as set out in the TEU and basing actions on a shared situational awareness both agreed among the Member States and corresponding to the needs of the concrete situation in hand.

[69] See K Härmä and T Minárik, *European Union Equipping Itself against Cyber Attacks with the Help of Cyber Diplomacy Toolbox* (CCDCOE, 2017) ccdcoe.org/incyder-articles/european-union-equipping-itself-against-cyber-attacks-with-the-help-of-cyber-diplomacy-toolbox/.

[70] Council, 'Draft implementing guidelines for the Framework on a Joint EU Diplomatic Response to Malicious Cyber Activities' 13007/17.

[71] Pawlak (n 44); European Council, *Meeting Conclusions, 18 October 2018. Draft Council conclusions on cybersecurity capability and cyber capacity building in the EU*, 15244/1/18 (2019); Council of the European Union, *EU External Cyber Capacity Building Guidelines*, 10496/18 (2018).

Both the Conclusions and Implementing Guidelines note that, since attribution remains 'a sovereign political decision based on all-source intelligence' best 'established in accordance with international law of State responsibility',[72] not all measures 'require attribution to a State or a non-State actor'. Following both documents the Council adopted a non-paper on 'Attribution of malicious cyber activities'[73] and legal acts on restrictive measures, to which I now turn.

i. Cyber-Related Restrictive Measures: Council Decision 2019/797 (RMDir) and Council Regulation 2019/796 (RMReg)

The EU can adopt autonomous RMs[74] under Article 29 TEU, which empowers the Council to adopt decisions, pursuant to Article 31(1) TEU, defining the approach of the Union to a particular matter of a geographic or thematic nature. Article 29 Decisions provide a framework but must be implemented by means of a Council Regulation adopted on the basis and in accordance with the procedures laid down in Article 215 TFEU[75] and accompanied by explanatory notes, also adopted in the guise of Council Implementing Regulations. Council Decisions and Regulations are legal (but not legislative) acts with binding effects on the EU and Member States[76] and in respect of which the CJEU has accepted jurisdiction.[77] Decisions and Regulations on restrictive measures are often adopted on the same day 'with nearly identical content'.[78] Such is the case of Council Decision 2019/797 (RMDir) and Council Regulation 2019/796 (RMReg) concerning restrictive measures against cyber-attacks threatening the Union and its Member States.

The RMDir and RMReg are thematic sanctions enabling the adoption of travel bans and freezing of assets against listed natural or legal persons found to have wilfully carried out[79] cyber-attacks with a significant effect, including attempted cyber-attacks with a potentially significant effect, which constitute an external threat to the Union or its Member States. The Council reviews the measures every 12 months with a view to their renewal and amendment.[80] The first sanctions were issued in 2020. In the following, I outline the contents of the RMDir and RMReg and highlight any relevant differences. I then proceed to analyse relevant definitions and scope, notion of security, presence of explicit cross-references, common logics as well as structures put in place to achieve their goals.

---

[72] Council 9916/17 (n 65).
[73] Council, 'Implementation of the Framework for a Joint EU Diplomatic Response to Malicious Cyber Activities. Non-paper on attribution of malicious cyber activities in the context of the framework for a joint EU diplomatic response to malicious cyber activities' 6852/1/19 (2019).
[74] As opposed to those giving effect to United Nations Security Council Resolutions: Sanctions Guidelines – update, 5664/18 (2018), 5.
[75] Council 9916/17 (n 65); Erlbacher (n 64); T Ramopoulos, 'Article 29 TEU', in M Kellerbauer (ed), *The EU Treaties and the Charter of Fundamental Rights: a Commentary* (Oxford, Oxford University Press, 2019).
[76] Ramopoulos (n 75), citing AG Wahl's Opinion in C-455/14.
[77] Erlbacher (n 64) 1641.
[78] ibid, 1635.
[79] RMDir, Rec 8. The advantage of these acts is that they provide a framework that can be easily activated at need.
[80] The Decision is renewed until May 2025; www.consilium.europa.eu/en/press/press-releases/2022/05/16/cyber-attacks-council-extends-sanctions-regime-until-18-may-2025/.

Recitals 1-7 RMDir clarify the lineage of the Decision, which is grounded in the Cyber diplomacy Toolbox and Implementing Guidelines. Recitals recall Council Conclusions adopted on 16 April 2018 on malicious cyber activities, as well as European Council Conclusions adopted on 28 June 2018 stressing the need to strengthen capabilities against cybersecurity threats and on 18 October 2018 calling for the work on the capacity to respond to and deter cyber-attacks through Union restrictive measures. Recitals 1-5 RMReg refer to the parent text and supplement the RMReg with references to the Charter and compliance with fundamental rights. Thus, Recital 3 RMReg establishes the respect for the rights to an effective remedy and to a fair trial which have taken centre stage in the case law on RMs, as well as respect for the protection of personal data. Recital 5 RMReg clarifies that publication of personal data is needed for legal certainty and must be processed in line with the GDPR and EDPSR2.

The RMDir has nine fewer Articles than the RMReg, but the contents relevant to this research broadly overlap.[81] Both texts contain an Annex listing natural or legal persons against whom restrictive measures have been taken. Articles 1 RMDir and RMReg define cyber-attacks and explain the meaning of significant effects, with criteria laid out in Articles 3 RMDir and 2 RMReg. Articles 4–5 RMDir outline the gamut of restrictive measures that Member States can adopt, and that third states can be encouraged to adopt, which are further specified in the RMReg with respect to the freezing of assets. Articles 6–7 RMDir and 13-14 RMReg concern the process of listing natural and legal persons to be targeted by restrictive measures. In particular, the Council establishes and amends the list, acting by unanimity upon a proposal from a Member State or from the High Representative of the Union for Foreign Affairs and Security Policy. The Annex includes the grounds for listing the natural and legal persons following the adoption of Council Implementing Regulations[82] and contains the information necessary to identify the natural or legal persons. The Commission is a data controller with respect to the processing activities necessary to comply the tasks entrusted to it.[83]

The RMDir and RMReg harbour an understanding of security that has internal and external connotations reflective of CFSP goals. Internal connotations relate to the integrity and security of the Union, which includes the thwarting of threats against, eg, health, safety and the economic and social well-being of people and critical state functions in the guise of 'internal security'.[84] External connotations refer to security and stability in cyberspace in pursuit of International Security.[85] Neither text refers to 'cybersecurity' or NIS as understood in the Digital Single Market.

In terms of goals, the RMDir and RMReg aim to deter 'cyber-attacks constituting external threats' as opposed to internal threats, which are dealt with under AFSJ legislation such as the Cybercrime Directive.[86] In the acts, cyber-attacks are

> actions involving any of the following: (a) access to information systems; (b) information system interference; (c) data interference; or (d) data interception, where such actions are not

---
[81] Except for the inclusion, in the RMReg, of additional definitions and data protection measures.
[82] Council Implementing Regulation (EU) 2020/1125 of 30 July 2020 implementing Regulation (EU) 2019/796 concerning restrictive measures against cyber-attacks threatening the Union or its Member States [2020] OJ L246/4 (RMs Implementing Regulation).
[83] RMReg, Art 16, as per EDPSR, Art 3(8)
[84] RMDir and RMReg, Rec 1, Arts 4(a), (c).
[85] RMDir and RMReg, Art 4(6), Rec 4.
[86] See ch 7.

duly authorised by the owner or by another right holder of the system or data or part of it, or are not permitted under the law of the Union or of the Member State concerned.

The definition of 'information system' is akin to that contained in the Cybercrime Directive, with the exception of computer data, called 'digital data' and left undefined, as is 'access to information systems'. However, the Acts contain no cross-references to the Cybercrime Directive, even though cyberattacks in the RMDir and RMReg broadly correspond to the offences laid down in the Directive, with a caveat.

The Acts seem to depart from the Cybercrime Directive in a way that challenges the coherence and consistency of EU action in this field. For instance, 'data interference' is broader than the relevant provision of the Cybercrime Directive. It includes theft of data, funds, economic resources or intellectual property,[87] offences that are defined in frameworks other than the Cybercrime Directive, such as the Fraud and Counterfeiting Directive (FCD).[88] The Acts also lack cross-references to the NISD with respect to the definition of incidents and to the Blueprint for coordinated response to large-scale cross-border cybersecurity incidents and crises.[89]

The immediate goals of the two Acts are to ban travel and freeze the funds of culprits under the logic of retribution for cyber-attacks. Furthermore, RMs leverage both the 'naming and shaming' logic of Network and Information Security (NIS) instruments discussed in this research and 'deterrence' and 'punishment' logics[90] shared by cybercrime instruments.[91] Although the Acts are silent as to the steps necessary to achieve their goals, Article 7 RMDir and 14 RMReg implicitly suggest how such goals may be achieved. Accordingly, the Annex must contain 'where available', information 'necessary to identify the natural or legal persons' concerned. The acts provide a non-exhaustive list of information for natural persons, such as 'names and aliases, date and place of birth, nationality, passport and identity card numbers, gender and address' and legal persons, such as 'names, place and date of registration, registration number and place of business'. The RMDir goes to great length to clarify that 'targeted restrictive measures should be differentiated from the attribution of responsibility for cyber-attacks to a third State' and that the 'application of targeted restrictive measures does not amount to such attribution, which is a sovereign political decision taken on a case-by-case basis'.[92] However, technical attribution is preliminary to apportioning state responsibility and sanctioning an entity. In practice, the entities listed in the Annex are the object of decisions by the High Representative to the effect of attributing attacks and apportioning responsibility to state proxies (with little regard for the presumption of innocence and defence rights).

---

[87] A baffling choice because there is no such EU offence of 'data theft' and the existence of such an offence in general is highly disputed. Moreover, the EU deals with intellectual property rights under the DSM, not the AFSJ.
[88] Directive (EU) 2019/713 [2019] OJ L123/18.
[89] Commission Recommendation (EU) 2017/1584 of 13 September 2017 on coordinated response to large-scale cybersecurity incidents and crises [2017] OJ C239/36.
[90] 'To prevent, discourage, deter and respond to continuing and increasing malicious behaviour in cyberspace', RM Implementing Regulation (n 82), Rec 4.
[91] See chs 6, 7.
[92] RMDir, Rec 9.

What of privacy and data protection? RMs are known to interfere with the right to private life. In *Sayadi and Vinck*[93] the HRC deemed that the dissemination of the United Nations Security Council's terrorist list containing full contact details about the applicants constituted an attack on their honour and reputation, in view of the negative association that some persons could make between the applicants' names and the title of the sanctions list. The same applies in the EU, where restrictive measures attracted particular attention after the *Kadi* ruling.[94] In *Ayadi*, the Court stated that being publicly identified as a person targeted by restrictive measures in light of one's association with a terrorist organisation attracts 'opprobrium and suspicion'.[95] Public recognition of the illegality of the association with terrorism constituted 'a form of reparation for the non-material harm' suffered by Mr Ayadi 'by reason of that illegality'.[96] Lock notes that in *Al Assad*, the General Court recognised that restrictive measures may interfere with the right to private life of the target, but that such measures are usually proportionate.[97]

The information published in the lists is personal data[98] and their processing must respect the principles established in Article 8 CFR. Even though we do not benefit from a Decision pursuant to Article 39 TEU, the Council must abide by the EDPSR2. The RMDir and RMReg are 'legal acts'[99] safeguarding objectives of the CFSP that lay down grounds justifying 'restrictions of the application of articles 14 to 22, 35, and 36, as well as Article 4 in so far as its provisions correspond to the rights and obligations provided for in Articles 14 to 22' pursuant to the EDPSR2.[100] Legal acts restricting principles and rights must contain specific provisions clarified by Article 25(2) EDPSR2. According to a 2015 EDPS 'umbrella opinion' covering 'future sanctions regimes imposing restrictive measures',[101] the restriction of data subjects' rights should be documented internally, by means of a note or file, at the time of applying the restriction. The RMDir and RMReg are accompanied by several notices for the attention of the data subjects to whom the

---

[93] *Sayadi and Vinck v Belgium*, no. 1472/2006, CCPR/C/94/D/1472/2006. See ch 3.
[94] *Kadi and Al Barakaat International Foundation v Council and Commission (Kadi I)*, C-402/05 P and C-415/05, EU:C:2008:461. For a literature review, see especially, S Poli and M Tzanou, 'The Kadi Rulings: A Survey of the Literature', in M Cremona et al. (eds), *Challenging the EU Counter-terrorism Measures through the Courts*, vol AEL 2009/10 (European University Institute Working Papers, 2009). See also Cremona et al (n 48); E Spaventa, 'Counter-Terrorism and Fundamental Rights: Judicial Challenges and Legislative Changes after the Rulings in Kadi and PMOI' in Antoniadis et al. (eds), *The European Union and Global Emergencies: A Law and Policy Analysis* (Oxford, Hart Publishing, 2011).
[95] *P Ayadi v Commission*, C-183/12, EU:C:2013:369, para 68.
[96] ibid, para 70.
[97] *Al Assad v Council*, T-202/12, EU:T:2014:113. See Lock (n 31) 2116–2117.
[98] European Data Protection Supervisor, Prior Checking Opinion regarding Restrictive Measures (Sanctions) of the European External Action Service (EEAS) (2014/0926), (2014).
[99] But *cf*, believing that such an act has not been adopted, F Dumortier and V Papakonstantinou et al., *EU Sanctions against Cyber-attacks and Defense Rights: Wanna Cry?* (European Law Blog, 2020) europeanlawblog.eu/2020/09/28/eu-sanctions-against-cyber-attacks-imposed-and-defense-rights-wanna-cry/.
[100] EDPSR2, Art 25(1)(c). These concern 'specific principles and the rights of information, access to and rectification or erasure of personal data, the right to data portability, confidentiality of electronic communications data as well as the communication of a personal data breach to a data subject and certain related obligations of the controllers, as far as necessary and proportionate in a democratic society to safeguard public security and for the prevention, investigation and prosecution of criminal offences or the execution of criminal penalties' (Rec 44).
[101] With the caveat that 'the processing operations foreseen are substantially identical to those analysed in this prior check' European Data Protection Supervisor (n 90) 4.

restrictive measures apply.[102] In general, the EDPS recommends evaluating on a case-by-case basis 'the need to process unique identifiers in case persons concerned can be easily identified without recourse to them'.

The procedures set out in the Sanctions Guidelines go to great lengths to respect the right to protection of personal data; however, the Acts are a form of restriction of the right pursuant to Article 25 (1)(c) EDPSR2. Furthermore, Article 7 CFR is overlooked in disregard of case law confirming its relevance and the observation that travel bans are capable of limiting the enjoyment of private and family life. Such findings, together with the outcome of the analysis of the definitions, scope, notion of security, presence of explicit cross-references, logics as well as structures put in place to achieve their aims, bring about the conclusion that the legal acts embody a weak form of reconciliation with data protection and privacy. I submit that, notwithstanding the efforts to protect personal data, compliance with primary law remains problematic as the Council has thus far failed to fulfil its positive obligations of adopting a Decision pursuant to Article 39 TEU.

Moreover, the analysis of the legal acts shows that the substantive functional interconnection to NIS and cybercrime is weakened by the absence of cross-references to NIS and cybercrime instruments. The acts are also functionally interconnected to cybercrime and NIS as to procedure because RMs implicitly rely on forensic analysis and technical attribution based on personal data processing and the analysis of communications, which I will discuss in section III.

C. Reconciliation of Cybersecurity, Privacy and Data Protection in EA Law

The findings of the high-level analysis of the RMDir and RMReg as flagship legal Acts within the Cyber Diplomacy Toolbox, whereby they lead to weak reconciliation between cybersecurity, privacy and data protection are not illustrative of the EA as a whole. The Toolbox is not carved in stone[103] and, as noted by Erlbacher, RMs 'are embedded in series of measures ... and must therefore be coordinated with other policy instruments'.[104] The mismatch between cybercrime definitions in the RMDir and RMReg and those contained in the AFSJ instruments potentially jeopardises cross-sectoral coherence. Erlbacher further notes that RMs 'often build upon existing legislation ... such as in particular the Dual-use Regulation'.[105] The Sanctions Guidelines note that 'the measures used in a specific situation will vary depending on the objectives of the restrictive measures' and can include export restrictions 'to prevent the misuse of equipment,

---

[102] Notice for the attention of the data subjects to whom the restrictive measures provided for in Council Decision (CFSP) 2019/797 and Council Regulation (EU) 2019/796 concerning restrictive measures against cyber-attacks threatening the Union or its Member States 2021/C 192/05 [2021] OJ C 192/6.

[103] With the French Presidency aiming to reform it. A Bendiek and M Schulze, *Attribution: A Major Challenge for EU Cyber Sanctions* (SWP Research Paper, 2021).

[104] Erlbacher (n 64) 1634. Such as neighbourhood policy instruments or Global Strategies, which contain relevant information on the mode of reconciliation for the triad.

[105] ibid.

technology or software for monitoring and interception'.[106] Indeed, export control to prevent the misuse of technology is among the measures mentioned in the 2020 Cybersecurity Policy and consequently the Dual-use Regulation acquires particular cybersecurity significance.

The Dual-use Regulation, adopted on the basis of Article 207 TFEU on the Common Commercial Policy, establishes a Union regime for the control of exports, brokering, technical assistance, transit and transfer of dual-use items. Such items are listed in an Annex implementing internationally agreed dual-use controls, including the Wassenaar Arrangement[107] for what concerns computers, telecoms and information security. Dual-use items such as those covered in 5A002.a. Note 2 can be used to undermine the integrity and confidentiality of personal data and communications and, as such, the instrument could offer prima facie strong reconciliation between cybersecurity and data protection.

The Dual-use Regulation is an example of the panoply of EA instruments with cybersecurity relevance.[108] To draw results as to the reconcilability between cybersecurity, privacy and data protection in the EA it would be necessary to jointly analyse EA-specific instruments and the extraterritorial dimension of NIS and cybercrime instruments discussed in chapters six and seven. While this is a task for the future, the findings of chapters six and seven hypothesise that the EA harbours the inherent contradictions of cybersecurity policymaking. Therefore, the EA effects changing forms of reconciliation, aligned along substantive and procedural functional interconnection mechanisms and potentially also along new policy dimensions.

III. Technology

Similar to chapters six and seven, this section elaborates on the findings of reconcilability between cybersecurity, privacy and data protection at a lower level of abstraction, by looking at the role of technology in EA legal acts (and policies) as a regulatory object and implementing tool. I begin by reflecting on the role of technical attribution in the RMDir and RMReg in the guise of cyber-forensic analysis, which benefits from deep packet inspection (DPI), a tool mentioned in the Dual-use Regulation for export controls. As an analysis of technology would substantially reproduce the findings of chapters six and seven, instead here I reason on the implications at EA level of the 'effacement of technology' from formal law,[109] and in particular the hiatus between the aspiration to pursue values and the concrete delivery on such values. Here, regulatory strategies informing international private regulatory law and particularly standardisation play a crucial role. The effacement of technology fosters the porousness of legislation enabling

---
[106] Sanctions Guidelines (n 74) 8.
[107] The Wassenaar Agreement on Export Controls for Conventional Arms and Dual-Use Goods and Technologies.
[108] Another relevant instrument is Regulation (EU) 2019/517 of the European Parliament and Council of 19 March 2019 on the implementation and functioning of the.eu top-level domain name and amending and repealing Regulation (EC) No 733/2002 and repealing Commission Regulation (EC) No 874/2004 [2019] OJ L91/25.
[109] See ch 5, section II.

the circulation of values, regulatory techniques and implementing tools with unpredictable effects. I will reason on whether the circulation of such values should be seen as cross-pollination or cross-contamination in the conclusion to this chapter.

A. The Importance of Technical Attribution for RMs and Some Considerations on Deep Packet Inspection

The RMDir and RMReg are among the Cyber Diplomacy Toolbox measures that require attribution, meaning the 'practice of assigning responsibility for malicious cyber activity'.[110] Such a practice is the 'result of a process'[111] consisting of a technocratic, political and legal assessment. The technocratic assessment draws on cyber-forensic analysis and intelligence assessment, coordinated at EU level by INTCEN. The political assessment is necessary because, as Bendiek and Schulze note, technical attribution cannot reveal the strategic and political motivation of actors[112] necessary to legally justify the adoption of RMs. The latter is part of the legal assessment and includes considerations on intent[113] and voluntary non-binding norms of state behaviour[114] as established by the UN GGE reports.

Similar to other cybersecurity instruments, the two legal acts on RMs do not contain references to technical attribution and related forensic requirements and also lack references to the Blueprint.[115] Such an omission stands in the way of redressing the great disparity of technical capabilities within the EU, greatly diminished with Brexit as noted by Bendiek and Schulze,[116] which in turn undermines the effectiveness of attribution[117] and the coherence of EU action. Bendiek and Schulze also point to mismatching technical and legal grounds for attribution – a problem not unique to RMs but rather common to the prosecution of cybercrime[118] and with due process implications. The removal of references to technological implementation in the law means that the legal Acts are only able to perform half the assessment necessary to establish the reconcilability of the triad in the EA.

That RMs require technical attribution means they rely on the implementation of IT forensics. At a lower level of abstraction, the RMDir and RMReg require the collection of e-evidence.[119] The identification of the necessary information for attribution

---

[110] Council (n 73) 3.
[111] ibid.
[112] Bendiek and Schulze (n 103) 10.
[113] RMDir, Rec 8 clarifies that RMs only attach to 'wilful' acts.
[114] Council (n 73).
[115] Rec (EU) 2017/1584 (n 89) contains technical and operations steps to deal with cross-border cyber-attacks. Blueprint on large-scale cybersecurity incidents.
[116] Bendiek and Schulze (n 103) 10.
[117] A strategy already questionable in light of the partial effectiveness of attribution, C Guitton, 'Criminals and Cyber Attacks: The Missing Link between Attribution and Deterrence' (2012) 6 *International Journal of Cyber Criminology* 1030–1043.
[118] On the disconnect between the technology and criminal law responses, see MG Porcedda, 'Sentencing data-driven cybercrime. How data crime with cascading effects is tackled by UK courts' (2023) 48 *Computer Law and Security Review*.
[119] See ch 7.

requires the analysis of communications and the processing of personal data interfering with Article 8 CFR and the confidentiality of communications enshrined in Articles 7 CFR and 8 ECHR. An explicit objective of general interest justifies such interferences, which are prima facie proportionate – that is, if we disengage from a thorough analysis of the essence of the two rights. The RMD and RMR may *de facto* espouse the findings of the ECtHR Grand Chamber in *Big Brother Watch* with respect to the bulk analysis of communications data, among others exactly to deal with cyber-attacks,[120] with extant implications for the essence of Articles 7 and 8 CFR.

Furthermore, the technology reviewed in chapters six and seven – DPI[121] – also plays a role here as a forensic (and intelligence) technique. Specifically within the EA, it is worth noting that the Dual-use Regulation places the export of 'certain non-listed cyber-surveillance items' under control for their ability to 'be misused by persons complicit in or responsible for directing or committing serious violations of human rights or international humanitarian law'.[122] Furthermore

> Associated risks relate ... to cases where cyber-surveillance items are specially designed to enable intrusion or deep packet inspection into information and telecommunications systems in order to conduct covert surveillance of natural persons by monitoring, extracting, collecting or analysing data, including biometrics data, from those systems. Items used for purely commercial applications such as billing, marketing, quality services, user satisfaction or network security are generally considered not to entail such risks.[123]

Recital 8 combined with Part VII, Category V of the Regulations' Annex[124] act as a reminder of the tensions sparked by DPI examined in chapters six and seven, which I will not retrace here.[125] Instead, I turn to the significance of the 'effacement of technology' for the hiatus between values that legislation aspires to uphold and is capable to concretise.

B. The Effacement of Technology: International Flow of Values, Norms, Ideas and Impact on the Triad

Debates concerning the role of value-based norm-setting and taking in power relations cut across many scholarly fields and branches of the law. Much has been written about the 'Brussels effect' and the global reach of EU law vis-à-vis the EU's principle of autonomy,[126] to the effect that norm-taking and norm-setting is bi-directional. Cremona notes the EA effects a complex web of international legal relations where the

---

[120] See ch 7, section III.B.ii.
[121] LF Pikos, 'Packet Analysis for Network Forensics: A Comprehensive Survey' (2020) 32 *Forensic Science International: Digital Investigation* 1–12; W Song, M Beshley et al., 'A Software Deep Packet Inspection System for Network Traffic Analysis and Anomaly Detection' (2020) 20 *Sensors*.
[122] Dual Use Regulation (n 37) Rec 8.
[123] ibid.
[124] ibid, Part VII – Category 5 – Telecommunications and Information Security.
[125] Chs 6, section III.B and 7, section III.B.
[126] A Bradford, 'The Brussels Effect' (2020) 107 *Northwestern University Law Review*. Cremona and Scott (n 4) 15.

EU engages in 'interactions which cannot be categorized simply as either norm export or import'.[127] For instance, Micklitz notes the tendency of regulatory private law to 'the export of internal procedural rules to the rest of the world and the impact of procedural rules into the EU'.[128] Flagship cybersecurity instruments offer examples of norm exports and imports.

The procedure whereby transborder data flows require a finding of adequacy of the recipient state under GDPR Title V procedures is a paradigmatic example of norms export. Through the adequacy procedure, the EU 'shield[s] its higher standards',[129] where standards are taken to mean norms and values. However, Bygrave notes that the GDPR also contains imported regulatory ideas and traditions, such as breach notification rules, data protection impact assessments, data protection by design and by default and certification schemes.[130] Similarly, Shackelford argues that the NISD follows in the steps of the US NIST Cybersecurity Framework.[131] These examples underline more than the import of rules: they underpin the import of regulatory philosophies and strategies capable of deeply influencing the fulfilment of values. At the heart of such strategies are standards.[132]

Standards are politically sensitive due to their ability to engender and reinforce dominant positions.[133] Whomever determines the dominant technology standards has immense power on the values that are to be prioritised and ultimately pursued. The EU 2020 Cybersecurity Policy shows awareness of the essential role of 'shaping international standards in the areas of emerging technologies' as well as (re)gaining technological sovereignty.[134] One cannot be a norm-setter as a standards adopter. And yet, this is what may have happened in the EU, to the ultimate detriment of the strong reconcilability of cybersecurity, privacy and data protection in practice.

In chapter five I introduced how standardisation rests on the work of SSOs and SDOs, including international organisations and private bodies. Part of global administrative law,[135] legislation incorporates standards, and co-opts the private sector involved in such policymaking, by means of co-regulatory approaches, which in the EU finds its

---

[127] Cremona (n 7).
[128] Micklitz (n 30) 17.
[129] ibid 27.
[130] LA Bygrave, 'The 'Strasbourg Effect' on Data Protection in Light of the 'Brussels Effect': Logic, Mechanics and Prospects' (2021) 40 *Computer Law & Security Review*.
[131] SJ Shackelford and S Russell et al., 'Bottoms up: A Comparison of Voluntary Cybersecurity Frameworks' (2020) 16 *UC Davis Business Law Journal* 217–260.
[132] Micklitz notes that standards, as the outcome of standardisation processes, are 'turned into code of practices' integrated into governance via contract or corporate governance: Micklitz (n 30) 25. In the GDPR and NISD, codes of practices are one of the ways to demonstrate the adoption of certification schemes and international standards, see ch 6, section III.A.
[133] S-y Peng, "Private' Cybersecurity Standards? Cyberspace Governance, Multistakeholderism and the (ir)relevance of the TBT Regime' (2018) 15 *Cornell International Law Journal*.
[134] JOIN (2020) 18 final (n 13) 20. JF Borrell, Answer given by High Representative/Vice-President Borrell on behalf of the European Commission to Parliamentary questions E-006876/2020 by Moritz Körner on the European Union position as regards cyber sovereignty (2021). See further: ec.europa.eu/commission/presscorner/detail/en/QANDA_22_662.
[135] B Kingsbury and N Krish et al., 'The Emergence of Global Administrative Law' (2005) 68 *Law and Contemporary Problems* 15–61.

expression in the New Approach/New Legislative Framework. The regulatory ecosystem epitomising such an approach and relying on technology neutrality, 'by design' requirements and reliance on the 'state of the art' effects the 'effacement of technology' from formal regulation, related case law and the interpretation of the essence of fundamental rights. 'By design' is an imported norm and preliminary research seems to show that technology neutrality is also an import,[136] through which the EU enjoys the simultaneous position of standards adopter and value-setter.

The fluidity of cybersecurity standards, characterised by multiple competing frameworks and especially the ISO 27000 family and the US NIST framework, has triggered what Shin-yi Peng describes as a 'standards jungle'.[137] This has immediate consequences for the essence of Article 8 CFR: what are the international standards determining the threshold for the integrity and security of personal data? The reality of international standards empties the significance of the essence of the right to data protection identified by the Court.[138] Disagreements at international level and discussions for a cybercrime Treaty at UN level show that no single actor has emerged as dominant yet, but that the competition is very fierce. International events also show that the relationship of the triad depends on external dynamics simultaneously activating multiple EU policy areas under the umbrella of the EA. As a result of such dynamics, the EA cannot foster a single mode of reconciliation of the triad. The question as to whether the EU can re-align values, design and delivery to foster a harmonious co-existence of cybersecurity, privacy and data protection in light of its constitutional constraints, historical dependencies and geopolitical contingency takes us to the conclusion.

IV. Conclusion: Weak Reconciliation of Cyber External Action, Privacy and Data Protection Challenged by Technology[139]

This chapter looked at the reconcilability of cybersecurity, privacy and data protection in the External Action – EA for short. Since the EA incorporates the trends and contradictions of internal policymaking, the analysis is in keeping with previous chapters: the EA does not effect a prevailing mode of reconciliation for the triad, so that we cannot say that cybersecurity, privacy and data protection are inherently complementary or at odds with one another.

Policy documents show how the geopolitical significance of cybersecurity determines the pre-eminence of traditional conceptions of 'security' overshadowing considerations specific to single rights, such as privacy and data protection. The simultaneous importance of values and interests in a post-Lisbon EA triggers a balancing act that engenders

---

[136] W Maxwell and M Bourreau, *Technology Neutrality in Internet, Telecoms and Data Protection Regulation* (Global Media and Communications Quarterly, 2014); C Reed, *Making Laws for Cyberspace* (Oxford, Oxford University Press, 2012). See ch 5, s II.A.
[137] Peng (n 133).
[138] See chs 4, 6–7.
[139] This chapter benefitted from comments by Marise Cremona; I am particularly grateful for comments at nn 26, 62, 79 and 104.

weak reconciliation of the triad, as exemplified by the analysis of restrictive measures (RMs) adopted against cyber-attackers.

Cybersecurity is a limitation of the two rights that must be procedurally respectful of fundamental rights, in a way that is evocative of counterterrorism policymaking. These considerations stem from formal law, examined at a high level of abstraction. In the EA as in the DSM and the AFSJ, formal law does not deal with implementing procedures and tools.

The 'effacement' of technology from legislation undermines the finding of weak reconciliation identified at a higher level of abstraction. The pursuit of RMs requires using technologies capable of undermining the essence of Article 7 CFR. As for Article 8 CFR, the bar for what constitutes the essence is so low and so dependent on international standards, as to be rendered insignificant. Analysis of policymaking at a lower level of abstraction shows how the EU's reliance on international standardisation can act as a boomerang against the EU's desire to be a norm-setter, thereby undermining the pursuit of fundamental rights, cybersecurity and their reconciliation. But this is for the overall conclusions of the book to address, to which I turn next.

Conclusion

I. Summary of Findings

How are cybersecurity, privacy and data protection (the triad) reconciled in EU law? This is the question I sought to answer with this book, a question that becomes more pressing by the day as our lives, society and democracy become intertwined with networked information technologies as critical infrastructure. Studying the relationship of the triad is no easy endeavour because in cyberspace, data and information can cause the triad to both clash and converge. To investigate the triad's relationship, I conceptualised the ambivalence caused by clash and convergence along an axis, shown in Figure 1, ranging from no to complete reconciliation and particularised by five relational modes.

Figure 1 Modes of reconciliation of the triad

		Reconciliation		
None	**Weak**		**Strong**	**Complete**
<-------	---------	----------	----------	------->
	Clash	Indifference	Complementarity	
		(non-interference)		
Zero-sum	Balancing		Convergence	Overlap

To the far right is strong reconciliation underscored by complementarity. 'Overlap' expresses the idea that cybersecurity, privacy and data protection are different facets of the same thing, thereby enjoying complete reconciliation. 'Convergence' points to the triad's shared goals and therefore underscores synergy and complementarity. To the far left is weak reconciliation underscored by clashes. 'Zero-sum' expresses the irreconcilability of the triad, while 'balancing' refers to the method of adjudication incorporated in the proportionality test characterising a mode of co-existence in which something has to give. An in-between state classed as 'indifference', for want of a better expression, points to reciprocal non-interference.

Some modes of reconciliation are not viable in all jurisdictions. The research question builds on the assumption that zero-sum outcomes are not compatible with EU law and the reasons why this is the case bring to surface elements for an analytical framework to investigate what other modes of reconcilability apply. To ascertain the modes of reconciliation, it is necessary to examine cybersecurity, privacy and data protection as: (i) techno-legal objects situated within the EU constitutional architecture or *ordre public* underpinned by the rule of law (RoL) and the EU multilevel system of protection of human rights; (ii) the values the triad expresses; and (iii) their concrete policy substantiation. The latter includes looking at the applicable laws (high level of abstraction) as well as their implementation (low level of abstraction) with an eye to technology. To treat cybersecurity, privacy and data protection as situated techno-legal objects of enquiry one must look at each separately and as they interact in the Digital Single Market (DSM), the Area of Freedom, Security and Justice (AFSJ) and External Action (EA) through policy, law and technology, bearing in mind the idiosyncrasies of such areas of EU decision-making.

In part one of the book (chapters one to four) cybersecurity, privacy and data protection were examined as self-standing regulatory objects. The analysis of cybersecurity in chapter two pointed to a framework still in the making and characterised by plasticity. The term 'cybersecurity' encompasses Network and Information Security (NIS), the fight against cybercrime, the collection of e-evidence, cyberdefence and cyberdiplomacy, cyber-exports and it can even incorporate elements of privacy and data protection. All dimensions of the Cybersecurity Policy come together, to the extent that treating them separately is an artificial exercise. Such plasticity is reflected in successive EU Cybersecurity Policies, with the 2020 Policy placing special emphasis on the synthesis of dimensions. However, the open-endedness of the concept of 'cybersecurity' betrays the cacophony of interests generated by communities animating its different facets. Moreover, as the development of the cybersecurity policy intersects with the peculiar evolution of the DSM, AFSJ and the EA, the result is a patchwork of instruments displaying both connections and clashes within and across areas of policymaking.

Privacy and data protection are treated as interlinked but independent rights enshrined in Articles 7 and 8 CFR,[1] each endowed with essential components and one or more core areas as identified by the CJEU. In both cases, essential components are enriched with findings from secondary law. Also in both cases, vagueness as to the essence favours an 'evolutive' interpretation of the two rights but weakens the possibility to understand whether measures stemming from legislation, including technologies, are proportionate and impose clear and strict permissible limitations.

Chapter three reviewed the connection between Articles 7 CFR and 8 ECHR[2] to identify privacy's essential components. The analysis points to a smaller scope of Article 7 CFR than Article 8 ECHR. The right's essential components are drawn from the four limbs of the right – private life, family life, home and communications. Private life is further conceptualised into physical and psychological integrity, personal social and sexual identity, and finally personal development, autonomy and participation ('outer circle'). The pronouncements of the CJEU point to three elements of the essence: [the revelation of] very specific information concerning the private life of a person, not limited to certain aspects of that private life; for a father, the possibility to apply for the right to custody; and the content of communications.

Chapter four looked at data protection as a self-standing fundamental right, the independence of which is worth defending even in the face of ambivalent case law of the CJEU. The right has four essential components roughly corresponding to the three

---

[1] Charter [2012] OJ L326/391 (CFR).
[2] Council of Europe, ETS no.° 005, 4 November 1950 (ECHR).

paragraphs of the right: protection, legitimate processing (fairness, lawfulness and purpose limitation), data subject rights and independent control. Essential components tend to have a manifest content but are also capable of subsuming other meanings, as found in secondary law or court decisions. For instance, protection reflects both the architecture of personal data protection and, in a more restrictive sense, the principles and related technical and organisational measures (TOMs) to safeguard individuals against harms that may derive from processing. The provision in the legal basis of measures protecting the integrity and confidentiality of data are an element of the essence, as are measures effecting purpose limitation. The overlap between independent control and data subject rights can give rise to a right to human oversight or intervention, at a minimum to explain the functioning of the processing so as to give meaning to the right to access to one's data.

In part two of the book (chapters five to eight), the common reference to confidentiality and, to a lesser degree, integrity across the triad emerging from the analysis offers the opportunity to investigate a possible overlap. This was done in chapter five through a techno-legal prism comparing both the technical understanding of the triad drawn from threat modelling – including security properties, protection goals and design strategies – and legal understanding of the rights as endowed with essential components and essence. If overlap appears to be a possible mode of reconciliation in theory, it is difficult to prove that in practice due to the lack of a common vocabulary between technologists and legislators, the misalignment between risk management and proportionality tests and some recurring features of (networked) information technology law.

Network and information technology as a regulatory target was dissected with a focus on two regulatory strategies, technology neutrality (TN) and 'by design'. Such regulatory strategies serve delegatory co-decision frameworks, which are studied by different bodies of literature. In a nutshell, secondary legislation creates the framework outlining the goals to be achieved and harms to be avoided[3] through the implementation of TOMs selected in accordance with a dynamic 'state of the art' (SoA) set by Standards Setting Organisations (SSOs) and Standards Developing Organisations (SDOs). Following the TN principle, the law only sketches the parameters of TOMs, which should abide by set principles 'by design'.

However, requirements couched in technology neutral terms frustrate efforts to align the design of TOMs to such requirements; furthermore, TOMs are destined for technology users rather than developers. The European data protection by design Standard adopted in 2022 notably 'provides voluntary tools to manufacturers and service providers to allow them to demonstrate to controllers'[4] compliance with 'by design' principles. The standard does not aim to provide a presumption of conformity and is not for publication in the Official Journal. The data processing, software-driven

---

[3] Developing the work of J Black 'The Emergence of Risk-Based Regulation' [2005] *Public Law* 512, see R Gellert, *The Risk-based Approach to Data Protection* (Oxford,Oxford University Press, 2020).

[4] European Commission, 'Commission implementing decision C(2015) 102 final of 20.1.2015 on a standardisation request to the European standardisation organisations as regards European standards and European standardisation deliverables for privacy and personal data protection management pursuant to Article 10(1) of Regulation (EU) No 1025/2012 of the European Parliament and of the Council in support of Directive 95/46/EC of the European Parliament and of the Council and in support of Union's security industrial policy. Mandate M/530', 5.

component of information technologies has further eluded stringent legislation on account of its misalignment with existing categorisations of product, process, service or system.[5] What is more, SSOs and SDOs are populated by actors that also happen to be among the major addressees of secondary legislation as technology users while also being information technology developers. Consequently, the law delegates to its most powerful addressees both the choice of what TOMs correspond to the SoA and what values are embedded in TOMs and how.

Such dynamics effect an ironic 'effacement of technology' from technology law and a 'technology indeterminacy loop'. Higher courts such as the CJEU and the ECtHR only review the legality of measures that are enshrined in law, so that the law's technological implementation disappears beneath the courts' radar and fails to contribute to the binding interpretations of the law. Thus, courts are not put in the position to supplement legislation with workable criteria that bridge law and technology; to the extent they ignore such dynamics, balancing formulas devised for the digital age are incapable of redressing the indeterminacy loop.[6] This, among other reasons, hampers the development of a common vocabulary between technologists and legislators and thus the demonstration of overlap. Such a finding also raises questions as to the possibility to define a default mode of reconciliation of the triad at high (applicable law) and low (technology implementation) levels of abstraction.

The investigation as to the mode of reconciliation of the triad continues with a study in chapters six to eight of the interaction of the triad in the DSM, AFSJ and EA, including the Common Foreign and Security Policy (CFSP) through policy, law and technology. In all areas, policy documents offer an overview of the context in which the relationship of privacy and data protection with NIS, the fight against cybercrime and collection of e-evidence as well as cybersecurity in the international arena play out.

The analysis shows substantive and procedural functional interconnection between NIS and cybercrime instruments in the AFSJ and EA. In particular, the pursuit of NIS and the response to cyber-dependent or 'narrow' cybercrime are functionally interconnected as to their substance, while the investigation and prosecution of all cybercrimes, collection of e-evidence and CFSP restrictive measures are functionally interconnected as to procedure. Such interconnections seem to relate to strong or weak reconcilability at a high level of abstraction. Instruments dealing with substantive matters point to strong reconcilability between the triad: frameworks converge on common goals and underpin the mutually beneficial nature of cybersecurity, privacy and data protection, although with caveats.[7] Conversely, rules enabling the collection of e-evidence point to weak reconcilability: frameworks pursue different goals, are fragmented and underpin the need to balance cybersecurity, privacy and data protection. And yet, such interconnections are not enough to determine the relationship of the triad.

---

[5] Regulation (EU) 1025/2012 [2012] OJ L316/12.
[6] M Susi, 'The Internet Balancing Formula' (2019) 25 *European Law Journal* 198–212; R Alexy, 'Mart Susi's Internet Balancing Formula' ibid 213–220.
[7] NIS instruments prioritise continuity of service, while fundamental rights prioritise fundamental rights. See ch 6, section III.D.

With respect to NIS, the analysis of policy and especially law showed strong reconciliation of the triad in the applicable law but not when considering technology as an element of implementation. Principles of EU policymaking informing the technological implementation of the applicable law and effecting the effacement of technology prevent strong reconciliation, as shown by the analysis of deep packet inspection. In the AFSJ, the analysis of policy and law underscored different degrees of reconcilability between measures addressing cybercrime, privacy and data protection depending on the goals of specific instruments. The spillover effect of the 'effacement of technology', if subdued on account of the reach of EU law in the AFSJ, prevents strong reconciliation, as shown by the analysis of deep packet inspection. Such variety, ranging from strong reconciliation to classic balancing, reflects the intrinsic complexity of cybersecurity as a policy area. Unresolved policy tensions reverberate through secondary law, to the detriment of coherence and legal certainty.

For both NIS and the AFSJ, the concept of the 'essence' appears unable to act as a fail-safe mechanism. The lack of technological specificity in the pronouncement of the CJEU creates a porous border between content and metadata, begs the question of whether there is a quantum of information capable of providing very specific information about one's private life, does not refer to a minimum threshold for confidentiality and integrity requirements and challenges the feasibility of stringent purpose limitation requirements in practice. With such loose parameters, the technological implementation of measures escapes a rigorous assessment; measures capable of infringing privacy and data protection and of constituting an 'attack' against network and information systems are not nipped in the bud. Rather, they are allowed to flourish until they become mainstream and too entrenched to be removed,[8] even if their use is not only capable of interfering with rights, but also of affecting their essence.

The analysis in chapters six and seven also draws a trajectory: reconciling cybersecurity, privacy and data protection becomes increasingly challenging as we move from older to newer EU policy areas, where integration is weaker and national variations are more entrenched.[9] Such dynamics affect external policymaking, with tensions that have been left unresolved internally likely to be replicated externally. The study of the EA proved more complex than NIS and cybercrime on account of the breadth of the area, the range of instruments and the need to consider the external dimension of NIS and cybercrime instruments. An analysis of restrictive measures points to the validity of functional interconnection in the EA; the examination of frameworks such as export controls on dual-use technology could further confirm the finding.

The analysis of the EA casts the 'effacement of technology' from technology law under new light. The ability to translate norms into practice depends on both standard setting and technology leadership. Standards, which are adopted by public or private international bodies, have gone from harbingers of international free trade to tools of political influence. Technology leadership over 'high-tech' products,[10] which has always

---

[8] Eg, following the Collingridge dilemma and similar arguments (see ch 5, sections III–IV).
[9] M Cremona, 'The Union as a Global Actor: Roles, Models and Identity' (2004) 41 *Common Market Law Review* 553–573.
[10] H Nau, *National Politics and International Technology* (Johns Hopkins University Press, 1974); J Lembke, *Competition for Technological Leadership* (Cheltenham, Edward Elgar, 2002).

been a field of geopolitical competition, is now fully concerned with data flows as crucial to innovation. The physical, logical and social components of cyberspace[11] have all become relevant to the maintenance and consolidation of state power, as exemplified by the mainstreaming of terms such as 'technology' and 'cyber' sovereignty.

The EU displays great influence as a norm-setter, especially for what concerns privacy and data protection, although a number of key regulatory principles including the TN and by design principles are normative imports. By contrast, the EU is a weak contributor to standards and a technology follower. Such a reality is painfully depicted in the 2020 Cybersecurity Strategy, with interventions that appear better suited to treat symptoms rather than cure causes. The causes of the hiatus between norm-setting and standards/technology-taking are rooted in dependence on technological systems provided by the market that are far removed from the norms enshrined in primary and secondary legislation and procedures unable to provide corrective measures because they assign the solutions to ... the market. What is more, Brenner notes how states turn to 'corporations as the twenty-first century "nobles" the resources of which nation-states employ to control cyber-threats'.[12]

In sum, the default mode of co-existence of the triad in EU law is weak reconciliation. Some technological applications are even capable of creating zero-sum games, which go undetected due to the effacement of technology from the law. Although overlap is difficult to achieve in light of the conflicting aims of cybersecurity, strong(er) reconciliation between the triad could still be possible if legislation consciously steered the technological choice and development of network and information technologies and cyberspace.[13] Such intervention concerns the entire lifecycle of a technical measure, from its design to its implementation and the applicable law under which the measure operates. The techno-legal analysis discussed in chapter five, which connects the essential components of rights with technological principles, could provide a first approach to operationalise values to embed in technology, to supplement fundamental rights impact assessments and to inform tests for permissible limitations that favour the most protective technologies.[14] But any method ultimately requires making technology 'reappear', by revisiting our legal analytical categories and our way of 'making laws for cyberspace'.[15]

Our way of making laws for cyberspace is possibly broken. The specifics of technology and possible usage are not subsumed under TN concepts such as state of the art, technical measure, organisational measure, content and monitoring; European judges are not put in the position to take responsibility to fill the vacuum and thus the test for permissible limitations, which is tech-agnostic, as are proposals for balancing in the digital

---

[11] MN Schmitt (ed), *The Tallin Manual 2.0 on the International Law Applicable to International Jurisdictions* (Caambridge, Cambridge University Press, 2017), 12.

[12] S Brenner, *Cyberthreats and the Decline of the Nation-state* (London, Routledge, 2014) 162.

[13] For those familiar with the etymological origins of cyberspace from cybernetics, drawn from the Greek kubernētēs 'steersman', the pun is intended.

[14] See also MG Porcedda, Cybersecurity and Privacy Rights in EU Law. Moving Beyond the Trade-off Model to appraise the Role of Technology (European University Institute 2017), ch 8; MG Porcedda, *Privacy by Design in EU law. Matching Privacy Protection Goals with the Essence of the Rights to Private Life and Data Protection* (Lecture Notes in Computer Science, 2018).

[15] Quoting C Reed, *Making Laws for Cyberspace* (Oxford, Oxford University Press, 2012).

age, provides little guidance; and rights are open-ended. What is more, these trends are mutually reinforcing. At the lower level of abstraction, courts do not perform an analysis of the technology involved because the applicable law is silent on that point; at a higher level of abstraction, courts do not provide a clear interpretation of rights, partly because of the 'living instrument' doctrine. While this enables adapting rights to changing times, it creates such a degree of uncertainty that can ultimately seriously undermine the enjoyment and substance of rights, without necessarily increasing the level of cybersecurity. Indeed, against this background, the market has free rein to identify sub-standard solutions that suit the agendas of different communities, whose interests may prevail over the reconciliation of the triad. As the cybersecurity market is notoriously characterised by a high degree of failure, it is unlikely that a solution will be found there, certainly not without remedial action.

What, then? Geopolitical and economic factors and extant technology law approaches affect political willingness and the options available to adopt interim solutions – be they technology-specific law, technological committees or specialised courts – and change the course of action. There is thus plenty of scope for further research to establish whether the triad could, with the right conditions in place, find a different default mode of co-existence, especially in light of upcoming legislation on data flows and streamlining automation.[16]

II. Research Trajectories and the Future of the Triad

To quote Brenner, 'it is much easier to criticize an existing system of [cyber] threat control than it is to develop a viable, effective alternative'.[17] This is especially the case at times of transition. While the search for new constitutional ways to deal with the digital unfold,[18] the pandemic and return of war in Europe may lend support to challenges to the neoliberal order.[19] We may be witnessing the waning of such an order and the waxing of contending alternatives. Some historical depth can help identifying root causes and areas for priority intervention.

The legal recognition of privacy emerged together with the evolution of modern technology in the nineteenth century and authoritarian regimes of the first half of the twentieth century. Both cybersecurity and data protection emerged with computing in the second half of the twentieth century, in a bipolar world order in which the fight over technological innovation was one of the many grounds on which the Cold War was contested. In both cases, the desire to innovate to serve defence, research, trade, or all

---

[16] Eg, European Commission, 'Proposal for a Regulation of the European Parliament and of the Council on contestable and fair markets in the digital sector (Digital Markets Act)' COM(2020) 842 final 2020/0374 (COD); Regulation (EU) 2022/868 of the European Parliament and of the Council of 30 May 2022 on European data governance and amending Regulation (EU) 2018/1724 (Data Governance Act) [2022] OJ L152/1; European Commission, Proposal for a Regulation of the European Parliament and of the Council laying down harmonised rules on Artificial Intelligence (AI Act) and amending certain Union legislative acts COM (2021) 206 final.

[17] Brenner (n 12) 167.

[18] Eg, under the banner of 'code is law' and digital constitutionalism, see ch 5, section IV.

[19] For a pre-pandemic critique of commercialisation: L Newlove-Eriksson et al. 'The Invisible Hand? Critical Information Infrastructures, Commercialisation and National Security' (2018) 53(2) *The International Spectator* 124–140; JE Cohen, Between Truth and Power (Oxford, Oxford University Press, 2019) introduction and ch 7.

of these at once prevailed over precautionary approaches. *'Laissez innover'*,[20] couched for data flows as *'laissez processer'*, has permeated first research, then the market and subsequently legislation. The neoliberal, new managerial turn that ushered in multi-stakeholderism and co-decision-making[21] gave the market an increasingly big say on regulation.

Such processes are deeply embedded in the fabric of EU law. Member States were utterly aware of the promises and challenges inherent in computing and data processing – in addition to longstanding privacy issues – as early as the 1960s. The European Commission pointed to the tech gap affecting Member States and potential interventions in the area,[22] but the times were politically unripe for joint action. Member States were protective of their monopolies and potentially in competition with one another in areas in which they had not given up sovereignty. In the words of former high-level EU official Heinrich Von Moltke, 'one tried to keep the best for oneself, even if it meant collaborating with US or Japanese corporations if necessary'.[23] Ironically, the EU could only become the norm-setter for privacy and data protection after the triumph of neoliberal capitalism, the end of the Cold War, the Treaty of Maastricht and the breaking of telecommunication monopolies. The same cannot be said for cybersecurity, possibly on account of its strong connection to traditional state functions that have not been transferred (yet?) to the EU.

The starting point is to see whether EU law – or any other jurisdiction – can withstand radical shifts, by questioning the goals and investigating the unintended effects of regulatory strategies, such as the effacement of technology from the law.[24] Regulatory strategies originally serving the de-politicisation of technology[25] for the sake of regulating it may now be favouring unbridled technological change instead. Technology neutrality can be made to exploit the law's mandate to be of universal application to serve market interests, interests advanced by the market thanks to its monopoly of innovation. 'Technology effacement' serves innovation, but what is innovation and just how fundamental is it? Is it an end in itself or a trope to evade legal constraints? And if it is the latter, is it worth it? The prioritisation of innovation, combined with the normalisation of technological change, has made it impossible for the law to keep up with the

---

[20] J McDermott, 'A Special Supplement: Technology – the Opiate of the Intellectuals' *The New York Review*.
[21] See generally S Borrás and J Edler (eds), *The Governance of Socio-Technical Systems. Explaining Change* (Cheltenham, Edward Elgar, 2014); H Wallace, MA Pollack et al. (eds), *Policy-making in the European Union* (Oxford, Oxford University Press, 2014).
[22] Council of the European Union, Ministers of the Common Market, 'Resolution of the Science Ministers of the Common Market calling Maréchal group to investigate EU cooperation in 7 fields, including data processing and telecommunications – Luxembourg Resolution (October 1967)'; Commission of the European Communities, 'European Society Faced with the Challenge of Information Technologies: a Community Response', COM (79) 650 final, (1979).
[23] '… on a essayé de garder le meilleur pour soi-même, quitte, le cas échéant, à coopérer avec des firmes japonaises ou américaines.' HV Moltke, *Interview with Moltke, Heinrich Von. The European Commission 1958–1973. Memories of an Institution* (2004).
[24] A similar investigation could be done for the organised and serious crime logics that characterise the approach to the AFSJ.
[25] Nau (n 13); J Kronlund, *Integration Through Depoliticization: How a Common Technology Policy Was Established in the EU* (CORE (Copenhagen Research Project on European Integration) Working Paper, 1995); C Colini and ED Pino, 'National and European Patterns of Public Administration and Governance' in Magone (ed), *Routledge Handbook of European Politics* (London, Routledge 2015).

pace of technology. But even when the law catches up, the market appropriation of law making corrodes the RoL from within. In agreement with Cohen, the law has evolved to meet the new economic demands; Cohen's invitation to consider the need for a RoL 2.0 is compelling.[26] This includes reconsidering 'slower, more atomistic, and more court-centered'[27] approaches.

Against this background, the current application of RoL-based proportionality enriched by the essence of the right may end up damaging rather than protecting rights. How exactly can the essence of the right to data protection be a fail-safe against powerful interests, when it is those powerful interests that determine the threshold for the essence? The example here is that of measures to safeguard the integrity and confidentiality of data, the significance of which is tied to standards. There is, at a minimum, the need to discuss how the essence works in a co-decision environment, whether it is a missed opportunity, and whether it could possibly backfire against rights holders.

This research focussed on the EU law in force at the time of writing. Important legislation affecting data flows and streamlining automation, which will soon enter into force or is in under discussion as part of the EU strategies for cybersecurity, for data and of the digital agendas,[28] may reinforce or alter the dynamics described in these pages, for instance by attributing legal personhood to technology,[29] making the conversation more pressing. The inclusion of the national implementation of EU law, including national case law, could point to a greater protection of rights, thanks to the availability of more tools drawn from Member States' *ordre public*.

Ultimately a change of course would have an impact on much more than the triad. At stake are not just cybersecurity, privacy and data protection, but the survival of democratic orders and the flourishing of human nature as we know it.

---

[26] Cohen (n 19).
[27] ibid, conclusions.
[28] European Commission and High Representative of the European Union for Foreign Affairs and Security Policy, 'The EU's Cybersecurity Strategy for the Digital Decade' (Joint Communication) JOIN (2020) 18 final; European Commission, 'A European Strategy for Data' (Communication) COM (2020) 66 final; European Commission, 'A Europe fit for digital age. Shaping Europe's digital future' (Communication) COM (2020) 67 final; European Commission, '2030 Digital Compass: the European way for the Digital Decade' (Communication) COM (2021) 118 final.
[29] Hildebrandt, M, *Law for Computer Scientists and Other Folk* (Oxford, Oxford University Press 2020), ch 9.

BIBLIOGRAPHY

Policy Documents

Council of Europe

Council of Europe, *Guidelines for the Cooperation between Law Enforcement and Internet Service Providers against Cybercrime*, Adopted by the Global Conference Cooperation against Cybercrime (2008).
——, Committee of Ministers of the Council of Europe, Reply of the Committee of Ministers to Parliamentary Assembly Recommendation 2067 (2015) on Mass Surveillance (CM/AS (2015)Rec2067-final, 2015).
——, The Modernised Convention 108: Novelties in a Nutshell (2018).
——, Division de la Recherche de la Cour Européenne des Droits de l'Homme, *Sécurité Nationale et Jurisprudence de la Cour Européenne des Droits de l'Homme* (2013).
——, European Commission for Democracy through Law (Venice Commission), *Rule of Law Checklist*, Study No 711 / 2013 (2016).
——, European Commission of Human Rights, 'Preparatory Work on Article 8 of the European Convention on Human Rights' www.echr.coe.int/library/COLFRTravauxprep.html.
——, Parliamentary Assembly, *Resolution 2045 (2015) on Mass Surveillance* (2015).
——, European Commission for Democracy through Law (Venice Commission), *Report on the Rule of Law*, Study No 512/2009 (2011).
——, *Update of the 2007 Report on the Democratic Oversight of the Security Services and Report on Democratic Oversight of Signals Intelligence Agencies* (CDL–AD(2015)006, Study N 719/2013 (2015).
Cybercrime Convention Committee (T-CY), *T-CY Guidance Note #2. Botnets. Adopted by the 9th Plenary of the T-CY (4–5 June 2013)* T-CY (2013) 6E Rev.
——, *T-CY Guidance Note #4. Identity Theft and Phishing in relation to Fraud. Adopted by the 9th Plenary of the T-CY (4–5 June 2013)* T-CY (2013) 8E Rev.
——, *T-CY Guidance Note #5. DDOS attacks. Adopted by the 9th Plenary of the T-CY (4–5 June 2013)* T-CY (2013) 10E Rev.
——, *T-CY Guidance Note #11. Aspects of Terrorism covered by the Budapest Convention. Adopted by the 16th Plenary of the T-CY (14–15 November 2016)* T-CY (2016) 11.
——, *T-CY Guidance Note#9. Aspects of election interference by means of computer systems covered by the Budapest Convention. Adopted by the 8th Plenary of the T-CY (8 July 2019)* T-CY(2019) 4.
Jurisconsult of the ECtHR, *Guide on Article 8 of the European Convention on Human Rights. Right to respect for private and family life (last updated 31 December 2020).*

European Union

Article 29 Data Protection Working Party, Opinion 4/2001 On the Council of Europe's Draft Convention on Cyber-crime (WP 41) (2001).
——, Opinion 9/2001 on the Commission Communication on "Creating a safer information society by improving the security of information infrastructures and combating computer-related crime" (2001).

——, Opinion 2/2006 on Privacy Issues related to the Provision of Email Screening Services (00451/06/EN WP 118, 2006).
——, Opinion 4/2007 on the Concept of Personal Data (01248/07/EN WP 136, 2007).
——, Opinion 03/2013 on Purpose Limitation (00569/13/EN WP 203, 2013).
——, Opinion 01/2014 on the Application of Necessity and Proportionality Concepts and Data Protection within the Law Enforcement Sector (536/14/EN WP 211, 2014).
——, Opinion 04/2014 on Surveillance of Electronic Communications for Intelligence and National Security Purposes (819/14/EN WP 215, 2014).
——, Opinion 05/2014 on Anonymisation Techniques (0829/14/EN WP216, 2014).
——, Guidelines on Personal data breach notification under Regulation 2016/679 (WP 250 rev.01 2018).
Article 29 Data Protection Working Party and Working Party on Police and Justice, The Future of Privacy: Joint Contribution to the Consultation of the European Commission on the Legal Framework for the Fundamental Right to Protection of Personal Data (WP 168, 2009).
Bangemann, M et al., The 'Recommendations to the European Council. Europe and the global information society'. The Bangemann Report (1994).
Body of European Regulators for Electronic Communications (BEREC), A Framework for Quality of Service in the scope of Net Neutrality, BoR (11) 53 (2011).
——, Guidelines on the Implementation by National Regulators of European Net Neutrality Rules, BoR (16) 127 (2016).
——, Report on OTT services, BoR (16) 35 (2016).
——, 'Response to the eprivacy Directive questionnaire, BoR(16) 133'.
——, 'Guidelines on the Implementation of the Open Internet Regulation, BoR(20) 112'.
Borrell, JF, Answer given by High Representative/Vice-President Borrell on behalf of the European Commission to Parliamentary questions E-006876/2020 by Moritz Körner on the European Union position as regards cyber sovereignty (2021).
Buttarelli, G, Convention 108: from a European reality to a global treaty (2016).
Commission of the European Communities, 'European Society Faced with the Challenge of Information Technologies: a Community Response' COM (1979) 650 final.
Council, Draft Internal Security Strategy for the European Union: Towards a European Security Model, 5842/2/10 (2010).
——, The Stockholm Programme. An Open and Secure Europe Serving and Protecting Citizens, OJ C 115 (2010).
——, EU Cyber Defence Policy Framework, 15585/14 (2014).
——, Draft Annex Conclusions on the Renewed European Internal Security Strategy 2015–2020, 9797/15 (2015).
——, 'Draft Council Conclusions on a Framework for a Joint EU Diplomatic Response to Malicious Cyber Activities ("Cyber Diplomacy Toolbox")' – Adoption, 9916/17, 7 June 2017.
——, Sanctions Guidelines – update, 5664/18 (2018).
——, Implementation of the Framework for a Joint EU Diplomatic Response to Malicious Cyber Activities. Non-paper on attribution of malicious cyber activities in the context of the framework for a joint EU diplomatic response to malicious cyber activities, 6852/1/19 (2019).
——, Council of the European Union Working Party on Information Exchange and Data Protection (DAPIX), 'Preview Towards the Next Generation Prüm on DNA Data Exchange in the EU' 13511/19 (2019).
——, Council Resolution on Encryption. Security through encryption and security despite encryption (2020).
Council of the European Union, Council Conclusions on Internet Governance, 27 November 2014, 16200/14 (2014).
——, Council Conclusions on implementing the EU global strategy in the area of security and defence, 14.11.2016, 14149/16 (2016).
Council of the European Union, 'Ensuring Protection-EU Human Rights Guidelines on Human Rights Defenders, 2008' (2008) eeas.europa.eu/sites/eeas/files/eu_guidelines_hrd_en.pdf.
——, EU Human Rights Guidelines on Freedom of Expression Online and Offline, Foreign Affairs Council Meeting, 12 May 2014 (2014).
——, Council Conclusions on Cyber Diplomacy, 11 February 2015, 6122/15 (2015).
——, EU Cyber Defence Policy Framework (2018 update) 14413/18 (2018).

——, EU External Cyber Capacity Building Guidelines, 10496/18 (2018).

——, Council Conclusions on EU priorities in UN human rights fora in 2019, 18 February 2019, 6339/19 (2019).

Council of the European Union, Ministers of the Common Market, 'Resolution of the Science Ministers of the Common Market calling Maréchal group to investigate EU cooperation in 7 fields, including data processing and telecommunications – Luxembourg Resolution' (October 1967).

Court of Justice of the European Union, Field of Application of the Charter of Fundamental Rights of the European Union (2021).

Dati, R, (Rapporteur), Draft Report on prevention of radicalisation and recruitment of European citizens by terrorist organisations (2015/2063(INI)) (European Parliament, Committee on Civil Liberties, Justice and Home Affairs, 2015).

European Commission, 'Proposal for a Directive Concerning the Protection of Individuals in Relation to the Processing of Personal Data; Recommendation for a Council Decision on the Opening of Negotiations With a View to the Accession of the European Communities to the Council of Europe Convention for the Protection of Individuals With Regard to the Automatic Processing of Personal Data; Commission Communication on the Protection of Individuals in Relation to the Processing of Personal Data in the Community and Information Security' (Communication) COM (90) 314 final.

——, 'White Paper on Growth, Competitiveness, Employment. The Challenges and Ways forward into the 21st Century' (Communication) COM (93) 700.

——, 'Creating a Safer Information Society by Improving the Security of Information Infrastructures and Combating Computer-Related Crime' (Communication) COM (2000) 890 final.

——, 'Network and Information Security: Proposal for a European Policy Approach' (Communication) COM (2001) 298.

——, 'A Comprehensive Approach on Personal Data Protection in the European Union' (Communication) COM (2010) 609 final.

——, 'Delivering an Area of Freedom, Security and Justice for Europe's citizens – Action Plan Implementing the Stockholm Programme' (Communication) COM (2010) 171 final.

——, 'Annexes to the Communication "A new EU Framework to strengthen the Rule of Law"' (Communication) COM (2014) 158 final.

——, 'Commission implementing decision C(2015) 102 final of 20.1.2015 on a standardisation request to the European standardisation organisations as regards European standards and European standardisation deliverables for privacy and personal data protection management pursuant to Article 10(1) of Regulation (EU) No 1025/2012 of the European Parliament and of the Council in support of Directive 95/46/EC of the European Parliament and of the Council and in support of Union's security industrial policy. Mandate M/530'.

——, 'A New EU Framework to Strengthen the Rule of Law' (Communication) COM (2014) 158 final.

——, 'A Digital Single Market Strategy for Europe' (Communication) COM (2015) 192 final.

——, 'The European Agenda on Security' (Communication) COM (2015) 185 final.

——, 'ICT Standardisation Priorities for the Digital Single Market' (Communication) COM (2016) 0176 final.

——, 'Report from the Commission to the European Parliament and the Council assessing the implementation of the measures referred to in Article 25 of Directive 2011/93/EU of 13 December 2011 on combating the sexual abuse and sexual exploitation of children and child pornography' (Communication) COM (2016) 872 final.

——, 'Strengthening Europe's Cyber Resilience System' (Communication) COM (2016) 640 final.

——, 'Assessment of the EU 2013 Cybersecurity Strategy' (Staff Working Document) SWD (2017) 295 final.

——, 'Building a European Data Economy' (Communication) COM (2017) 9 final.

——, 'Mid-Term Review on the implementation of the Digital Single Market Strategy. A Connected Digital Single Market for All' (Communication) COM (2017) 228 final (Staff Working Document) SWD (2017) 155 final.

——, 'Report from the Commission assessing the extent to which the Member States have taken the necessary measures in order to comply with Directive 2013/40/EU on attacks against information systems and replacing Council Framework Decision 2005/222/JHA' (Communication) COM (2017) 0474 final.

——, 'Report on the evaluation of the European Union Agency for Network and Information Security (ENISA)' (Communication) COM (2017) 0478 final.
——, 'Artificial intelligence for Europe' (Communication) COM (2018) 237 final.
——, 'Evaluation of Council Directive 85/374/EEC of 25 July 1985 on the approximation of the laws, regulations and administrative provisions of the Member States concerning liability for defective products' (Staff Working Document) SWD (2018) 157 final.
——, 'FinTech Action plan: For a more competitive and innovative European financial sector' (Commission) COM (2018) 109 final.
——, 'Liability for emerging digital technologies' (Staff Working Document) SWD (2018) 137 final.
——, 'Liability of defective products accompanying the document "Communication Artificial intelligence for Europe COM(2018) 237 final"' (Staff Working Document) SWD (2018) 137 final.
——, 'Recommendation for a Council Decision authorising the participation in negotiations on a second Additional Protocol to the Council of Europe Convention on Cybercrime (CETS No. 185)' (Communication) COM (2019) 71 final.
——, 'Proposal for a Directive of the European Parliament and of the Council on the resilience of critical entities' (Communication) COM (2020) 829 final.
——, 'A European Strategy for Data' (Communication) COM (2020) 66 final.
——, '2020 EU Strategy for a more effective fight against child sexual abuse' (Communication) COM (2020) 607 final.
——, 'EU Security Union Strategy' (Communication) COM (2020) 605 final.
——, 'A Europe fit for digital age. Shaping Europe's digital future' (Communication) COM (2020) 67 final.
——, 'Guidance on practical aspects of the implementation of Regulation (EU) No. 1025/2012 – Results of the consultation of stakeholders'.
——, 'On the European democracy action plan' (Communication) COM (2020) 790 final.
——, 'Way forward on aligning the former third pillar acquis with data protection rules' (Communication) COM (2020) 262 final.
——, '2030 Digital Compass: the European way for the Digital Decade' (Communication) COM (2021) 118 final.
——, 'Better Regulation Toolbox' (2021).
——, 'Protecting Fundamental Rights in the Digital Age' (Communication) COM (2021) 819 final.
——, 'Report from the Commission on the evaluation of Regulation (EU) No 910/2014 on electronic identification and trust services for electronic transactions in the internal market (eIDAS)' (Staff Working Document) SWD (2021)130 final.
——, 'Proposal for a Regulation on horizontal cybersecurity requirements for products with digital elements and amending Regulation (EU) 2019/1020 (Cyber Resilience Act)' (Communication) COM (2022) 454 final.
——, 'Proposal for a Directive on liability for Defective Products' (Communication) COM (2022) 495 final.
European Commission and High Representative of the European Union for Foreign Affairs and Security Policy, 'Cyber Security Strategy: An Open, Safe and Secure Cyberspace' (Joint Communication) JOIN (2013) 01 final.
——, 'Countering Hybrid Threats' (Joint Communication) JOIN (2016) 18 final.
——, 'Resilience, Deterrence and Defence: Building strong cybersecurity for the EU' (Joint Communication) JOIN (2017) 450 final.
——, 'EU Action Plan on Human Rights and Democracy 2020-2024' (Joint Communication) JOIN (2020) 5 final.
——, 'The EU's Cybersecurity Strategy for the Digital Decade' (Joint Communication) JOIN (2020) 18 final.
European Council, Report on the Implementation of the European Security Strategy – Providing Security in a Changing World (European Security Strategy) S407/08.
——, Meeting Conclusions, 18 October 2018. Draft Council conclusions on cybersecurity capability and cyber capacity building in the EU, 15244/1/18.
European Cyber Security Organisation, State of the Art Syllabus, Overview of existing Cybersecurity standards and certification schemes v2 (2017).
European Data Protection Board, 'Opinion 23/2018 of the EDPB on Commission proposals on European production and preservation orders for electronic evidence in criminal matters' (Art. 70.1.b) (2018).

——, Guidelines 2/2019 on the processing of personal data under Article 6(1)(b) GDPR in the context of the provision of online services to data subjects, v 2.0 (2019).
——, Guidelines 3/2018 on the territorial scope of the GDPR (Article 3), v 2.1 (2019).
——, Letter to BEREC. Data protection issues in the context of Regulation (EU) 2015/2120, OUT2019-0055, 3 December (2019).
——, Guidelines 3/2019 on processing of personal data through video devices (2020).
——, Guidelines 4/2019 on Article 25. Data Protection by Design and by Default, v 2.0 (2020).
——, Guidelines 04/2020 on the use of location data and contact tracing tools in the context of the COVID-19 outbreak (2020).
——, Guidelines 1/21 on Examples regarding Data Breaches, v1.0 (2021).
——, Guidelines 07/2020 on the concepts of controller and processor in the GDPR (2021).
——, Recommendations 01/2021 on the adequacy referential under the Law Enforcement Directive (2021).
——, Guidelines 01/2022 on data subject rights – Right of access v. 1.0 (2022).
European Data Protection Supervisor, Data Protection and Cloud Computing under EU Law, Speech by P Hustinx (2010).
——, 'Latest Developments in Data Protection' Speech by G Buttrelli at the meeting of the Heads of Agencies, Stockholm (19 October 2012).
——, Prior Checking Opinion regarding Restrictive Measures (Sanctions) of the European External Action Service (EEAS) (2014/0926) (2014).
——, Opinion 8/2015. Dissemination and use of intrusive surveillance technologies (2015).
——, Opinion on Net Neutrality, Traffic Management and the Protection of Privacy and Personal Data (OJ C 34, 1–17, 2011).
——, 'Opinion 5/2018. Preliminary Opinion on privacy by design' (2018).
——, Opinion 7/2019 on Proposals regarding European Production and Preservation Orders for electronic evidence in criminal matters (2019).
——, 'Opinion 5/2021 on the Cybersecurity Strategy and the NIS 2.0 Directive 6722/21' (2021).
European Parliament, LIBE Committee Inquiry on the Electronic Mass Surveillance of EU Citizens: Protecting fundamental Rights in a Digital Age. Proceedings, Outcome and Background Documents (2014).
——, Resolution on the US NSA Surveillance Programme, Surveillance Bodies in Various Member States and their Impact on EU Citizens' Fundamental Rights and on Transatlantic Cooperation in Justice and Home Affairs (2013/2188 (INI)) 2014 OJ C378/104.
——, European Parliament Resolution of 4 July 2017 on European standards for the 21st century (2016/2274(INI)) [2017] OJ C 334/2.
——, Resolution of 3 October 2017 on the fight against cybercrime (2017/2068(INI)) [2018] OJ C 346/04.
——, European Parliament Resolution of 25 November 2020 on addressing product safety in the single market (2019/2190(INI)) [2021] OJ 425/04.
European Parliament, LIBE Committee, Statement by Professor Martin Scheinin (Hearing within the Inquiry on Electronic Mass Surveillance of EU Citizens, 2013).
European Parliament, LIBE Secretariat, Background Note. The European Parliament's temporary committee on the ECHELON interception system (2014).
European Union Agency for Cybersecurity (ENISA), Actionable information for security incident response (2015).
——, ENISA 2014 Standards and tools for exchange and processing of actionable information (2015).
——, Guideline on assessing security measures in the context of Article 3(3) of the Open Internet Regulation (2018).
Europol, 'Internet Organised Crime Threat Assessment (IOCTA) 2019'.
——, 'Internet Organised Crime Threat Assessment (IOCTA) 2020'.
Fundamental Rights Agency, Using indicators to measure fundamental rights in the EU: challenges and solutions (2nd Annual FRA Symposium Report, 2011).
——, Surveillance by intelligence services: fundamental rights safeguards and remedies in the EU. Mapping Member States' legal frameworks (Publications Office of the European Union, 2015).
——, Ensuring Justice for Hate Crime Victims: Professional Perspectives (2016).
Hustinx, P (EDPS), Data Protection and Cloud Computing under EU Law (2010).
Reding, V, The Review of the EU Data Protection Framework, SPEECH/11/183 (2011).

———, The EU's data protection rules and cyber security strategy: two sides of the same coin. Speech before the NATO Parliamentary Assembly/Luxembourg, SPEECH/13/436 (2013).

United Nations

Cannataci, J, Right to privacy. Report of the Special Rapporteur on the right to privacy. A/HRC/40/63 (2019).
Committee on Economic, Social and Cultural Rights, *The Maastricht Guidelines on Violations of Economic, Social and Cultural Rights*. Background paper submitted by the International Commission of Jurists. E/C.12/2000/13.
Scheinin, M, Report of the Special Rapporteur on the Promotion and Protection of Human Rights and Fundamental Freedoms while Countering Terrorism, A/HRC/13/37 (2009).
Scheinin Martin, *Written testimony related to the surveillance program conducted under Section 702 of the FISA Amendments Act, LIBE Committee Inquiry on the investigation into the electronic mass surveillance of EU citizens* (2014), https://www.europarl.europa.eu/doceo/document/A-7-2014-0139_EN.html#_part2_def1.
United Nations, Economic and Social Council, Commission on Human Rights Drafting Committee. International Bill of Rights (E/CN4/AC1/3/ADD1 Part 1, 1947).
———, General Assembly, Declaration on Principles of International Law Friendly Relations and Co-Operation Among States in Accordance with the Charter of the United Nations (1970).
———, Report of the Group of Governmental Experts (GGE) on Developments in the Field of Information and Telecommunications in the Context of International Security A/68/98 (2013).
———, Report of the Group of Governmental Experts (GGE) on Developments in the Field of Information and Telecommunications in the Context of International Security, A/70/174 (2015).
———, Group of Governmental Experts on Developments in the Field of Information and Telecommunications in the Context of International Security A/72/327 (2017).
———, Open-ended Working Group on developments in the field of information and telecommunications in the context of international security. Final substantive Report, A/AC.290/2021/CRP.2 (2021).
———, Resolution 'The right to Privacy in the Digital Age', A/RES/68/167 (2013).
———, High Commissioner for Human Rights (OHCHR), Human Rights Indicators. A Guide to Measurement and Implementation (HR/PUB/12/5, 2012).
———, Human Rights Committee, Comments of the Human Rights Committee: United Kingdom of Great Britain and Northern Ireland (CCPR/C/79/Add 55, 1979).
———, International Human Rights Instruments, Report on Indicators for Monitoring Compliance with International Human Rights Instruments (HRI/MC/2006/7, 2006).
———, Office on Drug and Crime (UNODC), The Use of Internet for Terrorist Purposes (2012).
———, Comprehensive Study on Cybercrime (UNODC/CCPCJ/EG4/2013/3, 2013).
———, 'Vienna Declaration and Programme of Action adopted by World Conference on Human Rights in Vienna'.
———, Secretary General, The Rule of Law and Transitional Justice in Conflict and Post-conflict Societies. Report of the Secretary-General to the Security Council (S/2004/616, 2004).

Other Policy Sources

Irish Data Protection Commission, *Regulatory Strategy 2021–2026* (2021).
Commission Nationale de l'Informatique et des Libertés (CNIL), 'Délibération 2015-078 du 5 mars 2015 portant avis sur un projet de la loi relatif au reinsegnement'.
Independent International Fact-Finding Mission on the Conflict in Georgia, 'Report – Volume II'.
Information Commissioner's Office, *Investigation into the use of data analytics in political campaigns. A report to Parliament* (2018).
———, 'Update report into adtech and real time bidding'.
International Conference of Data Protection and Privacy Commissioners, *Joint Proposal for a Draft of International Standards on the Protection of Privacy with regard to the processing of Personal Data (The Madrid Resolution)* (30th International Conference of Data Protection and Privacy Commissioners 2009).

OECD, *Gaps in Technology, Analytical Report* (1970).
——, *OECD Digital Economy Outlook 2020* (2020).
White House, *International Strategy for Cyberspace. Prosperity, Security, and Openness in a Networked World* (2011).
Witness Statement of Erik King in Privacy International and Bytes for All v Secretary of State for Foreign and Commonwealth Affairs and Others (2015), https://www.privacyinternational.org/sites/default/files/2019-08/2015.01.19%20Eric%20King%20Witness%20statement.pdf.

Literature

Abelson, H and others, *Bugs in our Pockets: The Risks of Client-Side Scanning* (2021).
Abelson, H and others, 'Keys Under Doormats: Mandating Insecurity by Requiring Government Access to all Data and Communications' (2015) 0 *Journal of Cybersecurity* 1–11.
Adams, S and others, *The Governance of Cybersecurity: A Comparative Quick Scan of Approaches in Canada, Estonia, Germany, the Netherlands and the UK* (Tilburg, Tilburg University, 2015).
Aiken, M, *The Cyber Effect* (London, John Murray, 2016).
Akdeniz, Y, 'Media Freedom on the Internet: an OSCE Guidebook' (OSCE, 2016).
Alexy, R, *Theorie der Grundrechte* (Suhrkamp Verlag; Auflage, 1986).
——, 'Constitutional Rights and Legal Systems' in N Joakim (ed), *Constitutionalism – New Challenges: European Law from a Nordic Perspective* (Boston, Brill, 2008).
——, 'Mart Susi's Internet Balancing Formula' 25 *European Law Journal* 213–220.
Anderson, R, *Security Engineering. A Guide to Building Dependable Distributed Systems*, 2nd edn (New York, Wiley, 2011).
——, *Security Engineering. A Guide to Building Dependable Distributed Systems*, 3rd edn (New York, Wiley, 2020).
Anderson, R and Murdoch, SJ, 'Tools and Technology of Internet Filtering', in R Deibert, J Palfrey, R Rohozinski, and J Zittrain (eds), *Access Denied: The Practice and Policy of Global Internet Filtering* (Cambridge, MA, MIT Press, 2008).
Andrade, N, 'The Right to Personal Identity in the Information Age. A Reappraisal of a Lost Right' (PhD thesis, European University Institute 2011).
Angelini, F, *Ordine pubblico e integrazione costituzionale europea. I princìpi fondamentali nelle relazioni interordinamentali* (Cedam 2007).
Aplin, T, 'Trading Data in the Digital Economy: Trade Secrets Perspective' in L Stefan, S Reiner and S Dirk (eds), *Trading Data in the Digital Economy: Legal Concepts and Tools* (Oxford, Hart Publishing, 2017).
——, '"United Kingdom"' in B Lindner and T Shapiro (eds), *Copyright in the Information Society: A Guide to National Implementation of the EU Directive*, 2nd edn (Cheltenham, Edward Elgar, 2019).
Arendt, H, 'Freedom and Politics: a Lecture' (1960) 14 *Chicago Review* 28–46.
——, *The Human Condition*, 2nd edn (Chicago, The University of Chicago Press, 1998).
Bagnasco, A, Barbagli, M and Cavalli, A, *Sociologia, Cultura e Società. I concetti di base* (Il Mulino, 2001).
Baldwin, R, Cave, M and Lodge, M, *Understanding Regulation. Theory, Strategy and Practice (Second Edition)* (Oxford, Oxford University Press, 2011).
Bendiek, A and Schulze, M, *Attribution: A Major Challenge for EU Cyber Sanctions* (SWP Research Paper, 2021).
Bendiek, A, Bossong, R and Schulze, M, *The EU's Revised Cybersecurity Strategy. Half-Hearted Progress on Far-Reaching Challenges* (SWP Comments, 2017).
Bendrath, R, 'Global Technology Trends and National Regulation: Explaining Variation in the Governance of Deep Packet Inspection' (International Studies Annual Convention, New York City, 15–18 February 2009).
Bendrath, R and others, 'Governing the Internet: The Quest for Legitimate and Effective Rules', in H Achim and others (eds), *Transforming the Golden-Age Nation State* (Basingstoke, Palgrave, 2007).
Bendrath, R and Mueller, M, 'The End of the Net as We Know it? Deep Packet Inspection and Internet Governance' (2011) 13 *New Media and Society* 1142.
Bennett, C and Raab, C, *The Governance of Privacy. Policy Instruments in a Global Perspective* (Cambridge, MIT Press, 2006).

Bennett, ML, 'How to Think about Law, Regulation and Technology: Problems with 'Technology' as a Regulatory Target' (2013) 5 *Law, Innovation and Technology* 7.
——, 'Regulating in the Face of Socio-Technical Change', in R Brownsword, E Scotford and K Yeung (eds), *The Oxford Handbook of the Law and Regulation of Technology* (Oxford, Oxford University Press, 2017).
Berlee, A, Mak, V and Tjong, TTE, *Research Handbook on Data Science and Law* (Cheltenham, Edward Elgar, 2018).
Berners-Lee, T, 'No Snooping' www.w3.org/DesignIssues/NoSnooping.html.
Bieker, F and others, *A Process for Data Protection Impact Assessment under the European General Data Protection Regulation* (Cham, Springer, 2016).
Black, E, *IBM and the Holocaust: The Strategic Alliance between Nazi Germany and America's Most Powerful Corporation* (US, Dialog Press 2012).
Black, J, 'Critical Reflections on Regulation' (2002) 27 *Australian Journal of Legal Philosophy*.
Blair, J, *The International Covenant on Civil and Political Rights and its (First) Optional Protocol. A Short Commentary based on Views, General Comments and Concluding Observations by the Human Rights Committee* (Frankfurt, Peter Lang, 2005).
Bobbio, N, *L'Età dei Diritti* (Einaudi, 1997).
Boehme-Neßler, V, 'Privacy: a Matter of Democracy. Why Democracy Needs Privacy and Data Protection' (2016) 6 *International Data Privacy Law* 222–229.
Borrás, S and Edler, J (eds), *The Governance of Socio-Technical Systems. Explaining Change* (Cheltenham, Edward Elgar, 2014).
Borrus, M and Zysman, J, 'Industrial Competitiveness and American National Security', in W Sandholtz and others (eds), *The Highest Stakes. The Economic Foundations of the Next Security System* (Oxford, Oxford University Press, 1992).
Bourka, A and others, *Recommendations on Shaping Technology According to GDPR Provisions. Exploring the Notion of Data Protection by Default* (ENISA, 2019).
Bourreau, M and others, *The Future of Broadband Policy, Part 2: Technological Neutrality, Path Dependency And Public Financing* (Robert Schuman Centre for Advanced Studies (RSCAS) 2017).
Bradford, A, 'The Brussels Effect' (2020) 107 *Northwestern University Law Review*.
Bradley, C and Stringhini, G, *A Qualitative Evaluation of Two Different Law Enforcement Approaches on Dark Net Markets* (IEEE, 2019).
Bremer, ES, 'Government Use of Standards in the United States and Abroad', in JL Contreras (ed), *The Cambridge Handbook of Technical Standardisation Law* (Cambridge, Cambridge University Press, 2019).
Brenner, S, 'Is There Such a Thing as 'Virtual Crime'?' (2001) 4 *California Criminal Law Review*.
——, 'The Council of Europe's Convention', in JM Balkin et al (eds), *Cybercrime, Digital Cops in a Networked Environment* (New York, New York University Press, 2007).
——, *Cyberthreats and the Decline of the Nation-state* (London, Routledge, 2014).
Brenner, S and Koops, B-J (eds), *Cybercrime and Jurisdiction. A Global Survey* (The Hague, TMC Asser Press, 2006).
Brkan, M, *In Search of the Concept of Essence of EU Fundamental Rights Through the Prism of Data Privacy* (Maastricht Working Papers, Faculty of Law 2017-01, 2017).
——, 'The Concept of Essence of Fundamental Rights in the EU Legal Order: Peeling the Onion to its Core' (2018) 14 *European Constitutional Law Review*.
Burdon, M, Lane, B and von Nessen, P, 'Data Breach Notification Law in the EU and Australia. Where to Now?' (2012) 28 *Computer Law & Security Review* 296–307.
Buzan, B, Weaver, O and Wilde, JD, *Security: a New Framework for Analysis* (Boulder, CO, Lynne Rienner, 1998).
Bygrave, LA, *Data Privacy Law. An International Perspective* (Oxford, Oxford University Press, 2014).
——, 'The 'Strasbourg Effect' on Data Protection in Light of the 'Brussels Effect': Logic, Mechanics and Prospects' (2021) 40 *Computer Law & Security Review*.
Calderoni, F, 'The European Legal Framework on Cybercrime: Striving for an Effective Implementation' (2010) 54 *Crime, Law and Social Change* 339–357.
Candler, J, et al, *Human Rights Measurement Framework: Prototype Panels, Indicator Set and Evidence Base* (Equality and Human Rights Commission, 2011).
Cannataci, J (ed), *The Individual and Privacy: Volume I* (London, Routledge, 2015).

278 Bibliography

Carr–Chellman, A and Carr-Chellman, D, 'Special Issue: Technology Neutrality, Ethics, Values, and Human Social Systems' (2012) 52 *Educational Technology*.

Carrapico, H and Barrinha, A, 'The EU as a Coherent (Cyber)Security Actor?' (2017) 55 *Journal of Common Market Studies* 1254, 1272.

Carrera, S and Guild, E, *The European Council's Guidelines for the Area of Freedom, Security and Justice 2020: Subverting the 'Lisbonisation' of Justice and Home Affairs?* (CEPS Essay no. 13/14, 2014).

Cassese, A, *International Law*, 2nd edn (Oxford, Oxford University Press, 2005).

Cave, M and Shortall, T, 'How Incumbents can Shape Technological Choice and Market Structure – The Case of Fixed Broadband in Europe' (2016) 18(2) *Info* 1–16.

Cavoukian, A, *Privacy by Design … Take the Challenge* (2009).

Cayford, M, *Paper on Mass Surveillance by the National Security Agency (NSA) of the United States of America. Extract from SURVEILLE Project Deliverable D2.8* (2014).

Cayford, M, et al., *Consolidated Survey of Surveillance Technologies, SURVEILLE Project Deliverable D2.9* (2015).

Celeste, E, 'Digital Constitutionalism. A New Systematic Theorisation' (2019) 33 *International Review of Law, Computers & Technology* 76–99.

Chalmers, D, Davies, G and Monti, G, *European Union Law*, 4th edn (Cambridge, Cambridge University Press, 2019).

Chandler, JA, 'The Autonomy of Technology: Do Courts Control Technology or Do They Just Legitimize its Social Acceptance?' (2007) 27 *Bulletin of Science, Technology and Society* 339–348.

Christou, G, *Cybersecurity in the European Union. Resilience and Adaptability in Governance and Policy* (Basingstoke, Palgrave Macmillan, 2015).

Churchman, CW, 'Wicked problems' (2014) 14 *Management Science*, Guest Editorial.

Clarke, R, 'The Digital Persona and its Application to Surveillance' (1994) 10 *The Information Society*.

——, 'Introducing PITs and PETs: Technologies Affecting Privacy' Privacy Law & Policy Reporter, www.rogerclarke.com/DV/PITsPETs.html.

——, *Deep Packet Inspection: its nature and implications* (www.rogerclarke.com, 2009).

Clinton, W, 'A Framework for Global Electronic Commerce', in B Fitzgerald (ed), *Cyberlaw* (Farnham, Ashgate, 2006) clintonwhitehouse4.archives.gov/WH/New/Commerce/read.html or www.w3.org/TR/NOTE-framework-970706.

Clough, B, 'A World of Difference: The Budapest Convention on Cybercrime and the Challenges of Harmonisation' (2014) 40 *Monash University Law Review*.

Clough, J, *Principles of Cybercrime* (Cambridge, Cambridge University Press, 2010).

Cohen, JE, 'What Privacy is For' (2013) 126 *Harvard Law Review* 1094.

——, *Between Truth and Power* (Oxford, Oxford University Press, 2019).

Colini, C and Pino, ED, 'National and European Patterns of Public Administration and Governance', in JM Magone (ed), *Routledge Handbook of European Politics* (London, Routledge, 2015).

Collingridge, D, *The Social Control of Technology* (Pinter, 1980).

Connolly, L and Wall, DS, 'The rise of crypto-ransomware in a Changing Cybercrime Landscape: Taxonomising Countermeasures' (2019) 87 *Computers and Security*.

Contreras, JL (ed), *The Cambridge Handbook of Technical Standardisation Law* (Cambridge, Cambridge University Press, 2019).

Craig, P, *The Lisbon Treaty, Revised Edition: Law, Politics, and Treaty Reform* (Oxford, Oxford University Press 2013).

Craig, P and de Búrca, G, *European Union Law: Text, Cases and Materials* (Oxford, Oxford University Press, 2015).

Cremona, M, 'The Union as a Global Actor: Roles, Models and Identity' (2004) 41 *Common Market Law Review* 553–573.

——, *External Relations of the EU and the Member States: Competence, Mixed Agreements, International Responsibility, and Effects of International Law* (European University Institute Working Paper LAW 2006/22, 2006).

——, 'The EU and Global Emergencies: Competence and Instruments', in A Antoniadis, R Schutze and E Spaventa (eds), *The European Union and Global Emergencies: A Law and Policy Analysis* (Oxford, Hart Publishing, 2011).

——, 'Values in EU Foreign Policy', in P Koutrakos and M Shaw (eds), *Beyond the Established Orders. Policy Interconnections between the EU and the Rest of the World* (Oxford, Hart Publishing, 2011).
——, 'The Two (or Three) Treaty Solution: The New Treaty Structure of the EU', in A Biondi, P Eeckhout and S Ripley (eds), *European Union Law After the Treaty of Lisbon* (Oxford, Oxford University Press, 2012).
——, 'Who Can Make Treaties? The European Union', in D Hollis (ed), *The Oxford Guide to Treaties*, 2nd edn (Oxford, Oxford University Press, 2020).
——, 'A Triple Braid: Interactions between International Law, EU Law and Private Law', in M Cremona and H-W Micklitz (eds), *Private Law in the External Relation of the EU* (Oxford, Oxford University Press, 2016).
——, 'The Position of CFSP/CSDP in the EU's Constitutional Architecture', in S Blockmans and P Koutrakos (eds), *Research Handbook on the EU's Common Foreign and Security Policy* (Cheltenham, Edward Elgar, 2018).
——, 'Extending the Reach of EU Law: the EU as an International Legal Actor' in M Cremona and J Scott (eds), *EU Law Beyond EU Borders* (Oxford, Oxford University Press, 2019).
Cremona, M and Micklitz, H-W (eds), *Private Law in the External Relation of the EU* (Oxford, Oxford University Press, 2016).
Cremona, M, Monar, J and Poli, S (eds), *The External Dimension of the European Union's Area of Freedom, Security and Justice* (Brussels, Presses Interuniversitaires Europeennee, 2011).
Cremona, M and Scott, J (eds), *EU Law beyond EU borders* (Oxford, Oxford University Press, 2019).
Curtin, D, *Executive Power in the European Union* (Oxford, Oxford University Press, 2009).
Curtin, D and Dekker, IF, 'The European Union from Maastricht to Lisbon', in P Craig and G de Bùrca (eds), *The Evolution of EU Law* (Oxford, Oxford University Press, 2011).
Daly, A, 'The Legality of Deep Packet Inspection' (First Interdisciplinary Workshop on Communications Policy and Regulation 'Communications and Competition Law and Policy – Challenges of the New Decade').
Dambrine, B, *The State of French Surveillance Law (White Paper)* (2015).
Danezis, G et al., *Privacy and Data Protection by Design – from Policy to Engineering* (ENISA, 2014).
Dawson, M, Lynskey, O and Muir E (eds) 'Special issue: Interrogating the Essence of EU Fundamental Rights' 20 (2019) 6 *German Law Journal*.
De Hert, P, 'A Human Rights Perspective on Privacy and Data Protection Impact Assessments', in P De Hert and D Wright (eds), *Privacy Impact Assessment*, vol 6 (Dordrecht, Springer, 2012).
——, 'Data Protection as Bundles of Principles, General Rights, Concrete Substantive Rights and Rules. Piercing the Veil of Stability Surrounding the Principles of Data Protection (Foreword)' (2017) 2(3) *European Data Protection Law Review* 160–179.
De Hert, P and Gutwirth, S, 'Data Protection in the Case Law of Strasbourg and Luxembourg: Constitutionalism in Action', in S Gutwirth, Y Poullet, P De Hert, S Nouwt and C de Terwangne (eds), *Reinventing Data Protection?* (New York, Springer, 2009).
De Hert, P and Wright, D, *Privacy Impact Assessment*, vol 6 (Dordrecht, Springer, 2012).
Del Sesto, RW, Jr., and Frankel, J, 'How Deep Packet Inspection Changed the Privacy Debate', dpi.priv.gc.ca/.
Delrue, F, Kulesza, J and Pawlak, P, *The Application of International Law in Cyberspace: is There a European Way?* (Policy in Focus, 2019).
DeNardis, L, 'A History of Internet Security', in K de Leeuw and J Bergstra (eds), *The History of Information Security* (Oxford, Elsevier Science, 2007).
——, 'The Internet Design Tension between Surveillance and Security' (2015) 37 *IEEE Annals of the History of Computing* 72–83.
Diffie, W and Landau, S, 'Internet Eavesdropping: A Brave New World of Wiretapping' (2008) 299 *Scientific American Magazine* 4.
Dijk, P van, 'Article 8', in P van Dijk, F van Hoof and A van Rijn (ed), *Theory and Practice of the European Convention on Human Rights*, 4th edn (Cambridge, Intersentia 2006).
Donohue, LK, *The Cost of Counterterrorism. Power, Politics and Liberty* (Cambridge, Cambridge University Press, 2008).
Dragicevic, D, Kaspersen, H and Sherwa, J, *Conditions and Safeguards under the Budapest Convention on Cybercrime, Discussion Paper, EU/COE Joint Project on Regional Cooperation against Cybercrime* (Council of Europe, 2012).

Drewer, D and Ellermann, J, 'Europol's Data Protection Framework as an Asset in the Fight against Cybercrime' (Joint ERA-Europol conference Making Europe Safer: Europol at the Heart of European Security, The Hague, 18–19 June 2012).

Dumortier, F et al., 'La Protection des Données dans l'Espace Européen de Liberté, de Sécurité et de Justice' (2009) 166 *Journal de Droit Européen* 23.

Dunn Cavelty, M, 'Breaking the Cyber-Security Dilemma: Aligning Security Needs and Removing Vulnerabilities' (2014) 20 *Science and Engineering Ethics* 701–715.

——, 'From Cyber-Bombs to Political Fallout: Threat Representations with an Impact in the Cyber-Security Discourse' (2013) 15 *International Studies Review* 105.

Dunn, M, 'Securing the Digital Age. The Challenges of Complexity for Critical Infrastructure Protection and IR Theory' in J Eriksson and G Giacomello (eds), *International Relations in the Digital Age* (London, Routledge, 2007).

Dyzenhaus, D, 'States of Emergency', in M Rosenfeld and A Sajó (eds), *The Oxford Handbook of Comparative Constitutional Law* (Oxford, Oxford Handbooks Online, 2012).

E Silva, K, 'Europe's Fragmented Approach Towards Cyber Security' (2013) 2 *Internet Policy Review Journal on Internet Regulation*.

Edwards, L, '"With Great Power Comes Great Responsibility?": The Rise of Platform Liability', in L Edwards (ed), *Law, Policy and the Internet* (Oxford, Hart Publishing, 2018).

—— (ed), *Law, Policy and the Internet* (Oxford, Hart Publishing, 2018).

Edwards, L, Brown, I and Marsden, C, 'Information Security and Cybercrime', in L Edwards and C Waelde (eds), *Law and the Internet*, 3rd edn (Oxford, Hart Publishing, 2009).

Edwards, L and Waelde, C, *Law and the Internet* (Oxford, Hart Publishing, 2009).

Eichensehr, KE, 'Public-Private Cybersecurity' (2017) 95 *Texas Law Review* 467–538.

Eriksson, J and Giacomello, G (eds), *International Relations in the Digital Age* (London, Routledge, 2007).

Erlbacher, 'Article 215 TFEU', in M Kellerbauer, M Klamert and J Tomkin (eds), *The EU Treaties and the Charter of Fundamental Rights: a Commentary* (Oxford, Oxford University Press, 2019).

European Digital Rights (EDRI), *The Spanish Police Might use Spying Trojans on Individuals' Computers* (EDRI-gram newsletter, no. 11.12 2013).

——, *US Agencies Have Unlimited Access to Internet Data* (EDRI-gram newsletter, no. 11.12 2013).

——, *What Digital Rights Are at Imminent Risk? All of Them* (EDRi-gram newsletter no. 14.17 2016).

European Union Network of Independent Experts on Fundamental Rights, *Commentary of the Charter of Fundamental Rights of The European Union* (2006).

Fahey, E, 'The EU's Cybercrime and Cyber-Security Rulemaking: Mapping the Internal and External Dimension of EU Security' (2014) 5 *European Journal of Risk and Regulation* 46–60.

Finn, RL, Wright, D and Friedewald, M, 'Seven Types of Privacy', in S Gutwirth, R Leenes, P de Hert and Y Poullet (eds), *European Data Protection: Coming of Age* (Dordrecht, Springer, 2013).

Flanagan, A, 'The Law and Computer Crime: Reading the Script of Reform' (2005) 13 *International Journal of Law and Information Technology* 98.

Flanagan, A and Walden, I, 'Honeypots: a Sticky Legal Landscape?' (2009) 29 *Rutgers Computer and Technology Law Journal* 317.

Flear, M, 'Regulating New Technologies: EU Internal Market Law, Risk and Socio-technical Order', in M Cremona (ed) *New Technologies and EU Law* (Oxford University Press 2017).

Frediani, C, *Cybercrime. Attacchi Globali, Conseguenze Locali* (Milan, Hoepli, 2017).

Freedom House, *Freedom of the Net 2019. The Crisis of Social Media* (2019).

Galli, F and Weyembergh, A (eds), *EU Counter-terrorism Offences. What Impact on National Legislation and Case Law?* (Editions de l'Université de Bruxelles, 2012).

Geiger, C and Jütte Bend, J, 'Platform Liability Under Art. 17 of the Copyright in the Digital Single Market Directive, Automated Filtering and Fundamental Rights: An Impossible Match' (2021) 70 *GRUR International Journal of European and International IP Law* 517–543.

Gellert, R, 'Data Protection: A Risk Regulation? Between the Risk Management of Everything and the Precautionary Alternative' (2015) 5 *International Data Privacy Law* 3–19.

——, *The Risk-Based Approach to Data Protection* (Oxford, Oxford University Press, 2020).

——, 'Comparing Definitions of Data and Information in Data Protection Law and Machine Learning. A Useful Way Forward to Meaningfully Regulate Algorithms?' (2022) 16(1) *Regulation & Governance* 156–176.

Bibliography 281

Gercke, M, *Understanding Cybercrime: Phenomena, Challenges and Legal Response* (International Telecommunication Union, Geneva, 2012).

Ghernaouti, S, 'The Cyber Security Continuum to Enhance Cyber Resilience', in International Telecommunication Union (ed), *The Quest for Cyber Confidence* (International Telecommunications Union, 2014).

Giacomello, G, *National Governments and Control of the Internet. A Digital Challenge* (London, Routledge, 2005).

Gillespie, AA, *Cybercrime: Key Issues and Debates* (London, Routledge, 2019).

Global Alliance Partners, *Guiding Principles on The Global Alliance Against Child Sexual Abuse Online. Annex To the Declaration on Launching the Global Alliance Against Child Sexual Abuse Online* (2012).

González Fuster, G, *The Emergence of Personal Data Protection as a Fundamental Right in Europe* (Cham, Springer, 2014).

González Fuster, G and Gellert, R, 'The Fundamental Right of Data Protection in the European Union: In Search of an Uncharted Right' (2013) 26 *International Review of Law, Computers & Technology* 73–82.

González Fuster, G and Gutwirth, S, 'Opening Up Personal Data Protection: A Conceptual Controversy' (2013) 29 *Computer Law & Security Review* 531–539.

González Fuster, G and Jasmontaite, L, 'Cybersecurity Regulation in the European Union: The Digital, the Critical and Fundamental Rights', in M Christen (ed), *The Ethics of Cybersecurity* (Cham, Springer, 2020).

González Fuster, G et al., *Discussion Paper on Legal Approaches to Security, Privacy and Personal Data Protection*, PRISMS Project, Deliverable 5.1 (2013).

Goodwin, M, Koops, B- and Leenes, R, *Dimensions of Technology Regulation* (Nymegen, Wolf Legal Publishers, 2010).

Grabowski, M, 'Are Technical Difficulties at the Supreme Court Causing a "Disregard of Duty"?' [2011] *Journal of Law, Technology & Internet* 93–112.

Gravosto, A, 'Le Telecomunicazioni in Europa: Governance e Regulation', in F Passarelli (ed), *Unione Europea: Governance e Regolamentazione* (Il Mulino, 2006).

Greenberg, BA, 'Rethinking Technology Neutrality' (2016) 100 *Minnesota Law Review* 1495–1562.

Grief, N, 'EU Law and Security' (2007) 32 *European Law Review* 752–765.

Guinchard, A, 'The Computer Misuse Act 1990 to Support Vulnerability Research? Proposal for a Defence for Hacking as a Strategy in the Fight Against Cybercrime' (2017) 2 *Journal of Information Rights, Policy and Practice*.

Guitton, C, 'Criminals and Cyber Attacks: The Missing Link between Attribution and Deterrence' (2012) 6 *International Journal of Cyber Criminology* 1030–1043.

Gutwirth, S and Gellert, R, 'The Legal Construction of Privacy and Data Protection' (2013) 29 *Computer Law & Security Review* 522–530.

Hallinan, D, *Protecting Genetic Privacy in Biobanking through Data Protection Law* (Oxford, Oxford University Press, 2021).

Hallinan, D et, al, 'Neurodata and Neuroprivacy: Data Protection Outdated?' (2014) 12 *Surveillance & Society* 55–72.

Herrmann, D and Pridöhl, H, 'Basic Concepts and Models of Cybersecurity', in M Christen (ed), *The Ethics of Cybersecurity* (Cham, Springer, 2020).

Herron, P, 'Beyond Balance: Targeted Sanctions, Security and Republican Freedom', in E Orrù, MG Porcedda and S Volkmann-Weydner (eds), *Rethinking Surveillance and Control. Beyond the Security Versus Privacy Debate* (Baden-Baden, Nomos, 2017).

Hijmans, H, *European Union as Guardian of Internet Privacy: The Story of Art 16 TFEU* (Cham, Springer, 2016).

Hijmans, H and Scirocco, A, 'Shortcomings in EU Data Protection in the Third and the Second Pillars. Can the Lisbon Treaty be Expected to Help?' (2009) 46 *Common Market Law Review* 1485–1525.

Hildebrandt, M, *Law for Computer Scientists and Other Folk* (Oxford, Oxford University Press, 2020).

Hildebrandt, M and Tielemans, L, 'Data Protection by Design and Technology Neutral Law' (2013) 29 *Computer Law & Security Review* 509–521.

Hillion, C, 'Decentralised Integration? Fundamental Rights Protection in the EU Common Foreign and Security Policy' (2016) 1 *European Papers – A Journal on Law and Integration*.

Hinarejos, A, 'Law and Order and Internal Security Provisions in the Area of Freedom, Security and Justice: Before and fter Lisbon', in C Eckes and T Konstadinides (eds), *Crime within the Area of Freedom, Security and Justice: a European Public Order* (Cambridge, Cambridge University Press, 2011).

Hoepman, J-H, *Privacy by Design Strategies (The Little Blue Book)* (2022).
Holt, TJ, Smirnova, O and Chua, YT, *Data Thieves in Action: Examining the International Market for Stolen Personal Information and Cybercrime* (Basingstoke, Palgrave MacMillan, 2016).
Hosein, G and Eriksson, J, 'International Politics Dynamics and the Regulation of Dataflows. Bypassing Domestic Restrictions', in J Eriksson and G Giacomello (eds), *International Relations in the Digital Age* (London, Routledge, 2007).
Hunter, D, 'Cyberspace as Place and the Tragedy of the Digital Anticommons' (2003) 91 *California Law Review*.
Hunton, P, 'Data Attack of the Cybercriminal: Investigating The Digital Currency of Cybercrime' (2012) 28 *Computer Law & Security Review* 201–207.
Hustinx P, 'EU data protection law: the review of Directive 95/46/EC and the General Data Protection Regulation' in Cremona Marise (ed), *New Technologies and EU Law* (Oxford University Press 2017).
Hutchings, A and Holt, TJ, 'A Crime Script Analysis of the Online Stolen Data Market' (2015) 55 *British Journal of Criminology* 596–614.
——, 'The Online Stolen Data Market: Disruption and Intervention Approaches' (2017) 18 *Global Crime* 11–30.
Hutchins, E, Cloppert, M and Amin, R, *Intelligence-Driven Computer Network Defense Informed by Analysis of Adversary Campaigns and Intrusion Kill Chains* (Lockheed Martin, 2011).
Huysman, J, *The Politics of Insecurity* (London, Routledge, 2006).
Isenberg, D, 'The Dawn of the 'Stupid Network'' (1998) 2 netWorker 24.
IT Security Association of Germany (TeleTrust) and European Agency for Cybersecurity (ENISA), *IT Security Act (Germany) and EU Data Protection Regulation: Guidelines on 'State of the Art'. Technical and Organisational Measures* (2021).
Jakub, P, *Russia's war on Ukraine: Timeline of cyber-attacks* (2022).
Jasmontaite, L, and others *CANVAS – Constructing an Alliance for Value-driven Cybersecurity, White paper* (2020).
Jenkins, D, 'Introduction. The Long Decade', in D Jenkins, A Jacobsen and A Henrikens (eds), *The Long Decade: How 9/11 Changed the Law* (Oxford, Oxford University Press, 2014).
Jenkins, D, Jacobsen, A and Henrikens, A (eds), *The Long Decade: How 9/11 Changed the Law* (Oxford, Oxford University Press, 2014).
Kamara, I, 'Co-regulation in EU Personal Data Protection: The Case of Technical Standards and the Privacy by Design Standardisation 'Mandate'' (2017) 8 *European Journal of Law and Technology*.
Kaspersen, H, 'Jurisdiction in the Cybercrime Convention', in B-J Koops and S Brenner (eds), *Cybercrime and Jurisdiction: a Global Survey* (The Hague, TMC Asser, 2006).
Kilovati, I, 'Privatized Cybersecurity Law' (2020) 10 *UC Irvine Law Review*.
Kilpatrick, C, 'On the Rule of Law and Economic Emergency: The Degradation of Basic Legal Values in Europe's Bailouts' (2015) 35 *Oxford Journal of Legal Studies*.
Kim, NS, 'Online Contracting: Causes and Cures', in JA Rothchild (ed), *Research Handbook on Electronic Commerce Law* (Cheltenham, Edward Elgar Publishing, 2016).
Kingsbury, B, Krish, N and Stewart, RB, 'The Emergence of Global Administrative Law' (2005) 68 *Law and Contemporary Problems* 15–61.
Klimburg, A et al., *Synergies Between the Civilian and the Defence Cybersecurity Markets. Study for the European Commission's DG Communications Networks, Content and Technology* (Publications Office of the EU, 2016).
Klimburg, A and Tiirmaa-Klaar, H, *Cybersecurity and Cyberpower: Concepts, Conditions and Capabilities for Cooperation for Action within the EU* (Think Tank, European Parliament, 2011).
Kohl, U, 'The Rise and Rise of Online Intermediaries in the Governance of the Internet and Beyond – Connectivity Intermediaries' (2012) 26 *International Review of Law, Computers & Technology*.
——, 'Google: The Rise and Rise of Online Intermediaries in the Governance of the Internet and Beyond (Part 2)' (2013) 21 *International Journal of Law and Information Technology* 187–234.
Kohl, U and Fox, C, 'Internet Governance and the Resilience of the Nation State', in U Kohl (ed), *The Net and the Nation State Multidisciplinary perspectives on Internet Governance* (Cambridge, Cambridge University Press, 2017).

Bibliography 283

Kokott, J and Sobotta, C, 'The Distinction between Privacy and Data Protection in the Jurisprudence of the CJEU and the ECtHR' (2013) 3 *International Data Privacy Law* 222–228.

Koops, B-J, 'Should ICT Regulation be Technology Neutral?', in B-J Koops et al. (eds), *Starting Points for ICT Regulation* (The Hague, TMC Asser Press, 2005).

Koops, B-J and Kosta, E, 'Looking for Some Light Through the Lens of "Cryptowar" History: Policy Options for Law Enforcement Authorities Against "Going Dark"' (2018) 34 *Computer Law & Security Review*.

Koops, B-J and Leenes, R, 'Privacy Regulation Cannot be Hardcoded. A Critical Comment on the 'Privacy by Design' Provision in Data-Protection Law' (2014) 28 *International Review of Law, Computers & Technology* 151–171.

Koops, B-J et al., *Starting Points for ICT Regulation* (The Hague, TMC Asser Press 2005).

Kopp, C et al., 'The Role of Love Stories in Romance Scams: A Qualitative Analysis of Fraudulent Profiles' (2015) 9 *International Journal of Cyber Criminology* 205–217.

Kosta, E, 'Peeking into the Cookie Jar: The European Approach towards the Regulation of Cookies' (2013) 21 *International journal of law and information technology* 380–406.

Kranenborg, H, 'Access to Documents and Data Protection in European Union: on the Public Nature of Personal Data' (2008) 45 *Common Market Law Review* 1079–1114.

Kronlund, J, *Integration Through Depoliticization: How a Common Technology Policy was Established in the EU*. (CORE (Copenhagen Research Project on European Integration) Working Paper, 1995).

Kulesza, J, *International Internet Law* (London, Routledge, 2012).

Kuhen, A, and Mueller, M, 'Einstein on the Breach: Surveillance Technology, Cybersecurity and Organizational Change', in G Giacomello (ed), *Security in Cyberspace. Targeting Nations, Infrastructures, Individuals* (London, Bloomsbury, 2014).

Kulka, S and Zuiderveen, BF, 'Filtering for Copyright Enforcement in Europe after the Sabam Cases' (2012) 11 *European Intellectual Property Review* 54.

Kuner, C, 'The Internet and the Global Reach of EU Law', in M Cremona and J Scott (eds), *EU Law Beyond EU Borders* (Oxford, Oxford University Press, 2019).

Landau, S, *Surveillance or Security? The Risk Posed by New Wiretapping Technologies* (Cambridge, MA, MIT Press, 2010).

——, *Listening In. Cybersecurity in an Insecure Age* (New Haven, Yale University Press, 2017).

Lanier, J, *Who Owns the Future?* (London, Penguin Books, 2013).

Lavorgna, A and Sergi, A, "Serious', Therefore Organised? A Critique of the Emerging "Cyber-Organised Crime" Rhetoric in the United Kingdom' (2016) 10 *International Journal of Cyber Criminology* 1–23.

Leenes, R, 'Who Controls the Cloud?' (2010) 11 *Revista de Internet, Derecho y Política*.

——, 'Framing techno-regulation: an Exploration of State and Non-state Regulation by Technology' (2011) 5 *Legisprudence*.

Lembke, J, *Competition for Technological Leadership* (Cheltenham, Edward Elgar, 2002).

Lenaerts, K, 'The Contribution of the European Court of Justice to the Area of Freedom, Security and Justice' (2010) 59 *International and Comparative Law Quarterly* 255.

Lessig, L, *Code: And Other Laws of Cyberspace. Version 2.0* (New York, Basic Books, 2006).

——, The Law of the Horse: What Cyberlaw Might Teach 113 (1999) *Harvard Law Review* 501–549.

Leukfeldt, R, Lavorgna, A and Kleemans, ER, 'Organised Cybercrime or Cybercrime that is Organised? An Assessment of the Conceptualisation of Financial Cybercrime as Organised Crime' (2017) 23 *European Journal on Criminal Policy and Research* 287–300.

Levi, M and Wall, DS, 'Technology, Security and Privacy in Post-9/11 European Information Society' (2004) 31 *Journal of Law and Society*.

Lock, T, 'Article 7 CFR', in M Kellerbauer, M Klamert and J Tomkin (eds), *The EU Treaties and the Charter of Fundamental Rights: A Commentary* (Oxford, Oxford University Press, 2019).

——, 'Article 8 CFR' in M Kellerbauer, M Klamert and J Tomkin (eds), *The EU Treaties and the Charter of Fundamental Rights: A Commentary* (Oxford, Oxford University Press, 2019).

Lundqvist, B, 'Public Law, European Constitutionalism and Copyright in Standards', in JL Contreras (ed), *The Cambridge Handbook of Technical Standardisation Law* (Cambridge, Cambridge University Press, 2019).

Lynskey, O, *The foundations of EU Data Protection Law* (Oxford, Oxford University Press, 2015).

Maes, G and Ascensao, G, *Presentation 'Drafting standards for citation in OJEU'* (CEN and CENELEC, 2019).

Malone, EF and Malone, MJ, 'The "Wicked Problem" of Cybersecurity Policy: Analysis of United States and Canadian Policy Response' (2016) 19 *Canadian Foreign Policy Journal* 158–177.

Mankiw, G, *Principles of Economics*, 7th edn (Mason, OH, Cengage Learning 2013).
Marczak, B, Dalek J et al, *Bad Traffic. Sandvine's PacketLogic Devices Used to Deploy Government Spyware in Turkey and Redirect Egyptian Users to Affiliate Ads?* (Tspace, 2018).
Markatos, E and Balzarotti, D (eds), *The Red Book. A Roadmap for Systems Security Research* (The SysSec Consortium: A European Network of Excellence in Managing Threats and Vulnerabilities in the Future Internet: Europe for the World, 2013).
Marsden, C, Meyer, T and Brown, I, 'Platform Values and Democratic Elections: How can the Law Regulate Digital Disinformation?' (2020) 36 *Computer Law & Security Review*.
Marsden, C, 'Internet Service Providers. Content, Control and Neutrality (chapter 15)' in I Walden (ed), *Telecommunications Law and Regulation*, 4th edn (Oxford, Oxford University Press, 2012).
Mashaw, J and Harfst, DL, 'From Command and Control to Collaboration and Deference: The Transformation of Auto Safety Regulation' (2017) 34 *Yale Journal on Regulation* 167–278.
Mattioli, R, 'The 'State(s)' of Cybersecurity', in G Giacomello (ed), *Security in Cyberspace* (London, Bloomsbury, 2014).
Maxwell, W and Bourreau, M, *Technology Neutrality in Internet, Telecoms and Data Protection Regulation* (Global Media and Communications Quarterly, 2014).
McDermott, J, 'A Special Supplement: Technology – the opiate of the intellectuals', *The New York Review* (1969).
McIntyre, TJ, 'Child Abuse and Cleanfeeds: Assessing Internet Blocking Systems', in I Brown (ed), *Research Handbook on Governance of the Internet* (Cheltenham, Edward Elgar, 2013).
McKay, S, et al., *Reforming the Computer Misuse Act 1990* (2020).
Micklitz Hans-W, *La Mano Visibile del Diritto Privato Europeo in Materia Normativa – La Trasformazione del Diritto Privato Europeo dall'autonomia al Funzionalismo nella Concorrenza e nella Regolamentazione* (European University Institute, 2010).
——, 'The Internal Versus External dimension of European Private Law: a Conceptual Design and a Research Agenda', in M Cremona and H-W Micklitz (eds), *Private Law in the External Relation of the EU* (Oxford, Oxford University Press, 2016).
Micklitz, H-W and Tridimas, T (eds), *Risk and EU Law* (Cheltenham, Edward Elgar Publishing, 2015).
Milward, A, *European Rescue of the Nation State* (London, Taylor and Francis, 1999).
Moltke, H Von, *Interview with Moltke, Heinrich Von. The European Commission 1958–1973. Memories of an institution* (2004).
Moore, T, 'The Economics of Cybersecurity: Principles and Policy Options' (2010) 3 *International Journal of Critical Infrastructure Protection* 103–117.
Morsink, J, *The Universal Declaration of Human Rights: Origins, Drafting and Intent* (Pennsylvania, University of Pennsylvania Press, 1999).
Moss, K, *Balancing Liberty and Security. Human Rights, Human Wrongs* (Basingstoke, Palgrave Macmillan, 2011).
Mueller, M, *DPI Technology from the Standpoint of Internet Governance Studies: an Introduction (v1.1). The Network is Aware* (Syracuse University School of Information Studies, 2011).
Mueller, M, Kuehn, A and Santoso, SM, 'Policing the Network: Using DPI for Copyright Enforcement' (2012) 9 *Surveillance & Society* 348.
Mueller, RR (special Counsel), *Report On the Investigation into Russian Interference in the 2016 Presidential Election. Submitted Pursuant to 28 C.F.R. § 600.8(c)* (2019).
Mulligan, DK and Bamberger, KA, 'Saving Governance-by-Design' (2018) 106 *California Law Review* 697–784.
Mura, V, *Categorie della Politica. Elementi per una Teoria Generale* (Giappichelli Editore, 2004).
Murphy, RF, 'Social Distance and the Veil' (1964) 66 *American Anthropologist* 1257–1274.
Murray, A, 'Internet Regulation', in D Levi-Faur (ed), *Handbook on the Politics of Regulation* (Cheltenham, Edward Elgar, 2013).
——, *Information Technology Law. Law and Society*, 4th edn (Oxford, Oxford University Press, 2019).
Musotto, R and Wall, DS, 'Are Booter Services (Stressers) Indicative of a New Form of Organised Crime Group Online?' (UNODC Linking Organized Crime and Cybercrime Conference).
Nau, H, *National Politics and International Technology* (Johns Hopkins University Press, 1974).
Newlove-Eriksson, L et al. 'The Invisible Hand? Critical Information Infrastructures, Commercialisation and National Security' (2018) 53(2) *The International Spectator* 124–140.
Ni, LN, *EU Data Privacy Law and Serious Crime. Data Retention and Policymaking* (Oxford, Oxford University Press, 2021).

Nissenbaum, H, 'When Computer Security meets National Security', in JM Balkin (ed), *Cybercrime, Digital Cops in a Networked Environment* (New York, New York University Press, 2007).

Nissenbaum, H and Hansen, L, 'Digital Disaster, Cyber Security, and the Copenhagen School' (2009) 53 *International Studies Quarterly* 1155.

Nowak, M, 'Chapter on Article 17', in N Manfred and F Ermacora (eds), *UN Covenant on Civil and Political Rights, CCPR Commentary*, 4th edn (N.P. Engel, 2005).

O' Doherty M, *Internet Law* (Dublin, Bloomsbury 2020).

Ohm, P, *The Rise and Fall of Invasive ISP Surveillance*, Working Paper no. 8-22 (University of Colorado Law School, 2008).

Ojanen, T, 'Privacy Is More Than Just a Seven-Letter Word: The Court of Justice of the European Union Sets Constitutional Limits on Mass Surveillance. Case Note on Court of Justice of the European Union, Decision of 8 April 2014 in Joined Cases C-293/12 and C-594/12, Digital Rights Ireland and Seitlinger and Others' (2014) 10 *European Constitutional Law Review* 528–541.

Olster, J, 'Code is Code and Law is Law – the Law of Digitalization and the Digitalization of Law' (2021) 29 *International Journal of Law and Information Technology* 101–117.

Orrù, E, 'Minimum Harm by Design: Reworking Privacy by Design to Mitigate the Risks of Surveillance', in R Leenes et al (eds), *Data Protection and Privacy: (In)visibilities and Infrastructures* (Cham, Springer, 2017).

Ottis, R and Lorents, P, 'Cyberspace: Definitions and Implications' (Proceedings of the 5th International Conference on Information Warfare and Security, ICIW).

Pagallo, U, 'On the Principle of Privacy by Design and its Limits', in S Gutwirth et al (eds), *European Data Protection: in Good Health?* (Cham, Springer, 2012).

Pawlak, P, *Operational Guidance for the EU's International Cooperation on Cyber Capacity Building* (European Union Institute for Security Studies, 2018).

——, *Operational Guidance for the EU's International Cooperation on Cyber Capacity Building. A Playbook (Task Force for Cyber Capacity Building)* (European Union Institute for Security Studies, 2018).

Pawlak, P and Barmpaliou, P-N, 'Politics of Cybersecurity Capacity Building: Conundrum and Opportunity' (2017) 2 *Journal of Cyber Policy* 123–144.

Pech, L, *The Rule of Law as a Constitutional Principle of the European Union* (Jean Monnet Working Paper Series, New York University School of Law, 2009).

——, *Rule of law as a Guiding Principle of the European Union's External Action* (CLEER Working Papers, Centre for the Law of EU External Relations, TMC Asser Instituut Inter-university Research Centre, 2013).

Peers, S, *EU Justice and Home Affairs Law* (Oxford, Oxford University Press, 2011).

Peng, S-yi, "Private' Cybersecurity Standards? Cyberspace Governance, Multistakeholderism and the (ir)relevace of the TBT Regime' (2018) 15 *Cornell International Law Journal*.

Perdisci, R, Corona, I and Giacinto, G, 'Early Detection of Malicious Flux Networks via Large-Scale Passive DNS Traffic Analysis' (2012) 9 *IEEE Transactions on Dependable and Secure Computing* 714–726.

Peters, S, *The Chimp Paradox. The Mind Management Programme for Confidence, Success and Happiness* (London, Vermilion, 2012).

Pikos, LF, 'Packet Analysis for Network Forensics: A Comprehensive Survey' (2020) 32 *Forensic Science International: Digital Investigation* 1–12.

Piris, J-C, *The Lisbon Treaty. A Legal and Political Analysis* (Cambridge, Cambridge University Press, 2010).

Poldrack, R, 'Neuroscience: The Risks of Reading the Brain' (2014) 541 *Nature*.

Poli, S and Tzanou, M, 'The Kadi Rulings: A Survey of the Literature', in M Cremona, F Francioni and S Poli (eds), *Challenging the EU Counter-terrorism Measures through the Courts*, vol AEL 2009/10 (European University Institute Working Papers, 2009).

Porcedda, MG, 'Transatlantic Approaches to Cyber-security: the EU-US Working Group on Cyber-security and Cybercrime', in P Pawlak (ed), *The EU-US Security and Justice Agenda in Action*, vol No127 – 30 December 2011 (European Union Institute of Security Studies 2011) www.iss.europa.eu/publications/detail/article/the-eu-us-security-and-justice-agenda-in-action/.

——, *Data Protection and the Prevention of Cybercrime: the EU as an Area of Security?* (European University Institute Working Paper, Law 2012/25, 2012).

——, 'Lessons from PRISM and Tempora: the Self-contradictory Nature of the Fight against Cyberspace Crimes. Deep packet Inspection as a Case Study' (2013) 25 *Neue Kriminalpolitik* 305–409.

——, 'Public-Private Partnerships: A 'Soft' Approach to Cybersecurity? Views from the European Union' in G Giampiero (ed), *Security in Cyberspace: Targeting Nations, Infrastructures, Individuals* (London, Continuum Books, Bloomsbury Publishing, 2014).

——, 'Cybersecurity and Privacy Rights in EU Law. Moving Beyond the Trade-off Model to Appraise the Role of Technology' (PhD Thesis, European University Institute, 2017).

——, 'The Recrudescence of 'Security v. Privacy' after the 2015 Terrorist Attacks, and the Value of 'Privacy Rights' in the European Union', in E Orrù, MG Porcedda and S Volkmann-Weydner (eds), *Rethinking Surveillance and Control Beyond the "Security versus Privacy" Debate* (Baden-Baden, Nomos, 2017).

——, *Use of the Charter of Fundamental Rights by National Data Protection Authorities and the EDPS* (Robert Schuman Centre for Advanced Studies Working Paper, 2017).

——, *On Boundaries. In Search for the Essence of the Right to the Protection of Personal Data* (Oxford, Hart Publishing, 2018).

——, 'Patching the Patchwork: Appraising the EU Regulatory Framework on Cyber Security Breaches' (2018) 34 *Computer Law & Security Review*.

——, *Privacy by Design in EU law. Matching Privacy Protection Goals with the Essence of the Rights to Private Life and Data Protection* (Lecture Notes in Computer Science, 2018).

——, 'Regulation of Data Breaches in the European Union: Private Companies in the Driver's Seat of Cybersecurity?', in H Carrapico and O Bures (eds), *Security Privatization. How Non-security-related Private Businesses Shape Security Governance* (Cham, Springer, 2018).

——, 'Brexit, Cybercrime and Cyber Security. From en masse opt-out to Creative opt-in in the AFSJ and Beyond?', in H Carrapico, A Niehuss and C Berthelemy (eds), *Brexit and Internal Security. Political and Legal Concerns in the Context of the Future UK-EU Relationship* (Basingstoke, Palgrave Macmillan, 2019).

——, 'Sentencing Data-Driven Cybercrime. How Data Crime with Cascading Effects is Tackled by UK Courts' (2023) 48 *Computer Law and Security Review*.

Porcedda, MG, Vermeulen, M and Scheinin, M, *Report on Regulatory Frameworks Concerning Privacy and the Evolution of the Norm of the Right to Privacy. Deliverable 3.2, SurPRISE Project* (European University Institute, 2013).

Porcedda, MG and Wall, D, *The Chain and Cascade Effects in Cybercrime: Lessons from the TalkTalk Case Study* (IEEE, 2019).

——, 'Data Crime, Data Science and The Law', in V Mak, E Tjon Tjin Tai and A Berlee (eds), *Research Handbook on Data Science & Law* (Cheltenham, Edward Elgar, 2018).

——, 'Modelling the Cybercrime Cascade Effect in Data Crime' (3rd Workshop on Attackers and Cyber-Crime Operations (WACCO), held Jointly with IEEE EuroS&P, 2021).

Posner, E and Vermeule, A, *Terror in the Balance. Security, Liberty and the Courts* (Oxford, Oxford University Press, 2007).

Poullet, Y and Rouvroy, A, 'The Right to Informational Self-determination and the Value of Self-development. Reassessing the Importance of Privacy for Democracy', in S Gutwirth et al (eds), *Reinventing Data Protection?* (New York, Springer Verlag, 2009).

PricewaterhouseCoopers, 'Conti Cyber-attack on the HSE. Independent Post Incident Review' (2021).

Prosser, W, 'Privacy' (1960) 48 *California Law Review* 383–423.

Pugliese, G, 'Appunti per una Storia della Protezione dei Diritti Umani' (1989) 43 *Rivista Trimestrale di Diritto e Procedura Civile* 619–659.

Purtova, N, 'The Law of Everything. Broad Concept of Personal Data and Future of EU Data Protection Law' (2018) 10 *Law, Innovation and Technology* 40–81.

Rachovitsa, A, 'Engineering and Lawyering Privacy by Design: Understanding Online Privacy Both as a Technical and an International Human Right Issues' (2016) 24 *International Journal of Law and Information Technology* 374–399.

Rainey, S, et al, 'Brain Recording, Mind-Reading, and Neurotechnology: Ethical Issues from Consumer Devices to Brain-Based Speech Decoding' (2020) 26 *Science and Engineering Ethics* 2295–2311.

Ramopoulos, T, 'Article 29 TEU', in M Kellerbauer, M Klamert and J Tomkin (ed), *The EU Treaties and the Charter of Fundamental Rights: a Commentary* (Oxford, Oxford University Press, 2019).

Reed, C, 'Taking Sides on Technology Neutrality' (2007) 4 *Script-ed*.

——, *Making Laws for Cyberspace* (Oxford, Oxford University Press, 2012).

Rehof, LA, 'The Universal Declaration of Human Rights: A Commentary', in AEG Alfredsson, G Melander, LA Rehof and A Rosas, with the collaboration of T Swinehart, (ed), (Scandinavian University Press, 1992).

——, 'Universal Declaration of Human Rights – Common Standard of Achievement'. in A Eide and G Alfredsson (eds), (Zuidpoolsingel, Kluwer Law International, 1999).

Rehrl, J, *Handbook on Cybersecurity. The Common Security and Defence Policy in the European Union* (Federal Ministry of Defence of the Republic of Austria, 2018).
Reiman, JH, 'Privacy, Intimacy and Personhood', in FD Schoeman (ed), *Philosophical Dimensions of Privacy: an Anthology* (Cambridge, Cambridge University Press, 1984).
Renda, A, 'Quali Nuove Regole per la 'Information Superhighway' Europea?' in F Passarelli (ed), *Unione Europea: Governance e Regolamentazione* (Il Mulino, 2006).
Rieß-Marchive, V, *Vectra Networks veut Détecter les Signaux Faibles sur le Réseau* (2015).
Rodotà, S, *Elaboratori Elettronici e Controllo Sociale* (Mulino 1973).
——, 'Data Protection as a Fundamental Right', in S Gutwirth, Y Poullet, P De Hert, S Nouwt and C de Terwangne (eds), *In Reinventing Data Protection?* (New York, Springer, 2009).
——, *Il Diritto ad Avere Diritti*, vol Bari (Editori Laterza, 2012).
Romero, F, 'Antifascismo e Ordine Internazionale', in A De Bernardi and P Ferrari (eds), *Antifascismo e Identità Europea* (Carocci, 2004).
Rosario, M and Schimdt, S, 'Standardisation in the European Community', in C Freeman, M Sharp and W Walker (eds), *Technology and the Future of Europe. Global Competition and the Environment in the 1980s* (London, Cengage Learning, 1992).
Rosas, A and Armati, L, *EU Constitutional Law – An Introduction* (Oxford, Hart Publishing, 2010).
Sahakian, BJ and Gottwald, J, *Sex, Lies, and Brain Scans: How fMRI Reveals What Really Goes on in our Minds* (Oxford, Oxford University Press, 2017).
Sales, NA, 'Privatizing Cybersecurity' (2018) 65 *UCLA Law Review* 620.
Saltzer, JH and Schroeder, MD, 'The Protection of Information in Computer Systems' (1975) 63 *Proceedings of the IEEE* 1278–1308.
Sartor, G, 'Liabilities of Internet users and Providers' in M Cremona (ed), *New Technologies and EU Law* (Oxfod, Oxford University Press, 2017).
Savin, A, *EU Internet Law* (Cheltenham, Edward Elgar, 2013).
——, *EU Telecommunications Law* (Cheltenham, Edward Elgar, 2018).
Schaake, M, et al., *Software Vulnerability Disclosure in Europe. Technology, Policies and Legal Challenges. Report of a CEPS Task Force* (Centre for European Policy Studies (CEPS) 2018).
Schartum, DW, 'Making Privacy by Design Operative' (2016) 24 *International Journal of Law and Information Technology* 151–175.
Scheinin, M, *Terrorism and the Pull of 'Balancing' in the Name of Security. Law and Security, Facing the Dilemmas* (European University Institute Law Working Paper 11, 2009).
Schmitt, MN (ed), *The Tallin Manual 2.0 on the International Law Applicable to International Jurisdictions* (Cambridge, Cambridge University Press, 2017).
Schneier, B, *Beyond Fear: Thinking Sensibly about Security in an Uncertain World* (New York, Springer, 2003).
Shackelford, SJ, 'Should Cybersecurity Be a Human Right? Exploring the 'Shared Responsibility' of Cyber Peace' (2017) 55 *Stanford Journal of International Law* 155–184.
Shackelford, SJ, S Russell and J Haut, 'Bottoms up: A Comparison of Voluntary Cybersecurity Frameworks' (2020) 16 *UC Davis Business Law Journal* 217–260.
Sicilianos, L-A et al., *Respecting Human Rights and the Rule of Law when Using Automated Technology to Detect Online Child Sexual Exploitation and Abuse. Independent Experts Report* (Council of Europe, 2021).
Simitis, S, 'Privacy – An Endless Debate' (2010) 98 *California Law Review*.
Škorvánek, I, Koops B-J et al., '"My Computer Is My Castle": New Privacy Frameworks to Regulate Police Hacking' [2020] *Brigham Young University Law Review* 997–1082.
Smismans, S, 'Democratic Participation and The Search For an Institutional Architecture that Accommodates Interests and Expertise', in S Piattoni (ed), *The European Union Democratic Principles and Institutional Architectures in Times of Crisis* (Oxford, Oxford University Press, 2015).
——, 'Constitutionalising Expertise in the EU: Anchoring Knowledge in Democracy' in J Priban (ed), *The Self-Constitution of Europe* (Leiden, Brill, 2016).
Smismans, S and Minto, R, 'Are Integrated Impact Assessments the Way Forward for Mainstreaming in The European Union?' (2017) 11 *Regulation & Governance* 231–251.
Smith, RE, 'A Contemporary Look at Saltzer and Schroeder's 1975 Design Principles' (2012) 10 *IEEE Security & Privacy* 20–25.

Solove, D, 'I've Got Nothing to Hide' and Other Misunderstandings of Privacy' (2007) 44 *San Diego Law Review* 745.

——, *Nothing to Hide: the False Tradeoff Between Privacy and Security* (New Haven, Yale University Press, 2011).

Song, W et al., 'A Software Deep Packet Inspection System for Network Traffic Analysis and Anomaly Detection' (2020) 20 *Sensors*.

Spaventa, E, 'Counter-Terrorism and Fundamental Rights: Judicial Challenges and Legislative Changes after the Rulings in Kadi and PMOI', in A Antoniadis, R Schutze and E Spaventa (eds), *The European Union and Global Emergencies: A Law and Policy Analysis* (Oxford, Hart Publishing, 2011).

Stalla-Bourdillon, S, Papadaki, E and Chown, T, 'From Porn to Cybersecurity Passing by Copyright: How Mass Surveillance Technologies are Gaining Legitimacy ... The Case of Deep Packet Inspection Technologies' (2014) 30(6) *Computer Law & Security Review* 670–686.

Summers, S, et al., *The Emergence of EU Criminal Law. Cybercrime and the Regulation of the Information Society* (Oxford, Hart Publishing, 2014).

Susi, M, 'The Internet Balancing Formula' (2019) 25 *European Law Journal* 198–212.

Tanenbaum, AS and Wetherall, DJ, *Reti di Calcolatori (Quinta Edizione)* (Milan, Pearson Italia, 2011).

Taylor, C, *Sources of the Self. The Making of the Modern Identity* (Cambridge, Cambridge University Press, 1989).

——, *The Ethics of Authenticity* (Cambridge, MA, Harvard University Press, 1992).

Taylor, L, Floridi, L and Van der Sloot, B (eds), *Group Privacy: New Challenges of Data Technologies* (Cham, Springer, 2017).

Timmermans, C, 'The Specificity of Private Law in EU External Relations: The Area of Freedom, Security, and Justice', in M Cremona and H-W Micklitz (eds), *Private Law in the External Relations of the EU* (Oxford, Oxford University Press, 2016).

Tinoco-Pastrana, Á, 'The Proposal on Electronic Evidence in the European Union' (2020) 1 *Eurcrim* 46–50.

Toom, V, *Cross-Border Exchange and Comparison of Forensic DNA Data in the Context of the Prüm Decision. Study for the European Parliament's Committee on Civil Liberties, Justice and Home Affairs* (2018).

Tosza, S, 'All Evidence is Equal, but Electronic Evidence is More Equal Than Any Other: The Relationship Between the European Investigation Order and the European Production Order' (2020) 1 *New Journal of European Criminal Law*.

Tridimas, T, *The General Principles of EU Law* (Oxford, Oxford University Press, 2006).

——, 'Primacy, Fundamental Rights and the Search for Legitimacy', in MP Maduro and L Azoulai (eds), *The Past and Future of EU Law. The Classics of EU Law Revisited on the 50th Anniversary of the Rome Treaty* (Oxford, Hart Publishing, 2010).

Tsormpatzoudi, P, Berendt Bettina and Coudert Fanny, *Privacy by Design: From Research and Policy to Practice – the Challenge of Multi-disciplinarity* (Cham, Springer, 2015).

Tzanou, M, 'Data Protection as a Fundamental Right Next to Privacy? 'Reconstructing' a Not so New Right' (2013) 3 *International Data Privacy Law* 88–99.

——, *The Fundamental Right to Data Protection. Normative Value in the Context of Counter-Terrorism Surveillance* (Oxford, Hart Publishing, 2017).

Urquhart, L, 'Exploring Cybersecurity and Cybercrime: Threats and Legal Responses' in L Edwards (ed), *Law, Policy and the Internet* (Oxford, Hart Publishing, 2018).

Urquhart, L and McAuley, D, 'Avoiding the Internet of Insecure Industrial Things' (2018) 34 *Computer Law & Security Review* 450–466.

van de Poel, I, 'Core Values and Value Conflicts in Cybersecurity: Beyond Privacy Versus Security', in M Christen, B Gordijn and M Loi (eds), *The Ethics of Cybersecurity* (Cham, Springer, 2020).

Van der Kolk, B, *The Body Keeps the Score. Mind, Brain and Body in the Transformation of Trauma* (London, Penguin Books, 2014).

Van der Sloot, B, 'Legal Fundamentalism: is Data Protection Really a Fundamental Right?' in RE Leenes et al., (eds), *Data Protection and Privacy: (In)visibilities and Infrastructures* (Cham, Springer, 2017).

Van Schewick, B, *Internet Architecture and Innovation* (Cambridge, MIT Press, 2010).

Verbruggen, PWJ, et al., *Towards Harmonised Duties of Care and Diligence in Cybersecurity* (Tilburg University, 2016).

Verbruggen, PWJ, 'Tort Liability for Standards Development in the United States and European Union' in JL Contreras (ed), *The Cambridge Handbook of Technical Standardisation Law* (Cambridge, Cambridge University Press, 2019).
Vermeule, A, 'Critiques of the Trade-off Thesis', in D Jenkins, A Jacobsen and A Henrikens (eds), *The Long Decade. How 9/11 Changed the Law* (Oxford, Oxford University Press, 2014).
Viola de Azevedo Cunha, M, 'The Concept of Personal Data in the Post Lisbon Era: is there Need (and room) for Change?' in S Gutwirth et al. (ed), *Data Protection in Good Health?* (Doredrecht, Springer, 2012).
von Bogdandy, A, 'Founding Principles of EU Law: A Theoretical and Doctrinal Sketch' (2010) 16 *European Law Journal*.
von Grafenstein, M, 'Refining the Concept of the Right to Data Protection in Article 8 ECFR' (2020) 7 *Europeand Data Protection Law Review* 190–205.
Walden, I (ed), *Telecommunications Law and Regulation*, 5th edn (Oxford, Oxford University Press, 2018).
Waldron, J, 'The Concept and the Rule of Law' (2008) 43 *Georgia Law Review* 1.
——, *Torture, Terrore and Trade-offs. Philosophy for the White House* (Oxford, Oxford University Press, 2010).
Wall, DS, *Cybercrime: The Transformation of Crime in the Information Age* (Oxford, Polity, 2007).
——, 'Crime, Security and Information Communication Technologies: The Changing Cybersecurity Threat Landscape and Implications for Regulation and Policing', in R Brownsword, E Scotford and K Yeung (eds), *The Oxford Handbook of the Law and Regulation of Technology* (Oxford, Oxford University Press, 2017).
Wallace, H, Pollack, MA and Young, AR (eds), *Policy-Making in the European Union* (Oxford, Oxford University Press, 2014).
Ware, W (chair), *Records, Computers and the Rights of Citizens. Report of the Secretary's Advisory Committee on Automated Personal Data Systems* (1973).
Warren, SD and Brandeis, LD, 'The Right to Privacy' (1980) 4 *Harvard Law Review*.
Weber, M, *La Scienza come Professione. La Politica come Professione* (Einaudi, 2004).
Wertheim, M, *The Pearly Gates of Cybersapce. A History of Space from Dante to the Internet* (New York, WW Norton & Company Inc. 1999).
Westin, A, *Privacy and Freedom* (New York, Atheneum Press, 1967).
Wolters, PTJ, 'The Obligation to Update Insecure Software in the Light of Consumentenbond/SamsungR' (2019) 35 *Computer Law & Security Review* 295–395.
Wright, D et al., 'Minimizing Technology Risks with PIAs, Precaution, and Participation' (2011) 30 *IEEE Technology and Society Magazine* 47.
Wu, T, 'Network Neutrality, Broadband Discrimination' (2003) 2 *Journal on Telecommunications and High Tech Law*.
Wuyts, K, *LINDDUN: a Privacy Threat Analysis Framework*, https://www.linddun.org/.
Wylly, P, 'Evaluating the Costs of Technology Neutrality in Light of the Importance of Social Network Influences and Bandwagon Effects for Innovation Diffusion' (2015) 23 *NYU Environmental Law Journal* 298.
Yamaguchi, F, Liner, F and Rieck, K, 'Vulnerability Extrapolation: Assisted Discovery of Vulnerabilities using Machine Learning' (5th USENIX Workshop on Offensive Technologies (WOOT)).
Yar, M and Steinmetz, KFS, *Cybercrime and Society*, 3rd edn (London, Sage Publishing, 2020).
Yost, JR, 'A History of Computer Security Standards', in KMM de Leeuw and J Bergstra (eds), *The History of Information Security* (Oxford, Elsevier Science, 2007).
Zalnieriute, M, 'Towards International Data Privacy Cooperation: Strategies and Alternatives' (PhD thesis, European University Institute 2014).
Zeno-Zencovich, V, 'Articolo 8. Diritto al Rispetto della Vita Privata e Familiare', in SBB Conforti and G Raimondi (eds), *Commentario alla Convenzione Europea per la Tutela dei Diritti dell'Uomo e delle Libertà Fondamentali* (Cedam, 2001).
Zubik, M, Podkowik, J and Rybski, R (eds), *European Constitutional Courts towards Data Retention Laws* (Cham, Springer, 2021).
Zuboff, S, 'Big other: Surveillance Capitalism and the Prospects of an Information Civilization' (2015) 30 *Journal of Information Technology* 75–89.
——, *The Age of Surveillance Capitalism* (London, Profile Books, 2019).
——, 'Surveillance Capitalism and the Challenge of Collective Action' (2019) 28 *New Labor Forum* 10–29.

Blogs, Online Newspapers and Other Web Sources

'Hybrid CoE' (2019) www.hybridcoe.fi/what-is-hybridcoe/.
'Ep', *Deep Packet Inspection is Dead, and Here's Why'* (Institute for Advanced Studies – Network Security 2017).
Archambault, A, *Boites Noires: l'Utilisation de DPI Semble Inévitable* (2015) www.techniques-ingenieur.fr/actualite/articles/boites-noires-lutilisation-de-dpi-semble-inevitable-1696/.
Ball, J, Borger Julian and Greenwald Glenn, 'Revealed: how US and UK spy Agencies Defeat Internet Privacy and Security' *The Guardian* (6 Sep 2013) www.theguardian.com/world/2013/sep/05/nsa-gchq-encryption-codes-security.
Bogdanov, D and Siil, T, *Anonymisation 2.0: Sharemind as a Tool for De-Identifying Personal Data – Part 1: Definitions* (2018).
Brown, I, 'Internet Censorship: be Careful What you Ask for' (2008) /papers.ssrn.com/sol3/papers.cfm?abstract_id=1026597.
Chemla, L, Agent de double-langage Reflets Info (22 April 2015) https://reflets.info/articles/agent-de-double-langage.
Cluley, G, 'Government' Backdoor R2D2 Trojan Discovered by Chaos Computer Club' *NakedSecurity* (9 October 2011) nakedsecurity.sophos.com/2011/10/09/government-backdoor-trojan-chaos/.
Corfield, G, 'US Govt Accuses Four Chinese Army Soldiers of Hacking Equifax and Siphoning 145m Americans' Personal Info' *The Register* (20 February 2020) www.theregister.co.uk/2020/02/10/china_hacked_equifax_charges/.
Dodd, V and Gayle, D, 'Police to Hire Law Firms to Tackle Cyber Criminals in Radical Pilot Project' *The Guardian* (14 August 2016) www.theguardian.com/uk-news/2016/aug/14/police-to-hire-law-firms-to-tackle-cyber-criminals-in-radical-pilot-project?CMP=share_btn_link.
Donohue, LK, 'NSA Surveillance May Be Legal – but it's Unconstitutional' *The Washington Post* (21 June 2013) www.washingtonpost.com/opinions/nsa-surveillance-may-be-legal--but-its-unconstitutional/2013/06/21/b9ddec20-d44d-11e2-a73e-826d299ff459_story.html.
Dumortier, F, Papakonstantinou, V and De Hert, P, *EU sanctions against cyber-attacks and defense rights: Wanna Cry?* (European Law Blog 2020) https://europeanlawblog.eu/2020/09/28/eu-sanctions-against-cyber-attacks-imposed-and-defense-rights-wanna-cry/.
Eurojust, 'European Judicial Cybercrime Network' www.eurojust.europa.eu/Practitioners/Pages/EJCN.aspx.
European Commission, 'State of the Union 2017. Cyber Security Fact Sheet' (2017) www.consilium.europa.eu/media/21480/cybersecurityfactsheet.pdf.
——, State of the Union 2017. Cybersecurity: Commission scales up EU's response to cyberattacks (2017).
——, State of the Union 2018: European Commission proposes measures for securing free and fair European elections (2018).
——, 'European Defence Fund – factsheet' (2019) ec.europa.eu/docsroom/documents/34509.
European Defence Agency, *Cyber Ranges: EDA's First Ever Cyber Defence Pooling & Sharing Project Launched By 11 Member States* (2017).
European Network and Information Security Agency (ENISA), 'Glossary' (*ENISA*) www.enisa.europa.eu/topics/threat-risk-management/risk-management/current-risk/risk-management-inventory/glossary.
European Network of Forensic Science Institutes, enfsi.eu/.
European Union External Action Service, *ESDC/Cyber platform: Inauguration ceremony 'Cybersecurity will shape the pace and nature of our lives, work and consumption habits'* (2018).
——, *Towards a stronger EU on security and defence* (2018).
Federal Trade Commission, 'Equifax Data Breach Settlement' (2020) www.ftc.gov/enforcement/casesproceedings/refunds/equifax-data-breach-settlement.
Fung, B, 'The Aereo Case is Being Decided by People who Call iCloud 'the iCloud.' Yes, Really' *The Washington Post* (13 April 2014) www.washingtonpost.com/news/the-switch/wp/2014/04/23/the-aereo-case-is-being-decided-by-people-who-call-icloud-the-icloud-yes-really/.
Gallagher, S, 'NSA "touches" more of Internet than Google. In Deep Packet Inspection, it's not the Size of the Data that Matters' *Arstechnica* (13 August 2013) arstechnica.com/information-technology/2013/08/the-1-6-percent-of-the-internet-that-nsa-touches-is-bigger-than-it-seems/.
Gellman, B and Poitras, L, 'Documents: U.S. Mining Data from 9 Leading Internet Firms; Companies Deny Knowledge' *Washington Post* (6 June 2013).

Gellman, R, 'Fair Information Practices: A Basic History (Version 1.89)' (2012) Constantly updated at: bobgellman.com/rg-docs/rg-FIPShistory.pdf.
Greenberg, A, 'The Shadow Broker Mess is What Happens When the NSA Hoards Zero-days' *Wired* (17 August 2016) www.wired.com/2016/08/shadow-brokers-mess-happens-nsa-hoards-zero-days/.
Greenwald, G and MacAskill, E, 'NSA Taps in to Systems of Google, Facebook, Apple and Others, Secret Files Reveal' *The Guardian* (7 June 2013).
Griffiths, J, 'Chinese President Xi Jinping: Hands off our Internet' *CNN* (16 December 2015) edition.cnn.com/2015/12/15/asia/wuzhen-china-internet-xi-jinping/index.html.
The Guardian, 'The NSA files' (2013) www.theguardian.com/us-news/the-nsa-files.
Härmä, K and Minárik, T, *European Union Equipping Itself against Cyber Attacks with the Help of Cyber Diplomacy Toolbox* (CCDCOE 2017).
Karayan, R, 'Loi sur le Renseignement: ce que les Métadonnées Peuvent Dire de Vous' *L'express* (5 May 2015) lexpansion.lexpress.fr/high-tech/loi-sur-le-renseignement-tout-ce-que-les-metadonnees-peuvent-dire-de-vous_1677322.html.
Leiner, BM et al., 'A Brief History of the Internet version 3.2' (*Arxiv.org*, 1997) arxiv.org/html/cs/9901011; www.internetsociety.org/internet/history-internet/brief-history-internet/.
Loideain, NN, *Not So Grand: The Big Brother Watch ECtHR Grand Chamber Judgment* (2021) https://infolawcentre.blogs.sas.ac.uk/2021/05/28/not-so-grand-the-big-brother-watch-ecthr-grand-chamber-judgment/.
Maxwell, W, *French Surveillance Law Permits Data Mining, Drawing Criticism from Privacy Advocates* (Hogan Lovells, 2015) www.hldataprotection.com/2015/08/articles/international-eu-privacy/french-surveillance-law-permits-data-mining-drawing-criticism-from-privacy-advocates/.
McGowran, L, 'DPC Sued for 'failure to act' on Complaint Made against Google' *Silicon Republic* (15 March 2022) www.siliconrepublic.com/enterprise/dpc-high-court-iccl-gdpr-google-real-time-bidding.
McCollum, A, 'The Unavoidable Truth Of Moving Fast And Breaking Things' *TechCrunch* (New York, 10 March 2015).
Menn, J, 'Exclusive: Yahoo Secretly Scanned Customer Emails for U.S. Intelligence Sources' (4 November 2016) www.reuters.com/article/us-yahoo-nsa-exclusive-idUSKCN1241YT.
Michel, AH, 'There Are Spying Eyes Everywhere – and Now They Share a Brain' *Wired* (4 February 2021) www.wired.com/story/there-are-spying-eyes-everywhere-and-now-they-share-a-brain/.
Microsoft, 'Applying STRIDE' (*Microsoft*, 2005) msdn.microsoft.com/en-us/library/ee798544%28v=cs.20%29.aspx.
——, 'The STRIDE Threat Model' (*Microsoft*, 2005) msdn.microsoft.com/en-us/library/ee823878(v=cs.20).aspx.
Mueller, M, *The Narrative (March 16, 2021)* (Internet Governance, 2021) www.internetgovernance.org/2021/03/16/the-narrative-march-16-2021/.
Muižnieks, N, 'Human Rights at Risk When Secret Surveillance Spreads' (*The Council of Europe Commissioner's Human Rights Comment*, 2013) www.coe.int/en/web/commissioner/-/human-rights-at-risk-when-secret-surveillance-sprea-1.
Mullin, J, 'Privacy Lawsuit over Gmail Will Move Forward' (16 August 2016) arstechnica.com/tech-policy/2016/08/privacy-lawsuit-over-gmail-will-move-forward/.
Olenick, D, 'Data Breach Causes 10 Percent of Small Businesses to Shutter' *SC Magazine* (29 October 2019) www.scmagazine.com/home/security-news/data-breach/data-breach-causes-10-percent-of-small-businesses-to-shutter/.
Poe, R, 'The Ultimate Net Monitoring Tool' *Wired* (17 May 2006) www.wired.com/science/discoveries/news/2006/05/70914.
Ralston, W, 'The Untold Story of a Cyberattack, a Hospital and a Dying Woman' *Wired* (11 November 2020) www.wired.co.uk/article/ransomware-hospital-death-germany.
Riekeles, G, 'I saw first-hand how US Tech Giants Seduced the EU – and Undermined Democracy' *The Guardian* (28 June 2022) www.theguardian.com/commentisfree/2022/jun/28/i-saw-first-hand-tech-giants-seduced-eu-google-meta.
Sabbagh, D, 'Hackers Accessed Vaccine Documents in Cyber-attack on EMA' *The Guardian* (9 December 2020) www.theguardian.com/world/2020/dec/09/hackers-accessed-vaccine-documents-in-cyber-attack-on-ema.
Schneier, B, 'The NSA is Hoarding Vulnerabilities' (*CRYPTO-GRAM September 15*, 2016) www.schneier.com/crypto-gram/archives/2016/0915.htm.

Sharwood, S, 'US Declares Emergency after Ransomware Shuts Oil Pipeline that Pumps 100 million Gallons a Day' *The Register* (10 May) www.theregister.com/2021/05/10/colonial_pipeline_ransomware/.

Solon, O, 'Yahoo Confirms 'state-sponsored' Hackers Stole Personal Data From 500m Accounts' (23 September 2016) www.theguardian.com/technology/2016/sep/22/yahoo-hack-data-state-sponsored.

Stadnik, I, *Sovereign RUnet all the way down* (2019).

———, 'The Pegasus Project' (2022) www.theguardian.com/news/series/pegasus-project.

Tréguer, F, '*Surveillance: Petite Histoire de la Légalisation du Deep Packet Inspection*' *Le Club de Mediapart* (16 November 2017) https://blogs.mediapart.fr/felix-treguer/blog/161117/surveillance-petite-histoire-de-la-legalisation-du-deep-packet-inspection-0.

Tzanou, M, *Big Brother Watch and others v. the United Kingdom: A Victory of Human Rights over Modern Digital Surveillance?* (*Verfassungsblog* 2018) https://verfassungsblog.de/big-brother-watch-and-others-v-the-united-kingdom-a-victory-of-human-rights-over-modern-digital-surveillance/.

Volpato, A and Eliantonio, M, *The Butterfly Effect of Publishing References to Harmonised Standards in the L series* (European Law Blog, 2019).

von Appelbaum, J, et al., 'NSA Targets the Privacy-conscious' *Panorama 60 Jare* (Germany) daserste.ndr.de/panorama/aktuell/nsa230_page-5.html.

Wahl, T, *Progress on E-Evidence Package – Stakeholders Remain Critical* (Eucrim 2022) https://eucrim.eu/news/progress-on-e-evidence-package-stakeholders-remain-critical/.

Westby, J, "The Great Hack': Cambridge Analytica Is Just the Tip of the Iceberg' (*Amensty International*, 2019) www.amnesty.org/en/latest/news/2019/07/the-great-hack-facebook-cambridge-analytica/.

Zetter, K, 'A Cyberattack Has Caused Confirmed Physical Damage for the Second Time Ever' *Wired* (01 August 2015).

INDEX

abuse *see* child abuse
Action Plan to Combat Cybercrime   41
Alexy, R   24–5, 34
analytical framework of triad in EU law   5, 9–39
Anderson, R   138–9
Andrade, N   20
Angelini, F   31
Area of Freedom, Security and Justice (AFSJ) and cybercrime   3, 27, 195–239 *see also* Budapest Convention on Cybercrime (CoE); Cybercrime Directive; e-evidence, collection of; Fraud and Counterfeiting Directive (FCD); investigations
   Advanced Persistent Threats (APTs)   21
   aggravating factors   207, 209
   analytical framework   10, 32, 36–7, 39
   Budapest Convention   196–7, 200–1, 226–8
      2nd Additional Protocol   200, 220, 226–8
      Cybercrime Convention Committee (T-CY)   216–18
      legal status in EU law   201
      renvoi   203
   Charter of Fundamental Rights of the EU (CFR)   198, 220, 226, 228
   Child Sexual Abuse Material (CSAM)   195–6, 199, 202–3, 211–16, 230–1, 239
   CJEU, case law of   201, 219–26, 230
   comparative analysis   195
   complementarity   199–200, 211
   computer-related offences   20, 57–8, 201, 210
   confidential communications   200–1, 203, 206–10, 228–9, 238
   confidentiality, integrity and availability (CIA)   57–8, 61–2, 200–1, 203, 206–10
   confiscation and recovery of assets   59
   content-related offences   198–200, 218–19, 228, 230–1
   cooperation   58–60, 62, 99, 201–2, 206–7, 210, 212, 218–19
   copyright-related offences   57, 62, 200
   criminalisation   195, 205–6, 208–9
   cyber-attacks   207, 224, 229
   cybercrime, definition of   254

   Cybercrime Directive   57–8, 200–1, 205–11, 213, 226–7, 232, 239, 264
   data protection   43–4, 62, 99
   deep packet inspection (DPI)   6, 182, 196, 229, 232–8, 265
   definitions   6, 57–8, 61, 197, 203, 254
   Digital Single Market (DSM)   58, 190, 205–6, 213–14, 217–19, 232
   e-Commerce Directive (ECD)   217, 222, 226
   e-communication services (ECSs)   207, 222, 231
   effacement of technology   230, 239, 265
   electoral interference   58, 216–17
   emergency, times of   30
   e-Privacy Directive (EPD)   207, 213–15, 220–2, 226, 228
   e-Privacy Regulation (EPR)   220
   European Electronic Communications Code (EECC)   207, 213–14
   External Action (EA)   241, 244–5, 247, 260, 265
   forgery   57–8, 67, 201, 209–10, 232
   fraud   172, 174, 195–6, 201, 208–11
   functional interconnection   208–11, 217–19, 239, 264
   fundamental rights   61, 217, 225, 227, 239
   General Data Protection Regulation (GDPR)   199, 207, 211, 220–2, 226
   hacking   57, 91, 189, 203, 232–3, 237–9
   hate crime   61, 67
   identity theft   205–6, 209, 211
   illegal access to information systems   203, 206, 238
   illegal data interference   204, 206, 208
   illegal interception   204–5, 206
   illegal system interference   203–4, 205, 238
   information systems, attacks against   195–6, 200
   intermediaries, duty of care and liability of   218
   Internet   20, 42, 222
   law   6, 195, 200–29, 240
   Law Enforcement Directive (LED)   101, 195–6, 198, 206–7, 210–11, 215, 219–20, 222, 228–30

mass surveillance 198, 229
narrow or true cybercrimes 206, 264
network and information security (NIS) 43–4, 48, 61, 195–7, 202, 206–10, 214–16, 228, 230, 238–9, 264–5
overreach 198–9, 205
Payment Services Directive II (PSD II) 210–11, 218–19
police and judicial cooperation 58–60, 212, 219
policy 5–6, 36–7, 42–62, 64, 67, 195–239, 240, 262, 264–5
prevention 75, 207, 210–11, 225, 232–3
private and family life, right to respect for 220, 223–6
procedural functional interconnection 217–19, 239, 264
proliferation of cybercrimes 216–17
proportionality 212, 219, 221, 227, 238–9
prosecution 58, 201–2, 218, 264
public private partnerships (PPPs) 50, 55, 59, 213
ransomware 17, 172, 204
reconciliation of triad 4–6, 29, 195–219, 229–41, 244–5
restrictive measures 251–2
Rule of Law (RoL) 216–17, 227, 229, 238
Security Union Strategy 2020 198, 199–200
state of the art (SoA) 239
substantive cybercrime 60, 61
surveillance 61, 198, 218, 229, 237
techno-legal objects within EU, triad as 262
technology 6, 195, 229–38, 240
technology neutrality (TN), principle of 207, 210, 218–19, 227, 229–32, 239
tensions 240–1
terrorism 58, 59, 195–6, 198, 200, 216–17, 221, 227, 231
TEU 229, 240, 247
TFEU 195, 200, 202–3, 211–12, 214, 219–20, 240
three-pronged approach 197–8
tools, use of 230–2
Arendt, Hannah 13
artificial intelligence (AI) 49, 51, 183
authentication 11, 131–2, 135–6, 138, 166, 206
availability *see* **confidentiality, integrity and availability (CIA)**

Barlow, John Perry 19
Barrinha, H 47–8, 66
Bendiek, A 46, 256
Bennett, C 110
BEREC (Body of the European Regulators of Electronic Communications) 54, 55, 187, 189, 191–2, 232

Berners Lee, Tim 41
biometrics 82–3, 115, 153, 225–6
Bobbio, N 13
botnets 203–4, 205, 238
Bourreau, M 143, 146
Brandeis, Louis 14, 82
Brenner, S 233, 266, 267
Brexit 256
Brkan, M 33–4
Brownsword, R 156
Budapest Convention on Cybercrime (CoE) 29–30, 93, 196–7
  cookies 93
  Cybercrime Convention Committee (T-CY) 216–18
  e-evidence, collection of 59, 196, 220
  policy 43, 44, 52, 57–9, 61
  Second Additional Protocol 52, 59, 196, 200, 220, 226–8, 245, 247
Bygrave, LA 109–10, 124, 258

Cambridge Analytica 49, 217
capacity building 41, 50, 52, 64–6, 249
Carrapico, H 47–8, 66
Carrera, S 45
Cayford, M 16
Cavoukian, A 144
CERT-EU 54, 55
certification
  cloud services 182
  Cybersecurity Act (CSA) 166, 170, 176, 181
  data protection 110, 50, 159, 180, 258
  European Cybersecurity Certification Group (ECCG) 166, 181–2
  European Digital Identity Wallets, certification of 175–6
  General Data Protection Regulation (GDPR) 50, 180, 258
  national certification schemes 57
  technical and organisational measures (TOMs) 116–17, 170, 178
Chalmers, D 81
Chandler, JA 142, 152–3, 156
Charter of Fundamental Rights of the EU (CFR)
  see also **privacy in CFR/right to respect for private and family life in ECHR**
  clashes 26
  confidential communications 185–6, 188, 190, 228, 257
  cybercrime 198, 220, 226, 228
  data protection 32, 45, 97–126, 135–7
  deep packet inspection (DPI) 185–6, 188, 190–1, 193, 235–6
  emergency, times of 30–1
  essence of rights, notion of 33–5, 125–6

essential components   77–96, 111–26, 135–7, 262
Explanations   33, 69, 71, 74, 79, 97–100, 112
External Action (EA)   244–5, 247, 251, 259–60
extraterritoriality   244–5
general principles of EU law   33–4
horizontal provisions   33
identification of natural and legal persons   253
independent authority, control by an   123–5, 126
interpretation   33, 35, 97, 100, 102
legality, principle of   30–1
limitations   33–5
margin of appreciation   33
network and information security (NIS)   57
policy   46–7
privacy   32, 102–4, 135
proportionality   26, 33, 35
restrictive measures   251, 257, 260
Rule of Law (RoL)   33, 34
scope of rights   33
secondary law   99–101
sources   97–101, 109–10
standards   150, 259–60
techno-legal objects within EU, triad as   132, 135–7, 139
TEU   98–101, 103, 115
TFEU   37
child abuse
blocking access   230–1
Child Sexual Abuse Material (CSAM)   58, 61, 195–6, 199, 202–3, 212, 214–16, 230
Combating Child Sexual Abuse Directive (CSADir)   211–16, 227, 230–1, 239
Combating Child Sexual Abuse Regulation (CSAReg)   211–16, 230–1, 233
confidential communications   214–15
Law Enforcement Directive (LED)   215
procedural functional interconnection   211–16
China   51
Clarke, R   184–5
clashes
Charter of Fundamental Rights of the EU   26
constitutional architecture of EU   26, 27
Digital Single Market (DSM)   32
External Action (EA)   32
reconciliation of triad   9, 15–19, 22–4, 38, 129, 261
techno-legal objects within EU, triad as   129
CleanFeed   213
Client-Side Scanning (CSS)   213, 237
Clinton, Hillary   217
cloud computing   41, 182, 185, 197–8

Cohen, JE   87, 156, 269
Cold War   12, 267–8
Collingridge, D   141
Common Commercial Policy (CCP)   240, 255
Common Foreign and Security Policy (CFSP)   62–3, 65, 99, 241, 243, 244, 246–8, 264
Common Security and Defence Policy (CSDP)   62–4, 241, 244, 246–7
communications, definition of   162–4
complementarity   2, 9, 15–18
clashes, reconciliation with   22–3
cybercrime   199–200, 211
Digital Single Market (DSM)   157, 167, 176–82, 194
indeterminacy loop   177, 194
network and information security (NIS)   158–9
reconciliation of triad   22–3, 129, 138, 167, 261
Rule of Law (RoL)   28
techno-legal objects within EU, triad as   129, 138
computer-related offences   57, 62, 201, 210
confidential communications *see also* confidentiality, integrity and availability (CIA)
Charter of Fundamental Rights of the EU   185–6, 188, 190, 228, 257
Child Sexual Abuse Material (CSAM)   214–15, 228
communications, definition of   163
cybercrime   200–1, 203, 206–10, 228–9, 238
data protection   116–18, 120–1, 139–40, 263
deep packet inspection (DPI)   185–6, 188–90, 193, 235
definition   139
disclosure   131
illegal interception   206
Law Enforcement Directive (LED)   228–9
privacy   91–3, 95, 135–6, 139–40, 262
security, definition of   166
standards   269
techno-legal objects within EU, triad as   129, 130–1, 135–6, 138–9
confidentiality, integrity and availability (CIA)   200–1, 203, 206–10
authentication   11, 131–2, 166, 206
continuity of services   165
Cyber Diplomacy Toolbox   248
data protection   103, 116–18, 121, 263, 265
deep packet inspection (DPI)   185–90, 232
Digital Single Market (DSM)   166–7
European Electronic Communications Code (EECC)   164
External Action (EA)   243

illegal data interference   206, 208
incidents   206
network and information security (NIS),
   interconnection with   158–9, 166, 208, 210
overlaps   129
policy   57–8, 61–2
protection goals (PGs)   138
security properties (SPs)   131, 138
standards   269
techno-legal objects within EU, triad as   129–31, 132, 138–40
constitutional architecture of EU, triad within the   9, 22–3, 25–39
law analysis   26–38
legally situated objects, triad as   26, 36–8
ordre public in EU   25–6, 27–8, 36–7
policy analysis   26–38
Rule of Law (RoL)   3, 9, 27–32
situated objects, triad as   36–8
techno-legal objects within EU, triad as   3, 156, 261
technology analysis   26–38
constitutional rights   24–5
content-related offences   57–8, 198–201, 218–19, 228, 230–1
control   11–13, 123–5, 126, 131
cooperation
Cyber Diplomacy Toolbox   249
cybercrime   58–60, 62, 99, 201–2, 206–7, 210, 212, 218–19
Cybersecurity Act (CSA)   181
data protection authorities   206–7
ENISA   147
incidents   173
international cooperation   50, 110
NIS Directive (NISD)   167
PESCO   50, 63, 64
police and judicial cooperation   58–60, 99, 201–2, 212, 219
policy   50, 58–60, 62
copyright   62, 122, 158, 177, 188–90, 193, 200
corporate social responsibility (CSR)   13
Council of Europe (CoE) *see also* **Budapest Convention on Cybercrime (CoE); Council of Europe Convention for the Protection of Individuals with regard to Automatic Processing of Personal Data (Convention 108)**
data protection   97–8, 101–10
Human Rights and Biomedicine Convention   74
interpretation   110
Parliamentary Assembly   17
Venice Commission (CoE)   28

Council of Europe (CoE) Convention for the Protection of Individuals with regard to Automatic Processing of Personal Data (Convention 108)   108–12
accession of EU   109, 248
Convention 108+   109–10, 112, 115, 122–3, 247–8
direct effect   248
External Action (EA)   245, 247–8
fair information practice principles (FIPs)   108–9
interpretation   29–30, 110
OECD Privacy Guidelines   101–2, 108, 110–11
rectification   122–3
TEU   248
counterfeiting *see* **Fraud and Counterfeiting Directive (FCD)**
Covid-19   51, 166, 203
Craig, P   76, 79
Cremona, M   240, 241–2, 246, 248, 257–8
crime *see* **cybercrime**
Critical Infrastructure (CI)
Critical Information Infrastructure (CII)   12, 51, 54–5, 166, 175, 196, 229
   foreign entities, concentration in hands of   51
   users, definition of   166
critical information infrastructure protection (CIIP)   42
cyber-attacks   166
Digital Single Market (DSM)   160
economic and monetary Union (EMU)   27
information systems, reliance on   21–2
network and information security (NIS)   53–4
terrorism   44
CSIRTs network   54
customary international law   29, 110–11
cyber-attacks   1, 12, 16–17, 196, 225 *see also* **Cybercrime Directive; restrictive measures (RMs) against cyber-attacks**
AFSJ   207, 224, 229
Critical Information Infrastructure (CII)   166
Critical Infrastructure (CI)   27
cyberspace   20–1
data minimisation   159
deep packet inspection (DPI)   185, 232–4
definition   251–2
democracy, interference with   224
denial of service attacks (DoS)   57, 131, 189, 203–4, 232–3
dependency   169
External Action (EA)   241–2, 247
Fraud and Counterfeiting Directive   230
investigations   229
IP addresses   191
large-scale cyber-attacks   49, 207

legality, principle of   30
national security   30, 44, 224
network and information security (NIS)   50, 55, 166
ordre public   31
policy   40, 43–4, 45, 57, 67
security by design (SbD)   170
terrorism   44, 58, 216, 219, 234
warfare, as precursor to   242
zero-days attacks   16–17, 20–1, 238
Cyber Diplomacy Toolbox   52, 63, 241, 245, 248–54, 256
cyber-exploits   197, 229
cyber incidents *see* incidents
Cyber Industry, Technology and Research Competence Centre (CCCN)   52
cyber sovereignty   51, 184, 242, 266, 268
cyber-terrorism *see* terrorism
cybercrime *see* Area of Freedom, Security and Justice (AFSJ) and cybercrime; Budapest Convention on Cybercrime (CoE); child abuse; e-evidence, collection of; investigations; terrorism
Cybercrime Directive   200–2, 205–10, 226–7, 239
    Budapest Convention   61
    confidentiality, integrity and availability (CIA)   203
    Digital Single Market (DSM)   205
    External Action (EA)   245
    Fraud and Counterfeiting Directive (FCD)   208–11, 239
    Global Alliance   213
    large-scale cyber-attacks   207
    network and information security (NIS)   206, 264
    policy   57–8
    prevention   207, 232
    prohibited conduct   205
    reconciliation of triad   202, 206–8, 239
    renvoi or connection clause   201
    restrictive measures   251–2
    revision   208
    security, notion of   206
    tools for commission of offences   205
Cybersecurity Act (CSA) (Regulation (EU) 2019/881)
    addressees   161
    certification   166, 170, 176, 181
    cooperation   181
    Digital Single Market (DSM)   157, 161–2, 165–76, 178, 181
    digital services providers (DSPs)   161
    External Action (EA)   245
    operators of essential services (OESs)   161

Payment Services Directive II (PSD2)   171–2
personal data breaches   173–4
risk assessment and management   168–9
security, notion of   165
state of the art (SOA)   178
technical and organisational measures (TOMs)   170
users, definition of   166
Cybersecurity Competence Centre (3C)   54, 55
cybersecurity, nature of   10–13, 46, 262
cyberspace environment   9, 18–22, 37–8, 52
    cyberspace, definition of   18–19
    physical world laws, application of   46–7

data, definition of   21, 112, 162–4, 177
data protection   5, 97–126 *see also* Council of Europe (CoE) Convention for the Protection of Individuals with regard to Automatic Processing of Personal Data   108; General Data Protection Regulation (GDPR)
    access to data, right of   122–3, 126, 263
    accuracy, principle of   122
    active, as   15
    anonymisation   114
    applicable law   112–15
    automated processing   112–13, 124
    autonomy   102, 107
    breaches   168–74, 176, 178–82, 206
    categories of personal data   115
    certification   110, 50, 159, 180, 258
    Charter of Fundamental Rights of the EU (CFR)   32, 45, 97–126, 135–7
    CJEU, case law of   100, 104–8, 111, 115, 119–26, 262
    confidential communications   116–18, 120–1, 263
    consumer right, as   106
    cooperation   50, 206–7
    Council of Europe (CoE)   97–8, 101–10
    cyberspace   21–2
    data, definition of   112
    Data Protection Directive (DPD)   42, 99–102, 105–6, 108–9, 119, 122–3, 132
    data subjects   114–21, 126
        identifiers   114
        rights   119–21, 126, 263
    deep packet inspection (DPI)   186–7
    democracy   15, 16
    derogations   99, 105
    design, by   170, 178
    Digital Single Market (DSM)   157–94
    ECtHR, case law of   102–4, 108, 110
    Electronic Privacy Directive (EPD)   101, 105–6, 111

Electronic Privacy Regulation (EPR)   101
essence of rights, notion of   115–18, 121,
   125–6, 265
essential components   97, 111–18, 123–6, 262–3
everyone has a right to, meaning of   111–12
fair information practice principles (FIPs)   101,
   108–9, 112–13, 136
fairly, obligation to process data   119–21, 125
free movement of personal data   98–9
fundamental rights   15, 50, 100, 108, 110, 115,
   123–4, 262
general principles of EU law   36, 97, 101
him or her, meaning of personal data
   concerning   112–15
human oversight   124, 126
identity   15, 107, 114, 122
inclusive right to data protection   111–18
independence of data protection from
   privacy   102–8, 263
independent authority ensuring compliance,
   control by an   123–5, 126
instrumentality to privacy, data protection as   107
integrity   103, 116–18, 121, 263, 265
interpretation   97, 99–106, 108–15, 119–21, 125
Law Enforcement Directive (LED)   101, 111,
   122–3
legitimate processing   125, 263
list of international organisations and
   supervisory authorities outside
   EU with international cooperation
   frameworks   110
manual means   113
network and information security (NIS)   42,
   46, 48, 57
OECD Privacy Guidelines   101–2, 108, 110–11
personal data   5, 97–126, 263
   breaches   168–74, 176, 178–82, 206
   definition   112–13
personality, preservation of   13, 107
policy   43–6, 50, 62, 66–7
positive obligations   99
primary law   98–101, 103–5, 123
principles   97, 101–2, 106, 115–26, 263
privacy/private and family life, right to respect
   for   92–3, 97–9, 101–10, 120
procedural right, as   106
protection of, meaning of   115–18
pseudonymisation   119
purpose limitation   115–18, 120–1, 126, 263
rectification, right to   122–3
retention of data
   cybercrime   198
   Data Retention Directive (DRD)   44, 153,
      219–20
   privacy   92–3

secondary law   98–101, 104–5, 108–11, 120,
   124, 263
sensitive data   86, 92, 103, 105, 115, 118, 172
Single Market   102
soft law   110–11
sources   97–101, 109–11
special categories of personal data, prohibition
   of automatic processing of   108
specified purposes, fair processing for   120–1
such data must be processed, definition
   of   119–20
supervisory authority   123–5, 137
surveillance in the workplace   103–4
technical and organisational measures
   (TOMs)   116–18, 263
TFEU   98–103, 115
de Hert, P   75, 106, 124
deep packet inspection (DPI)   157–8, 178,
   182–93, 257
ambiguity of DPI for the Triad, implications
   of   190–3
Charter of Fundamental Rights of the EU
   185–6, 188, 190–1, 193, 235–6
CJEU, case law of   191–2, 234–5
Combating Child Sexual Abuse Regulation
   (CSAReg)   233
compliance with legal obligations   185–90
confidential communications, principle
   of   185–6, 188–90, 193, 235
confidentiality, integrity and availability
   (CIA)   232
content of a packet, meaning of   190–1
copyright infringement   188–90
cyber-attacks   185, 232–4
cybercrime   6, 182, 196, 229, 232–8, 265
data protection, interference with   186–7
definition   183
denial-of-service (DOS) attacks   232–3
Digital Single Market (DSM)   6, 157–8, 178,
   182–93, 235
e-Commerce Directive (ECD)   188–9, 234–5
ECtHR, case law of   233
Electronic Communications Services
   (ECSs)   234–5
e-evidence, collection of   232
External Action (EA)   6, 241
integrity, preserving   185–90
illegal access   232–3
illegal data interference   232–3
Internet Service Providers (ISPs)   182–5, 234–5
keywords   236
malware   185–6, 189, 232
manipulation or active DPI   183
metadata/content divide   192
monitoring   182, 185–93, 232–4

network and information security (NIS)   182, 185–6, 189–93
Open Internet Regulation (OIR)   232, 234–5
passive engines   183
permissibility of DPI with regard to the Triad   185–90
prevention of crimes   232–3
proportionality   193, 235–6
pros and cons   182–5
reconciliation of triad   232–7
restrictive measures   257
security, preserving   185–90
signatures   236
significance for the Triad   234–7
standard-setting organisations (SSOs)   182
state of the art (SoA)   182–93
surveillance   184, 234, 237
tensions   234–7
terminal equipment of end-users   189
terrorism   233–4
traffic management techniques   187, 189, 192
usage   182–5
defence   53, 62–6
Common Security and Defence Policy (CSDP)   62–4, 241, 244, 246–7
Cyber Defence Joint Program   63
Cyber Defence Policy Framework (CDPF)   62–3
cybersecurity, definition of   262
diplomacy   50–1, 53, 66
European Defence Agency (EDA)   47–8, 62, 244
European Defence Fund   50, 63
European Security and Defence College   63
exercises   63
objectives   62–3
overlaps   66–7
PESCO   63, 64
policy   47–8, 50, 53, 62–7
trade, tensions with   66
democracy   1, 4, 15–16, 18, 261
cyber-attacks   224
deficit   149–50
electoral interference   1, 58, 216–17
External Action (EA)   246
modulated democracy   156
policy   46–7
Rule of Law (RoL)   28–9
surveillance   87, 91, 156
DeNardis, L   11, 61, 229
denial of service attacks (DoS)
confidentiality, integrity and availability (CIA)   131
deep packet inspection (DPI)   232–3
distributed denial of service attacks (D(DoS))   203–4

monitoring   189
policy   57
design *see also* **security by design (SbD)**
data protection   170, 178
privacy by design   139
strategies   130–5, 140, 155, 263
techno-legal objects within EU, triad as   129–35, 139–40, 144–5, 155, 261, 263
values   37–8
digital rights management (DRM)   153–4
Digital Single Market (DSM) Strategy (Commission)   3, 6, 157–94
analytical framework   9–10, 32, 36–7, 39
certification   166, 170, 175–6, 181–2
CJEU, case law of   161–3, 182
clashes   32
Combating Child Sexual Abuse Directive (CSADir)   214
communications, definition of   162–4, 177
comparative analysis of selected instruments   157, 162–76
complementarity   157, 167, 176–82, 194
confidentiality, integrity and availability (CIA)   166–7
continuity of services   165, 193
convergence   157, 180
cybercrime   58, 205–6, 213–14, 217–19, 232
Cybersecurity Act (CSA)   157, 161–2, 165–76, 178, 181
data, definition of   162–4, 177
data protection, concept of   157–94
deep packet inspection (DPI)   157–8, 178, 182–93, 235
definitions   6, 162–8
effacement of technology   177, 178–82, 193–4
eIDAS Reg   157, 160–2, 165–7, 170–6
Electronic Communications Services (ECSs)   161–3
ENISA   167, 169, 171, 173, 181
e-Privacy Directive (EPD)   157, 160–4, 169–71, 173–6
European Electronic Communications Code (EECC)   157, 160–6, 170–2
External Action (EA)   241, 244–5, 260
fragmentation   160–1, 174–5, 264
General Data Protection Regulation (GDPR)   157, 160–2, 164–5, 170–4, 178, 180
incidents   171–4, 176, 178–82
information, definition of   162–4, 177
Information Society Services (ISSs)   161–2
innovation   27, 36
law and reconciliation of triad   6, 157, 160–77
legislative instruments and implementation   6, 157, 160–78

network and information security (NIS)   50, 53–7, 157–94, 264
operators of essential services (OESs)   161
overlaps   162, 167, 176, 193
packet inspection techniques   6, 157–8
Payment Services Directive II (PSD2)   157, 160–1, 171–4
personal data breaches   168–74, 176, 178–82
policy   5–6, 36–7, 50, 52–8, 157–88, 262, 264, 265
prevention   168–74
privacy, notion of   157–94
proportionality   157, 176
reconciliation of triad, modes of   4–6, 157–94, 240–1, 244–5
regulation of ICT products, services and processes   178–82
risk   168–76
security, notion of   6, 164, 165–8, 175–6
signals, definition of   162–4, 177
standards   178–82
state of the art (SoA)   175, 177, 178–94
technical and organisational measures (TOMs)   157–8, 168–94
technology   6, 157–8, 177–94
tensions   240–1
terminal equipment, entities accessing   161, 174
TEU   240
TFEU   240
triad   157–94
trust service providers   167–8, 173
values   244
dignity   13, 33–4, 81, 107, 246
diplomacy   1–2, 27, 62–6
  cyber dialogues   63
  Cyber Diplomacy Toolbox   52, 63, 241, 245, 248–54, 256
  cybersecurity, definition of   262
  defence   50–1, 53, 66
  External Action (EA)   27, 53, 62–7
  Joint EU Diplomatic Response on Malicious Cyber Activities   63
  multi-stakeholder governance   63
  policy   53, 62–6, 67
  trade, tensions with   66
domain names   52, 187
dual-use technology   64, 241, 245, 254–5, 257, 265
Dual-use Regulation   241, 245, 254–5, 257
Dunn Cavelty, M   18

e-Commerce Directive (ECD)   188–9, 217, 222, 226, 234–5
e-communication services (ECSs)   161–3
  cybercrime   207, 222, 231
  deep packet inspection (DPI)   234–5

NIS Directive (NISD)   161
Over-The-Top (OTT) services   163
privacy   69, 78, 80, 91–3
economic and monetary Union (EMU)   27
Edwards, L   188
e-evidence, collection of
  AFSJ   195–229, 238–9, 264
  biometrics   225–6
  Budapest Convention   59, 196, 220
  CJEU, case law of   219–26
  Data Retention Directive (DRD), invalidity of   219–20
  deep packet inspection (DPI)   232
  ECtHR, case law of   223–6
  e-Privacy Directive (EPD)   220–2, 226
  European Investigation Order Directive (EIOD)   219–20, 226
  European Production and Preservation Orders (EPPOR)   220, 226–8
  General Data Protection Regulation (GDPR)   220–2, 226
  intelligence-gathering   223–5
  Law Enforcement Directive (LED)   219–20, 222, 228–9
  policy   43, 50, 52–3, 57–62, 262
  private and family life, right to respect for   223–5
  proportionality   221
  reconciliation of triad   195–200, 219–38, 264
  Regulation of Investigatory Powers Act 2000   223–5
  restrictive measures   256–7
  seriousness of interferences   221–3
  technology   229–38
  TFEU   219
  zero-sum game between surveillance and security   228–9
effacement of technology
  complementarity   178–82
  cybercrime   230, 239, 265
  digital rights management (DRM)   153–4
  Digital Single Market (DSM)   177, 178–82, 193–4
  External Action (EA)   241, 255–60, 265–6
  indeterminacy loop   3, 152–4, 155, 230, 239, 264
  regulation   268
  spillover effect   265
  techno-legal objects within EU, triad as   129, 141–54, 155, 264
  zero-sum outcomes   266
e-Identity and Assurance Services Regulation (eIDAS Reg)   170–6
  addressees   161
  Digital Single Market (DSM)   157, 160–2, 165–7, 170–6

European Digital Identity Wallets, certification of 175–6
Fraud and Counterfeiting Directive (FCD) 211
incidents 171, 173–5
liability 173–4
network and information security (NIS) 166, 175
pseudonyms 167
reform 174–6
technical and organisational measures (TOMs) 170
trust services 161
electoral interference 1, 58, 216–17
Electronic Frontier Foundation 19
Eliantonio, M 148
emergency, times of 24, 26, 29–32
Emergency Response Coordination Centre (Commission) 54
ENISA (European Network and Information Security Agency) (European Union Agency for Cybersecurity)
cooperation 147
deep packet inspection (DPI) 192
Digital Single Market (DSM) 167, 169, 171, 173, 180–1
network and information security (NIS) 47, 54, 55
prevention 169
privacy by design 131, 132
state of the art (SOA) 147, 179
technological and organisational measures (TOMs) 171
environmental rights 73, 74
epistemic communities 19, 36, 67
e-Privacy Directive (EPD) 69, 78, 86, 91–3, 105–6, 111
addressees 161
confidential communications 139–40
cybercrime 207, 213–15, 220–2, 226, 228
deep packet inspection (DPI) 185–7
Digital Single Market (DSM) 157, 160–3, 173–4
e-evidence, collection of 220–2, 226
E-Privacy Regulation (EPR), replacement with 174
national security 69, 101, 221
technical and organisational measures (TOMs) 170
terminal equipment, entities accessing 161
e-Privacy Regulation (EPR) 78, 88, 90, 92–3, 101, 160, 220
Erlbacher, F 254
essence of rights, notion of 3, 5, 33–5, 37–8
Charter of Fundamental Rights of the EU 33–5, 125–6

cybercrime 265
network and information security (NIS) 265
privacy 94–6, 135–6
proportionality 26, 34, 37
purpose limitation 115–18, 121, 265
techno-legal objects within EU, triad as 130, 132, 135–7, 263
vagueness 262
zero-sum outcomes 240
essential components of rights 130, 132, 135–7, 140–1, 266
data protection 97, 111–18, 123–6, 155, 190, 262–3
private and family life, home and communications, right to respect for 68, 77–96, 155, 163, 190, 262–3
secondary law 35
Estonia, cyber-attacks on 45, 203–4, 242
EU cybersecurity policy 3, 40–67
2013
after 40, 46–8, 49, 50, 58, 266
before 40–5
2017 update 48–50, 52
2020 policy 50–2, 66
adoption of policy 45–8
AFSJ 5, 50, 53, 57–62, 64
Budapest Convention 43, 44, 52
capacity building 50, 52, 64–6
Commission 42–4, 46–8, 52
Common Commercial Policy (CCP) 240, 255
Common Foreign and Security Policy (CFSP) 62–3, 65, 99, 241, 243, 244, 246–8, 264
Common Security and Defence Policy (CSDP) 62–4, 241, 244, 246–7
competences 40–1
constitutional architecture of EU 26–38
cooperation 50, 58–60, 62
cyber-attacks 40, 43–4, 45, 57, 67
cybercrime 6, 36–7, 42–5, 48–50, 53, 57–62, 67, 195–240, 262, 264–5
cybersecurity, definition of 262
data protection 42–3, 45–6, 48, 50, 66–7
defence 47–8, 50, 53, 62–7
deterrence 50, 52
development of policy 40–52
Digital Single Market (DSM) 5–6, 36–7, 50, 52–8, 157–88, 262, 264, 265
diplomacy 53, 62–6, 67
emergency brake 28
encryption 42, 50
External Action (EA) 5–6, 36–7, 50, 53, 62–6, 240–4, 255, 258–60, 262, 264, 265
future 66–7

implementation 265
independent policy, as 40
Internet 41–2
JHA-related measures 41, 43, 45
legal certainty 61, 265
national security 44, 67
network and information security (NIS) 42–57, 61, 64, 67, 158–77, 262
policy and law landscape 52–66, 262
principles 46–8, 50
privacy 43, 46, 50, 52, 66–7
proportionality 262
resilience 46, 47–8, 50
security by design 42, 55
Stockholm Programme 45
tensions within cybersecurity 66–7
TEU 45, 50, 62
TFEU 45, 50, 57
Eurojust 59
European Banking Authority (EBA) 55
European Centre of Excellence for Countering Hybrid Threats 64
European Convention on Human Rights (ECHR) *see also* **privacy in CFR/right to respect for private and family life in ECHR**
accession 104
External Action (EA) 245, 247–8
interpretation of EU law 29–30
mass surveillance 18
national security 31
European Data Protection Board (EDPB) 54, 55, 110–12, 114, 187, 189–91, 227, 235
European Data Protection Supervisor (EDPS) 54, 55, 111, 189, 227, 254
European Data Protection Supervisor Regulation (EDPSR) 99–101, 111, 247
European Digital Identity, framework for 211
European Electronic Communications Code (EECC) 157, 160–4, 171, 189, 207, 213–14
European External Action Service (EEAS) 62, 64, 244, 247
European Investigation Order Directive (EIOD) 219–20, 226–7
European Judicial Cybercrime Network (EJCN) 59
European Medicines Agency (EMA), cyber-attacks on 203
European Parliament 16–18, 50, 67, 229
European Production and Preservation Orders (EPPOR) 220, 226–8
European Security Strategy 44
Europol's Cybercrime Centre (C3) 47, 58–9
evidence *see* **e-evidence, collection of**
export control 254–5, 257, 265

External Action (EA) 3, 4, 240–60 *see also* **restrictive measures (RMs) against cyber-attacks**
AFSJ 241, 244–5, 247, 260
analytical framework 10, 36–7, 39
capabilities, developing 62–3, 66
Charter of Fundamental Rights of the EU (CFR) 244–5, 247, 251, 259–60
CJEU, case law of 248
clashes 32
Common Commercial Policy (CCP) 240
Common Foreign and Security Policy (CFSP) 62–3, 65, 241, 243, 244, 246–8, 264
Common Security and Defence Policy (CSDP) 241, 244, 246–7
confidentiality, integrity and availability (CIA) 243
constitutional architecture of EU 27
Convention 108 245, 247–8
cyber-attacks 241–2, 247
Cyber Diplomacy Toolbox 241, 245, 248–54, 256
defence 53, 62–6, 241, 244, 246–7
Digital Single Market (DSM) 241, 244–5, 260
diplomacy 27, 53, 62–7
Dual-Use Regulation 241, 245, 254–5, 265
effacement of technology 241, 255–60, 265–6
European Convention on Human Rights (ECHR) 245, 247–8
European External Action Service (EEAS) 62, 64, 244, 247
fundamental rights 246–9, 260
General Data Protection Regulation (GDPR) 244–5, 247–8, 258
Law Enforcement Directive (LED) 247–8
legislative instruments and implementation 6, 65
mass surveillance 243–4
mutual legal assistance 240–1
network and information security (NIS) 244–5, 255, 258–9, 264, 265
norms and ideas, international flow of 257–9
policy 5–6, 36–7, 50, 53, 62–6, 240–4, 255, 258–60, 262, 264, 265
reconciliation of triad, mode of 5–6, 240–60
regulation 241, 244–5, 255–9, 264
Restrictive Measures Regulation (RMReg) 245, 250–7
standards 241, 243, 255–6, 258, 260, 265–6
techno-legal objects within EU, triad as 262
technology 6, 241, 255–60, 265–6
tensions 240–1
TEU 240, 242, 244–6, 254
TFEU 240, 247–8, 255

trade   53, 62–6
treaty-making   240–1
umbrella nature   241
values   27, 241–3, 245–6, 255–60

Fahey, E   46, 48
fair information practice principles (FIPs)   101, 108–9, 112–13, 136
fairly, obligation to process data   119–21, 125
family, concept of the   135
family life, respect for *see* privacy in CFR/right to respect for private and family life in ECHR
Flear, M   155
forgery   57–8, 67, 201, 209–10, 232
forum shopping   123–4
France   231–2, 237
fraud   172, 174, 195–6, 201, 208–11 *see also* Fraud and Counterfeiting Directive (FCD)
Fraud and Counterfeiting Directive (FCD)   208–11, 226–7, 239
   Cybercrime Directive   208–11, 239
   European Digital Identity, framework for   211
   identity theft   209
   policy   58
   restrictive measures   252
   substantive functional interconnection   208–11, 264
   technology neutrality   230
   weak reconciliation   208–11
freedom of expression   51, 64, 67, 80
freezing of assets   250, 252
fundamental rights   26, 28, 32–5 *see also* Charter of Fundamental Rights of the EU (CFR); privacy in CFR/right to respect for private and family life in ECHR
   Child Sexual Abuse Material (CSAM)   215
   data protection   15, 50, 100, 108, 110, 115, 123–4, 262
   diplomacy   63–4
   emergency, times of   30
   External Action (EA)   246–9, 260
   Fraud and Counterfeiting Directive (FCD)   211
   freedom of expression   51, 64, 67, 80
   Fundamental Rights Agency (EU)   73
   general principles of EU law   26
   Human Rights Measurement Framework (HRMF) (EHRC)   73, 77
   ICCPR   69–71, 77–80, 85–6, 111, 139
   impact assessments   266
   permissible limitations   32–5
   policy   61

proportionality   5, 32–5
restrictive measures   251
Rule of Law (RoL)   26, 28, 32
techno-legal objects within EU, triad as   3, 261–2, 266
zero-sum outcomes, fail-safe against   32–5
future of the triad
   policy   66–7
   research trajectories   267–9

Geiger, C   193
Gellert, R   106–7, 164
General Data Protection Regulation (GDPR)   101–3, 111–15, 136
   addressees   161
   burden of proof, reversal of   174
   certification   50, 180, 258
   Charter of Fundamental Rights of the EU   108
   confidential communications   139–40
   Convention 108   109
   cybercrime   199, 207, 211, 220–2, 226
   deep packet inspection (DPI)   186–7
   design, data protection by (DPbD)   170, 178
   Digital Single Market (DSM)   157, 160–2
   e-evidence, collection of   220–2, 226
   e-Privacy Regulation (EPR)   174
   External Action (EA)   244–5, 247–8, 258
   extraterritoriality   244–5
   guidelines   112
   interpretation   106, 111–12, 114, 119–21
   personal data breach   171, 173–4
   privacy   78, 86
   purpose limitation   121
   rectification   122–3
   restrictive measures   251
   security by design (SbD)   170
   standards   150, 180
   state of the art (SOA)   178
   technical and organisational measures (TOMs)   170–1
   terminal equipment, entities accessing   161
   transborder data flows and requirement for findings of adequacy   258
general principles of EU law
   data protection   36, 97, 101
   emergency, times of   31
   essence of rights, notion of   33–4
   privacy   26, 36, 70–1
   Rule of Law (RoL)   26, 28, 32
Gercke, M   57
Germany
   automatic processing of data   112–13
   Charter of Fundamental Rights of the EU   33–4
   cyber-attacks   166

German Federal Constitutional Court   13, 237–8
  investigations   237
  secret monitoring and reconnaissance on Internet   237–8
González Fuster, G   76, 107, 112, 115
Grabowski, M   152–3
Greece and Athens Affair   236
Greenberg, A   152
Greenleaf, G   109
Guild, E   45
Gutwirth, S   75, 106–7, 112, 115

hacking   57, 91, 189, 203, 232–3, 237–9
HAS Consultants Framework   150
hate crime   61, 67
Herrmann, D   130–1, 185
High-Performance Computing infrastructure   54
High Representative for Foreign Affairs and Security Policy   46–8, 50–2
Hildebrandt, M   144, 146
Hinarejos, A   31
Hobbes, Thomas   25
home, concept of the   73, 90–1, 95, 135–6, 262
honour and reputation   80, 84–6
human rights *see* fundamental rights
Human Rights and Biomedicine Convention (CoE)   74
human trafficking   59, 218
Hybrid Fusion Cell (EU)   64

ideal of life (*vouloir-vivre*)   25, 31–2
identity   13–14
  autonomy and self-determination   15
  biometrics   82–3, 115, 153, 225–6
  data protection   15, 107, 114, 122
  EIDAS Reg   157, 160–2, 166, 170, 173–6, 211
  European Digital Identity Wallets, certification of   175–6
  personal social and sexual identity   73, 77, 82, 83–6, 95–6, 135, 262
  personality, preservation of   13
  political identity   25
  restrictive measures   252–4
  theft   205–6, 209, 211, 232
illegal access to information systems   203, 206, 232–3 *see also* hacking
illegal data interference   204, 206, 208, 232–3
incidents
  confidentiality, integrity and availability (CIA)   206
  cooperation   173
  definition   171–3
  Digital Single Market (DSM)   171–4, 176, 178–82

eIDAS Reg   171, 173–5
ENISA   171
media   12
network and information security (NIS)   173
notification   173, 178
response   64
state of the art (SoA)   178–82
indeterminacy loop   3, 129–30, 152–4, 155, 177, 194, 230, 239, 264
information, definition of   21, 162–4, 177
Information Society Services (ISSs)   80, 112, 161–2, 222
infrastructure *see* Critical Infrastructure (CI)
integrity *see* confidentiality, integrity and availability (CIA)
Intelligence and Situation Centre (INTCEN)   64, 66
interception of communications   44, 87, 91–2, 198, 204–5, 206
International Covenant on Civil and Political Rights (ICCPR)   69–71, 77–80, 85–6, 111, 139
International Standardisation Organisation (ISO)   12, 131, 140, 147
International Telecommunications Union (ITU)   12–13, 130, 140, 147
Internet   19–21
  access to Internet and information flows   46–7
  Artificial Intelligence   49
  boom and bust/dot.com crash   41–2
  cybercrime   20, 42
  data protection   102
  early security   11
  Internet Access Services (IASs)   222
  Internet Engineering Task Force (IETF)   131–2, 139
  Internet of Things (IoT)   49, 204
  Internet Service Providers (ISPs)   182–5, 234–5
  interoperability   11
  IP addresses   59, 114, 186, 189–92, 222, 232–4
  net neutrality   20
  Open Internet Access Regulation (OIR)   187–9, 192
  policy   41–2
  privatisation   12
  processing   119
  World Wide Web   12, 41, 49, 184–5
interpretation
  Budapest Convention   29–30
  Charter of Fundamental Rights of the EU   33, 35
  Convention 108   29–30, 110
  data protection   97, 99–106, 108–15, 119–21, 125
  evolutive   262

General Data Protection Regulation
 (GDPR)   106, 111–12, 114, 119–21
ICCPR   111
international law   29
living instrument doctrine   267
personal data, definition of   112–13
private and family life, right to respect for
 69–72, 76–8, 90, 96, 101–2, 109, 120
purposive interpretation   35, 96
secondary law   99–102, 104–5, 111, 248
techno-legal objects within EU, triad as   140–1
investigations
 AFSJ   198, 201–2, 217–19, 226, 228–32, 237–9, 264
 cyber-attacks   229
 cyber-exploits   229
 European Investigation Order Directive (EIOD) 219–20, 226–7
 hacking   237–9
 human trafficking   218
 mutual legal assistance   218
 network and information security (NIS)   177
 policy   58–9
 protection goals (PGs)   228
 security properties (SPs)   228
IP addresses   59, 114, 186, 189–92, 222, 232–4
Isenberg, D   19–20

judicial cooperation   99, 201–2, 212, 219
Justice and Home Affairs (JHA)
 (third pillar)   41, 43, 45
Jütte, BJ   193

Kilpatrick, C   28
Klimburg, A   48
Kohl, U   218
Koops, BJ   144, 146
Kranenborg, H   103

laissez innover   11, 12, 14–15, 120, 268
laissez processer   120, 268
Landau, S   61, 229, 236
law   3, 200–29
 AFSJ   6, 195, 200–29, 240
 constitutional architecture of EU   26–38
 cybercrime   6, 195, 200–29, 240
 network and information security (NIS)   6, 157, 160–77
 pace of technology   268–9
 reconciliation of triad   6, 157, 160–77
 vulnerabilities   179
Law Enforcement Directive (LED)
 Child Sexual Abuse Material (CSAM)   215
 cybercrime   101, 195–6, 198, 206–7, 210–11, 215, 219–20, 222, 228–30
 data protection   101, 111, 122–3
 e-evidence, collection of   219–20, 222, 228–9
 External Action (EA)   247–8
 Fraud and Counterfeiting Directive (FCD)   211
 privacy   69
 rectification   122–3
 technology neutrality   230
Leenes, R   19, 156
legal certainty
 coherence   32
 data protection   120–1
 deep packet inspection (DPI)   193
 emergency, times of   32, 156
 policy   61, 265
 restrictive measures   251
 Rule of Law (RoL)   28
 secondary law   265
 standards   150
 techno-legal objects within EU, triad as   156
legality, principle of   28, 29–32
legally situated objects, triad as   26, 36–8
 see also **techno-legal objects within EU, triad as**
legitimate expectations   32
let alone, right to be   14
LINDDUN project   131–2, 136
living instrument doctrine   81, 267
Lock, T   253
Lorents, P   18
Lundqvist, B   149
Lynskey, O   35, 100, 106, 108

McDermott, J   11, 120
malicious activities *see* **Cyber Diplomacy Toolbox**
malware   185–6, 189, 204, 232, 238
mass surveillance   1, 9, 15–18
 back doors   17
 clashes   38
 data protection   16, 198
 European Parliament   16–18, 229
 External Action (EA)   243–4
 national security   15–18
Micklitz, H-W   244, 258
Microsoft STRIDE model   131
military   11, 13, 20, 44, 46–7, 52, 62–4, 66–7
monitoring
 BEREC   187, 189, 191–2, 232
 deep packet inspection (DPI)   182, 185–93, 232–4
 Open Internet Access Regulation (OIR)   187–9, 192
Morsink, J   77
multi-stakeholder governance   12, 46–7, 63, 243
mutual legal assistance (MLA)   218, 240–1

national security
  confidentiality 228
  cyber-attacks 30, 44, 224
  data protection 99, 101
  emergency, times of 30–1
  e-Privacy Directive 69, 101, 221
  mass surveillance 15–18
  ordre public 25, 31
  policy 44, 67
  privacy 69, 75, 76, 99, 101, 221
  restrictive measures 251
  serious interferences 221–4
NATO 64
neoliberalism 267–8
network and information security (NIS)
  confidentiality, integrity and availability (CIA) 158–9, 166, 208, 210
  c-PPP (cybersecurity public private partnerships) 159
  Critical Infrastructure (CI) 53–4
  cyber-attacks 50, 55, 166
  cybercrime 43–4, 48, 61, 195–7, 202, 206–10, 214–16, 228, 230, 238–9, 264–5
  data, definition of 162–4
  deep packet inspection (DPI) 182, 185–6, 189–93
  data protection 46, 57
  definition 42
  Digital Single Market (DSM) 50, 53–7, 157–94, 264
  eIDAS Reg 166, 175
  electronic communications networks and associated facilities 161
  ENISA 47, 54, 55
  essence of rights, notion of 265
  External Action (EA) 244–5, 255, 264, 265
  extraterritoriality 255
  Fraud and Counterfeiting Directive (FCD) 209–10
  hacking 238
  incidents 173
  information, definition of 162–4
  investigative tools 228
  law 6, 157, 160–77
  legal vulnerabilities 179
  networks, definition of 162–4
  NIS Directive (NSID)
    addressees 161
    cybercrime 206, 210
    deep packet inspection (DPI) 186
    Digital Single Market (DSM) 157, 160–2, 164, 167
    External Action (EA) 244–5
    NIS Directive II 175
    policy 49, 53
  operators of essential services (OESs) 161
  overlaps 167
  policy 42–57, 61, 64, 67, 158–77, 262
  privacy 46, 57, 160
  reform 174–6
  resilience 48, 50, 55
  restrictive measures 252, 254
  security, definition of 165–6
  technical and organisational measures (TOMs) 170
  tensions between NIS dimension 55–7
  three-pronged approach 42–3, 48, 158–9
  tools, use of 230
neutrality *see* **technology neutrality (TN), principle of**
New Approach to Harmonisation and Standardisation 180–1
New Legislative Framework (NLF) 146–52, 154, 155, 180, 259
Nissenbaum, H 61

OECD Privacy Guidelines 101–2, 108, 110–11
Olster, J 114
Open Internet Access Regulation (OIR) 187–9, 192
operators of essential services (OESs) 161
opinio juris 110–11
ordre public 5, 9, 33, 39
  composite EU 29–32
  constitutional architecture of the EU 25–6, 27–8, 36–7
  emergency, times of 26, 29–32
  legality, principle of 29–32
  national implementation of EU law 269
  national security 25, 31
  policy 36
  reconciliation of triad 26, 37, 39
  Rule of Law (RoL) 3, 27–8, 29–32, 39
  techno-legal objects within EU, triad as 3, 156, 261
Organization for Security Co-operation 63
Ottis, R 18
overlaps 2–4
  complementarity 22
  defence 66–7
  Digital Single Market (DSM) 162, 167, 176, 193
  network and information security (NIS) 167
  reconciliation of triad 38, 129, 138–41, 155, 261
  techno-legal objects within EU, triad as 129, 130, 138–41, 152, 155, 263

pacing problem 32, 35, 156, 268–9
packet inspection techniques *see* **deep packet inspection (DPI)**

Pagallo, U 146
Pauletto, C 109
Payment Services Directive II (PSD II) 157, 160–1, 171–4, 210–11, 218–19
Pegasus software 1
personal data breaches 168–74, 176, 178–82, 206
personal social and sexual identity 73, 77, 82, 83–6, 95–6, 135, 262
personality, preservation or development of 13, 14, 107
personhood, development of 15, 73, 77, 81, 86–8, 95, 135, 262
PESCO (Permanent Structured Cooperation) 50, 63, 64
Pikos, LF 191, 193
Poland 27–8
police and judicial cooperation 58–60, 99, 201–2, 212, 219
policy *see* EU cybersecurity policy
politics
  agendas 52
  aim (resolution of conflict) 23
  de-politicisation 268
  geopolitics 40, 241–2
  identity 25
  interim solutions 267
  means towards the aim (binding collective decisions) 23
  policy 40
  politicisation 19
  scope (organised community) 23–4
  technological sovereignty
Posner, E 23
Poullet, Y 106
prevention
  averting incidents 168–74
  capacity building 52
  Cyber Diplomacy Toolbox 249
  cybercrime 75, 207, 210–11, 225, 232–3
  dependency 169–70
  Digital Single Market (DSM) 168–74
  ENISA 169
  e-Privacy Directive 169
  intermediary services, exploiting vulnerable 169–70
  personal data breaches 168–74
  security by design 207
  signatures, checking known 232–3
  technical and organisational measures (TOMs) 168–74
Pridöhl, H 130–1, 185
PRISM programme (US) 229, 231
privacy *see* e-Privacy Directive (EPD); privacy in CFR/right to respect for private and family life in ECHR

privacy in CFR/right to respect for private and family life in ECHR 68–96
  autonomy 73, 77, 81, 86–8
  breadth of protection, divergence on 72–5
  CJEU, case law of 74, 81–95, 262
  confidential communications 91–3, 95, 135–6, 262
  correspondence, concept of 73, 163
  cybercrime 220, 223–5
  damages 77
  data protection 78, 86, 97–8, 101–9, 120, 263
  deep packet inspection (DPI) 185, 191
  democracy 15, 16, 87, 91
  depth of protection, divergence as to the 75–7
  Digital Single Market (DSM) 52, 157–94
  dignity, right to 13
  discrimination 89–90
  ECtHR, case law of 68, 70–2, 77–94
  e-evidence, collection of 223–5
  electronic communications services (ECSs) 69, 78, 80, 91–3
  environmental rights 73, 74
  e-Privacy Directive (EPD) 69, 78, 86, 91–3, 101, 105–6, 111
  e-Privacy Regulation (EPR) 78, 88, 90, 92–3, 101, 160, 220
  essence of rights, notion of 94–6, 135–6
  essential components of CFR 77–96, 135–6, 262
  everyone has a right to, meaning of 77–8
  Explanations (CFR) 69, 71, 74, 79
  family life (inner circle) 73, 88–90, 95, 135, 262
  general principles of EU law 26, 36, 70–1
  his or her private life, meaning of 80–8
  home, concept of the 73, 90–1, 95, 135–6, 262
  honour and reputation 80, 84–6
  horizontal obligations 78–80
  Human Rights Measurement Framework (HRMF) (EHRC) 73, 77
  ICCPR 69–71, 77–80, 85–6
  in accordance with the law, interferences must be 75, 76
  independence of privacy from data protection 101–8
  interception of communications 87, 91–2
  interpretation 69–72, 76–8, 90, 96, 101–2, 109, 120
  intimacy 14
  legitimate aims 75
  let alone, right to 14
  limitations, test for permissible 75–7
  margin of appreciation 75, 224
  minimum threshold of protection 71–2, 78
  national security 69, 75, 76, 99, 101, 221
  necessary in a democratic society 75
  negative obligations 78

network and information security (NIS)   46, 57
OECD Privacy Guidelines   101–2, 108, 110–11
personal data   86, 88
personal development, autonomy and participation (outer circle)   73, 77, 81, 86–8, 95, 135, 262
personal information and surveillance   73, 74
personal social and sexual identity   73, 77, 82, 83–6, 95–6, 135, 262
personality, development of   14
physical and psychological integrity   73–4, 77, 81–2, 85, 87, 94, 96, 135, 262
policy   43–4, 46, 50, 52, 62, 66–7
positive obligations   78–9
prevention of disorder or crime   75
primacy of CFR   71
primary law, interpretation of   70–1
private life, notion of   73, 77–88, 90–4, 262
proportionality   75, 94
protection of health and morals   75
qualified right, privacy as a   75
reasonable expectation of privacy   185
residence, right of   71–2
respect for, meaning of   78–80
restrictive measures   257
retention of data   92–3
secondary law   77–9
sexual orientation   74, 77, 81–6, 89, 94–6
sources for interpretation   69–71
surveillance   16, 18, 86–7, 91–3, 96
TEU   70, 76
vertical obligations   78–80
Product Liability Directive (PLD)   150–1
proportionality
  assessments   138, 140, 157, 263
  Charter of Fundamental Rights of the EU   26, 33, 35
  Child Sexual Abuse Material (CSAM)   213
  cybercrimes   212, 219, 221, 227, 238–9
  deep packet inspection (DPI)   193, 235–6
  Digital Single Market (DSM)   157, 176
  e-evidence, collection of   221
  essence of rights, notion of   26, 34, 37
  fundamental rights   5, 32–5
  monitoring   189
  policy   262
  privacy   73, 77–88, 90–4, 262
  reconciliation of triad   9, 26, 35
  Rule of Law (RoL)   28, 269
  surveillance in the workplace   104
  values   25
protection goals (PGs)
  definition   133–4
  ENISA study on engineering privacy by design (PbD)   131, 132

Internet Engineering Task Force (IETF)   131–2, 139
investigations   228
LINDDUN project   131–2, 136
Microsoft STRIDE model   131
plausible deniability   131–2, 136, 138
security properties (SPs)   132, 136
techno-legal objects within EU, triad as   130–6, 138, 140, 155, 263
pseudonymisation   119, 167
public interest   27, 203
public private partnerships (PPPs)   50, 55, 59, 159, 213
Pugliese, G   13
purpose limitation   115–18, 120–1, 136, 190, 263, 265
Purtova, N   113–14

Raab, C   110
Rachovitsa, A   139
ransomware   17, 172, 204
reconciliation of triad   2–6, 9–10, 22–6, 38–9
  abstraction   157–8, 262
  balancing exercise   3, 25, 38, 129, 157, 229, 259–61, 265
  Child Sexual Abuse Material (CSAM)   211–16
  clashes   9, 15–19, 22–4, 38, 129, 261
  complementarity   22–3, 129, 138, 167, 261
  complete reconciliation   129, 261
  constitutional architecture of EU   9, 25–6
  convergence   38, 261
  cybercrime   4–6, 29, 195–219, 229–39, 241, 244–5
  deep packet inspection (DPI)   232–7
  Digital Single Market (DSM)   5–6, 157–94, 240–1, 244–5
  e-evidence, collection of   195–200, 216–38, 264
  External Action (EA)   5–6, 240–60
  Fraud and Counterfeiting Directive (FCD)   208–11
  indifference/non-interference   38, 129, 261
  network and information security (NIS)   158–93
  ordre public   26, 36–7, 39
  overlaps   38, 129, 138–41, 155, 176, 261
  proportionality   9, 26, 35
  Rule of Law (RoL)   28
  strong reconciliation   22, 38–9, 129, 261, 265
    complementarity   129
    cybercrime   195, 206, 240
    Digital Single Market (DSM)   157–8, 161, 174, 176–82, 193, 240
  techno-legal objects within EU, triad as   129, 130–41, 155, 263–4
  technical and organisational measures (TOMs)   157–8

technology   177–93, 255–9
values   262
weak reconciliation   22, 38–9, 129, 261, 266
   cybercrime   216–19, 239, 240
   External Action (EA)   241, 254, 259–60
   Fraud and Counterfeiting Directive
      (FCD)   208–11
   prospective   216–17
   reconciliation of triad   157, 240
   zero-sum outcomes   23, 35, 38–9, 261
rectification   122–3
Reding, V   159
Reed, C   156
regulation
   Better Regulation agenda   141, 180
   co-decision delegatory forms of
      regulation   142, 147, 155
   co-regulation   180, 258–9
   effacement of technology   268
   External Action (EA)   241, 244–5, 255–9
   New Approach/New Legislative Framework
      259
   policy   51
   reconciliation of triad   178–82, 241
   state of the art (SoA)   259
   targets   38, 129, 141–52, 263
   technology as a regulatory object   9–10
   vested interests   156
   weak regulation   245, 264
**Regulation of Investigatory Powers
      Act   2000**   223–5
Rehof, LA   70
**Renewed European Internal Security
      Strategy**   199
research trajectories   267–9
resilience   12–13, 159, 211
   network and information security (NIS)   52, 210
   policy   46, 47–8, 50
   technical and organisational measures
      (TOMs)   117
   third countries, in   66
resources   23–4
**restrictive measures (RMs) against
      cyber-attacks**   247–57
   attribution of attacks to third states   252, 256–7
   Blueprint for coordinated response to large-scale
      incidents and crises   252, 256
   Charter of Fundamental Rights of the EU   247,
      251, 257, 260, 264
   Common Foreign and Security Policy
      (CFSP)   247, 264
   cyber-attack, definition of   251–2
   Cyber Diplomacy Toolbox   241, 245, 248–54,
      256
   deep packet inspection (DPI)   257

Dual-use Regulation   241, 245, 254–5, 257, 265
e-evidence, collection of   256–7
export control   254–5, 257, 265
forensic analysis   255–7
Fraud and Counterfeiting Directive (FCD)   252
freezing of assets   250, 252
functional interconnection   254–5, 265
fundamental rights   251
General Data Protection Regulation (GDPR)
   251
identification of natural and legal persons
   252–4
network and information security (NIS)   252,
   254
private and family life, right to respect for   257
proportionality   253
reconciliation of triad   241
Restrictive Measures Directive (RMDir)   245,
   250–7
Restrictive Measures Regulation (RMReg)   245,
   250–7
Sanctions Guidelines   254–5
technical attribution, importance of   256–7
technocratic assessment   256
terrorism   253
TEU   250, 253
TFEU   248, 250
travel bans   250, 252
Rodotà, S   107
Rouvroy, A   106
Rule of Law (RoL)
   authoritarianism   26
   Charter of Fundamental Rights of the EU   33, 34
   complementarity   28
   constitutional architecture of EU   3, 9, 27–32
   cybercrime   216–17, 227, 229, 238
   democracy   28–9
   emergency, times of   24, 29–32
   executive powers, arbitrariness of   28
   fundamental rights   26, 28, 32
   general principles of EU law   26, 28, 32
   independent and impartial courts   28
   judicial review   28
   legal certainty   28
   legality, principle of   28, 29–33
   market appropriation of law   269
   ordre public   27, 28, 29–32, 39
   policy choices, emergency brake on   28
   proportionality   28, 269
   reconciliation of triad   28
   standards   149–50
   techno-legal objects within EU, triad as   136,
      261
   value-principle, as   27–9
   zero-sum outcomes   3, 22

310   *Index*

Saltzer, JH   145
Schartum, DW   146
Scheinin, M   34, 78–9
Schroeder, MD   145
Schulze, M   256
security by design (SbD)
 General Data Protection Regulation (GDPR)   170
 network and information security (NIS)   180
 New Approach/Legislative Framework   146–51
 policy   42, 55
 prevention   207
 regulation   259
 standards   146–51
 state of the art (SOA)   146–51
 techno-legal objects within EU, triad as   141–2, 144–51, 263
 technology neutrality (TN), principle of   142, 146–51
security, definition of   6, 164–8, 175–6
security properties (SPs)
 confidentiality, integrity and availability (CIA)   131, 138
 definition   133–4
 family, concept of the   135
 home, concept of the   136
 investigations   229
 protection goals (PGs)   132, 136
 techno-legal objects within EU, triad as   130–6, 138, 140, 155, 263
Security Union Strategy 2020   198, 199–200
Shackelford, SJ   13, 258
Shin-yi Peng   259
signals   9, 162–4, 177
Simitis, S   115
situated objects, triad as   36–8
Škorvánek, I   91
Smismans, S   149
Smith, RE   131
Snowden, Edward   1, 10, 15–18, 48–9, 110, 139, 198, 205, 219, 223, 228, 236–7, 243
solidarity, principle of   246
Solove, D   25, 132
Song, W   192
sovereignty
 cyber sovereignty   51, 184, 242, 266, 268
 technological sovereignty   51, 243, 258
spoofing   131
spyware   1, 189, 204–5, 232
standards   11
 CEN, CENELEC and ETSI
  Commission mandate   147–8
  MoU between   57
 Charter of Fundamental Rights of the EU   150, 259–60

 CJEU, case law of   148–50
 confidentiality   269
 conformity, of   150, 170
 definition   181
 democratic deficit   149–50
 Digital Single Market (DSM)   178–82
 European Harmonised Standards (EHS)   147–8, 154
 External Action (EA)   241, 243, 255–6, 258, 260, 265–6
 General Data Protection Regulation (GDPR)   150, 180
 governmental standards   12
 integrity   269
 legal certainty   150
 minimum security standards   13
 national certification schemes   57
 New Approach to Harmonisation and Standardisation   180–1
 New Legislative Framework (NLF)   148–50, 152, 154
 norm-setting   266
 political agendas   52
 primary law   150, 152
 Product Liability Directive   150–1
 protectionism   148–9
 publication   154
 regulation   255–6
 Rule of Law (RoL)   149–50
 security by design   146–51
 Standardisation Regulation   149
 Standardisation Strategy   52
 Standards Developing Organisations (SDOs)   51, 149, 151–2, 182, 243, 258–9, 263–4
 Standards Setting Organisations (SSOs)   51, 131, 149, 151–2, 243, 258–9, 263–4
 state of the art (SOA)   147
 techno-legal objects within EU, triad as   141–2, 146–51, 155, 263–4
 technical and organisational measures (TOMs)   151, 178–82
 technology neutrality (TN), principle of   146–51
state of the art (SoA)
 cybercrime   239
 Cybersecurity Act (CSA)   178
 deep packet inspection (DPI)   182–93
 Digital Single Market (DSM)   175, 177, 178–94
 General Data Protection Regulation (GDPR)   178
 incidents   178–82
 New Approach/Legislative Framework   148
 regulation   259
 security by design   146–51
 standards   147

techno-legal objects within EU, triad as 141–2, 146–51, 155, 263–4
technical and organisational measures (TOMs) 152
technology neutrality (TN), principle of 146–51, 266–7
Steinmetz, KFS 200
Stockholm Programme 45
Stuxnet 20–1, 45
Summers, S 203, 205–6
surveillance *see also* **interception of communications; mass surveillance**
  abuse of power 61
  cybercrime 198, 218, 229, 237
  data protection 103–4
  deep packet inspection (DPI) 184, 234, 237
  democracy 87, 91, 156
  interception of communications 44, 87, 91–2, 198, 204–5, 206
  personal information 73, 74
  privacy 86–7, 91–3, 96
  proportionality 104

Taylor, C 13
technical and organisational measures (TOMs)
  certification 116–17, 170, 178
  Cybersecurity Act (CSA) 170
  data protection 116–18, 170–1, 263
  Digital Single Market (DSM) 157–8, 168–78, 193–4
  prevention 168–74
  privacy 93
  reconciliation of triad 157–8
  risk 168–74
  standards 151
  state of the art (SOA) 152, 175, 177, 178–94
  techno-legal objects within EU, triad as 141–2, 146–51, 263–4
  technical, operational and organisational measures (TOOMs) 175
  technology neutrality (TN), principle of 146–51
techno-legal objects within EU, triad as 9–10, 22–3, 129–56
  applicable law 139–40
  authorisation 131
  authentication 131, 138
  availability 131, 132, 138–9
  Better Regulation toolbox 141
  Charter of Fundamental Rights of the EU 132, 135–7, 139
  CJEU, case law of 132, 135–6, 139–40, 153–4, 264, 266–7
  co-decision delegatory forms of regulation 142, 147, 155

complementarity 129, 138
confidentiality 129, 130–1, 135–6, 138–40
constitutional architecture or *ordre public* 3, 156, 261
design 129–35, 139–42, 144–51, 155, 263, 266
Digital Single Market (DSM) 262
disappearance of technology 129
ECtHR, case law of 140, 264, 266–7
effacement of technology from the law 129, 141–54, 155, 264
engineering/computer science approach 129, 130
essence of rights, notion of 130, 132, 135–7, 263
essential components 130, 132, 135–7, 155–6, 263
External Action (EA) 262
fundamental rights 3, 261–2, 266
indeterminacy 129–30, 141–2, 152–4, 155, 264
integrity 129, 130–2, 138–40
interpretation 140–1
leveraging technology 130–41
linking technological and legal notions of triad 132–8
New Approach/Legislative Framework 146–52, 154, 155
non-repudiation 131, 132, 138
overlaps 129, 130, 138–41, 152, 155, 263
privacy by design 139
private and family life, right to respect for 139
proportionality assessments 138, 140, 157, 263
protection goals (PGs) 130–6, 138–40, 155, 263
reconciliation of the triad 129, 130–41, 155, 263–4
regulatory target, technology as a 129, 141–52, 263
reliability 131
risk assessment and management 131, 138, 140–1, 263
Rule of Law (RoL) 136, 261
secondary law 147, 263–4
security by design, principle of 141–2, 144–51, 263
security properties (SPs) 130–6, 138, 140, 155, 263
standards 141–2, 146–52, 154–5, 263–4
state of the art (SOA) 141–2, 146–52, 155, 263–4
technical and organisational measures (TOMs) 141–2, 146–51, 263–4
technology law techniques 129, 266
technology neutrality (TN), principle of 129, 141–4, 146–52, 155–6, 263, 266–7
tensions 129
threat modelling 130–2, 263
values 141, 145, 154–6, 266

technology   3, 26–38 *see also* **effacement of technology; techno-legal objects within EU, triad as; technology neutrality (TN), principle of**
  analysis   26–38
  cybercrime   6, 195, 229–38, 240
  Digital Single Market (DSM)   6, 157, 177–94
  dual-use technology   64, 241, 245, 254–5, 257, 265
  e-evidence, collection of   229–38
  External Action (EA)   6, 241, 255–60, 265–6
  gap   14–15, 268
  law techniques   129, 266
  leadership   265–6
  policy   40
  reconciliation of triad   177–93, 229–38, 255–9
  restrictive measures   241
technology neutrality (TN), principle of   146–51
  cybercrime   207, 210, 218–19, 227, 229–32, 239
  deep packet inspection (DPI)   184
  Digital Single Market (DSM)   177, 193–4
  External Action (EA)   259
  Fraud and Counterfeiting Directive (FCD)   230
  Internet   20
  Law Enforcement Directive (LED)   230
  market interests   268
  New Approach/Legislative Framework   146–51
  security by design   142, 146–51
  state of the art (SoA)   146–51, 266–7
  techno-legal objects within EU, triad as   129, 141–4, 146–51, 155–6, 263
  technical and organisational measures (TOMs)   152
technological sovereignty   51, 243, 258
TeleTrust   147, 179
Tempora   231
terrorism
  Combating Terrorism Directive (CTDir)   58, 59, 216–17, 227, 234
  Combating Terrorism Regulation (CTReg)   216–17
  critical infrastructure (CI), attacks on   44
  cyber-attacks   44, 58, 216, 219, 234
  cybercrime   195–6, 198, 200, 216–17, 221, 227, 231
  deep packet inspection (DPI)   233–4
  cyberspace   21
  London bombings   44
  Madrid bombings   44
  personal social and sexual identity   85
  restrictive measures   253
  September 11, 2001, attacks on US   44, 216
  terminal equipment, location of   221
  UN Security Council list of terrorists   253
  war on terror   1, 3, 9, 40, 44, 197–8
  zero-sum outcomes   9

threats
  assessments   207
  modelling   130–2, 263
Tielemans, L   144, 146
Tiirmaa-Klaar, H   48
trade
  defence and diplomacy, tensions with   66
  dual-use technology   64
  External Action (EA)   53, 62–6
transparency   29, 120–1, 136–7
travel bans   250, 252
Tribe, L   141
Trojans   204, 238
Trotter, S   81
trust services   161, 167–8, 173
Tzanou, M   106

United Nations (UN)
  Charter   246
  Group of Governmental Experts (UN GGE)   63, 243, 246, 249, 256
  Rule of Law (RoL)   28
United States
  Covid-19, cyber-attacks on health care system during   166
  electoral interference   217
  high-tech products, dominance in   11
  investigations   229
  National Security Agency (NSA)   15–17
  network and information security (NIS)   258–9
  September 11, 2001, attacks on US   44, 216
  standards   11
  Stuxnet   20–1, 45
  terrorists, Security Council list of   253
  war on terror   1, 3, 9, 40, 44, 197–8
Universal Declaration of Human Rights (UDHR)   70, 77–80

values   3, 255–60
  choice   25
  constitutional rights   24–5
  design-based legislation   37–8
  Digital Single Market (DSM)   52, 244
  economic concerns   51
  epistemic communities   36
  essence of rights, notion of   38
  External Action (EA)   27, 241–3, 245–6, 255–60
  ordre public   25
  policy   47, 262
  political identity   25
  principles, collision with   24–5
  reconciliation of triad   262
  Rule of Law (RoL)   27–9
  security and rights, relationship between   26

security concerns 51
TEU 29
techno-legal objects within EU, triad as 141, 145, 154–6, 266
Van der Sloot, B 100, 106, 119
variable geometry security 177–8
Venice Commission (CoE) 28
Vermeule, A 23
Vermeulen, M 76
viruses 204
Volpato, A 148
vouloir-vivre (**ideal of life**) 25, 31–2
von Grafenstein, M 106–7
Von Moltke, Heinrich 268

WannaCry ransomware 17
Ware, Willie 101, 136
Warren, Samuel 14, 82
Westin, A 13
Wikileaks 238
worms 204

Wolters, PTJ 179
World Wide Web 12, 41, 49, 184–5

Yar, M 200
Yost, JR 10–11, 136

Zalnieriute, M 110
zero-days attacks 16–17, 20–1, 238
zero-sum outcomes 3–5, 9, 26, 38–9
  effacement of technology 266
  essence of rights, notion of 240
  e-evidence, collection of 228–9
  fundamental rights as a fail-safe 32–5
  Law Enforcement Directive (LED) 229
  pendulum argument 25
  reconciliation of triad 23, 35, 38–9, 261
  Rule of Law (RoL) 3, 22
  techno-legal analysis 3, 6
  trade-offs 22–3, 25
zombies 203–4, 238
Zuboff, S 87